GOKHALE

The Indian Moderates and the British Raj

Gokhale in England, 1912

GOKHALE

THE INDIAN MODERATES
AND THE BRITISH RAJ

B. R. NANDA

PRINCETON UNIVERSITY PRESS
PRINCETON, NEW JERSEY

To Baba

Preface

When I started working on a biography of Gopal Krishna Gokhale, I had no idea of the time and labour it would involve. It did not take me long to discover that the transformation in the Indian political scene, which came with the emergence of Gandhi after the First World War, had obscured the role not only of Gokhale, but of almost the entire leadership of the Moderate era. Gandhi himself was, of course, not responsible for this, as he never ceased to pay tributes to the Moderate veterans, and especially to Gokhale whom he acknowledged as his political mentor. However, the 'generation gap' impeded the understanding of the social and political environment in which the early leaders of the Congress had to function.

With the passage of time and the availability of fresh sources, it is now possible to take a more balanced view of this period, and especially of the milieu in which Gopal Krishna Gokhale worked. We have a huge mass of material, published and unpublished, including memoirs, diaries, unpublished official records and private papers of Indian leaders as well as of Viceroys, Secretaries of State, Governors and other participants as well as observers of the political scene, for a study in depth.

Gokhale's political career practically coincided with the first thirty years of the Indian National Congress. He was much younger than its founding-fathers, but it was his good fortune to come into intimate contact with them, to win their confidence, and to become their ablest spokesman. While he was still in his thirties, he became the authentic spokesman of his country's aspirations both in India and England. As a leader of the Indian National Congress, as a member of the Imperial Legislative Council, as the confidant of the British Committee of the Congress in London, as India's unofficial envoy to England, Gokhale occupied a unique vantage point in Indian politics. He belonged to a not-too-common species—an intellectual in politics. He was not only one of the main actors in the Indian political drama, but one of its shrewdest and most vocal observers. The study of his life thus offers valuable insights into the history of Indian nationalism and Indo-British relations.

I have drawn upon a mass of unpublished materials, including the correspondence of Gokhale, his associates and critics among the Indian leaders, and of British Viceroys, Secretaries of State, Governors and other administrators, and the official records. I have tried to understand and interpret, rather than to uphold and condemn. I hope the diversity of sources will contribute to a well-proportioned and objective account of Gokhale's life and times.

My thanks are due, for their unfailing courtesy and assistance, to the Librarian and staff of the Gokhale Institute of Politics and Economics, Poona, the National Library, Calcutta, the National Archives of India and the Nehru Memorial Museum & Library, New Delhi. I am grateful to the Rockefeller Foundation, which made it possible for me to travel to the U.K. in 1964, and consult unpublished records and papers in various repositories, such as the India Office Library and the British Museum in London, and the National Library in Edinburgh. The Bibliography at the end of the book includes collections of unpublished records and papers, to the owners or donors of which I acknowledge my debt of gratitude. I have kept references in the notes to the minimum, and as a rule have cited them only for direct quotations.

That I write a biography of Gokhale was first suggested to me by Pandit H. N. Kunzru and Shri B. Shiva Rao. Pandit Kunzru, Shri D. V. Ambekar, Shri S. R. Venkataraman and the late Shri S. G. Vaze were kind enough to provide me with their reminiscences of Gokhale and his times. I had very valuable interviews with Professor N. R. Phatak, the late Shri R. P. Paranjpye and Justice Dhavle, the son-in-law of Gokhale. My thanks are due to Shri S. G. Gokhale and Shri S. R. Venkataraman for the photographs which appear in the book.

I am grateful to Dr S. R. Mehrotra and Shri V. C. Joshi for reading through the entire manuscript and making useful suggestions. Finally, I am indebted to my wife for her constant understanding, encouragement and support, without which I could hardly have completed this work.

B. R. N.

Contents

PREFACE   vii

ABBREVIATIONS   xii

BOOK I: FORMATIVE YEARS   1

1   EARLY LIFE   3
2   FERMENT IN MAHARASHTRA   9
3   EMERGENCE OF THE EDUCATED ÉLITE   14
4   THE INDIAN JESUITS   26
5   APPRENTICED TO RANADE   39
6   THE YOUNG POLITICIAN   51
7   PROFESSOR GOKHALE   60
8   ON THE CONGRESS PLATFORM   67
9   THE GREAT SPLIT   72
10 THE RISING STAR   88
11 ECLIPSED   102
12 THE CLOUDS LIFT   118
13 TRIUMPH   133

BOOK II: SPOKESMAN FOR THE MODERATES   143

14 GOKHALE COMES OF AGE   145
15 WANTED, A LEADER   154
16 SERVANTS OF INDIA   169
17 CLASH WITH CURZON   177
18 ENVOY EXTRAORDINARY   187
19 CONGRESS PRESIDENT   202
20 ADVOCATE FOR INDIA   212

BOOK III: CONFRONTATIONS, WITHIN AND WITHOUT   221

21 MORLEY'S DILEMMA   223
22 THE EXTREMIST CHALLENGE   241
23 THE WIDENING RIFT   253
24 CRISIS IN THE RAJ   268

x *Contents*

25 Road to Surat   279
26 Reforms on the Anvil   296
27 Climax   314
28 Origins of Muslim Separatism   320
29 Gokhale and the Communal Problem   337
30 Separate Electorates   344
31 Anticlimax   354
32 A House Divided Against Itself   361
33 Détente   372
34 Leader of the Opposition   378
35 Educating the Masses   386

BOOK IV: THE LAST PHASE   395

36 Educating the British   397
37 Gandhi and Gokhale   407
38 Crisis in South Africa   422
39 The Last Battle   435
40 No Reunion   451
41 Last Days   461
42 'The Greatest Indian'   471
43 The End of an Era   480

    Bibliography   495

    Index   507

List of Plates

Frontispiece

Gokhale in England, 1912

Between pages 216 and 217

Gokhale with the members of the Deccan Education Society,
Poona, 1902

Leaders of the Indian National Congress, Bombay,
December 1904

Gokhale with Gandhi, Kallenbach and members of the
Reception Committee, Durban, 1912

Gokhale with Dadabhai Naoroji (sitting) and D. E. Wacha,
London, 1897

A. O. Hume

Sir William Wedderburn

Lord Curzon

John Morley

Lord Minto

Lord Hardinge

Pherozeshah Mehta

Bal Gangadhar Tilak

Mahadev Govind Ranade

Abbreviations

B.P.	— Butler Papers
C.P.	— Curzon Papers
D.N.P.	— Dadabhai Naoroji Papers
E.P.	— Elgin Papers
F. Wilson P.	— Fleetwood Wilson Papers
G.P.	— Gokhale Papers
H.P.	— Hardinge Papers
L.P.	— Lytton Papers
M.P.	— Morley Papers
P. Mehta P.	— Pherozeshah Mehta Papers
S. Ray P.	— Sarla Ray Papers
V. S. Sastri P.	— V. Srinivasa Sastri Papers
AIR	— All India Radio
confdl.	— confidential
G.O.I.	— Government of India
hony.	— honorary
I.N.C.	— Indian National Congress
IOL	— India Office Library
Jud.	— Judicial
NAI	— National Archives of India
NMML	— Nehru Memorial Museum & Library
Pol.	— Political
prob.	— probably
proc.	— proceedings
P.S.	— Private Secretary
Pub.	— Public

Book I

FORMATIVE YEARS

1

Early Life

It is now 10.30 p.m., and I am writing in a train after a long and exhausting day. I have presided for six hours at the budget meeting of the Legislative Council. The only speaker of the slightest merit whom we possess in Council is Mr Gokhale from Bombay. He is a very able and courageous person, a Mahratta Brahmin, a Congressman, as you remember, connected with Poona affairs. . . . But he is not, I believe, disloyal; he represents a very important stratum in Native thought and opinion; he is highly cultivated and not unreasonable. . . .

The date was 25 March 1903. Lord Curzon, the Viceroy of India, was travelling from Calcutta to Simla, and writing his periodic letter to Secretary of State, Lord George Hamilton. It was unusual for Curzon—who was conscious of his own exceptional intellectual gifts —to pay a compliment to anyone around him, and especially to a thirty-five year-old 'native' politician of the Indian National Congress, a political body which in his eyes was synonymous with sedition. During the next two years, as Gokhale assailed one official measure after another in the Imperial Legislative Council, Curzon's admiration for him turned to suspicion, irritation and indignation. Gokhale aroused ambivalent feelings not only in Curzon, but in his successors on the Viceregal throne and most British officials in India. They were attracted by his ability, but exasperated and repelled by his lack of amenability. They could not quite square his professions of loyalty with his aspirations for Indian self-government. They liked his simple, direct, guileless manner, but wondered whether it was a mask for some sinister design to undermine the Raj. They found it hard to accept that so much ability, integrity, acumen and naïveté could co-exist in an Indian politician. Their bewilderment would have been less if they could have realized the significance of the intellectual, social and political ferment which had been changing the face of Maharashtra, and indeed of India in the last quarter of the nineteenth century, of which Gokhale was the product.

2

Gopal Krishna Gokhale was born on 9 May 1866 in the little village of Kotluk in the Ratnagiri district of, what was then, the Bombay Presidency. This was the village to which his mother Satyabhama belonged. Not far from Kotluk was Tamhanmala, the native village of his father Krishnarao Gokhale. The Gokhales were Chitpavan Brahmans who had once commanded considerable prestige, perquisites and power in the days of the Peshwas, and one of them had received the enviable appellation of *Raste* ('True'). But this could scarcely have been a consolation to Krishnarao, who owned a small plot of land in Tamhanmala and enjoyed the *Khot* right as a rent-collector. Unfortunately in Tamhanmala, as indeed in the greater part of Ratnagiri district, the soil was poor, the rain water drained off the hills into the Arabian Sea, and the peasant's lot was hard. Krishnarao needed a job to eke out a living. In his youth he had been ambitious, and had tried to learn English. He had gone to a school at Kolhapur, where Mahadev Govind Ranade was his classmate, but poverty had forced him to give up his studies and take up the post of a low-paid clerk at Kagal. Krishnarao rose to be a sub-inspector of police, but salaries in the Indian States were pitifully low, and he had to struggle hard to provide the barest subsistence for his large family of two sons and four daughters. In this struggle he was supported by his deeply religious, hard-working and self-effacing wife, Satyabhama.

Krishnarao's chief ambition was to give to his sons, Govind and Gopal, what had been denied to him—English education. In 1876 both the boys, who had completed the elementary course in the rural surroundings of Kagal, were sent to the high school at Kolhapur. They were intelligent, eager, industrious and responsible boys, determined to make the most of the opportunity their self-sacrificing parents provided them. But they had hardly been in Kolhapur for three years when their luck ran out. Krishnarao died in 1879 and the two boys were left to fend for themselves. The elder boy, Govind, who was eighteeen years old and already married, now became the head of the family. He gave up his studies and returned to Kagal where he took a job carrying a monthly salary of Rs 15. On this paltry sum, Govind decided to support his wife, mother, brother and four sisters. Young Gopal, who was only thirteen years old at the time, recognized the harsh realities of his domestic situation, and offered to leave school and take up a job to do his bit for the family. The elder brother would not, however, hear of Gopal giving up his studies, and went on remitting half of his meagre salary of fifteen rupees to maintain him in school at Kolhapur. On his part, Gopal led a hard and frugal existence, paring down his expenses to the minimum, cooking his own meals and saving kerosene by reading under the street lamp.

In 1881, Gopal passed the matriculation examination of Bombay University. He wondered whether he had any right to study for a degree and thus add to his brother's burden. Govind, however, insisted that Gopal must receive the best education available in the country. Had not their father looked forward to the day when his sons would qualify as graduates? Was not a university degree a passport to a well-paid post and to higher status in the new society which was emerging? Was it not foolish of Gopal to throw away almost the only chance he had of lifting his family from poverty and oblivion? These arguments of the elder brother were dramatically clinched by his wife's offer to pawn her jewellery to enable her young brother-in-law to go to the university.

In 1881, Gopal joined the Rajaram College at Kolhapur. The college did not have arrangements for the full B.A. course and Gopal had to go to Poona to continue his studies at the Deccan College. Not much is known about his college days, but it seems he was exceedingly ambitious with an almost obsessive desire to excel. Many years later, in a triumphant moment in his political career—his election to the Imperial Legislative Council—one of his classmates reminded him of an incident which had taken place in April 1883, immediately after a college terminal examination in which a very stiff question paper had been set.

D. H. Waknis to G. K. Gokhale, 2 September 1901: The Terminal [examination] was proceeding. It was Trigonometry paper. At about 10 you entered my room. I asked you how you had done in the paper. Let me tell you by the way I had stolen away from the Hall without handing over my answer papers. Needless to say they were blanks. To resume the narrative—in answer to my interrogatory you called yourself a thousand names for being able to secure only 90 out of a hundred marks. 'A monstrously ambitious soul', I uttered to myself.[1]

This competitive spirit had characterized Gokhale even in his

[1] Waknis to Gokhale, 2 Sept. 1901 (G.P.).

school days at Kagal. In one of the school examinations the first place in the class had gone to another boy, Salvedekar. Gokhale's reaction was explosive: 'He tore up his own textbook and then borrowed Sanvaldekar's book and learnt it off by heart in order to make himself independent of it altogether.'[2]

Gokhale returned from the Deccan College, Poona, to Rajaram College at Kolhapur for a while, but in 1884, he joined Elphinstone College, Bombay, for the final year of the degree course. In retrospect, it seems fortunate that he did not remain confined in these impressionable years to the backwaters of Kolhapur, but was able to attend the two colleges in western India, the Deccan College and the Elphinstone College, which offered the best that was available in India in the way of English education.

Gokhale had taken mathematics for the degree course at the Elphinstone College. There were only six students in his class. One of them was D. K. Karve, who was to be honoured as a renowned centenarian and social reformer in our own day. Gokhale and Karve both secured only a second division in 1884; a first division in mathematics was rarely awarded. Karve recalled later that Gokhale had 'a pushing nature and an impressive personality'.[3] It is, however, doubtful if this poor, shy, secretly ambitious and highly-strung Chitpavan boy left any great impression on his teachers. It is possible that mathematics did not offer the fullest scope for his intellectual gifts, which were to find a more congenial outlet in literature, history, economics and politics. Or perhaps his intellect had not yet fully flowered. His chief asset at the time seems to have been his keen memory. He sharpened it by practice; he learnt passages, chapters and even whole books by heart. Gokhale showed off his retentive powers by offering to pay an anna for every mistake in recalling what he had memorized. 'Nobody', Srinivasa Sastri wrote, 'made a fortune out of his mistakes.'[4] Gokhale is stated to have memorized the whole of Scott's *Rokeby*, Milton's *Paradise Lost* and the speeches of Edmund Burke and John Bright. Later, when he became a teacher in Poona, he recalled and dictated to his class without any obvious effort passages from newspaper editorials he had glanced through earlier in the day.[5]

[2] Reminiscences of S. B. Dhavle (formerly of the I.C.S., who married Gokhale's daughter, Kashibai) recorded by A.I.R. (tape in NMML).
[3] Reminiscences of D. K. Karve recorded by A.I.R. (tape in NMML).
[4] V. S. S. Sastri, *Life of Gopal Krishna Gokhale*, Bangalore, 1937, p. 5.
[5] R. P. Paranjpye, *Gopal Krishna Gokhale*, Poona, 1915, p. 4.

Gokhale may not have left a lasting impression upon his teachers in Elphinstone College, but they seem to have made a deep impression on him. The lectures on English literature by Principal Wordsworth, the grandson of the poet, and on mathematics by Professor Hawthornwaite fascinated Gopal Gokhale. These two were among the finest Englishmen who ever came out to India; they inspired in their students not only love of English history and literature, but respect for English character. It was in Elphinstone College that Gokhale acquired a taste for English poetry, and cultivated an elegant English style which was to prove a great asset to him in public life.

In the last year of his college career, Gopal won a scholarship of Rs 20 a month. Immediately after taking his B.A. degree, he began to coach students. He utilized his earnings to pay back the loan his brother had incurred to support him in college. The straitened condition of the family finances required that Gopal should stand on his own feet as early as possible. The choice of a profession was, however, not easy. Since Gopal had taken mathematics for his degree course, engineering seemed a logical choice. He joined the engineering college in Bombay, but left it when he found that there were a few brilliant boys in his class. 'There are some devils here', he is reported to have said, 'with whom I may not compete.'[6] This remark could be laughed away as an example of youthful humour, if we did not know that at this stage in his life young Gopal was consumed with a burning desire to excel in everything he attempted with almost a morbid spirit of competition.

A more glittering prize than the engineering profession was the membership of the Indian Civil Service, the *El Dorado* of every ambitious young man in India. The 'heaven-born service' offered Gokhale a dazzling career, but to enter it his family would have to borrow money to enable him to proceed to England for a stiff competitive examination, in which success was by no means certain. The plan for the Civil Service seemed attractive, but impracticable. Gopal's mind then turned to the practice of law. He started attending the law classes at Bombay University. At the end of 1885 he had passed the first law examination and may have qualified as a lawyer, or become a judge, were it not for a sudden and unexpected development which was to alter the course of his life.

In January 1885, Gopal joined the New English School in Poona

[6] Sastri, op. cit., p. 6.

as an assistant master. This school had been set up only five years earlier by a group of young Chitpavan Brahmans who were fired with a missionary zeal to carry English education to the people. The 'Indian Jesuits'—as these young men styled themselves—had taken a vow of lifelong service to the cause of education on what was no more than a subsistence allowance.

The acceptance of a teacher's job in a school at a paltry salary of Rs 35 a month struck Gopal's family as an insane act. Was it for this that his brother, and indeed the whole family, had stinted themselves, suffered hardships and incurred debts? Were Krishnarao Gokhale's hopes for his children to end up in smoke after all? Was Poona to open no more attractive prospects to Gopal than Kagal had done to Govind? Was Gopal to resign himself, his university degree notwithstanding, to that poverty to which his father and brother had been condemned for want of an English education?

Gopal did not take this crucial step of joining the New English School without the deepest heart-searching. While he was a student in the Deccan College, he and his friend, Hari Narayan Apte, had once confided to each other their most cherished ambitions. Apte said he aspired to be a great novelist. 'My ambition', remarked Gokhale, 'is to become a Cabinet Minister so as to be able to serve my country.'[7] For a young man who had set his sights so high, to accept a teacher's post on a pittance would seem utterly incongruous if one did not take into account the new spirit that was animating the mind of Maharashtra in the 1880s under the impact of British rule.

[7] B. M. Ambekar, *Hari Narayan Apte Yanchen Sankshipt Charitra*, Poona, 1922, pp. 91–2.

2

Ferment in Maharashtra

Nearly fifty years before Gokhale's birth the Maratha Confederacy had been overthrown and its territories had passed under the control of the East India Company. The successors of Shivaji lacked the qualities which had enabled him to carve out a kingdom in the Deccan. The Peshwas, who wrested power from the House of Shivaji, made themselves a power in the land, but could not sustain a strong, stable and well-knit administration. In the last phase of the Anglo-Maratha wars the actions of almost all the Maratha chiefs seemed to be dictated more by personal and dynastic ambitions than by patriotism or loyalty to their nominal Chief in Poona. No wonder the Maratha chiefs were defeated one after another and the East India Company emerged as the supreme political power in the Indian sub-continent.

Mountstuart Elphinstone, the British Resident at the Peshwa's court at Poona, who played a prominent part in the concluding stages of the struggle between the British and the Marathas and became the first administrator of the conquered territories, had seen too much of the martial spirit and tenacity of the Marathas to imagine that they would be quickly reconciled to British rule. It was easy enough to depose the Peshwa and pack him off to the village of Bithur on the bank of the Ganges near Kanpur, but it was more difficult to deal with the large ruling caste of Chitpavan Brahmans to which the Peshwas belonged. The Chitpavans had basked in the sunshine of the Peshwas' rule. They had monopolized the best land and the most coveted posts in the state. Since they were also the hereditary religious leaders of the community, they came to dominate the political, religious and social life of Maharashtra. The British were anxious to avoid gratuitous offence to the Chitpavans. Not only were they allowed to keep their lands and given employment under the government, but their peculiar prejudices and vested interests were respected. Nevertheless, throughout the nineteenth century, the British had an almost obsessive fear of an armed rising in Maharashtra. That this fear was not entirely groundless was proved by some of the insurrections which actually occurred.

The first uprising occurred in 1844 at Kolhapur, where the garrison, provoked by an Anglophile but unscrupulous minister, refused to pay revenue. The young princes, the descendants of Shivaji, fearing for their own safety, cast in their lot with the rebels. 'The [East India] Company have taken my Raj [kingdom]', said the Raja, 'and I am to be put under restraint. . . . Therefore now let happen what will, I will not abide under the area of the Company's Sirkar.'[1] The rising was a tame affair. The British Resident was ambushed on his way to Kolhapur, captured by the rebels, but released when British batteries were trained on the fort. Princely pique and the impulsive action of a small garrison proved powerless against the vastly superior British power and organization.

Thirteen years after this short-lived insurrection came the revolt of 1857 which shook the foundations of British rule in northern India. The echoes of the Mutiny were heard in Kolhapur on 31 July 1857 when about two hundred men of the 27th Native Infantry plundered the treasury and attacked the living quarters of British officers. The Europeans in Bombay panicked and some of them even sent their families to England. There was, however, no threat to the British in western India. The Maharaja of Kolhapur remained ostentatiously loyal and the British Resident confidently reported to his superiors: 'In no case has the population or the native chiefs of the Southern Mahratha Country evinced any sympathy with the mutinous spirit which has unhappily pervaded a portion of the native troops in this quarter.'[2] A second uprising a few months later proved no more successful.

A more serious challenge to the British in that critical summer of 1857 came from Nana Saheb, the adopted son of the last Peshwa, who was living at Bithur near Kanpur. He had a long list of personal grievances. His pension had been stopped; he was not allowed to use the seal or title of the Peshwa and was in fact reduced to the status of a commoner, Shrimant Nana Dhondu Pant. He was at first hesitant to join the rebels at Kanpur but later drifted into their leadership; it was perhaps his lack of a firm grip on the situation rather than any calculated cruelty which resulted in the horrible holocaust that ensued at Kanpur. His position as the legal heir of the last

[1] *Source Material for a History of the Freedom Movement in India*, Bombay, 1957, vol. I, p. 66.   [2] Ibid., p. 262.

Peshwa made him the natural leader of a popular uprising in the Deccan. In one of his proclamations he promised to come 'to the Hoozoor at Poonah' and to 'recover the country below the Sahyadree Range (Concan) and the Bombay Presidency and to protect the cows and Brahmins'.[3] His call remained unheeded: the Maratha chiefs, softened by the *Pax Britannica*, were more anxious to safeguard their titles and lands than to embark on risky ventures. Oddly enough, the deposed Peshwa evoked greater sympathy in Kanpur and Gwalior than in Poona and Kolhapur. He ended his days not in the Peshwa's palace at Poona but in the jungles of Nepal.

2

The old feudal order of Maharashtra was played out. The last armed revolt, twenty-two years after the Mutiny, was led not by a member of the princely order but by an obscure Brahman youth, Wasudeo Balwant Phadke. An insight into the working of his mind is given by his autobiography and diary captured by the British. 'My mind turned against the English, and I wished to ruin them. From morning to night, bathing, eating, sleeping, I was brooding over this, and I could get no proper rest. At midnight I used to get up and think how this ruin might be done until I was as one mad.'[4] Phadke learnt to ride, to fence, and to shoot at targets. He collected 'swords, spears, guns, gunpowder, lead and chain armour'. He planned to raise an army and to support it by organizing raids on *banias* and other rich men in the villages. For these raids he formed gangs of Ramoshis, a low-caste tribe which was scattered in parts of Poona and Satara districts—a strong, hardy race, who had in the early days of Maratha power distinguished themselves in forays and sudden attacks on forts and arsenals of the Muslim rulers in the Deccan. Phadke soon discovered that the Ramoshis' motives were different from his own: after they had cut off the ears of the *banias* and looted their cash and silver, they seemed less concerned with the destruction of British rule than with the division of the booty. The hapless Phadke, who was all the while being pursued by a sizable police and military force, sought refuge in a temple. He knew success had eluded him in this world: he prayed for an opportunity to plead for his country in the next.

The robberies organized by Phadke created a considerable stir in

[3] Ibid., p. 256.   [4] Ibid., pp. 82–3.

the Deccan, already in the grip of a serious famine. The Anglo-Afghan war and the events in Europe had created a vague sense of unease and expectancy not only in India but in Whitehall.

Lord Cranbrook, Secretary of State for India to Viceroy, Lord Lytton, 31 March 1879: . . . Sir R. Temple [Governor of Bombay] speaks of some disloyalty at Poona, but I hope it is nothing serious. . . . It must be expected that with such a number of newspapers and rumours our difficulties in Africa and Afghanistan will be exaggerated . . . may indicate a shaken allegiance. . . . Are there any extraneous agencies at work to affect the minds of the natives adversely?[5]

The anxiety of the government was accentuated by the burning of the Peshwa's palace in Poona, a fine historic building which was being used as a public office. There was no knowing what would happen next.

On 21 July 1879 Phadke was arrested, sentenced to transportation for life, taken to Yeravda gaol in Poona and finally to Aden where, after a vain attempt to escape, he died in 1883. His was an extraordinary career. There is no doubt that he had long nursed a personal grievance: the refusal of his superiors in the Military Accounts Office at Poona to grant him leave to see his dying mother. This grievance alone may not, however, fully account for the fierce hatred of British rule which pervaded the words and deeds of this 'mad patriot'. He displayed amazing courage and stamina against heavy odds. Nevertheless, the whole idea of overthrowing the British empire in India with chain-armour, swords and old muskets was quixotic. Phadke was vainly trying to repeat against the British, in the nineteenth century, tactics which two hundred years before had been successfully employed against the Deccan States and the Mughals. Being a 'lone wolf', he posed no real military threat to the British, but he was none the less a disturbing portent. The fact remained that a young unknown Brahman, an ex-accounts clerk with no military experience whatsoever, had been able to hold the Deccan countryside to ransom and tie up sizable police and military forces for nearly three months. What would happen if a more intelligent, resourceful or popular leader emerged and exploited some transitory but real grievance, stirred Maratha pride and harnessed it to a well-designed plot to overthrow British rule? The ovation Phadke had received at Poona railway station[6] in the course of a train journey had alarmed the

---

[5] Cranbrook to Lytton, 31 March 1879 (L.P.).
[6] *History of the Freedom Movement*, p. 77.

authorities. Sir Richard Temple, the Governor of Bombay, under-scored the deeper implications of the Phadke affair:

Sir Richard Temple to Lord Lytton, 3 July 1879:

But nothing that we do now, by way of education, emolument, or advancement in the public service at all satisfies the Chitpavans. They will never be satisfied till they regain their ascendancy as they had it during last century. . . . They esteem it their charter from on high to rule over the minds of the Hindoos. . . . Their past to them—their glorious past—survives in their minds. . . .[7]

9 July 1879

. . . barely sixty years have elapsed since the Chitpavans ceased to be rulers—the memory of all this is still to this day comparatively fresh in the minds of the Natives, fresher far than the memory of most of the great political events of Indian history.

Now the Chitpavan tribe still exists in vigour and prosperity. They are inspired with national sentiment and with an ambition bounded only with the bounds of India itself. . . .

Temple went on to express the fear that gnawed at his heart: just as the Marathas under Brahmanical guidance 'beat the Mahomedan conquerors bit by bit, inch by inch, out of the Deccan', so some day the British would be made 'to retire into that darkness where the Moguls have retired'. Shortly afterwards, in his *Men and Events of My Time in India*, he recalled how with a history book in hand he used to inspect the Western Ghats, 'the lairs, the retreats and strong-holds, in this mountain range', which had sustained Maratha resis-tance, and 'baffled the armaments of the Afghan horse or the artillery of the Great Mogul'.[8] Temple wondered whether these fortresses would one day harbour rebels against the British Raj.

The Phadke rebellion was evidently on Sir Richard's brain, and misled him into looking for rebels against the Raj in the wrong place. The real challenge to the British was to come not from the secret 'lairs, the retreats and strongholds' in the Western Ghats, but from the schools and colleges which were instructing the people in western learning. It is a strange irony that English education, which had been deliberately introduced in Maharashtra by Elphinstone and his successors to wean the people from the old feudal order and to strengthen their loyalty to British rule, produced the very class which was to challenge that rule.

[7] L.P.
[8] *Idem, Men and Events of My Time in India*, London, 1882, pp. 470–1.

3

Emergence of the Educated Élite

Mountstuart Elphinstone, who, as the Commissioner of the Deccan and later as the Governor of Bombay, administered the territories conquered from the Peshwa, was no stranger to the Deccan. For ten years he had served as the British Resident at Poona. He had seen at first hand the authority and prestige enjoyed by the Brahmans, especially the Chitpavan Brahmans, who had a virtual monopoly of the best land and the best jobs under the Peshwas. Elphinstone had little love for the Brahmans. He was sceptical about their loyalty to the new regime and, as a good Christian, detested Brahmanical domination and the 'heathen values' it symbolized. 'I consider', he wrote in 1819, 'the Hindoo religion to be one great cause of the people of this country being so far behind Europeans in laws and morals and I should be very glad to see that obstacle to their improvement removed.'[1] He would have liked the Chitpavans, and indeed the whole Hindu community, to be weaned from ancient beliefs, rituals and traditions which bound them to their political past. Nevertheless, as a seasoned administrator, he knew well the dangers of precipitate action.

Elphinstone tried to make the transition from the old to the new order as painless as possible. He did not go so far as Malcolm, who suggested that the East India Company should declare itself the Peshwa in the Deccan just as sixty years before it had proclaimed itself the Dewan in Bengal. But he did a great deal to placate the upper classes which had directly suffered from the ruin of the Maratha empire. He guaranteed the *watans*, *inams* and allowances already in existence. He did not withdraw temple lands; he continued cash payments to temples and even to individual Brahmans of note who had been patronized by the Peshwa.[2] He decided not to discontinue the annual *Dakshina* festival in which impecunious Brah-

[1] K. Ballhatchet, *Social Policy and Social Change in Western India, 1817–1830*, London, 1957, p. 248.
[2] R. Kumar, *Western India in the Nineteenth Century*, London, 1968, p. 49.

mans assembled in Poona once a year to pass a test in Hindu philosophy and ritual, and receive cash awards from the State. All these concessions derived from a shrewd political calculation.[3] The retention of *Dakshina*, Elphinstone hoped, would attach a powerful group to British rule.

The maintenance of *Dakshina* put the seal of British approval on the privileged status of the Brahmans. The opening of the Poona Hindu College in 1821 was a further sop to them. The professed object of the Hindu College was to educate 'young men of the caste of Brahmins' in the 'several branches of science and knowledge'. Apart from some junior professorships for the Vedas, the college had chairs in *advaita* (philosophy), *shastras* (religion), *vyakaran* (grammar), *nyaya* (logic), *vydic* (medicine), and *alankar* (belles-lettres). That a British administration should set up a college to cater to the needs of the dominant caste of one community and that its curriculum should be exclusively based on Hindu religious and classical learning seemed incongruous, almost incredible, to Elphinstone's critics. He received a sharp rebuke from his superiors in London, but he had his own reasons for appeasing the Brahmans. The Hindu College, he argued, was being set up 'among a most bigoted people whose knowledge has always been in the hands of the priesthood, and whose science itself is considered a branch of religion'.[4] The teaching of Hindu theology in the new college was intended to serve the same purpose as the disbursement of the *Dakshina* funds, i.e. to soothe the wounded pride of the Brahmans, who until recently had been the most privileged class in the land, to disarm their suspicions and assure them that their special status and vested interests would be safeguarded in the new order ushered in by the British.

One of Elphinstone's successors, Robert Grant, complained that the Hindu College preserved and cherished 'the old Brahmanical interest, which is anti-British in all its tendencies'.[5] Elphinstone would not have disputed this verdict, but he considered these arrangements transitional and believed that they could be modified or revoked later. As the memories of the Maratha empire faded and the British grip on the Deccan tightened, Hindu theology could be replaced by western learning, and the *Dakshina* doles could be diverted to scholarships for students of schools and colleges set up

[3] Ballhatchet, op. cit., p. 84.   [4] Kumar, op. cit., p. 50.
[5] Ibid., p. 266.

on the western model. All this had, however, to be done gradually, unobtrusively, almost imperceptibly, so as not to provoke the Brahmans.

The next quarter of a century bore testimony to Elphinstone's prescience. The *Dakshina* and the Hindu College went through the metamorphosis anticipated by him. This metamorphosis was assisted by the opening of the Poona English School in 1832, the products of which became the allies of the British Government in seeking the disestablishment of the institutions preserved by Elphinstone for political expediency. In September 1849 the Bombay Government received a representation from a number of liberal Brahmans protesting against

the old illiberal and barbarous prejudice of confining learning to the Brahmin caste and locking it up in stores which the great mass of the people will never be able or hope to open. . . . What the nation most wants is useful arts, science and morals and they should find them not certainly in the dead Sanskrit, but in the animated English literature.[6]

This protest was reminiscent of Raja Rammohun Roy's famous letter to Lord Amherst in 1823 against establishing 'a Sanskrit School under Hindu Pandits to impart such knowledge as is already current in India . . . to load the minds of youths with grammatical niceties and metaphysical distinctions of little or no practical use to the possessors or to society'. In Maharashtra, as in Bengal, western education found its ardent advocates among its own first beneficiaries.

In the Hindu College, with successive reviews of the curriculum, the emphasis gradually shifted from the metaphysical to the practical. In 1850 it was thrown open to all castes and the Sanskrit professorships were replaced by chairs in English, Marathi and the Sciences.[7] In 1864, forty-three years after it was founded, the Hindu College was renamed the Deccan College, and transformed into an institution wholly devoted to the dissemination of western learning. The *Dakshina* funds, or whatever remained of them, had already been turned over to the Education Department of the Bombay Government for the creation of fellowships to be awarded irrespective of caste and community. The wheel had turned full circle. Secular education had replaced the special provisions for Brahmanical education made in the years immediately after the British conquest, and might

[6] Ibid., p. 272.
[7] *Report of the Board of Education of Bombay for 1850–51.*

well be expected to dry up the dark and mysterious springs from which the Brahmans seemed to draw their unique hold over the minds and hearts of the people. What could be a better lever for detaching the people of Maharashtra from their political past than a secular and western-oriented education, imparted not through the powerful priestly caste but through state-owned schools?

2

The career of Sardar Gopal Hari Deshmukh (1823–83) illustrates the influence of the new education on the first generation of Maharashtrians brought up under British rule. His family of Chitpavan Brahmans, one of the greatest beneficiaries of the Peshwa regime, had suffered heavily from the British conquest and lost its extensive estate. Deshmukh passed through the Poona English School, began life in a humble post under the government and rose to be a judge. The misfortunes of his family did not sour him, nor did they alienate him from the new order. On the contrary, he tried to hasten the process of reconciliation to British rule. One of the founders of the *Dnyanaprakash* of Poona, he was a pioneer of Marathi journalism. He considered the British conquest of Maharashtra fundamentally different from the earlier conquests: the British had finally put an end to anarchy and introduced standards of administration and public life far superior to those of the autocratic and feudal regimes under which the country had suffered for centuries. In *Shatpatre*, a collection of a hundred letters, addressed to the people and published during the years 1848–50 in the columns of the *Prabhakar* of Bombay, Deshmukh expressed his admiration for the new concepts introduced into Indian polity by the British, namely, equality before the law, freedom of speech and worship, and, above all, the maxim that the State existed for the welfare of the people and not for the aggrandizement of a family or a caste. Foreign rule, with all its faults, struck Deshmukh as a necessary stage in the training of the country for self-government. He held up before his compatriots the vision of an Indian parliament, but he argued that the political forms of the West could not be adopted without purging Indian society of outdated ritual, glaring caste inequalities and grievous disabilities imposed on women. If the people of India earnestly set about this task of reformation he predicted that in two to five hundred years India would become an independent nation.

'Lokahitwadi' (the well-wisher of the people), as Gopal Hari Deshmukh came to be called, was not a bold or brilliant thinker. Nevertheless, he represented the first generation of English-educated Maharashtrians who had the courage to reassess traditional concepts and institutions in the light of western ideas.

A more notable product of early western education was Vishvanath Narayan Mandlik (1833–89). Ten years younger than Gopal Hari Deshmukh, he was also well-born: his family was related to the last Peshwa and his ancestors had held high office in the Maratha empire. He learnt English in the school at Ratnagiri and at the age of fourteen, joined the Elphinstone Institution in Bombay. His English teachers were impressed by his exceptional intelligence and advised him to go to England and sit for the Indian Civil Service examination. Foreign travel was, however, severely frowned upon by the Chitpavan community and Mandlik had to start his career with a low-paid job in the office of the British Agent in Sind. He won the instant appreciation of his superiors and held a number of responsible posts. By 1862 he felt he had had enough of government service, resigned from it, qualified as a lawyer and forged his way to the forefront of the Bombay Bar. In 1877, he was appointed to the coveted post of 'Government Pleader', which he continued to hold till his death in 1896.

Mandlik was not merely a successful lawyer. At twenty-six, he started *Native Opinion* and edited it for seven years. He had a flair for languages; during his stay in Sind he picked up enough of the local language to publish a grammar of Sindhi dialects. He acquired enough Gujarati to translate into it Elphinstone's *History of India*. In his native Marathi he published a great deal of original work as well as translations. His manual of Hindu Law included an authentic edition of *Yajnawalkya Smriti* and *Nilakantha*—the two authorities on the Hindu civil law of western India—with English translations and notations, and was a notable contribution to Hindu jurisprudence. He built up a splendid library of his own and published, at his own expense, a selection from the transactions of the Bombay Literary Society, which later developed into the Royal Asiatic Society. He became the first Indian Fellow of the Bombay University, a member of the Governor of Bombay's Legislative Council and of the Governor-General's Legislative Council. In the council chamber he was noted for his dignity and independence; he dealt with each bill on its merits, criticizing the government when it was necessary.

As a 'Government Pleader', he could not take part in nationalist politics, and his political views were somewhat subdued. On issues of social reform, such as the Age of Consent Bill, he took a conservative stand diametrically opposed to that of many leaders of the educated classes.

One of Mandlik's younger contemporaries, Kashinath Trimbak Telang (1850–93), resembled him in combining a first-rate intellect with prodigious industry, but unlike Mandlik, he was a protagonist of social reform and (until his appointment as a judge of the Bombay High Court) an ardent and vocal nationalist. Telang was a child prodigy; when he joined the Elphinstone High School at the age of nine, his proficiency in chess was as remarkable as his scholastic attainments. At fourteen he entered the Elphinstone College and instantly won the high appreciation of his English professors. He was an outstanding member of the debating society and a voracious reader; rumour had it that he knew the position of every book on the shelves of the college library. He never forgot the debt he owed to Principal Jefferson of the Elphinstone School and Professor Chatfield of the Elphinstone College. He put himself through a rigorous intellectual regimen. He devoured the works of Plato, J. S. Mill and Herbert Spencer. After taking his Master's degree, he qualified as a lawyer and started practice at the Bombay Bar, of which he came to be recognized as one of the leaders. He succeeded in combining a lucrative legal career with scholarly pursuits. Elected president of the Bombay branch of the Royal Asiatic Society, he contributed papers to the *Indian Antiquary*. He made a name for himself as a Sanskrit scholar, translated the *Bhagavad Gita* into English verse, and refuted the thesis of a European scholar that the story of the *Ramayana* was derived from Homer. On social reform, he took up a militant line, favouring legislative action to curb chronic evils like infant marriage. He wrote on political and economic issues, and during the bitter controversies of the Ripon regime, supported the Ilbert Bill. He was the secretary of the Bombay Association and one of the founders of the Bombay Presidency Association as well as of the Indian National Congress, in the proceedings of which he took a prominent part.

A distinguished scholar and man of letters, a brilliant lawyer and speaker, a shrewd politician and an able legislator, Telang towered above his contemporaries. We have a remarkable pen-picture of him drawn by Chief Justice Westropp of the Bombay High Court in a letter to the Governor of Bombay in 1880 when Telang had not yet turned thirty.

An Advocate of the High Court, an accomplished scholar and a thorough gentleman, a favourite of the Bar and Bench and a Brahman, who is in short the best native gentleman whom we know. He is a sound lawyer and especially well versed in Hindu Law which his wide knowledge of Sanskrit has enabled him to study in its original sources. . . . He is a good and candid logician, and so perfect in his knowledge of English, that in addressing the Court he surpasses several of our English Barristers in the style and choice of his language—yet he has never been out of India . . . .[8]

Telang, like Gopal Hari Deshmukh and Mandlik, represented the cream of the educated élite of Maharashtra. They came from different social strata: Deshmukh and Mandlik from old aristocratic families, Telang from the middle class. But they found in education a social leveller. They drank deep from the fountain of western culture and found it an exhilarating experience. It sharpened their consciousness of the past, shed a new light on some of the age-old evils and enabled them to take a fresh and critical look at the social problems of their time; it inspired in them the vision of a bright future for their country. To their credit it must be said that they were not so intoxicated by western ideas as to be alienated from their ancestral religion and culture. Unlike some of their counterparts in Bengal, the educated classes of Maharashtra did not ape western dress, food or mode of life. Their appreciation of western literature did not affect their attachment to Sanskrit classics; they read the *Ramayana* with the same enthusiasm as the *Odyssey*; they enjoyed the *abhangas* of Tukaram and the poetry of Tennyson with equal gusto. English education they found to be a liberating force. English philosophers, particularly John Stuart Mill and Herbert Spencer, armed them with arguments with which they could challenge the shibboleths of an entrenched priesthood and the claims of an alien and all-powerful bureaucracy. Herbert Spencer with his revolutionary theory of social change derived from Darwin, and J. S. Mill with his advocacy of popular education, emancipation of women, and state-intervention in social and economic spheres provided to Indian intellectuals growing up in the 1860s and 1870s the same inspiration which Marx, Lenin and Sartre have provided to the intellectual *avant-garde* in our time.

[8] Home Dept., Jud., Aug. 1880, Nos. 203–5 (NAI).

3

The path of the educated élite, lying as it did between the Scylla of popular opposition and the Charybdis of official distrust, was not easy. This is best illustrated by the career of Mahadev Govind Ranade (1842–1901), the maturest, the most prescient and probably the most influential Maharashtrian of his time.

Born in 1842, Ranade went to school at Kolhapur. His luckiest break came when he was sent at the age of fourteen to the Elphinstone High School in Bombay. For the next ten years he was nurtured on the best fare that western education in India could provide. His intellectual appetite seemed insatiable; in the words of D. E. Wacha, a contemporary at the Elphinstone Institution, he was seen 'wholly absorbed in writing his weekly essay or reading aloud his Grote and Gibbon, his Hume and Macaulay, his Locke and Hamilton'.[9] His English professors were delighted to see a young Indian scholar acquire a quick proficiency in subjects which were being taught for the first time in western India and in a foreign language. He was one of the twenty-one students who passed the first matriculation examination held by Bombay University in 1859.

Ranade's college record was outstanding. Even before he graduated in 1862, he had become a Fellow of Elphinstone College: the annual report of the College for 1862–3 referred to him as 'a Hindu student of superior calibre'. For a few months, while a student, he edited the English section of the *Indu Prakash*, an Anglo-Marathi paper of Bombay. In 1864 at the age of twenty-two he was awarded his M.A. degree. The following year he was appointed a Fellow of the Bombay University. Two years later he passed the law examination with flying colours, but decided to take a job under the government rather than practise at the Bar. He held a number of appointments: oriental translator to the Government of Bombay, administrator of Akalkot, judge in Kolhapur State, professor of English and History in the Elphinstone College, judge of the Small Causes Court at Bombay. And finally, in 1871, at the age of twenty-nine, he was posted at Poona as 'First Class First Grade Sub-Judge'. About this time he wrote an introduction to the speeches of Sir Bartle Frere, a former Governor of Bombay, in which he paid a tribute to him as one of the few British rulers of India who had in the post-Mutiny decade given proof of the 'generous ambition to help the native population to

[9] J. Kellock, *Mahadev Govind Ranade*, Calcutta, 1926, pp. 10–11.

elevate themselves, to teach them self-reliance and the strength of lawful combination'.[10] To Ranade the British conquest of India was not a calamity to be lamented, but an opportunity to be seized. Under foreign rule, the scope for individual ambition had undoubtedly narrowed, but opportunities for realization of national aspirations had immeasurably widened. The British nation, argued Ranade, had its own 'faults and foibles', but its character had been 'formed by ages of struggle and self-discipline which illustrates better than any other contemporary power the supremacy of the reign of law'.[11] He discerned a 'moral element' in the British people which 'inspires hope and confidence in colonies and dependencies of Great Britain that whatever temporary perturbation may cloud the judgment, the reign of law will assert itself in the end'.[12]

Looking back at the history of his own country, Ranade could not help feeling that both Hindus and Muslims lacked many of those 'virtues represented by the love of order and regulated authority'. Both had been lacking in the 'love of Municipal freedom, in the exercise of virtues necessary for civic life, and in aptitudes for mechanical skill, in the love of science and research, in the love and daring of adventurous discovery, the resolution to master difficulties, and in chivalrous respect for womankind'.[13] The British connection was thus part of a disciplining process, coming as it did through 'the example and teaching of the most gifted and free nation in the world'.[14] Under the impact of the forces released by English rule, India was being roused from the stupor of the ages; there were forces at work for social, economic and political reconstruction which could bring her on a level with the advanced countries of the West. In this reconstruction Ranade saw the guiding hand of God in history.[15]

We may smile today at this belief in a 'Divine dispensation' linking the destinies of India and England. But to the English-educated who had grown up in the middle of the nineteenth century, British imperialism did not appear in the same light as it does to us. They were close enough to the pre-British era in India not to romanticize it. The divisions and disorders of the eighteenth century were hard

---

[10] B. N. Pitale (ed.), *Speeches and Addresses of Sir H. B. E. Frere*, Bombay, 1870, pp. vii–viii.

[11] *The Mahratta*, 4 July 1897.   [12] Ibid.

[13] *The Miscellaneous Writings of the late Hon'ble Mr. Justice M. G. Ranade*, Bombay, 1915, p. 226.

[14] Ibid., p. 117.   [15] Ibid., p. 126.

facts in the living memory of men who had seen them, or heard about them from their parents. Bipin Chandra Pal, the fiery leader of Indian nationalism in the first decade of the twentieth century, has left it on record that in the 1860s village urchins in Bengal, when attacked by their playmates, used to cry out for protection from the East India Company: 'Dohai Company Bahadur'.[16] *Pax Britannica* in its literal sense was not just a British conceit but an article of faith with many educated Indians in the latter half of the nineteenth century.

It is significant that during the Phadke 'rebellion' in the summer of 1879, far from encouraging subversion (as suspected by British officials) Ranade detected and handed over to the authorities the young man who had set fire to the Peshwa's palace. Ranade, and indeed the entire educated class whom he represented, was convinced that violence could do India no good. They had no desire to return to what they believed to be the bad old days of the eighteenth century. They pinned their hopes for progress on the gradual extension of education and the adoption of western political methods rather than on the incalculable hazards of a violent upheaval.

Foreign rule appeared to them not only the cause but the consequence of the evils from which India had suffered in the past. The problem, as they saw it, was one of reactivating an ancient but ossified civilization which had been cut off for centuries from an invigorating contact with the rest of the world. In Gokhale's words, Ranade saw that

An ancient race had come in contact with another; possessing a more vigorous, if a somewhat more materialistic, civilization, and if we did not want to be altogether submerged or overwhelmed, it was necessary for us to assimilate what was noble and what was vigorous in the new influences operating upon us, preserving at the same time what was good and noble in our own system.[17]

The transition was to be (to quote Ranade) 'from constraint to freedom, from credulity to faith, from status to contract, from authority to reason, from unorganized life to organized life, from bigotry to toleration, from blind fatalism to a sense of human dignity'.[18] This was an ambitious programme. Its pursuit was to

[16] B. C. Pal, *Memories of My Life and Times*, Calcutta, 1932, p. 292.
[17] D. G. Karve & D. V. Ambekar (eds.), *Speeches and Writings of Gopal Krishna Gokhale*, Bombay, 1967, vol. III, pp. 295–6.
[18] *Miscellaneous Writings of M. G. Ranade*, pp. 116–17.

bring Ranade into collision not only with his own people, but with the British authorities.

Ranade thought deeply and wrote copiously on the history, economic conditions and politics of his country. He did not however live in an academic ivory tower. He had a strong practical bent and recognized that no real progress was possible without the right men and the right institutions. During the twenty years he spent in Poona he founded, inspired or supported a number of organizations. These included a girls' high school, a library, a town hall, a museum, a bank, a paper mill, a cotton and silk factory, an arbitration court for the settlement of disputes and a society for the encouragement of Marathi literature. He was one of the founders of the Indian National Congress and attended its sessions even though his position as a judge prevented him from openly participating in its proceedings. In the inner circle of the Congress leadership, he was a highly respected figure. He was the founder of the Indian Social Conference and its chief inspiration for more than fourteen years. He guided the Poona Sarvajanik Sabha, wrote most of the articles published in its quarterly journal and drafted most of its memorials and representations. He was active in the Bombay University, in the Deccan Education Society, and in the Industrial Conference.

Not all of these activities were palatable to British officials. His presence in Poona gave a new lease to political life in that historic town; his intellect, industry and integrity combined to give him a unique influence. He seemed indefatigable, incorruptible and imperturbable. The interest which the Sarvajanik Sabha took in investigating and ventilating the grievances of the Deccan peasantry in 1873 made the government suspect that a new and powerful weapon of political agitation was being forged under Ranade's inspiration. The fact that he was a Chitpavan Brahman was enough to cast doubts on his bona fides; these doubts were the deepest during the disturbances of 1879 when he was transferred in quick succession from Poona to Nasik and from Nasik to Dhulia.

How deep the official distrust of Ranade was may be judged from the comments made on 16 June 1880 by E. W. Ravenscroft, a member of the Executive Council of the Governor of Bombay, when Ranade was being considered for promotion as the 'Joint Judge' of Thana.

This gentleman [wrote E. W. Ravenscroft] is well-known as a man of acute intellect and deep reading and as a man who performs his

judicial work to the full satisfaction of the High Court. He is, however, much better known amongst his educated countrymen and
those officials whose duty it is to make themselves acquainted with
the feelings and sentiments of men of notoriety, as a man possessed
of very strong, national patriotic feelings in the native acceptance
of the term, which he is at no pains to conceal. The position which
in fact he holds amongst his countrymen here and the views he
entertains are professed by Mr Parnell in Ireland, and in short he is
in the Deccan what Mr Parnell is in Ireland, a strong Home Ruler.[19]

Ravenscroft went on to describe Ranade as the 'Hampden of the
Deccan', and quoted the opinion of a former Governor of Bombay,
Sir Richard Temple, of Ranade as a 'dangerous man'. The danger
was (wrote Ravenscroft) that 'dozens of Ranades possessed of his
strong nationalistic feeling, but without his polished intellect and
prudence, would spring up like mushrooms and sooner or later,
sentimental patriotism and ardent love of the "good old days" of
the Peshwas would develop in the person of a second Wassudeo
Balvant Fadke into active widespread treason'. Ravenscroft's strictures seem to have had their effect; the recommendation of the Chief
Justice of the Bombay High Court for Ranade's promotion, even
though it was backed by Sir James Fergusson, the Governor, was
rejected by the Government of India.

To senior British officials, Ranade was a 'dangerous man', and a
serious political risk. Curiously enough, to the rising generation of
Maharashtrian youth in the late 1870s it appeared that Ranade and
his friends were not going far or fast enough. English education and
knowledge of public affairs were still confined to a microscopic
minority; the mass of the people remained almost untouched by the
new ideas; if there was progress, it was at a snail's pace. It was this
feeling of dissatisfaction with the existing state of affairs that drove
a few angry young men of Poona to take an initiative which was to
profoundly influence the public life of Maharashtra and the career
of Gopal Krishna Gokhale.

[19] Home Dept., Jud., Aug. 1880, 203–5 (NAI).

4

The Indian Jesuits

The summer of 1879 was a turbulent one for India. A terrible famine, the result of repeated failures of the monsoon, was ravaging the land; the pent-up tensions of the viceroyalty of Lord Lytton seemed to have reached the breaking point. There was a crisis in Anglo-Afghan relations; three British armies were in Afghanistan, heading for a disaster, the echoes of which were to reverberate throughout the sub-continent. The imperial bombast of Lord Lytton was wearing thin; the racial slant of his policies particularly towards the vernacular press was too obvious to be missed by the Indian educated classes.

Throughout the summer, a series of mysterious dacoities had been taking place in the villages of Maharashtra; the troops and the police were hot on the trail of the 'rebels' led by Phadke; the countryside was tense.[1] It was during these anxious weeks that a group of young men were seen engaged in heated discussions in the hostel of Poona's Deccan College. One of them was Bal Gangadhar Tilak. His family had come to Poona in 1867 from Ratnagiri—the home town of Chitpavan Brahmans. He had lost his father in 1872; four years later in 1876 he graduated in the first division with mathematics as one of his subjects. He was an intelligent student, but no bookworm; he seemed more in his element in the gymnasium and in the swimming pool than in the classroom. Robust and radiant, he cut lectures when he pleased, ate heartily and seemed to enjoy himself thoroughly. He was rather taciturn and had a caustic wit which could cut his victims to the quick. His friends nicknamed him Mr Blunt.

One of Tilak's best friends in the Deccan College was Gopal Ganesh Agarkar. They were of almost the same age, but life had treated them differently. Unlike Tilak, Agarkar had a poor physique and was subject to bouts of illness. Unlike Tilak, who had inherited a sizable patrimony from his father, Agarkar had lived in grinding poverty from early childhood. At the age of twelve, Agarkar had to give up school and take up a job. Indeed, were it not for the generos-

[1] See chap. 2, pp. 3–6.

ity of a relative at Akola, he would not have been able to resume his studies. He passed the matriculation examination in 1875; three years later he graduated. While at the Deccan College, he possessed just one shirt which he washed every night.

Despite the differences in their background and temperament, Tilak and Agarkar felt very close to each other. They shared a spirit of adventure as they stood on the threshold of life. Unlike most young men of their age, they were preoccupied not with their own future, but with the future of their country. They were 'men with their brains in fever heat with the thoughts of the degraded condition of the country'. They felt the humiliation of foreign rule, criticized the policies of British officials, and had nothing but scorn for (what seemed to them) the halting and feeble policies of the leaders of the educated classes in India. They felt outraged by the subservience of the titled gentry, the diffidence of the intelligentsia, the passivity of the masses and the conceit of the Anglo-Indian administrators. They were convinced that India could build a future for herself by the efforts of her own people, and that the initiative for this had to come from the educated classes. The government had done something for English education; it had opened schools and colleges, but they were too few, and already there were signs that its commitments, particularly for higher education, might be reduced. Moreover, how could western education be a liberating force in India if it was directed by the officers of an alien government? The obvious solution was to provide Indian enterprise and management in education, to design it solely for Indian needs and interests, and to free it from the fetters of official control.

Tilak and Agarkar persuaded two other young men, Bhagwat and Karandikar, to join them in opening a private school in Poona. A high school unaided by the government seemed a risky, almost quixotic venture. Where was the money to come from? Even if the financial difficulty was partly solved by the teachers agreeing to work at a subsistence rather than at the market wage in the spirit of Jesuit missionaries, could parents be persuaded to send their children to a new school started by impecunious and inexperienced young men whose prime asset seemed to be their optimism? Clearly, without influential auspices, the school could not even be started. Tilak and Agarkar decided to canvass support for their project. They approached Ranade and found him sympathetic. Ranade's friends warned him of the risks of backing raw young men whose sense of

responsibility was an unknown quantity; at least one of whom—
Tilak—had been connected with the *Deccan Star*, a Poona paper,
which specialized in sniping at British officers and Indian social
reformers. Would it not be embarrassing if the new school revealed
a similar bias? Ranade's reply to his sceptical friends was characteristic: for the first time a few young men had come forward to devote
themselves wholly to public work; what they deserved was hearty
approbation and not a critical appraisal of their possible shortcomings.[2] Had Ranade himself not been under a cloud in the summer
of 1879, it is possible he would have given more tangible assistance
to Tilak and Agarkar.

Fortunately for Tilak and Agarkar, Vishnu Chiplunkar, an experienced teacher and well-known Marathi journalist, had at almost
the same time decided to resign his job in the Ratnagiri Government
School and to open a publishing house, a printing press and a school
in Poona. The son of Krishna Shastri Chiplunkar, an eminent Maharashtrian scholar and social reformer, Vishnu Chiplunkar was born
in 1850, graduated in 1871, and, thanks to his father's influence,
secured a job in the Poona High School. As a teacher, he was a
square peg in a round hole; he lectured over the heads of his students;
his unpunctuality and disregard of the school curriculum were the
despair of his headmaster, M. M. Kunte. A friend tried to console
Kunte by pointing out that Vishnu Chiplunkar, though an indifferent
teacher, was a great scholar. 'Some people pass for scholars', replied
Kunte, 'because their fathers are learned.' Kunte paid heavily for
this *bon mot*; he became a butt of ridicule in the *Nibandh Mala*, a
Marathi magazine, which Vishnu Chiplunkar had started. For the
first few years the magazine, almost entirely written by Chiplunkar,
dealt only with literary themes. Chiplunkar fancied he was doing
for Marathi literature in the nineteenth century what Dr Samuel
Johnson had done for English literature in the eighteenth. His
Marathi style, with its rhetorical and colourful prose, was consciously modelled after Macaulay. He wanted to infuse something of
the sharpness, vigour and flexibility of the English language into
Marathi prose. 'The English language', he wrote, 'is the nourishing
mother of the Marathi tigress.'

In one of his essays on the poet Moropant, Chiplunkar hit out at
all those who had criticized the poet: these critics included not only

[2] N. Chandavarkar's reminiscences, 'An Appreciation', pub. in *Indian Social
Reformer*, 20 Aug. 1920.

European missionaries, Indian social reformers, but even his own father, Krishna Chiplunkar, and the great Ranade. The barbed wit of Vishnu Chiplunkar delighted his readers: he discovered a short-cut to popularity in Marathi journalism. The *Nibandh Mala* gained in prestige and influence. The magazine acquired an aggressively nationalistic slant. Chiplunkar lamented the condition of India and her progressive deterioration under foreign rule. He recognized that a successful armed revolt was impossible, but trusted to the power of 'the pen and the tongue' to rouse the people of India from their stupor. He rejected the thesis that there was no alternative to British rule and that the British alone could teach the arts of peace and war to the Indian people. He deplored the tendency of English education to sap the faith of the people in their inherited religion and culture. He appealed to the conservative instincts of the people, recalled the glorious days of Maratha hegemony, and ridiculed those who had been swept off their feet by alien influences and presumed to reform Hindu society. His reasoning, anti-British and anti-reformist, laced with biting irony, formed a delectable mixture which made *Nibandh Mala* the most popular journal and Vishnu Chiplunkar the most admired editor in Maharashtra.

For Tilak and Agarkar the availability of a man of Chiplunkar's status and experience was a godsend. Though he spoke of 'kicking off the chains', Chiplunkar's reasons for resignation from government service were largely personal. He was unhappy with his posting to the school at Ratnagiri, and wanted to settle in Poona. He had thought of opening a school, though not one run in a missionary spirit. However, when Agarkar and Tilak placed their proposal before him, he readily agreed to join them. It was Chiplunkar who issued the prospectus of the new school. As an experienced teacher and noted writer, his association with the new institution was a decided asset to it.

2

On 1 January 1880, the New English School was opened at Poona. Such was the scepticism about the success of the venture that the two young graduates, Bhagwat and Karandikar, who had agreed to join Agarkar and Tilak, backed out at the eleventh hour; they were not sure that the school would be able to provide them with even a bare subsistence. These misgivings were belied by events. The school charged lower fees than its established rival, the Government-owned Poona High School, but it was soon able to pay its way. It started with 35 pupils; the number rose within a year to 336; in 1882 it was 501, and reached the impressive figure of 1009 in 1885.[3] The examination results were highly satisfactory. The Jugonnath Sunkersett Sanskrit Scholarships were consistently won by the students of the New English School. In September 1882, Dr W. W. Hunter, who headed the Bombay Provincial Committee of the Education Commission, paid an extraordinary compliment to the school after an inspection: 'Throughout the whole of India, I have not yet witnessed a single institution of this nature. Without receiving any aid from the Government, it can rival and compete with success not only with Government High Schools in this country but with other countries as well.' The Private Secretary to Sir James Fergusson, the Governor of Bombay, congratulated the school on its excellent results in the matriculation examination. In February 1884, Fergusson himself presided over the annual prize-distribution ceremony and personally endowed a prize.

The credit for the success of the school was really due to V. S. Apte (1858–92), a brilliant scholar and a capable administrator, who was the first superintendent of the school. V. K. Chiplunkar was of course the nominal head of the institution. 'A man with a large turban and short phrases' (as an old student recalled him), Chiplunkar had little aptitude for teaching, and even less for administration. We have it on the authority of his brother that he did not even read the *Times of India*, and that all the knowledge of the outside world he possessed was derived from the columns of the Poona Marathi paper, the *Dnyan Prakash*. Chiplunkar was not cut out for a role in public life. Even in the New English School he had taken a back seat before his untimely death in 1882.

The success of the New English School encouraged its founders to establish 'the Deccan Education Society' to administer it and to set up more schools and colleges on similar lines. On 24 October 1884, at a meeting held in Poona, it was resolved:

As the managers of the New English School and other sympathizers with private education think it desirable to have a society to promote the cause of private education and to put it on a more extended basis in order to give permanence to it, it is desirable that

---

[3] P. M. Limaye (ed.), *The History of the Deccan Education Society, 1880–1935*, Poona, 1935, pt. I, pp. 5–6.

a society should be established for the aforesaid purpose, and that it be called the Deccan Education Society.[4]

The society was intended to promote 'the cause of private independent education, adapted to the wants of the community, and so cheapened as to come within the reach of children of even the lower middle class'. The first Governing Council of the Society included such well-known figures as Ranade, Telang, Bhandarkar and William Wedderburn of the Indian Civil Service. On 2 January 1885 a college was formally inaugurated under the auspices of the Deccan Education Society by Wordsworth, the Principal of the Elphinstone College, Bombay. It was named after the retiring Governor, Sir James Fergusson, who laid the foundation-stone of the building on 5 March 1885.

The formation of the Deccan Education Society and the opening of the Fergusson College were important landmarks not only in the history of education in Maharashtra, but also in the life of Gopal Krishna Gokhale. We have already seen how, soon after his graduation, he had weighed his prospects in different professions—in law, engineering and the civil service—and finally opted in January 1885 for the humble post of a teacher in the New English School. In June 1886 he enrolled himself as a life-member of the Deccan Education Society and thus pledged himself to serve it for twenty years at a subsistence wage.

There was a strong streak of personal ambition in Gokhale since his childhood, but it was also accompanied by a strong susceptibility to hero-worship. The trial and imprisonment of Agarkar and Tilak in the Barve case[5] thrilled him in 1882, while he was still a student; he acted in a benefit performance in his college to raise funds for the defence of these two brave men whose names had become household words in Maharashtra.

In the latter half of 1884 when Gokhale was in Poona, he saw something of Agarkar and Tilak at work; his admiration for them fanned his youthful idealism and drowned the voice of his own ambition and the warnings of his family.

The decision to turn his back on personal ambition and to embrace

[4] Ibid., pt. I, p. 54.
[5] Certain letters purported to have been written by Barve, the Diwan of Kolhapur State, published in the *Mahratta*, proved to be forgeries. Barve, assailed in the *Mahratta* and *Kesari* for irksome restrictions on the freedom of the Kolhapur prince, sued Agarkar and Tilak for defamation. They apologized, but were sentenced to four months' simple imprisonment.

a life of voluntary poverty as a member of the Deccan Education
Society could not have been easy for the twenty year-old Gokhale.
There were of course possible compensations in such an act of renunciation, which a friend of Gokhale discerned with remarkable
prescience even at that time.

V. H. Kanilkar to G. K. Gokhale, 20 September 1886: . . . I am very
glad to learn too that a friend of mine, spurning at [*sic*] wealth and
power and such other things . . . has placed himself into the most
honourable pursuit of serving one's country. . . . In my opinion
. . . you have made good choice. . . . I hope I shall live to see you
in possession of that distinction which men like you are destined to
attain and which you have already given some promise of attaining
in the world . . . . [6]

Gokhale's own letter to which this was a reply has not survived. But
it is significant that his friend recognized not only Gokhale's immediate sacrifice, but the new vistas which were to open to him in the
not too distant future.

3

The cooperation of Agarkar and Tilak was a vital factor in the
foundation of the Deccan Education Society. The two friends jointly
ran the *Kesari* and the *Mahratta*; and were co-accused in a suit filed
by Barve, the Diwan of Kolhapur. The three months they spent together in Dongri Jail seemed to have set the seal of common suffering, almost of martyrdom, on their heads. They were honoured as
young men who had the courage of their convictions. At the annual
function of the Deccan College in 1885, Agarkar, supported by Tilak,
assailed the plea of the learned orientalist R. G. Bhandarkar for a
'culture of religion'. Religion, argued Agarkar, was not an essential
part of culture; it was no use frittering away energy on such discussions. Ranade intervened in the debate, and, without naming Agarkar
and Tilak, deplored the tendency in the younger generation to be
misled into agnosticism under the influence of western writers, such
as Mill and Spencer.

Agarkar made no effort to conceal his agnosticism. One of his
students has recorded how, in the course of a lecture on logic, he
explained anthropomorphism. 'If the donkeys were to paint their own
God,' he asked the students, 'what do you think the picture would be

[6] V. H. Kanilkar to Gokhale, 20 Sept. 1886 (G.P.).

like?' Without waiting for an answer, he raised both his hands above his ears and shook them, 'suggesting the long shaky ears of a donkey God!'[7] It is not surprising that the students of the Fergusson College should have acquired among the devout an odour of irreligion. V. R. Shinde, who was in the college in the early 1890s, recalled many years later that when he introduced himself as a 'Fergussonian' to Pandita Ramabai, the Christian reformer, she exclaimed, 'Oh! you come from that atmosphere of Atheism'.[8]

Agarkar's was a rational mind, nurtured on Mill and Spencer. He would not accept a compromise on principle, however uncomfortable the repercussions might be. When his mother died in November 1890, he defied the time-honoured custom of shaving his head and moustaches as a mark of mourning. 'It would be a shame', he wrote, 'for the editor of the *Sudharak* to do so.'[9] He made a frontal assault on Hindu orthodoxy, challenged its cherished beliefs and questioned the value of its ancient rituals. His denunciations of the caste system, untouchability and infant marriage were merciless. He could not see why a Hindu widow should be denied the privilege of putting the 'kumkum' mark on her forehead. He advocated co-education and jobs for women on the same terms as for men. He died young in 1895 at the age of 39, but so modern was his outlook that he would have felt perfectly at home in contemporary India.

In politics Agarkar was a thoroughgoing radical. 'If the greed of the Government grows boundless', he wrote in the *Sudharak*, 'and the poverty of the people becomes unbearable, the grand superstructure of the Government built by the English in India is sure to tumble down.'[10] In 1891, he suggested that the Indian National Congress should demand an Indian House of the People on the model of the British House of Commons.[11] He conceded that it was not easy to shake off the foreign yoke, but predicted that if the worst came to the worst, the English would rather renounce political control than lose their trade with India.[12] He did not set much store by the English Liberals, who seemed to him as much committed to the cause of the empire as the Tories. He was convinced that the people of India would have to depend upon themselves for their salvation:

[7] Limaye (ed.), op. cit., pt. II, p. 130.
[8] Ibid., pt. II, p. 131.
[9] G. G. Agarkar to his uncle, 25 Nov. 1890 (Agarkar P.).
[10] M. D. Altekar (ed.), *Sampuran Agarkar, Nibandh Sangraha*, pt. III, Poona, 1940, p. 137.
[11] *Sudharak*, 28 Dec. 1891.
[12] G. P. Pradhan (ed.), *Agarkar Lekh Sangraha*, New Delhi, 1960, p. 297.

'their own prejudices were to be uprooted, their superstitions eradicated, their courage strengthened, their weaknesses conquered—in fact their character re-formed so as to suit the spirit of the age'.[13]

Agarkar's political views were radical, but he exercised little political influence. His poor health barely enabled him to cope with his teaching and journalistic chores. He rarely attended a public meeting; his attendance at the annual Congress session was erratic, and he made little impression on the politics of his time.

In education and social reform, where Agarkar's interest chiefly lay, he was embroiled in bitter controversies which sapped his strength and shortened his life. His chief antagonist was Tilak, fellow-founder of the New English School; Tilak endorsed Agarkar's radicalism in politics, but not in social matters. The *Kesari*, the editing of which was their joint responsibility, began to reflect their differences in signed articles. However, the arrangement did not work, and in 1887 Agarkar broke off his connection with the *Kesari* and the *Mahratta*. He started a new paper, the *Sudharak* (The Reformer), in the following year. The *Sudharak* was bilingual: the Marathi section was edited by Agarkar, and the English section by Gokhale, who by then had become a close friend and *protégé* of Agarkar. The war of words which had first started in a subdued tone in the columns of the *Kesari* henceforth raged with unmitigated fury in the rival papers. Agarkar and Tilak were both masters of Marathi prose, and especially of the hard-hitting phrase. Tilak described Agarkar as a 'dog in the neighbouring haystacks'. Agarkar in 'an open letter to the orthodox' in the *Sudharak* in 1892 charged that Tilak did not believe in the social orthodoxies to which he paid lip service, and was only trimming his sails to catch the winds of popularity.

From Agarkar's personal papers it appears that he had developed a deeply ingrained distrust of his former friend and colleague. When the *Kesari* criticized the activities of Pandita Ramabai's 'Sharda Sadan', Agarkar confided to a relative: 'It is very unfortunate that an intelligent man like Tilak swayed by other motives has been doing everything to malign that most useful institution.'

Serious as the differences on problems of social reform were, the rupture between Tilak and Agarkar would not have occurred but for the personal antagonism which made it impossible for them to co-exist in the Deccan Education Society.

[13] Limaye (ed.), op. cit., pt. III, app., pp. 1–29.

4

We have Tilak's version of the dispute in the long letter he wrote on 15 December 1890,[14] two months after he resigned from the Deccan Education Society. He took his position on the high ground of principle. He protested against the tendency of the members to deviate from the ideals for which the Society had been founded. He accused his colleagues of supplementing their income by 'outside sources', and of succumbing to temptations, such as writing textbooks and dabbling in journalism and politics.

Agarkar did not accept that most of the members of the Deccan Education Society were guilty of backsliding. It was all very well for Tilak to speak of the original founders of the New English School and the Deccan Education Society as 'Jesuits', but the analogy could not be pushed too far.

The vow of Jesuitic poverty [wrote Agarkar] is impracticable for married men belonging to the Hindu community, with their un-defined family obligations to relations far and near, and in claiming for life members the freedom to supplement their salaries, by extra earnings, they were facing the situation in a spirit of realism. No Jesuit is a married man; no Jesuit has private property, nor is he allowed to have any; the Jesuits have a common mess and they lodge in a common house. Above all, they are a religious body in which free thought is strictly forbidden.

Agarkar believed that Tilak was animated less by principles than by personal animosities. Tilak's opposition to Agarkar's proposal for an increase of Rs 5 per month in the salary of the life-members of the Deccan Education Society left a bad taste in his mouth. Agarkar suspected that Tilak had gone out of his way to deprive him of his share in a purse of Rs 700 granted by Maharaja Holkar of Indore. As for the charge of supplementing income from 'outside sources', Agarkar argued that Tilak could well deprecate it as he was quite well off, having inherited property from his father. As for textbooks, almost all members who could, had tried their hands at writing them. Apte had compiled a Sanskrit dictionary, Agarkar had written on Marathi syntax, Gokhale on arithmetic, and Tilak himself had writ-ten a textbook on mechanics. The writing of textbooks has always been a popular pastime for ambitious school-teachers; the 'Young Jesuits' in the 1880s were in this respect probably abler and more needy than most of their successors.

[14] N. C. Kelkar, *Life and Times of Lokamanya Tilak*, Madras, 1928, p. 160.

It seemed to Tilak's colleagues that he was protesting too much. He was already a popular journalist and before long was to be in the forefront of politics in Maharashtra. In the light of later history, it is difficult to imagine him entirely occupied in teaching the students of the Fergusson College. His talents needed a better medium than a blackboard, and a larger audience than the undergraduates of Poona. Indeed, if the reminiscences of his contemporaries and students are to be believed, Tilak was not an outstanding success as a teacher. There is no doubt, however, that he was a born politician and a gifted journalist.

Under the impact of western education, public life in Poona in the 1880s was stirring and the atmosphere was charged with an air of expectancy. In this atmosphere the more energetic members of the Deccan Education Society and teachers of the Fergusson College— Apte, Agarkar, Tilak, Gokhale and Namjoshi—were not content only to be teachers: they wanted at the same time to be authors, social re- formers, orators, politicians. In seeking this versatility, they were following in the footsteps of such veterans as Gopal Hari Deshmukh, V. N. Mandlik, K. T. Telang and M. G. Ranade, who had not let their professional obligations (even when they were in government service) interfere with their intellectual and political interests.

Tilak's pleas left his colleagues cold. Nor did he impress such members of the Governing Body as Justice Ranade and Principal Selby of the Deccan College, who could be expected to take an objec- tive view in the feud between the rival factions. Tilak's fears that the Society and its institutions were losing their missionary zeal proved groundless; the Fergusson College kept up its high reputation, and the spirit of self-sacrifice of its teachers was long held forth as an ideal to others.

In after years there was an understandable tendency to play down the Agarkar–Tilak feud. In the words of N. C. Kelkar, Tilak's lieu- tenant and biographer, despite the 'yawning gulf of differences be- tween them, Tilak and Agarkar met together at a high point with an eternal sunshine settling upon it, like two cliffs rising on two sides of a valley and, joining heads to create an arch . . . beneath which the shrubbery of differences might freely luxuriate and streams of invec- tives flow as turbulently as ever. They had a supremely sublime regard for each other.' This analysis is more amusing than accurate. A striking feature of the controversy between Tilak and Agarkar was the deep distrust and bitterness it generated at the time. The two antagonists saw each other without the haze of hero-worship, which has clouded the vision of later writers. Agarkar charged Tilak 'with the superlative self-conceit that the little world by which you are surrounded is full of gulls and that you alone amongst them have all the shrewdness, the disinterestedness, and intellectual perspicacity'.[15] 'Tilak must leave the body [the Deccan Education Society]', wrote Agarkar, 'or there will be no progress and no peace in it.' 'He is so violent and obstinate.'[16] Tilak's language was more restrained: 'I have all along been afraid', he wrote to Agarkar, 'that our private relations may break sometime and I shall not be much pained if they do so a little too soon, though I shall be extremely glad to have them restored.'[17] Tilak admitted that he occasionally used 'strong and cutting language . . . giving sharp and stinging replies and being unsparing in my criticism'.[18] Tilak's ruthless logic and biting irony were more effective in the editorial columns of his journals than in exchanges across the table in committee meetings at the College and the Deccan Education Society. His exit from the Deccan Education Society proved an asset to him in the long run; it enabled him to devote all his energies to the more congenial spheres of journalism and politics.

Gokhale was at first not directly involved in this conflict between the two men whose example had first attracted him to the teaching profession. As an intimate friend of Agarkar, he had incurred Tilak's distrust, and as one of the editors of the *Sudharak*, he found himself in the thick of the fray. He figured several times in the factional dispute within the Deccan Education Society. His request for a loan of Rs 500, his textbook on arithmetic, his election as secretary of the Poona Sarvajanik Sabha, and his appointment as editor of its journal added to the heat of the controversy between Agarkar and Tilak. It is significant that on 14 October 1890, when Tilak handed in his letter of resignation, Gokhale also offered to resign. 'I want to say', he wrote, 'that if my withdrawal from the Body can induce Mr Tilak to remain, I hereby offer my resignation as a life-member.'[19] Gokhale was informed that Tilak's resignation had nothing to do with his (Gokhale's) connection with the Society.

[15] Agarkar to Tilak, 25 Dec. 1888 (Agarkar P.).
[16] Agarkar to his uncle, 25 Nov. 1890 (Agarkar P.).
[17] Tilak to Agarkar, 24 Dec. 1888, in M. D. Vidwans (ed.), *Letters of Lokamanya Tilak*, Poona, 1966, pp. 243–4.
[18] Tilak's letter of resignation, 15 Dec. 1890, in Limaye, op. cit., pt. III, p. 28.
[19] Limaye (ed.), op. cit., pt. I, p. 119.

Two years after Tilak's exit, Agarkar became the Principal of the Fergusson College. Three years later, in 1895, he died. A condolence meeting was convened in the College hall and Gokhale rose to address it. He was unable to speak, and with tears in his eyes abruptly left the College hall.

Gokhale owed much to Agarkar. It was Agarkar who had first evoked his youthful enthusiasm and hero-worship. It was Agarkar who had initiated him into journalism and imbued him with respect for western thought and culture. But it was also Agarkar who had inspired in him an inveterate distrust of Tilak. This distrust was of course heartily reciprocated by Tilak. In his letter of resignation, Tilak had deplored the tendency in 'some of the new members' to indulge in activities unconnected with the Society. 'They appear to believe', he wrote, 'that the membership of the Deccan Education Society is a good start for a beginner in Poona and that if one has energy and ambition, he can use it as a stepping stone for personal distinction and gain.' Tilak's shaft was apparently aimed at Gokhale. Gokhale was, however, not the only teacher in the New English School and Fergusson College who had political ambitions.

The feud in the Deccan Education Society ended with Tilak's departure from it, but its memories were to poison the politics of Maharashtra and indeed of India for a long time.

5

Apprenticed to Ranade

'There are not half a dozen towns in India', Allan Octavian Hume, the 'Father of the Indian National Congress', said in 1893, 'that surpass Poona in intellectual development. There are thousands of men and women in Poona qualified to understand every particle of the Congress programme.'[1] In the spring of 1880, I. P. Minayeff, the Russian Indologist, had visited Poona and noted in his diary that the town was regarded a hotbed of treason by the British, that legends about its glorious past were still current in Maharashtra, that Phadke's 'rebellion' was secretly admired even by those who considered it an ill-conceived venture.[2] We know now that British officials had begun to look askance at the political consciousness of the Poona Brahmans even in the 1870s. Soon after the Phadke affair, the Governor of Bombay, Sir Richard Temple, had confided to the Viceroy:

That such discontent exists has long been known; it should rather be called disaffection, because it arises not so much from any specific causes which could be overtly alleged, probed, and perhaps remedied, but rather from causes inevitably incidental to a foreign rule like ours, and which could not be set forth categorically by the disaffected. . . . [The Chitpavans] are inspired with national sentiment and with an ambition limited only with the bounds of India itself.

Of Poona and its Brahmans, Sir Richard was especially suspicious; 'Any fine morning an observant visitor may ride through the streets of Poona and mark the scowl with which so many persons regard the stranger . . . the bearing of the inhabitants of Poona—the head and centre of political Brahminism in Western India—towards European civil officers was becoming very uncomfortable, but changed like magic when the Native troops sailed for Malta.'[3]

Sir Richard was right in recognizing the existence of political discontent in Poona, but wrong in imagining that it would lead to a

[1] Speech at Poona on 27 Nov. 1893, *Quarterly Journal of the Poona Sarvajanik Sabha*, Jan. 1894, p. 95.
[2] I. P. Minayeff, *Travels and Diaries of India and Burma*, Calcutta, n.d., pp. 52–4.
[3] Temple to Lytton, 3 July 1879 (L.P.).

rebellion on the pattern of Shivaji's struggle against the Mughals. Thanks to western education, the thoughts of the rising generation of Chitpavan Brahmans were turning not towards a violent upheaval, but towards greater participation in the government of their own country through representative institutions. With its small but vocal educated élite, Poona enjoyed a political prestige which rivalled that of the presidency towns in the last quarter of the nineteenth century. Indeed, but for the sudden outbreak of cholera in the closing weeks of 1885, Poona, and not Bombay, would have had the honour of holding the first session of the Indian National Congress.

The memory of past greatness sharpened the political consciousness of Poona. But no less important was the happy coincidence that for more than twenty years the town was served by a remarkable institution and by a remarkable man. The institution was the Sarvajanik Sabha, and the man Mahadev Govind Ranade.

2

The Poona Sarvajanik Sabha was founded on 2 April 1870—the Hindu New Year's Day—the first *Chaitra* of the Saka year 1792. On 'that auspicious day', its ninety-five founding members assembled at Poona. Elected by nearly six thousand people from different parts of Maharashtra, they regarded themselves as 'delegates'. The elective principle was a distinctive feature of the new organization. No-one could be a member unless he had been elected by fifty persons inhabiting a particular place or locality. Its constitution deliberately excluded from its purview the religious and personal problems of its members.

The first president of the Sabha was the Chief of Aundh, and its patrons included several members of the titled and landed gentry of the Deccan. That the Sabha did not become a mouthpiece of the old feudal order was largely due to the fact that, within a year of its establishment, Mahadev Govind Ranade was posted to Poona. The twenty-nine year-old Ranade, whose intellectual zest and patriotism needed a larger outlet than his judicial office, found a handy instrument in the Sarvajanik Sabha. Ganesh Vasudeo Joshi, one of the founders and working secretaries of the Sabha, quickly recognized the exceptional ability of the young judge and cheerfully accepted his lead. A government servant, Ranade could not hold an office in a political body, but this did not prevent him from quietly directing the policies of the Sarvajanik Sabha and doing most of its work. Almost all important letters or memorials issued by the Sabha were drafted or revised by him. A diligent student of politics and economics, he insisted that facts should be carefully investigated, collated and interpreted. He would not let the local leaders function from an ivory tower; the facts about Indian economics and administration were to be found not only in British Blue Books, but in the towns and villages of Maharashtra. At his instance the Sarvajanik Sabha conducted an economic survey in 1873, which brought into sharp relief the heavy burden of land revenue on the peasantry in the districts of Ahmednagar and Sholapur. During the terrible famine of 1877–8, the agents of the Sabha toured the famine-stricken districts and brought to light facts which could hardly have been revealed through the normal official channels.

In 1874, the Sarvajanik Sabha had petitioned the British Parliament to grant India the right to send fifteen representatives to the House of Commons. The same year the Sabha announced that it would collect funds for the defence of the Gaikwad of Baroda, who had been charged with an attempt to poison the British Resident. These were bold moves, but they were not calculated to endear the Sabha to the government. 'The conduct of the association of the Deccan landholders called the "Surva-Janik Sabha" ', wrote Sir Richard Temple to Lord Lytton, 'has long been, as Your Lordship well knows, regarded with suspicion—which suspicion continues . . . its wires are believed to be pulled by men with tainted views.'[4]

That the Sarvajanik Sabha, which was wholly wedded to constitutional methods, could be mistaken for a subversive body may seem absurd today. No less absurd would be the view that the Sabha represented only a small middle-class coterie, intent on promoting its class interests. The Sabha started with a membership of 95 in April 1870; during the next five years the number rose to 132. The president and the vice-president of the Sabha belonged to the aristocratic families of the Deccan, but the real power rested in the hands of the Managing Committee, which included the representatives of almost all important classes, castes and interests of Poona. If the Brahmans predominated in the Committee of the Sabha, and there were only a couple of Muslims and Parsis, it was because Poona's population was predominantly Hindu, and among the English-speaking Hindus, the Brahmans were in a majority.

[4] Ibid.

The day-to-day work of the Sarvajanik Sabha was carried on by its secretary and a couple of other workers who took their cue from Ranade. Ranade was not the man to work for any clique. He had drunk deep at the fountain-head of western culture; he had dreams of a new India, rejuvenated by contact with the West. He loved Poona, where he spent the best years of his life. He loved Maharashtra, whose history and literature he sought to interpret. His patriotism was not confined to Poona and Maharashtra. As one reads the proceedings and memorials of the Sarvajanik Sabha drafted or vetted by him a hundred years ago, one cannot but be impressed by the absence of any narrow, sectarian or parochial approach. It is true that occasionally the Sabha took up local issues, such as the introduction of window delivery at the Poona Post Office or the allotment of an elective seat to the Central Division in the Bombay Legislative Council. Most of the causes championed by the Sabha, however, transcended the interests of any particular caste, community or region. In agitating for the reform of the legislative councils, the holding of the I.C.S. examination simultaneously in England and India, easier credit facilities for the peasant, and protection for Indian industry, the Sarvajanik Sabha followed the line adopted by Dadabhai Naoroji and A. O. Hume, and embodied in the resolutions of the Indian National Congress from year to year. The Sabha gave its wholehearted support to measures conceived in the interest of the poorer classes, even though they were not directly represented on the Sabha. The lowering of the salt duty, the lenient administration of the forest laws, the improvement in famine administration, the reduction in land revenue, the introduction of Marathi in schools and colleges were all demands from which the English-speaking middle class had little to gain for itself.

That the educated middle class of Poona, which controlled the Sarvajanik Sabha, resisted the temptation to seek its own self-interest is not at all surprising, if we remember that it was led by men who were conscious of the duty they owed to their country as a whole rather than to their particular community or region. It is also important to remember that in the last quarter of the nineteenth century the lines of class cleavage were not sharply drawn in Maharashtra. The *Bhakti* movement in the seventeenth century and the memories of Shivaji and the Peshwas had prevented the erection of emotional barriers which had fragmented Hindu society of other provinces, such as Bengal and Madras. The educated men of Poona did not have the hauteur of some of their anglicized counterparts in Calcutta and Bombay. In dress, mode of life or style of conversation, Ranade, Gokhale and Tilak would have been indistinguishable from hundreds of their neighbours in the streets of Poona. In the educated élite in that town there were many who had tasted poverty in their early days, and maintained links with their native villages where many of their relatives and friends still lived.

Much of the credit for keeping the politics of the Sarvajanik Sabha and indeed of Poona on a national, secular and progressive plane was due to Ranade, whose capacity for taking pains was only equalled by his self-effacement. He kept political controversy above personalities, and tried to prod the government without provoking it. He knew that British officials did not like the courage and candour with which the Sarvajanik Sabha spoke up on political issues. He also knew that the Sabha was not strong enough to survive open official antagonism. Between the Scylla of quiescence and the Charybdis of open defiance, the course was precarious, but Ranade managed to steer the Sabha along it successfully.

3

In Poona, as in other Indian towns, hundreds were ready to flock to a public meeting, but there were few who were willing to part with money for political activities, and fewer still who could be persuaded to take on that daily drudgery behind the scenes which alone keeps a political organization or a journal alive. Ranade did not spare himself, but his official position prevented him from functioning openly. He needed reliable assistants to run the Sabha and its *Quarterly Journal*. He was fortunate in the successive secretaries of the Sabha: Ganesh Vasudeo Joshi who held the office until his death in 1880, S. H. Chiplonkar,[5] Shivram Hari Sathe,[6] and Gokhale. Gokhale had first seen Ranade at a function arranged by the New English School in 1885. Their first encounter was somewhat awkward; Ranade did not have his invitation card with him, and was stopped at the gate by Gokhale. S. H. Sathe introduced Gokhale to Ranade.[7] Agarkar had already spoken highly of Gokhale's ability to Ranade, who took an instant liking to the young professor-politician and appointed him

[5] S. H. Chiplonkar (1851–94), lawyer and journalist of Poona.
[6] S. H. Sathe (1836–1912), lawyer of Poona.
[7] T. V. Parvate, *Gopal Krishna Gokhale*, Ahmedabad, 1959, p. 24.

editor of the Sabha's *Quarterly Journal*. Gokhale, only twenty-three at the time, was conscious of the high honour conferred on him despite his youth and inexperience. In a letter to Ganesh Vyankatesh Joshi, a confidant of Ranade and an expert on economic problems, Gokhale expressed his feelings towards Ranade.

G. K. Gokhale to G. V. Joshi, 17 October 1889: . . . The Sabha has conferred on me an honour of which I am conscious I am quite unworthy. . . . The opening afforded me to endeavour to cultivate relationships of acquaintance, if nothing higher, with one for whom I had all along cherished the deepest regard, whose earnest and unassuming exertions for the welfare of the country. . . . I must content myself with only admiring from respectful distance. Mr Ranade at whose feet I am at present and hope to always sit as a very humble pupil was kind enough to show me your last letter to him in connection with your article on the Economic situation. . . .[8]

Besides the proceedings of the Sarvajanik Sabha, the *Quarterly Journal* published articles on current issues. Its editorship gave Gokhale his first lessons in political journalism and an opportunity of seriously studying problems which were exercising the minds of educated India. We have it on Gokhale's authority that almost two-thirds of the *Quarterly Journal* was written anonymously by Ranade and the rest was vetted by him before publication.[9] Ranade was a hard task-master who would never allow an unchecked fact or a careless statement to be printed. Gokhale had sometimes to re-write an article several times before it received Ranade's approval.

Ranade was a confidant of A. O. Hume, Dadabhai Naoroji, William Wedderburn and Pherozeshah Mehta. Such was the respect in which he was held by the Congress leaders that it was a decided advantage for the young Gokhale to be known as his protégé. Gokhale's apprenticeship to Ranade lasted for nearly fourteen years. It had a profound effect upon him. Indeed, it is impossible to understand the further development of Gokhale's personality and politics without understanding the intellectual make-up and character of his mentor.

4

We have already seen* how, soon after being posted to Poona as a judge in 1871, Ranade acquired a pivotal position in the public life of

---

* See Chapter 3, *supra*.
[8] G.P.
[9] Karve & Ambekar (eds.), *Speeches and Writings of Gokhale*, vol. III, p. 288.

that town. When Gokhale fell under his spell, Ranade was in his late forties and at the height of his intellectual powers and political influence. In Poona he was the brain behind the principal political body, the Sarvajanik Sabha. In all public movements in western India he was (in the words of Surendranath Banerjea) 'the power behind the throne'.[10] Of the social reform movement, he was the moving spirit as well as the 'one-man secretariat'.

The image of Ranade as a leader of the rational, progressive and west-oriented educated class could be misleading, if it conjured up the figure of an anglicized Maharashtrian. Unlike some of his friends and contemporaries, such as Surendranath Banerjea, Pherozeshah Mehta, W. C. Bonnerjee and Dadabhai Naoroji, Ranade's dress, food habits, and mode of life betrayed little western influence. Visitors who called at his house in Poona would often find him seated on the floor, chewing a betel-nut and writing at a low desk. When he was not humming a verse from Tukaram, he was probably meditating on an aphorism of Emerson's. His rugged appearance, with one eye continually drooping, his frayed linen projecting from under the sleeves of his long black coat, his inordinately short, ill-cut crumpled trousers, the knotted stick on which he leant while speaking and his icy reserve, all served to put off English officers who commented on his 'unprepossessing appearance and uncouth manners'. Neither personal grievances nor official displeasure soured Ranade, whose admiration for English character and English institutions remained unabated till the very end. Gokhale has recorded how 'Rao Saheb' (as Ranade was affectionately called in his intimate circle) 'delighted us in the course of our evening walks and after-dinner conversations with comparisons of Englishmen and other people, both ancient and modern, and in which comparisons he would pay ungrudging tribute to the highest qualities of the English nation'. Ranade had no doubt that India could go forward only along the road which England herself had traversed—that of constitutional and peaceful evolution. It was a tribute to his foresight that, as early as 1870, he recognized that British rule could be turned into an instrument of Indian resurgence; that India must turn her gaze to the future rather than to the past, that her new leaders would emerge from the new educated class reared by the recently established universities rather than from the decadent feudal aristocracy.

Ranade was in his teens when he heard the distant rumbles of the

[10] S. Banerjea, *A Nation in Making*, Calcutta, 1963, p. 128.

Mutiny of 1857; he was in his thirties when he saw at close quarters Balwant Rao Phadke's brave but suicidal gesture of defiance. Ranade had a keen sense of history, and a great pride in the past of Maharashtra. He called for the celebration of Shivaji's festival long before young men like Tilak did so. Ranade did not, however, delude himself into thinking that Maharashtra or India could manage in the nineteenth century with the political ideas or institutions of the seventeenth century.

Like Rammohun Roy before him, and Gandhi after him, Ranade tried to see the Indian predicament as a whole. He did not draw a rigid line between politics and economics, society and religion. He told the Bombay Social Conference in 1900:

You cannot have a good social system when you find yourself low in the scale of political rights, nor can you be fit to exercise political rights and privileges unless your social system is based on reason and justice. You cannot have a good economical system when your social arrangements are imperfect. If your religious ideals are low and grovelling, you cannot succeed in social, economical or political spheres. This inter-dependence is not an accident but is the law of our nature.[11]

Ranade sought to open the western window for a gust of fresh air to blow away the cobwebs of custom and superstition which were asphyxiating Hindu society. But he was not a blind admirer or imitator of the West. He did not imagine that an idea or institution which suited England would necessarily suit India. He was, for example, all for representative institutions and a free press on the British model, but not for the doctrine of *laissez-faire*, which was an article of faith with most Englishmen but was really detrimental to India's economic development.[12]

Ranade was not content with writing articles and making speeches. He knew that political, social, economic and even religious ideals required men and institutions to realize them. The first task was to analyse and pose the problems of India in the right perspective. It was a hard task. The walls of official obstinacy and public apathy were difficult to pierce. An unremitting campaign to educate both the government and the people was necessary. This campaign required not only institutions, but dedicated men to run them. All his life Ranade remained on the look-out for able young men. His greatest find was Gokhale.

[11] *Miscellaneous Writings of M. G. Ranade*, pp. 231–2.
[12] M. G. Ranade, *Essays on Indian Economics*, 2nd ed., Madras, 1906, pp. 45–6.

Gokhale has recorded that young men who came into personal contact with Ranade felt 'as in a holy presence, not only uttering "nothing base" but afraid even of thinking unworthy thoughts'.[13] The reverence and awe in which Gokhale held Ranade were expressed on several occasions. Ranade was one of 'the chosen instruments of God to work out His beneficent purpose in this world'.[14] If Ranade had been born a few centuries earlier, he would have been 'counted among the divine incarnations'.[15] These tributes are the more striking because Gokhale was not given to hyperbole and was indeed noted for a tendency towards understatement. He did not have a strong religious streak, nor did the religious idiom easily come to him; if he used it for Ranade this must have been because it alone could express his deep feeling for his master. Gokhale was fascinated by Ranade's patriotism, integrity, industry, perseverance and freedom from egotism. The first person singular, as Gokhale said, did not exist for Ranade. Nor did he seek the limelight. It is significant that Ranade's name scarcely figures in the records of the organizations which he founded and ran almost single-handed. He had a keen sense of responsibility, and approached public life with high seriousness. He wrote and spoke with great deliberation; behind his articles and speeches there were long hours of research and reflection. He wrote his speeches, even when he spoke without notes.

Gokhale never tired of acknowledging his debt to Ranade. In the moment of his greatest triumph, immediately after his evidence before the Welby Commission in 1897, he described himself as a mere 'conduit pipe' who had transmitted[16] what Ranade had given him. This humility was appropriate in a devoted disciple towards his mentor. If Gokhale was a conduit pipe, he contrived not only to transmit but to transform what he had received. The disciple, as we shall see later, was destined in some ways to surpass the master.

Ranade's political views were basically the same as those of other leaders of the first generation of Congressmen. It was in the sphere of economic and social reform that he made his most significant contribution. He drew attention to some of the fallacies in the economic orthodoxies of the territorial division of labour which condemned India for ever to the production of raw materials and to the doctrine of *laissez-faire* which was held forth as a justification for the lack of

[13] *Speeches of Gopal Krishna Gokhale*, 3rd ed., Madras, 1920, p. 781.
[14] Ibid., p. 789.
[15] R. Ranade, *Ranade: His Wife's Reminiscences*, Delhi, 1963, p. 9.
[16] Gokhale to G. V. Joshi, 16 April 1897 (G.P.).

official initiative in developing Indian agriculture and industry. The Anglo-Indian administrators and publicists, who questioned the application of English political ideas and institutions to Indian conditions, glibly invoked English economic principles to justify British policies towards the Indian economy.[17] Ranade held that the experience of the United States and the continent of Europe was more relevant to Indian economic conditions than that of Britain, which was 'proud of its position, strong in its insularity, and the home of the richest and the busiest Community in the modern industrial World'.[18]

The great Indian Dependency of England [he wrote] has, during the century, come to supply the place of the Old Colonies [and] ... come to be regarded as a Plantation, growing raw produce to be shipped by British Agents in British Ships, to be worked into Fabrics by British skill and capital, and to be re-exported to the Dependency by British merchants to their corresponding British Firms in India and elsewhere.[19]

He did not see why the Government of India, which guaranteed a fixed return to British investors in railway projects in India, could not help the Indian farmer or entrepreneur. Indo-British economic relations constituted 'a struggle of a very unequal character, a struggle between a Giant and a Dwarf, and yet the struggle has to be maintained against great odds'.[20] The results of this struggle could be seen in the manipulation of the Indian tax-structure to maintain the imports of British textiles into India.

Ranade was too sophisticated a thinker to seek a single short-cut to Indian progress. He recognized that economic problems were complex and could be tackled only in their causal structure, in which psychological and institutional factors interacted. India's poverty appeared to him the result not only of British economic policies, but of other factors as well: her dependence on agriculture as the main resource, her archaic social system which throttled the acquisition of new skills and the mobility of labour, her want of enterprise and

[17] 'Great Britain is most peculiarly circumstanced, and its economic history furnishes no guide for dealing with the difficulties of the situation in India, where, except in a few provinces, the State claims to be the sole landlord, and agricultural classes form 80 per cent of the total population, and there is no accumulation of capital, and manufactures and commerce are in their rudimentary stage, and in that stage also chiefly monopolized by strangers.' Paper read by M. G. Ranade on 'The Reorganization of Rural Credit in India' at the Industrial Conference and printed in *Sarvajanik Sabha Quarterly Journal*, Oct. 1891.
[18] Ranade, *Indian Economics*, p. 36.
[19] Ibid., p. 106.   [20] Ibid., p. 107.

capital, and lack of an efficient credit system.[21] Ranade was ruthless in his analysis of the economic shibboleths, and the vested interests of British administrators, but he knew he could not demolish these interests at a blow. All he could do immediately was to offer palliatives and 'reforms'. He initiated the campaign for India's economic emancipation, which Gokhale was destined to pursue vigorously.

Though Ranade was a friend and admirer of Dadabhai Naoroji, he did not set the same store by the 'drain theory'. The central problem did not seem to him simply as that of a foreign power bleeding Indian resources, but of 'the competition of Nature's powers against man's Labour,—it is the competition of organized skill and science against Ignorance and Idleness,—transferring the monopoly not only of wealth, but what is more important, of skill, talent, and activity to others'.[22]

Ranade was not dismayed by the resistance his ideas encountered from the British. This resistance seemed to him a blessing in disguise: the very process of wresting concessions from the British could generate in the Indian people the strength for exercising new responsibilities. Nor did he believe in the possibility of a single explanation for Indian poverty, or of a single sovereign remedy for eradicating it. He preferred to investigate problems and to analyse them with facts and figures. He sought to build up a well-informed public opinion on issues of crucial importance to the country. He clearly saw and defined the goals for his country in all fields: political, social and economic. But he knew that to define a goal was not the same thing as to reach it. Himself a cog of the British administrative machine in India, he knew how powerful and well-entrenched it was, and how difficult it was to shake it out of the ruts of complacency, vested interests and self-righteousness. At the same time he was conscious of the inertia, apathy and prejudice which paralysed his own people. The modernization of India, the reform of the administration, society and economy of the country, were not tasks which could be completed in a year, or even in a generation. The phrase 'robust optimism' was often used of Ranade by his contemporaries and colleagues. It must have required tremendous courage and optimism to continue the battle with the British bureaucracy and Brahman orthodoxy, when it was obvious that the victory would come, if at all, to a future generation.

In the last quarter of the nineteenth century, progress seemed by

[21] Ibid., pp. 23–4.   [22] Ibid., p. 197.

no means assured; there were hurdles all along the line. These hurdles could be surmounted or side-stepped, but they could not be wished away. It was part of Ranade's strategy to keep on hammering against these obstacles. Sometimes, as in 1891, 1895 and 1896, the opposition seemed so strong that Ranade decided to give in, rather than seek a head-on collision with the opponents of reform. Did this smack of pusillanimity? Was it an evidence of 'lack of iron' in his soul?

In a revealing passage in her reminiscences, Ranade's widow, Ramabai, quoted Shankar Pandurang Pandit, a close friend of her husband, whose motto was: 'I would sooner break than bend.' Her husband's motto, Ramabai wrote, was just the opposite; he was prepared to bend rather than break.[23]

This willingness to compromise may have been due to the temperament of a scholar and a man of religion who hated bitterness and strife. We should also remember that Ranade was not a full-time politician. He was a busy judge and could hardly have had the time or even the inclination to indulge in prolonged polemics. His authority in Maharashtra, as in the rest of the country, was intellectual and moral. He did not have to maintain his grip on a journal or an organization in order to keep himself in the public eye. If he was abused, he could afford to be silent; if a colleague deserted him, he could look for another; if any institution was taken out of his hands, he could set up another. These Fabian tactics were especially suitable for the times in which Ranade's lot was cast. They made it possible for the process of political education and propaganda to be kept up at a time when the government was too powerful and public opinion too feeble or too disorganized to be effective.

Gokhale spent the most formative years of his life under Ranade's direction. These years brought him excruciating toil and some shocks. But he had his rewards too, not the least of which was an intimate association with one of the greatest Indians of his time.

[23] R. Ranade, op. cit., p. 150.

6

The Young Politician

Eighteen eighty-nine, the year of Gokhale's entry into the politics of
Poona, was the last year of the administration of Lord Reay, Governor of Bombay. Lord Reay was a friend of Gladstone. He was by no
means a pro-Congress Governor, but he had an easy and friendly
manner with Indians and did not think the I.C.S. impeccable and
infallible. Some of his early decisions, such as the raising of school
fees and the refusal to transfer the Deccan College to Indian control,
were unpopular, but he more than made up for them by conceding
a liberal constitution to the municipality of Poona and permitting
it to elect its own president. He sanctioned generous grants to the
Fergusson College and the Poona High School for Girls. He had the
courage and wisdom to nominate to his Legislative Council such distinguished and independent Indians as Dadabhai Naoroji, M. G.
Ranade, K. T. Telang, Badruddin Tyabji and Pherozeshah Mehta.

In the last months of his administration, Reay's popularity with
the Indian intelligentsia almost rivalled that of his friend Ripon. The
Crawford case did for Reay what the Ilbert Bill controversy had done
for Ripon. Crawford, a senior member of the Civil Service, who had
risen to the rank of Commissioner, Central Division, had long had
a shady reputation; his venality had been the subject of cynical
comment in Indian bazaars as well as in English clubs. He had
evolved a sordid technique for extorting bribes from his subordinates
by threatening to demote, dismiss, or transfer them to inconvenient
places. Successive Governors of Bombay had shrunk from exposing
him, but Reay decided to prosecute him, and refused to accept the
verdict of the British judges when they declared him 'not guilty'.
The Government of India felt deeply embarrassed. 'The undoubted
corruption of Mr Crawford,' wrote the Viceroy in a letter to the
Secretary of State, 'one of our very highest dignitaries . . . words cannot express how tormented I have been by the evidences of frailty in
the ruling race.'[1]

[1] Dufferin to Cross, 24 Aug. 1888 (Dufferin P.).

In the course of the trial, confessions of some *mamlatdars*—junior Indian officers who had been victims of Crawford's extortions—were obtained on the understanding that they would not be used against them. When Crawford's guilt was proved to the hilt, his friends launched a smear campaign not only against Lord Reay, but against the *mamlatdars*. With righteous indignation, Anglo-Indian newspapers argued that Indian officers who, on their own confession, had been parties to the corrupt practices of Crawford, should not be retained in the service of the state. *The Times* [London] joined Anglo-Indian papers in demanding the dismissal of the *mamlatdars*, the official pledge of immunity notwithstanding.

This new twist to the Crawford case created a sensation. That the pledged word of the Bombay Government was about to be broken seemed incredible. In Poona there was widespread sympathy with the aggrieved *mamlatdars*, many of whom had friends and relations in that town. A meeting was convened on 1 September 1889 to express popular feeling on this case. Tributes were paid to Lord Reay for his courage and fair play, but the mood of the audience was well expressed by Rao Bahadur K. L. Nulkar, C.I.E., a former Dewan of Cutch, who presided over the meeting: 'It is well-nigh hopeless for the ruled to expect prompt and ready justice against a powerful and influential member of the ruling race.'[2]

Both Gokhale and Tilak spoke at this meeting. Gokhale moved a resolution denouncing the 'persistent and factious misrepresentations' of the Crawford case in the English press. He expressed astonishment that *The Times* [London] had swallowed 'with remarkable simplicity all the trash' which its correspondent at Calcutta had sent it, and 'the small band of traducers of Lord Reay' had succeeded in provoking the intervention of the Secretary of State and setting at nought Lord Reay's 'struggle for removing a foul stain from the brow of England'. Gokhale's sharpest attack was reserved for the *Times of India*, which had been reviling not only Indian officers, but also Indian character. After quoting Sir William Harcourt's remark: 'If you have abuses to defend or good measures to abuse, you may rely on the universities', Gokhale said: 'We here can say a similar thing of the *Times of India*—that if you have Anglo-Indian misconduct to defend or natives or their sympathisers to abuse, you may rely on the *Times of India*.'[3]

[2] *The proc. of a public meeting of the citizens of Poona*, Bombay, 1889, p. 12.
[3] Ibid., p. 55.

From the Crawford case, the *Times of India* had drawn its own inference about the lack of integrity in educated Indians and their unfitness for higher responsibilities. 'In my opinion', Gokhale declared, 'it is not for these persons who are themselves living in glass houses to throw stones at us. . . . It is unwarrantable to draw any conclusions in the Crawford case, and if unfortunately they are to be drawn, let them be drawn in a fair manner; I am afraid no community will have a case for rejoicing.'

This was not Gokhale's first public speech. A few months earlier, in November 1888, he had spoken at the Bombay Provincial Conference at Poona. There is no doubt, however, that his speech on the Crawford case with its pointed thrusts at the British bureaucracy and the Anglo-Indian press was his first notable performance and marked him out as a promising politician.

2

The Crawford case reached its climax when Lord Reay was about to retire. Gokhale's early political career and secretaryship of the Poona Sarvajanik Sabha thus coincided with the administration of Lord Harris, who succeeded Lord Reay. A fine cricketer who had captained the English team against Australia, Harris had served as Under-Secretary of State for India and Secretary of State for War, before his appointment as Governor of Bombay. He had a deep distrust of the Indian educated classes. His complacency and conceit could be compared with those of Lord Curzon, and may be sampled in his correspondence with the Secretary of State for India.

Lord Harris to Lord Cross, 4 June 1891: You asked me what I think . . . the feelings of the people to us are. . . . I should say that ninety per cent of the population, i.e. the agricultural class—don't care two pence to what nationality the Sircar [i.e. Government] belongs as long as the [revenue] assessment is a fair one . . . and that a large proportion of that percentage is quite in the dark as to who the English are, or where they came from. . . . I should say that they don't hate us more than they hate each other. . . . Hindus hate Muhammedans and Parsis hate both. Each is ready to get up a free fight about nothing at all. . . . We can do infinitely more work in their climate than they can, and they get fat and lazy as they rise in rank whilst our civilians are as active as young men.[4]

---

[4] Papers of the fourth Baron Harris.

To Lord Harris Indian politics seemed a mixture of ignorance, prejudice and self-interest. When there was an agitation in Poona, he ascribed it to the machinations of its Brahman clique.[5] When the bill for regulation of traffic in mhowra flowers met with opposition in his Legislative Council, he blamed it on the Parsi liquor contractors.[6] When the press criticized him, he attributed it to the malice of European journalists and the sedition of Indian editors. For the few Indian members of the Civil Service under him, 'Babu Collectors and Babu Superintendents of Police', as he called them—he had nothing but contempt. When communal riots broke out in Bombay in 1893, he hastened to censure the Hindu community without waiting for the result of the official inquiry. When communal disturbances spread to Poona and other places in Maharashtra in the succeeding year, his overheated imagination read into them a Brahman conspiracy. 'It is monstrous', he wrote to the Viceroy, 'that the whole of Maharashtra should be convulsed by the machinations of a few fanatical Brahmins.'[7] Even after the bubble of the Brahman conspiracy had been pricked by the courts, he continued to single out the Brahmans for public censure. 'An unsympathetic and reactionary administration', was how Gokhale described Lord Harris's regime in an article in the *Quarterly Journal of the Poona Sarvajanik Sabha* (April 1895). Earlier he had written a letter to the editor of the *Times of India* under the pseudonym 'A Poona Brahmin'.[8] This was a 2000-word, well-informed and closely reasoned commentary on the course of events in the Deccan, and ended on a note of passionate indictment of the British officials, and in particular of Governor Harris:

A great deal has recently been said of a conspiracy in the Deccan. Yes, I too believe that there is a conspiracy, but it is for discrediting not the Government, but the people of Deccan in general and the Poona Brahmins in particular. . . . I admit that some of the vernacular papers in the Deccan write much too strongly. Did they write like that during Lord Reay's time? Has Lord Harris ever shown the least regard for the press of the Presidency? But is there no provocation to write strongly? Has he ever moved, even so much as by the breadth of a hair, to conciliate public opinion? The entire press opposed the Mhowra Bill; the entire press disapproved the exclusion of the Central Division from the elective franchise. The entire press condemned the Provincial Service rules. Has Lord Harris

[5] Harris to Lansdowne, 7 July 1892 (Lansdowne P.).
[6] Ibid.
[7] Harris to Elgin, 1 Oct. 1894 (Harris P.).
[8] *Times of India*, 10 Nov. 1894.

shown the least shred of respect for these unanimous expressions of opinion?

Gokhale concluded this trenchant indictment of the Harris administration by affirming that his criticism of Harris was no more a 'systematic attempt to render the task of Government difficult' than had been the violent denunciations of Lords Ripon and Reay by the Anglo-Indian press.

3

In the eighteen-eighties and early nineties, politics in Poona were primarily the affair of a small group of teachers, journalists, merchants and retired government servants. A serious local grievance, a provincial conference, or a distinguished visitor could, however, stir almost the entire educated class of the town, and bring it to a public meeting under the auspices of the Sarvajanik Sabha. As the secretary of the Sabha, Gokhale had a prominent role on such occasions. It was his privilege to read out the address of welcome to the distinguished visitor, to move a resolution or to deliver a speech. Short, fair, with his intellectual forehead covered with the red Maratha turban, a frank open countenance with a slight moustache fringing his upper lips, and kindly eyes that shone through his glasses, Gokhale's was a familiar figure on the political stage of Poona in the 1890s.

On 20 March 1892, Allan Octavian Hume, the 'Father of the Indian National Congress', visited Poona just before his departure for England. He received a hearty welcome, and was taken in a procession to Hirabag, where a public meeting was held in his honour. More than five thousand persons were present and Sardar Gopal Hari Deshmukh, one of the oldest and most respected citizens of Poona, who was in the chair, declared that Hume was leaving India to disprove the charge of the Anglo-Indian detractors of the Congress that it could not survive without him. It was for the Indian people to give the lie to this statement. The government was bad, argued Hume, because it was ignorant, and it was the fault of the people that their government was so ignorant, 'for the people did not honestly speak out their view'. He urged them to keep up the tempo of their agitation. Their fault as a nation was that they were 'very enthusiastic today, but forgot everything on the morrow'. They had to shed the fear of authority. 'There was no one whom an Englishman despised more than one who bowed down to him. There was no one an Englishman respected more than the man who was able to stand up to him and fight him.'[9]

Hume received a great ovation. He was garlanded, and the meeting terminated with the singing of 'God Save the Queen' and 'three enthusiastic cheers for Mr Hume'. An evening party followed in the brightly illuminated Town Hall. As Hume left, an Indian band played 'Auld Lang Syne'.

In November 1893, Hume again visited Poona and was given a public reception. In an eloquent address, Gokhale expressed feelings of 'gratitude and admiration and veneration and love'.

For Mr Hume [said Gokhale] had enabled India for the first time in her history, to breathe and feel like one nation by bringing together men of enlightenment and patriotism from the various parts of the country to work in a common cause. He had tried to steady their faltering footsteps and turn their weak accents into firm speech. He had toiled for them in the midst of calumny and contumely of every kind. . . . [For their sake he had] denied himself the comforts which old age demanded and to their service he had devoted his time, his energy, his talents, his purse, his all.

Gokhale wished him a well-earned retirement in words which Hume himself had used for Lord Ripon ten years before:

> Farewell, farewell, a nation's love
> A nation's prayers watch o'er thee
> Nor space nor time can part thee e'er
> From hearts that here adore thee.[10]

This was Hume's last visit to Poona, but Gokhale was to see a great deal of him during the next two decades.

In 1892, another British friend of India, William Digby, paid a brief visit to Poona. Gokhale was again the principal speaker at the public meeting called by the Poona Sarvajanik Sabha to honour the distinguished guest. Gokhale assailed the policies of the government: 'A wave of retrogression' was affecting the relations of the rulers and the ruled throughout the country; the government was daily viewing the public with 'increasing jealousy and distrust' and the people in their turn were 'returning in full measure these feelings'. He described the orders of the Government of India on the report of the Public Service Commission as 'an insult to the intelligence of the country',

[9] *Sarvajanik Sabha Quarterly Journal*, April 1892, pp. 51–2.
[10] *Speeches of Gokhale*, pp. 755–6.

and its educational policy as 'unsympathetic and short-sighted'. Referring to a notification of the Government of Bengal on the jury system, Gokhale said that he could not conceive 'a more wanton, a more mischievous, a more stupid, and a more precipitately introduced measure'.[11]

In 1893, Poona had the honour of welcoming Dadabhai Naoroji, a few days before he presided over the annual Congress session at Lahore. Dadabhai was visiting India after an absence of six years and had at this time the halo of a double triumph. He had recently been elected a member of the British Parliament, and his friends had succeeded in piloting a resolution through the House of Commons in favour of holding the I.C.S. examination simultaneously in India and England.

The citizens of Poona warmly welcomed the 'Grand Old Man'. Gokhale sat in the coach-box of the carriage in which Dadabhai was taken in a triumphal procession through the streets of Poona to Hirabag, where every one of the two thousand chairs was occupied. Gokhale welcomed Dadabhai on behalf of the Sarvajanik Sabha and congratulated him on his success in entering the British Parliament:

We all remember how for six long years a whole nation's eyes were watching with anxious suspense the unequal and unprecedented struggle which Mr Dadabhai was carrying on in England on India's behalf, and how our hearts constantly rose or sank according as we heard that his prospects were getting brighter or darker. . . . And gentlemen, to my mind, it has always appeared that the one secret of the unique, the unparalleled success which he has achieved has been the great faith that is in him—the faith that if only he did his duty honestly and manfully, success must follow no matter when it came.[12]

Gokhale referred to the resolution on the I.C.S. competitive examination passed by the House of Commons and said: 'The work which Mr Dadabhai has done for us in one brief year in Parliament demonstrates the necessity of a few representatives at least in the House of Commons.'

The young Gokhale had a profound reverence for the sixty-eight year-old Dadabhai Naoroji who was Ranade's idol, and could, therefore, be described as the mentor of Gokhale's mentor.

In thanking the citizens of Poona, Dadabhai gave a speech which summed up not only the creed of the Indian National Congress at

[11] *Sarvajanik Sabha Quarterly Journal,* Jan. 1893, p. 53.
[12] Ibid., Jan. 1894, p. 109.

the turn of the century, but also the aspirations, assumptions and illusions of its leadership.

Citizens of Poona, I wish to address to you a few words. . . . Here I observe with the greatest pleasure and gratification that you, from one end of this ancient city to the other, the lowest to the highest, not only from one class or creed, but from every class and creed, all have welcomed me; . . . the lesson to be learnt from this is that whatever be the faith . . . there is a national life beyond a sectarian life and that we are all really the children of India. We must work together, we must stand foot to foot for the progress and amelioration of our country . . . unite in perfect harmony among ourselves in loyalty to the British people who have produced this phenomenon, and to whom, therefore, all the glory is due rather than to me, the child of that British work. . . . Until we are able to satisfy the British people that what we ask is reasonable and that we ask it in earnest, we cannot hope to get what we ask for, for the British are a justice-loving people, and but for that conviction I should not have worked on as I have done for forty years, and I shall go on cherishing that idea. . . . At their hands we shall get everything that is calculated to make us British citizens. But it all rests on ourselves. We must satisfy them that we are in earnest, we must work, we must struggle, we must make self-sacrifice, and when that has been done, we shall be in a position to ask all and get all we may reasonably ask. What can better illustrate it? What better proof can you have? Here I stand and you welcome me as a Member of the British Parliament and a Member of a British constituency.[13]

4

In October 1896, M. K. Gandhi, a twenty-seven year-old Gujarati barrister, came to Poona. No one in his wildest dreams would have classed him with Naoroji, Hume, or Digby. His youth, inexperience, innocence and humility were touching. He was in dead earnest about the cause nearest his heart, that of the Indian immigrants in South Africa. In Bombay, he succeeded in arranging a public meeting under the auspices of the Bombay Presidency Association at which Pherozeshah Mehta himself presided. In Poona he called upon Tilak and sought his support. Tilak was sympathetic, but asked him if he had met Gokhale.

'I have not yet seen him', replied Gandhi; 'I know him by name and mean to see him.'[14]

[13] Ibid., p. 111.
[14] M. K. Gandhi, *Satyagraha in South Africa*, 2nd ed., Ahmedabad, 1950, p. 50.

'You do not seem to be familiar with Indian politics', said Tilak, and went on to explain that Poona politicians were divided into two parties, and that if Gandhi wanted the support of both for a public meeting on South Africa, he should request a 'neutral' like Professor Bhandarkar, who did not take part in politics, to preside.

Tilak and Bhandarkar were both kind to Gandhi, but it was Gokhale who won his heart. Gandhi's autobiography contains a vivid picture of the first meeting in the Fergusson College grounds with the man whom he was later to call his political *guru*: 'Gokhale closely examined me, as a schoolmaster would examine a candidate seeking admission to a school. He told me whom to approach and how to approach them. He asked to have a look at my speech. He showed me over the college, assured me that he was always at my disposal. . . .'[15]

'Love at first sight', was Gandhi's description of his first encounter with Gokhale. Gokhale was only three years older, but this was not the only reason for the obvious respect, almost reverence with which Gandhi treated him. In 1896 both of them were young; Gandhi was twenty-seven, and Gokhale thirty. While Gandhi was a little-known, diffident champion of the small Indian minority in distant Africa, Gokhale was a prominent educationist, editor and politician, in the centre of provincial and national affairs. The first letter written by Gandhi immediately after leaving Poona indicates that he had cheerfully accepted the role of a disciple. He requested Gokhale to form 'a committee of active, prominent workers for our cause'. He sought Gokhale's co-operation in raising the problems of Indians overseas in the Imperial Council at Calcutta and in the House of Commons, if the 'Indian enterprise outside India' was not to come to nought.[16]

The first meeting in 1896 was the beginning of a lifelong collaboration and friendship which was to affect not only the political careers of both Gokhale and Gandhi, but also the history of India.

---

[15] *Idem, An Autobiography*, 2nd ed., Ahmedabad, 1940, p. 129.
[16] Gandhi to Gokhale, 18 Oct. 1896, in *Collected Works of Mahatma Gandhi*, vol. II, p. 90.

7

Professor Gokhale

For the first ten years of its existence the Fergusson College was located in the old Gadre Wada in Shaniwarpeth with its old-world ornamental arches and overcrowded benches. It offered a complete contrast to the government-owned Deccan College. It could not boast of a hostel, a library or even a playing field; its teachers were young, inexperienced and without the high qualification and prestige of the English Principal and professors of the Deccan College. 'A tinpot college' was how the students of the Deccan College described the Fergusson College. However, the Fergusson College more than made up for what it lacked in amenities in the enthusiasm of its teachers and students; they were proud that theirs was a wholly 'indigenous institution', run entirely by Indians fired with a missionary zeal.

Sir James Fergusson, the Governor of Bombay, after whom the college was named, had encouraged its promoters; he visited the New English School and presided over its prize-distribution ceremony in 1884. There was even a proposal to turn over the management of the government-owned Deccan College to the Deccan Education Society, formed to run the New English School, the Fergusson College and other such institutions. Anglo-Indian critics, however, did not take long to scent the dangers inherent in colleges run entirely by Indians. 'The minds of the present generation of educated natives', wrote the *Times of India*, on 10 March 1895, 'have been moulded by European scholars with whom they have been associated. The minds of future generations will be moulded by men who have founded a college on the historic site of the Peshwa's palace and have strong views about patriotism.' The official attitude towards the Fergusson College gradually changed from one of sympathy to suspicion, and in August 1890 we find Governor Harris confiding to the Secretary of State that the Fergusson College was a 'nest of disaffection'.[1] Seven years later, the Bombay Government openly frowned on the

[1] Harris to Lord Cross, 2 Aug. 1890 (Harris P.).

Fergusson College and sought to clip the wings of its teachers.

Gokhale started his career at the Fergusson College as a lecturer in English literature. When Tilak resigned in 1890, Gokhale was asked to take the mathematics classes. The following year, D. K. Karve, who was Gokhale's classmate in Elphinstone College, joined Fergusson College and relieved him of the mathematics classes. Gokhale seems to have found little difficulty in switching from literature to mathematics and from mathematics to history and political economy. A little book he wrote on arithmetic for schools proved extremely popular, and did for him what the *Autobiography* did for Jawaharlal Nehru:[2] it made him financially secure. The study of mathematics was a useful discipline for Gokhale; it gave a statistical bias to his study of economic and financial problems and lent clarity and trenchancy to his criticisms of official policies. The close reasoning and the great precision which were to characterize his writings and speeches on economic matters may have owed something to his training in mathematics in his youth. But he also had unique opportunities for intimate discussion with two of the most knowledgeable critics of the Indian economic scene: G. V. Joshi and M. G. Ranade. From them Gokhale learnt the value of the Blue Books and official reports for analysing and assailing the policies of the government. For an admirer of Edmund Burke and Robert Browning, wading through statistical tables and official verbiage may not have been a wholly pleasant pastime, but, as we shall see later, it paid rich dividends.

Gokhale was an exceedingly conscientious teacher. If we are to believe the recorded recollections of some of his students, he hardly ever laughed in the classroom. Lack of humour does not, however, seem to have been a serious handicap to him. He was well liked by his students, who found him accessible and helpful. They were spellbound by his clear and eloquent exposition in the classroom. 'The bell that tolled the close of the period', recalled one of them many years later, 'often came as a deep disappointment'.[3] Gokhale did not treat the study of history and economics merely as an intellectual exercise; he made it a key to the understanding of contemporary problems. In his lectures on economics, he stressed the necessity of a

---

[2] *Arithmetic For High Schools* by Gopal Krishna Gokhale, B.A., originally published by Arya Bhushan Press, and reprinted by Macmillan in 1896. Macmillan sold 312,000 copies. *Arithmetic for Lower Secondary Schools* was published in 1902. There were also several Indian-language translations.

[3] M. V. Bhide, recollections *in* Limaye (ed.), op. cit., pt. II, p. 149.

protective tariff for India's nascent industries. In his lectures on history, he drew telling parallels between Ireland and India; he felt sure that the tide of liberalism and democracy which had swept across nineteenth century Europe was bound to reach Asia. Dhavle, who graduated from the Rajaram College at Kolhapur and attended some of Gokhale's lectures on Indian history at the Fergusson College, recalls: 'He spoke on the Peshwas. He marshalled his facts with great skill, gave opinions of Marshman, Hunter and Grant Duff, but said that the opinions of these English historians should not be considered the last word on the subject.'[4] Gokhale wanted his students to prepare themselves for the great responsibilities which awaited them. Such was his preoccupation with the political and economic problems of India that he went out of his way to discourage promising students from taking up the study of science. Conditions in India, he told them, were not propitious for specialization in industrial and scientific studies. 'The study of history, economics and politics', he argued, 'would balance our judgements, widen our sympathies and broaden our vision . . . and if we have a large class of men well-read in these subjects, the level of public life will, of necessity, be raised.'

As a teacher, Gokhale never seemed to be in a hurry. He explained every passage and argued every problem from different angles. Though he spoke and wrote chaste Marathi, his real medium was English, which he wielded with an uncommon facility and elegance. He had closely studied the works of Edmund Burke, John Stuart Mill and John Morley. Such was his sensitivity to a good English style that he tended to form a favourable first impression of any unknown correspondent who sent him a well-composed letter. For this weakness he had sometimes to pay dearly, by being saddled with 'the company of undesirable persons who first approached him by means of a fluent letter in imitation of Macaulay or Burke'.[5]

Gokhale was never slipshod in his thinking or expression. Sometimes he would walk up and down the room ('like a tiger in a cage' as his friend and pupil R. P. Paranjpye once put it) to think out the precise word or phrase he wanted to use. His speeches and articles were well-argued and compact. As a student, Gokhale was nervous and halting in his speech, but he resolved to overcome this handicap after he became a teacher. He memorized many famous speeches.

[4] Dhavle's interview with the author in Dec. 1963.
[5] Paranjpye, *Gopal Krishna Gokhale*, p. 15.

While at the Deccan College, he is reputed to have committed to memory portions of Burke's *Reflections on the French Revolution*. The result was that in his early twenties he was able to make a mark as a speaker, and was much in demand at meetings organized in Poona by the Fergusson College, the Deccan Education Society, and the Sarvajanik Sabha—and later at the annual sessions of the Indian National Congress. In 1896, he was invited to deliver the annual address of the Bombay Graduates Association. This was a signal honour, as among the speakers in previous years had been such eminent figures as Pherozeshah Mehta and Ranade. Like Ranade, Gokhale usually wrote his speeches; with his excellent memory he could, however, effortlessly deliver them without any notes. His close reasoning, polished diction, poetical allusions and apt quotations delighted a generation of educated Indians who studied English classics with greater care and enjoyment than we can imagine today.

It did not take Gokhale long to discover that it was not easy to be at once a conscientious teacher, journalist and politician. What it meant in terms of hard work may be gathered from a letter which he wrote to G. V. Joshi in 1891. He was lecturing twenty hours a week and also correcting students' notebooks. His week-ends were almost entirely taken up by the editing of the *Sudharak* and the *Quarterly Journal* and by the secretarial work of the Sarvajanik Sabha. In addition to this back-breaking schedule, he had to keep himself posted with current affairs in India and abroad, and to read the *Kesari*, *Mahratta*, *Dnyanaprakash*, the *Times of India* and other newspapers and magazines. He subscribed to the Dublin *Freeman*, and *The Times* [London]. He read the proceedings of legislative councils, and official reports, without which it would have been impossible for him to function effectively as an editor and politician. In 1895, Gokhale was elected to the senate of the Bombay University of which he remained a member for nearly twenty years. He was appointed the examiner in history and political economy by the Bombay University, an honour then rare for an Indian professor. It brought him an additional burden, but gave much satisfaction to the Indian academic community which resented the virtual monopoly of examinerships by European professors. 'I have heard of grumblings in some Anglo-Indian newspapers', wrote Paranjpye to Gokhale, 'about some of these appointments [of Indians] owing to their being natives, but they are incomparably better than insulting us by appointing the average two-penny, half-penny Englishmen whose only qualification is their white skin as examiners in all conceivable subjects.'[6]

All this added up to a heavy load, but in 1892 Gokhale also became the secretary of the governing body of the Council of the Deccan Education Society. It was a great honour, but it brought additional worries. A new building for the Fergusson College was planned; the foundation stone had been laid in 1892. Funds had to be raised, and Gokhale had to spend some week-ends and summer vacations contacting potential donors in Bombay and Gujarat. Thanks largely to Gokhale's efforts, Fergusson College moved into the new building in 1895. His health was nearly shattered in the process, but the experience was useful. Many years later when he was called upon to collect funds for the Indian National Congress or the Servants of India Society, the contacts he had made in the *mofussil* stood him in good stead.

When Gokhale was the secretary of the Council of the Deccan Education Society, its president was F. G. Selby, Principal of the Deccan College. Selby was a remarkable Englishman who had come to India in 1877 after taking his degree from the University of Oxford. He had edited Bacon's *Essays* and Aristotle's *Ethics*, but his popularity with the Indian élite in Poona was due less to his scholarship than to his great amiability and complete freedom from racial prejudice. To many Indians he seemed the epitome of the best qualities of an Englishman. Even though he was the Principal of the rival Deccan College, he was elected to preside over the governing body of the Fergusson College.

Gokhale's friendship with Selby was long and fruitful. What it meant to Gokhale may be gathered from a letter he wrote to Selby on 4 January 1905:

Throughout these years, I have felt for you the reverence and affection that one feels for a teacher, and if my attitude of mind towards Englishmen generally is today more friendly and more appreciative than that of many of my colleagues, it is largely due to what I have seen of Englishmen in you. The thought that what I said or wrote would perhaps meet your eye has always increased my sense of responsibility and exercised a sobering and restraining influence on my thoughts and words.[7]

2

Gokhale had inherited a good constitution. As a student he was no bookworm. He took long walks and played cricket and tennis.

[6] Paranjpye to Gokhale, 3 Oct. 1901 (Paranjpye P.).   [7] G.P.

He enjoyed a good game of cards, billiards or chess. If he had continued to balance mental toil with physical exercise and recreation, all would have been well. The seduction of politics and his youthful ardour, however, made him careless of his health. He tended to take too much upon himself and to take everything too seriously. If there was an important speech or article to prepare, he postponed it till the last day, and then sat up the whole night to complete it. He did not realize the risks he was running by curtailing his sleep. His food habits were also not very admirable. He disliked ghee, but could hardly resist food seasoned with chillies. His hair-trigger sensitivity to criticism added an emotional strain to the burden of his work and responsibility. An uncharitable comment in the *Kesari* or the *Times of India*, a careless remark by a friend, or a malicious innuendo by a political opponent could throw him into a fit of despair. Politics is a rough game and requires, even from its luckiest practitioners, not only intellectual toughness but a thick skin. It is a strange paradox that Gokhale, who was initiated into journalism and politics almost in his teens, should have remained all his life so sensitive and vulnerable to criticism.

So much of a prominent politician's life is sometimes lived in public that one may be tempted to imagine that he has no life of his own apart from politics. In India there is the further difficulty that we know very little about the private lives of our public figures; it is not part of decorum to talk or write about one's intimate life even to one's closest friends. The barest facts of Gokhale's domestic life have therefore to be pieced together from stray references in his correspondence, and the recorded recollections of his friends and relatives. He was married early (at the age of fifteen) as was customary at that time among the Brahmans of Maharashtra. About his first wife, Savitribai, we know little except that she suffered from leprosy and never lived with her husband. In 1887, at twenty-one, Gokhale was persuaded by his mother and elder brother to marry again. Savitribai, whose malady was incurable, is said to have given her consent. Her gesture was reciprocated by Gokhale and his second wife, Radhabai, both of whom treated Savitribai with much kindness and arranged for her treatment and care until she died a few years later.[8]

Gokhale's second marriage was a happy one. Radhabai gave birth

[8] Information supplied to author by S. R. Venkataraman, Sec., Servants of India Society, Madras. Venkataraman got it from D. P. Velankar, husband of Gokhale's niece.

to a daughter, Kashibai, in 1893. Three years later, in 1896, another girl, Godavari, was born. It is doubtful if Radhabai knew more than the rudiments of Marathi, or understood the great world of literature and politics which absorbed her husband. To live with a man who was wedded to intellectual pursuits, voluntary poverty and political ambition could not have been easy. The relentless schedule which Gokhale imposed upon himself left him little time to spend with his family. This may not have weighed heavily on Radhabai; a Hindu wife of her age and class could fulfil herself by serving her husband and children, dividing her time between the home and the temple, and remain remarkably undemanding and uncomplaining. One wonders if Radhabai sensed the special position that her young husband occupied not only in the Fergusson College but in Poona. There is some evidence that she tried to share her husband's responsibilities. Dr Krishnabai Kevalkar, the first girl to join the Fergusson College in 1894, recalled many years later that Gokhale had helped her in securing admission and that 'Mrs Gokhale was very sympathetic towards me throughout my career'.[9]

Politics brought to Gokhale moments of great excitement and exaltation as well as of disillusionment and despair. Of his attachment to his wife and children, we get brief but revealing glimpses in the recollections of Wacha, who accompanied him to London in 1897, and of Mrs Congreve, who nursed him back to health after a serious illness in England. For a man who was so earnest, so ambitious, and so sensitive, that little house in Bhatwadekar Wada in Poona, where Radhabai was bringing up their two little daughters, must have been a little haven. The haven was not to last long. On 18 October 1900, Radhabai gave birth to a child. Neither the mother nor the child lived.

[9] Limaye (ed.), op. cit., pt. II, p. 139.

8

On the Congress Platform

The visits of Hume and Naoroji were reminders of the ties between
Poona and the Indian National Congress. It was at the annual sessions
of the Congress that Gokhale experienced a sense of participation in
national politics.

In November 1888, even before he was elected secretary of the
Sarvajanik Sabha, Gokhale attended the first Provincial Conference
at Poona, which elected delegates to the Allahabad Congress. He
moved one of the important resolutions at the Provincial Conference
and was elected its joint secretary.[1] Gokhale could not, however,
attend the Allahabad Congress. The following year, in the Christmas
week of 1889, when the Congress met at Bombay with Sir William
Wedderburn in the chair, the large contingent of fifty-nine delegates
from Poona included (to quote from the official report of the proceedings) 'Mr Gopal Krishna Gokhale, B.A., Brahmin, Teacher and
Professor, Fergusson College, Joint Secretary, Provincial Congress,
Joint Editor, *Sudharak*, Editor, *Quarterly Journal*, Sarvajanik Sabha'.
Among his fellow delegates were three of his colleagues in the
Fergusson College, B. G. Tilak, V. S. Apte and G. G. Agarkar.

Gokhale's maiden speech on the Congress platform was delivered
on 27 December 1889. He spoke in support of an amendment moved
by Tilak to a resolution on the reform of the Governor-General's
Legislative Council. It was an uninspiring performance, but on the
following day when Gokhale criticized the Government of India's
action on the report of the Public Service Commission, he gave ample
proof of his gifts as a speaker. Recalling the 'noble promises' of the
Charter of 1833 and the Queen's Proclamation of 1858, he argued
that those who shrank from fulfilling them 'must be prepared to face
the painful dilemma of hypocrisy or treachery, must be prepared to
admit that England was insincere when she made those promises or
that she is prepared to break faith now'. He compared 'the present
struggle' between Anglo-Indians and Indians to the struggle between

[1] *Sarvajanik Sabha Quarterly Journal*, Jan.–April 1889, pp. 12–13.

the 'patricians and plebians' in ancient Rome and between 'the classes and the masses' in modern Britain. He reiterated the demand that the I.C.S. examination should be held simultaneously in India and England: 'For posts in our own country, if we are not to be examined in our own country, I do not know what justice and equity are.'[2]

The young professor-politician was developing his style as a speaker: mastery of facts, marshalling of arguments, a repertoire of literary and historical allusions and a felicitous English style which was calculated to fascinate a generation of educated Indians. His diction was elegant, but he did not hesitate to call a political spade a spade.

The January 1890 issue of the *Quarterly Journal of the Poona Sarvajanik Sabha* carried an article on the Bombay Congress which was evidently from Gokhale's own pen: 'The Fifth National Congress was in many ways the most remarkable of all the Congresses hitherto held. In point of number—nearly 1900 delegates—and in point of the variety of subjects on which resolutions were passed, no other Congress has approached it; while in regard to the eloquence displayed on the platform and enthusiasm pervading the general ranks of the delegates, it has, to say the least, fully maintained its traditions of previous years.' With Sir William Wedderburn in the chair and with Charles Bradlaugh on the platform, the atmosphere of the Bombay Congress was charged with great enthusiasm. In half an hour, a sum of Rs 63,000 was raised for the work of the Congress.

Gokhale's article stoutly defended the representative character of the Congress. He analysed the motives of its detractors. Foremost among them were the Anglo-Indian gentlemen, 'whose illiberality of mind and narrowness of vision are equalled only by the selfishness of their aims and the elasticity of their conscience, and who are therefore bitter and uncompromising foes of all political and educational progress of the Natives of this country'. Then there were those 'well-meaning but timid souls, who can never contemplate the prospect of any change in the constitution without trembling'. Finally, there were the 'aspiring officials, and self-seeking sycophants, and spiteful cavillers and misguided simpletons . . . fit only to be tools in the hands of the designing persons'. Gokhale refuted the charge that Muslims and Parsis were keeping away from the Congress. A few Parsis had been critical, but the Parsi community—on the basis of its popula-

---

[2] *Report of the Fifth Indian National Congress,* Bombay, 1889, p. 50.

tion—was well-represented in the rank and file of the Congress as well as in its leadership. As for the Muslims, they had so lagged behind in education that the wonder was 'not that more Mahomedan delegates are not seen in the Congress, but so many are'.

Gokhale also answered the charge that the Congress did not represent the interests of the mass of the people. He could not see how the Congress demands were opposed to the real interests of the Indian masses. How could the masses be hurt by election, rather than nomination of some of the members of the Legislative Councils? In whose interest, if not that of the masses, was the reduction of the salt duty, the establishment of technical schools, the separation of the judiciary and the executive, and the reform of the police and revenue administration?

Gokhale affirmed that the interests of the educated and uneducated classes were not basically antagonistic. Education had 'merely put a tongue into the mouths that were dumb before'; the educated classes were merely the spokesmen of their countrymen. In any case it was presumptuous on the part of 'Anglo-Indian administrators, whose life passes in the seclusion of their bungalows or in the exclusive atmosphere of their offices, or in the *shikar* of wild beasts', to claim that they knew more of the wants and wishes of the masses of India than educated Indians who were in daily contact with their countrymen.[3]

A year later, when the Indian National Congress met at Calcutta, Gokhale spoke eloquently in favour of reducing the salt tax. The tax which had been increased pressed heavily on the Indian peasantry, living on the 'borderland of famine', to whom Gokhale applied (with a slight alteration) the lines of the Corn Law poet:

> Landless, joyless, helpless, hopeless,
> Gasping still for bread and breath;
> To their graves, by troubles haunted,
> India's helots toil till death.

He reminded the delegates of the Calcutta Congress that the poor people in the villages had 'as much right to the comforts of this God's earth as you or I or anyone else'. 'I dare say', he said, 'there is not a single person present, not a single member of those who are called the middle and upper classes who have consumed during the last three years, one grain of salt less than he would have done if there

[3] 'Reflections Suggested by the Fifth Indian National Congress', in *Sarvajanik Sabha Quarterly Journal*, Jan. 1890, p. 8.

had been no enhancement [of the salt tax].' He recalled that when
the income-tax was imposed, official spokesmen had argued that the
poorer classes were already bearing more than their share of the tax
burdens. Why was the salt tax raised? asked Gokhale. Was it because
'the masses were almost certain to suffer silently without protest . . .
whereas their wealthier brethren were . . . certain to denounce any
taxation on them in the public press and at St. Andrew's dinner
speeches?' 'We are appealing', declaimed Gokhale, 'to the sense of
justice of the Government of India. We are appealing to their states-
manship, to their righteousness, and I even go further and say, to
their mercy. . . .'

As Gokhale spoke at Congress sessions year after year, he gained
in self-confidence. Whatever the subject under discussion he gave a
good account of himself. He appealed to the better side of the ruling
race, but was unsparing in his criticism of the authorities. Speaking
at the Allahabad Congress (December 1892) on the Indian share in
the higher ranks of the administration, he burst out: 'If ever a
mountain was in labour and brought forth a mouse, it was in the
present instance of the Public Service Commission. . . . I say it would
be well for them [the British] to openly and publicly fling into flames
all these promises, and pledges as so much waste-paper and tell us
once for all that after all we are a conquered people and can have no
rights or privileges.'

At the Lahore Congress (December 1893), Gokhale charged the
Government of India with pursuing 'a policy of retrogression', and
treating the educated classes 'with increasing jealousy'. He criticized
the rules for the Legislative Councils framed under the Act of 1892
and dwelt on the inequitable distribution of financial burdens between India and England. A recent debate in the House of Commons
had revealed the raw deal India had received at the hands of the
British War Office and the Treasury. 'If ever the Government of the
country were put on its trial', said Gokhale, 'I should be content to
frame the indictment on those admissions [of responsible British
statesmen].' The financial and economic partnership between India
and England reminded him of the dwarf and the giant in Goldsmith's
The Vicar of Wakefield.[4]

From 1889 onwards Gokhale attended the Congress sessions re-
gularly. At the Nagpur Congress (1891), he was elected a member of
the 'Subjects Committee', the inner forum for the selection of subjects

[4] *Report of the Ninth Indian National Congress*, Lahore, 1893, pp. 141–2.

and speakers for the plenary session of the Congress. It was in the Subjects Committee that he had opportunities of meeting the senior leaders who decided the strategy and commanded the patronage of the Indian National Congress. As the secretary of the Poona Sarvajanik Sabha and the editor of its journal, he was already acquainted with the leaders of western India; but it was at the annual Congress gatherings that he came to know the leaders from other provinces and acquired the reputation of a young, able and eloquent politician who was deferential towards his seniors but in dead earnest about politics.

In 1895, when the Indian National Congress met at Poona, Gokhale was one of the secretaries of the Reception Committee. The Poona Congress brought into the open a bitter rift in the body politic of Maharashtra, the roots of which lay in personal and social rather than in political issues.

9

The Great Split

In the long-drawn-out controversy between Agarkar and Tilak differences on social reform had not figured prominently, though they undoubtedly contributed to mutual misunderstanding and bitterness. After Tilak was forced out of the Deccan Education Society in 1890, social reform increasingly became a wedge in the public life of Poona.

It is not easy for us to imagine the feelings of those who attacked and those who defended orthodox customs and ritual eighty years ago. Under Muslim rule, Hindu society had developed a defensive dogmatism and rigidity. As a system of thought Hinduism continued to be liberal, but as a social system it became increasingly exclusive and intolerant. Caste distinctions hardened; the professional priestly caste gained in authority; religion tended to be reduced to mechanical formulae; superstition and fatalism were at a premium. A contemporary of Gokhale, G. S. Sardesai, the historian, has recorded how as a child he was required to take a bath if he happened to touch a person of the lowest caste, to wear at meal-times clothes made only of 'pure textiles' (silk or wool) and to have a hair-cut only on an 'auspicious' day.[1] Little boys had to get their ear-lobes pierced; such was the importance attached to this custom that in Marathi non-Hindus were often referred to by a term (*avindh*) meaning 'without the pierced ear-lobe'.[2] Instructions on what, how and where to eat were carried to ludicrous lengths, not only by unsophisticated people in the villages but by the educated élite. Some of the delegates to the meetings of the Indian National Congress carried or cooked their own food and ate behind closed doors to avoid the unholy gaze of their colleagues. The more prosperous of them asked not only for Brahman cooks, but for Brahman cooks of particular sub-castes.[3] In

[1] G. S. Sardesai, 'The Pilgrimage of My Life', in D. D. Karve (ed.), *The New Brahmans, Five Maharashtrian Families*, Berkeley, California, 1963, p. 118.
[2] D. K. Karve 'My Life Story', in D. D. Karve (ed.), op. cit., p. 50.
[3] 'We may provide Brahman cooks', R. Sapru wrote from Allahabad to Gokhale on 11 April 1908, a few days before the Congress Convention, 'but it will be better for those who insist upon any particular class of Brahman cooks that they should bring their own cooks.' (G.P.).

Bengal the eating of biscuits was at one time a serious enough trans-
gression to merit excommunication from the caste.[4] Excommunication was a deadly weapon, a sword of Damocles hanging over the
head of anyone who dared to defy the canons of Hindu orthodoxy.
In 1883 no Hindu youth in the whole of Bombay Presidency came
forward to avail of a Parsi magnate's generous offer of a scholarship
for qualifying as a barrister in England. The taboo on foreign travel
was so strong that even Tilak, a devout and scholarly Hindu, had to
undergo a penance when he returned from a visit to Burma in 1899.

It was quite natural that contact with the West should have produced impatience with the strait-jacket of caste, custom and superstition. 'Our system is to a great extent become petrified . . .', complained Telang;[5] 'the moral conceptions which once informed it have
long since vanished and . . . we are now hugging the mere outer shell
as if that were all in all.' 'A kind of death-in-life' was how N. G.
Chandavarkar, another prominent figure in the social reform movement, described the state of Hindu society.[6] 'We are neither Vedant-
ists . . . nor Pauranics nor Tantrics', declared Swami Vivekananda.
'We are just "Don't-touchists". Our religion is in the kitchen. Our
God is the cooking-pot, and our religion is "Don't touch me, I am
holy." If this goes on for another century, every one of us will be in
a lunatic asylum.'[7]

Of the evils which were corroding Hindu society, none seemed
graver than those which stunted the growth of Indian womanhood.
Ranade's wife has recorded[8] how as a child she was forbidden to
enter the front apartments of her own home and be seen in the presence of even her father. Singing and playing were unthinkable for
girls, and so were reading and writing. One of her sisters was married
at the age of five, another at seven; she was lucky to be married relatively late, at eleven. Pandita Ramabai, the Christian missionary
who founded the Sharda Sadan in Poona, told the Education Commission that no more than one in five hundred Indian women was
literate. Early marriage was the root cause of illiteracy; it also resulted in another terrible institution; that of the child widow. Little
girls, who hardly knew the meaning of marriage, were condemned to

[4] B. C. Pal, *Memories of My Life and Times*, Calcutta, 1932, p. 370.
[5] K. T. Telang, *Select Writings and Speeches*, Bombay, n.d., vol. II, p. 549.
[6] L. V. Kaikini (ed.), *The Speeches and Writings of Sir Narayan G. Chandavarkar*, Bombay, 1911, p. 97.
[7] *The Complete Works of Swami Vivekananda*, 9th ed., Calcutta, 1964, vol. III,
p. 167.   [8] R. Ranade, *Ranade*, pp. 37–8.

lifelong mourning when their boy-husbands, on whom they had hardly set their eyes, died. The condition of the infant widows, Ranade wrote in 1886, was 'a scandal and a wrong which is a disgrace to any well-regulated society'.

The efforts of the great Bengali reformer, Iswarchandra Vidyasagar, culminated in the passage of the Hindu Widows Remarriage Act of 1856, but it afforded little real relief to the widows. Thirty years after the passage of the Act, a child-widow, Godubai (who later married D. K. Karve—the centenarian reformer of Poona), discovered that she was virtually a slave in the home of her deceased husband. To expiate the alleged sins of a past life which had robbed her of her husband, her head was shaved; she was made to wear a red sari, the widow's garb; she had to do all the menial tasks in the house, and on the farm. That the unfortunate victims of this tyranny were not few was shown by a statistical analysis in the *Quarterly Journal of the Poona Sarvajanik Sabha*. The article showed that among the Deccan and Konkani Brahmans, one woman out of five was a widow, and one out of every thirty widows was under nine years of age.[9]

The biggest hurdle in the way of reforms was the intimate connection between marriage customs and religious beliefs: suggestions for reform instantly evoked the cry of 'Hinduism in danger'.

The social reformers of western India were usually good and even devout Hindus. Unlike most of their counterparts in Bengal, they did not take to European ways. Nor did they cut themselves off from the common people. K. T. Telang, a distinguished Sanskrit scholar, affirmed with all sincerity that he was first and last a Hindu. Ranade was deeply religious, and anxious to conserve the best elements in Hindu thought and practice. In March 1875, he took a prominent part in the organization of a public debate in Poona on the religious validity of widow remarriages. The fact that the verdict of the Hindu Pontiff, the Sankaracharya, went against the reformers was less important than that the reformers had sought scriptural sanction for reform instead of basing it entirely on the rational and humanitarian ethic of the West.

Curiously enough, the head-on collision between the champions and opponents of social reform in Maharashtra was provoked not by the reformers, but by a Parsi journalist, Behramji Merwanji Malabari (1853–1912). His famous *Notes on Infant Marriage and Enforced*

[9] *Sarvajanik Sabha Quarterly Journal*, April 1895, p. 35.

Widowhood, published in August 1884, suggested, among other things, that child marriages should be denounced in school textbooks, that married students should not be allowed to take university examinations, that preference in government employment should be given to bachelors, that child-widows should be protected by the state against 'social ill-usage', that priests should be prohibited from excommunicating anyone who assisted in the remarriage of a widow.

Malabari's proposals touched off a fierce controversy. British officials in India professed sympathy with his aim, but were loath to meddle in the religious beliefs and superstitions of an alien race. A resolution of the Government of India in 1886 ruled out official initiative in a matter which required reform from within the Hindu society rather than coercion from without.[10]

Frustrated in India, Malabari took his crusade to England. His appeal on behalf of the 'Daughters of India' struck responsive chords in former Viceroys and Governors, the Bench of Bishops, the Roman Catholic Episcopacy, the non-conformists, and the universities. It won the sympathy of Tennyson, the poet-laureate; Herbert Spencer, the most influential philosopher of the time; and of Max Müller, the Indologist. A largely attended meeting was held in London on 18 July 1890, with Lord Reay in the chair. In the face of the mounting pressure of public opinion in England, the Viceroy, Lord Lansdowne, felt that the Government of India had to do something. 'It seems to me', he wrote on 15 September 1890, 'that the law as it stands does not afford protection to children of tender age.'[11] The outcome of the deliberations which followed was the introduction of the Age of Consent Bill in the Governor-General's Legislative Council.

2

The Age of Consent Bill sought to raise the age for the consummation of marriage from ten years (as fixed by the Act of 1860) to twelve years. It fell short of what Malabari had been asking for, and it did not even touch the problem of enforced widowhood. All it did was to make mating with a girl below twelve years equivalent to rape. It was a conservative, and as it turned out, ineffective measure, but it raised a terrific storm. The press in Bengal thundered against

[10] G.O.I., Home Dept., Pub. Proc., Nov. 1886, nos. 131–138E.
[11] Lansdowne's Minute on 'The Age of Consent', 15 Sept. 1890, circulated to Members of Executive Council (Lansdowne P.).

it. A mammoth meeting was held in the *maidan* at Calcutta on 25 February 1891 to protest against the intervention of the Government. Handbills announcing the meeting screamed: 'Brethren! The danger is serious! Total destruction is imminent. Government, without understanding the Hindu religion, are about to interfere with it! The honour of our mothers and wives is about to be destroyed.'

This hysterical reaction had its counterpart in Maharashtra where the Age of Consent Bill led to a major collision between the forces of Hindu orthodoxy and the party of social reform. Tilak headed the orthodox party. He questioned the right of Malabari, a Parsi, to tell the Hindus what was good for them; he disputed the competence of a foreign government to legislate on social and religious issues; he charged the Hindu reformers with ignorance of their scriptures. When R. G. Bhandarkar, the orientalist, affirmed that marriages after puberty did not violate the Hindu religious law, Tilak retorted: 'If you don't know how to interpret the *Shastras* correctly, then at least try to remain silent.'

Bhandarkar and Ranade were not ignorant of their religious heritage; they were well-versed in Hindu law; they knew how the ancient texts had been twisted in the past by an unscrupulous priesthood. They claimed 'not to revolutionize, but only to lop off the diseased overgrowth and excrescences'.[12] As Ranade explained, state intervention was not necessarily an evil. 'The State in its collective capacity represents the power, the wisdom, the mercy and charity, of its best citizens.'[13] If Hindu society was to free itself from the bondage of the past, it was necessary to withdraw one by one the fetters of the so-called religious injunctions and turn them into civil restraints which were more amenable to change and adaptation. The initiative for reform was almost wholly Indian; all that was sought at the hands of the foreign government was that the reform should be given the force and sanction of law.

It is over three-quarters of a century since India was convulsed with the agitation over the Age of Consent Bill. It is not easy to understand the fierce emotions aroused by a measure which seems almost innocuous today. The motives of some of those who participated in this controversy were not as unmixed as they made out at the time. The Government of India under Lord Lansdowne was not

[12] M. G. Ranade, 'The Sutras and Smriti dicta on the age of Hindu Marriage', *Sarvajanik Sabha Quarterly Journal*, Jan.–April 1889, p. 20.
[13] M. G. Ranade, *Religious and Social Reform*, Bombay, 1902, p. 103.

at all eager to jump into the fray. But for Malabari's propaganda in England, they would probably have continued to profess neutrality in social and religious controversies. Malabari's humanitarianism, stimulated as it was by Christian and philanthropic influences of the West, was probably sincere, but he could not have been unaware that his crusade was being exploited by Anglo-Indian apologists, anxious to divert public opinion from political questions. 'The Indian press', wrote Sir Auckland Colvin, the Finance Member of the Viceroy's Council, 'should confine itself to social reform, the merits of which it thoroughly understands than in wasting itself in barren philippics against English rule and English character.' Malabari's close contacts with high British dignitaries and the scornful tone he adopted in private towards the aspirations and the leaders of the Congress suggest that he was not wholly the disinterested philanthropist he professed to be. In fairness to Malabari, it must, however, be said that among his opponents there were several who had their own axes to grind.[14] A. O. Hume, the founder of the Indian National Congress, observed that Motilal Ghose, the proprietor of the *Amrita Bazar Patrika*, had been deliberately whipping up opposition to the Age of Consent Bill to gather public support for the conversion of his newspaper from a weekly into a daily.[15]

Unfortunately for Maharashtra, the controversy on the Age of Consent Bill became involved in the factional feud in Poona, which had split the Deccan Education Society, and was before long to wreck the Sarvajanik Sabha. Agarkar, one of the leaders of the reform party, alleged that Tilak was deliberately pampering the ignorant masses to win cheap popularity, and leading a crusade in which he did not believe. Tilak denounced the superior, almost supercilious attitude of Agarkar and his fellow-reformers towards the common people. The battle of words between the *Kesari* and the *Sudharak* raged fiercely. Both Tilak and Agarkar were born journalists and could wield their native Marathi with deadly effect. The reformers were, however, at a disadvantage: they were a tiny minority and could be represented as renegade Hindus, guilty of outraging the cherished sentiments of their community. Agarkar had to face a continuous barrage of ridicule and invective: his effigy with an egg in one hand and a bottle of liquor in the other was taken in a procession through the streets of Poona and ceremoniously consigned to

[14] A. O. Hume to Lansdowne, 10 Feb. 1891 (Lansdowne P.).
[15] *Idem*, 21 Feb. 1891 (Lansdowne P.).

flames on the outskirts of the town.

Early in 1891, the excitement in Poona reached its peak. To rally its forces, the reform party summoned a meeting at Kridha Bhawan. The meeting was broken up by local rowdies while the police looked on apathetically. It was only after the arrival of a posse of European constables that the trouble-makers dispersed. Most of them were student-admirers of Tilak, who was present at the meeting.

The Kridha Bhawan fiasco was a frustrating experience for the reformers in Poona. They felt powerless between the invective in the local press and the threats of physical violence in the town. Gokhale was not yet senior enough to be counted among the leaders of the party, but he was close to both Ranade and Agarkar, and was editing the English section of the *Sudharak*, the mouthpiece of social reform in Poona. This was his first introduction to the rough and tumble of politics. What he saw in Kridha Bhawan did not exactly correspond to the image of political life which he had learnt to cherish. He unburdened himself in a letter to Ranade's friend, G. V. Joshi.

G. K. Gokhale to G. V. Joshi, 3 March 1891: . . . The conduct of 'leading men' of Poona which culminated in the disgraceful rowdyism of Wednesday last has fairly sickened me. It has exercised a deciding influence on my wavering mind and I am now most exceedingly anxious to be relieved of the necessity of keeping up any kind of connection with them. . . . I am longing for the time when I shall have nothing to do directly with these people. . . .

To the young politician, not yet twenty-five, disenchantment had come a little too soon.

Gokhale and his friends of the reform party could not see that their opponents had the advantage of riding on the tide of a Hindu revival. The fact that the Age of Consent Bill passed through the Viceroy's Legislative Council with the support of its official majority did not alter this fundamental fact.

3

'A dozen years ago', wrote the *Amrita Bazar Patrika* on 14 October 1895, 'when educated men sat together they talked of politics; now, generally speaking, they talk of religion.' Oddly enough, it was the nationalist sentiment which fostered a reaction against the West. The symptoms of this reaction were noted by the young Jadunath Sarkar, the future historian: 'Twenty years ago to discredit a reformer with a Hindu audience it was enough to call him a Christian at heart. Now you have to call him a Sahib at heart.'[16] Sarkar noted that leaders of Hindu opinion, who had 'been the men of light and learning' in the 1870s, had reverted to orthodox ways in the 1890s, and the Bengali stage turned the laugh against the reformers by making them ape Europeans on the stage.

The reversion to orthodoxy was to some extent a natural reaction against the earlier indiscriminate admiration for everything western. The rationalism and individualism of the early Victorian era had swept many educated Indians off their feet; the Brahmo Samaj and other 'progressive' groups had fallen under the intellectual and cultural spell of the West and declared total war on caste and custom. Christian missionaries heaped ridicule on Hindu beliefs and ritual. Hinduism seemed to be on the defensive, almost defenceless, but, as the century wore on, it showed signs of recovery. The feeling of inferiority *vis-à-vis* the West was offset by the tributes paid to Indian philosophy, art and religion by western scholars like F. Max Müller. The emergence of theosophy on the Indian scene stimulated this process: the uncritical enthusiasm of Annie Besant and her friends for Hindu tenets and ritual proved infectious; on the authority of western observers, Hinduism turned out to be not only ancient but scientific. Bankim Chandra Chatterji, one of the foremost Bengali writers of his time, sought a re-interpretation of Hindu theology in the light of 'new rules of literary criticism and scriptural interpretation'. The reconciliation of western-educated intelligentsia to the faith of their forefathers was accelerated by that gentle prophet of the Vedanta, Ramakrishna Paramahansa, and his dynamic disciple, Swami Vivekananda.

In north India Swami Dayananda offered, in the Arya Samaj, a purified, almost puritanic, version of Hinduism, which appealed not only to the English-educated Hindu's rationalistic ethic, but also to his idealistic image of the pristine purity of the Vedic age, unsullied by the encrustations of later times. The Arya Samaj was the Church Militant; it claimed that India was the chosen land, the Aryans were the chosen people, and the Vedas were the chosen gospel.

This religious revival in the closing decades of the century was not merely an urban or middle-class affair. One of its significant manifestations, which caused the government much concern, was the

[16] *Indian Nation*, 10 Aug. 1896.

phenomenal growth of the 'cow protection' movement. The Governor of the North-West (the United) Provinces, where the movement was most vigorous, was convinced that it was anti-British as well as anti-Muslim; he urged the Viceroy, Lord Lansdowne, to enact a new law to suppress it.[17] 'I doubt', wrote Lord Lansdowne on 28 December 1893,

> whether, since the Mutiny, any movement containing in it a greater amount of potential mischief has engaged the attention of the Government of India. The magnitude of the danger arises from this, that the agitation has supplied the whole of the disloyal elements to be found in the Indian community with a popular backing which they could not have obtained from another source . . . a common ground has been found upon which the educated Hindus and the ignorant masses can combine their forces.[18]

Western India did not remain immune from the religious revival which swept over the rest of the country. The Hindu community was pulsating with a new vitality, confidence, even a new and unwonted aggressiveness. Tilak sensed the new mood of the community, to which the Bombay riots in August 1893 were a pointer. The riots were touched off by a minor incident of 'music before a mosque', but the Hindu mill-hands of Bombay, who had heard of rumours of ill-treatment of Hindus in the neighbouring Muslim state of Junagadh, were in an angry mood, and struck fiercely. There were heavy casualties; sixty persons were killed and three hundred injured; shops were plundered, places of worship were desecrated; the police lost control of the situation, and British troops had to be called in. Appeals for the restoration of peace emanated from Queen Victoria downwards. The Anglo-Indian papers laid the blame on the Hindu community, and the British officials, led by the Governor, Lord Harris, did not conceal their sympathy for the Muslims. The official reaction to the Bombay riots made Tilak's blood boil. Writing in the *Kesari*, he rejected the thesis that the riots were due to the cow protection movement, and the Hindus were the guilty party. He asserted that Muslims had attacked first and Hindus had only acted in self-defence: 'They [the Hindus] waited for a day; they could not get protection from the police, and then they had to resort to retaliation for self-protection.'

[17] Crosthwaite, Lt-Gov. of N.W.P. & Oudh to Lansdowne, 26 Sept. 1893 (Lansdowne P.).
[18] Lansdowne's Minute on 'Anti Kine Killing Agitation' (Lansdowne P., vol. XIII).

It was at this juncture when the Hindus in Poona were excited over the riots in Bombay that Tilak gave a new complexion to the Ganapati festival, the annual celebration of the 'elephant-headed god' which had long been a gay family affair. From 1893, under his inspiration, the festival acquired a congregational aspect: the numerous little processions for the immersion of the image of Ganapati were coordinated and combined for a common massive celebration. In 1894, Tilak commented upon the success of the festival he had inspired: 'the excellent arrangements for the *melas* [music and singing parties] . . . the attractive dresses . . ., the parties marching in measured steps, the delightful voice of the singers, the songs full of devotion, the notes of songs full of praise for our religion, and the enthusiasm of the heroic zeal of our Maratha brethren'.[19] The ten-day Ganapati festival, argued Tilak, simply sought to unite the Hindus on a platform of religious piety and innocent gaiety. This was not how it struck British officials and Muslim critics, whose worst suspicions were confirmed by the riots which broke out in Poona on 13 September 1894. On that day, a *mela* (singing party) led by Sardar Tatya Sahib Natu, an orthodox leader of Poona, marched past a mosque near Daruwalla's bridge with his musicians. There was a clash which left a trail of tension and bad blood not only in Poona, but in other towns of Maharashtra.

The government was inclined to blame the majority community for these disturbances. The social reformers, who took their inspiration from Ranade, were anxious to play down the riots and to avoid any provocation to the government and the minority community. Ranade did not like the congregational twist to the Ganapati festival, which weaned the Hindus from their traditional participation in the *Muharrum* festival and aroused the fears and suspicions of the Muslim community. To Tilak the attitude of the government seemed partisan, that of Ranade and his friends pusillanimous. When Ranade opposed the proposal to hold a meeting of the Hindus of Poona to discuss the communal riots in Bombay, Tilak taunted: 'As Rao Bahadur [Ranade] has been bound by silver chains [as a government servant], we cannot say that his opinions on political matters must always be to our good.'

Ranade and his friends feared that the Ganapati festival by sharpening the communal consciousness of the Hindus was bound to provoke a reaction from the Muslim community. Tilak was not im-

[19] *Kesari*, 18 Sept. 1894.

pressed by this argument. He protested that the government was not holding the scales even between the two communities on such contentious questions as processions in public places, music before mosques, and cow-slaughter. He did not see the logic of the Hindus being asked to throw away their legitimate rights simply because they were in a majority. He did not see why congregational worship should be barred to Hindus, when Muslims and Christians were free to practise it.

Tilak did not give up his interest in the organization of the Ganapati festival; indeed, he developed another great celebration, the Shivaji festival. The initial impulse for the renovation of Shivaji's *Samadhi* had come from an Englishman, James Douglas, who in *A Book of Bombay* (1883) pointed out: 'Over all those wide domains, which once owned him Lord and Master . . . not one man now contributes a rupee to keep or repair the tomb of the founder of the Mahratta Empire.' In 1885, Ranade supported a fund-raising campaign for Shivaji's memorial, but it was Tilak who focused the limelight on Shivaji. It was under Tilak's inspiration that on 5 April 1896 the first Shivaji festival was organized at Raigarh, a place consecrated by Shivaji's coronation and death. The following year, the festival was celebrated in June on the anniversary of Shivaji's coronation. His heroic struggle against the Muslim rulers of the Deccan and the Mughal empire, and his success in carving a Maratha kingdom were recalled to inspire the people of Maharashtra with a new pride and enthusiasm. The festival had the usual features of a Hindu religious celebration: songs, dances, readings from the scriptures and distribution of sweets. Ballads exalting Shivaji's heroic deeds were sung, and lectures on Maratha history delivered. Huge portraits of Shivaji were carried in procession to the accompaniment of devotional hymns and shouts of 'Shivaji Maharaj ki jai'. Tilak was criticized for playing on the emotions of the masses. He retorted that there was 'no greater folly than the educated people thinking themselves to be a different class from the rest of the society. . . . The educated people can achieve through these national festivals results which would be impossible for the Congress to achieve.' The festivals 'could carry political activities to the humblest cottages in the villages'. Tilak did not consider English education a *sine qua non* for political capacity, and looked forward to the day when the *telis* (oil vendors) and *tambolis* (betel-leaf sellers) would understand political questions.

Ranade's cautious, pragmatic and rational approach to political questions clashed with Tilak's emotional and bold stance. The Age of Consent Bill, the Ganapati and Shivaji festivals, and the communal riots revealed the basic differences between the rival parties in Poona which looked up to Ranade and Tilak. So strained were the relations between them that almost any issue could become a *casus belli*. The final breach came on an issue which should really have united them: the decision to hold the Congress session in Poona in December 1895.

4

Ranade was well aware of the factional and personal rivalries in Poona, and had, therefore, supported Tilak's appointment as a joint secretary of the committee which was to raise funds and make arrangements for the Congress session. The two parties could not, however, work together on the committee. A fierce controversy broke out over the propriety of holding the National Social Conference in the Congress pavilion. The National Social Conference, of which Ranade was the founder, had, ever since its inception in 1887, held its annual session after the conclusion of the Congress session at the same place and in the same pavilion in which the Congress held its deliberations. The two organizations were of course entirely distinct; the resolutions of one did not commit the other. But the practice of holding the Indian National Congress and Social Conference meetings at the same place and around the same time had the merit of saving trouble and expense to scores of delegates who were interested in both the organizations. This was not how Tilak and his friends viewed the problem; they saw the social 'reformers' pitted against the vast majority of their countrymen. To use the Congress pavilion for the Social Conference was, therefore, unjust to those Congressmen who did not subscribe to the policies of the Social Conference. 'The use of the Congress pavilion for ventilating social grievances', wrote Tilak's paper, the *Mahratta* (8 December 1895), 'is very likely to make Congress itself unpopular.'

Social reform was an explosive subject in Poona; it revived something of the deep emotions of 1890–1 over the Age of Consent Bill. A local firebrand, S. V. Date, threatened that it would be 'murderous' if the 'Sudharaks' (reformers) were permitted to hold the Social Conference in the Congress pavilion. The reformers saw that efforts were being made to cow them down by press attacks and public demonstrations. They felt that on the issue of the use of the Congress pavilion for the Social Conference, justice and precedent were on their side; why could Poona not do what other principal towns in India (which played host to the Indian National Congress) had done for seven successive years? The reformers suspected that the pavilion controversy was merely another stick with which their opponents sought to beat them out of the political life of Poona. The very existence of the reform party seemed at stake. Gokhale's friends remonstrated with him for not hitting back at Tilak. The contest, however, was not really between Tilak and Gokhale, but between Tilak and Ranade. 'We do not desire the struggle', Ranade confided to K. Subba Rao on 16 October 1895, 'but it can't be helped . . . the small band of workers [of the Social Reform Party] scattered in every town . . . are being cried down and abused by the other side. . . .'[20]

The reformers sought to resolve the problem by seeking the views of the Provincial Congress Committees. Of the replies received, almost two-thirds supported Ranade's stand, but they urged that a split in the Congress must be avoided. Even Ranade's supporters did not desire a show-down with the orthodox party in Poona which could jeopardize the success of the Congress session. He decided to hold the Social Conference in a separate pavilion. This was Tilak's victory but it was a pyrrhic one. By driving Ranade to the wall, he alienated the Pherozeshah Mehta–Dinshaw Wacha group in the Bombay Congress, which controlled the party organization. This group turned on Tilak and hamstrung him by appointing additional secretaries to the Reception Committee of the Poona Congress; one of these secretaries was Gokhale. Tilak did not take the affront lying down. He resigned from the Reception Committee.

Tilak was present and even spoke at the Poona Congress in December 1895. But it was Gokhale who was in the centre of the political stage; it fell to him to read the welcome address to the Congress delegates on behalf of Moreshwar Bhide, the chairman of the Reception Committee, who was too old and feeble to perform this duty.

5

The controversy on the use of the Congress pavilion for the Social Conference in Poona was complicated by another development which

[20] K. Subba Rao, *Revived Memories*, Madras, 1933, p. 249.

undermined the position of Ranade's adherents. For nearly a quarter of a century the Sarvajanik Sabha had functioned under his direction. For the last five years Gokhale had been its secretary and the editor of its quarterly journal. The Sabha had acquired a certain standing not only with the people, but with the authorities; it was one of the foremost political associations in India. Its statements and representations, thanks to their association with Ranade, carried weight. But Ranade's influence over the Sabha came to a sudden end on 14 July 1895, after the annual general meeting of the Sabha. His adherents found themselves for the first time in a minority in the Sabha. Tilak and his friends had enrolled new members just before the meeting and outvoted their opponents. The new managing committee of thirty-four members included ten of the outgoing committee and Gokhale was elected one of the secretaries. But there was no doubt that the control of the committee had passed to Tilak. The complexion of Poona politics changed overnight. Well might Tilak and his friends say that what had happened was the perfectly constitutional process of 'converting minorities into majorities'. To Gokhale, and other members of the Ranade group, all this was specious reasoning; the truth was that Tilak and his friends had effected a *coup d'état*. The majority of the members of the new managing committee were opponents of social reform; one of them, Krishnarao Bapu Mande, who was appointed assistant secretary, had even tried to get Ranade into trouble with the government.[21]

Gokhale did not wish to continue as secretary of the Sabha when its managing committee was dominated by the rival party. However, he was prevailed upon by Pherozeshah Mehta and Ranade not to press his resignation till the Poona Congress session was over. Gokhale himself had no doubt that the 'revolution' in the affairs of the Sarvajanik Sabha was directed against Ranade. In a letter to Dadabhai Naoroji, he explained its implications:

G. K. Gokhale to Dadabhai Naoroji, 3 September 1896: Developments of a distressing character have already taken place in the political life of this city. God's curse seems to be resting on this country, else how should it always be that directly some good and useful work is begun, dissensions arise to undo it! The Sarvajanik Sabha —a child of Mr Justice Ranade's—for which he has worked so nobly now for a quarter of a century, has been taken out of his hands and for a whole year the Sabha has done absolutely no work. The whole attempt here is to drive out of public life all workers who

[21] Gokhale to G. V. Joshi, 8 Feb. 1896 (G.P.).

sympathize with the cause of social reform by discrediting them with the masses by all manner of means. . . . [22]

These events revived Gokhale's disgust with politics in his home town. 'I have grown', he wrote to G. V. Joshi on 8 February 1896, 'absolutely sick of public life in Poona. Recent events have opened my eyes very wide indeed. . . . I wish now to wash my hands of all political work in Poona. There is so much that is selfish and ignoble here that I would fly from it to the furthest extremities of the world if I could.'

Gokhale's pessimism was evidently not shared by Ranade, who took the initiative in starting a new political body in Poona. At Ranade's instance, a meeting was called in the historic Kiba Wada in Poona. Attended by 101 prominent citizens it decided to found the Deccan Sabha. The manifesto of the new organization, drafted by Ranade, emphasized that it would represent

moderate and liberal public opinion. . . . The spirit of liberalism implies a freedom from race and creed prejudices and a steady devotion to all that seeks to do justice between man and man, giving to the rulers the loyalty that is due to the law they are bound to administer, but securing at the same time to the ruled the equality which is their right under the law. Moderation imposes the condition of never vainly aspiring after the impossible, or after too remote ideals, but striving each day to take the next step in the order of natural growth by doing the work that lies nearest to our hands in a spirit of compromise and fairness.

The foundation of the Deccan Sabha brought the conflict between the two parties in Poona to a head. Tilak was furious. What did Ranade mean by professing to be the embodiment of moderation and liberalism? Did he imply that Tilak and his friends were immoderate and illiberal? Was not such a stance an invitation to the government to visit official displeasure on the Sarvajanik Sabha under its new management? The *Kesari* denounced Ranade, labelled him a Kautilya and even the 'meanest of men'. 'Is it dotage or puerility?' asked Tilak in the *Kesari* in an article which, in the words of N. C. Kelkar, would 'go down in the history of Marathi journalism as a classical example of invective'.[23]

This bitterness boded ill for nationalist politics in Poona. Without the guiding hand of Ranade and the tireless industry of Gokhale, the Sarvajanik Sabha could not maintain its position for long. Its

[22] G.P.   [23] Kelkar, *Lokamanya Tilak*, p. 322.

relations with the government, even during the last few months of Gokhale's secretaryship, had been strained. Local officials were probably waiting to pounce on the Sabha; its new management easily provided an opportunity. One of the agents of the Sabha was accused of making unverified statements in the countryside about the remission of land revenue. The Bombay Government called for an explanation, and after the exchange of a few letters, curtly informed the Sabha that its representations would no longer be entertained. For a political body which was founded to 'mediate between the rulers and the ruled', and functioned only constitutionally, this act of de-recognition was a crippling blow. No wonder Dadabhai Naoroji, writing from England, remonstrated with Tilak for destroying an institution built up with infinite patience and dedicated labour over several decades.

The Sarvajanik Sabha lost its effectiveness. The Deccan Sabha did not prove a reasonable substitute, or alternative; its politics were much too tame. Tilak's description of it 'as a *pinjrapole* [stable] of Rao Bahadurs' in his characteristic satirical vein was not altogether unjust. So long as Ranade lived the Deccan Sabha could muster strength for sporadic fits of activity, but after his death it was practically dormant. Gokhale made an attempt to give it another lease of life in 1908 but failed.

The events in Poona during 1895–6 seemed catastrophic not only for the causes for which Gokhale stood, but for his own political future. He and his friends had been outwitted and outmanoeuvred. He had lost control of the Sarvajanik Sabha, and its quarterly journal. When the first issue of the journal under the new management announced that Gokhale had resigned, and proposed to devote all his time to his duties as a teacher, his political opponents were serving a notice on him that he would henceforth be on the shelf.[24] Things looked pretty bleak for Gokhale in 1896. Luckily for him, however, events were conspiring to bring him back into the limelight not only of local, but national politics.

---

[24] *Sarvajanik Sabha Quarterly Journal*, July & Oct. 1896, p. 4.

10

The Rising Star

Within three years of the foundation of the Indian National Congress, A. O. Hume had come to the melancholy conclusion that it was futile to address petitions and protests to the Government of India in Calcutta or Simla. He decided to appeal to public opinion in India and England over the head of the bureaucracy. The unchanging and unchangeable bureaucracy in India was impervious to Congress agitation; if any reforms were to come at all, it was obvious they would have to be through the pressure of public opinion in England. Distinguished parliamentarians such as Burke, Bright, Fawcett and Bradlaugh had occasionally voiced Indian grievances, but to put across the Indian view of Indian affairs to the British press, parliament and people, systematic work was necessary. Hume and his friends, therefore, made a beginning in 1888 with the setting up of an 'Indian Agency' in London. The following year the British Committee of the Indian National Congress came into being with Sir William Wedderburn as its chairman. For the next thirty years the British Committee was the pivot of Congress propaganda in Britain. Sir William Wedderburn was its moving spirit, and the journal *India* its mouthpiece. Dadabhai Naoroji and Wedderburn, who were elected to Parliament in 1892 and 1893 respectively, formed the 'Indian Parliamentary Committee'.

The Indian Parliamentary Committee was an amorphous body, its size fluctuating with the fortunes of the Liberal Party from which it drew almost all its members. Most of them had only a superficial acquaintance with Indian affairs, but the Committee had a small dedicated core, which functioned as a pressure group on behalf of the Indian National Congress. This group at first met with a quick and astonishing series of successes. In 1893 it carried through the House of Commons a resolution in favour of holding the I.C.S. examination simultaneously in India and England. The following year it pressed for a parliamentary inquiry into Indian expenditure, and an equitable redistribution of financial burdens between India and Britain. A parliamentary enquiry had long been demanded by Indian leaders, and resisted by the Anglo-Indian officials, who felt safer with a Royal Commission than with a parliamentary inquisition into Indian affairs. Sir Henry Fowler, the Secretary of State, had promised a Select Committee, but was persuaded in favour of a Royal Commission. The Royal Commission on Indian Expenditure, which was announced in 1895, was headed by the sixty-three year-old Lord Welby, a former Permanent Secretary of the British Treasury. The thirteen members of the Commission included M.P.s as well as veterans of the civil and military services in India.

From the Indian point of view, the most heartening aspect of the Royal Commission was that Dadabhai Naoroji and two of his closest colleagues in England, William Wedderburn and W. S. Caine,[1] were appointed to it. Their appointment was hailed in India as a promise of better things to come. The pro-Indian trio knew that there was no cause for immediate rejoicing. Not only was the Commission heavily weighted with British officials, but its terms of reference enjoined it only to go 'into the administration and management of the military and civil expenditure of India and into the apportionment of charges between the Governments of the United Kingdom and of India'. The scope of the inquiry was thus circumscribed so as to exclude matters of high policy. But could the line between finance and administration be rigidly drawn? Were financial inequalities not really the result of economic policies? Could economic ills be cured without administrative and political remedies? The fact that an enquiry had been conceded at all was in itself an achievement. It was obvious that the Indian nationalists' case needed to be put forward by the ablest Indians available, the more so because the Government of India, the India Office and the British Treasury were likely to marshal a formidable array of witnesses on behalf of the 'Establishment'. 'A supreme effort is to be made now in this Commission', wrote Dadabhai Naoroji to D. E. Wacha; 'we may not get another opportunity of the kind for a generation.' He pleaded with Ranade to come to England and appear before the Commission. 'Dear Ranade,' he wrote on 18 June 1896, 'you have an opportunity now to do the greatest service you can to our poor country that you will have in your lifetime. Come and support me in your own able way. . . .'[2]

---

[1] W. S. Caine (1842–1903), temperance reformer and Liberal M.P.; delegate, Indian National Congress, 1890. Visited Poona, Feb. 1897.

[2] R. P. Masani, *Dadabhai Naoroji*, London, 1939, pp. 379–80.

Ranade was willing to go, and Lord Welby, the Chairman of the Commission, was ready to invite him, but the Government of India blocked the way.[3] The Viceroy's advisers argued that Ranade was 'an unfortunate selection', that as a judge he was supposed to be above politics, that he was unacceptable to Europeans in India, and that he was 'a puller of strings'.[4] In the event, D. E. Wacha was selected as a representative of the Bombay Presidency Association, G. Subramania Iyer on behalf of the Mahajan Sabha, Madras, and Surendranath Banerjea on behalf of the Indian Association, Calcutta. Himself thwarted, Ranade decided to depute Gokhale as a representative of the Deccan Sabha. He arranged for funds from the rulers of Baroda and Kolhapur. Gokhale took the assignment earnestly; he spent ten days at Sholapur discussing economic and financial matters with G. V. Joshi, and before embarking from Bombay received a final briefing from Ranade himself.

While Gokhale was on the high seas, Ranade commended his young disciple to the care of his friend Sir William Wedderburn.

Ranade to William Wedderburn, 19 March 1897: . . . Prof. Gokhale is a young man who has been very useful as Honorary Secretary to the Poona Sarvajanik Sabha. . . . He has been acting under my advice for the last ten years and I have found that he possesses a very high order of natural talents and scholarship. He is a Professor of English & History in the Fergusson College, being one of the life-members. He is also one of the few good speakers we have on this side of India. . . . Prof. Gokhale goes fully equipped on the points on which he gives evidence. He is, however, a young man and you, Mr Caine and Prof. Dadabhoy shall have to do your best to see that his examination is conducted in a spirit of fairness. . . .

As he is a good speaker, I would very much like that some arrangement be made to enable him to visit the chief towns where he might speak with great freedom on general questions. . . . [5]

The encounter between Gokhale and Wedderburn was fateful for its effect on them and on Indo-British relations. It was the beginning of a lifelong friendship between two men belonging to different races and generations, but sharing a common purpose. From this moment it is impossible to understand the course of Gokhale's political career without understanding the personality and politics of William Wedderburn.

The Wedderburns of the Scottish border were a family of great

[3] Telegram, Viceroy to Sec. of State, 30 June 1896 (Hamilton P.).
[4] J. Westland to Elgin, 29 June 1896 (E.P.).   [5] G.P.

antiquity, but since the beginning of the nineteenth century they had served in India's Civil Service. 'I can say', Sir William Wedderburn wrote, 'that I always regarded this [I.C.S.] a profession, which was also a profession of my choice, the noblest career open to youthful talent.' His father, Sir John Wedderburn (1789–1862), retired as Accountant-General, Bombay. Sir William's elder brother, John, was the Magistrate and Collector of Hissar in the Punjab and lost his life in the Mutiny of 1857. Sir William's career in the I.C.S. began in 1860 when, at the age of 23, he landed in Bombay. He held a number of administrative and judicial appointments, officiating as Secretary to the Government of India, Judicial Commissioner Sind, Judge of the Bombay High Court, and Member of the Governor's Council.

William Wedderburn did not wholly fit in the official grooves. He was no self-conscious sahib. He worked out schemes for rural credit, and interested himself in education, particularly girls' education. The Poona meeting which resolved upon the formation of the Deccan Education Society in 1885 was presided over by him. Unlike most of his colleagues in the Indian Civil Service, he did not give the leaders of educated India a wide berth. Early on, he helped Pherozeshah Mehta become a Justice of the Peace. In Poona, he made friends with Ranade, and in Bombay, with Dadabhai Naoroji. He was present at the first meeting of the Indian National Congress held in the Gokuldas Tejpal Sanskrit College, Bombay, in 1885. The following year when he officiated as the Chief Secretary to the Government of Bombay, an Indian paper wrote: 'Sir William Wedderburn's presence in the secretariat will be a guarantee that the popular side of the question will not be unrepresented.'[6] Such a close association with Indian opinion was not calculated to make him a favourite of the government. In November 1885, Lord Randolph Churchill, the Secretary of State for India, told the Viceroy that Sir William Wedderburn could not be given a permanent seat on the bench of the Bombay High Court, because 'he was crotchety and also to a great degree a political incendiary. He . . . never loses an opportunity of associating himself with native political movements.'[7] Wedderburn's promotion was thus blocked; this, coupled with the fact that the Indian climate did not agree with his wife, led him to seek premature retirement.

When Wedderburn returned to England in 1887 he was only fifty.

[6] *Indu Prakash*, 15 March 1886.
[7] R. Churchill to Dufferin, 27 Nov. 1885 (Dufferin P.).

He could have led a quiet life. He loved gardening; he was fond of travel; he had a baronetcy and could well have hoped for a seat in Parliament. The twenty-seven years he had spent in India did not, however, allow him rest. He had seen something of the poverty of the country; he had also seen from the inside the working of the efficient but unfeeling bureaucratic machine. His ingrained liberalism, his sympathy with the Indian educated classes, his impatience with the ruling caste in India—so confident, so smug and so superior—made it impossible for him to live the life of a retired English gentleman. He decided to back up the efforts of his friend A. O. Hume in India. He threw himself into the work of the British Committee of the Congress and its journal *India*. In December 1889, two years after his retirement, he had the honour of being invited to preside over the fifth session of the Indian National Congress. 'I have been in the service of the people of India', he said in the course of his presidential speech, 'and have eaten their salt. And I hope to devote to their service what still remains to me of active life.'[8]

During the years 1890–2, when the reform of the Indian councils was on the parliamentary anvil, Wedderburn was continually in touch with Bradlaugh, Ripon and other Liberal statesmen. In 1893, he was elected to the House of Commons and took the lead in organizing the Indian Parliamentary Committee. From the first he assumed the role of a fearless critic of the 'Simla Clique', as he called the Indian administration. He affirmed that the interests of the British officials in India ('repression at home and aggression abroad') were at odds with those of the Indian tax-payers. He pleaded for the employment of Indians in senior posts in the interests of efficiency as well as economy. He denounced military expeditions beyond the Indian frontier for the burdens they imposed on an already impoverished country. He pleaded for a parliamentary enquiry into Indian affairs. 'I affirm', he told the House of Commons in 1893, 'that every good thing done for the people of India has arisen out of an inquiry in this House for reform.'[9]

These criticisms did not endear Wedderburn to his former colleagues in the Indian Civil Service or to the British non-officials in India. He was called a faddist, a crank, and even a traitor. His presidential address at the Bombay Congress was described by the British-owned *Pioneer* of Allahabad as a

[8] *Speeches and Writings of Sir William Wedderburn*, Madras, 1918, p. 1.
[9] Ibid., p. 49.

piece of sophistical impertinence rarely equalled and never surpassed in the annals of political clap-trap. Sir William Wedderburn's speech in short was a simple appeal to the cupidity and vanity of his audience. There are those who may wonder at an Englishman hinting to an assembly of natives that the English army of occupation is a pure element of turbulence far more costly than it is worth; and that all the work of the Government could be done as well and more cheaply than it is at present by native machinery; but then to be at once a professional agitator and an Englishman is undoubtedly hard.[10]

No-one could be less like a professional agitator than Sir William Wedderburn. The epithet was belied by his benign face, his modest, almost shy demeanour, his habit of balancing the rights and wrongs of every situation, his ingrained caution and deep consideration for others. Long years in the civil service had taught him to look at the practical rather than the ideological aspect of public affairs; he was incessantly engaged in tackling specific issues: finding funds for a girls' school in Poona, improving the clauses of a measure for legislative reform, extending famine relief in an Indian district, or softening the rigour of a discriminatory law against Indian immigrants in Natal. He had seen the Indian bureaucratic apparatus; he knew how difficult it was to change its direction. But as a civil servant he had also learnt the value of tenacity and was not discouraged by rebuffs, nor daunted by obstacles. Pragmatic, patient, plodding, tireless, incorrigibly optimistic, he was an epitome of moderation, conciliation, and compromise. In 1897 his chief interest was the Welby Commission of which he was a member. It was for this Commission that his friend Ranade had sent Gokhale to England.

2

Gokhale does not seem to have enjoyed his first voyage to England. From the familiar routine in Poona, the cosmopolitan atmosphere on a modern steamer was a tremendous change; English dress and manners did not sit easy on him, and his vegetarianism was an additional embarrassment. To the amusement of his senior and well-travelled companion, Wacha, Gokhale nervously scanned the menu card at each meal to make sure that he did not order anything that contained eggs or meat. He was also worried about the important assignment at hand. Would he be able to acquit himself well? It was difficult for him to take his mind off the ordeal that awaited him in

[10] *Pioneer*, 28 Dec. 1889.

London; like a student preparing for a stiff test, he pored over the Blue Books he had brought with him and puzzled out the problems of Indian finance. As ill-luck would have it, he received a serious injury in the P & O train between London and Calais when a door struck against his chest. He arrived in London in great pain, but such was the reverential awe in which he held his host, Dadabhai Naoroji, that he did not breathe a word of his suffering to him or to anyone else. It was only when the pain became unbearable that Gokhale took Wacha into confidence. A doctor was summoned at once, and it was found that he had suffered a severe concussion of the heart which could have proved fatal. He was ordered complete rest in bed, and slowly nursed back to health by a friend of Dadabhai's, Mrs Congreve, 'a highly polished lady . . . exceedingly sympathetic and full of humanity'. Testimony to her devoted nursing has been left by Wacha: 'No sister could have nursed better. And none could have kept Mr Gokhale so cheerful and bright all through that serious illness. In a way it was a fortuitous circumstance that the friendship of Mrs Congreve dispelled to a considerable extent his shyness. . . .'[11]

As he lay convalescing, Gokhale was visited by his former pupil, R. P. Paranjpye, who was a student at Cambridge. Gokhale dictated to him part of his evidence for the Welby Commission. Fortunately, he felt well enough to appear before the Commission on 12 and 13 April. His written statement was a sober and effective presentation of the nationalist case on the financial and economic grievances of India. That the distribution of burdens between Britain and India was inequitable, that there was discrimination in favour of British and against Indian industries, that there was a heavy 'drain' from India in the interest of the British garrison and capital. This was a familiar charge-sheet against British rule; it was embodied in Congress resolutions, and was the recurrent theme of Congress publicists such as Dadabhai Naoroji, R. C. Dutt and William Digby. Gokhale made use of the 'drain theory' in his criticisms of British economic policies, but he did not make it the main plank of his argument. Nor did he confine himself only to financial issues. Subtly and effectively, he built into his evidence a reasoned denunciation not only of the economic, but the social and political policies of the Government of India as well. His lucid arguments were supported by facts and figures, drawn for greater effect from official publications. Only occasionally did his passionate nationalism break the self-imposed re-

[11] D. E. Wacha, *Reminiscences of Gokhale*, p. 27.

straint of the scholar: 'For years past we have been treated as a vassal dependency bound to render services to the suzerain power and to place our resources, whenever required, at its disposal. As a result, millions upon millions have been spent on objects which have not advanced the welfare of the Indian people so much as by an inch —even the empty sense of glory, which is a kind of barren compensation to self-governing nations for such a large expenditure of money, is not available to us as a consolation.'[12]

Gokhale went on to voice a grievance which rankled in the breasts of three generations of educated Indians from Naoroji to Nehru: 'We must live all the days of our life in an atmosphere of inferiority, and the tallest of us must bend, in order that the exigencies of the existing system must be satisfied. . . . Our administrative and military talents must gradually disappear owing to sheer disuse, till at last our lot as hewers of wood and drawers of water in our country is stereotyped.'

It is important to remember that these words were addressed in London in 1897 by a young Indian to a Royal Commission. Lord Welby and his British colleagues could not of course be expected to let Gokhale get away with this massive indictment. Besides the Chairman, he was cross-examined by a former Bombay civilian, the sixty-seven year-old Sir James B. Peile, who had served as the Director of Public Instruction, Bombay, Political Agent, member of the Famine Commission, Vice-Chancellor of the Bombay University, and member in turn of the executive councils of the Governor and the Viceroy. 'Was it not a fact', asked Lord Welby, 'that the working expenses of the Indian railways were the lowest in the world and that as a Government speculation, it was a beneficial one?' 'I do not think so, my Lord,' replied Gokhale, 'our wages are very low and therefore the working expenses must be low. If the Indian Railways on the whole are a profitable undertaking, why do English investors, with all their enterprise, almost invariably insist on a Government guarantee of interest in one form or another?' The Indian people felt, Gokhale added, that railway construction was undertaken principally in the interests of the English commercial and moneyed classes.

On the explosive issue of Indian poverty and famines, Gokhale

[12] For Gokhale's evidence see *Indian Expenditure Commission*, vol. 3, *Minutes of evidence taken before the Commission on the administration of the expenditure of India with index, analysis and appendices*, London, 1900. The written and oral evidence reprinted in R. P. Patwardhan & D. V. Ambekar (eds.), *Speeches and Writings of Gopal Krishna Gokhale*, vol. I, Bombay, 1962, pp. 456–671.

clashed head-on with Sir James Peile, who cited the import of bullion into India as evidence of increased prosperity in India.

SIR JAMES PEILE: . . . You accept those facts, I think?

GOKHALE: I accept the figures from you.

SIR JAMES: Are not these facts that I have mentioned signs of decreasing rather than of increasing poverty?

GOKHALE: I do not think so.

SIR JAMES: You do not; can you tell us why?

GOKHALE: It all depends on what classes all these things go to . . . you must also be able to show that these increased imports of precious metals found their way into the pockets of the agriculturists—into the pockets of these poor people. . . .

CHAIRMAN: Perhaps you hesitate to accept proofs of prosperity?

GOKHALE: I am quite open to correction, but I do not quite see clearly how the mere fact of the imports of gold and silver being so and so can mean that the country is increasing in prosperity. This is a fallacy of the mercantile system long regarded as exploded.

Sir James Peile suggested that famines, such as the one in the Deccan which Gokhale had seen at first-hand before embarking for England, were a mere adjunct of an agricultural economy, largely attributable to the vagaries of the monsoon and the follies of a thriftless peasantry.

SIR JAMES PEILE: Well, if you take farm labourers and mill-hands in England, supposing that a great calamity fell upon England and the food supplies were suddenly stopped, do you think that the farm labourers and weavers and mill-hands and so on, would have resources which would enable them to live over the period of high prices which would result?

GOKHALE: That is a very hypothetical case, because such a calamity never seems to come to England.

The fact that the peasants had sold their gold and silver ornaments was, according to Sir James, a sign that they had a resource to draw upon. 'Is it not then a resource?' asked Sir James. 'It is a resource,' retorted Gokhale, 'but it is a very cruel resource to use.'

Lord Welby, the Chairman, intervened to suggest that the import of gold into India showed 'the great taste of the Indian people for ornaments which is a form of luxury'. 'Just in the same way', replied Gokhale, 'they [Indians] have to spend large amounts on funerals. They groan under the system and have to go to the money-lender, but they must do it, it is the social life of the people.'

Lord Welby had no more success than Sir James Peile in browbeating the young politician from Poona. When reminded that he was no military expert to comment on military expenditure in the Indian budget, Gokhale replied, 'I admit that, but it is not our fault . . . we are non-official critics and all the information that is available to us, we utilize.'

One of the tensest moments in the cross-examination came when Lord Welby suggested that it could be an advantage to a country to borrow capital cheaply in another country to help the development of its resources. This provoked Gokhale into an outburst which could have been echoed many years later by young radicals of a later generation. 'If I had a vast property myself, I would rather allow that property to remain as it is with the consciousness that I may make full use of it when I have the means, rather than allow somebody else to come and use it and give me only a pittance, the outsider getting all the rest.'[13]

Gokhale's cross-examination continued for two days, 12 and 13 April. 'You have done most splendidly', Wedderburn assured him. 'Your evidence will be much the best on our side.' Caine, Wedderburn's colleague on the Royal Commission, described Gokhale's evidence 'as the most masterly exposition of the views of an educated Indian reformer on all the subjects dealt with'. These compliments pleased Gokhale, but he hastened to acknowledge his debt to Ranade and G. V. Joshi, who had briefed him before he left India. His role, he wrote to Joshi, was 'no more than that of a conduit pipe and Edison's phonograph'.[14] This was becoming modesty in a young man, but it underrated his own contribution to the final result. His mentors had supplied him with Blue Books, statistical tables and much useful advice. But it was Gokhale who had drafted the memorandum of his evidence, which won such high praise, after his arrival in England. What distinguished Gokhale's evidence was its skilful presentation and lucid exposition. More important than his memorandum was the oral examination which gave Gokhale's performance the quality of a triumph. To be cross-examined by old India hands like Sir James Peile was no trifling matter. Backed by the massive resources of their archives and their lifelong experience of Indian administration, the British officials were eager to explode what they considered the myths of Congress propaganda. When the Government of India were considering the selection of Indian witnesses for the Royal Com-

[13] *Indian Expenditure Commission,* op. cit., p. 220.
[14] Gokhale to G. V. Joshi, 16 April 1897 (G.P.).

mission, Lord Elgin was told by his Finance Member that he 'thought it might be an instructive lesson if a man like Mr [Pherozeshah] Mehta could be subjected to the cross-examination of a Royal Commission'.[15] It was to Gokhale's credit that he succeeded not only in parrying the thrusts of Lord Welby and his colleagues, but even in hitting back at them. A new confidence and militancy surged in Gokhale as he faced the Commission, which was sitting in judgement on the affairs of his country.

There was probably no-one in England whom Gokhale's performance pleased more than Sir William Wedderburn. For ten long years Sir William had been trying to educate English opinion on Indian affairs. In this task he had been assisted by the Congress veterans—Dadabhai and W. C. Bonnerjee. But these veterans were getting on in years. Sir William saw in Gokhale a new ally for the British Committee of the Congress; able, urbane, earnest and with a gift for exposition, which made him equally at home in the committee room and on the public platform. Sir William invited Gokhale to his house in Meredith, Gloucestershire, initiated him into the mysteries of British politics, and introduced him to prominent British politicians and Anglo-Indian officials. Gokhale was touched by the kindness of Sir William, who was his senior by thirty years, but he was not awed by him as he had been by Ranade and Dadabhai Naoroji. From the first Gokhale treated Sir William more like an elder colleague than as a mentor.

Ranade had suggested to Sir William that Gokhale be given a chance to address meetings in Britain. A lecture tour had in fact been organized by the British Committee for the Indian witnesses before the Welby Commission. Gokhale spoke at Lambeth on 13 May, at Hastings on 26 May, at Dublin on 4 June, at Gloucester on 16 June and at Acton on 20 June. The summer months were not the ideal period for public meetings. Gokhale noted that the people were more attracted by cricket and the preparations for Queen Victoria's Diamond Jubilee than by the affairs of a distant dependency. Nevertheless he made the most of his opportunity. Speaking at Hastings on 26 May, he referred to the partnership between India and Britain as that 'of the giant and the dwarf, where everything went to the giant and what was left went to the dwarf'.[16] On 16 June, when he addressed a meeting at Gloucester, he was in his native dress. He

[15] Elgin to Westland, 28 June 1896 (E.P.).
[16] *India*, July 1897, pp. 214–15.

acknowledged the efforts being made by the Government of India to relieve famine, but pointed out that the famine had been brought on by its own mistakes: the government, he argued, by merely 'palliating the efforts of their unsympathetic administration, did not get rid of their responsibility in the matter'. 'No people', said Gokhale, 'could be so well governed as by men who knew them well . . . but the Indian people were living under a despotic and perfectly irresponsible government by . . . officials, whose interests were to take care of their own positions, . . . who . . . did not care to know the language and did not mix with the people.'[17] The Charter Act of 1833 had promised equality to the people of India with the other subjects of the British Empire, but even after sixty years the promise remained unrealized and the people of India were 'merely hewers of wood and drawers of water. In questions of legislation and taxation they had practically no voice. Their laws were made for them by officials.'

It is difficult to gauge the effects of this lecture tour on British public opinion, but there is evidence that it nettled the authorities. A letter written by Lord George Hamilton, the Secretary of State for India, appeared in the *Standard* (24 May 1897) criticizing the Indian speakers and warning 'that to introduce a system of representative government would be fatal to the external safety of the country and the maintenance of order internally . . . it is useless to eulogize in the abstract the blessings of the British rule in India and then propose to destroy that which alone makes British rule possible and beneficent.'

The intervals between lectures enabled Gokhale to do some sight-seeing and to visit some educational institutions. His initial self-consciousness and diffidence had worn off; he had shed the courtly manners which had at first amused his companion, Wacha. He was learning to move freely in English society. He took lessons in French, frequented the theatre, and on one occasion, pulled his fellow-delegate Surendranath Banerjea out of his bed to show him Sir Henry Irving play the part of Napoleon.[18]

Gokhale made a good impression in England as a speaker. He was invited to a garden party by the Countess of Warren where he spoke on 'Female Education in India'. At the annual general meeting of the Indian National Association he was present on the platform. In the National Liberal Club, he was introduced to a number of leading politicians, including T. P. O'Connor. He met Sir William Hunter to

[17] Ibid., p. 215.
[18] S. Banerjea, *A Nation in Making*, Calcutta, 1963, p. 364.

discuss educational problems. He visited Eton, Cambridge, Dulwich College and the Bedford College for Women. At the Educational Congress in the Women's Section of the Victorian Era Exhibition, he read a paper in which he lamented the 'enforced ignorance and over-done religion which had made India's women willing victims of custom and formidable opponents of reform'.

It was only natural that as a teacher Gokhale should have been interested in educational problems, but his heart really lay in politics. He was pleased at the notice which Hume, Naoroji and Caine took of him. Wedderburn missed no chance of paying a compliment to Gokhale and of improving his knowledge of English politics. He gave him letters of introduction to the leading politicians and officials who mattered in Indo-British relations. It was at Wedderburn's instance that Gokhale went to see John Morley, the distinguished writer and a prominent member of the Liberal Party.

Gokhale to Morley, 9 May 1897: I beg to send herewith a letter of introduction which Sir William Wedderburn has kindly given me . . . your teachings next after John Stuart Mill have been for years past largely moulding the thought of New India, and there are, I believe, many young men like my humble self in my country who are greatly indebted for the main inspiration of their life. Under the circumstances I thought it as much a duty as a privilege not to leave this country without paying my respects to you. . . . [19]

The meeting took place on 12 May 1897 and lasted half an hour. Morley's reactions are not known, but Gokhale returned to his lodgings, 'overjoyed like a grown-up schoolboy who had gratified the inmost desire of his heart'.[20] Gokhale wrote home that Morley had been

very kind and sympathetic, and expressed a wish that I should see him again before leaving England. My object in going to him was to enlist his sympathy on the side of our aspirations to which he has been unaccountably cold. He spoke to me very frankly on the subject and said that somehow or other he had an impression that a terrible catastrophe was in store for England in connection with India. . . . It was merely a vague instinctive presentiment.[21]

In May 1897 neither Gokhale nor Morley could have foreseen the chain of events which was to bring them together again nine years later in critical discussions on India's constitutional future.

'Overjoyed like a grown-up schoolboy' was a pardonable hyper-

[19] G.P.   [20] Wacha, op. cit., p. 34.
[21] Gokhale to G. V. Joshi, 14 May 1897 (G.P.).

bole of Wacha's, but there is no doubt that Gokhale was in high spirits in the summer of 1897. His evidence before the Welby Commission had raised his political stock; compliments were showered upon him. 'Our rising man' was Ranade's description of him. One of Gokhale's friends, more enthusiastic than the rest, compared his performance before the Welby Commission with Benjamin Franklin's deposition before the House of Commons: 'You have made a name for yourself in the history of India when words instead of swords are to be wielded.'[22] Gokhale could not but notice the extremely favourable impression he had made on Naoroji, Hume and Wedderburn whom he had so far dared to admire only from a distance. As he attended the meetings of the British Committee, addressed English audiences, talked to well-known English politicians, heard debates in the House of Commons, and paced its corridors, the flame of his political ambition which had been flickering under the wet blanket of Poona's factional politics began to burn brightly. Was it too much to hope that the mantle of Dadabhai Naoroji would fall on him? The words 'G. K. Gokhale, M.P.' had a pleasant ring. New vistas were suddenly unfolded to him. He saw himself pleading for his country from a seat in the House of Commons. Little did he know that six thousand miles away in his home town there were rumblings of a storm which would wreck all these fancies.

[22] V. G. Bijapurkar to Gokhale, 2 June 1897 (G.P.).

11

Eclipsed

In his evidence before the Welby Commission Gokhale had referred to the terrible famine of 1896–7, officially described at the time as the most disastrous in a century[1] which was no stranger to famines in India. An area of more than half a million square miles, inhabited by nearly 97 million people, was affected. Some of the worst-affected districts were in the Deccan. Wedderburn, Naoroji and their friends of the British Committee of the Congress, who kept a watching brief for India in England, were naturally anxious about conditions in India; it was their pressure which led to the foundation of Lord Mayor's Fund for famine relief. No less important than immediate relief was the problem of focusing attention on the basic economic issues of India, of breaking through the spell of official optimism to the terrible poverty which made it impossible for the hard-pressed peasantry to withstand a single crop failure.

In western India, to the rigours of famine had been added the terrors of bubonic plague. Its first assault on India, like the one on Hongkong two years earlier, was particularly fierce. When Gokhale left for England early in March 1897, several towns in western India, including Karachi, Bombay, Surat and Poona, were in the grip of the epidemic. Mortality was heavy; medical science had yet much to learn about the prevention and treatment of this scourge. Those were the days when, in the words of the poet Gadkari, one had to be more afraid of a dead rat than of lions and tigers.[2]

With the spread of plague in India, European ports threatened to shut out British ships bearing produce from India. Claims of commerce no less than those of humanity dictated urgent measures for the suppression of the epidemic.[3] Hamilton, Secretary of State for India, pleaded with Elgin, the Viceroy, to stamp out the dreadful disease, and not to allow the sanitary considerations to be subordi-

[1] B. M. Bhatia, *Famines in India*, Bombay, 1963, p. 239.
[2] D. D. Karve (ed.), *The New Brahmans*, Berkeley, 1963, p. 141.
[3] Hamilton to Elgin, 21 Jan. 1897 (Hamilton P.).

nated to the political. This was no time to be squeamish about caste and social prejudices.[4] After some initial misgivings, the Government of India joined in the pressure on the Bombay Government for a more drastic campaign against the plague.

In March 1897, the Bombay Government decided to form a Plague Committee, with W. C. Rand, i.c.s., as Chairman, and Lt-Colonel C. R. Phillipps and Surgeon-Captain W. W. O. Beveridge as members. Consisting of a senior civilian, a military officer and a doctor, the committee was well-equipped to combat the epidemic in Poona.

The Plague Committee was authorized to supervise, and in some respects almost to supersede, the local bodies exercising jurisdiction over the city, cantonment and suburban areas, to amend municipal bye-laws, to incur expenditure, to search and fumigate buildings, to segregate persons suspected of the disease, and even to demolish or burn infected huts or temporary structures. It became obligatory to register every death; in case of default, any member of a funeral party could be detained by the police!

Sandhurst, the Governor of Bombay, who had taken much of the initiative in this campaign, called a meeting of the leaders of various communities and parties in Poona, informed them that stringent measures were proposed, including the house-to-house search for patients for isolation and treatment in hospitals. There was an air of expectancy and even apprehension in Poona, but there was at first little disposition to criticize measures which were obviously in the interest of the people. Even Tilak's newspapers pointed out the cruel necessity of these steps if the town was to be purged of the epidemic.[5]

The 'Operation Plague' started in Poona, rather dramatically. In the early hours of a March morning, the Budhwarpeth and part of Shukrawarpeth were taken up by the military—about 200 cavalry and 100 infantry—for inspection. The streets were blockaded. At that early hour, some of the shop-keepers who lived in outlying parts of the town had not arrived. Their shops were forced open, disinfected, and left unattended. Between the British and Indian soldiers there seemed to be a division of labour; the former confined themselves to 'inspection' and the latter to disinfection of buildings. The medical

[4] 'I am sorry to hear', Elgin wrote to Hamilton on 7 April 1897, 'that Dr Lowson was not satisfied with the measures taken at Bombay to stamp out the plague. . . . I venture to say that he was rash in assuming that the advisers of the Governor were "unduly afraid of exciting caste or religious prejudice". It is true that our Home Department were inclined to think that the risk must be run, and we urged the Bombay Government to take a stronger line. . . .' Elgin to Hamilton, 7 April 1897 (Hamilton P.).   [5] *Kesari*, 30 March 1897.

member of the Plague Committee, Dr Beveridge, who had been well acquainted with the course of plague operations in Hongkong, felt that a native agency for inspection was likely to fail in Poona as it had done in Hongkong, and that only the British soldiers were capable of strict impartiality in segregating the sick. Whatever the reason for employing British soldiers for house-to-house searches, it was a tactical blunder of the first magnitude. The soldiers could hardly be expected to realize that if an Englishman's house is his castle, the Brahman's house is his temple. The young Tommy who stepped with his shoes on into rooms reserved for offering worship or eating did not even know that he had committed a sacrilege. Nor could he see any harm in the mild pleasantry of lifting a flower from an idol to throw it on a trembling young Brahman maiden.[6] Nevertheless, these were heinous offences in the eyes of the people of Poona. The Poona press at once became critical of the Plague Committee; there were numerous allegations; soldiers were alleged to have opened metal safes and cash-boxes in search of patients, and to have burnt not only the personal belongings and beddings of diseased persons, but even their account books and sewing-machines.

Complaints were carried to Rand, but without much effect. 'If anyone takes a complaint to Mr Rand orally,' said a local newspaper, 'he simply laughs and sends the complainant away. If anyone sends a written petition, he gets the stereotyped reply that his allegations are false.'[7] The same paper accused Rand of behaving 'like the Sultan of Turkey'. Tilak, who had been present in a deputation which waited on Rand, castigated him in the *Kesari* and asked indignantly, 'Which people on earth, however docile, will continue to submit to this sort of mad terror?' Though Rand may not have been 'one of the most courteous and kindly men', it is not necessary to assume that he was trying deliberately to oppress the people. He knew he had a disagreeable and thankless job to do, and he was determined to do it quickly. His reputation with the people of Poona was not high; the convictions in the *Wai* case had shown that he was no friend of the Brahmans or the educated community. Indeed, in common with most of his British colleagues in the civil service, he entertained a lively distrust of Poona Brahmans, whom the germs of sedition seemed to have infected long before the plague came to Poona. Inspection and segregation, if they were to be effective, were processes which could hardly be popular; it was not easy to distinguish between a really

[6] *Dnyanaprakash*, 19 April 1897.   [7] Ibid., 22 April 1897.

aggrieved person and one who was out to sabotage the operations, and Rand had no intention of getting involved in a long argument.

Failing to secure redress through representations, deputations and complaints in the press, the people of Poona sent up a memorial to the Governor of Bombay. The initiative was taken by the Deccan Sabha, which had been founded only in November 1896 under the inspiration of Ranade to serve as the mouthpiece of the moderate politicians of Poona, who were pledged to constitutional methods. The memorial, which also bore the signatures of some leading members of the Anjuman Association, the premier organization of the local Muslims, referred to the 'irregular and oppressive high-handedness of the special agency employed by the Plague Committee', which had resulted 'in a reign of terror' in Poona. Among the grievances were the rough and ready methods used by the soldiers who carried off to hospitals not only patients, but even their relatives and passersby; the indignity of public stripping of men and women for 'inspection'; the disregard of social and religious susceptibilities; the forcible opening of houses and business premises, and the wanton destruction of property. The enclosures to the memorial cited specific cases in support of the allegations. Finally, there was a demand for the redress of grievances, and the substitution of the Plague Committee by 'such other agency as will be more amenable to control, on the plan followed in Bombay with such success'.

The memorial was dated 10 May 1897; the next ten days were spent in collecting signatures, and the memorial was submitted to Lord Sandhurst on 21 May. Gokhale read it in London when he was engaged in the lecture tour organized by the British Committee. He knew some of the important men who had signed the memorial. There was V. M. Bhide, president of the Deccan Sabha (of which Gokhale himself was a secretary), a retired judge, a former head of the Poona Sarvajanik Sabha, and a highly respected spokesman of the moderate and reforming party in the town. There was Koopooswamy Mudaliar, elevated by the government to the rank of the 'First Class Sirdar of the Deccan', a popular figure among the local Europeans, and one of the richest men in Poona, who took little interest in politics. Then there was Nawab Abdul Ferojkhan, president of the (Muslim) Anjuman Association. That Hindus and Muslims, despite recent communal tension in the town, should have agreed on a joint representation was a measure of the resentment roused by the operations of the Plague Committee.

The memorial was mailed to Gokhale by his friend H. N. Apte, a famous Marathi novelist, at the time one of the secretaries of the Deccan Sabha. When Gokhale left Poona early in March, Apte had promised to keep him posted about developments at home, but he left the town just before the Rand Committee went into action:

I was compelled [he wrote to Gokhale] to leave the place bag and baggage. A rumour was afloat that military search-parties were to make house-to-house visitation in the city, and this terrified me as I had at that time in my house my sister suffering from fever for several months. It was no doubt an act of cowardice thus to take to one's heels at that time, but I preferred to discharge the duty of looking after those in my charge, to remain[ing] wilfully indifferent to their interest.[8]

Apte's letter made ominous reading, but the Deccan Sabha in its memorial to Governor Sandhurst had also mentioned that in 'a few cases the modesty of Native Ladies has not been respected'. There were other complaints of alleged misconduct by soldiers. Pandita Ramabai, a prominent Christian social worker of Poona and Bombay, complained in the *Bombay Guardian* how one of her girls had been taken to the Plague Hospital, and had not been heard of again. 'God knows', she wrote, 'how many young girls of good character have been . . . obliged to go to the Plague Hospital and Segregation Camp and been ruined and lost for ever.'[9]

The contents of the Deccan Sabha memorial were disquieting but, by the time Gokhale read them in England, 'Operation Plague' in Poona was over; the house-to-house inspection for isolation of the sick had been completed; the soldiers were withdrawn; the mortality had perceptibly declined; the epidemic—deceptively, as it turned out—seemed to have been suppressed; the people of Poona could breathe again. But just as the end of this unhappy chapter was in sight, a tragedy occurred which brought fresh trials to Poona and its leaders, including Gokhale.

2

The tragedy occurred on the midnight of 22 June 1897. It had been a crowded and memorable day, marking as it did the sixtieth anniversary of Queen Victoria's reign. There could be little real rejoicing for a people afflicted by famine and plague, but there was a

---

[8] H. N. Apte to Gokhale, 27 May 1897 (G.P.).
[9] Letter, 18 May 1897, to editor, *The Bombay Guardian*, in *India*, Aug. 1897.

reservoir of real reverence and affection for the Great White Queen. Colour and pageantry were much in evidence in the European quarter of the town. In the afternoon Governor Sandhurst held a levee which was attended by high European officials, the principal chiefs of the Deccan and 'some Native Gentlemen', including 'the Hon'ble B. G. Tilak, Member of the Governor's Legislative Council'. 'Ganesh Khind', the Poona residence of the Governor, which had been brilliantly illuminated, was the scene of a state banquet and a reception. Huge fires on the hills beyond blazed merrily, lighting up the country-side for many miles. And finally, as a fitting close to a day of joyous celebration, came a spectacular display of fireworks.

Soon after midnight a string of carriages began to file out of the gates of 'Ganesh Khind'. Among these was one carrying Mr W. C. Rand to the Western India Club; it had gone only a few hundred yards when at a spot lined by an avenue of trees, somebody climbed onto his carriage from the back, and fired with a pistol. Almost simultaneously, Lt O. E. Ayerst, whose carriage immediately followed Rand's, had his brains blown out. Ayerst died on the spot, but Rand lingered on for a few days.

It is not easy today to realize the impact this outrage made on European opinion in India and Britain. The attack on the twenty-seven year-old Lt Ayerst, a junior officer in the Commissariat Department, seemed a case of mistaken identity, but in the case of Rand, there was immediately a suspicion of a political motive. The European community was deeply stirred; sympathy for the victims of the tragedy mingled with indignation against native, particularly Brahman, wickedness. Memories of 1857 flooded back. In European clubs, offices and homes there were whispers of the gravity of the crisis; everyone seemed to agree that this was no time for weakness or misplaced kindness. The Bishop of Bombay, preaching in St. Paul's Church, Poona, on the Sunday following the tragedy, sensed the feeling of his audience and tried to assuage it: 'it was unjust to lump all Natives together in our loathing of those who are guilty. . . . After all these years . . . do they [the natives] suppose us capable today of letting loose a military vengeance, indiscriminately for the shedding of Christian blood.'[10]

The news of the Poona murders was serious enough to earn head-lines and editorial comment in the British press. 'Poona', wrote the *Daily Mail* (1 July), 'of course has long been notorious as the hotbed

[10] *India*, Aug. 1897.

of Southern India fanaticism; a town and district where the crafty, mutinous, semi-educated Brahmin walked at large, and freely propagated in newspaper and bazaar his faith in the liberation and regeneration of India on high caste lines.' Two days later, the *Morning Post* (3 July), after darkly hinting at the possibility of a 'Second Mutiny', ascribed the 'disturbances' in India to the fact that, 'for twenty years all sorts of *Babus* have been allowed by the special permission of Lord Ripon to scatter broadcast whatever venomous lies it occurred to them to utter'. The *Daily Mail* (1 July) held the 'Brahmin editor' responsible for the Poona outrages, and observed that 'assassination by the pen may, in the long run, prove a deal more formidable to British rule in India than assassination by the sword'.

'Assassination by the pen' was no journalistic hyperbole. Within a few hours of the shooting of Rand and Ayerst, Hamilton, Secretary of State for India, enquired telegraphically from Governor Sandhurst, 'Do you connect these outrages with the incendiary tone of the press?'[11] Ten days later, Hamilton urged the Viceroy to take strong measures as 'public opinion in the Parliament and press and elsewhere' was 'uneasy'.[12] Hamilton had good reasons for anxiety. The year 1897 was 'full of the tricks of malevolent fortune'.[13] Famine and plague had ravaged large parts of India, and strained local administration to the limit. A surprise raid on an armed escort accompanying a Political Officer on 10 June had not only resulted in the loss of British lives,[14] but had the ominous ring of a tribal rising on the north-west frontier. On 16 June Assam and Bengal were rocked by a terrible earthquake. In Shillong, the capital of Assam, most of the buildings and private houses were razed to the ground; in Cooch Behar only one house was left standing, and in Calcutta, the damage to buildings was considered so serious that it was considered unsafe to fire a sixty-gun ceremonial salute on the Queen's Jubilee.[15] It was on the very night of the Jubilee that Rand and Ayerst had been shot down at Poona. A week later there was a riot at Calcutta in which local Muslims, outraged by nothing more than the execution of a legal process (which put a Hindu landlord in possession of property on which a mosque had been constructed), vented their fury on the European inhabitants in Calcutta.

---

[11] Sec. of State to Gov. of Bombay, 23 June 1897 (Hamilton P.).
[12] Sec. of State to Viceroy, 3 July 1897 (Hamilton P.).
[13] Elgin to Hamilton, 17 Aug. 1897 (Hamilton P.).
[14] Station Staff Officer B. Khel to Military, Simla, 10 June 1897 (E.P.).
[15] Elgin to A. Mackenzie, Lt-Gov. of Bengal, 17 June 1897 (E.P.).

It is not surprising that, overwhelmed by bad news in such quick succession, Hamilton should have hastened to enquire from the Viceroy about the 'disposition of native troops', and whether there was any connection between the tribal trouble in the north-west, the riot in Calcutta, and the assassinations in Poona. The Viceroy consulted his Executive Council and sounded the provincial Governors, but discounted dangers of a mutiny. Nor did he favour hasty legislation against the Indian press or grant of more executive powers to the Bombay Government to deal with the emergency. 'Sandhurst', wrote the Viceroy about the Bombay Governor, 'has such ample military and police resources at his command that he can enforce anything which he thinks necessary, while in the Regulation of 1827 he has summary powers of arrest and imprisonment which . . . probably exceed those of the Czar of Russia.'[16]

As the police were unable to lay their hands on the assassins of Rand and Ayerst immediately, the Bombay Government announced a reward of Rs 10,000 for clues leading to their arrest. The Governor of Bombay wrote to the Viceroy:

Investigations are proceeding and, so far as we have got indications, point to Brahminism as being at the bottom of the plot. . . . My colleagues and I are unanimous in thinking strong action most necessary. We have resolved as a beginning to put into Poona a punitive police force of 50 Europeans and 150 Natives. We are further considering the desirability of disarming Poona City, . . . while it might be necessary to put into force the power to arrest and detain persons as state prisoners.[17]

3

The imposition of the punitive police on Poona, the smear campaign against educated Indians as a class, the outcry in the Anglo-Indian and Tory press for repressive measures and hints from the Secretary of State for India in the Parliament that legislation to curb the 'native' press was being contemplated, were developments which caused Wedderburn much concern. The question was not merely of affording some relief to the unfortunate people of Poona who had been harassed by famine, plague, house-searches—and now by punitive police. Efforts were clearly necessary to prevent new chains being forged for the Indian press. If the Poona assassinations could be

[16] Elgin to Hamilton, 6 July 1897 (Hamilton P.).
[17] Sandhurst to Elgin, 25 June 1897 (E.P.).

shown in the local context of plague-operations, and the bubble of a widespread conspiracy and an imminent mutiny pricked, the threatened legislation against the Indian press might perhaps be staved off. Wedderburn decided to campaign for a public and impartial inquiry into Poona affairs. He convened a meeting of the Indian Parliamentary Committee in the Conference Room of the House of Commons on 1 July, and invited to it the four Indian delegates who had appeared before the Welby Commission. It fell to Gokhale, as the representative of the Deccan, to provide most of the briefing to the M.P.s on the background of events in his home town and on the reasons which made a public enquiry imperative. After the meeting Gokhale gave an interview which appeared the following day (2 July), and constituted a sharp and unequivocal indictment of the entire Plague Administration; it had the air of certainty and the fighting spirit which had marked his cross-examination by the Welby Commission a few weeks earlier. British soldiers (the *Manchester Guardian* quoted Gokhale as saying), 'ignorant of the language and contemptuous of the customs, the sentiments and the religious susceptibilities of the people', had been 'let loose' upon the town; they had wantonly destroyed property, appropriated jewellery, burnt furniture, entered kitchens and places of worship, contaminated food, spat upon idols or broke them by throwing them on the ground, and dragged women into the streets for inspection before removal to hospitals. 'My correspondents', added Gokhale, 'whose word I can trust absolutely, report the violation of two women, one of whom is said afterwards to have committed suicide rather than survive her shame.'

The Wedderburn–Gokhale strategy of highlighting the local significance of the Poona murders by seeking a public enquiry was a rational one, but in the irrational, almost hysterical, atmosphere created by the murders, it had no chance of success. A public enquiry into Poona affairs at any time would have been difficult to secure; but after 22 June it was ruled out. For the government to concede such an inquiry would have been to cast a slur on the record of Rand (who was lying in hospital in a grave condition when Gokhale gave his press interview), to question the honour of the British soldiers, and even to impugn the administration of Governor Sandhurst, who was closely associated with the direction of plague operations.

Hostile critics at once seized upon that part of Gokhale's indictment which was the most difficult to prove: the alleged violation of women by the British soldiers. The major issues of the conduct of plague-operations in Poona and the justification for a public enquiry were relegated to the background, and Wedderburn and Gokhale became the chief targets of a scathing press campaign. Meanwhile, on the very day Gokhale addressed the Indian Parliamentary Committee, the Secretary of State telegraphed the Governor of Bombay for information. Sandhurst's reply of 4 July was emphatic: 'Gokhale is Poona Brahmin, his associates are known to be disaffected, and to have done much to obstruct and defame plague operations. Probably question in Parliament is prompted by desire to gain some sympathy with Poona Brahmins, a section of whom are suspected to be promoters of Poona assassinations.'[18]

On 13 July, in reply to a question by Sir James Fergusson, the Secretary of State read a telegram sent by Lord Sandhurst: 'Regarding Gokhale's letter alleging violation of women, from all inquiries I have made, I am convinced this is still more gross and malevolent invention than that about stripping of women.' Wedderburn, who was not present in the House of Commons when this question was answered, at once wrote a letter to *The Times*[19] bearing personal testimony to Professor Gokhale's 'highest character for integrity' and his public spirit, and justifying a public enquiry into Poona affairs. Gokhale himself wrote to the *Manchester Guardian* on 14 July, explaining the context of the allegation about the misconduct of the soldiers and the grounds on which he had based it.

Gokhale's letter to the *Manchester Guardian* was published on 15 July. The following day he left for India. However, he already had some idea of the severity of the storm which had broken over his head. Not only was he being branded an arch-liar and slanderer, but a campaign of vilification had opened against Poona Brahmans, indeed against educated Indians as a class whose claims for greater association with the administration of the country he had so ably advocated before the Welby Commission. If (as seemed likely) the allegation about the violation of women by the soldiers could not be proved, would it not give a handle to Anglo-Indian opponents of Indian reform who never lost an opportunity of denouncing Indian politicians as untrustworthy and irresponsible? Would it not make the task of good old Hume, Wedderburn, and Naoroji in putting across the Indian case to the British people even more difficult?[20]

[18] Gov. of Bombay to Sec. of State, 4 July 1897 (Hamilton P.).
[19] *The Times*, 17 July 1897.
[20] This opinion was later expressed by Subramania Iyer, editor of *The Hindu*, who had also appeared before the Welby Commission: 'I cannot but think that

When Wacha joined Gokhale aboard the s.s. *Caledonia*[21] at Brindisi, he found him in the midst of a deep depression.[22] With his head stooped low, the young professor paced the deck, brooding on the cruel turn of events which had brought his triumphant trip to England to a disastrous conclusion. A group of Europeans from Aden recognized Gokhale and went out of their way to insult him. Wacha and Lawrence (a British civilian who was on his way to India) did their best to comfort Gokhale. Before landing in Bombay, Gokhale had an unexpected visitor. Vincent, the Commissioner of Police, came aboard to probe Gokhale for fuller details of the allegations, and if possible, for the names of his correspondents in Poona. Gokhale was polite but firm; he would not oblige the Commissioner of Police, though he assured him that he proposed to act in a straightforward manner.

After meeting Ranade and his other friends in Bombay and Poona, Gokhale realized that there was no chance of his being able to substantiate the allegations. In the peculiar conditions of Indian social life, two months after the completion of the plague operations, production of evidence would have been difficult under the best of circumstances. But after the imposition of the punitive police on Poona, the arrest of Tilak, and the deportation of the Natu brothers, few people dared to defy the authorities. Though it was impossible to be sure, the chances of Gokhale being prosecuted were remote; his allegations had been made in England in good faith in general terms and avowedly on the basis of reports received from correspondents in India; moreover, he could not be charged with defaming a particular individual. Even if the case against him was legally untenable, did he not have a moral duty? 'The very fact', he recorded later, 'that the injured parties had no legal redress against me made my responsibilities as a gentleman all the greater.'[23] The moral argument was reinforced by a political one: if the controversy on Rand and the soldiers continued, it could only further stoke up the fires of racial antagonism in Poona. If by a frank withdrawal of the charges, Gokhale could close the controversy, would it not lower the political temperature and afford a sorely needed respite to that hapless town?

Within five days of landing in Bombay, Gokhale mailed to Gover-

on the whole we have received a heavy blow.' Iyer to Gokhale, 21 Sept. 1897 (G.P.).

[21] On 28 July 1897.
[22] Wacha, *Reminiscences of Gokhale*, p. 45.
[23] Gokhale's letter to the *Times of India*, 8 Jan. 1898.

nor Sandhurst 'a full statement containing explanation, full retraction' and 'an unqualified apology' which was directed to all, 'to H.E. the Governor, to the members of the Plague Committee, and to soldiers engaged in plague operations'. The draft had been vetted by Ranade.

For Gokhale, the 'apology' was a bitter cup of humiliation. He drained it to the dregs, but it seemed to do him little good. The wrath of the government did not visibly abate. On 4 August, Lord Sandhurst spoke in the Bombay Legislative Council in terms of irony and scorn about 'the apology and withdrawal made by a gentleman, whose name was prominently for a few days before the public'. On 5 August, M. Bhownaggree, an Indian member of the British Parliament, who usually toed the Anglo-Indian line, made a stinging attack on Gokhale in the House of Commons: 'There had appeared before them the precious Mr Gokhale, who under the guidance of the Hon. Member for Banff [Sir William Wedderburn] defiled the threshold of this building.' Nor did the apology go down well with the Indian press. A few papers, such as the friendly *Dnyanaprakash* (9 August), or the *Indian Spectator* (8 August) praised Gokhale for acting like a gentleman, but many papers were frankly critical. 'Whatever may be said in favour of the rising publicist', wrote the *Kaiser-i-Hind* (8 August), 'this much is certain that he has much compromised his reputation.' The *Gujarati* (8 August) referred to Gokhale's 'absolute, frank, and helpless self-condemnation'. Tilak's papers were far from sympathetic. The *Mahratta* (8 August) could not appreciate why 'the humiliated professor' had withdrawn all the charges, when he was unable to substantiate one of them. The *Kesari* expressed the fear that Gokhale's 'overwhelming apology' and the repudiation by the Muslims of Poona of the joint memorial had lent support to Governor Sandhurst's charges against the people of Poona.[24] In a letter to Motilal Ghose, Tilak, who had meanwhile been arrested and placed on trial for seditious writings, made a disparaging reference to Gokhale: 'I think in me they [government] will not find a *kutcha* [raw] reed as they did in Professor Gokhale.'[25]

With political factionalism developed to a high degree in Poona, there was no dearth of men willing to embroider on the story of the apology. It was suggested that Gokhale had agreed to apologize under a threat from the Commissioner of Police who had met him

[24] Kesari, 10 Aug. 1897.
[25] P. Dutt, *Memoirs of Motilal Ghose*, Calcutta, 1935, p. 98.

on arrival at Bombay, and that the letter of apology had been drafted
by Bennet, the editor of the *Times of India*. It was argued that
Gokhale had lowered the prestige of his country, that he had shown
want of courage, and irretrievably damaged the Indian cause in
England.

Gokhale was very lonely and unhappy, talked of retiring from
public life and wrote long letters to Hume, Wedderburn, Naoroji,
and Caine to whom he opened out his heart. They were all sympathetic and realized his predicament. Caine,[26] Naoroji[27] and even Hume[28]
pointed out that the apology was much too long and much too
humble, but they admired his public spirit and did not see why he
should talk of retiring from politics. 'We look upon you', wrote
Hume to Gokhale, 'as a martyr to the cause', and advised him to
'disregard the ravings alike of the Anglo-Indians and Indian lick-
spittles'.[29] Naoroji urged him to remain 'cool and calm'. Wedderburn acknowledged his own part in the affair: he had failed to foresee
the risks of mentioning anything that was not capable of legal proof.
'Among us', he told Gokhale, 'we made the mistake—it was a venial
one—we were trying to protect the weak against the strong, and in
such work we must expect sometimes to get hard knocks . . . the very
ferocity of the attack upon you testifies to the importance and value
of the work you did in England on behalf of your countrymen.'[30]

These were comforting words, but they could not solve Gokhale's
immediate difficulties. On his return from England, he was excom-
municated from the Chitpavan Brahman community for breaking the
taboo on foreign travel. Thus he became a social outcaste, just when
he was being reduced to a political outcaste. He feared his opponents
would go to any length to discredit him; he was haunted by the fear of
a public affront which would only rub salt into his wounds. In the
last week of August, the Bombay Presidency Association[31] called a
special public meeting to honour him and Wacha for their work in
connection with the Welby Commission. Gokhale was proud of his
work in England, and would have loved to be present at the meeting,
but thought it prudent to stay away.

As the Amraoti session of the Indian National Congress ap-

[26] Caine to Gokhale, 29 Oct. 1897 (G.P.).
[27] Naoroji to Gokhale, 27 Aug. 1897 (G.P.).
[28] Hume to Gokhale, 24 Aug. 1897 (G.P.).
[29] Ibid.
[30] Wedderburn to Gokhale, 24 Aug. 1897 (G.P.).
[31] Letter from Secs. of the Bombay Presidency Assoc. to Gokhale, 2 Aug. 1897
(G.P.).

proached, Gokhale's friends urged him to attend it; to deliberately avoid it would be an act of cowardice, perhaps of political suicide. Gokhale was not well; the pain in his heart, caused by the accident at Calais in March, had recurred, and the week's quarantine for plague before entering Amraoti was something of an ordeal.[32] Nevertheless he persevered in his resolve to attend the Congress. Unfortunately for him his worst fears were confirmed. The hostile demonstration which he had dreaded all along came when his name was proposed to be included in the list of speakers. He was denounced as a traitor by some delegates from Bengal who were being egged on by their friends from the Deccan.

Gokhale's cup of humiliation and sorrow brimmed over; once again he reviewed the whole course of events which had led to the fatal interview and the apology in a letter to the press. It was a long, eloquent and even moving document; its concluding paragraph affirmed:

Public duties, undertaken at the bidding of no man, cannot be laid down at the desire of anyone. . . . One is always glad of the approbation of the public of what one has done. . . . But it is not the highest purpose of existence, nor nearly the highest. If it comes—to use the words of Herbert Spencer—well, if not, well also, though not so well.[33]

He was indeed hungering for public understanding, if not public appreciation. It might seem at first that he was wallowing in self-pity. Those who told him to lie low and let the incident be forgotten did not know Poona; he knew his home town too well to cherish any such illusion. Not the least disconcerting aspect of the situation was the attitude of students of Fergusson College. 'By the way, is it true', V. V. Khatidarkar wrote to Gokhale on 24 August 1897, 'that students of your own college treat you with hisses?' The cold war of Poona politics had swept over the Fergusson College and even three years later a devoted pupil and friend, R. P. Paranjpye, writing from Cambridge could tell Gokhale: 'You may complain perhaps rightly that your students don't appreciate your work and sacrifice as well as that of the other life-members, that they are ever ready to pick holes in your coats & are always loud in the praises of the people who are doing their little best to pull the college down.'[34]

[32] Gokhale to G. V. Joshi, 9 Dec. 1897 (G.P.).
[33] *Times of India*, 8 Jan. 1898.
[34] 2 Nov. 1900 (Paranjpye P.).

The apology was going to be a very handy stick to beat Gokhale with. It is true that in his statements and letters to his friends he preferred to put the matter on a public plane, but he would have been more than human if he had not been conscious of the personal aspect of the crisis. Only two years earlier, he and his friends had been squeezed out of the Poona Sarvajanik Sabha. With the foundation of the Deccan Sabha in November 1896 his party had made a fresh start. It was, however, the visit to England in 1897 which had really put fresh heart into him. But suddenly, after that fatal meeting of the Indian Parliamentary Committee and the interview to the correspondent of the *Manchester Guardian*, his fortunes had suffered a drastic reversal. The high praise he had earned for his evidence before the Welby Commission was forgotten; in the eyes of the Europeans he was a slanderer; in those of his own countrymen he was a coward. 'You must be prepared,' W. S. Caine wrote to Gokhale on 29 October 1897, 'if you came to settle in this country [England], to be constantly spoken of as the fellow who slandered the British soldiers.'[35]

It was at the Amraoti session of the Congress that Gokhale's fortunes touched their nadir. He saw the virulence of his opponents. They had edged him out of the Poona Sarvajanik Sabha. Would they also hound him out of the Indian National Congress?

This was Gokhale's moment of truth. His extreme sensitivity, and disdain for the rough and tumble of politics wrestled with his sense of self-preservation. 'The best part of our nature', he wrote to a correspondent in January 1898, 'is manifested not in what we enjoy, but what we endure. There is a sublimity and moral elevation in undeserved suffering, which nothing can equal, and which is almost its own reward.'[36] This was what we may call the Gandhian approach, but high idealism alone was not enough to sustain Gokhale against the vicissitudes of politics. The flame of ambition had to be rekindled. During these weeks he did much heart-searching but emerged a stronger, if sadder, man. On 5 February 1898, he committed to his diary a remarkably ambitious programme. 'By the grace of Sree Guru Dattatreya', he solemnly recorded, he 'would endeavour humbly but firmly to acquire or achieve yoga, knowledge of History, Philosophy, Astronomy, Geology, Physiology, Psychology and French', and would 'try to become a member of Bombay Legislative Council, the Supreme Legislative Council and the British Parliament. In all these

[35] W. S. Caine to Gokhale, 29 Oct. 1897 (G.P.).
[36] Gokhale to A. K. Ghosh, 15 Jan. 1898 (G.P.).

assemblies I will try to do good to my country by all means in my power.'[37]

Though the diary entry goes on to include even the preaching of a new religion, what is really important is the reassertion of Gokhale's intellectual and political ambition. He was no longer thinking of retiring from the field of battle; he was bracing himself to face the obduracy and malice of his opponents and the fickleness of public opinion. Though he never acquired the cool assurance of a political gladiator who emerges completely unruffled from the heat and dust of political controversy, he was able to shed some of his ultra-sensitivity. He also realized that knowledge and courage were not enough; they needed to be tinged with caution if the struggle for Indian reform was to be waged on a long-term basis.

Henceforth Gokhale's speeches and writings, though firmly based on facts and figures, acquired a marked tendency to understatement; this proved a great asset to one whose best political work was to be done in legislative chambers or in private negotiations with British statesmen. The crisis in 1897, which had threatened to sweep him off the political stage, provided the dynamic for his spectacular come-back and for the important role he was to play in the political evolution of India.

[37] Sastri, *Life of Gokhale*, pp. 32–3.

12

The Clouds Lift

Eighteen ninety-seven had been a trying year for Poona and its leaders. It had brought famine, plague, search parties of soldiers and the punitive police. To Gokhale it had brought public humiliation and political eclipse; to his rival, Tilak, it had brought arrest and imprisonment. Tilak was prosecuted for the 'seditious' tone of certain articles in the *Kesari*; but it was obvious to all that he was being made a scapegoat for the authorities' failure to capture Rand's assassins. Governor Sandhurst and his officers were resolved to make an example of Tilak who appeared to them the epitome of the defiant Brahman élite of Poona. A series of repressive measures revealed the temper of the authorities. Tilak was sentenced to eighteen months' imprisonment. The Natu brothers, men of high lineage and influence in Poona, were deported under the emergency regulations of 1818. The government barred teachers in government-aided schools and colleges from taking part in politics. The Deccan Education Society was directed by the Education Department to completely dissociate education from politics. Three professors of the Fergusson College, Bhanu, Patwardhan and Gokhale, were especially singled out for official displeasure. Bhanu had written a textbook with patriotic overtones; Patwardhan was the editor of the *Sudharak*, and Gokhale the author of allegations against British soldiers. The Fergusson College and Gokhale were denounced not only in the Anglo-Indian press, but also in *The Times* [London].[1]

The two succeeding years were bleak for Poona. 'We are passing through fearful times here', Gokhale wrote to Dadabhai Naoroji, 'and the insolence and ill-treatment with which nearly all of us have at present to put up is something of which you have no idea.'[2] Political life was at a low ebb, but Gokhale found plenty of work to do. Besides his considerable teaching work, he was the secretary of the governing body of the Deccan Education Society. He plunged him-

[1] Paranjpye to Gokhale, 30 Sept. 1897 (Paranjpye P.).
[2] Gokhale to Naoroji, 16 Sept. 1897 (G.P.).

self into the campaign against the plague in Poona with utter disregard for his own safety. All this activity, however, did not really satisfy him. He missed the excitement of politics to which he had vibrated for a decade. In December 1898, he was present at the Madras Congress, but did not address it. He had become, thanks to the events of 1897, a back-bencher. Almost overnight he had been reduced to a political outcast, having alienated the government as well as the politically conscious class. He did not, however, throw up his hands. 'The day will come', he told a critic of his role in the apology incident, 'when I shall cover my country with glory by way of compensation for the wrong I have [been] alleged to have done.'[3] Gokhale's friend, D. G. Vaidya, pleaded with him to transfer the scene of his activity to England and enter the House of Commons. 'The Indian atmosphere', wrote Vaidya, 'seems to be utterly vitiated; everything around is rotten to the core. So the sooner you carry out your determination of going to England the better.'[4] Vaidya did not know, what Dadabhai Naoroji had learnt at a great cost, that a parliamentary seat required a heavy investment of time and money. After the stigma of irresponsibility which Gokhale had incurred in 1897 it was doubtful if any political party in England would be willing to sponsor him. Gokhale realized that if he was to recover the ground he had lost, a parliamentary seat was the last and not the first political outpost to be captured. Indeed, in an entry in his diary on 5 February 1898, he had correctly recorded the sequence: a seat in the Bombay Council, followed by a seat in the Imperial Council and finally in the House of Commons.

2

In 1899, when Gokhale told his friends that he proposed to stand for the Bombay Council from the district boards of the Central Division, it looked a courageous, almost rash act. This seat, created in 1895, had been filled for the first two years by B. G. Tilak. Tilak was re-elected in 1897, but had to resign after his conviction for sedition. D. S. Garud, who succeeded Tilak, had a good deal of local influence but little political stature. The election was due again in 1899; it was known that both Tilak—who had been prematurely released from prison on 6 September 1898—and Garud intended to

[3] Quoted in T. V. Parvate, *Gopal Krishna Gokhale*, Ahmedabad, 1959, p. 84.
[4] D. G. Vaidya to Gokhale, 20 Jan. 1898 (G.P.).

contest this seat. A tough fight was in store for Gokhale. Tilak's political stock had risen after his trial; he had the halo of a martyr about him. W. S. Caine, a member of the British Parliament and a friend of both Gokhale and Tilak, warned Gokhale that Tilak would be a 'most formidable opponent to you. . . . I hope that the political acrimony which has been the curse of Poona for many years past will not be aggravated by a contest between you and Tilak.'[5] Gokhale's friends were worried. Would he be able to ignore, if not parry, the attacks of his opponents and to take the cut and thrust of political debate in his stride? Or, would he relapse into that bottomless depression of melancholy in which he had sunk under adverse criticism in the summer of 1897? These misgivings were frankly expressed by Ranade.

M. G. Ranade to G. K. Gokhale, 6 February 1899: The risk of failure in your case is not the ordinary risk of failure, but of many other things besides. . . . In the struggle [of the election] all sorts of offensive weapons will be used and you will have to be thick-skinned. Your temperament is naturally sensitive and you are so easily depressed that . . . those who like me know the worth in you & the value of retaining your health and coolness of mind, have to think twice before they give you much advice. . . . [6]

Ranade did not realize that the apology incident had not only hardened the fibre of his disciple, but rekindled his ambition. Gokhale planned his election strategy with great skill and determination. He endeavoured through Ranade to persuade Garud to withdraw from the contest. Garud was evasive. Gokhale suspected collusion between Garud and Tilak to keep him out of the Council. The electoral college was small and the members of the district boards were highly susceptible to local pressures. T. J. Bennett, the editor of the *Times of India*, who was well disposed to Gokhale, interceded on his behalf with the European chairmen of some of the district boards. Gokhale knew that any display of enthusiasm by Bennett would be a liability rather than an asset. He urged Bennett to desist from attacks on Tilak in the *Times of India* which could only have the effect of swinging some of the voters in his favour.[7]

Gokhale toured his constituency intensively. However, the election was indirect and the franchise restricted. There were no public meetings and what was needed was more the practice of diplomacy than

[5] W. S. Caine to Gokhale, 22 Sept. 1899 (G.P.).   [6] G.P.
[7] T. J. Bennett to Gokhale, 28 Sept. 1899 (G.P.).

a political campaign. The fact that Gokhale and Tilak were pitted against each other seems to have aroused the interest of the highest British authorities in India. 'There are rumours', Governor Sandhurst wrote to Lord Curzon, 'that he [Tilak] is going to stand (he is most likely to be successful); should they turn out to be true, I don't think I ought to accept the recommendation. Tilak's seat may be contested by another Brahmin named Gokhale. He and Tilak are bitter opponents and Gokhale was a man who, in England two years ago, told outrageous falsehoods about the soldiers at Poona. Since then he has done everything to redeem his position, and has been one of the most ardent plague workers in Poona.'[8] The Viceroy endorsed the Governor's suggestion that if Tilak was successful, his election should be vetoed by the Bombay Government.[9]

It is possible that Tilak may have got wind of the intention of the Government to disqualify him. On the other hand he may have realized that, by intensively canvassing voters in the districts, Gokhale had stolen a march over him. Whatever his reasons, Tilak withdrew from the contest. He switched his votes to Garud against Gokhale, but the latter won. The formal announcement appeared in the *Bombay Government Gazette* of 21 December 1899: 'On the recommendation of the District Local Boards of the Central Division of the Presidency the Government has nominated Mr Gopal Krishna Gokhale, B.A., to be an additional member of His Excellency's Council for the purpose of making laws and regulations.'

Today, with the numerous legislatures in India elected on adult franchise, it is not easy for us to imagine the prestige which attached to a seat in the Bombay Council at the turn of the century. The whole of Bombay, Maharashtra, Gujarat and Sind were represented in the Governor's Legislative Council by only eight members through an indirect election. Gokhale's victory would in any case have been a triumph, but it was doubly so in December 1899, marking as it did the dissipation of the black cloud which seemed to have settled over his political life in 1897. He had at last found the forum where he could show his talents to the best advantage. 'I fully expect', a friend wrote to Gokhale, 'that your career in the Council will be a brilliant one, that the "Rising Star of the Deccan" of former years will shine in all genuine glory.'[10] Another friend reminded Gokhale of a strange

[8] Sandhurst to Curzon, 2 Aug. 1899 (C.P.).
[9] Curzon to Sandhurst, 10 Aug. 1899 (C.P.).
[10] H. S. Dickshit to Gokhale, 21 Dec. 1899 (G.P.).

incident which had occurred three years earlier at Karachi. 'I asked you casually when you intended to be a member of the Legislative Council. I cannot say why, but you got wild at me and about that question of mine.'[11] It almost seems that for years Gokhale had cherished the ambition of a parliamentary career at heart but was reluctant to avow it. In 1896, having been pushed off the political stage in Poona by the rival party, a legislative career may have seemed beyond his grasp. In 1897 his hopes had risen dramatically and then been dashed to the ground. Not until 1899 did his luck turn.

3

So different was the Bombay Legislative Council in January 1900 when Gokhale first took his seat in it, from Maharashtra's 'Vidhan Sabha' of today, that it requires an effort of imagination to realize its peculiar composition and limitations. Its twenty-four members included three of the Governor's Executive Council, the Advocate-General and twelve nominees of the Government, mostly European officers and a few non-officials. The word 'election' was not mentioned in the Indian Councils Act of 1892; the rules framed under it had, however, stipulated that members for eight seats were to be first elected and recommended by certain constituencies and then nominated by the Governor. The eight elective seats had been allotted to the Bombay Corporation, the Bombay University, the Bombay Chamber of Commerce, the district boards of the Northern Division, the 'Sardars' (chiefs) of the Deccan, the municipalities of the Northern Division, the zamindars of Sind, and the district local boards of the Central Division. The last of these constituencies was represented by Gokhale.

The majority of the members in the Bombay Council, which was presided over by the Governor, the head of the provincial administration, were British officers. The Council met at long intervals and for short periods. The non-official members could not initiate proposals though they could participate in the discussion. Most of the members read out their speeches. The *Times of India* once likened the Bombay Council to 'a suburban literary society at whose meetings a number of earnest people read elaborate essays on the same subject'.[12] The official attitude to Indian members oscillated between patronage and

[11] L. R. Gokhale to G. K. Gokhale, 27 Nov. 1899 (G.P.).
[12] *Times of India*, 26 Aug. 1901.

petulance. After the budget debate in 1897, Governor Sandhurst told the Viceroy:

We had our Legislative Council meeting on August 4th for the discussion. There was not very much to discuss, as there is no money in the till, and those who generally make long speeches were absent, such as Mehta and Tilak, and we got through easily in 5 hours, though I took up an hour and 20 minutes. There were 3 new Members—Chandvarkar, a pleader, a very good man I am told and certainly of very pleasant address, a pleader, Dr Bhalchandra Krishna . . . and a third, an old bore from Gujarat . . . The tone throughout was very good & the expression of appreciation about famine unanimous.[13]

Governor Sandhurst was in the chair, when at noon on 24 January 1900 the Honourable Mr G. K. Gokhale took his seat for the first time at the Council table. On the first day he asked eight questions, most of them on famine and plague; at the next two meetings on 14 February and 26 March, he asked twelve questions. His maiden speech was not delivered until 24 August, when the Finance Statement of the Bombay Government for the year 1900–1 was debated. John Nugent, the Revenue Member of the Governor's Executive Council, who had prepared the budget statement, passed away before he could present it to the Legislative Council. Gokhale paid a tribute to 'Mr Nugent's clear and vigorous grasp of principles, his quaint humour, his directness and force,' and expressed the hope that 'the service, of which Mr Nugent was so distinguished a member, is not poor in men of his calibre', and that his successor would exhibit 'a generous spirit' and 'earn for the Government the abiding gratitude of the people'.[14]

From these preliminary and conciliatory remarks, Gokhale passed on to a calculated attack on the economic and political policies of the Bombay Government: 'Famine and plague, plague and famine, these have been our lot without intermission.' He acknowledged the efforts of the district officers to save life and mitigate suffering, but felt that the relief measures had been inadequate. He cited figures from the *Government Gazette*, and the Blue Books to prove the niggardliness of the famine relief in Bombay as compared with that in the Central Provinces. He pleaded for a new deal for the peasant:

Whoever, therefore, among the Indian people may be lightly taxed, the peasant is surely the most heavily burdened among them all. In

[13] Sandhurst to Elgin, 6 Aug. 1897 (E.P.).
[14] *Proc. of the Council of the Gov. of Bombay*, Bombay, 1901, vol. XXXVIII, 1900, p. 84.

the best of times his lot is hard, and when mother nature grows un-kind, not all the efforts of a benevolent Government save him from immense misery. He, however, endures all meekly, patiently, without a word of complaint. Surely, it will be a mark of the highest states-manship to introduce a ray of hope and light into the gloom which generally surrounds his life.[15]

An indication that Gokhale's criticism had gone home came in the official spokesman's reference to Gokhale's 'accusations' and 'fine disregard for actual circumstances'. Another, and more important, indication was Gokhale's appointment to the Select Committees ap-pointed to consider the amendment of the Municipal Act, the Bombay Abkari Act, and the Land Revenue Code of 1879.

4

It was the amendment of the Land Revenue Code which brought a head-on clash between the official bloc and the elected Indian mem-bers of the Council. The object of the bill was to amend the Land Revenue Code Bill of 1879 to permit the Bombay Government to let out waste, unoccupied or forfeited lands for short terms, and to re-strict the holder's power of transferring his land. The restricted tenure was intended *inter alia* to arrest the process of alienation of land from the peasantry to money-lenders. The subject of land rights was a delicate and explosive one. In this case Governor Northcote, who had succeeded Lord Sandhurst, aroused further suspicions by what ap-peared to be an indecent haste in pushing the bill through the Council. Under the rules of business a minimum notice of fifteen days was necessary before the Council could discuss the bill. The Governor used his special powers to waive this notice, and on 30 May 1901 the Council met, in a special session, and despite the opposition of the elected Indian members, referred the bill to a select committee. The committee met for the first time on 31 May, and for the second and last time on 24 June, before a single comment from the public had reached it. On 23 August the bill came back from the select committee to the Council when it met in Poona.

The object of the bill, Governor Northcote explained to the Vice-roy, was to protect the peasants '[to some extent] from themselves and their own folly as a class who are not fit to have uncontrolled possession of their lands'.[16] This was not how the measure appeared

[15] Ibid., p. 94.   [16] Northcote to Curzon, 13 July 1901 (C.P.).

to its Indian critics. R. C. Dutt, who had made a close study of land revenue problems, wrote to Gokhale, describing the bill

as a reactionary piece of legislation. The bones of Cornwallis, Thomas Munro, Elphinstone, Canning and Lord William Bentinck must rattle in their graves at this 20th century idea of helping the cultivators of India by depriving them of their tenant rights which have been recognized and fostered since the commencement of British rule in India.[17]

In the Bombay Council the opposition to the bill was led by Pherozeshah Mehta, who proposed that the bill be returned to the select committee for six months to consider the criticism received from the public. He charged that the government was establishing 'the absolute right of the State as sole landlord of all the soil in the Presidency', and achieving this purpose by a 'flank[ing] movement'. He counselled 'caution and patience, justice and sympathy'. He ridiculed the claim of the official spokesman—James Monteath—that British officials were better able to represent the interests of the peasantry than educated Indians.

Now, my Lord [said Pherozeshah], let us examine the claim which has been set up for the European official. In many respects, I have very great respect for him. I appreciate highly many good and great qualities which distinguish him. But he is generally totally unable to get over what are conveniently called his insular proclivities and his insular stiffness. . . . The continental languages are bad enough for him; but when he comes to Indian languages and dialects, his jaws are absolutely unmanageable . . . the English official moves among the natives, isolated even when not unsympathetic, ignorant even when not uninquisitive, a stranger and a foreigner to the end of the chapter . . . it is I and my native colleagues who can claim to speak at first hand and out of our own personal and intuitive knowledge and experience of the feelings and thoughts of the ryot, his prejudices, his habits of thought, his ways of life, his ambitions and his aspirations.[18]

Pherozeshah Mehta wound up his speech with a threat: 'My Lord, if this amendment fails, I do not see how we non-official elected members can make ourselves useful in the subsequent stages of the bill.'

Pherozeshah had spoken in his characteristic, hard-hitting style, and assailed the government with scorn and sarcasm. Gokhale's

[17] R. C. Dutt to Gokhale, 15 Aug. 1901 (G.P.).
[18] *Proc. of the Council of the Gov. of Bombay*, Bombay, 1902, vol. XXXIX, 1901, p. 358.

speech was in a different key. He had studied the problem in detail. He had served on the select committee, and recorded his dissenting minute. In the Council Chamber he spoke more as an economist than as a politician. He recognized the evil of land transfers to money-lenders, but argued that the problem of rural indebtedness needed to be tackled systematically. He wondered if a mere substitution of short leases for perpetuity of tenure could solve the difficulties of the peasant. It was not possible, argued Gokhale, 'to improve the position of the agriculturist by a mere manipulation of the legislative machine'. If the government really wanted to experiment, they could select a small area, take on in that area the debts of the ryots to the 'sowcars' (money-lenders), effect a settlement of some sort, start agricultural banks to provide for the ordinary needs of the agriculturists (thus freeing them from the rapacity of the 'sowcars') and then declare their lands inalienable.

The charge that the opposition to this bill was got up by money-lenders provoked Gokhale into a confession of faith:

It was my privilege to receive my lessons in Indian Economics and Indian Finance at the feet of the late Mr Justice Ranade who . . . was always a friend of the poor ryot. . . . It is not, therefore, possible, unless I am prepared to prove false to the teachings of my departed master, that in any agrarian discussion I should range myself against the interests of the ryot, or be swayed by a special feeling of partiality for the money-lender.[19]

The official members, nettled by the criticism of the Indian members, tended to dismiss them as impractical, academic and irresponsible critics. One of the official members, Lely, had lamented that men of education and of undoubted patriotism 'should confine themselves to the work of mere criticism and should oppose so small a measure framed in the interests of their poorer brethren!' This elicited a retort from Gokhale.

What opportunities have we [he asked] for initiating important measures? Put men like the late Mr Ranade or my honourable friend Mr Mehta on your Executive Councils. Place them in a situation of real power and responsibility and then we undertake to show that we can initiate measures as well as anyone else. It is because you have power to carry out your ideas and we have not, that we appear to you to be engaged in unpractical or academic discussions.[20]

To Gokhale and his colleagues the bill did not seem to be only an

[19] Ibid., p. 340.   [20] Ibid., p. 346.

agrarian issue. The way it was being pushed through the Council in the face of their united opposition reminded them of the obvious political impetus behind the measure.

We, the elected members of this Council [declared Gokhale], are absolutely unanimous in resisting this Bill, and though our voting power is not large enough under the constitution of this Council to prevent the passing of any measure which Government are determined to carry, we represent, when we are unanimous, a moral force, which it is not wise to ignore. For better, for worse, you have introduced the elective element into your Councils, and according to your own English ideas, you must now accept us as speaking not for ourselves individually, but in the name of those who have sent us here. . . . [21]

Gokhale's gentle pleading had no more effect on the government than the barbed shafts of Pherozeshah Mehta whose amendment was defeated by the official bloc with its standing majority. Mehta, Bhalchandra Krishna, Parekh and Khare left the Council Hall as a protest. Gokhale followed them, but before doing so he addressed Governor Northcote, who was in the chair: 'I think it my duty, my Lord, now to say that I must follow the course which has been taken by some of my honourable colleagues . . . I mean no disrespect to Your Excellency or your colleagues personally. It is only an overwhelming sense of duty which urges me to take this step.' The walk-out by the Indian members was a bold act of defiance. The *Times of India* described it as 'the exhibition of petty temper'. Northcote suggested to the Viceroy an amendment of the rules of local legislatures to check 'disorderly conduct' on the part of the members.[22]

The dramatic walk-out on 23 August 1901 was not at all typical of the temper of the Bombay Council or of Gokhale's style as a legislator. Indeed, Gokhale decided on a walk-out after a great deal of deliberation, and against his better judgement. He was in favour of moving amendments which could improve the bill from the cultivators' point of view. He failed to convert Pherozeshah Mehta, but decided to follow his lead. 'I would rather be in the wrong with you', he wrote to him, 'than be in the right by myself.'[23] The Council was in fact a fairly staid assembly, with few pyrotechnics. And in any case the official bloc, with its standing majority, could carry through any measure it wanted. Nevertheless, it was a useful training ground for Gokhale. He cultivated a winsome parliamentary manner and pre-

[21] Ibid., p. 347. [22] Northcote to Curzon, 27 April 1901 (C.P.).
[23] Gokhale to P. Mehta, 9 Aug. 1901 (P. Mehta P.).

pared his brief carefully before challenging official spokesmen in the Council chamber or in the select committee. He brought the same industry and earnestness to bear on his legislative work as he had applied to the work of the Fergusson College and the Sarvajanik Sabha.

5

Just as Gokhale's political star was beginning to rise a shadow fell over his domestic life. His wife Radhabai died after giving birth to a son. Gokhale, who was only thirty-three, was left with two young daughters and a baby son. The baby did not survive either. Ranade sought to console his disciple.

M. G. Ranade to G. K. Gokhale, 26 October 1900: It is indeed a great trial for one in your place, and you have . . . young children left on your hands to be cared for only as a mother can care. The trial will be a very heavy one. We can only submit to God's decree.

Ranade's own health had been failing for some time; he had long been suffering from heart trouble and passed away on 16 January 1901. The depth of Gokhale's grief may be gauged from a letter he wrote to R. P. Paranjpye twelve weeks after Ranade's death.[24] 'Since I wrote to you last, my great master Mr Ranade has passed away! What his death means to me is more than I can tell you. I feel as though a sudden darkness has fallen upon my life and the best part of the satisfaction of doing public work is, for the present at any rate, gone.'

Gokhale bore his bereavements with fortitude. They do not seem to have deflected him from the political career on which he had embarked. Indeed, it is possible that the loss of his wife and his political mentor stimulated, rather than weakened, his political ambition. After his wife's death, he was less trammelled by domestic ties, and after the death of Ranade, he was compelled to exercise greater initiative. It is perhaps not a mere coincidence that Gokhale's letter to Paranjpye, lamenting Ranade's death, also included a reference to his election to the Imperial Council.

Of the four elective seats in the Governor-General's Legislative Council—or the Imperial Council as it was popularly known—one had been allotted to the Presidency of Bombay, and was occupied by Pherozeshah Mehta, the foremost Indian politician of the day. Early

[24] Paranjpye, *Gopal Krishna Gokhale,* facsimile opp. p. 44.

in 1901, it became known that Pherozeshah Mehta was thinking of resigning his seat on grounds of health. Some of Gokhale's friends in Bombay—Vishnu Bhatvadekar, H. S. Dickshit and Lalubhai Samaldas—urged him to seize this opportunity of getting into the Imperial Council. Under the Act of 1892, the decision rested with the twelve non-official members of the Bombay Council. Gokhale was only thirty-four years old and had been a member of the Bombay Council for barely a year. Was it not too much to expect that his non-official colleagues would elect him to the highest office in their gift? Would not some of them like to advance their own claims? The Indian members did not form a party, nor did they have an elected leader, but Pherozeshah Mehta's opinion carried weight with most of them. Gokhale realized that the key to success lay in Pherozeshah's support.

Gokhale to Pherozeshah Mehta, 15 January 1901: I assure you it is not mere personal ambition which is urging me to seek the honour. My reasons are different. . . . In 1897 when a perfect storm of fierce criticism broke over my head in connection with my unhappy share in the incidents of that year, nothing wounded me deeper than Bhownagri's denunciation of me in the House of Commons as a 'despicable perjurer'. The words burnt into my heart, & the night I read them, I made up my mind to devote my life, as soon as I was free from my pledge, to the furtherance of our political cause in England, to which I had, without meaning it, done such serious injury. And for this work a brief period of membership of the Viceroy's Council will be very useful.

The principal affair of 1897 will perhaps be brought against me again and again, but the testimony of Lord Sandhurst himself and my membership of the Bombay and Supreme Councils subsequent to that incident will go a long way towards silencing my critics. . . .

I myself feel that I am too young for the position, but the fierce mental anguish which I have had to endure since 1897, has made me older in judgement and experience, and in any case it is not wholly a disadvantage that I shall begin the new career at a comparatively young age.[25]

The letter to Pherozeshah Mehta had been drafted with consummate skill. It approached him with due deference and even played upon his vanity. Gokhale frankly avowed his ambition to step not only into Mehta's shoes in Calcutta, but into those of Dadabhai Naoroji in London. He took care to stake his claims on a public rather than on a private plane. He was simply volunteering for full-time service in the cause of the country. He did not slur over the

[25] P. Mehta P.

stigma of the apology incident, but turned it into an argument in his favour: for the wrong he had unwittingly done to the nationalist cause in 1897 he wanted to make amends by serving India as a member of the Imperial Council and later of the House of Commons.

Gokhale was no stranger to Pherozeshah Mehta. Pherozeshah was a shrewd judge of men; he had watched Gokhale at work in the Sarvajanik Sabha, in the Indian National Congress, and in the Bombay Council. He knew how able and earnest the young professor from Poona was; indeed, Pherozeshah himself occasionally sought facts and figures from Gokhale for preparing his speeches. Whatever Pherozeshah's reasons, he threw his weight in favour of Gokhale.

On 1 March 1901 it was made known that Pherozeshah Mehta would resign from the Imperial Council. A fortnight later, Vishnu Bhatwadekar, who was lobbying for Gokhale in Bombay, cheerfully informed him that the rival candidates, Ibrahim Rahimatoola and Bomanji Dinshaw Petit, had withdrawn: 'So, Mr Mehta's tactics in first asking you to occupy the field before his resignation was announced have succeeded admirably without causing a split. The rival competitors have probably given up the struggle as hopeless by your anticipating them by a long distance.'[26]

Pherozeshah Mehta's support was a great asset to Gokhale, but he had also played his cards skilfully. He took no chances. He canvassed the support of each of his fellow legislators in the Bombay Council, and won over six of them. Thanks to Bennett of the *Times of India*, he was promised the support of S. M. Moses, one of the European members. This gave him a decisive majority, and finally led to the withdrawal of his opponents from the contest.

Bennett, who had earlier helped Gokhale in his election to the Bombay Council, had again used his influence in Gokhale's favour. This was not because he hoped to exercise any direct influence over Gokhale. Gokhale's record in the Bombay Council was proof enough that he had a will of his own. Still, from Bennett's point of view, it was something of an advantage that an able Indian had succeeded Pherozeshah Mehta, and the seat had not fallen to an adherent of Tilak.

Gokhale's meteoric rise in 1899–1901 was due not only to luck and Pherozeshah's patronage, though these undoubtedly played their part. Gokhale's own determination and shrewdness helped him to outwit his rivals. So long as Ranade was alive, most people saw in

[26] V. K. Bhatwadekar to Gokhale, 14 March 1901 (G.P.).

Gokhale only a pale reflection of his master. The factionalism of Poona politics had obscured his real worth, and the apology incident had clouded his prospects. He had little chance so long as he fought for a place in the sun in Poona. If he was to make an impression, it could only be on the provincial or the national stage. His election to the Bombay Council in 1899 and the Imperial Council in 1901 gave him opportunities which he turned to excellent account. His success aroused mixed feelings amongst older politicians. Some in Poona and Bombay were frankly envious; others were happy to see on the Indian political horizon a young man with energy, ability and vision. To these latter Gokhale brought at the turn of the century what Nehru brought to a later generation in the late 1920s, a breath of fresh air. R. C. Dutt, who had retired from the Indian Civil Service, specialized in the study of economic problems and presided over the 1899 Congress session, saw Gokhale's victory in 1901 as the precursor of even greater triumphs.

R. C. Dutt to G. K. Gokhale, 16 May 1901: Ever since I saw you in London some 4 years ago, I have marked and sincerely admired your single-minded devotion to our country, your zealous determination to place all your talents, all your industry, all your life in the service of our country. You have outlived prejudices and hostilities. You have proved your worth, your virtues and your patriotism, and you stand forth today, what you have always been, one of the best and foremost and noblest of the young sons of India devoting their lives to the cause of India.[27]

6

A year after Gokhale's election to the Imperial Legislative Council, he had an unexpected compliment from his home town. In July 1902, he was invited by all the parties in the Poona City municipality to be its president, filling the vacancy caused by the death of Dorabji Padumji. That the sole elected representative of the Bombay Presidency in the Imperial Legislative Council should have been asked to head a municipality did not sound so odd in 1902 as it may seem today. A certain prestige attached to work in local bodies at that time; among those who had served the municipal corporations in their home towns were Pherozeshah Mehta, Surendranath Banerjea and Tilak. Those who pressed the honour on Gokhale in Poona in 1902 included N. C. Kelkar and other adherents of Tilak. Gokhale's

[27] G.P.

new eminence in national politics evidently tickled Maharashtrian pride. The offer to Gokhale was really a tribute to the new status he had recently acquired as a national leader.

Gokhale headed the municipal administration of Poona for nearly four years. He proved a competent president, but he had his hands too full with his responsibilities as a legislator, Congress leader and First Member of the Servants of India Society to do justice to local affairs. He took special interest in the expansion of educational facilities. The number of municipal schools and pupils, which was 28 and 1316 respectively in 1903–4, rose to 33 and 1733 in the following year. Gokhale's friend, H. N. Apte, was the chairman of the Municipal School Board. The resources of the Poona City municipality were, however, limited, and the small margin of income over expenditure was used up by the campaign against plague, which afflicted Poona as an epidemic for several months every year. The fight against plague required additional expenditure on sanitary and medical facilities at a time when, because of the epidemic, the yield from municipal taxes fell off. The Poona municipality had also to pay a heavy annual instalment towards the repayment of a 'plague loan', for expenditure incurred by the provincial government some years earlier in combating plague in Poona.

The brief experience of municipal administration gave Gokhale an insight into the actual working of local self-governing institutions. He discovered that, with inelastic revenues, they could achieve little. Though he continued vigorously to advocate a pyramid of elective local bodies—with panchayats in the villages, municipalities in towns, and advisory councils in the districts—he came to the melancholy conclusion that 'local self-government continued to be where it was carried by the late Marquis of Ripon about 30 years ago'.[28]

[28] Patwardhan & Ambekar, op. cit., vol. I, pp. 369–70.

13

Triumph

On 20 December 1901, 'the Hon'ble Mr Gopal Krishna Gokhale' took his seat in the Council of the Governor-General as 'an Additional Member'. The 'Supreme Council' or the 'Imperial Council', as it was called, had been set up under the Indian Councils Act of 1892. The word 'election' did not figure in the Act of the British Parliament nor in the regulations issued under it. Of the twenty-four councillors, nineteen were officials of the government or its nominees. Of the remaining five, one represented British commercial interests through the Calcutta Chamber of Commerce, and four were appointed by the Governor-General on the recommendation of a majority of non-official members in each of the four legislative councils of Bombay, Calcutta, Madras and North-West (later, United) Provinces. Since the recommendation was invariably accepted, the procedure in fact amounted to indirect election. The four Indian members sat at one end of the table, facing a permanent majority of European officials. They could ask questions, but the Viceroy, who was in the chair, could disallow any question. It was rarely that more than ten questions were asked in a session. The great event of the year was the presentation of the financial statement in the last week of March by the Finance Member of the Viceroy's Executive Council. The debate on the budget usually took place on the day of the Governor-General's departure for Simla, and lasted four to five hours. One by one, the members read out their speeches, the Finance Member replied, and after the Viceroy's address, the Imperial Council adjourned. The budget was not submitted to the vote of the Council: indeed there would have been no point in doing so, as the official majority would in any case have ensured its passage.

The official reaction to criticism by Indian councillors was usually one of condescension or annoyance, depending upon whether the criticism was attributed to ignorance or perversity. Of Sri Ram Bahadur, one of Gokhale's colleagues in the Imperial Council, a senior British official wrote: 'he talks nonsense elsewhere than in this province'.[1] Another member, B. K. Bose, sent drafts of his speeches to the members of the Viceroy's Executive Council before they were delivered.[2] In a small body of this kind, presided over by the head of the Indian administration, and packed with his own subordinates and nominees, it was not easy for a tiny group of Indian members to assert themselves, even if they had the will to do so. Indeed, the Indian members could hardly be called a group; most of them seemed to have no opinion of their own, and realized the hazards of alienating the Viceroy and senior officials. These hazards ranged from a stinging rebuke at the council table to the possible denial of a knighthood. With rare exceptions, such as that of Pherozeshah Mehta, most Indian members went through the budget debate, gingerly touching upon minor local grievances, or readily joining in a chorus of praise for the Finance Member.

2

When the Budget debate opened on 26 March 1902, it seemed that the same old scene would be re-enacted. The Finance Member, Sir Edward Law, patted himself on the back for a surplus of seven crores in the previous year's budget. 'Fortune', declared Sir Edward Law, 'has given us unique opportunity and we have spared no pains to make the best of it. I gratefully acknowledge that this indeed is the case.' The official members, non-official European members and even some of the Indian members offered their meed of praise. 'My Lord,' said the Maharaja of Darbhanga, 'it is hardly necessary for me to assure Your Excellency that there is universal and genuine satisfaction throughout the country at the prosperous financial circumstances revealed by the Budget Statement.' B. K. Bose thanked the government on behalf of the Central Provinces and expressed his 'delight and thankfulness'.

The debate was running in its well-worn grooves until Gokhale rose to speak.

I fear [he began] I cannot conscientiously join in the congratulations which have been offered to the Hon'ble Finance Member on the huge surplus which the revised estimates show for the last year. The successive surplus budgets of the Government of India illustrate the utter absence of a due correspondence between the condition of the

[1] J. D. Latouche, Lt-Gov. N.W.P., to Curzon, 1 April 1905 (C.P.).
[2] D. Ibbetson to W. Lawrence, P. S. to Viceroy, 22 March 1902 (C.P.).

country and the condition of the finances of the country. . . . [the surpluses] constitute a . . . wrong to the community. They are a wrong in the first instance that they exist at all—that Government should take so much more from the people than is needed in times of serious depression and suffering. . . .

Gokhale pointed out how in the preceding sixteen years the income tax, the salt tax, the excise duty and the cotton duties had gone up; even the collections of land revenue had registered an upward trend at a time when drought and famine afflicted large parts of the country. He referred to the apparent 'paradox of a suffering country and an overflowing treasury'. He called for a relief in tax burdens, for a cut in the salt duty, and an increase in the taxable minimum for income tax to one thousand rupees a year. He suggested that the excise duty on cotton yarn be abolished. The government could afford to give all this relief and still retain a surplus of receipts over expenditure. He pleaded for more funds for education, particularly technical education, and the development of industry. The Viceroy, Lord Curzon (who was in the chair), had challenged the advocates of technical education in India to make definite proposals. 'I do not see', said Gokhale, 'how such responsibility can be sought to be imposed on our shoulders. Government have command of vast resources and they can produce without difficulty the required expert advice on the subject.' He proposed that a small committee of competent Englishmen and Indians should be asked to visit foreign countries, particularly Japan, which had made significant progress in the field of technical education and industrial growth.

Gokhale argued that it was possible to reduce taxation and to undertake constructive activities if military expenditure was reduced. The Viceroy had declared that so long as he was at the helm of affairs in India, no suggestion for reduction of the army would be entertained. If that was the inflexible position of the government, said Gokhale, was it not possible to take part of the Indian military expenditure to the English estimates? Was not England as 'interested in the maintenance of this rule here as we are?'

From a critical analysis of the budget estimates, Gokhale passed on to an attack on the policies of the government. He alleged that the Indian finances were so managed as to lend support to the view that foreign interests took precedence over Indian interests. Large sums had been spent on territorial expansion beyond the borders of India, which had brought no benefit to the country. The interests of the

English mercantile class had been conciliated by the construction of the railways, and those of the civil service by sanctioning additional allowances to its members at a time when India was passing through difficult times.

Gokhale refuted the argument of the Finance Member[3] that the increase in the customs returns was a sign of the advancing prosperity of the people. The import of sugar, fine cloth and silver had little relation to the condition of the masses who were suffering from the rigours of a widespread famine. In Gokhale's opinion only two taxes could be considered reliable indices of the condition of the Indian people: the income tax of the condition of the upper and middle classes, and the salt tax of the poorer classes. The fact that both these taxes had remained stationary testified to the stagnation of the Indian economy. He referred to the controversy on 'the Condition of India' in which Curzon had asserted that the *per capita* income was Rs 30 a year and not Rs 19 a year as computed by Dadabhai Naoroji. Apart from the fact that the *per capita* estimates gave a 'statistical', and not a dynamic view of the situation, was not the Viceroy's own figure, Gokhale asked, pitifully small? Gokhale went on to quote figures of salt consumption, agricultural output, imports and exports, to suggest that the mass of the people were not only not prospering, but were actually growing poorer.

The 'Condition of India' was a controversial issue on which Curzon had crossed swords with Indian nationalists. Gokhale brought it to the Council Chamber: his criticism of the government acquired a sharper edge, partly because it was based on the government's own Blue Books, and partly because it added up to an assault not only upon the budget for that year, but upon the political and economic polices of the Government of India. With great skill, Gokhale laid bare the connection between economic and political reform: 'If we had any votes to give and the Government of the country had been carried on by an alteration of power between two parties, both alike anxious to conciliate us, and bid for our support, the Hon'ble Member [for Finance] would assuredly have told a different tale.' What India required was not 'efficiency merely, but bold and generous statesmanship'. But the government was so constituted that it favoured a policy of drift. The members of the Civil Service, said Gokhale, were 'able and conscientious men', but they did not command the prestige

[3] For budget debate see *Proc. of the Gov.-Gen.'s Council*, 1902 vol. XLI, pp. 85–213.

to launch any large schemes making a departure from the established order of things. The administrators—the Viceroy and some of the important Governors—came out directly from England, and did not have the opportunity, even if they had the will, to tackle basic issues. The result was that there was 'an inveterate tendency to keep things merely going . . . as though everyone said to himself: "This will last my time".'

Gokhale concluded his speech with an appeal to the ruling race: 'Let Englishmen exercise a certain amount of imagination and put themselves into our place, and they will be able to better appreciate our feelings. . . .' He invoked a 'true spirit of Imperialism, not the narrower Imperialism which regards the world as though it was made for one race only and looks upon subject races as if they were intended to be mere footstools of that race—but that nobler Imperialism which would enable all who are included in the Empire to share equally in its blessings and honours'.

3

Gokhale had not been too well during the weeks preceding the budget debate. On the advice of his doctor, he went to Darjeeling for a change, but the budget speech was never off his mind. He was conscious that he would have to speak in the presence of a Viceroy, 'who is always on the look-out for a chance to smash the critics of the Government in argument'.[4] He gave much thought to what he should say, and sought the advice of his old friend G. V. Joshi, who had, jointly with Ranade, briefed him in 1897 for the Welby Commission. Joshi sent some notes for which Gokhale thanked him profusely. It would, however, be rash to conclude that Joshi was 'ghosting' for Gokhale. 'The reason why I so constantly trouble you', wrote Gokhale, 'for notes is that anything you send [me] proves useful by suggesting to me much else.'[5] Joshi's real role, as Ranade's in the past, was that of a catalytic agent, providing Gokhale with intellectual stimulus and moral support at a time when he had not acquired sufficient confidence in himself.

Gokhale was no stranger to the problems of Indian economics and finance: for fourteen years he had pondered, spoken and written upon them. His brief term in the Bombay Council had taught him an

[4] Gokhale to G. V. Joshi, 24 Jan. 1902 (G.P.).
[5] *Idem*, 17 Jan. 1902 (G.P.).

effective parliamentary style, and the art of saying the hardest things in the gentlest manner.

Gokhale's speech in the Imperial Council on 26 March 1902 had an electrifying effect upon the Indian intelligentsia. Like Byron, he could have said that he woke up one fine morning and found himself famous. The *Amrita Bazar Patrika*, in an editorial, expressed the thoughts which were uppermost in many minds:

We had ever entertained the ambition of seeing some Indian member openly and fearlessly criticizing the Financial Statement of the Government. But this ambition was never satisfied. When members had ability, they had not the requisite courage. When they had the requisite courage, they had not the ability. . . . For the first time in the annals of British rule in India, a native of India has not only succeeded in exposing the fallacies which underlie these Government statements, but has ventured to do it in an uncompromising manner.[6]

Letters of congratulation poured in from friends and admirers, from M. K. Gandhi, who was on a brief visit in India from South Africa, from Akbar Hydari, a young civil servant, and C. Y. Chintamani, then a little-known journalist. R. C. Dutt, the veteran civilian and publicist, was delighted.

R. C. Dutt to G. K. Gokhale, 8 April 1902: I am not in the habit of saying more than I mean;—and I can honestly assure you that I consider your Budget speech to be the ablest and best that has ever been made from our point of view in the Viceroy's Council.

More than this, it discloses the sad truths which the officials try to conceal, and does this so effectively, so clearly, and so convincingly that there is no answer to it. Your cogency of reasoning is admirable, and your conclusions come with irresistible force of a sledge-hammer and pound the official sophistries into atoms!

. . . The Viceroy must feel today—strong and self-willed as he is,—there are stronger forces arraigning themselves in India in the popular cause. . . . Ten years hence these forces will be stronger than they are today; and I dare prophesy—knowing all the eminent public men in India,—that you will be the strongest, the foremost and the most irresistible leader among them, because you are inspired by the truest and the honestest zeal for our country.[7]

Thoughtful Europeans, not blinkered by racial prejudice, were quick to perceive the talents of the youngest member of the Imperial Council. W. S. Caine reported from London that the speech received a good coverage from the British press. L. G. Fraser, the editor of the *Times of India*, did not agree with everything that Gokhale had

[6] *Amrita Bazar Patrika*, 29 March 1902.   [7] G.P.

said, but expressed the pride of 'western India in possessing [in Gokhale] a representative of so much distinction and individuality'.[8]

The *Indian Daily News*, a British-owned paper of Calcutta, drew the best pen-picture of Gokhale's impact on the Imperial Council:

Mr Gokhale, a member from Bombay, made a slashing attack on the whole financial position of the Government, and the explosion of a bombshell in their midst could hardly have created greater surprise and consternation in the midst of that sedate assembly. With the daring of youth, Mr Gokhale expounded . . . the views of the Digby School . . . with singular lucidity. His command of nervous English, his fluency of delivery, and his logical arrangement of his argument made it a pleasure to listen to him. . . .[9]

4

The official reaction to Gokhale's speech was a mixture of irritation and bewilderment. The Finance Member, Sir Edward Law, frankly admitted that he had not had time to prepare the answers to the many questions which the Honourable Member from Bombay had raised. Curzon did not counter Gokhale's arguments and contented himself with the facetious remark: 'If the Hon'ble Member were to transfer his residence to any European country, he would soon be back again here with altered views about fiscal matters.' The following day, on 27 March, in a confidential letter to the Secretary of State, Lord George Hamilton, Curzon referred to 'Mr Gokhale from Bombay' who 'had made a very strong speech of the Congress type denouncing our currency policy and our fiscal policy in unmeasured terms. I should like to have had an hour in which to answer him, but he was hardly worth the powder and shot.'[10]

This superior air of condescension did not last long. An able man himself, Curzon could recognize and occasionally admire ability in others. The following year, on 25 March 1903, while winding up the budget debate, Curzon observed that Gokhale's speech was 'characterized by the great ability which we have learnt to associate with his utterances'.[11] The same night, while travelling from Calcutta to Simla, Curzon gave Hamilton an assessment of Gokhale which was markedly different from that he had made a year earlier.[12]

[8] L. G. Fraser to Gokhale, 31 March 1902 (G.P.).
[9] Quoted in *Amrita Bazar Patrika*, 29 March 1902.
[10] Curzon to Hamilton, 27 March 1902 (C.P.).
[11] *Proc. of the Gov.-Gen.'s Council*, 1902, vol. XLI, p. 201.
[12] *Supra*, chap. 1, p. 3.

The budget statement presented by the Finance Member in 1903 conceded some of the demands Gokhale had made in the previous year's debate. The salt duty had been reduced and the taxable minimum for income tax raised. Gokhale's speech on this occasion was, however, no less vigorous, but the official reaction was more sympathetic. Acknowledging an error in the budget statement which Gokhale had pointed out, Sir Edward Law, the Finance Member, said: 'I am much obliged to him and I can only beg to be excused.'[13] Sir Edward seemed to be making a conscious effort to conciliate and, if possible, to win over Gokhale.

Sir Edward Law to G. K. Gokhale, 7 August 1903: Lady Law has been suggesting that possibly when you are free from your present labours, after the rains, you may be inclined to pay a visit to Simla for a few days, and that if so, we might offer to put you up. . . .
I am greatly interested in your idea of travelling, and I should very much like to talk over with you your plans in this direction if you choose to give me the opportunity. . . . I should be really happy if before leaving this country, I could get you to accept my views on the real needs of the country.[14]

The deference with which high dignitaries now began to treat Gokhale was indicated by an incident in April 1902. A young British officer, Lieutenant Goldingham, was rude to him when he was boarding the train for Poona from Nagpur, and would not let him enter a first class compartment. However, as soon the train left and Goldingham discovered that his fellow-passenger was a member of the Imperial Legislative Council, he apologized. So far as Gokhale was concerned, the matter was closed. But it had received publicity in the press, and Lord Northcote, the Governor of Bombay, hastened to express his regret. Northcote had good reasons to deplore this incident. Convinced that Gokhale's political star was in the ascendant, he was out to cultivate Gokhale. In a letter to the Viceroy, he pleaded for a title for Gokhale.

Northcote to Curzon, 7 February 1903: You have seen something of Gokhale now. I consider him to be able and, on the whole, well-affected, though not a strong character. He is now, I think, at the parting of the ways. He is President of the Poona Municipality, not a well-disposed body on the whole, and he is acknowledged to be one of the leaders of the less extreme Native Reform Party. The Tilak section will do all they can to capture him; and he is in a position where he can do a great deal of service on the one hand or some

---

[13] *Proc. of the Gov.-Gen.'s Council*, 1902, vol. XLI, p. 190.   [14] G.P.

harm on the other, to Government. If a C.I.E. will secure him to us, it would be well disposed, I think at the proper time. . . .[15]

Curzon agreed with Northcote that Gokhale was 'worth keeping on our side', but wondered whether such honours as the C.I.E. should be 'won so much more cheaply by Natives than by Europeans'.[16] Undaunted by this rebuff, Northcote pressed his recommendation until it was accepted. The day before the *Government of India Gazette* was to announce the bestowal of a C.I.E. on Gokhale, Curzon wrote to him that the honour was in 'recognition of abilities which are freely bestowed upon the service of your countrymen and of which I would ask no more than that they should continue to be so employed. I only wish that India produced more such public men.'[17]

Not to be outdone in courtesy and literary grace, Gokhale at once wrote to the Viceroy: 'No words that I can employ will adequately express the feelings which this letter has aroused in me. . . .' He undertook 'to continue his efforts to bring the two races together in this land so that the purpose of the Providence in bringing India under British rule may best be realized by both'.[18]

The bestowal of the C.I.E. was well received in India. Scores of Indian princes, landlords, and officials had received this honour before. It was however noted that Gokhale had earned this distinction even though he was an outspoken critic of the government. The award proved, wrote old Woomes Chunder Bonnerjee, the first President of the Indian National Congress, 'that it is not necessary to be subservient to the Government for them to recognize true merit. You have always been independent, and never gave in to the powers that be.'[19] Bonnerjee was reading too much into the bestowal of the decoration, just as Gokhale had read too much into the felicitous diction of Curzon's letter of congratulations.

The first of January 1904 may be considered the high-water mark in the relations between Curzon and Gokhale. Curzon could appreciate ability in an opponent, but could not appreciate patriotism— except, of course, in true-born Englishmen. During the next three months, as the government initiated legislation which was to alienate it from public opinion, it fell to Gokhale to lead the opposition with a mixture of courage, tenacity and ability which delighted Indian nationalists, upset the calculations of Northcote and infuriated Cur-

[15] C.P.   [16] Curzon to Northcote, 3 April 1903 (C.P.).
[17] Curzon to Gokhale, 31 Dec. 1903 (C.P.).
[18] Gokhale to Curzon, 1 Jan. 1904 (C.P.)
[19] W. C. Bonnerjee to Gokhale, 1 Jan. 1904 (G.P.).

zon. The C.I.E. failed to buy off Gokhale. Many years later, after the heat and dust of debate had subsided, Curzon recalled the qualities of the man who had dared to stand up to him in the Imperial Legislative Council at Calcutta.

Mr Gokhale was a member of my Legislative Council during a period of, I suppose, five or six years. During that time he was, I think, I may almost say, in invariable opposition to the Government. He was, if I may so describe him, the leader of the Opposition in the Imperial Legislative Council over which I presided. In that capacity I often had to suffer from the weight of Mr Gokhale's blows, but I should like to say this, that I have never met a man of any nationality more gifted with what one could describe in this country as Parliamentary capacities, than was Mr Gokhale. I truly believe . . . [he] would have attained a position of distinction in any Parliament in the world.[20]

[20] *Debates on Indian Affairs*, House of Lords Session, 1914–16, 5 and 6 George V, London, 1916, p. 119.

Book II

SPOKESMAN FOR THE MODERATES

14

Gokhale Comes of Age

The Imperial Council met in Calcutta during the last week of December and adjourned at the end of March when the Viceroy and his colleagues left for Simla for the summer. From 1902 onwards Gokhale was to spend the best part of winter not in Poona, but in Calcutta. Calcutta was the seat of the provincial and the central governments and the heart of commerce of the 'Indian Empire'. The gulf between Indians and the Europeans was much wider in Calcutta than in Bombay. Gokhale's privileged position as a member of the Imperial Council gave him access to the highest official quarters, but there were hardly any Europeans with whom he could make friends. It was in the Indian—or rather in the Bengali—society of Calcutta that he received respect, warmth and affection.

At the turn of the century Bengal was pulsating with a new vitality. She was proud of her pre-eminent place in the country, in literature, music, drama, painting and politics. Calcutta was indeed the intellectual and cultural capital of Bengal. For Gokhale Calcutta was a refreshing contrast to Poona. For the first time in his public life he was spared for a few months at a time the tension of the factional politics of his home town. His social and political horizons widened, and he acquired a new insight into the minds and hearts of the Bengalis, who were soon to set a new pace for nationalist politics.

Among those who became Gokhale's friends in Calcutta there were some remarkable men and women. There was Motilal Ghose of the *Amrita Bazar Patrika*. Thin and erect, with his mass of grey hair surmounting a face in which pathos, humour and subtlety were mingled, he was a friend of Tilak, but his occasional, exuberant professions of loyalty to the British Crown could have shamed the most sentimental royalist in England. This did not however prevent Motilal Ghose from directing the guns of the *Amrita Bazar Patrika* at the Viceroy, the Governor of Bengal and other high officials, to the great amusement of its readers and the great annoyance of its victims.

For Gokhale, Motilal Ghose had a particularly soft corner. One of the finest tributes to Gokhale on his first budget speech in the Imperial Council was paid by the *Amrita Bazar Patrika*: 'Mr Gokhale has demonstrated . . . that the members of the Council have their duties towards their country, and in performing them they must not think of self.'[1]

Less ebullient than Motilal Ghose, but not less cordial to Gokhale were Nilratan Sircar, the eminent physician, Prafulla Chandra Ray, the pioneer chemist, and Jagdish Chandra Bose, the famous botanist. Bose, who was on the faculty of the Presidency College, had published thirty-one research papers between 1895 and 1903, and addressed some of the foremost associations of scientists in the world. The government had sent him twice on deputation to Europe and honoured him with a C.I.E. Nevertheless, he had to wage a continual battle with bureaucratic obstruction, and could rarely get anything important done without the intercession of a high British dignitary, such as the Governor of Bengal or the Viceroy.[2] Gokhale met Bose in January 1903. A few days later he sought the Viceroy's intervention to ensure better facilities for Bose. In a letter to Sir Walter Lawrence, Private Secretary to Curzon, he wrote:

I address you not because I am a friend of Dr Bose—I made his acquaintance only in January last . . . but as an Indian I feel proud of the position which he has achieved for himself in the world of science in the face of overwhelming difficulties. . . .
What Dr Bose needs is a properly equipped laboratory and sufficient leisure for pursuing his studies and research work without interruption. The Presidency College Laboratory is already a large one; but a heavy additional outlay—about three lakhs of rupees or so—is necessary to bring it up to the requirements of Dr Bose. . . . He has at present to do about 18 hours' lecturing work a week—for the most part on very elementary portion of physics. . . . I would therefore respectfully repeat the suggestion . . . that Government should be pleased to relieve Dr Bose of all lecturing work. . . .[3]

It was through J. C. Bose that Gokhale met Rabindranath Tagore. 'I want you to see my friend Mr Rabindranath Tagore', Bose wrote to Gokhale; 'I wish I could have taken you to see his school. It is an experiment from which I expect much . . . next time I want you to know more of my friend.'[4] Bose also introduced Gokhale to a re-

[1] 29 March 1902.
[2] See P. Geddes, *The Life and Work of Sir Jagdish C. Bose*, London, 1920, pp. 40–3.   [3] G.P.   [4] 14 April 1903 (G.P.).

markable woman, a disciple of Swami Vivekananda and an evangelist of a resurrected Hinduism. Margaret Elizabeth Noble, better known as Sister Nivedita, was an Irish lady of Scottish descent, who had come to India in 1898 and was on the friendliest of terms with some of the foremost families of Calcutta, the Boses, the Ghosals and the Tagores. To her house at 17 Bosepara Lane came not only scientists like J. C. Bose, but eminent politicians like R. C. Dutt, Anand Mohan Bose and Bipin Chandra Pal. Her politics were radical and strongly anti-British. What impressed her was Gokhale's sincerity and ability rather than his political moderation. On 29 March 1903, we find her congratulating Gokhale on his 'recent [budget] speech in Council. . . . It is an infinite joy to me to know that a Maharatta is loved in Bengal as you have caused yourself to be by our finest men here, and when that love is joined with such respect for your intellect & such implicit trust in your courage & disinterestedness, it is beyond all praise.' A few years later we find her pleading with Gokhale not to give up his seat in the Imperial Council:

That seems to me to be your place, where you are invaluable. Besides, you are some day to be in India what Lamartine was in Paris, in the Great Crisis. I have always thought this was your destiny. Still that will come to you whether you remain on the Council or off. Thy place in life is seeking after thee. Therefore be thou at rest from seeking after it.[5]

The low-key politics and the constitutional methods of the Indian National Congress, of which Gokhale was an ardent advocate, left Nivedita cold. Though her principal preoccupation was with reforms in the religious, cultural and social spheres, she made no secret of her political views which were aggressively pro-Hindu and pro-Indian. She doubted the bona fides of the British in India. 'Can the robbers teach her [India] anything?',[6] she asked and answered: 'No, she [India] has to turn them out and go back where she was before. Something like that, I fancy, is the true programme for India. And so I have nothing to do with Christians or Government agencies as long as the government is foreign.' She implored Gokhale not to be taken in by a 'few saintly or exquisite persons' in England, but to 'judge my people as they really are—often blood-thirsty, always money-thirsty—degraded by unjust wars. . . .'[7]

[5] 28 March 1907 (G.P.).

[6] Pravrajika Atmaprana, *Sister Nivedita of Ramakrishna-Vivekananda*, Calcutta, 1961, p. 125.

[7] Nivedita to Gokhale, 20 Sept. 1905 (G.P.).

It was not easy even for Nivedita with her missionary zeal to wean Ranade's disciple from political moderation. On the contrary, there is evidence that Gokhale tried to instruct Nivedita and her friend Sister Christina[8] in the virtues of the constitutional method.

Gokhale's politics were proof against the mystical fervour of these nuns of the Ramakrishna Mission, but his religious beliefs were not. The agnosticism of his early years, which he had shared with Agarkar, soon became a thing of the past; it was eroded by his exposure first to theosophy, and then to the teachings of Swami Vivekananda and the Ramakrishna Mission during his periodical visits to Calcutta. 'I wanted to write and tell you some time ago', Gokhale confided to his friend K. Natarajan, the editor of the *Indian Social Reformer*, 'that I read your article on Vivekananda with great pleasure. During my stay in Calcutta I came to understand his aims and aspirations much better than before.'[9] Some years later Natarajan found in Gokhale's study in Calcutta a glass paper-weight with an inscription in bold letters: 'God is Love.' Gokhale did not wear his religious beliefs on his sleeve, and had little time and aptitude for theological disputation, but there is no doubt that the contacts he made in Calcutta anchored him firmly to the religion of his birth.

Of Gokhale's life in Calcutta, we have a vivid pen-portrait by Gandhi, who spent a month with him in January 1901: 'To see Gokhale at work was as much a joy as an education. He never wasted a minute. His private relations and friendships were all for public good. All his talks had reference only to the good of the country and were absolutely free from any trace of untruth or insincerity. India's poverty and subjection were matters of constant concern to him.'[10]

It was this feeling, that Gokhale had given his all to the country and was wholly devoted to its service, which made him the idol of not only Gandhi in South Africa, but of practically the entire educated élite in India. Thirty-two year-old Sarla Ghosal, the daughter of J. Ghosal, Calcutta's leading Congressman, and a niece of Rabindranath Tagore, typified the new generation of young Bengalis pulsating with patriotic fervour. Long before the partition of Bengal, she had been advocating *swadeshi*, reviving national festivals, staging patriotic plays, helping to run a girls' school, publishing the journal

[8] Christina Greenstidel, born in Germany. Her parents migrated to the U.S. where she met Swami Vivekananda in 1894. She came to India in 1902.
[9] Gokhale to K. Natarajan, 26 July 1902 (G.P.).
[10] M. K. Gandhi, *An Autobiography*, 2nd ed., Ahmedabad, 1940, p. 169.

Bharati to promote the national spirit, and organizing athletic and music clubs in her home in Ballygunj. She was deeply stirred by Gokhale's first budget speech in the Imperial Council.

Sarla Ghosal to Gokhale, 31 March 1902: Allow me to congratulate you on your beautiful speech. I read it with the greatest interest in the papers. Lord Curzon's reply after yours is such a frivolous thing. It proves more emphatically what a cry in the wilderness even the sober and just utterances of the conquered are. Still the nation should profit more by men like you and more speeches like yours.

I was thinking of what you had said once, that of your resolution to devote yourself solely to politics after you had served your term at the Fergusson College. The moral strength which can enable a few men to give the best years of their life to a fixed cause, to sacrifice themselves singly for the mass . . . it is this habit of sacrifice that we want cultivating in Bengal. . . . What men have done in one part of the country could at any rate be attempted in another part. . . .[11]

2

Gokhale had pledged himself to serve the Deccan Education Society for twenty years. He joined it as a life-member in 1886, but since his service as a teacher in the New English School from 1 January 1885 was reckoned as part of the service of the Society, he could retire at the end of 1904. It had not been easy to combine teaching and politics, and overwork had begun to tell on his health. In 1895 he went through a serious illness; two years later he had, on his way to England, suffered a concussion of the heart in an accident at Calais. Early in 1900, his friends were deeply concerned about his health. One of them, V. G. Bijapurkar, urged him to give up either teaching or politics. Some of his colleagues feared that if he left the Fergusson College, 'it would be a great blow to the efficiency and prestige of the college throughout the country'.[12] Professor Selby, the president of the Deccan Education Society, in fact urged Gokhale to agree to serve as principal of the College. Gokhale declined the offer. He was keen on completing the twenty years' service to which he had pledged himself when he had joined the New English School in 1884. His earlier associates, Agarkar, Apte and Kelkar, had died with the twenty years' service still uncompleted. But what with the Congress, legislative work and teaching, the load had become unbearable by 1902. Gokhale applied for two years' furlough from the college. The

[11] G.P.   [12] Paranjpye to Gokhale, 17 Jan. 1901 (G.P.).

request was acceded to by the Governing Body of the Deccan Education Society,[13] and on 19 September 1902 the students and staff of the Fergusson College assembled to formally bid him farewell. Gokhale delivered an eloquent and moving speech on this occasion. He was leaving, he said, the best work of his life behind him. He was leaving the safe haven of his college to enter the stormy sea of politics. Public life in India had 'few rewards and many trials and discouragements'. He recalled the folly of a man 'who lived by the side of the sea', who had a nice cottage and fields that yielded him their abundance, and who was surrounded by a happy family. The world thought he was very happy, but to him the sea had a strange fascination. 'When it lay gently heaving like an infant asleep, it appealed to him; when it raged like an angry and roaring lion, it still appealed to him, till at last he could withstand the fascination no longer. And so having disposed of everything and put his all into a boat he launched it on the bosom of the sea.'

Gokhale was launching forth on the stormy sea of Indian politics and wondered whether he would be able to press onward or 'return a weather-beaten, tempest-torn and shipwrecked mariner'.

It is surprising that in the autumn of 1902, after his triumphant début in the Imperial Council, Gokhale should still have spoken in such a hesitant vein. Was he deliberately feigning humility? Was he still suffering from the hangover of the apology incident? Was he still haunted by the fickleness of public opinion and the vindictiveness of political opponents?

Gokhale's tone may have been hesitant, but his actions were not. There was a refreshing touch of self-assurance in his handling of men and events. In 1903, several months before his two-year term in the Imperial Council was to end, he made careful soundings for his re-election. When Ibrahim Rahimatoola, a member of the Bombay Council, complained that Gokhale had once again 'stolen a march over him', he received a stinging rebuke.

I cannot understand how you should take it upon yourself to address such a letter to me. Our relations are not of a character to permit of your charging me in a reckless fashion with breach of faith or stealing a march over you, or things of that kind. There never was any understanding between you and me, express or implied. You know quite

[13] The resolution of the Governing Body of the Deccan Education Society: 'Mr Gokhale's letter of resignation was read. A pension of Rs 27 was admissible to him under the rules of 1898. But in recognition of his special services a full pension of Rs 30 was voted to him.'

well that you retired from the contest last time because you had not the ghost of a chance against me. . . .[14]

It was presumptuous on the part of a political light-weight like Ibrahim Rahimatoola to challenge Gokhale; but there was some force in his argument that Gokhale had originally sought a seat in the Imperial Council for a short period and as a prelude to a seat in the House of Commons. It was not entirely Rahimatoola's fault that in the meantime Gokhale had changed his mind about seeking a parliamentary career in England.

3

The exchanges with Ibrahim Rahimatoola revealed the self-confidence Gokhale had developed. He was now able to handle his rivals with surer skill and firmness. No longer did he sink into a depression at the first touch of hostile criticism or adverse circumstance. This confidence had not been acquired without a price. It was to stand him in good stead in coming years.

The death of Ranade in January 1901 seems to have accelerated the process of Gokhale's political maturity. Ranade's death had been a stunning blow to him. 'I feel', he wrote, 'as though a sudden darkness has fallen upon my life.' His feelings towards his master may be gauged from what he wrote to Dr Bhandarkar of Poona in 1896:

As regards Mr Justice Ranade, my relations with him are such that any proposal emanating from him must, more or less, inevitably presuppose me in [its] favour. I have now sat for eight years at Mr Ranade's feet as a pupil & I feel that for the greater part of what real education I have received in the world, I am indebted to him. I know no man more selfless or more earnestly devoted to the service of his country. Add to this tie of gratitude & admiration, my respect for his commanding intellect & it ought not to be difficult for anyone to understand why ordinarily I should be disposed to distrust my own judgement if it came into conflict with his.[15]

These sentiments may have been admirable in a *chela* (disciple) towards his guru, but they were hardly the stuff of which political leadership is made. Moreover, in politics as in any other sphere, apprenticeship must end one day, and the apprentice must stand on his own feet. Ranade was continually advising Gokhale, instructing

[14] Gokhale to Rahimatoola, 26 March 1903 (G.P.).
[15] Gokhale to R. G. Bhandarkar, 24 Jan. 1896 (G.P.).

him on political issues, and correcting the drafts of his articles and speeches. Gokhale had to outgrow this tutelage if he was to carve a place for himself in national politics. It is not surprising that Gokhale's rise to eminence in national politics should only have come soon after Ranade's death.

In December 1900, when his failing health prevented Ranade from attending the annual session of the All India Social Conference at Lahore, he had asked Gokhale to deputize for him. Ranade was happy to learn that the Conference was a success and pleaded with Gokhale to take up the work of the Social Conference.

Ranade to Gokhale, 3 January 1901: I hope that this practical acquaintance with the silent work of the conference has satisfied even your high standard of earnest devotion & that year after year, your love for the work will increase. Our great want is that young men with great promise and usefulness do not step in the place of the older men who are disabled for active duties in the political as also in the social sphere . . . this want is much felt & in my moments of self-communion, I feel that you have it in your power to console any passing despondency one might feel on this account.[16]

Ranade was offering the leadership of social reform movement on a silver platter to Gokhale, but he did not accept it. This was not because Gokhale's social conscience was not sufficiently developed. Indeed, on the few occasions when he expressed himself on social issues, he did so even more trenchantly than Ranade. During his visit to England in 1897, Gokhale had spoken on female education. Six years later at the Dharwar Social Conference, he denounced untouchability in the strongest terms. It was 'absolutely monstrous', he said, 'that a class of human beings with bodies similar to our own, with brains that can think and hearts that can feel, should be perpetually condemned to a low life, utter servitude and mental or moral degradation'.[17] Gokhale's views on caste, marriage and untouchability were thus radical enough, but he had no intention of becoming a social reformer. It was not only because, as he once told Paranjpye, his second marriage, while his first wife was still alive, had made him vulnerable to criticism. What kept him away from the social reform movement, besides this skeleton in his domestic cupboard, was that his real interest lay in politics. As the joint editor of the *Sudharak*, he preferred to write on political questions and left social problems to the caustic pen of Agarkar. His attendance at the annual sessions of

[16] G.P.   [17] *Speeches of Gokhale*, p. 898.

the National Social Conference was erratic even though it was run by Ranade. He was not present at the session held in Bombay in December 1889. In the 1890 session at Calcutta he was seen on the dais with the prominent social reform leaders, but his name does not figure in the reports of the conference for 1894, 1895 and 1899. In December 1900 he had, at Ranade's request, deputized for him, but during the next fourteen years he attended only three meetings of the conference—in 1901, 1902 and 1908.

Gokhale had reasons for his lukewarm interest in social reform. He had seen how, in the early 1890s, the orthodox fury in Maharashtra had turned upon the social reform party, and damaged its political influence. In the cold-war politics of Poona one false step could result in political *harakiri*. The storm which broke over Gokhale's head after the apology incident in 1897 had chastened him. It had taken him nearly five years to rebuild his position, which was not to become really invulnerable until 1905. The leadership of the social reform movement, which Ranade pressed upon Gokhale from his death-bed, could have been a dangerous distraction for him. It was not Gokhale, but N. G. Chandavarkar, who was to inherit Ranade's mantle of social reform.

15

Wanted, A Leader

The nineteenth session of the Indian National Congress was held in Madras during the last week of December 1903. 'The Congress was a great failure', Lord Ampthill, the Governor of Madras, reported to Lord Curzon, 'and it is a question whether the President's speech or the cyclone storm administered the greatest douche of cold water to the assembled delegates.'[1] Lord Ampthill was by no means a sympathetic observer, but his verdict was endorsed by friendly critics. The *Hindustan Review* distinguished the Madras session from all its predecessors as a 'distinct and dismal failure'.[2]

Gokhale did not go to Madras, but received a full report from his friend Hari Narayan Apte.[3] Apte noted an undercurrent of discontent among the delegates, who seemed to be disappointed and bored with the proceedings. Gone were the days when Congressmen from various provinces vied with each other for the honour of holding the Congress session. No province seemed eager to invite the 1904 Congress until Pherozeshah Mehta offered to hold it at Bombay, even though the Congress had already met in that province as recently as December 1902.

The Madras Congress reflected the change in the mood of the Indian intelligentsia between 1885 and 1904. The initial mood of the founders of the Congress had been one of faith, hope and innocence. Dadabhai Naoroji had avowed his unshakable faith in the English character for fairness and desire to do good to India. Bipin Chandra Pal, who was to be one of the leaders of the Extremist Party, affirmed in 1887 that he was

loyal to the British Government, because with me loyalty is identical with loyalty to my own people and my own country; because I believe that God has placed this Government over us for our salvation; because I know that without the help and tuition of this Government,

[1] Ampthill to Curzon, 9 Jan. 1904 (C.P.).
[2] *Hindustan Review & Kayastha Samachar*, Jan. 1904.
[3] H. N. Apte to Gokhale, 6 Jan. 1904 (G.P.).

my people shall never be able to rise to their legitimate place in the commonwealth of free nations; because I am convinced that there is no other Government on the face of the earth which so much favours the growth of infant nationalities, and under which the germs of popular government can so vigorously grow as under the British Government.[4]

The *Amrita Bazar Patrika*—no friend of the government or of the European community—wrote of the Madras session (1887) that it had drawn 'the hearts of the people towards the Governor as their own real ruler. In short the European community in general at Madras seemed to sympathize with the movement like true and genuine Britons.'[5] The *Patrika* added that 'an institution like the National Congress implies, in fact requires, the permanent existence of the British rule in India'.

Eight years later, Surendranath Banerjea, while speaking at the Poona Congress, appealed to England,'august mother of free nations', to gradually change the character of her rule in India, to liberalize it, to shift its foundations, 'so that in the fullness of time, India may find her place in the great confederacy of free States, English in their origin, English in their character, English in their institutions, rejoicing in their permanent and indissoluble union with England, a glory to the mother country, and an honour to the human race'.[6]

The Congress leaders had set their sights high. They had read British history, and did not expect a sudden transition from British rule to Indian self-government. They were conscious of their limitations. They realized that political awakening was not only of recent origin in India, but also confined to a small minority of the population. Hume wrote in 1888:

So far as I know, no leading member of the National Congress thinks that for the next twenty years at any rate the country will require or be fit for anything more than the mixed councils that have been advocated at the Congress. . . . No one expects that a full parliamentary system can possibly be introduced here under 50 years.

Hume, however, looked forward to the day,

say 50, say 70 years hence, when the Government of India will be precisely similar to that of the Dominion of Canada; when, as there, each province and presidency will have its local Parliament for provincial affairs and the whole country will have its Dominion

[4] B. C. Pal, *The National Congress*, 1887, p. 9.
[5] *Amrita Bazar Patrika*, 12 Jan. 1888.
[6] *Report of the Eleventh Indian National Congress*, 1895, p. 51.

Parliament for national affairs, and when the only officials sent out to India from England would be the Viceroy and the Governor-General of India.[7]

For the founders of the Congress, self-government was a distant goal, but the way for it had to be paved by immediate legislative and administrative reforms; the enlargement of the size, elective proportion, and functions of the legislative councils; the extension of trial by jury, the grant of commissions to Indians in the army, the reduction in military expenditure; and a more equitable adjustment of financial burdens between India and Britain. Neither the ideal of self-government nor the modest reforms claimed as steps towards it evoked a sympathetic chord in the British Government and its representatives in India. Lord Dufferin, during whose viceroyalty the Congress was founded, came to doubt the possibility of applying constitutional reforms to a conquered country 'inasmuch as self-government and submission to a foreign sovereign are incompatible terms'.

Dufferin's attitude towards the Congress changed from the initial benevolent neutrality to a prickly intolerance. The reaction of his successors varied. Lansdowne exhibited a good-humoured indifference to the Congress at least for the first few years of his viceroyalty, Elgin wavered between indulgence and opposition, Curzon was implacably hostile. To most British officials in India the Congress leaders were a small selfish minority who were out to feather their own nests, and did not really mean what they said, and whose demands in any case could not be entertained without shaking the foundations of British rule. The representatives of the Raj were not moved by eloquent appeals to British constitutional history, or to past pledges of equal and just treatment to the Indian people. A Tory Secretary of State, Lord George Hamilton, privately lamented that the principle of perfect equality between the European and the Indian should have been included in Queen Victoria's Proclamation in 1858. To this guardian of the British Empire, the introduction of a free press, civil codes, literary education, and competitive examinations in India seemed a series of blunders. The brief interlude of Sir Henry Fowler's tenure (1894–5) as Secretary of State for India showed that the Liberal Party was no more sympathetic to Indian aspirations than the Tories.

---

[7] Letter of 17 May 1888 to editor, *Morning Post*, Allahabad, in S. R. Mehrotra, *India and the Commonwealth*, 1965, p. 33.

With this built-in resistance in the guardians of the Raj, there was hardly any chance of a major concession being made to the Congress during the first fifteen years of its existence. Indeed, the early optimism of the Congress leaders would have been quickly dissipated but for two measures which raised false hopes. One was the reform of India's legislative councils, which had remained on the parliamentary anvil for several years, until it was carried through in 1892. The other was the appointment in 1895 of the Welby Commission on Indian Expenditure, which included three champions of the Indian viewpoint in England: Dadabhai Naoroji, William Wedderburn and W. S. Caine. This pro-Indian trio found itself in a minority in the Commission, whose report, published in 1900, gave India only a paltry relief of £250,000 a year and did not even touch on the major grievance of the inequitable burdens borne by India.

Congress leaders were not daunted by these setbacks. 'We will have dissensions and difficulties', Dadabhai Naoroji had once told Gokhale, 'but we must be prepared to surmount them, not be beaten by them. The Irish have been struggling for 800 years and here they are struggling all the same.'

Eight hundred years may not have exhausted the stamina of the Irish in their struggle against British rule, but fifteen years of sporadic effort had begun to tell on the Indians. At the turn of the century many Congressmen were asking, 'What has the Congress achieved?' The Congress seemed to be repeating the same demands every year, and doubts began to be voiced about the wisdom of its strategy. The critics wondered, in the words of the *Amrita Bazar Patrika*, if there was any point in petitioning 'from the Chota Sahib to the Burrah Sahib'.[8] A new generation which refused to take British tutelage or good faith for granted was growing up. In a series of articles published in 1893–4 in the *Indu Prakash* entitled 'New Lamps for Old', the twenty-one year-old Aurobindo Ghose, who was one day to shape into a great revolutionary and savant, charged the leaders of the Indian National Congress with lack of vision, courage and earnestness, and pronounced the Congress an utter failure.

A similar scepticism was voiced by a rising Punjabi politician, the thirty-seven year-old Lajpat Rai. 'No nation', he wrote in August 1902, 'was worthy of any political status if it could not distinguish between begging political rights and claiming them.'[9] During the same year,

[8] *Amrita Bazar Patrika*, 19 Aug. 1886.
[9] Quoted in V. C. Joshi (ed.), *Lala Lajpat Rai, Writings and Speeches*, vol. 1, 1966, p. 28.

the *Indian Social Reformer* of Bombay referred to the 'tide of pessimism' and the paralysis of public life and sought to connect them with the fact that 'our public movements are so entirely controlled by men past the prime of life'.[10] To the British, the increasing scepticism of the Congress rank and file and the waning popular enthusiasm for its annual meetings were a welcome development. In 1896 Secretary of State Hamilton noted that 'the Congress as a political power had gone steadily down during the last few years'.[11] Four years later Curzon cheerfully recorded that the strategy of the Congress had failed, and it was heading to its fall, and 'one of my ardent desires is to lay it to a peaceful demise'. The wish may have been father to the thought, but the condition of the Congress was causing anxiety even to its well-wishers. Its initial enthusiasm had worn off; it was ceasing to be interesting even as a three-day national festival; it had not struck roots in district towns, much less in the villages; its leaders betrayed apathy and inertia between the annual sessions; many of its adherents had melted away. Unfortunately the small coterie which controlled the organization from Bombay did not seem to be sensitive to the discontent in the rank and file.

2

While the Congress organization in India was afflicted by doubt and demoralization, its branch in London was on the brink of collapse. The British Committee of the Indian National Congress was plagued by what Wedderburn, its chairman, described as 'the want of pence'. Every year the Indian National Congress at its annual session voted thanks and funds to its British Committee, but between promise and performance, there was a yawning gap. Between 1894 and 1900, a total of £25,833 was voted for expenditure of the British Committee; the remittances totalled £15,908, the actual expenditure was £22,608. The difference of £6,700 was largely made up by Hume and Wedderburn from their private savings. Frantic appeals by the British Committee could not improve the remittances from the provincial Congress committees in India. The financial position of the British Committee at last became so desperate that it thought of closing down its office in London, and discontinuing the publication of *India*. This would have been an ignominious end to

[10] *Indian Social Reformer*, 29 June 1902.
[11] Hamilton to Elgin, 11 Dec. 1896 (Hamilton P.).

Congress propaganda in England, which was bound to delight its Anglo-Indian critics who asserted that the British Committee and its principals in India lacked real popular support. Dadabhai Naoroji, a member of the British Committee in London, posed the dilemma to Gokhale:

Dadabhai Naoroji to Gokhale, 27 September 1901: I view with the greatest misgiving the discontinuance of the journal 'India'. It was established and has been carried on as an organ of the Congress in in this country . . . without such an organ the cause could not be pushed on and all our efforts in India would be vain. To end such an organ is like cutting off the right arm. I therefore appeal to you to do all in your power to maintain the committee and the journal. . . .

Sir William Wedderburn and Mr Hume . . . have devoted the best years of their lives and, what is more, their purse to the cause of India. Sir William Wedderburn has, I think, spent not less than £10,000 or perhaps up to £15,000 in various ways in the furtherance of the cause of our country. But his personal work is of far more value and the Congress cannot afford to lose it. His earnestness and experience cannot be provided by any new organization. Trusting you will . . . do your best to lighten my responsibility . . . and adopt some mature plan for future financial requirements.[12]

There were good reasons why Dadabhai should have sought Gokhale's help. For several years as secretary of Poona's Sarvajanik Sahba, Gokhale had taken the lead in remitting contributions to the British Committee from the Deccan.

Though it may not have been obvious at the time, the crisis in the fortunes of the British Committee was the direct result of the malaise from which the parent body was suffering in India. The Congress committees in the provinces were unable to meet their obligations to the British Committee, because they lacked proper organization and earnest workers. Suggestions had been made at the Congress sessions and in the press for a constitution for the Indian National Congress to infuse new life into it. But these suggestions were resisted by the leadership. A constitution, it was argued, could be useful only after the diffusion of public spirit in the rank and file. The experiment of the Indian Congress Committee had not proved a success. There were whispers that this Committee had been killed by the Congress leaders themselves, headed by Pherozeshah Mehta. After Hume's departure from India in 1894, there had been no full-time secretary of the Congress. If Ranade had not been appointed a judge of the

[12] G.P.

Bombay High Court, he might have served as secretary. As it was, Congress work remained a spare-time activity for its leaders, who were busy professional men. Dinshaw Wacha had a job in a Bombay mill; Surendranath Banerjea ran a newspaper; W. C. Bonnerjee lived in London apart from occasional trips to India for legal work. Lala Murlidhar in the Punjab, Munshi Ganga Prasad Varma in the United Provinces, and R. N. Mudholkar in the Central Provinces succeeded in keeping their local organizations functioning, and taking delegations to the annual sessions, but their interest in politics was tepid and fitful.

The reins of the Congress at this time were in the hands of Pherozeshah Mehta, a contemporary of Bonnerjee, Ranade, J. N. Tata, Manmohan Ghose and Badruddin Tyabji. He belonged to the first generation of English-educated Indians which not only did very well out of western education for themselves, but also learnt to challenge the Anglo-Indian monopoly of power in India. A graduate of the Elphinstone College in Bombay, Pherozeshah qualified as a barrister in England in 1869, and soon forged his way to the forefront of the Bombay bar. He dominated the Bombay Corporation, the Bombay University and the Bombay Legislative Council. He was elected to the Imperial Legislative Council thrice, and could have continued had he wished. In the Indian National Congress, he exercised a tremendous, and on occasions, decisive influence. His fabulous practice at the Bombay bar, his princely mode of life and travel at home and abroad marked him out from his contemporaries. He was intolerant of criticism, quick to take offence and did not know how to apologize. He was also susceptible to flattery, and after the day's work was over, he sat in his chambers in the 'Fort'—opposite the University Clock Tower—discussing legal and political affairs with friends and admirers. Occasionally, after making a point, he would turn to Wacha and ask: 'Wacha, what do you say?' Wacha invariably nodded his assent.

Pherozeshah was of medium height, had a strong constitution and good looks. He could assume a winsome manner and enliven any company with the charm and versatility of his conversation. But he could also be roused to fits of indignation, when he was 'Pherozeshah the ferocious', roaring like a lion, making menacing gestures, scaring away friend and foe alike.

British dignitaries, including several Governors of Bombay, learnt to their cost that it did not pay to provoke Pherozeshah. They disliked him and tried to discredit and dislodge him, but Pherozeshah knew how to turn the tables on them. When he was outvoted by the permanent official majority in the Legislative Council, or in the Corporation meetings, he pursued the controversy into the columns of the daily press, where he made his opponents look ridiculous. On the floor of the legislative chamber, he asked for no quarter and gave none. 'Two minutes more, Sir Pherozeshah', Sir George Clarke, the Governor of Bombay, once told him from his presidential chair. 'Two minutes, Your Excellency,' retorted Pherozeshah before resuming his seat, 'I cannot use those two minutes better than by recording an emphatic protest against the way you use your power! You will hear more of this.'[13] On another occasion, cut to the quick by the arrogance of an official member in the Bombay Legislative Council, Pherozeshah exclaimed: 'The Hon. Mr Logan has expressed offensive statements in particularly offensive language . . . I resent it strongly and I throw it back in his face.'[14] In the eyes of the educated class in the last decade of the century, Pherozeshah Mehta epitomized national self-respect. They admired him for his grasp of constitutional law, his command of the English language, his strong commonsense, unquestioned integrity and freedom from religious or regional partisanship. It is significant that during his long sway over the Bombay Corporation even his worst critics did not accuse him of nepotism.

Srinivasa Sastri has left a graphic description of Pherozeshah as a speaker:

Sir Pherozeshah seemed to dominate you. When you saw him full in the face there was a squint in his eye which fixed you almost. You felt you were in his power. I have seen him in the Legislative Council speak with authority and with vigour that drew everybody's attention to him; and I have seen how when any member of the Council spoke, every two minutes or three minutes he turned to him to glance at him to know what impression he was producing on the master of the House.[15]

Whatever their true feelings, Pherozeshah's critics took care to behave with great decorum in his presence. At the turn of the century even firebrands like Tilak and Lajpat Rai approached Pherozeshah with due deference.

[13] Sastri, *Life and Times of Sir Pherozeshah Mehta*, 1945, p. 145.
[14] Ibid., p. 93.
[15] Ibid., p. 49.

3

The courage and stubbornness which Pherozeshah Mehta employed against the British bureaucracy were also on occasions used against such of his countrymen as dared to differ from him. He was called 'the uncrowned King of Bombay', and he did indeed on occasions behave as if he were a king. In 1903 he resembled King Canute, vainly trying to hold back the tides of change. Of his older colleagues of the Congress, Hume, Dadabhai Naoroji and Bonnerjee were in London, and Surendranath Banerjea was in Calcutta. Pherozeshah was, therefore, almost in exclusive control of the office of the Indian National Congress in Bombay. His friend and protégé, Dinshaw Wacha, was secretary of the Congress. Pherozeshah's control of the central Congress organization during the years 1894–1904 was almost as effective as Gandhi's in the 1920s and 1930s. At the annual sessions, Pherozeshah's lead was followed, whether or not he was himself present.

At the Madras session in December 1903, several delegates, especially from among those of the Punjab, Bengal, and Madras, demanded a constitution for the Congress, but Pherozeshah silenced them. The critics were silenced, but not convinced. H. N. Apte, one of the delegates from Poona, confided to Gokhale that he

heard an amount of grumbling the next day. Some even threatened that Bengal would send no delegates next year. . . . However, one thing was quite apparent at the Madras session—the younger generation was not satisfied with the working of the Congress and there was the hankering after something new—some new element being put into it—although nobody could say what it was that was wanted.[16]

The view that the Indian National Congress was a sick organization was widely shared, but opinions differed on the remedy. It was suggested that if the founding fathers of the Congress, Hume, Dadabhai Naoroji, Bonnerjee and Wedderburn could visit India, the Congress would receive a fresh lease of life. Nothing, however, came of this proposal. Bonnerjee was fighting a losing battle with diabetes, complicated by Bright's disease; Hume was so ill that he considered a journey to India 'tantamount to committing suicide';[17] Dadabhai, intent on re-entering the House of Commons, was busy nursing a constituency which his friends knew he could never win. While the

[16] H. N. Apte to Gokhale, 6 Jan. 1904 (G.P.).
[17] Hume to Gokhale, 24 Sept. 1904 (G.P.).

veterans in London were thus immobilized, Pherozeshah and his friends, whose control of the Congress in India was unquestioned, were averse to new ideas. To Pherozeshah any innovation—such as a constitution for the Congress—must have seemed a nuisance; apart from the risk of upsetting established procedures, it was bound to make demands on his time. He was already one of the busiest men in the country, rationing his time between his legal practice, work in the Bombay Corporation, the Bombay University and the Legislative Council, besides the Indian National Congress. He did not like murmurs of dissent whether in the Subjects Committee or at the plenary sessions of the Congress. He was insensitive, even hostile, to the new forces emerging in the country; he looked askance at the new men and their ideas; they threatened to disturb the harmony of the Congress organization and his hegemony over it. He had no patience with the nostrums put forward by Aurobindo Ghose, Lajpat Rai and Bal Gangadhar Tilak. He had no doubt that he could out-argue, outwit and outvote them in the Congress. Well may his critics call him overweening; some even described him as a 'dead-weight', but nothing could make him budge from the view that the Congress should continue to work on the lines it had followed since 1885.

Gokhale was twenty-one years younger than Pherozeshah, and his admiration and respect for him bordered on awe. In 1895 he had paid a public tribute to 'the grasp and vigour of Mr Mehta's intellect, his wide culture, and his fearless independence coupled with dignity and judgment'.[18] Six years later, in a letter dated 15 January 1901, Gokhale told Pherozeshah, 'Everyone feels—I state what I honestly think—that on the score of gifts, natural and acquired, on the score of prestige, on the score of these numerous qualities which are indispensable in a political leader, there is no equalling you or even coming near you'.[19] True, in this very letter, Gokhale sought Pherozeshah's support for his election to the Imperial Council, and his words may therefore be discounted as coming from a suppliant for a favour. But three years later we find Gokhale's close friend Lallubhai Samaldas writing to him after attending the Madras Congress: 'I can now appreciate your remark that you had taken measure of all public men in the country and found that Mr Mehta was head and shoulders above the rest.'[20]

[18] *Speeches of Gokhale*, p. 797.
[19] G.P.   [20] L. Samaldas to Gokhale, 6 Jan. 1904 (G.P.).

On his part, Pherozeshah had a high opinion of Gokhale, whom he had seen at work in the Poona Sarvajanik Sabha, in the Indian National Congress and in the Bombay Legislative Council. Had it not been for Pherozeshah's support, Gokhale could never have been elected to the Imperial Council. The two men were, however, divided not only by twenty years of age, but by differences in temperament and methods of work, which were soon to become apparent.

By 1903–4, Pherozeshah had been in public life for more than thirty-five years. He had always been in the forefront, and was the dominant figure in and outside the legislature. His views had become stereotyped; he repeated the same old phrases, the same formulae which he had learnt in his youth. Impatient of criticism, irascible, inaccessible, forbidding, he failed to discern the new forces emerging in the Congress and the country. He was allergic to the proposals for reform which some of his colleagues considered essential.

4

In February 1903, R. C. Dutt was corresponding with Gokhale on the possibilities of reinvigorating the Congress. Gokhale pleaded with him to help put new life into the Congress and to lift it from academic discussions into the sphere of practical work. Dutt responded enthusiastically, and suggested a small executive committee for carrying on the work of the Congress throughout the year.

R. C. Dutt to Gokhale, 23 February 1903: You have pointed out to me a new path of usefulness and fired in me a new ambition. And the last years of my life shall not be lived in vain if I succeed in organizing our work in India and leading all the patriotic aspirations. . . .

Let us suppose the next Congress creates an Executive Committee consisting of Mehta,[21] Charlu[22] and myself for organizing and conducting Congress work in India. I was even thinking of adding the names of Malaviya[23] of Northern India and Mudholkar[24] of the C.P. and Berar to make a Committee of five members . . . a central place for a permanent office (Bombay, Amraoti and Allahabad). . . .

I will in the course of 3 winter months visit all the provinces, create

[21] Pherozeshah Mehta (1845–1915), eminent lawyer, legislator and Congress leader of Bombay; president of Indian National Congress, 1890.

[22] P. Ananda Charlu (1843–1908), lawyer, president of Indian National Congress, 1891.

[23] Madan Mohan Malaviya (1862–1946), lawyer, president of Indian National Congress in 1909, 1918 & 1933.

[24] R. N. Mudholkar (1857–1921), lawyer and prominent (Moderate) politician of Berar; president of Indian National Congress, 1912.

50 affiliated Congress Associations, frame rules for them, explain their work to them . . . and inspire in them a new life. More than this —we will train these associations to work along the same channel, we will focus all the forces of the country in the same centre, and we will work and speak on every question with the united voice of a nation.

We will create a moral power which the Administration will soon enlist in the cause of good government.[25]

12 November 1903:

The Congress works for four days in the year. The Executive Committee should work throughout the year with the authority of the Congress, making that body a living power in the country . . . Pherozeshah Mehta and myself, if the Congress appoints us, will work very well together, sometimes meeting, and always corresponding, so that every action taken shall be our joint action. To some extent Mehta represents Southern India, I represent Northern India. The Congress should also provide for a paid secretary, and personally I know of no better and efficient man in India than yourself. We shall make a capital working committee with your help.[26]

The proposals for a new constitution and a committee for the Congress could make no headway at the Madras Congress session in December 1903. Well might Lal Mohan Ghose, the president of the session, murmur against 'autocracy' within the Congress, but Pherozeshah had no intention of sharing his authority in the Congress with either a small or a large committee.

R. C. Dutt's suggestion for the appointment of Gokhale as a 'paid secretary' of the Indian National Congress was intended to put its work on a sound footing. Gokhale was prepared to give all his time, but he was not prepared to accept any remuneration for political work. Honorary work seemed to him more honourable. Moreover, with his monthly pension of Rs 30, and another Rs 170 from royalties on his arithmetic book coupled with his allowances as a member of the Imperial Legislative Council, Gokhale was not in want. In the autumn of 1903, the Congress Committee at Madras (where the Congress session was to be held) proposed that Gokhale and Wacha should be appointed joint general secretaries of the Congress. Dadabhai Naoroji, Hume and Wedderburn in England and Pherozeshah in India all welcomed the proposal, and its passage at the Madras session was a foregone conclusion.

This was just the time when Gokhale's friends were debating whether he should move the scene of his political activity to England.

[25] G.P.   [26] Ibid.

Two of them, Lallubhai Samaldas and H. A. Wadya, even explored the possibilities of financing his parliamentary career in England. There was no doubt that Gokhale's talents especially fitted him for advocating the cause of his country from a seat in the House of Commons. Stepping into the shoes of Dadabhai Naoroji had a certain glamour about it. As against this, a long absence from the country would cut him off from Indian public life. If he went over to England, would he not become like W. C. Bonnerjee, a back-number in Indian politics?

That Gokhale should have finally decided to continue to work in India is not surprising. Though he had once cherished the idea of entering the British Parliament, he now knew how much there was to do in India. As early as 1898, R. P. Paranjpye, then a student at Cambridge, had shrewdly summed up the pros and cons of a parliamentary career in England for Gokhale. 'I for myself do think that any agitation in England would only lead to personal fame, but any real solid work can only be done in India.'[27]

As joint general secretary of the Congress, Gokhale did not consider it his duty merely to carry on the routine work of the Congress; that was being ably handled by Wacha. Gokhale's immediate task was to collect funds to save the British Committee from insolvency, and also to inject some energy into the Congress committees in the provinces.

During the three months which followed the Madras Congress, Gokhale was in Calcutta for the winter session of the Imperial Council. It was one of the busiest and stormiest sessions in the history of the Council; for Gokhale it was a long and bitter confrontation with Curzon. Nevertheless, he found time to attend to Congress work. On 7 April 1904, he remitted £400 to Wedderburn as share capital for a new company 'India Limited' which had been floated in London to recoup the finances of *India*, the journal of the British Committee of the Congress. Gokhale enrolled 215 shareholders; as many as 185 potential shareholders had not yet returned the forms and paid the money, but Gokhale borrowed from friends to send the remittance to the British Committee. He was heartened by the results of his first effort at fund-raising in Bengal.

Gokhale to William Wedderburn, 7 April 1904: I propose to spend August, September and October of this year in Bengal and hope to secure annual contributions to the extent of about forty thousand

[27] Paranjpye to Gokhale, 18 March 1898 (Paranjpye P.).

rupees and at least one thousand subscribers to *India*. The present number is 200, and I think, with proper work, 800 more ought to be secured without much difficulty. . . . My work in Bengal this year will be directed towards

(1) securing annual contributions . . .

(2) reorganizing Congress committees in all important centres with active earnest-minded men as secretaries,

(3) securing for the Congress the services of at least half a dozen earnest, devoted, self-sacrificing young men in Bengal, working all the year round in the spirit in which my colleagues in the Fergusson College are working for that institution, and

(4) securing at least one thousand reliable subscribers to the *India*.

When this is done in one province, similar work in other provinces will be comparatively easy and next year, I shall take in hand N.W. Provinces, and Madras, reserving Bombay, Punjab and Central Provinces for the third year. . . .[28]

Gokhale's 'Operation Congress Revival' delighted Wedderburn and the British Committee. With the funds for *India* in their hands, they knew that Gokhale's was not a mere empty boast. 'You are working on the best possible lines', Wedderburn wrote to him. Even Hume, who tended to take a gloomier view of things than Wedderburn, expressed his gratitude and gratification to Gokhale. 'You did not sit in vain at dear Ranade's feet—and were he still with us, he would be proud of his disciple as I am of having long worked alongside of you. You have, I hope, many happy busy years and many triumphs for India's cause before you.'[29]

Hume, Wedderburn, Dutt and many others were thus looking up to Gokhale as the man who would rescue the Congress in India and the British Committee in England from stagnation. By a strange coincidence just at the time when the political situation called for a new leadership, Gokhale's personal life took a turn which led to his deeper involvement in national politics. His wife's death in 1900 snapped such bonds of settled life as he had. A few months later, the death of his mentor, Ranade, compelled him to shake off some of his diffidence and to stand on his own feet; his election to the Imperial Council brought him to a forum where he could display his talents to the best advantage and, finally, his retirement from the Fergusson College enabled him to give his undivided attention to politics. Few of those who elected him joint general secretary by acclamation at

[28] G.P.   [29] Hume to Gokhale, 24 Sept. 1904 (G.P.).

the Madras Congress in December 1903 could have foreseen that within two years this young Maharashtrian, still in his thirties, would be invited to preside over the Indian National Congress.

At the end of 1903, Gokhale's stock stood high. It was to rise still higher because of two important developments: one was his determined opposition to Curzon's unpopular measures, and the other was the establishment of the Servants of India Society, which stamped Gokhale's brow with the mark of a political *sanyasin* (monk).

16

Servants of India

By 1904 it was clear to Gokhale that the Indian National Congress was losing its influence in India, and its branch in England, the British Committee, was on the verge of insolvency and collapse. The apathy of the Congress organization between the annual sessions was deplorable enough, but even the 'three-day Congress festival' was ceasing to be impressive. Many of the Congress leaders were well-meaning and patriotic, and some of them were really able and elo-quent, but they tended to treat politics as an occasional diversion from their personal and professional preoccupations. Indian univer-sities turned out every year hundreds of young men who had all the zest and time in the world for politics, but lacked the knowledge, training and experience. Gokhale had long been wondering whether it was possible to harness the energy and enthusiasm of these young men for national regeneration. From time immemorial India had furnished the highest example of self-abnegation in her *sanyasins*, who renounced the world and its material interests, subjected them-selves to a rigorous discipline and consecrated their lives to the service of God and man. Could this ancient ideal of renunciation be adapted for secular ends? What if a few young men turned their backs upon personal ambition, and made the social and political uplift of their country their sole mission in life? At the Dharwar Social Conference in April 1903, while urging a crusade against untouchability, Gokhale had asked,

Cannot a few men—five per cent, four per cent, three, two, even one per cent—of hundreds and hundreds of graduates that the University turns out every year, take it upon themselves to dedicate their lives to this sacred work of the elevation of low castes? My appeal is not to the old or the middle-aged—the grooves of their lives are fixed—but I think I may well address such an appeal to the young members of our community. . . . What the country needs most at the present moment is a spirit of self-sacrifice on the part of our educated young men.[1]

[1] *Speeches of Gokhale*, p. 902.

Few among India's politicians were better qualified to make such an appeal than Gokhale. For eighteen years he served the Deccan Education Society at a pittance. In his farewell address to the Fergusson College in 1904 he said:

The principal moral interest of this institution is in fact that it represents an idea and embodies an ideal. The idea is that Indians of the present-day can bind themselves together, and putting aside all thoughts of worldly interest, work for a secular purpose with the zeal and enthusiasm which we generally find in the sphere of religion alone.[2]

The idea that dedicated workers were required in the sphere of politics and social reform no less than in that of education had occurred to Gokhale many years before, but he did not—perhaps could not —give practical shape to it until his retirement from the Fergusson College. Though he had spoken about a new organization for training young men for public life to his young friend R. P. Paranjpye as early as 1897,[3] he took it up in right earnest only in 1904–5. Early in 1905, he sounded his friends on the aims and rules of a new society he proposed to set up. The venture seemed to him at once fascinating and awesome. He wondered whether he would be able to attract enough able young men who had the spirit of self-sacrifice. Would he be able to train them for the tasks of nation-building? Would he be able to inspire, guide, and control the young men who placed themselves under his charge? Would he be able to find the money for building the headquarters of the society and running it from month to month? And finally, would the government allow him to go ahead with this scheme of training 'national missionaries'?

These and other doubts assailed Gokhale as he formulated the constitution of the 'Servants of India Society' in the early months of 1905. At first he thought of apprenticing young men for five or ten years, and then allowing them to go back to their professions. Life-membership was a stiffer condition, but Gokhale finally preferred it to short-term membership. He decided to recruit university-educated 'young men with intellectual capacity, devotion to duty and mental elevation'. There was to be a period of probation during which the new entrants were to be under the immediate supervision of the First Member (as Gokhale designated himself). Not until the young missionaries had completed their training and acquired a degree of maturity were they to be allowed to act on their own. Gokhale was

[2] Ibid., p. 897.   [3] Paranjpye, *Gopal Krishna Gokhale*, pp. 64–5.

acutely conscious of 'the disorganized and undisciplined public life and the want of self-restraint' which characterized most young men.[4] Article 5 of the constitution of the Servants of India Society, as originally drafted, had laid down that every member on admission would be under a vow of 'absolute obedience' to the First Member for five years. The idea of 'absolute obedience' jarred on many of his friends. 'The Society of Jesus', he reminded one of them, 'enjoined strict obedience on some members for a period of 31 years.' Though Gokhale was not wholly convinced by the criticism that Article 5 posed a danger to individual liberty, he agreed to tone it down. In its revised form it read: 'Every member shall during the time that he is under training place himself under the entire guidance and control of the First Member and shall do such studies as the First Member may direct.' 'I am hopeful', Gokhale wrote to Krishnaswami Aiyer, 'that young men will be forthcoming in sufficient numbers. For the rest everything must depend upon the personal influence which I am able to exert on these men. The time to speak of that will be, say, five years hence, not now.'

2

The preamble to the constitution of the Servants of India Society, drafted by Gokhale, was a confession of his political faith. He acknowledged the 'startling' growth during the preceding fifty years of the feeling of common nationality in India, based upon common tradition, common disabilities and common hopes and aspirations. There was a growing realization that they were 'Indians first, and Hindoos, Mahomedans, Parsees or Christians afterwards' and 'the idea of a united and renovated India, marching onwards to a place among the nations of the world, worthy of her great past, is no longer a mere idle dream of a few imaginative minds, but is the definitely accepted creed of those who form the brain of the community—the educated classes of the country'.[5] A new life was coursing in the veins of the people. The foundations of national regeneration had been laid, but the 'great work of rearing the superstructure had yet to be taken in hand'.[6] The rules framed by Gokhale required members to live on a modest allowance: Rs 30 p.m. for a trainee;

[4] Gokhale to K. Aiyer, 31 July 1905 (G.P.).
[5] Karve & Ambekar (eds.), *Gokhale's Speeches and Writings*, vol. II, p. 181.
[6] Ibid., p. 181.

Rs 50 for a full member. They were forbidden to earn for themselves, or to engage in personal quarrels. Thus cut off from material pursuits and personal ambition, they were to give their undivided attention to public affairs. The Servants of India Society was being established, Gokhale wrote, 'to train men, prepared to devote their lives to the cause of the country in a religious spirit, for the work of political education and agitation, and will seek to promote, by all constitutional means, the national interests of the Indian people'.[7] Gokhale held forth a lofty ideal before these young missionaries of Indian nationalism, the 'ascetic pilgrims of politics', as H. W. Nevinson, the British journalist, once described them. 'Love of country', Gokhale wrote,

must so fill the heart that all else shall appear as of little moment by its side. A fervent patriotism, which rejoices at every opportunity of sacrifice for the motherland, a dauntless heart, which refuses to be turned back from its object by difficulty or danger, a deep faith in the purpose of Providence that nothing can shake—equipped with these, the worker must start on his mission, and reverently seek the joy which comes of spending oneself in the service of one's country.[8]

As the appointed day—12 June 1905—for the establishment of the Society approached, and Gokhale thought of its tremendous possibilities and problems, he was swayed by feelings of anxiety, hope, and exaltation. Whether he succeeded or failed, he was conscious that he was on the brink of the most important decision of his life.

Gokhale to Sarla Ray, 3 June 1905: In about a week or ten days from today, the three men who have agreed to join, and myself will take the requisite vows and start the society and after that there will be only one purpose and one meaning to my existence. As I stand on the shore, ready to take the plunge, the immensity of the ocean in front of me overwhelms me. And various emotions crowd into my heart—a feeling of awe at the responsibility I am undertaking, a vague unstilled regret at the farewell I am bidding to all purely personal life, a sense of realization too at the thought that I have probably attained the purpose of my existence—for I feel profoundly that all my past has tended towards this consummation. If I live ten years more, I feel confident that my Society will by the end of that time have become a great power for good in the land. If I die before that, well, I shall have done my best for my country within the limitations within which work has to be done—and no one can do more than his best.[9]

[7] Ibid., p. 182.   [8] Ibid.   [9] S. Ray P.

On the morning of 12 June 1905, Gokhale took the 'seven vows', and then swore in G. K. Devadhar, A. V. Patwardhan and N. A. Dravid—all in their thirties—as members of the Servants of India Society. Gokhale was already acquainted with these three men who, informally, were already working under his direction. From the outset Gokhale set his heart on quality rather than on numbers. The care he took in selecting new members is shown by the experience of V. S. Srinivasa Sastri. A school teacher from Madras, the thirty-seven year-old Sastri succeeded in getting himself elected as a delegate to the Benares Congress in December 1905 over which Gokhale was to preside. At Benares, he wrote a letter requesting Gokhale for an interview. The interview did not, however, take place until February 1906 when Gokhale was in Calcutta for the meetings of the Imperial Council. And it was not until January 1907 that Sastri was administered the vows. 'Gokhale's deportment', Sastri recalled, many years later, 'was solemn and inspired me with . . . awe. As I pronounced the phrases of each vow after him, I was seized with terrible misgivings as to my being able to keep them in a tolerable degree.'[10]

The experience of Hriday Nath Kunzru was no different.[11] The son of Pandit Ajudhianath, a leading figure of the early Congress and a friend of Allan Hume, Kunzru offered to join the Servants of India Society when Gokhale visited Allahabad in April 1908. Gokhale was about to leave for England and told Kunzru to wait for his return. Kunzru attended the Madras Congress in December 1908, but Gokhale was too busy to meet him and invited him to Calcutta. At Calcutta, Kunzru had to undergo a searching cross-examination by Gokhale and was even asked to write an essay on the Madras Congress. Not until 1909 did Gokhale admit Kunzru into the Society. Two years later, he sent him to England to attend lectures at the London School of Economics.

Several members of the Servants of India Society were destined to make a mark in the public life of India. Srinivasa Sastri was to distinguish himself as a legislator, envoy and Privy Councillor; Kunzru was to shape into an outstanding parliamentarian; A. V. Thakkar ('Thakkar Bapa') was to make his mark as a great social reformer and N. M. Joshi, as an eminent labour leader; N. A. Dravid was to serve as the editor of the *Dnyanaprakash*, and A. V. Patwardhan as

[10] Sastri, *My Master Gokhale*, Madras, 1946, p. 82.
[11] Interview with the author.

the manager of the Arya Bhushan Press, which was eventually to become the mainstay of the Society. Hardly any of these 'Servants of India' could have foreseen the vistas which were to open to them in future. To the new entrants in the years before the First World War, the Society must have seemed the gateway to a monastery, rather than to honour, fame or influence. Renunciation of all personal ambition and the acceptance of voluntary poverty evoked feelings of shock and disbelief amongst relatives and friends. The case of A. V. Thakkar, who resigned his job to join the Society, was probably not atypical.

Dear Brothers, [he wrote in his farewell letter to his family]
It pains me to write this letter and I believe it will pain you all very deeply to read its contents.
I have resigned my service from the Bombay Municipality... and shall immediately join the Servants of India Society. I have consulted no one in this matter, and have acted entirely according to the dictates of my own conscience. I may have erred, if the voice of my conscience errs. Whatever it may be, I can ignore the voice no longer. . . .[12]

Not everyone had the courage of Thakkar Bapa. C. Y. Chintamani, the young journalist from Andhra, the editor of the *Indian People*, who was one day to win his laurels as the editor of the *Leader*, pleaded his inability to join the Servants of India Society. He wrote to Gokhale:

I curse myself that God has not placed me in a position to have the privilege of being trained under you. I have a mother who has suffered more than her fair share of misfortunes, a widowed sister and a motherless son to look after. . . . My eldest brother has been an insolvent and we are scattered with not a rupee to our credit in this wide world.[13]

A similar plea was offered by young Rajendra Prasad, a promising lawyer from Patna, who was destined to be the first President of the Indian Republic. The thirty-two year-old M. R. Jayakar, who had met Gokhale three weeks before the Society was founded, wrote in his diary:

Gokhale spoke very enthusiastically about his scheme. The veteran patriot was aglow. His face shone brightly in the morning sun. . . . I gave him a complete picture of my present situation and some idea

[12] T. N. Jagadisan & Shyamlal (eds.), *Thakkar Bapa Eightieth Birthday Commemoration Volume*, Madras, 1949, p. 17.
[13] C. Y. Chintamani to Gokhale, 11 July 1905 (G.P.).

of the difficulties which confronted me. He felt very disappointed. . . .
I pleaded for time to get over my family difficulties. On that he
rightly observed: 'My mind may change or I may not live long
enough to receive you at a later date. Besides, ten years of your
present age are worth twenty a decade hence.'[14]

Jayakar did not join the Society, but begged Gokhale to understand,
if he could not forgive, one to whom 'the tears of his dearest relatives
are more than the censure of the motherland'.[15]

3

One of Gokhale's worries, while he made preparations for the
launching of the Servants of India Society, was the possibility of
suspicion and even hostility on the part of the government. The con-
stitution of the Society avowed 'frankly' the acceptance 'of the
British connection as ordained, in the inscrutable dispensation of
Providence, for India's good', and held out 'self-government on the
lines of English Colonies', as the goal. The guardians of the British
Raj were not won over by felicitous phrases. The Indian National
Congress had at several of its sessions professed its loyalty to the
'Throne' and concluded its meetings with three cheers for Her
Majesty the Queen of England, but it had nevertheless remained on
the wrong side of her government and her agents in India. Few
British statesmen or civil servants at the turn of the century would
have conceded even the remotest possibility of India becoming a
self-governing colony like Canada or Australia. There was no getting
away from the fundamental fact that Gokhale was setting up an
organization for systematically training full-time politicians who
were likely to follow in his footsteps. One Gokhale was bad enough;
a battalion of young Gokhales could hardly be a welcome prospect
to British officials.

Anticipating possible obstruction from the government, Gokhale
was inclined to present it with a *fait accompli*. He deliberately
avoided publicity. His friend V. Krishnaswami Aiyer, however,
advised him to take the government into confidence. 'They are sure
to disapprove of your scheme', Aiyer wrote, 'but they will know
what it is, and won't suspect. Secrecy engenders suspicion and
suspicion of authorities in India means danger to individuals.'

[14] M. R. Jayakar, *The Story of My Life*, Bombay, 1958, vol. I, pp. 65–6.
[15] Ibid., p. 67.

Gokhale took the cue, and called on Du Boulay, the private secretary to Lord Lamington, the Governor of Bombay. He explained the objects of the Servants of India Society. Lamington hastened to take the Viceroy into confidence.

Lamington to Curzon, 8 July 1905: I enclose a copy of the Rules of a Political Brotherhood, which Gokhale is starting. . . . Gokhale came to see Du Boulay, to impress upon him that the object of the Society was to agitate upon constitutional lines for fuller rights of citizenship and larger political powers for natives of India: and that one of its principal aims was to counteract the growing tendency of the rising generation to adopt the seditious attitude and wild language of such papers as the *Kal* and the *Kesari*. Gokhale said . . . that he had a firm faith in the ultimate, if deferred, realization of his political aspirations! that he was convinced that a real national spirit would eventually be born: but that it would not come until the people saw that their political leaders were animated by a spirit of self-sacrifice and devotion to their country such as underlies the code of rules of his new brotherhood. His particular object in seeking an interview was doubtless to discount the suspicions attached towards the movement which he anticipated on the part of the Police.

The City Magistrate—one Carvalho—says he cannot help thinking that Gokhale is becoming more advanced in his opinions and fears that in time he will become a violent opponent of Government.[16]

Curzon had never been able to understand, much less sympathize with, Indian political aspirations. His admiration for Gokhale's ability had from the first been tempered by a deep suspicion of his motives. This suspicion turned to active hostility during the winter session of the Imperial Council in 1904–5, when Gokhale stoutly fought one unpopular measure after another brought forward by the Government of India. It is therefore not surprising that Curzon's comments on the Servants of India Society should have been caustic:

I do not believe in the least [he replied in a letter to Governor Lamington] either in Gokhale or in his new brotherhood. Gokhale either does not see where he is going, or if he does see it, then he is dishonest in his pretensions. You cannot awaken and appeal to the spirit of nationality in India and at the same time, profess loyal acceptance of British rule.[17]

[16] C.P.
[17] Curzon to Lamington, 24 July 1905 (C.P.).

17

Clash with Curzon

Gokhale's election to the Bombay Council in 1899 had marked the beginning of his political rehabilitation after his eclipse over the 'apology incident'. Six years later, when he presided over the Benares session of the Indian National Congress, he may be said to have climbed the top rung of the political ladder. His rise to political eminence thus almost exactly coincided with the term of Lord Curzon as the Viceroy of India.

The viceroyalty of India was a prize which Curzon had long coveted. He had formed a romantic image of the Indian Empire in his schooldays at Eton; he had been thrilled by a lecture delivered by Sir James Fitz-James Stephen, a former member of the Viceroy's Executive Council, who told the boys that there was 'in the Asian continent an empire more populous, more amazing, and more beneficent than that of Rome; that the rulers of that great dominion were drawn from the men of our own people; that some of them might perhaps in the future be taken from the ranks of the boys who were listening' to these words.[1] In his day-dreams young Curzon imagined himself being summoned and told by the Queen-in-Council: 'Young fellow, if there do lie in you potentialities of governing, of gradually guiding, leading and coercing to a noble goal. . . . See, I have scores on scores of colonies. One of these you shall have as vice-king. Go you and buckle with it in the name of Heaven, and let us see what you will build it to.'[2]

India thus figured in Curzon's imagination not only as a land of oriental mystery and romance, but as a field for the exercise of his talents. She was not merely 'a magnificent jewelled pendant hanging from the Imperial collar capable of being detached therefrom without making any particular difference to its symmetry or strength', but 'the strategic centre' of imperial defence, the granary of Britain, the

[1] *Lord Curzon in India: Being a Selection from His Speeches as Viceroy & Gov.-Gen. of India*, 1898–1905, London, 1906, p. 4.
[2] Ibid., pp. 2–3.

source of plantation labour for the colonies, and of raw materials for the home industries, and an outlet for British capital and manufactures and a training ground for young Britons in the arts of peace and war.[3]

Commenting on Curzon's appointment as Viceroy of India, the *Spectator*[4] wrote that he was 'inclined to ambition and . . . is delighted by personal victories. He takes pleasure, that is, in being visibly the instrument by which a great service is rendered to his country.' The *London Review*, after acknowledging the Viceroy-designate's gifts of 'reckless courage, honeyed eloquence, indomitable industry, subtle courtesy, comprehensive intellect, encyclopaedic knowledge, and ubiquitous travel', wrote: 'Of late years, a general murmur has arisen to the effect that it was really too absurd that he should not be made governor of the world.'[5]

Incredible as it may seem in the light of later events, Curzon began his term with a vast fund of goodwill in India. His farewell speech to Old Etonians, in which he felt that 'the mission of the British . . . is to maintain with justice what has been won by the sword', made an excellent impression upon Indian opinion which had been outraged by the indiscreet outburst of Elgin, the outgoing Viceroy, that 'India had been won by the sword and, if necessary, must be held by the sword'. The *Bengalee* noted a similarity between the early speeches of Lord Curzon and the first utterances of Lord Ripon in India.[6] R. C. Dutt went so far as to express the hope that the regime of Lord Curzon, despite his conservative predilections, would be a 'pleasant change after that of Lord Elgin'.[7]

Curzon did not think much of his predecessors, who had managed to just 'slide along with smooth words, raising nothing new, deciding nothing old and only trying to get out of it all with a whole skin'.[8] He was resolved to shake the bureaucracy in India out of its slow and dilatory ways and its addiction to 'leisurely argument in manuscript or in print . . . as if Government were a sort of badminton in which the only object is to hit the shuttlecock over the net without it ever falling to the ground'.[9] There was hardly a department of the

---

[3] Lord Curzon, *The Place of India in the Empire: Being an address presented before the Philosophical Institute of Edinburgh on 19 Oct. 1909*, London, 1909.
[4] *Spectator*, 13 Aug. 1898.   [5] *London Review*, 22 Oct. 1898.
[6] *Bengalee*, 7 & 28 Jan. 1899.
[7] Quoted J. N. Gupta, *Life and Work of Romesh Chunder Dutt*, London, 1911, p. 239.
[8] Curzon to C. E. Dawkins, 24 Jan. 1901 (C.P.).
[9] Minute, 12 May 1899 (C.P.).

Government of India which escaped Curzon's reforming vigour. He
appointed a Famine Commission to formulate a new policy for
famine relief. He set up a central agricultural research institute at
Pusa and planned agricultural colleges and research centres in different parts of the country. He appointed an Inspector-General of
Irrigation and constituted an Irrigation Commission which recommended additional outlay on both productive and 'protective' works.
He sanctioned an addition of six thousand miles to the railway
network and set up a Railway Board to supervise the administration
of the railways. He had the courage not only to institute an inquiry
into the working of the police force, but to publish its strictures to
the whole world. He took steps to protect the peasantry from the
clutches of money-lenders by promoting legislation for co-operative
credit, and for preventing transfer of cultivable land to non-agri-
culturist classes. He founded the Departments of Commerce and
Industry, and Mines. He braved unpopularity with employers—
British and Indian—by trying to restrict hours of work in mines and
factories. The preservation of the ancient monuments and historic
buildings of India owed much to his initiative. His championship of
the village handicrafts has a strangely modern ring. He wrote on
21 October 1900:

There does, I believe, exist a wide external market which it is still
possible to recover or to capture. Without organization of some sort
this is not likely to be done. There is not, in my judgment, the slightest
objection, in a country like India—where the sole fountain of initiative is the Government—to the latter interesting itself and even
directing such a venture. Nor do I see any objection to our finding
within reasonable limits and possibly losing money on it.[10]

All through his viceroyalty Curzon maintained a back-breaking
schedule of twelve to fourteen hours a day. He was incessantly
travelling, ploughing through official files, writing minutes, dictating
memoranda, drafting bills for the legislature, making speeches, and
writing long letters to his colleagues and friends in England. 'My first
duty lies in my judgment', he wrote on 17 December 1903, 'to my
constituents and they are the people of India. I would sooner retire
from my post than sacrifice their interests.'[11] Coming from a Tory
Viceroy, whose name was to become a byword for reactionary
imperialism, this assertion may seem odd. Nevertheless it is true that

[10] Curzon's minute, 21 Oct. 1900, on the revival of village industries and handicrafts in India (C.P.).
[11] Curzon to A. Godley, Under-Sec. of State for India, 17 Dec. 1903 (C.P.).

in the allocation of financial burdens as between Britain and India,[12] unlike most of his predecessors and successors, Curzon often argued for India. He would have preferred the purchase of stores for the Indian army in India, rather than in Britain, if he had not been overruled by the Secretary of State.[13] And he denounced—of course privately—the selfishness of Lancashire and Dundee manufacturers in promoting their interests at the expense of India.[14]

Curzon's severest strictures were reserved for a section of his own countrymen, soldiers, planters, merchants; the 'inferior class of Englishmen', as he called them, who were guilty of assaults on Indians. Most of them got away with a paltry fine or simple imprisonment for a few weeks. Curzon did what he could to break this conspiracy of connivance to which almost all Europeans in India seemed to be privy: commanding officers, police superintendents, merchants, magistrates, juries, high courts and provincial governments. He was not far wrong when he wrote that he was 'almost the only white man in this country who at all seriously deplored these monstrous miscarriages of justice, and tried to bring the criminals to book'. He incurred the implacable hatred of thousands of British Tommies and hundreds of 'pudding-headed subalterns'[15] in India, in whose eyes he was guilty of lowering the prestige of the ruling race. The fact is that Curzon was personally freer from race prejudice than most of his colleagues in the government and countrymen serving or residing in India.

'A great era in Indian progress' was how Lovat Fraser, the editor of the *Times of India*, described the first five years of Curzon's rule from 1899 to 1904,[16] graphically summing up how Curzon would have liked to figure in history. His Indian viceroyalty was intended to be a prelude to still greater triumphs in British politics, but it ended on a melancholy note in the midst of bitter recriminations with his colleagues in the government, and mounting unpopularity with the Indian intelligentsia.

2

Rarely was the road to failure paved with better intentions and harder toil than in the case of Curzon. One need not doubt the

[12] Curzon to Hamilton, 2 April 1902 (C.P.).
[13] Military Dept. Proc. A, Jan. 1902, Nos. 2313–28 (C.P.).
[14] Curzon to Dawkins, 15 Feb. 1905 (C.P.).
[15] *Idem*, 24 Jan. 1901 (C.P.).
[16] L. Fraser to Curzon, 19 Nov. 1904 (C.P.).

sincerity of his claim at the end of his term that he had 'loved India'.[17] His love for India, however, seems to have identified itself with his will to power. He set out to make the viceroyalty 'a personal force instead of a constitutional formula in India'.[18] No problem was too large or too small for his personal attention. Elaborate and well-phrased minutes flowed from his pen, whether the question under consideration was that of Anglo-Afghan relations or a memorial to Queen Victoria at Calcutta, the formation of a new province in the North-West Frontier or the selection of a clock for the Golden Temple at Amritsar,[19] the formulation of anti-plague measures or the employment of European barmaids in Calcutta hotels.[20] Even the Delhi Durbar of 1903 seemed to have been staged by Curzon less to mark the coronation of Edward VII, than as a splendid apotheosis of his own viceroyalty.

As Curzon gained more experience of India, his innate confidence and complacency swelled into conceit and arrogance; his facile pen acquired the sharpness of a rapier, which wounded friends and foes alike. He did not heed the advice of his friend Lord George Hamilton, Secretary of State for India, to 'suffer fools gladly'. He pulled up members of his Executive Council, and Governors of presidencies and heads of departments, as if they were errant schoolboys and he was the headmaster. He loved to dole out what he called 'home-truths', which only irritated, when they did not amuse, his European subordinates, but stung members of an alien race.

It is characteristic of Curzon that he should have looked upon the administration of India as a piece of gigantic machinery. 'We are all concerned', he told the Governor of Bombay, 'in propelling the same vast and wonderful machine; and the several engineers must understand what each other is about. . . .'[21] Thus viewed, the problem of India reduced itself to the tasks of toning up the bureaucratic apparatus, extending the railway and irrigation networks, evolving a new famine-code and administering even-handed justice between the British and Indians, and between Muslims and Hindus. Of the deeper aspirations of the people, Curzon had hardly any inkling. This is not surprising, for, as a British writer[22] points out, Curzon in

---

[17] *Lord Curzon in India*, p. 588.
[18] Curzon to Dawkins, 24 Jan. 1901 (C.P.).
[19] Curzon to G. Birdwood, 18 June 1900 (C.P.).
[20] Curzon wrote a trenchant minute running to 1000 words on barmaids in Calcutta hotels (C.P.).
[21] Curzon to Northcote, 26 Oct. 1899 (C.P.).
[22] L. Mosley, *Curzon: the End of an Epoch*, London, 1960, p. 87.

his heart did not believe in democracy and equality for his fellow-countrymen in Britain, and there was no question of his conceding liberty and equality to Indians.

In the early years of Curzon's viceroyalty, before he had alienated educated India, William Wedderburn, as Chairman of the British Committee of the Indian National Congress, addressed him on the possibilities of 'a reconciliation between the great official dominant power and those popular forces, which in Russia are a danger, but are in India really an element of safety by reason of the spirit which dictated the Queen's Proclamation of 1858'.[23] Wedderburn suggested 'a friendly, though perhaps informal, recognition of the purposes of the Congress as a constitutional means of laying before the Government responsible expression of the Indian view of Indian affairs'.[24] To these overtures Curzon responded with mingled ridicule and contempt. 'Government patronage,' he replied in a letter to Wedderburn on 15 August 1902, 'I should have thought, should be the last thing that it [the Congress] would desire.'[25] He doubted whether the Congress possessed any very strong vitality, or was capable of doing much good. 'The fact is', Curzon wrote, 'that the Congress party are trying to do two incompatible things: to retain the respect and to guide the counsels of the respectable reforming party; and at the same time to keep in with the extreme men, who want something very different. Parnell made the same attempt in Ireland and failed utterly. I do not think that the enterprise is likely to be more successful in India.'[26] The Congress movement, Curzon told Governor Ampthill of Madras, was 'superfluous' in so far as it was innocent, and a 'natural danger' in so far as it was seditious or hostile.[27] When the Congress met at Madras in December 1903, the Governor was advised to 'studiously' keep away from it. 'My policy, ever since I came to India', Curzon confided to Ampthill, 'has been to reduce the Congress to impotence.'[28] He had no use for the educated 'natives' who ran the Congress and seemed to him 'utterly' divorced from the people. He pinned his faith for the security of the British Raj on 'the Princes, the landholders and other classes with a stake in the country'.[29]

Given Curzon's general antipathy to the educated classes and his hostility to their political aspirations, he was bound sooner or later

[23] Wedderburn to Curzon, 10 July 1902 (C.P.).   [24] Ibid.
[25] Curzon to Wedderburn, 15 Aug. 1902 (C.P.).   [26] Ibid.
[27] Curzon to Ampthill, 15 June 1903 (C.P.).   [28] Ibid.
[29] Curzon to Low, June 1905 (C.P.).

to clash with them. The clash was precipitated by his plans for the reform of the universities.

3

On 2 September 1901, a 'private' conference of educational officers met at Simla. Among those who were present were some members of the Executive Council, the Director of Public Instruction and the Vice-Chancellors of the Bombay and Madras universities, Principal Selby of the Deccan College, Poona, and Principal Chatterton of the Madras School of Arts. None of these high officials was an Indian, and no Indian non-official had been invited to the conference. Curzon's inaugural speech was an elaborate, critical and, on the whole, not an unjust commentary on the Indian educational system. Nearly seventy years after Macaulay's famous minute on western education in India and fifty years after Sir Charles Wood's despatch on university education, the time was certainly propitious for a review of the educational structure. University education in India had undoubtedly suffered, as Curzon pointed out, by a too slavish imitation of English models, and particularly of the London University: 'In India, the university has no corporate existence . . ., it is not a collection of buildings, it is scarcely even a site. It is a body that controls courses of study and sets examination papers to the pupils of affiliated Colleges' in different towns, even in different provinces.[30] The whole system was examination-ridden and entailed tremendous waste. Of the candidates taking the Entrance Examination of the Calcutta University nearly half failed; in Madras, the failures rose to eighty per cent. The universities had scarcely any teaching functions. The standards in most of the private colleges were absurdly low; many of them were poorly housed, ill-equipped and inadequately supervised. Primary education had been woefully neglected, and the government's own educational policy had been confused and erratic.

The Simla Conference, which met for six hours daily for sixteen days, discussed the problems of Indian education threadbare. Curzon found time in the midst of his busy routine to take the chair at all the sessions, and to personally draft all the 150 resolutions passed by the conference. For this Herculean labour, which nearly broke his health, he received no thanks. On the other hand there

[30] *Lord Curzon in India: A Selection from his Speeches*, p. 320.

was a demonstration at Calcutta when the Town Hall and the Senate Hall of the University were 'packed with shouting and perspiring graduates' and his name was 'loudly abused as the author of the doom of higher education'.[31] For this dénouement Curzon himself was largely responsible. The absence of any Indian at the Simla educational conference and the secrecy which surrounded its proceedings had lent it a conspiratorial air, and fostered the suspicion that a plot was afoot to cripple higher education in India. The inclusion of an Indian, Justice Gurudas Banerjee, in the Universities Commission at almost the last moment had somewhat mollified Indian opinion. But the failure to publish the report of the University Commission with Banerjee's note of dissent, on the flimsy pretext of economy, strengthened the impression that the real aim of the government was not so much to raise the level of university education as to discourage western education, and thus to dry the springs which nourished the incipient national feeling. Both the government and the intelligentsia seemed to be conscious that political awakening and western education in India had gone hand in hand. Gokhale told the Imperial Council:

The greatest work of Western education in the present state of India is not so much the encouragement of learning as the liberation of the Indian mind from the thraldom of old-world ideas and the assimilation of all that is highest and best in the life and thought and character of the West. I think Englishmen should have more faith in the influence of their history and their literature.[32]

Curzon protested against the imputation of ulterior motives: he was merely trying to streamline university education as he had sought to streamline the departments of irrigation, railways and mining! Of the political implications of his educational reforms, Curzon and his colleagues were, however, not as innocent as they professed to be. 'In India', wrote Sir Edward Law, the Finance Member, 'the university system must lead to the same class of results as in Russia though it will take some time before it shows any acute and violent forms. . . . The situation can be remedied by raising fees so that only the richer classes could afford to send their sons to a university.'[33] E. R. Ellis, another Executive Councillor, saw the parallel between Russia and Bengal so far as higher education was concerned,[34] and agreed that high fees could get rid of the 'riff-raff'.

[31] Curzon to Hamilton, 10 Sept. 1902 (C.P.).
[32] Karve & Ambekar (eds.), *Gokhale's Speeches and Writings*, vol. III, pp.11–12.
[33] Minute, 23 July 1903 (C.P.).   [34] Minute, 25 July 1903 (C.P.).

The bill, in its final form, did hardly anything to expand the teaching functions of the universities. Nor did it really touch the problems of elementary, technical or scientific education. Government control on the affiliation and inspection of private colleges was, however, tightened, and the government was given a greater say in the nomination of senates and syndicates. All the European official and non-official members—who between themselves accounted for the majority of the Imperial Legislative Council—lined up behind the Viceroy. Two Indian members, R. G. Bhandarkar (who was specially nominated to the Council) and B. K. Bose, voted with the government, but the others followed Gokhale, who moved a string of amendments which were rejected. Finally, as the bill went through, Gokhale put in a final word of protest: 'My Lord, the struggle is over. The opponents of the Bill have lost all along the line. . . . Let those who will, say what they will; this Bill amounts to an emphatic condemnation, as unmerited as it was unnecessary, of the educated classes of this country.'[35]

A few days earlier, Gokhale had led the opposition to the Official Secrets Bill. Government spokesmen asserted that it was modelled on the British Act of Parliament, but unlike that Act it covered civil as well as naval and military matters, which roused the suspicion of the press, both Indian and European. Gokhale told the Imperial Council:

This is the first time within my experience that a legislative measure has been opposed by all classes and all sections of the public in this country with such absolute unanimity. . . . never before did the Government dissociate itself so completely from all public opinion —including Anglo-Indian public opinion—as it has done on the present occasion.[36]

Curzon was furious at the determined opposition to the Official Secrets Bill and the University Bill led by Gokhale. He wrote off the young Maharashtrian leader as an implacable opponent of the government.

Gokhale had lost the unequal battle in the Imperial Council, but it had its reverberations in the country. The mood of nationalist India was mirrored in a letter written by the veteran R. C. Dutt to Gokhale, immediately after the passage of the University Bill.

R. C. Dutt to Gokhale, 22 March 1904: You have performed a noble

[35] Karve & Ambekar (eds.), op. cit., vol. III, p. 55.
[36] *Speeches of Gokhale*, p. 223.

and a patriotic duty, both with regard to the Official Secrets Bill & the University Bill—and a grateful country will not forget your services. You have lost all along the line, as you yourself put it, but there are defeats which are more brilliant and more honourable than victories —and the fight that you have made during the last and worst years of a heartless and ungenerous Imperialism will be historic and will never be forgotten by our countrymen. . . .

A Nation becoming more and more conscious of its just rights and of the strength of its endeavours *cannot* be repressed. I have faith in my countrymen—more than you have—they have within the last 30 years done more to unite and strive for progress than any other nation in the world has done, or could have done, and God helping, they *shall* win in the long run when a blatant Imperialism shall perish in shame. . . .

And even if this be not so,—if this Imperialism gathers force in England and makes administration more and more despotic in India —even then, we have the proud consciousness of having done our duty. It is better to fight and fail in such a cause, than not to fight at all.[37]

[37] G.P.

18

Envoy Extraordinary

By the summer of 1904 Indian nationalists had despaired of a favourable response to their demands from Lord Curzon or the Conservative Government in Whitehall. Things looked really bleak, but fortunately, as the year wore on, British politics took a hopeful turn. The Conservative party found itself in difficulties; it was split down the middle by Joseph Chamberlain's campaign for 'imperial preference'; it lost the goodwill of the nonconformists on temperance and of the working class on the import of Chinese labour to work in South African mines. The days of the Balfour ministry seemed numbered, and a general election was on the cards when William Wedderburn and Henry Cotton, two members of the British Committee of the Congress in London, arrived in Bombay in December 1904 for the annual session of the Indian National Congress. 'It is not in India itself', said Henry Cotton in his presidential speech to the Congress, 'that the fate of India will ultimately be determined.'[1] He referred to the coming 'upheaval' in party politics in England: the likelihood of a general election and a Liberal victory, and 'the beginning of a period during which it is reasonable to expect, not only the undoing of many of the mistakes committed during the ten dark years of reaction, but also some definite advance in the work of reconstruction'. A thrill of hope ran through the Bombay Congress when it unanimously decided to depute Congress representatives to bring the claims of India 'before the electors, before the Parliamentary candidates and before the political leaders' in England.

On their return to England, Wedderburn and Cotton stressed the urgency of the despatch of the Congress delegates; among these were Surendranath Banerjea, M. A. Jinnah, Lajpat Rai and Gokhale. 'Last night', Wedderburn wrote to Gokhale on 3 March 1905, 'the Government majority went down on one division to 24, and the Tory Party is so demoralized that anything may happen at any

---

[1] *Congress Presidential Addresses*, 1885–1910, Madras, 1935, p. 666.

moment. . . . If I telegraph the word "come" to Mr Wacha, it will mean that in our opinion the delegates should start at once.'[2]

The imminence of the general election offered an excellent opportunity for focusing attention on Indian affairs in England. Unfortunately, at this critical juncture, the British Committee of the Indian National Congress in London was in disarray. Two of its members, Allan Hume and W. C. Bonnerjee, had been incapacitated by illness, and Dadabhai Naoroji was wholly absorbed in nursing North Lambeth, a constituency from which he had really little chance of being elected to the House of Commons. The weekly *India*, the Congress organ in England, also needed to be put on a sound footing. Wedderburn had no doubt that Gokhale alone could come to the rescue of the British Committee, conduct its publicity campaign in England, educate the British electorate, and brief prominent members of the Liberal party, who in the event of a Liberal victory were likely to hold office. Wedderburn wrote to Gokhale:

Your first interviews should be with Lord Ripon & Lord Reay, who will both welcome you. I enclose a note from the former. As regards your future rulers, the names of Lord Elgin & Mr Bryce have been mentioned to me as possible Secretaries of State. I should best like Mr Leonard Courtney, but it seems doubtful whether he will win West Edinburgh. As Viceroy, Lord Crewe is spoken of. We know little about him. I should like Lord Reay or Lord Tweedmouth. I think a strong protest from India might keep Sir H. Fowler out of India Office, though he might claim to go back there.

Wedderburn advised Gokhale to reach England by the end of May. Early in April it was agreed that Lajpat Rai, who was to represent the Indian Association of Lahore, and Gokhale, who was to represent the Bombay Presidency Association, should sail on 13 May. In the event only Lajpat Rai was able to leave. Gokhale's departure was blocked by Pherozeshah Mehta, who interpreted the resolution of the Bombay Congress to mean that Congress delegates could leave for England only when Parliament had been actually dissolved and a general election announced. Whatever the validity of this interpretation, it ignored the realities of British politics. Pherozeshah may have had the satisfaction of scoring a point over the British Committee in London, but he nearly drove it to despair. Wedderburn had planned Gokhale's programme so that he could spend the entire month of June in addressing political organizations, and July in

[2] G.P.

briefing members of Parliament before the presentation of the Indian budget in the House of Commons. August and September, believed to be unsuitable for public meetings, were reserved for interviews with leading politicians, who were likely to be inaccessible once Parliament was actually dissolved. Seeing his plans go awry, Wedderburn sent frantic letters and cables to Wacha in Bombay, urging the immediate departure of Gokhale. Gokhale decided to call on Pherozeshah. The interview was a disaster. We have a first-hand account of it from one of Gokhale's closest friends.

Lallubhai Samaldas to Gokhale, 10 May 1905: We were both so much excited last night that I did not like to add fuel to the fire by speaking out my mind about the disgraceful (I use the word in a calm state of mind) conduct of Sir Pherozeshah. . . .

You should not give up the idea of going as a delegate to England. The public have elected you, and you should not disappoint the public. . . . I feel that an apology or at least explanation is due to you from him—You may treat him formally as the recognized leader of the party; the private relations will of course cease. . . .[3]

Gokhale's cup of humiliation was full. He had not gone to seek a personal favour from Pherozeshah. He had been elected as a delegate by the Bombay Presidency Association and was going to England in accordance with the mandate of the last plenary session of Congress. It was easy enough for Gokhale to abandon the trip altogether, but would he not be letting down good old Sir William and the British Committee? On the other hand, if he openly defied Pherozeshah, would he not incur his implacable hostility? Pherozeshah had it in his power to retaliate: he could withdraw his support and jeopardize Gokhale's re-election to the Imperial Legislative Council. Little did Pherozeshah realize that by delaying the Congress delegates' departure for England, he was playing into the hands of Anglo-India. In 1904, the Viceroy had warned Sir Arthur Godley of the India Office of the impending visit of the

Congress deputies . . . Gokhale . . . and that . . . vitriolic windbag Surendranath Banerjea. . . . Their object in proceeding to England now is purely electoral. They want to secure pledges from the Radical Party to give them a Viceroy like Lord Ripon and a Secretary of State of the type of Sir Henry Cotton. They will coo like sucking doves in London. But on provincial platforms their roars will awaken an echo in Hades.

[3] G.P.

It required strong pressure from the Congress veterans in London, Dadabhai Naoroji, Hume, and Wedderburn, to make Pherozeshah relent. On 16 September 1905 Gokhale was able to sail for England.

2

Just when Gokhale was preparing to leave for England, two events took place which added to the importance as well as the delicacy of his mission. One was his election to the presidency of the annual Congress session to be held at Benares in December 1905; the other was the partition of Bengal.

The Congress president was chosen every year by the Congress committee of the province which was playing host to the session, but the choice was, as a rule, informally discussed and approved by prominent all-India leaders. In 1905 Congress leaders of the North-West (United) Provinces had a wide choice: among the names mentioned were those of Lord Ripon, Rash Behari Ghosh, Kali Charan Banerji, R. N. Mudholkar, Sir Gurudas Banerjee, Nawab Syed Mohammed Bahadur and Eardley Norton. Southern India strongly favoured Eardley Norton, Syed Mohammed Bahadur or someone else from Madras Presidency. Bombay leaders, including Pherozeshah, wanted the honour to go to a south Indian or to someone from the Central Provinces and Berar.[4] Local Congress leaders in Benares and Allahabad, however, favoured Gokhale. Gokhale was conscious of the great honour, but pleaded that he was relatively young and could make room for a senior Congress leader. Gokhale's admirers, however, insisted on electing him. 'I have told them', Chintamani wrote to Gokhale from Allahabad, 'that you may not be available, but they are in hopes that they can secure you.'[5] Three weeks later the opinion in the U.P. Congress had crystallized in favour of Gokhale.

C. Y. Chintamani to Gokhale, 27 August 1905: I am glad to inform you that at the meeting of the Congress Committee held on the 20th August you have been elected president of the next Congress with practical unanimity. There was such commendable anxiety on the part of nearly everyone to get you in preference to all other possible men that no other name was so much as proposed. *After you were elected*, one member proposed the election of Dr Rash Behari Ghosh,

[4] N. V. Gokhale to G. K. Gokhale, 31 Aug. 1905 (G.P.).
[5] C. Y. Chintamani to Gokhale, 2 Aug. 1905 (G.P.).

but there was not even a seconder. All the leading men of these provinces and our Chairman of the Reception Committee more than any other man were from the first of one mind that it should be you and nobody else.[6]

It was not modesty alone that impelled Gokhale to wish to forgo the Congress presidency in 1905. The fact was that he had already bitten off more than he could chew. He had been busy for months in raising funds for a memorial to Ranade. In June 1905, he had founded the Servants of India Society, and undertaken to build a home for its members for whose training and political education he had assumed a personal responsibility. As if this was not enough, he was committed to a hectic tour of Britain during the autumn. No one could foresee precisely when the general election in Britain would actually take place. It was obvious that during the few months which remained before the Benares Congress, Gokhale would have little time to devote to Congress affairs. So overwhelming, however, was the warmth of his friends and admirers in the North-West (United) Provinces that Gokhale could not decline the invitation. One of the last things he did before sailing for England was to telegraph his acceptance. Whatever the additional burdens this decision might bring in future, immediately the fact that he was the president-elect of the ensuing Congress session added to the importance of his visit to England.

The other important event which was to affect Gokhale and change the course of Indian politics was the partition of Bengal. The decision was not really as sudden as it seemed. It had long been the subject of an earnest debate among high officials of the Government of India. That a province consisting of the present-day West Bengal, Bangladesh, Bihar, Chota Nagpur and Orissa was unwieldy in size was clear enough. What was, however, not so clear was how the provincial boundaries were to be re-drawn. Various permutations had been suggested from 1854 to 1902—the year in which Curzon first examined the problem. The original impulse behind this 'reform' was doubtless administrative convenience, but political considerations soon supervened. When it was suggested that Berar should be merged in the Bombay presidency, Curzon at once objected that he could not contemplate 'with anything but dismay any proposal which would add to the strength or solidarity of the Mahratta community . . . the most able and the most dangerous of the opponents of our

[6] G.P.

rule in India'.[7] The very argument which ruled out the addition of Berar to Bombay dictated the bifurcation of the Bengali-speaking areas, and the division of the Hindu *bhadralok* which formed the backbone of the nationalist forces in eastern India. Two senior civil servants, Sir Andrew Fraser, the Governor of Bengal, and Sir Herbert Risley, the Home Secretary to the Government of India, won Curzon over to the idea of detaching Dacca and Mymensingh from Bengal, and attaching them to Assam; this would at once strengthen the administration of Assam and cut Bengal and Hindu nationalists down to size.

The partition scheme was announced on 12 December 1903. It evoked a storm of protest. 'To a Dacca man', wrote the *Bengalee*, 'the very thought that he was to cease to be a Bengali and become an Assamese is little short of maddening.'[8] Early in 1904, Curzon toured the eastern districts of Bengal, noted the widespread opposition to the scheme of partition, but decided to ignore it:

The Bengalis, who like to think themselves a nation and who dream of a future when the English will have been turned out, and a Bengali Babu will be installed in Government House, Calcutta, of course, bitterly resent any disruption. . . . If we are weak enough to yield to their clamour now, we shall not be able to dismember or reduce Bengal again; and you will be cementing and solidifying on the eastern flank of India a force already formidable, and certain to be a source of increasing trouble in future.[9]

In April 1904, before a final decision could be taken, Curzon went home on leave. During the next eight months, while he was away, and Lord Ampthill, the Governor of Madras, was acting as the Viceroy, the partition of Bengal was discussed threadbare by the officials of the Government of India. Bampfylde Fuller (who later was to win much notoriety as the first Lt-Governor of the new province of East Bengal & Assam) came out with a solution, which could have solved the administrative problem, staved off the partition and perhaps changed the course of events. Fuller suggested that the integrity of the Bengali-speaking areas need not be disturbed, but the load on the Governor of Bengal could be reduced by constituting a separate province of Bihar and Orissa, and transferring only the Chittagong district to Assam. In the event, it was not the view of Fuller but that of Andrew Fraser and Herbert Risley which pre-

[7] Curzon's minute, 6 March 1903, Notes Pub. A, 1903, Territorial Changes in India (C.P.).   [8] *Bengalee*, 13 Dec. 1903.
[9] Curzon to St J. Brodrick, Sec. of State, 17 Feb. 1904 (C.P.).

vailed: the temptation of creating a separate Muslim-majority province in East Bengal as a counter-weight to the Hindu nationalists proved irresistible. 'Fuller's scheme', wrote Risley, 'would be welcomed by the Bengalis as involving a practical surrender.' Curzon himself seemed at this time to take a peculiar, almost perverse, pleasure in provoking Indian nationalism.

Curzon to St John Brodrick, Secretary of State, 2 February 1905: We are sending off to you by the present mail our final despatch about the so-called partition of Bengal. . . . the opposition to our scheme . . . is now in relation to our final plans, an outcry of Congress party alone, inspired by political motives and directed to a political end. Calcutta is the centre from which the Congress party is manipulated throughout the whole of Bengal, and indeed the whole of India. . . . The whole of their activity is directed to creating an agency so powerful that they may one day be able to force a weak Government to give them what they desire.

Any measure in consequence that would divide the Bengali-speaking population, that would permit independent centres of activity and influence to grow up; that would dethrone Calcutta from its place as the centre of successful intrigue, or that would weaken the influence of the lawyer class, who have the entire organization in their hands, is intensely and hotly resented by them.

The outcry will be very loud and very fierce, but as a Native gentleman said to me: 'My countrymen always howl until a thing is settled; then they accept it.'[10]

The howl was louder and lasted longer than Curzon imagined. There were hundreds of protest meetings in Bengal. Memorials poured in upon the Viceroy. The Secretary of State for India was implored to withhold his sanction to the scheme. A monster petition with sixty thousand signatures was sent to the British Parliament. Questions were asked in the House of Commons. It was all in vain. Curzon was determined to make the partition a *fait accompli* before he laid down the viceroyalty. The prospect of a general election in England drove him to hasten the enforcement of the scheme. He was not prepared to risk its being jettisoned by his successor or by a Liberal ministry in England. On 16 October 1905, within two months of its publication, the scheme was carried into effect. Meanwhile, Curzon had been involved in a bitter controversy with Kitchener, Commander-in-Chief of the British-Indian army, which led to a clash with the authorities in England and brought Curzon's vice-

[10] Curzon to Brodrick, 2 Feb. 1905 (C.P.).

royalty to an abrupt end. In November 1905, Curzon sailed from India.

Seventy years after the partition of Bengal it is possible to argue that the agitation against it did not draw its inspiration from the pure springs of patriotism, that the lawyers and journalists and merchants of Calcutta were worried as much about their own business interests as the integrity and unity of their province. On the other hand, we know now that no mere administrative expediency drove Curzon and his advisers to flout public opinion. Never since the Mutiny had any event in India exercised such a traumatic effect on such large sections of the population as did the partition of Bengal. The tremendous upsurge in Bengal found expression not only in demonstrations in the streets of Calcutta and other towns, but also in the emergence of new slogans, new methods of agitation and a new leadership. The intelligentsia of Bengal, consisting mostly of the Hindu *bhadralok*, was jolted out of the political groove in which it had moved for two decades. 'Swadeshi', 'Boycott', 'National Education', 'Passive resistance', suddenly became the battle-cries of a resurgent and embattled nationalism, the significance of which was to sink slowly into the minds not only of the British rulers, but also of the leaders of the Indian National Congress.

Having spent the winter in Calcutta since 1902, Gokhale had acquired an insight into the politics of Bengal. This stood him in good stead in the autumn of 1905. He was better able than most of his friends in western India to gauge the intensity of the Bengali feeling on the partition, though even he could hardly have foreseen in September 1905 the impact that the partition would make on Indo-British relations and on alignments within the Congress.

'My dear Gokhale,' Surendranath Banerjea wrote on 8 September 1905, 'Do help us in this hour of our sorest trial. You will have to see Brodrick, Fowler, Balfour & Campbell-Bannerman and impress upon them the outrage that has been done to public sentiment by the partition of Bengal . . . Farewell, Bengal's best interests are confided to you.'[11]

3

The S.S. *Caledonia* left Bombay on 16 September 1905. It was the slack season for British tourists and civil servants going home; there

[11] G.P.

were barely twenty first class passengers as against two to three hundred in the summer months. 'I . . . have the greatest possible quiet about me', Gokhale wrote from Aden, 'and you can easily imagine how after the hurry and rush of things at Poona, I must be enjoying it. The sight of the sea also on all sides is most soothing to the eye and spirit, and altogether I am better than I have been for some time past. I spend my time reading, walking about and thinking and I have never enjoyed my reading so well as I am doing here. I read about ten hours a day and don't feel the strain at all.'[12]

On 2 October 1905, Gokhale arrived at London's Charing Cross station and was received warmly by a large number of Indians headed by Dadabhai Naoroji. His arrival did not go unnoticed in the British press. The *Westminster Gazette* described him 'by caste a Mahratta Brahmin, by profession an educationist and by birth a statesman and leader of men'.[13] The *Daily News* referred to him 'as the leader of the people of India in the Legislative Council of the Viceroy of India'.[14] The best pen-portrait of Gokhale was, however, drawn by the correspondent of the *Morning Leader*:

The Hon. Mr Gopal Krishna Gokhale is a much younger man than the majority of the political leaders of India whose names are more or less known in England. There are people in India and in England, who have a notion that a Mahratta Brahmin, especially if he comes from Poona, is a monster of a terrible kind. Mr Gokhale is a Mahratta and a Brahmin and he comes from Poona. Yet he is to be seen among the elect at the Government House, and in the social atmosphere of the cold-weather session in Calcutta, you may hear of him playing billiards with the Finance Member or some other overpowering official. Still young in years—he can hardly be more than 35—he looks with a calm and somewhat shy gaze upon a world which politically he seems not greatly to approve. No man in the Viceroy's Council has his facts so well in hand; none is so keen in debate; none during the years of Lord Curzon's ascendancy has stood up to the Viceroy with anything like Mr Gokhale's force and overmastering conviction . . . He fought the Universities Act almost single-handed and it will be long before the encounter between Lord Curzon and his 'Hon'ble colleague' over the Universities Validation Bill is forgotten.[15]

'My principal plea', Gokhale told a correspondent of the *Daily News* at Charing Cross station, 'will be for self-government for India. That in a word will be the keynote of our new campaign.'[16]

[12] Gokhale to N. A. Dravid, 21 Sept. 1905 (G.P.).
[13] Quoted in *India*, 6 Oct. 1905.   [14] Ibid.
[15] *India*, 13 Oct. 1905.   [16] *India*, 6 Oct. 1905.

The British Committee of the Congress had engaged an 'expert', S. S. Campion, to plan its campaign under the guidance of Sir William Wedderburn. Since Gokhale had to return to India by the end of November to preside over the Benares Congress, he had no more than seven weeks during which he was scheduled to speak at forty-five meetings. One of his most successful visits was to Cambridge where, at a meeting of the Union, he moved a resolution: 'That the House would welcome the introduction in India of government on more popular lines.' Those who supported the resolution included J. M. Keynes. The opposition was led by an ex Anglo-Indian official, Sir Edward Candy. The resolution was carried by 161 to 62 votes. An Indian student, C. R. Reddy, who was later to distinguish himself as a politician and educationist, was swept off his feet by Gokhale's performance.

C. R. Reddy to S. S. Campion, 2 November 1905: He [Gokhale] impressed everyone with his high abilities, massive and well-cultivated intellect and keen power of analysis and criticism. As Mr J. M. Keynes, ex-President of the Union Society, said, he has feeling, but feeling guided and controlled by thought, and there is nothing in him which reminds us of the usual type of political agitators. I am sending you papers which will give you a fair—but certainly not an adequate impression of his tremendous success at the Union Society. He gave a rousing address to the Indians, another very helpful speech to the I.C.S. men and finished his triumphal progress with the most cogent speech I have ever heard at the Liberal Club. The power and directness of his appeal was impossible to resist. One of my friends remarked that they had listened not to a politician but to a statesman of the first degree, who knew how much was to be achieved under the present conditions and by what practical way. His constructive skill is the theme of universal laudation. My happiness is too great for prose and I curse my fate I am not a poet.

C. R. Reddy's enthusiastic account of the debate was confirmed later in the tribute paid to Gokhale by the *Granta*: 'It is impossible to give a fair report of the hon. proposer's speech. It was one of the finest we have ever heard, and although it lasted nearly an hour, and was full of statistics, it was delivered entirely without the aid of any notes.'[17]

Gokhale had been warned that the agitation against the partition of Bengal and particularly the threat of boycott of British manufactures had roused angry feelings in Manchester. This did not deter

[17] C. R. Reddy to S. S. Campion, 2 Nov. 1905 (G.P.); extract from *Granta* quoted in *Bengalee*, 30 Nov. 1905.

him from visiting Manchester, and explaining the political context of the boycott movement. He attributed the tension in India to ten years of Tory Imperialism which had swept the whole British Empire. He told the people of Manchester:

You here have suffered from that wave and you can imagine how much more people have suffered who in their own country are more or less at the mercy of the officials whom you send out to govern them. . . . The Government has taken it into its head to think that if the people are not disloyal today they may be disloyal tomorrow, and so they are saying: 'Let us cripple them for once and all, so that they shall be incapable ever of rising against our rule.'[18]

Under the regime of Lord Curzon the universities had been 'official-ized', the press fettered by the Official Secrets Act, opportunities for Indians to enter higher services in their own country curtailed, and local self-government whittled down. The partition of Bengal was thus only the last of a series of reactionary and repressive measures which had driven the people of Bengal to a state of utter despair. 'The Bengalis', said Gokhale, were 'the most influential community in India' and 'as intellectually among the finest people in the world'. Therefore, more than any other community, they had been 'marked out for Government disapproval and displeasure, and there were officials who thought if these people [the Bengalis] could be gagged the work of administration would be easier'.[19]

Gokhale did not deny that the movement for boycott of British goods in Bengal, if successful, would hurt the textile industry in Manchester.

But what were the people [of Bengal] to do? They had tried to move the government on the spot and failed. They had tried to approach the Secretary of State for India and failed. They had tried to approach the British Parliament and failed. They knew from bitter experience, how difficult it was to get you . . . to take any real interest in the affairs of India. I say this not to blame anybody. The situa-tion is difficult. There are six thousand miles between us, and you have your own problems. We know that you do not wish that India should be badly governed, and all we ask is that she shall be governed in accordance with the English traditions of constitutional liberty. Therefore I am sure that when the whole position is brought home to you, you will rise as one man and put an end to these Russian methods of administration. . . . 'Why, then, you ask, have we taken up a step against Manchester?' Well, what else could the people do? The

---

[18] Karve & Ambekar (eds.), *Gokhale's Speeches and Writings*, vol. II, pp. 321–2.
[19] Ibid., p. 322.

Manchester trade was the only vulnerable point at which we could strike against the Government of India, and we struck not with the object of injuring you in your pockets . . . but because you are in the position to call this reactionary Government to account. . . . I was even told in London that it would not be a pleasant thing to come to Manchester to address a meeting because people were embittered against the Indians for the boycott. But I said I would take the risk. I am not sorry that you are angry, because I want you to be angry, but I want you to turn your anger not against the helpless people, who have been driven to the last possible measure that they could take in an extremity but against those officials of yours who are responsible for the unhappy situation that has been brought about.[20]

Gokhale's speeches in Britain were variations on one major theme: that all was not well with India, that the British people and Parliament had been guilty of a grave dereliction of duty in leaving India to a coterie of professional administrators, that the people of India had grievances which cried for immediate redress as well as for fundamental changes.

The system of Indian administration, Gokhale told the Fabian Society, was 'unworthy of free England', being largely based on 'confidential police reports, . . . and on hostility towards the educated classes'.[21] Some of the British officials were no doubt very conscientious men, but the evils of the system could not be avoided 'even if they could import angels from heaven to fill these posts'.[22]

An extremely lucid exposition of Indian aspirations was given by Gokhale to the Political Committee of the National Liberal Club on 15 November 1905, when he addressed it on the 'Awakening of India'. He traced the root cause of the ills from which India suffered to the fact that the British bureaucracy in India was 'absolutely uncontrolled in its actions'.[23] It consisted of men who were birds of passage, and had little incentive to launch long-term measures for the permanent good of the country. In consequence, the Indian economy was in a bad way; village industries languished, the soil was exhausted, the peasantry was hopelessly in debt and the people were desperately poor. Yet, there was 'the extraordinary spectacle of a thriving treasury and a starving peasantry'. There were, he argued, two ways in which the British bureaucracy in India could be controlled: either from England, or on the spot in India. Even if the former were practicable, he would object to it, because the aim

[20] Ibid., p. 325.   [21] Ibid., p. 328.   [22] Ibid.
[23] *The Awakening of India*, published by the Political Committee of the National Liberal Club, London, 1905, I.O.L. Tracts, Pol. 993, p. 3.

of British rule had been 'declared . . . to be to train the people of India for self-government'. The British Parliament had neither the time nor the knowledge to exercise effective control. The remedies for the ills of India could only be applied by the people of India. To enable them to do so, they needed greater control of the government of their own country. The Indian people asked for self-government on colonial lines. They desired to remain within the British Empire, but they wished such a share in the government of the country 'as would be worthy of their self-respect, and which would make them worthy of the respect of others'. They recognized that the transition to self-government could not be made in a day, but what they did ask was that their faces should be set in the direction of self-government.

Gokhale offered concrete suggestions for reform. The proportion of elective Indian seats in the Imperial Council should be raised to half of its total strength. The budget should be formally presented to the Imperial Council, and members allowed to move amendments, though the Viceroy's power of veto could remain. Of the members of the Secretary of State's Council in London, at least three should be Indians. In the House of Commons at least six seats should be allotted to India. 'Six in a House of 670', argued Gokhale 'will not introduce any disturbing factor and certainly shall not affect the fate of ministries. . . . But the House will have an opportunity to know at first hand the Indian view of things.'

Lord Coleridge, the Liberal peer who presided at the meeting at the National Liberal Club, paid a tribute to 'the extraordinary moderation of Mr Gokhale's speech'.[24] He confessed that if he were in the same position as Mr Gokhale, he should not be so moderate. He wished the House of Commons had members like Mr Gokhale. He had no doubt that 'arguments so reasonable, so moderate, so fair, would be irresistible to the great common sense of the British legislature'.

It was part of Wedderburn's strategy that, besides delivering public lectures, Gokhale should have opportunities of privately briefing the leading lights of British politics, and particularly of the Liberal Party. Among those whom Gokhale met were Lords Ripon and Reay who were traditionally friendly to Indian aspirations, Herbert Gladstone, H. H. Asquith, John Morley, Leonard Courtney, Arthur Godley, St John Brodrick, Richard Haldane, Lloyd George and Winston Churchill. No one could say for certain who was to be the Secretary of

[24] Ibid., p. 5.

State for India if the Liberals won. John Morley was one of those tipped for the job: Gokhale had a pleasant interview with him.

'I trust', Wedderburn wrote to Gokhale, 'that both strength and voice are holding out under the severe strain to which you are being subjected.' They held out, but not for long. By the middle of November, the burden of work and anxiety had become unbearable. Gokhale wrote to his faithful disciples in Poona:

As the time of my departure approaches, the pressure of work here is proving so terrible as to drive me almost mad. During the last five days, would you believe it, I have been working seventeen and eighteen hours a day . . . [holding] meetings and interviews with prominent men of both sides. . . . I have to be rushing about from one place to another, sometimes without breakfast or lunch or both and the anxiety of keeping an appointment punctually causes a great worry during the long and unfamiliar distances. Then there is heavy urgent correspondence and finally there are visits from Anglo-Indians and others.[25]

This Herculean labour was, from the point of view of the British Committee of the Congress, well worth it. Gokhale made an excellent impression on the British public in lectures and on politicians in private meetings. Wedderburn, who treated Gokhale like a son as well as a friend and comrade, was delighted, and was already looking forward to another visit by him in the following year. Henry Cotton, the most radical member of the British Committee, who privately wrote off most of his colleagues as 'extinct volcanoes', described Gokhale as one 'who most accurately and thoroughly represented the feelings of the educated classes of the peoples of India'. Old Dadabhai Naoroji was so impressed that he advised Gokhale to forgo the presidency of the Benares Congress, and to stay on in England for electioneering work.[26] Even the militant radical, H. M. Hyndman of the Social Democratic Federation, paid a tribute to Gokhale's ability and courage. 'I think it was very plucky of Mr Gokhale', Hyndman wrote to Naoroji, 'to speak on the same platform with myself and I told him so.'[27]

Reports of Gokhale's English tour appeared in the Indian press and more information must have trickled through letters to Indian politicians from friends and relatives. The courage, clarity and eloquence with which he championed the cause of his country in

[25] Gokhale to Dravid, 17 Nov. 1905 (G.P.).
[26] Naoroji to Gokhale, 9 Oct. 1905 (G.P.).
[27] H. M. Hyndman to Naoroji, 9 Oct. 1905 (G.P.).

Britain raised his stock in his homeland. 'The whole Indian world', a friend wrote to Gokhale on 2 November 1905, 'is at your feet at present.'[28]

Gokhale could look back on this tour with some satisfaction, but he was also exhausted by it. The return voyage gave him a little respite, but there was no rest for him after he landed at Bombay. There was just a fortnight before the Benares Congress was to meet. Thanks to the partition of Bengal, the Congress presidency had become a crown of thorns.

[28] S. Ray to Gokhale, 2 Nov. 1905 (S. Ray P.).

19

Congress President

Gokhale had been elected president of the Benares Congress only a few days before he sailed for England. 'The Presidential speech', he wrote to N. A. Dravid from s.s. *Caledonia* on 26 September 1905, 'is fermenting in the head and some of the ideas are already taking a definite shape. But the thought of the responsibility is oppressive and God alone knows how it will be discharged in the end.'[1] How oppressive the responsibility was to be was mercifully hidden from him at that time. During the next three months, while he campaigned on behalf of the Congress in England, the Indian political scene underwent a radical transformation.

The transformation was caused by Curzon's persistence in enforcing the partition of Bengal in the teeth of popular opposition. Criticism in newspapers, protest meetings, petitions and deputations failed to deflect him from the 'collision course' on which he had embarked. The Bengali *bhadralok* felt (in the words of Surendranath Banerjea) that they had been 'insulted, humiliated and tricked'.[2] The sixteenth of October 1905, when the partition actually took effect, was observed as a day of mourning; in Calcutta thousands abstained from food, suspended business and walked barefoot to the banks of the Ganges for a dip in the holy river amidst deafening cries of 'Bande Mataram'. The same day Anand Mohan Bose, the veteran Bengali nationalist, was carried in an invalid's chair to a moving ceremony for laying the foundation-stone of the 'Federation Hall', which was to symbolize the indissoluble bond between the two parts of Bengal.

The official reaction to the agitation was characteristic; efforts were made to silence the critics and particularly to curb students, who were in the vanguard of the agitation. Repressive measures had, however, just the opposite effect. With the rising crescendo of popular indignation, the anti-partition agitation became more vehement.

[1] Gokhale to Dravid, 26 Sept. 1905 (G.P.).
[2] Banerjea, *A Nation in Making*, p. 173.

The boycott of British manufactures and the use of 'swadeshi' (India-made goods) were advocated to bring the government to heel. Traditional Congress policies seemed ineffective in the new political context, and there was a clamour for new methods and a new leadership. The older Congress leaders like Surendranath Banerjea at first tried to keep pace with popular feeling, but soon found that they were being led by, instead of leading, public opinion and that the reins of the movement were slipping from their hands.

The new mood of Bengal was reflected in an 'open letter' to the leaders of the Indian National Congress published in the *Amrita Bazar Patrika*. It affirmed that:

the country in general has grown almost impatient of your tinkering Congress politics. It seems to have realized that the most successful of your Congresses cannot secure permanent good for the country simply by a policy of what is called begging. . . . The Congress must . . . adapt itself to the changed conditions of life. . . . Places in Government service, shadowy representation in the Legislative Councils, this or that makeshift in the policy of the Government are not exactly the things the people want at present. True self-government . . . is the new creed. . . .[3]

The feeling that old methods would not do was also voiced by Lala Lajpat Rai, Gokhale's fellow-delegate to England in 1905. 'What Bengal has done', wrote Lajpat Rai, 'should be done by every province in ventilating its grievances.'[4] He proposed a monster demonstration against the policies of Lord Curzon by a hundred thousand men in Benares to coincide with the Congress session. Such a demonstration, Lajpat Rai told Babu Ganga Prasad Varma, a prominent Congress leader of the North-West (later, United) Provinces,

will carry more weight & will impress the people in England more than any number of your Congresses. . . . People are just now fairly well-excited & you should not fail to take advantage of this. Unless you are prepared to change the nature of your movement in this direction, you are not likely to make any progress towards political freedom at all, and I am sure that if the Congress will not take the initiative in this matter, some other movement may have to be set up to do the same and the Congress will dwindle into insignificance.[5]

Lajpat Rai may have been in tune with the new spirit in Indian politics, but unlike Gokhale, he was not in the inner counsels of the

---

[3] Quoted in *India.*, 29 Dec. 1905.
[4] *Hindustan Review*, Oct.–Nov. 1905, p. 355.
[5] L. Rai to G. P. Varma, 8 Aug. 1905 (G.P.).

Congress leaders in Bombay or in the confidence of the British Committee in London, who between themselves determined the Congress strategy. Pherozeshah Mehta and his adherents in Bombay did not like much that was being said and done in Bengal in the wake of the partition. Wedderburn, Hume and Dadabhai Naoroji were extremely critical of Curzon's decision to partition Bengal, but they saw it only as the crowning blunder of a reactionary Tory regime which was on the way out. By the end of the year Curzon had left India, and a Liberal ministry was in office in England. 'I think', wrote Dadabhai Naoroji to Gokhale on 26 November 1905, 'our day of emancipation is much nearer than many of us imagine'[6] Wedderburn was more explicit. He wanted the Benares Congress 'to take full advantage of the great upheaval in this country [Britain] which has suddenly placed in power the friends (& some very advanced ones) of progress and popular aspirations', and expressed the hope that the Benares Congress would be guided by Gokhale.[7]

Gokhale's task as president of the Congress was more difficult than Wedderburn and Dadabhai Naoroji knew. The aftermath of the partition had strengthened the hands of extremist elements in the Bengal Congress. These elements found allies in like-minded men in Maharashtra and the Punjab, who had been chafing under the inaction of the Congress leadership. The anti-British upsurge in Bengal had given a temporary spurt to 'swadeshi' and the boycott of British goods, and there was even talk of passive resistance. Gokhale saw that it was not going to be easy to keep the Congress at Benares in the grooves within which it had moved for twenty years. He looked around for allies. If only he could persuade Pherozeshah Mehta to go to Benares, all might be well. Pherozeshah knew how to handle dissidents and rebels; he had silenced his critics in 1903 at the Madras Congress, and deftly managed the Bombay Congress the following year; he could be relied upon to ensure a smooth session at Benares. But Pherozeshah declined to attend the session with a single peremptory sentence: 'We shall not go to Benares.' It was not only his sore throat which held him back. In recent months, Pherozeshah had not been able to see eye to eye with Gokhale on several matters. He had a lurking feeling that Gokhale had not been ruthless enough in his criticism of the Universities Bill. Pherozeshah did not like the way he had been pushed by the British Committee into

[6] *India*, 26 Jan. 1906.
[7] Wedderburn to Gokhale, 14 Dec. 1905 (G.P.).

sanctioning Gokhale's departure for England in September 1905. Some of the radical stuff in Gokhale's speeches in England also seems to have jarred on Pherozeshah. It seemed to him that Ranade's disciple was going off the track. Even the foundation of the Servants of India Society had struck Pherozeshah as a presumptuous if not futile exercise. Would not Gokhale's 'political missionaries' with their emphasis on renunciation develop a supercilious attitude towards their colleagues in the Congress?[8] The fact that, on his return from England, Gokhale had been taken out in a huge procession in Poona (in which Tilak's adherents had enthusiastically joined) and that he had even spent an hour at Tilak's house in Gaikwad Wada struck Pherozeshah as odd. Indeed, the *Kesari* and the *Mahratta* were already hinting at an estrangement between Pherozeshah and Gokhale, commending Gokhale's views on the partition of Bengal and the boycott, and denouncing Pherozeshah as the major reactionary influence in the Congress. The editor of the *Gujarati*, who was close to Pherozeshah and also a friend of Gokhale, thought it prudent to warn Gokhale of the pitfalls which awaited him at Benares.

N. V. Gokhale to G. K. Gokhale, 22 December 1905: Please do not get offended, because I can mean no offence to you. But Sir P.M.M. [Pherozeshah M. Mehta] thinks that you are, in spite of yourself, about to play into hands of men, who until recently persecuted & denounced you, & who, you declared, were not gentlemen to be argued with & were irreconcilable. This was said to a few select friends who have a high regard for both of you. The situation is very delicate and difficult, and I only hope everything may pass off successfully.[9]

2

The choice of Benares as the venue for the annual Congress session had struck some observers as a 'daring' one. The ancient city of Benares was the principal seat of Sanskrit learning and a stronghold of Hindu orthodoxy, but its citizens were not much concerned with politics. Nevertheless, during the Christmas week of 1905 Benares was agog with excitement. Besides the Congress session, an industrial conference was being held for the first time to coincide with the industrial exhibition. There was a 'Ladies Conference', besides 'caste'

[8] Sastri, *Pherozeshah Mehta*, pp. 58–9.   [9] G.P.

gatherings of Gaur Brahmans, the 'Rajput Sabha' and the 'Kalwar Sabha', in addition to a meeting of scholars presided over by R. C. Dutt to consider the question of a uniform script for the whole of India.

The citizens of Benares gave a splendid welcome to Gokhale. He was taken in a huge procession from the railway station to the venue of the Congress and was deeply moved by the popular enthusiasm. At the plenary session on the afternoon of 27 December, Gokhale's name was formally proposed for the presidency by Pandit Bishambhar Nath, one of the oldest Congressmen of U.P. and seconded by R. C. Dutt and G. Subramania Iyer. Bishambhar Nath, in traditional Congress oratory, described the Congress as 'the crowning triumph of *Pax Britannica* with its untold numerous blessings'.[10] Munshi Madholal, the Chairman of the Reception Committee, also repeated the old clichés about the Congress being 'the intellectual product of British rule and English education'.[11] Earlier, in a telegram to the Viceroy, the Munshi had 'respectfully' pleaded for an alteration in the Prince of Wales' tour programme, enabling him to see the industrial exhibition organized by 'the Indian National Congress, a loyal body representing all sections of His Majesty's Indian subjects'.[12] The sedate tone of these speeches was to some extent a part of the ritual at Congress sessions, but it was also a reminder that the North-West (United) Provinces continued to be a political backwater, barely ruffled by the storm of the partition of Bengal. Gokhale had a keen sense of political realities; he perceived the beginning of the process of polarization in the Congress; and the belligerent mood of Bengal had struck sympathetic chords in the Central Provinces, Berar, Maharashtra and the Punjab. These provinces accounted for more than half of the delegates present at the session and two-thirds of the delegates from outside the United Provinces. It was obvious that an inter-provincial group, visibly impatient with old leaders and old slogans, was emerging at Benares, informally evolving a common approach to controversial issues, and trying to push forward the Congress in opposition to the government. This group by and large admired and respected Gokhale, who himself took care not to gratuitously offend it. Indeed, in his presidential address, which usually set the tone for the Congress session, Gokhale shrewdly took

[10] *Report of the Proc. of the Twenty-first Indian National Congress*, Benares, 1905, p. 3.   [11] Ibid., p. 2.

[12] Telegram, 20 Dec. 1905, from Madholal, Chairman, Congress Art Exhibition, to P. S. to Viceroy (Minto P.).

a position half-way between the Congress Establishment and the new radicals.

Gokhale's presidential address included an appraisal of the political situation at the end of 1905, a historical retrospect and a forecast of the future. It also contained a reiteration of his own political faith and a restatement of the ideals and policies of the Indian National Congress. He recalled the days when the Congress had first met at Bombay in 1885, when 'hope was warm and faith shone bright', and the founders of the Congress believed that they would secure a steady advance 'in the direction of the political emancipation of the people'. Twenty years had elapsed and much had happened to chill that hope and dim that faith. It was true the Congress had succeeded in making only meagre political gains and latterly stagnation, even reaction, had set in. Nevertheless, the Congress was resolved to attain its goal 'that India should be governed in the interest of the Indians themselves, and that in course of time a form of Government should be attained in this country similar to what exists in self-governing colonies of the British Empire'. The advance to such a goal could only be gradual, for it was a 'reasonable proposition, that the sense of responsibility required for the proper exercise of the political institutions of the West can be acquired by an Eastern people through practical training and experiment only'. To admit this was not to question the fitness of the Indian people for self-government. Had not Mr Gladstone 'in words of profound wisdom' pointed out that 'it is liberty alone which fits men for liberty'?

Gokhale made a scathing attack on the monopoly of power by the British bureaucracy in India. The gulf separating British officials from educated Indians had widened; the bureaucracy was growing 'frankly selfish' and 'openly hostile' to the national aspirations of India. The domination of one race over another inflicted great injury on a subject race, which faced not merely demoralization, but also impoverishment. For a century or more, India had been for the British 'a country where fortunes were to be made to be taken out and spent elsewhere'. As in Ireland, the evil of absentee landlordism had in the past aggravated the racial domination of the English over the Irish, so in India, 'absentee capitalism has been added to the racial ascendancy of Englishmen'.

Self-government was the only real and permanent remedy for the evils from which India suffered. The time had come for the British bureaucracy in India to part with some of its powers in favour of the educated classes. The argument that the educated classes were as yet a very small fraction of the community was unconvincing. At the end of the eighteenth century, not one man in ten or one woman in twenty knew how to read and write in England, and yet there was a House of Commons. In India about fifteen million could read and write, and a million of them had come under the influence of some kind of English education. It was true that the educated class was still small in size, but in the circumstances prevailing in India, they were the natural leaders of the people. They controlled the vernacular press which reached the masses; in a hundred ways they had access to the latter's minds, and 'what the educated Indians think today, the rest of India thinks tomorrow'.

Gokhale called for a beginning, even a modest beginning in administrative and constitutional reforms: the enlargement of the size, elective element and powers of the legislative councils, the appointment of Indians to the councils of the Secretary of State, the Viceroy and the provincial Governors, the formation of advisory boards at the district level, the separation of the judicial from the executive functions, the reduction of military expenditure, and the expansion of primary, technical and industrial education. These demands, many of which were embodied in Congress resolutions from year to year, may not sound revolutionary today, but in 1905 few Britons (or even Indians) considered them immediately attainable. What lent special significance to the reiteration of these demands in 1905 was the exit of the Tory Government in England. 'For the first time since the Congress movement began', said Gokhale, 'the liberal and radical party will come into real power.' He described the Liberal Prime Minister, Sir Henry Campbell-Bannerman, as 'a tried and trusted friend of freedom', and referred to John Morley, the new Secretary of State for India, as 'the reverent student of Burke, the disciple of Mill, the friend and biographer of Gladstone', to whom large numbers of educated men in India felt 'as towards a Master and the heart hopes and yet it trembles as it had never hoped or trembled before'.

'A more gratifying combination of circumstances', declared Gokhale, 'could not be conceived and it now rests with us to turn it to the best advantage we can for our motherland.' Though he ended on a note of cautious optimism, he had earlier in his address bluntly analysed the great ferment caused by the partition of Bengal. The partition was a cruel wrong inflicted on our Bengali brethren . . . a complete illustration of the worst features of bureaucratic rule in India, its utter contempt for public opinion, its arrogant pretensions to superior wisdom, its reckless disregard of the most cherished feelings of the people . . . and its cool preference of Service interests to those of the governed.

Gokhale's tribute to 'Bengal's heroic stand', his support for *swadeshi* and even for boycott as a political weapon in extreme cases were not merely sops to Bengali delegates at the Benares Congress. There was hardly anything in his address which he had not expressed a few weeks before in England in even stronger language.

Khaparde, an associate of Tilak, grudgingly confided to his diary on 27 December 1905: 'Mr Gokhale's speech as president was not quite in the ultra moderate style and was cheered in its stronger parts.' F. J. Bennett of the *Times of India* regretted that Gokhale had ceased to be 'a steadying force' on public feeling.[13] 'The Mr Gokhale who presided over the Benares Congress yesterday', wrote the *Times of India* on 28 December 1905, 'will seem to many readers of his inaugural address to be a different person from the Mr Gokhale whom they knew some years ago as a sober and dispassionate critic of the acts and policy of the Government.'[14] It seemed to this Anglo-Indian paper that Gokhale had fallen into 'the wild ways of the perfervid orators and writers of the Deccan who, in the days when he was much more restrained in utterance than he is now, seemed to move him to remonstrance'.

3

The presidential speech was a great occasion at the annual Congress session, but the crucial decisions which determined its success or failure were taken in the meetings of the Subjects Committee. The Subjects Committee, which met after the presidential speech on the evening of 27 December, got bogged down on the very first resolution, one welcoming the Prince of Wales (later King George V) to India. Lajpat Rai raised objections to the resolution on the ground that the country, suffering from famine and the after-effects of Curzon's repressive policies, was in no mood to stage pageantry for the royal couple. The Prince had been invited to Benares, but had not responded. In fact, the Congress could express its regret that

[13] F. J. Bennett to Gokhale, 29 Dec. 1905 (G.P.).
[14] *Times of India*, 28 Dec. 1905.

the Prince had not found it possible to see the Congress session and the exhibition. Tilak supported Lajpat Rai, but the original resolution was passed by a majority. A threat was then held out by Lajpat Rai and his supporters that they would oppose the resolution in the plenary session.

The Congress leaders had so far scrupulously kept the royal family above politics; the debate on the Prince of Wales was inadvisable, an ill-chosen phrase could do much harm by tarnishing the image of the Congress in England just when the Liberal Government had come into office. There was much excitement in the Congress camp on the night of 27 December, and Munshi Madholal and his friends in the Reception Committee even feared a riot. Gokhale did not, however, lose his nerve; he preferred quiet diplomacy to an acrimonious public debate. Just before the Congress session was scheduled to begin on 28 December, he sent for Lajpat Rai and made a 'personal appeal' to him not to oppose the resolution on the Prince of Wales and sought his assistance in persuading Tilak and the Bengali extremists to exercise similar restraint. While the controversial resolution was debated in the plenary session, the opponents of the resolution stayed out of the Congress pavilion; some of the Bengali delegates had to be forcibly kept out by Lajpat Rai and S. B. Bapat, an adherent of Tilak. On his part Gokhale was sporting enough to agree that the Congress records would not show the resolution as having been passed unanimously.[15]

The other resolution which caused some anxious moments at the Benares session was on the boycott of foreign goods 'as a last protest, and perhaps the only constitutional and effective means left to them [the people] of drawing the attention of the British public' to the iniquity of the partition of Bengal. The remaining twenty resolutions, such as those on the expansion of the Councils, the public service question, military expenditure, police and land revenue reforms, were hardy annuals. One of the resolutions recorded the appreciation of the work done by Gokhale in England; another enjoined him to visit England again 'to urge the more pressing proposals of the Congress on the attention of the authorities'.

To have emerged unscathed from the Benares Congress was no mean achievement for Gokhale. The tensions released by the partition of Bengal had fortunately been contained within the Subjects Committee, and not allowed to spill into the plenary session. The

[15] V. C. Joshi (ed.), *Lajpat Rai: Autobiographical Writings*, Delhi, 1965, p. 111.

battle lines between the Congress Old Guard led by the adherents of Pherozeshah Mehta and the emerging Bengali–Maharashtra–Punjab alliance had been drawn, but a clash had been avoided, thanks to Gokhale's acumen, patience, and tact. In his presidential address he succeeded in treading the tight rope between the old Congress orthodoxy and the new radicalism. The absence of Pherozeshah Mehta, whose sledge-hammer tactics could crush, but also incite opposition, Gokhale's personal equation with Lajpat Rai, and the latter's influence over Tilak had helped to stave off a show-down at Benares and to maintain the façade of Congress unity. This unity was essential if Gokhale was to plead for a new deal for his country under the new regime in India and England.

20

Advocate for India

In the last months of his viceroyalty, Curzon had so thoroughly alienated large sections of Indian opinion that almost any Viceroy following him would have been popular. Lord Minto did not have Curzon's dominating personality, intellectual stamina and demoniac energy, but he was also free from his predecessor's flamboyance, conceit and irascibility. Soon after his arrival in India, the new Viceroy stumbled upon the key to popularity which had eluded Curzon for six years. 'It takes a very short time in this country', Minto wrote, 'to realize how much may be done by a sympathetic appreciation of existing conditions.'[1] He noted how 'the excitable and impressionable leaders of India are curiously amenable to personal influence'.[2] A year later, Motilal Ghose of the *Amrita Bazar Patrika*, a caustic critic of Curzon and official policies, was assuring Dunlop-Smith, the Viceroy's private secretary, that 'it would take two Curzons in succession to disturb the calm Lord Minto had brought'.[3]

Minto seems to have tried his charm on Gokhale. Their meeting on 30 January 1906 went off very well. 'I had a long and most cordial interview yesterday with the Viceroy', Gokhale confided to Krishnaswami Aiyer. 'He had sent for me himself and asked my opinion about several important matters, including the Partition and expressed himself in very flattering terms about my Congress [presidential] address.'[4]

A few days later, Gokhale used his influence in the viceregal camp to intercede on behalf of his friend Samuel Ratcliffe, the editor of the *Statesman*, who had got into trouble with the Home Department of the Government of India for publishing one of Curzon's minutes

[1] Minto to Morley, 3 Jan. 1906 (M.P.).
[2] Ibid., 19 March 1906.
[3] Note, 15 March 1907, of J. Dunlop-Smith, forwarded by Minto to Morley (M.P.).
[4] Gokhale to Aiyer, 31 Jan. 1905 (G.P.).

on the partition of Bengal.[5] Enraged by this breach of the Official Secrets Act, the Home Department had barred the *Statesman* from government advertisements and other privileges. Gokhale spoke to Dunlop-Smith, who helped in arranging an interview between Samuel Ratcliffe and Arundel, the Home Member. A compromise was reached, the *Statesman* published an apology and the government withdrew the ban.

Gokhale's first impressions of Minto as a cool and sympathetic ruler were confirmed during the winter session of the Imperial Legislative Council. Aware that 'no Viceroy of recent times has had to succeed to a greater legacy of difficulties than Lord Minto',[6] Gokhale was anxious not to embarrass him. In his budget speech on 28 March, he concentrated on economic rather than political issues. He outlined a comprehensive scheme of state action for improving the condition of the masses: the reduction in the salt duty and land revenue at least in the famine-stricken areas, the amortization of rural debts, the provision of funds for local bodies, particularly for rural water supply and drainage, the extension of primary education and the establishment of a technological institute. The additional funds for this programme were to be found partly by financing railway construction through loans rather than through taxation, and partly by scrapping the costly military reorganization scheme prepared by the Commander-in-Chief, Lord Kitchener, before the Japanese victory over Russia altered the balance of power in Asia. 'The power of Russia has been broken', Gokhale argued. 'Her prestige in Asia is gone. She has on her hands troubles more than enough of her own to think of troubling others for years to come: and thus a cloud that was thought to hang for twenty years and more over our north-western frontier has passed away.'[7]

Gokhale cited the example of Japan to expose the 'un-national character of the Indian army'. With an expenditure of 37 million yen, or a little under six crores of rupees, Japan had a standing army of 167,000 men with reserves which could be raised to 600,000 men. 'We spend', Gokhale reminded the Imperial Council, 'six times as much money a year and yet in return for it we have only an inexpansive force of about 230,000 men with about 25,000 Native reservists and about 30,000 European volunteers!' Indians were

[5] Gokhale to Dunlop-Smith, 1 Feb. 1906, A. T. Arundel to Dunlop-Smith, 5 Feb. 1906 (Minto P.).
[6] Karve & Ambekar (eds.), op. cit., vol. II, p. 354.
[7] Patwardhan & Ambekar (eds.), op. cit., vol. I, p. 94.

barred from the officers' cadre. The exclusion of the people of India from all honourable participation in the defence of their own country was, said Gokhale, 'a cruel wrong to a whole people— one-fifth of the entire population of the world'.

In a telling comparison with Japan, Gokhale pointed out that though the Japanese people had come under the influence of western ideas only forty years before, they had, under the fostering care of their own government, taken their place by the side of the proudest nations of the West. Indians had been under English rule much longer, and yet continued 'to be mere hewers of wood and drawers of water in our own country and, of course, we have no position anywhere else'.

'What the country needs at this moment above everything else', Gokhale told the Imperial Legislative Council, 'is a government, national in spirit, even though it may be foreign in personnel—a government that will enable us to feel that *our* interests are the first consideration with it, and our wishes and opinions are to it a matter of some account.'[8] Gokhale concluded: 'My Lord, I have ventured to make these observations because the present situation fills me with great anxiety. I can only raise my humble voice by way of warning, by way of appeal. The rest lies on the knees of the gods.'[9]

Gokhale's speech had ended on an ardent note. It included a trenchant criticism of the government, but it did not refer to the controversial issues of the partition of Bengal and the boycott. This studied restraint could not have passed unnoticed by Minto, who presided over the deliberations of the Imperial Council. The Viceroy and his Finance Member, E. N. Baker, seemed to have made an earnest effort to win over Gokhale, who returned to Poona from the winter session of the Imperial Council with high hopes.

Gokhale to G. A. Natesan, 2 April 1905: You will be glad to know that my budget speech this year was extremely well received in the Council. The Viceroy specially sent for me at the conclusion of the proceedings and congratulated me in very flattering terms. He further assured me that it would be his ambition to advance to some extent at any rate, to work on the lines indicated by me during his regime.

Mr Baker [Finance Member], with whom I had a long interview at his special request the next day, assured me that he would provide funds in next year's budget for making a beginning in the direction of free Primary Education. He said very kind things, which I need not repeat here, but you will judge how friendly he is when I tell you

[8] Ibid., p. 99.   [9] Ibid., p. 107.

that he made an earnest appeal to me not to retire from the [Imperial Legislative] Council next year, as he knows it is my intention to do. He said, 'Give me two to three years and I will make a beginning in regard to most of the things you are advocating, only you must be in the Council to back me up by your criticism and your demands.' He explained to me confidentially his difficulties, but with the retirement of two of his senior colleagues, his voice will prevail more and more on the Executive Council and you may rest assured that that voice will be raised wholly in our interest. . . .

Altogether, I feel the situation is most hopeful and I have never returned from Calcutta with such a sense of satisfaction within me as this year. Now that the Government of India have themselves taken up the question of a further reform of Legislative Council, my hands will be immensely strengthened in pressing the question forward during my forthcoming visit to England.[10]

Gokhale was in a buoyant mood when he sailed for England from Bombay in the s.s. *Egypt* on 14 April. This was his fifth sea voyage, but the first which he really enjoyed. In 1897, the thought of the ordeal awaiting him before the Welby Commission had weighed on him; the return voyage had been clouded by the 'apology incident'. In 1905, the breeze with Pherozeshah Mehta, the aftermath of the partition of Bengal and the critical responsibility of having to preside over the Benares Congress had kept his nerves on edge. In the spring of 1906 he was happily free from such anxieties, and cheerfully looked forward to being in England. He wrote from Aden on 18 April:

I am enjoying the voyage immensely. The sea so far has been calm and there is a beautiful breeze all day long on the deck. . . . I spend my time mostly in walking and reading, with a little conversation with fellow-passengers by way of variation. . . . The Aga Khan is also with us and I am delighted to find that he is coming over to our way of thinking in politics more and more.[11]

The Aga Khan expressed his happiness at the formation of the Servants of India Society, offered to contribute Rs 5000 to its funds, and invited Gokhale to stay with him in Switzerland for a month to improve his health. As we shall see later, the Aga Khan's cordiality was not as disinterested as it seemed at the time; these conversations on the s.s. *Egypt* were exploited to embarrass Gokhale's mission in England.

On the evening of 30 April Gokhale reached London. The train

[10] G.P.   [11] Gokhale to Dravid, 18 April 1906 (G.P.).

was two hours late, but about fifty Indians, headed by Dadabhai Naoroji, were waiting at Victoria station to receive him. On 1 May he met the British Committee of the Indian National Congress. The next day he called on J. E. Ellis, the Under-Secretary of State for India. On 3 May he addressed about fifty M.P.s at a meeting of the Indian Parliamentary Committee. Two days later he was Wedderburn's guest at Gloucester where he spoke on temperance. He returned to London to address the Indian Parliamentary Committee and a meeting convened to protest against the 'Barisal Incident' in East Bengal. He visited Cambridge and Oxford, attended a peace conference at Birmingham, and addressed the East India Association.

The paper that Gokhale read before the East India Association on 11 July 1906 was one of the clearest and most forthright expositions of the Indian case for self-government which he had ever attempted. It was sporting of the East India Association—comprising predominantly former governors, judges, generals, bankers and planters —to invite him to speak. The consciousness of an unsympathetic or even hostile audience seems to have put Gokhale on his mettle. He asserted that the faith of the people of India in the character and ideals of British rule had been shaken, and its place was being taken by 'a conviction that, however great England may be, she is not great enough to forgo voluntarily the gains of power from considerations of mere justice or national honour'.[12] He admitted that the English-educated class in India numbered merely a million in a population of three hundred millions. There was, however, no greater mistake than to imagine that 'the influence of this class was proportionate only to its numbers'. The members of this class 'constituted the brain of the community'; they did the thinking not only for themselves, but also for their ignorant brethren. They controlled the Indian language press, which shaped the thoughts and swayed the feelings, not only of the fifteen million literates in vernaculars whom it reached directly, but also of many more who were indirectly under its influence.

It was possible, argued Gokhale, that 'bureaucracies like the Bourbons' never learnt, but it should not be difficult for Englishmen to realize that

you cannot have institutions like the universities working for more than half a century in India, and then expect to be able to govern the people, as though they were still strangers to ideas of constitutional

[12] Karve & Ambekar (eds.), op. cit., vol. II, p. 351.

Gokhale with the members of the Deccan Education Society, Poona, 1902
(Gokhale sitting fifth from left)

Leaders of the Indian National Congress, Bombay, December 1904
(Gokhale standing fifth from left)

Gokhale with Gandhi, Kallenbach and members of the Reception Committee, Durban, 1912
(Gandhi sitting fourth and Gokhale fifth from left)

Gokhale with Dadabhai Naoroji (sitting) and D. E. Wacha, London, 1897

A. O. Hume

Sir William Wedderburn

Lord Curzon

John Morley

Lord Minto

Lord Hardinge

Top Left   Pherozeshah Mehta
Top Right Bal Gangadhar Tilak
Bottom   Mahadev Govind Ranade

freedom or to the dignity of national aspirations. Those who blindly uphold the existing system, and resist all attempts, however cautious and moderate, to broaden its base, prefer practically to sacrifice the future to the present. The goal which the educated classes of India have in view is a position for their country in the Empire worthy of the self-respect of civilized people. They want their country to be a prosperous, self-governing, integral part of the Empire, and not a mere poverty-stricken, bureaucratically-held possession of that Empire. The system under which India is governed at present is an unnatural system, and however one may put up with it as a temporary evil, as a permanent arrangement it is impossible. . . .[13]

Gokhale conceded that since self-government for India had to be on western lines, the steps by which the goal was to be reached would be slow. But there was all the difference between cautious progress and no progress at all. The bureaucracy which stood in the way of all reasonable instalments of reform was 'undermining its own position by such a short-sighted and suicidal policy'.[14] It had been argued by British officials that India would have to wait till the mass of the people had been qualified by education to take an intelligent part in public affairs. But was it not the fault of the government that after a century of British rule, seven children out of eight in India continued to grow up in ignorance and darkness? In any case, what he was asking for immediately was a voice in the administration only for those who were qualified by education to exercise their civic responsibilities.

One can only guess how the audience, consisting mostly of old India hands, must have squirmed when Gokhale told them that 'the efficiency attained by a foreign bureaucracy, uncontrolled by public opinion' was bound to be of a 'strictly limited character',[15] that as things were, there was 'no one ever in the Indian Government who is permanently interested in the country as only its own people can be interested . . . the true well-being of the people is systematically subordinated to militarism, service interests of English mercantile classes. . . .' Gokhale denounced the virtual British monopoly of the higher posts in the administration in India. He warned that unless the educated classes were conciliated, 'England will find on her hands before long another Ireland, only many times bigger, in India'. 'I cannot say', Gokhale concluded, 'that I have much hope that any such policy will be at once adopted. The struggle before us is, I fear, a long one, and, in all probability, it will be a most bitter one. The

[13] Ibid., p. 354.   [14] Ibid., p. 355.   [15] Ibid., p. 353.

flowing tide, however, is with us, and such a struggle can have but one issue.'[16]

3

In the summer of 1906, as in his earlier visits, Gokhale's mentor in England was Sir William Wedderburn. Sir William's watchword was 'moderation'. 'The object should be', he told Gokhale, 'to show the moderation and practicality of our proposals.'[17] Despite occasional tours and public meetings, the emphasis during this visit was on quiet diplomacy rather than on overt propaganda. Sir William introduced Gokhale to a number of M.P.s, including Ramsay MacDonald, Sir Charles Dilke, Keir Hardie, C. P. Trevelyan and G. P. Gooch. Some of them drew upon him for facts and figures for asking questions or moving amendments to official resolutions. Many years later, G. P. Gooch, in his memoirs, described Gokhale as the most eminent Indian statesman of his time, with 'mellow wisdom and quiet strength'.[18] Ellis, the Under-Secretary of State for India, was extremely well-disposed to Gokhale and invited about forty members of Parliament to meet him at breakfast. The Inter-Parliamentary Conference invited Gokhale to attend the conference. From the 'Anti-Imperialist League' of America came a request that Gokhale should visit the United States and deliver a series of lectures on India.

All this was very flattering, but somewhat irrelevant. The main purpose for which Gokhale had come to England was to persuade the new Liberal Government to recognize the gravity of the crisis in India and to reverse the process of alienation of the people which Curzon had set in motion. There was no time to lose. 'Now is the time for work,' R. C. Dutt wrote to Gokhale from Baroda on 24 May 1906, 'now or never. If this Liberal Govt. fails to give a more representative character to the Indian administration, we shall never get anything by peaceful methods, and England will be teaching us to pursue Irish methods in a country which has more than 50 times the population of Ireland.'[19]

The central figure in the Liberal Government, who needed to be educated from the Indian point of view, was John Morley, the Secretary of State. Gokhale had met him during his earlier visits to

[16] Ibid., p. 357.   [17] Wedderburn to Gokhale, 2 May 1906 (G.P.).
[18] G. P. Gooch, *Under Six Reigns*, London, 1958, p. 127.
[19] R. C. Dutt to Gokhale, 24 May 1906 (G.P.).

England in 1897 and 1905. These visits made it somewhat easier for Gokhale to approach Morley, who received from the young Indian politician a full exposition of Indian grievances and aspirations. 'I made a passionate appeal to Mr Morley yesterday', Gokhale wrote home on 10 May 1906, 'to realize the great responsibility of his teachings in his present office. And he was much moved and he spoke freely of his difficulties and intentions.'[20] Eight days later, Gokhale felt that Morley was 'at last waking up to the situation and we may expect further developments yet'.[21] 'I may tell you privately', Gokhale confided to Krishnaswami Aiyer, 'that I have been able to establish excellent personal relations with Mr Morley.'[22]

Wedderburn and his colleagues in the British Committee were glad that Gokhale was hitting it off so well with Morley. In India hopes rose high. 'You have secured the ear of Mr Morley', Gokhale's friend R. N. Mudholkar wrote to him. 'You have opened his eyes. Through him you have moved that immovable barrier, the India Office.'[23] Another friend, Hari Narayan Apte, was delighted when he was approached on behalf of an English Radical, J. Seymour Keay, to secure Gokhale's help in finding him a safe seat in the House of Commons:

When my friend . . . asked me to write to you in this connection [Apte told Gokhale] I was not a little overjoyed—for this shows that making India a plank in their platform has been considered advantageous by some [British] politicians at least. This gives me hope that the time is not far distant when there will be an India Party—as strong as the Labour Party in the British Parliament. I only hope you will be there to lead it.[24]

This optimism was racing ahead of events. Soon Gokhale was complaining of 'adverse influences' being at work. The anticlimax came with Morley's long-awaited speech on the Indian budget on 20 July.

Three months of silent and strenuous diplomacy had nearly broken Gokhale's health, but they had not brought him visibly nearer the constitutional reforms he had been advocating. Some of the obstacles to the reforms were inherent in the structure of the British Raj; others arose at the time from conflicting pressures on John Morley.

[20] Gokhale to Dravid, 10 May 1906 (G.P.).
[21] *Idem*, 18 May 1906 (G.P.).
[22] Gokhale to Aiyer, 8 June 1906 (G.P.).
[23] R. N. Mudholkar to Gokhale, 10 Aug. 1906 (G.P.).
[24] Apte to Gokhale, 5 May 1906 (G.P.).

Book III

CONFRONTATIONS, WITHIN AND WITHOUT

Morley's Dilemma

The victory of the Liberal party in the general election of 1905 thrilled the Indian intelligentsia. Reared on the works of Burke, Macaulay and Mill, it tended to see English history as a triumphal procession from autocratic and feudal rule to constitutional government and democracy. It associated the Liberal party with the best in English politics and indeed in English character. Few educated Indians could speak of Lord Ripon without emotion, and for many years it was not unusual for the annual Congress sessions to conclude with three cheers for the Queen or for Mr Gladstone. When a collection of Pherozeshah Mehta's speeches and writings was published in 1905, its editor, C. Y. Chintamani, could not think of a better tribute to his hero than to compare him with Gladstone.[1] When Gokhale told the Benares Congress that large numbers of educated Indians felt towards Mr Morley 'as towards a master', he was speaking not only for himself, but for thousands of his countrymen, who had learnt to equate English liberalism with 'peace, freedom, economy and reform'.

The fact that the Indian National Congress had been able to win few tangible concessions in the first twenty years of its existence was attributed by its leaders to the long Tory ascendancy throughout this period, except for a brief interval from 1892 to 1895, when a shaky Liberal ministry (compared to 'Polar explorers marooned on a melting icefloe'[2]) was in office. The general election of 1905 reduced the strength of the Conservative party in the House of Commons to 157 members. The Liberals captured 401 seats and could, in addition, count upon the support of the 83 Irish nationalist and 29 Labour members.[3] Indian observers of the British scene were agog with excitement and felt that the day of India's deliverance was at hand.

---

[1] C. Y. Chintamani (ed.), *Speeches and Writings of the Honourable Pherozeshah M. Mehta, K.C.I.E.*, Allahabad, 1905, p. ii.
[2] A. P. Thornton, *The Imperial Idea and Its Enemies*, London, 1966, p. 62.
[3] C. Cross, *The Liberals in Power 1905–1914*, London, 1963, p. 23.

This optimism was due to the facile assumption that the generous and sympathetic attitude towards India of a few Liberals such as Charles Bradlaugh, Henry Fawcett, Charles Dilke, Allan Hume, Henry Cotton and William Wedderburn was typical of the Liberal party as a whole. In fact, neither the leadership nor the rank and file of that party were deeply concerned about India. Despite its sweeping victory in 1905, the Liberal party was really not so dynamic or coherent as it seemed at first sight. *Justice*, the organ of the Marxist Social Democratic Federation, had shrewdly predicted just before the election that 'the Liberals would win, but it would be for the last time. Liberalism as a creed and as a force is played out and it only lives on its past credit.'[4] 'Your coach', Joseph Chamberlain is said to have told Mrs Asquith, 'has about twelve horses and will require skilful driving.'[5] More than half the Liberal M.P.s in the new Parliament were non-conformists, animated by a deep antagonism to the established Church and Balfour's Education Act. Quite a few of them were industrialists and financiers who had helped to fill the coffers of the Liberal party, but had little interest in India, except perhaps to ensure that it continued to be an outlet for the export of British capital and manufactures.

Lajpat Rai, when he toured England with Gokhale in 1905 as a Congress delegate, was astonished at the absorption of the British electorate in domestic issues and the general indifference of the Liberal party to India.[6] However hard Wedderburn and the British Committee of the Congress might try, it seemed impossible to turn Indian reform into a live issue in a British general election: it did not move the people at large, and it touched too many pockets.

The rising tide of imperialism in Britain in the last quarter of the nineteenth century had been attributed by Indian leaders—somewhat naïvely—solely to the wickedness of the Tory politicians. In fact the supporters of Imperial ventures in Africa and South-East Asia in the nineteenth century included not only the aristocratic classes (for whose younger sons the colonies were alleged to be 'a vast system of outdoor relief') but also Liberal politicians such as Rosebery, Chamberlain and Grey, adventurers like Cecil Rhodes, administrators like Milner and Cromer, explorers like Livingstone, and merchants and manufacturers eager for markets and raw materials, and missionaries

---

[4] W. S. Adams, *Edwardian Portraits*, London, 1957, p. 22.   [5] Ibid.
[6] L. Rai to G. P. Varma, 8 Aug. 1905 (G.P.). See also H. W. Nevinson, *The New Spirit in India*, London, 1908, p. 297.

anxious to save the souls of the heathens. Between 1870 and 1900, the European powers had succeeded in parcelling out Africa among themselves. Britain's gains had been the most spectacular: 4.5 million square miles and a population of 66 million. France had secured an addition of 3.5 million square miles and a population of 26 million and Russia had annexed half a million square miles and a population of 6.5 million. Indeed, at the turn of the century, 'empire' was a status symbol among European nation-states. In Britain, no major political party, least of all the Liberal party, thought in terms of 'decolonization'. Far from being a dirty word, 'imperialism' epitomized national pride and affluence, not guilt for exploitation of alien races. Kipling's image of the 'white man's burden' and the ignorant native, 'half-devil and half-child', was not a mere poetical invention; it reflected the prejudices of the late Victorians reared on 'Darwinism', exalting the survival of the fittest among races and nations.

Of the leaders of the British Liberal party in 1906, Lord Ripon was the most respected in India, but he had not visited the country since 1884. Lord Elgin and Sir Henry Fowler, who were both in the Liberal Cabinet, had been connected with Indian administration, the former as Viceroy, the latter as Secretary of State, but were far from being friends of nationalist India. It was Henry Fowler who had declined to carry out the resolution of the House of Commons in favour of simultaneous examinations to the Indian Civil Service and declared in January 1897: 'I have a strong opinion of the goodness of the Government of India . . . I think it a wise, a strong, and an economical Government—a Government which has conferred upon India untold blessings.'[7]

In the first few months following the formation of the Liberal Government, hopes were running high in India. In February 1906 Wedderburn reconstituted the Indian Parliamentary Committee in the House of Commons. It claimed a membership of nearly 150 M.P.s, belonging mostly to the Liberal party, but the hard core of the committee, consisting of men like Henry Cotton, C. J. O'Donnell and Herbert Roberts, was small. Before the new government was formed, Wedderburn ventured to address Henry Campbell-Bannerman, the leader of the Liberal party, on the selection of the Secretary of State for India. Wedderburn took Ripon into his confidence.

[7] Parliamentary Debates, House of Commons, 4th Ser., vol. XLV, 1897, col. 544.

Wedderburn to Ripon, 7 December 1905: I am so anxious as to the fate of India that I have taken the liberty of writing to Sir H. C. B. who is a very old friend of mine. I have besought him not to send either Sir H. Fowler or Lord Elgin to the India Office. They are both hopelessly in the hands of the officials. With further audacity I have said that if you did not come to the rescue of poor India (which Lord Curzon had almost driven to despair) any of the following would be acceptable: Leonard Courtney, Sir Charles Dilke, Lord Reay, John Morley, Lord E. Fitzmaurice, James Duce.[8]

2

Morley himself was not keen on the India Office; he would have preferred a more important portfolio, such as that of the Chancellor of the Exchequer. He had never visited India; in fact his interest, like that of his master Gladstone, lay in Irish rather than in Indian affairs. A radical in his youth and middle years, he had once been called 'the St Just of the English Revolution',[9] but was far from being a fanatical doctrinaire; indeed the greatest formative influence in his life was that of John Stuart Mill from whom he imbibed a coherent liberalism based on reasoned optimism and generous humanity.

In 1906 Morley was sixty-seven. The idealism of his youth had been somewhat tempered by the caution and cynicism of age. The lavish compliments showered on him by Indian nationalists at once flattered and embarrassed him: they exposed him to the Tory taunt of being a theorist, a philosopher, even a gullible tool in the hands of Indian agitators.

Mr Morley [wrote the *Englishman* of Calcutta], though a rabid radical, and a convinced and avowed Little Englander, is nevertheless too reasonable a man ... to deliberately put his ill-informed Radicalism against the knowledge of the Government of India, under such an able and trusted administrator as Lord Minto, reinforced by the experience of the India Council.[10]

Morley's task, as Secretary of State, was not as simple as it seemed to his Indian admirers. He had yet to grasp the intricacies of Indian administration, foreign policy, finance, defence and politics. He had to establish an understanding with Minto, who had recently succeeded the controversial Curzon as Viceroy of India. He had to carry with him his own Council in London, a traditional stronghold of

[8] Ripon P.
[9] G. P. Gooch, *Under Six Reigns*, London, 1958, p. 187.
[10] Quoted in *India*, 5 Jan. 1906.

Anglo-Indian conservatism. In the British Parliament he had to reckon not only with the prejudices of ex-Viceroys such as Lansdowne and Curzon in the Conservative Opposition, but also of a small, but vocal section in his own party, led by Sir Henry Cotton, which functioned as a pressure group on behalf of the Indian National Congress.

It did not take Morley long to realize that India could not be governed from London, and that the Viceroy was the focal point of the Indian administration. However, as his correspondence with Minto shows, Morley tried to imbue the Viceroy with some of his liberal ideas and to inject a fresh impulse into the Indian administration which seemed frozen under bureaucratic complacency. This correspondence relating to the years 1905–10 is an interesting commentary on Indian affairs by two men occupying points of vantage. It throws much light on the shaping of the official policies and on the motives of the main actors on both sides of the water. It does not, however, provide an entirely true picture of the political problem on which both Minto and Morley had good reasons for not being entirely frank with each other. So far as Minto was concerned, he was for the most part retailing the fears and prejudices of his subordinates in Simla, in order to dampen the ardour of the reputedly innovating Secretary of State for India. Morley's liberalism was not of a radical brand, especially on imperial issues, but his experience of Ireland and sense of history enabled him to see some aspects of the Indian situation which were beyond the ken of the blinkered Anglo-Indian bureaucrats in Simla and London.

'Cut him open', George Meredith had once said of Morley, 'and you will find a clergyman.'[11] Morley, the moralist, can be easily discerned in his correspondence with Minto. He was continually throwing feelers, offering suggestions, persuading, prodding and pushing the Viceroy towards reforms. At the same time he was anxious not to alarm Minto, and adopted the stance of a practical statesman rather than that of a philosopher. During his first few months at the India Office, Morley went out of his way to make allowances for the difficulties, the limitations and even the prejudices of the conservative Viceroy. He phrased his references to Gokhale and the Congress carefully so as to reassure the Viceroy and his colleagues that he had no intention of walking into the 'enemy's camp'. On his part Minto seems to have quickly sensed that the new Secretary of State for

[11] Gooch, op. cit., p. 188.

India, with his radical past and the pressures in the Commons, was likely to lend a sympathetic ear to the advocates of popular aspirations in India. Minto, therefore, took care to refer to the Congress and its leaders in terms which concealed his real feelings about them. Reading between the lines of the two men's correspondence, one cannot resist the impression that while Morley was discreetly pushing Minto into a recognition of the political ferment in India and the need for reforms, Minto was using all his ingenuity and skill to delay or dilute them.

3

In May 1906, after meeting him, Gokhale had come to the conclusion that Morley's mind was still 'fluid'.[12] Ever since he had taken office in December 1905, Morley had been groping his way towards a sympathetic reorientation of the Indian administration. He had taken the earliest opportunity of warning the new Viceroy that the Liberal Cabinet had no use for the Curzonian policy of extending protectorates and spheres of influence in Afghanistan, Tibet or Persia. He exhorted Minto to give 'a general cue' to Englishmen all over India to treat Indians civilly. He wondered whether the salt duty, which bore hard on the poorest in the land and their half-starved cattle, could be reduced or even repealed.[13] He had the courage to acknowledge to the Viceroy that he agreed with the minute of dissent recorded by Dadabhai Naoroji, Wedderburn and Caine in the Report of the Royal Commission on Indian Expenditure.[14] He rejected the proposal for celebration of the fiftieth anniversary of the Indian Mutiny which was to fall in 1907;[15] he saw that whatever satisfaction it might give to Anglo-Indian pride, it was bound to hurt Indian feelings. He sought a modicum of relief through the Colonial Office for the Indian minority in South Africa struggling for elementary rights under the leadership of Gandhi.[16]

There is thus plenty of evidence to indicate that Morley was anxious to placate educated India, but on broader issues of Indian politics, he could not but tread warily. Privately, he acknowledged that the partition of Bengal was an 'administrative operation, which went wholly and decisively against the wishes of the people con-

---

[12] Gokhale to Dravid, 25 May 1906 (G.P.).
[13] Morley to Minto, 19 April 1906 (M.P.).   [14] *Idem*, 2 Jan. 1907 (M.P.).
[15] *Idem*, 15 Aug. 1906 (M.P.).   [16] *Idem*, 2 May 1907 (M.P.).

cerned', but in his first public reference to it in February 1906, he described it as a 'settled fact'. This statement came as a shock to Indian nationalists, who had hoped that the Liberal Government would lose no time in reversing the most unpopular decision of their Tory predecessors. They did not realize that even a Liberal Secretary of State could hardly begin his term with a row with the Viceroy and Government of India. Indeed, during his first months in the India Office, Morley was consciously trying to achieve a *rapport* with the Conservative Viceroy.

4

We have already seen how cordial Minto was to Gokhale during the budget session of the Imperial Legislative Council at Calcutta in the spring of 1906. This cordiality may have been no more than studied courtesy to the ablest and most eloquent Indian member of the Council; a little flattery and patronage by British dignitaries had been known to work wonders on Indian politicians. On the other hand, it is possible that in the first few months of his viceroyalty Minto was under the relatively liberal influence of E. N. Baker, his Finance Member, who seems to have been less hidebound than most of his colleagues on the Executive Council. The budget session was as usual followed by the annual exodus to the hills. Minto's acclimatization to Simla was extraordinarily rapid. Baker's benign influence declined, and Minto's initial sympathy seems to have quickly changed into scepticism. This metamorphosis is not difficult to explain. Not only was Minto new to his job, he lacked the quick grasp, energy and versatility of his predecessor. General Barrow's verdict on Minto's administration that 'K[itchener] and the Secretaries run the government, Lady Minto runs the patronage and H.E. [His Excellency] runs the stables',[17] was undoubtedly malicious, but it had a modicum of truth. Senior civil servants and particularly those like Harvey Adamson, Herbert Risley and Dunlop-Smith, the Private Secretary to the Viceroy, who enjoyed his confidence, had a share in shaping matters of high policy that they could not have dreamt of under Curzon.

'When I wish to be misinformed about a country', Palmerston had once said, 'I ask the man who has lived there thirty years.'[18] The

[17] E. Barrow to Curzon, 27 July 1907 (C.P.).
[18] Quoted in Thornton, op. cit., p. 41.

truth of this dictum was confirmed by Minto's experience in the summer of 1906. It was not long before he was repeating the shibboleths of his Anglo-Indian subordinates. The British in India were (Minto wrote) 'a small British garrison surrounded by millions composed of factors of an inflammability unknown to the western world, unsuited to western forms of government', and had to 'be physically strong or go to the wall'.[19] British rule in India was 'no doubt a bureaucratic administration', but it possessed many great administrators 'of whom we may well be proud'.[20] There was a 'change in the air in India, the Indian National Congress being one of the chief factors in the change; but the real danger to the Raj lurked not in the Congress party, but in England where its supporters in the British Parliament managed to keep the pot of disaffection boiling'.[21]

How far and fast Minto imbibed the Anglo-Indian ethos is shown by his eager acceptance and transmission to Morley of the assertion of loyalists like Raja Partab Singh that India was unfit to govern herself. He also repeated with obvious relish extracts from the speech of Bharucha, a Parsi broker of Bombay, assailing Gokhale and the Indian National Congress. Minto passed on to Morley even the fatuous comment of Sir T. Bhashyam Iyengar, a retired judge of the Madras High Court, who claimed to have discovered sanctions for British rule in the Hindu *shastras*:

Current events afford ample proof day after day how unsuitable many of the English institutions are to India. . . . In spite of its cumbrous form of government, England is by far the best-governed country in the world. Why? It is because of the high character and good sense of the British nation . . . my idea as a true Hindu is that God has blessed India by relieving Indians from the most difficult and painful task of governing themselves, and God has conferred a still greater blessing on India by entrusting that task to the English nation.[22]

In recent years attempts have been made to depict Minto as a far-sighted and liberal Viceroy, who recognized the aspirations of educated India and willingly went forward to meet them.[23] Stray quotations from Minto's letters to Morley have been cited as proof of the

[19] Minto to Morley, 20 May 1906 (M.P.).
[20] *Idem*, 27 June 1906 (M.P.).
[21] Minto to Prince of Wales, 6 June 1906 (Minto P.)
[22] Enclosure to letter from A. T. Arundel, Member, Executive Council, to Minto, 14 May 1906 (M.P.).
[23] E.g., Syed Razi Wasti, *Lord Minto and the Indian Nationalist Movement, 1905 to 1910*, Oxford, 1964.

liberal outlook of the conservative Viceroy. The fact is that though Minto was eager to project himself as a sympathetic ruler, responsive to the winds of change in India, he had no intention of making any substantial concession to nationalist elements. He was conscious of the intellectual and temperamental gulf which separated him from Morley who seemed—at least in some of his letters—hypersensitive, wilful and domineering. Minto was too discreet to antagonize Morley; he preferred half-hearted agreement to an acrimonious debate on paper in which he could only come off second best. It was not in his letters to the Secretary of State, but to his colleagues and friends in India and England that Minto laid bare his real aims and motives. His attitude to the Indian National Congress and the constitutional reforms is, for example, revealed in a letter to Lt-Governor Hewett of the North-West Provinces, written while Gokhale was in England.

Minto to J. P. Hewett, 11 July 1906: Personally I am very doubtful as to the honesty of the aims of the Congress leaders . . . Native representation on the Viceroy's Executive Council I put out of court. The advisability of it is doubtful and even if we agreed to attempt it, it would in no way satisfy the advanced party here unless we appointed a man such as Gokhale, who is the last sort of man we want on the Viceroy's Council . . .

An increase of representation on the Legislative Council is a different thing. . . . Of course anything like popular representation in the home [English] sense is quite out of the question, and the increase would have to come from certain recognized bodies, authorized to nominate representatives. The bodies that occurred to me are the Universities, with perhaps some selected colleges as Aligarh, but I should be afraid that their representation would be tinged with Congress aspirations and their influence would require to be balanced somehow, possibly by representation of the Oudh Taluqdars. . . .[24]

Minto's response to the double pressure from the nationalists in India and the Liberal Secretary of State in England was thus to concede as little as possible, and to hedge what was conceded with safeguards for the Raj. His favourite stratagem for counteracting nationalist elements was a 'Council of Princes' presided over by the Viceroy. The Prince of Wales, the future King George V, who had visited India towards the end of 1905, also commended the proposal for a Council of Princes to 'take the wind out of the sails of the National Congress'.[25]

Within four months of his arrival in India, Minto was expounding

[24] Minto P.   [25] Prince of Wales to Minto, 1 Jan. 1907 (Minto P.).

the political philosophy—which pervaded not only the major and minor bureaucrats of Simla, but even the patrician governors of three presidencies directly appointed from England. One of them, Lord Lamington of Bombay, advised Morley not to yield to Indian agitators.

Lamington to John Morley, 6 April 1906: Undoubtedly the spirit of disaffection is confined to the high educationists and Brahmins. . . . The favourite proposed panacea of opening more higher appointments [to Indians] would certainly impair the efficiency of the administration, but might have compensating advantages were it to allay the spirit of unrest. But I have never heard anyone with experience of this country suggest that it would be worth trying.

We suffer a great deal for our virtues and in endeavouring to give the people good government in all its branches. We distrust their national craving for repose and conservatism. The real guarantees of our stay in India remain as strong as ever, viz. the caste system, the diversity of nationalities and creeds and the lack of confidence and trust of one native for another.[26]

Lamington's was the classic defence of *status quo*. Minto himself was prepared to go a little farther and accept minor changes, but even he would not tinker with the power-structure of the Raj. What galled the educated Indian, he assured Morley, was not the humiliation of foreign subjection, but the frustration of personal ambition. A judicious distribution of more and better-paid jobs could thus turn malcontents into allies of the Raj. Representative government for India was unthinkable, but the British could invite the Indian educated classes 'to rule with us'. There were certain departments of government, such as that of public works, which could certainly do with a few more Indians. 'I believe', Minto wrote, 'we shall derive the greatest assistance from this [educated] class if we recognize its existence, and that if we do not, we shall drive it into the arms of the Congress leaders.'[27]

Of the Congress politicians, and particularly of those who belonged to Bengal, Minto had no very high opinion. 'If British influence was withdrawn, what would become of Bengali ideas and Bengali eloquence!' he asked, and himself answered: 'The population of India is a conglomeration of races, the majority of whom would not put up with Bengali superiority for five minutes.'[28] Unlike his predecessor, Minto did not publicly slight Congress leaders, and very occasionally

[26] Lamington P.   [27] Minto to Morley, 27 Feb. 1907 (M.P.).
[28] Minto to Prince of Wales, 6 June 1906 (Minto P.).

in his letters to Morley he even let fall compliments to Congress leaders such as Gokhale. These compliments were, however, grudging and half-hearted, and usually carried a sting in the tail. When Sir Arthur Lawley, the Governor of Madras, wrote to Minto that he intended to receive a Congress deputation, the Viceroy's comment was characteristically equivocal:

The Congress is a factor we must be prepared to recognize in the future. The best of their representatives I believe to be honest, though they advocate much that is not adaptable to India—the worst of it is that they are taken at a far higher valuation at home than they deserve. But we must recognize them and it would be the greatest mistake to attempt to ignore them. Still one cannot disguise from oneself the danger ahead. . . . I know you will be careful in any reply you make to a deputation. They will be ready to twist anything they can.[29]

It was not only the Extremist politician who was the Viceroy's *bête noire*. 'I like Gokhale', Minto wrote to the Prince of Wales on 6 June 1906, 'and believe him to be honest, but I am sure no one knows better than Your Royal Highness that it would take countless Gokhales to rule the Punjab and the N.W.F.P., to say nothing of the rest of India.'[30]

In his letters to the Secretary of State, Minto's references to Gokhale were usually double-edged: praise was judiciously balanced with criticism. This ambivalence—which was shared by most British officials—was not unnatural towards a critic of the government who was at once brilliant, irrepressible and incorruptible. Minto did not question Gokhale's ability, but cast doubts on his motives. 'I like what I have seen of Gokhale', he wrote on 20 May 1906, 'but he is playing with dangerous tools.'[31] Again, on 22 August Minto wrote to Morley: 'He is all you say about ability, but whether he is a really genuine article I can't tell.'[32]

5

Gokhale's presence in England was as much of an eyesore to Minto in the summer of 1906 as it had been to Curzon a year before. Indeed, with a Liberal Secretary of State, the risks of Gokhale's lobbying in London seemed infinitely greater. Minto sought to

---

[29] Minto to Lawley, 29 June 1906 (Minto P.). [30] Minto P.
[31] Minto to Morley, 20 May 1906 (M.P.).
[32] *Idem*, 22 Aug. 1906 (M.P.).

counteract Gokhale's efforts by supplying the Secretary of State with a critical commentary on him, the Congress and the Indian nationalists. Dunlop-Smith, the Viceroy's knowledgeable and influential Private Secretary, noted in his diary that such information should prove a useful 'antidote to the vapourings not only of Gokhale, but Cotton, Smeaton and other radicals in England'.[33] Referring to a talk with Asutosh Mukherjee, the Vice-Chancellor of the Calcutta University ('who I suppose probably stands higher than any other Indian gentleman in the position he occupied both as a judge and a deep thinker'), Minto wrote to Morley: 'I was a little bit surprised, in his unwillingness to express much appreciation of Gokhale'.[34] In his anxiety to prejudice Morley's mind against Gokhale, Minto was not even above retailing vague and wild allegations by the ruler of Kolhapur that seditious leaflets were circulated among the troops in his state and arms collected for a popular rising, and that Gokhale was aware that this was happening.[35]

Far from advocating constitutional reforms, as some historians would have us believe, it is doubtful if Minto would have taken any initiative on his own. It was only when he saw Morley determined to make a move that he decided to sponsor the reforms so that the Government of India might have a major say in the final decision, and did not seem to have acted under duress from London. The diary (17 August 1906) of Dunlop-Smith provides an insight into the working of the Viceroy's mind: 'Mr Morley was anxious to do all kinds of things, but the Viceroy, while agreeing to discuss the most radical proposals, insisted on moving cautiously.'[36] Ten days later Dunlop-Smith wrote:

When Morley wrote and said he thought the [Legislative] Council might be enlarged, the representative element increased, etc., etc., Lord Minto replied that he thought it a bit early in the day for either Morley or himself to venture to tackle subjects, but he would take them up, only the thing must be done deliberately and in a constitutional way. Morley didn't like this at all but gave in. . . .[37]

Morley got little inspiration or support from the Viceroy or the Government of India for any major initiative in conciliating India in 1906. At home, he had even less backing for such an initiative. Arthur Godley, the Permanent Under-Secretary of State, who had

---

[33] Martin Gilbert, *Servant of India*, London, 1966, p. 49.
[34] Minto to Morley, 16 May 1906 (M.P.).
[35] *Idem*, 10 Sept. 1906 (M.P.).
[36] Gilbert, op. cit., p. 52.   [37] Ibid., pp. 52–3.

for twenty years, and under seven successive Secretaries of State, really run the India Office, was a zealous partisan of the bureaucracy in India. And the member of the India Council who seems to have carried a great deal of weight with Morley at this time was Sir William Lee-Warner—a retired civil servant, who had in the course of his long service in Bombay presidency acquired an obsessive hatred of Indian nationalists and especially of Maharashtrian Brahmans. But the man who exercised probably a crucial influence over Morley during these early months of his tenure in the India Office was his private secretary, F. A. Hirtzel. 'To me Hirtzel means life and death',—this was how Morley recommended Hirtzel for a decoration to Prime Minister Campbell-Bannerman.[38] Hirtzel's diaries reveal how, in the summer of 1906, he became a willing party to a concerted move—almost a conspiracy—to spike Gokhale's guns.

To Hirtzel, Godley and Lee-Warner the spectacle of an Indian politician, the president of the Indian National Congress, being closeted week after week in confidential parleys with the Secretary of State for India must have seemed scandalous. They knew that an outright refutation of Gokhale's arguments might not go down well with Morley. It was much easier to sow seeds of suspicion in Morley's mind about the aims and methods of Indian politicians in general and of Gokhale in particular. Could a Maharashtrian Brahman, and a Chitpavan Brahman at that, be trusted? Was it possible that Gokhale was double-faced? Was a sly and seditious conspirator lurking behind the façade of an Indian parliamentarian? Was it possible that Gokhale was exploiting his contacts with the Secretary of State to further his own personal and party ends in India? There was no lack of opportunities for denigrating Gokhale or casting doubts on his motives. In June 1906, Morley cabled Simla that he proposed to invite Gokhale to the King's birthday party. 'I said', Hirtzel noted in his diary, 'if G. [Gokhale] is invited, he ought to be diluted with other natives.'[39] A few days earlier, Lee-Warner got the Aga Khan to discuss Gokhale with the Secretary of State. The Aga Khan, who had travelled with Gokhale on s.s. *Egypt* in April 1906, had come to the fantastic conclusion that if the Servants of India Society (the 'Brotherhood' as he called it) could be infiltrated with elements loyal to the British Raj, Gokhale could be diverted from political agitation into the innocuous by-ways of social reform. The

[38] Morley to Campbell-Bannerman, 14 June 1907 (C.-Bannerman P.).
[39] Diary of F. A. Hirtzel. 14 June 1906 (IOL).

Secretary of State's advisers had begun to doubt the bona fides not only of Gokhale, but of the Aga Khan as well. Hirtzel noted in his diary that Lee-Warner 'regarded the said Brotherhood (which was to unite Hindus and Muslims) with great suspicion, and thought that the Aga had somehow got into G's [Gokhale's] power and was really playing his game. He [Lee-Warner] had an interview with J. M. [John Morley] before the Aga in order to suggest this possibility.'[40]

6

Gokhale's first interview with Morley, which took place on 9 May, went off very well.

You will be able to judge how cordial and satisfactory the interview was [he wrote home] from the fact that when I expressed the hope before parting that if Bengal affairs took much of our time at the next interview . . . he would give me a third chance of seeing him, he said: 'It is not a question, Mr Gokhale, of how many interviews I will grant you, but of how many *you* would give. And if you are equal to ten interviews, I would like to have all ten of them.[41]

A fortnight later, after the second interview, Gokhale felt grateful for having come to England 'at a time when Mr Morley's . . . opinions on India are in the process of forming'.[42]

Gokhale kept Wedderburn posted with the progress of his conversations with Morley, and Wedderburn took Ripon into his confidence. 'I am very glad', Ripon wrote to Wedderburn, 'that he [Mr Gokhale] found Mr Morley's views so consonant with his own.'[43] Wedderburn felt so optimistic that he advised Gokhale to start cultivating some of the experts of the Conservative party on India such as Lord George Hamilton and St John Brodrick and the editors of *The Times* and *The Spectator*, for 'if any Indian legislation were introduced it would be well that they should not be very antagonistic'.[44]

By the end of June, Gokhale had had five interviews and talked with Morley for seven and a half hours. Morley invited him to spend a day with him at his house. Gokhale felt confident and predicted an important statement by the Secretary of State when the Indian estimates came up before the House of Commons on 20 July. A fresh start in India seemed on the cards. If only Morley would transfer Sir

[40] Ibid., 1 June 1906.
[41] Gokhale to Dravid, 10 May 1906 (G.P.).   [42] Ibid., 25 May 1906.
[43] Ripon to Wedderburn, 6 June 1906 (Ripon P.).
[44] Wedderburn to Gokhale, 2 June 1906 (G.P.).

Bampfylde Fuller, the unpopular Governor of East Bengal, make R. C. Dutt a member of the India Council in London, and promise the reform of the legislative councils, the political climate would be transformed. It all seemed too good to be true. Would Morley be able to contend with the contrary influences around him? Would he really be allowed to open a new chapter in Indo-British relations? Torn between hope and anxiety, Gokhale found the strain of the weeks preceding the budget debate almost unbearable. He had already driven himself too hard, and his health had visibly suffered, but he did not mind paying this penalty, 'as such opportunities of work did not recur again and again'. On the eve of the budget debate, he assured his disciples in Poona, 'You will see how true is the interest aroused in the minds of some of the members of the present House [of Commons]'.[45]

Meanwhile Gokhale had a vague premonition that 'adverse influences' were at work to frustrate his mission. 'My principal work has now resolved itself', he wrote on 6 July 1906, 'into a kind of tug of war between the officials of the India Council & myself as to whose views will prevail with Mr Morley. They are so many & I am only one & moreover my opportunities of access to Mr Morley are more restricted than theirs.'[46] We know that the Godley–Lee-Warner–Hirtzel group, which had the ear of Morley and was in sympathy and even in secret correspondence with the Viceroy and senior civil servants in India, was subtly but vigorously undermining Gokhale's position, in order to avoid a dent in the bureaucratic monopoly of power.

In the second and third weeks of July the pace of events quickened. We learn from Hirtzel's diary that on 13 July 1906 Morley expressed his determination to act quickly as he 'did not want it said that with all his Liberal principles, he had done nothing' for India; one of the immediate steps he planned was the appointment of an Indian to his own Council. Hirtzel cautioned his chief against precipitate action. Three days later, he noted in his diary that after seeing Godley, the Secretary of State was inclined 'to say nothing definite in budget speech about proposed reforms but to wait for another year'. The same evening Lord Cromer met Morley at a dinner and referred to the anti-English feeling in Egypt. This set Morley thinking about a similar possibility in India. On 17 July Hirtzel cheerfully wrote in his diary: 'J. M. discussed with Lee-Warner the scheme of putting an

[45] Gokhale to Dravid, 19 July 1906 (G.P.).   [46] G.P.

Indian on his Council, and abandoned it, being greatly impressed by what L. W. [Lee-Warner] said about their [Indians'] total lack of sense of honour. . . .'

On 20 July came the long-awaited budget speech. Morley obviously spoke from the official brief, and announced no major departure in policy. The partition of Bengal remained unaltered; and there was not a word on the appointment of an Indian member to the Secretary of State's Council. During the debate Morley exhibited great impatience with the knot of radicals in his own party, Henry Cotton, O'Grady and others who had demanded swift, concrete and conciliatory measures to placate Indian discontent.

The budget debate showed that Hirtzel and his friends had won the first round in the tug-of-war for Morley's mind. They pressed their advantage home. A batch of inflammatory writings, judiciously extracted from the Indian press, was placed before the Secretary of State. Morley's reaction was on predictable lines; he was alarmed at 'disaffection' in India and saw the wisdom of supporting the man on the spot—the Viceroy. 'I seized this admission', Hirtzel gleefully recorded in his diary, 'and rubbed the idea well in and pointing out that the same principle applied to the Lieut.-Governor and the District Officer. He [Morley] said he was beginning to realize that too.'[47]

Gokhale had not been particularly happy with Morley's budget speech, and in a conversation with an officer of the India Office he said so. His remarks, possibly with some embellishments, were relayed to the Secretary of State, who was (recorded Hirtzel) 'greatly annoyed and began to suspect Gokhale of not running straight'.[48] A few days later, Godley drew Morley's attention to Gokhale's criticism. Morley burst out: 'I can forgive him [Gokhale] for being double-faced, but I can't forgive him for being so stupid.'[49]

Morley's irascibility was understandable. Hirtzel and his friends had succeeded, at least for the time being, in convincing him that the English-educated Indians were a tiny, vociferous and selfish minority, that the Congress was unrepresentative, and that Gokhale could not be trusted. Morley had been brought to a standstill by two opposing forces; his own instinct to live up to his Liberal principles, and his ambition to project himself as a practical statesman rather than a theorist. He was not an unqualified admirer of the Anglo-Indian

[47] Diary of F. A. Hirtzel, 3 Sept. 1906.
[48] Ibid., 23 June 1906.   [49] Ibid., 28 July 1906.

bureaucrats ('Risley & Co.', as he called them), but they had so over-whelmed him with the hazards of any advance that he could hardly make a move.

Morley to Lamington, 24 August 1906: . . . I believe that you appre-ciate the case as clearly as anybody. We are obliged to make a move in a liberalizing direction, whether we are particularly partial to such a move in such a country as India or not (when I said country, I ought to have said continent). The risks are pretty plain, and they may be rather formidable.

An atmosphere of general excitement may be created, with all sorts of vague expectations, aspirations and violent nonsensical babble.

The European population may fly into an angry panic, and won't forget that we are only fifty years from the Mutiny.

The Mahomedans may show their teeth against changes that they may regard as too favourable to the Hindoos.

The Hindoos, or at any rate the Bengalis, may lose their heads—not very solid heads at the best, some say.

The Princes may turn glum, for they are not really in love with the Raj, whatever they may profess.

In short the cauldron which is simmering may begin to boil.[50]

So nervous was Morley at this time that he toyed with the idea of extending Lord Kitchener's term as Commander-in-Chief of the Indian Army. He wrote to Prime Minister Campbell-Bannerman protesting against the grant of an interview to Gokhale without prior consultation with the Secretary of State for India.[51] When the Prime Minister retorted that his half an hour's interview with Gokhale mainly concerned the partition of Bengal and was 'innocent',[52] Morley pleaded that the ground of Indian affairs was tricky:

I never dreamt that your conversation with our Indian friend was other than innocent. Unimportant, a conversation between G [Gokhale] and a Prime Minister can hardly be, because it is in the interest of G to make much of it, never intended by the P.M. . . . I have to keep friends with the Viceroy, with the Civil Servants, with my own Council, with the Congress party etc. etc. Hence my anxiety lest anything should be said by you without my knowing it.[52]

Morley's last interview with Gokhale on 1 August 1906 was half an appeal and half a threat. If the Liberal Secretary of State and Minto were 'to have any chance of carrying out any reforms during

[50] Lamington P.
[51] Morley to Campbell-Bannerman, 2 Aug. 1906 (C.-Bannerman P.).
[52] *Idem*, 4 Aug. 1906 (C.-Bannerman P.).

the next two years or so, G. must keep his people quiet. If native press kept attacking them and belittling all that was done and if agitation were kept up in East Bengal [the] only result would be that they would get back into old ruts.'[53]

The possibility of a political 'truce' in India, suggested by Morley, had been spoilt by his own wobbling in the summer and autumn of 1906. True, he had postponed and not abandoned constitutional reforms, but the delay was to fatally accentuate tensions and deepen the crisis in India.

[53] Morley to Minto, 2 Aug. 1906 (M.P.).

22

The Extremist Challenge

There was little to cheer Gokhale when he left England at the end of August 1906. Not only had Morley failed to rectify the mistakes of the Tory regime in India; he had asked for a moratorium on all political agitation for a couple of years so that he and Minto could work out a scheme of reforms. Little did Morley realize that the mood of Indian nationalists, sick with hope long deferred, was already turning into one of weariness, frustration and even bitterness. The impression was growing that constitutional reforms would not be conceded by Britain and would have to be extorted from her. Shyamji Krishnavarma, who ran the India House in London and edited the *Indian Sociologist*, poured ridicule on Dadabhai Naoroji, Gokhale and other Moderate leaders for wasting time and money on the hopeless venture of converting the ruling race. Similar ideas were being propagated on the continent by the Paris India Society. Early in 1906, one of its prominent members, S. R. Rana, a scion of the ruling family of Limbdi State in western India, wrote to Wedderburn, accusing *India*, the journal of the British Committee of the Congress, of consistent hypocrisy and of betrayal of the cause of Indian nationalism. It was foolish, Rana argued, to judge the English people by the example of exceptional men like Burke, Bright and Bradlaugh. The Indian people had to rely on their own efforts and 'not to put their faith in the Englishman's vaunted justice and fairplay which was only a mockery and sham'.[1] The Liberal and Conservative parties, whatever their differences, were at one in their 'resolve that India shall be permanently under British rule'.[2] British rule had sometimes been described as a divine dispensation for India's good.

In a sense [wrote Rana] it is. Not that the Rule in itself is good, but ... it has given India a common foe to fight against. ... The last battle therefore cannot be fought in England in the House of Commons as Mr Dadabhai believes, but it shall be fought like the first one

[1] S. R. Rana to Wedderburn, 24 Jan. 1906 (G.P.).
[2] Ibid., 4 Feb. 1906.

in India, on the shores of the Arabian Sea on the island of Bombay between the plucky Tommy Atkins on one side and the gallant Gurkhas, the fiery Sikhs and the sturdy Marathas on the other side, standing shoulder to shoulder for their country, their honour and their freedom. . . .[3]

A shiver ran down Wedderburn's spine as he read Rana's letters. He passed them on to Allan Hume, his colleague on the British Committee. Hume's comments were characteristically blunt:

I understand Rana's position, but none the less agree with you that he is foolish. . . . If there were only 3 or 4 hundred thousand of them [Indians] out of 270 millions ready to sacrifice their own interests, ready to fight—ready to die nobly in the cause, I should agree with him—but there are only at most a dozen, who are ready to do even as much as Gokhale does—& not one who is ready to fight to the death—our line of proceeding is the only possible one. . . .[4]

S. R. Rana also corresponded with Gokhale and commended to him an article in the *Indian Sociologist*, in which Shyamji Krishna-varma had ridiculed the Congress aspiration for a self-governing colony and demanded an 'absolutely free and independent form of national government'. The letter arrived as Gokhale was about to leave for India. Rana and his friends met Gokhale at the Paris railway station. There was not enough time for a full discussion, but Gokhale promised to write to them, and to send them the prospectus of the Servants of India Society.

Had it been possible for me [he wrote to these Indian revolutionaries in Paris] to spend some time in Paris, it would have given me great pleasure to discuss the subject with you and other friends. But it is too large for letters. I consider Mr Shyamji's views . . . altogether crude, such as an unpractical man, living at a distance of six thousand miles from his country, where all work of regeneration has to be done, dreaming dreams without thought of the [human] material available, and the difficulties to be overcome, may find it delightful to express. My life is given to humble practical work in India and not until Mr S[hyamji] returns to India and tries to put his theories into practice need I or any other Congress worker trouble to consider what he thinks of our work.[5]

2

Scepticism about the efficacy of the Congress aims and methods was not confined to the knot of Indian revolutionaries in London

[3] Ibid.   [4] Hume to Wedderburn, 30 Jan. 1906 (G.P.).   [5] G.P.

and Paris. In the summer of 1906, while Gokhale was in England, the political temperature had risen in India, and especially in Bengal. In April there was a clash at Barisal between a Congress procession and the police, which had objected to the shouting of ' *bande mataram*'. Among those arrested was the veteran Surendranath Banerjea, a former president of the Indian National Congress. Sir Bampfylde Fuller, Governor of the new province of East Bengal and Assam, seemed eager to establish a reputation as a strong man. He tightened official control over schools and colleges, and sought to crush the *swadeshi* and boycott movements. 'I am not given to using unduly strong language', Gokhale told a London audience on 5 May 1906, 'but I feel bound to say . . . that Sir B. Fuller's Government has in six months done more to discredit the character of British rule in India than have all the denunciations of the worst critics of that rule, Indian and European, ever done during a hundred years.'[6] The students, who were in the vanguard of the anti-partition agitation, especially incurred the wrath of Fuller's government. 'A Government commanding 260,000 or 500,000 soldiers', observed Lajpat Rai, 'stooping to strike us by striking at our boys. . . . What would people conclude that this mighty government, with so many guns and cannons, with so many armies and with such an array of statesmen, have begun to fight with boys?'[7] Even the British-owned *Statesman* thought the East Bengal Government had 'blundered apparently into a childish and futile policy which can only have the effect of manufacturing an army of martyrs'.[8]

In his *A Nation in Making* Surendranath Banerjea has left a graphic account of the emotional upsurge in Bengal in the wake of the partition. 'A strange atmosphere is created. Young and old, rich and poor, literate and illiterate, all breathe it, and all are swayed and moved and even transported by the invisible influence that is felt. Reason halts; judgment is held in suspense; it is one mighty impulse that moves the heart of the community and carries everything before it.' Banerjea's description faithfully portrays the mood, if not of the whole of Bengal, at least that of an important section of it, the Hindu *bhadralok*. Almost overnight *swadeshi* and boycott movements received the stamp of patriotism, and the use of foreign cloth, foreign salt, foreign sugar and even foreign drugs

[6] Karve & Ambekar (eds.), op. cit., vol. II, p. 358.
[7] L. Rai's speech at the Benares Congress, in V. C. Joshi (ed.), *Lala Lajpat Rai: Writings and Speeches*, vol. I, Delhi, 1966, p. 99.
[8] Banerjea, *A Nation in Making*, p. 182.

acquired a touch of odium. Old habits of thought received a sudden jolt. Surendranath Banerjea, who dressed, spoke, wrote and even looked like an Englishman, has recorded how, 'on an impulse of the moment', he administered to a gathering in the courtyard of a village temple, 'the religious vow' to use only goods made in India.[9]

This was Banerjea's triumphant hour. The College Square in Calcutta resounded with his oratory, admiring crowds followed him, and his feet ached with hundreds reverentially taking the dust off them. It soon became obvious that he had drifted into a radical posture not so much from conviction as from a craving for popularity. Before long his leadership was to be challenged by others who could outbid him in radicalism and even in eloquence.

Throughout 1906 Banerjea's position in his own province was being undermined by Bipin Chandra Pal and Aurobindo Ghose, who had begun to question the aims and methods of the Congress. What had the Congress achieved, they asked, by twenty years of constitutional agitation? Had not the British bureaucracy mistaken the restraint of the Congress for cowardice? Had not the excellently-worded resolutions of the Congress found their way into the official wastepaper basket? Had not the representatives of the Crown in India even declined to receive the deputations of the Congress leaders? Bipin Chandra Pal had no doubt that 'the ideal of self-government within the Empire, this [Congress] policy of association with and opposition to the Government, this policy of helping to smooth down the rough places of the administration'[10] was doomed to failure. Aurobindo Ghose (whom the British journalist Nevinson described as 'grave with intensity, careless of fate, one of the most silent men I have known, he was of the stuff that dreamers are made of, but dreamers who will act their dream, indifferent to the means'[11]) considered that the ideal of colonial self-government for India was a political monstrosity and a negation of Indian patriotism. The only worthwhile ideal for India, argued Aurobindo, was absolute autonomy, unqualified *swaraj*. He regarded the expansion of legislative councils, and the appointment of Indians to the Executive Council of the Viceroy or the India Council in London as red herrings across the path of nationalism. Such 'reforms' could do little good to a subject people; in fact the worse the government, the better it was

[9] Ibid., p. 212.
[10] *Speeches of Bipin Chandra Pal Delivered at Madras*, Madras, 1907, p. 48.
[11] Nevinson, op. cit., p. 226.

for the cause of political emancipation. Thus viewed, the partition of Bengal was the best thing that could have happened to India, for it had stirred national feeling and dissipated the lethargy of decades.

Aurobindo Ghose took a year's leave from Baroda, where he was employed in the Gaikwad's service, came down to Calcutta, and joined the *Bande Mataram*, a weekly paper started by Bipin Chandra Pal. Aurobindo's eloquent English prose turned *Bande Mataram* into a heady wine for the 'New Party', which was now openly questioning not only the right of the British Government to rule India, but also the right of the veteran leaders of the Congress to speak for the Indian people.

3

Of the Congress leaders outside Bengal, Tilak was the first to recognize the potential of the ferment in Bengal for the cause of Indian nationalism. The partition struck him not so much as a British blunder as an Indian opportunity. He extended his support to the anti-partition agitation and the new Extremist leaders emerging in Bengal. Gokhale had seen the beginnings of this alliance at Benares in December 1905. In the following year, it became closer. One of its first fruits was the celebration of the Shivaji festival in Bengal. When Tilak arrived for the celebration in June 1906, he received a thunderous welcome. He drove through the streets of Calcutta amidst deafening cries of '*bande mataram*' and '*Shivaji ki jai*', and with banners and drums; his carriage was unhorsed and drawn by wildly cheering students. He addressed crowded meetings, some in English and the others in Hindustani, and impressed Bengalis and Marwaris alike. When he went for a 'public bath' to the Ganges, the scene (Khaparde wrote in his diary) was 'unique, and they worshipped Tilak like a god. Part of the worship was transferred to us also. They touched our feet, put the mud of our feet on their heads. . . .'[12]

The Tilak–Bipin Chandra Pal alliance caused deep concern not only to the government, but also to the Congress leadership. In the Indian National Congress Tilak's position had long been that of a dissident, if not of a thinly disguised rebel. Pherozeshah Mehta, Wacha, and indeed the entire Bombay group of Moderates had a lively distrust of Tilak. This distrust dated back to the controversies

[12] Diary entry, 10 June 1906.

which raged in Poona in the 1890s; its origins lay partly in ideological and partly in temperamental differences. For at least fifteen years there had been a sort of cold war, which hindered not only mutual understanding, but even mutual comprehension between the Congress Establishment in India—of which Pherozeshah Mehta was the virtual chief—and Tilak.

Tilak suffered greatly from the malignant hostility of the British while he lived. After his death he has probably suffered no less at the hands of uncritical admirers, who have tended to present him not as a flesh-and-blood politician, but as a mythical hero. The image of Tilak as an uncompromising champion of *swaraj*, a reckless patriot hurling defiance at the mighty British raj, while the craven Moderates lay low, does less than justice to the subtlety, stamina and flexibility of a consummate politician who managed to survive the bitter hostility of the government for nearly forty years.

As we have already seen, Tilak had all along an anti-British, almost an anti-western streak: how far this was due to his attachment to the tenets and traditions of his ancestral faith it is difficult to say. Agarkar, once a comrade and then a bitter critic, alleged that Tilak's conservatism was the result of calculation, rather than of conviction; that he trimmed his sails to catch the winds of popularity. We have already seen Tilak's attitude to the Age of Consent Bill.[13] No less astonishing was his opposition to inoculation against plague. The idea, he wrote in the *Kesari*, 'that many infectious diseases occurred when some sort of very small germs enter the body is only about twenty-five years old. . . . Simply because the people of India are very poor and tolerant, it is very hard to try to test half-baked scientific discoveries on them.'[14]

The love of Maharashtra and Hinduism were primary ingredients in Tilak's philosophy. In the early years he often wrote and spoke of the 'Mahratta nation', and was not very vocal about the common nationality of the Mahrattas, the Punjabis and the Bengalis.[15] His work on the antiquity of the *Vedas* and his commentary on the *Gita* gave him the status of a scholar-statesman and made him the idol of the Hindu community. In 1893–4 when riots broke out in Bombay and Poona he accused the local officials, with some justification, of partisanship towards the Muslim community; Tilak's role was more that of an advocate of his own community than that of an objective

---

[13] *Supra*, chap. 9.   [14] *Kesari*, 25 Sept. 1901.
[15] Ibid., 25 April 1901.

observer. It was only from 1905 onwards that Tilak tended to shed his regional and religious prepossessions and to grow into a national leader.

Tilak refuted the charge that his propagation of the Shivaji festival or the congregational twist he had given to the Ganapati celebrations had an anti-Muslim inspiration. These festivals, he affirmed, were intended to give to the masses a sense of belonging and to evoke in them a pride in their past. Tilak argued that it was the peculiar predicament of Maharashtra in the seventeenth century that had led to the emergence of Shivaji. A great future leader of India could be born anywhere in India 'and who knows, may even be a Muhammadan'.[16] Tilak dismissed the idea that the polity of Shivaji or of the Peshwas could be restored in twentieth-century India. 'We Indians', he wrote, 'have learnt at our own cost the lesson of the importance of popular and representative government, and that is exactly the reason why our aspirations seem to be different from the patent oriental ideal.'[17]

Tilak was, in the eyes of the British officials, the archetype of the subtle, seditious Poona Brahman. In 1882, he had been convicted for publishing defamatory articles against Barve, the minister of Kolhapur State. In 1897 he received a sentence of twelve months for 'seditious writings' in the *Kesari*. Three years later he was implicated in the Tai Maharaj case, which dragged its weary course for several years. Indeed, the Damocles' sword of prosecution often hung over Tilak's head when he was out of prison. His worst ordeal came in 1908 when he was deported to Burma and lodged in the Mandalay fort for six years. British officials in India learnt to equate Tilak with sedition and subversion. In July 1899 the British General commanding the Poona garrison wrote to the Viceroy: 'I do not think you need fear any rising yet, though I know for a fact that Tilak is working hard, preaching the doctrine of unity amongst all Mahratta Brahmins.'[18] Fifteen years later, immediately after Tilak's release from Mandalay, the Bombay Government directed all its officers to regard him 'as an enemy of the British Government' and to consider people who associated with him to be 'unfriendly'.[19]

---

[16] *Mahratta*, 24 June 1906.
[17] *Bal Gangadhar Tilak, His Writings and Speeches*, Appreciation by Aurobindo Ghose, Madras, 1918, p. 80.
[18] C. J. Burnett to the P.S. to Viceroy, 13 July 1899 (C.P.).
[19] Confdl. Circular No. S.D. 1137 of 26 June 1914, File 1703 of 1914, Jud. Dept., Bombay Govt.

Despite—and perhaps because of—this persistent and vindictive pursuit by the authorities, Tilak was neither a reckless politician nor a careless journalist. Aurobindo Ghose, who knew and admired him, testified to his 'conservative temperament, strongly in touch with the sense of the people',[20] and suggested that in a free country he would probably have figured as an

advanced liberal statesman . . . careful of every step . . . always seeking to carry the conservative instinct of the nation with him in every change. . . . [he] will take willingly half a loaf than no bread, though always with a full intention of getting the whole loaf in good time. . . . Such a man is no natural revolutionary, but a constitutionalist by temperament.[21]

Training in law and a lifelong study of Hindu religious and philosophical texts had taught Tilak the art of logic-chopping and hair-splitting which reduced his opponents to despair. He knew how to adapt his language to his audience. He had a gift for the deadly metaphor, especially in Marathi, and drew his illustrations not from the writings of Burke and Macaulay, but from the *Ramayana* and the *Mahabharata*; his irony gave a sharp edge to his speeches and writings. 'God has not conferred upon foreigners', he once wrote, 'the grant inscribed on a copper plate to the kingdom of India.'[22] On another occasion, he argued, 'as men have not given up building houses for fear that rats should dig up holes, so we should not give up our aims for fear of government displeasure'.[23] 'What was sedition?' he once asked. 'Was there not treason to the people in the Penal Code of God, who is the king of kings?'[24] He agreed that political revolution in India should be bloodless, but added: 'The path of duty is never sprinkled with rose-water nor do roses grow on it.'[25]

In the 1880s and 1890s Tilak occasionally criticized particular policies of the Indian National Congress, but not until 1906 did he challenge its broad strategy or its leadership. A few weeks before the Bombay Congress (December 1904) rumours reached Dadabhai Naoroji in England that Tilak was restive and might create difficulties for the Congress leadership. Dadabhai at once wrote to Tilak not to

---

[20] *Tilak's Writings and Speeches*, p. 12.   [21] Ibid., p. 14.
[22] *Kesari*, 15 June 1897, quoted by Wolpert in *Tilak and Gokhale*, Berkeley, California, 1961, p. 87.
[23] *Tilak's Writings and Speeches*, p. 88.
[24] Quoted by Wolpert, op. cit., p. 218.
[25] *Tilak's Writings and Speeches*, p. 76.

take any hasty step and to help maintain the unity of the Congress.[26] Tilak immediately reassured Dadabhai.

B. G. Tilak to Dadabhai Naoroji, 6 December 1904: . . . First of all let me assure you, once for all, that I have never been, nor am I in any way against the Congress. Constitutional agitation, I shall be the last person to decry. But I am rather sanguine by temperament, and think that we must push our efforts to their logical extreme. I firmly believe—and let me tell you that you yourself have been the principal cause of this belief—that if we wish to get any rights or privileges we must agitate in England in a missionary spirit. The Anglo-Indians here won't listen to what we say. The pressure must come from England. . . . I do maintain that without persistent work in England carried on by our own men, mere annual gathering in India would be of no avail. What a grand thing it would be . . . if Sir P. M. Mehta, Mr Surendranath Banerjea or Rai Bahadur Ananda Charlu were to go to England and stay there for some years agitating the Indian questions like your noble self?

. . . I have attended most of the Congress sessions and I am going to attend the coming one also.[27]

Tilak attended the Bombay Congress in December 1904 and favoured the stationing of a permanent Congress delegation in England. A few months later, he was ridiculing the Congress leadership for seeking concessions from the British Government and accusing it of 'mendicancy'.

4

Tilak's volte-face was due to the change in the political situation in the wake of the partition of Bengal. The storm of protest in Bengal and its repercussions in other provinces created the climate in which political consciousness could be sharpened. 'If you forget your grievances', Tilak told a Calcutta audience on 7 June 1906, 'by hearing words of sympathy, then the cause is gone. You must make a permanent cause of grievance. Store up the grievances till they are removed. Partition grievance will be the edifice for the regeneration of India.'[28] The grievance was not merely against an unpopular act of the alien regime, but against the alien regime itself. 'The point is', Tilak told a Calcutta meeting in January 1907, 'to have the entire control in our hands. I want the key of my house and not merely one

[26] Naoroji to Tilak, 2 Nov. 1904, in N. C. Kelkar, op. cit., vol. II, 4, p. 83.
[27] M. D. Vidwans (ed.), *Letters of Lokamanya Tilak*, Poona, 1966, pp. 253–4.
[28] *Tilak's Writings and Speeches*, p. 26.

stranger turned out of it.'[29] He discounted the possibility of converting the British people by sending deputations to England or pleading at the bar of English opinion. 'Our object', he said, 'is to attract the attention of England to our wrongs by diverting trade and obstructing the government.'

Long before the partition of Bengal, Tilak had criticized the narrow base of the Congress and suggested the induction into it of the semi-literate and even some of the illiterate millions in the towns and villages of India. It was true that they did not understand the niceties of constitutional problems, but without their backing the Congress could hardly hope to be a power in the land. 'Just as without gun-powder, bullets can do nothing,' wrote Tilak, 'so too, so long as the peasants, artisans and merchants are not in agreement with you, nothing can come out of your learning.'[30] Tilak's faith in the masses was not shared by most of the older Congress leaders, who viewed political education as a slow and gradual process. Pherozeshah Mehta had stated in 1890:

If the masses were capable of giving articulate expression to definite demands then the time would have arrived not for consultative Councils, but for representative institutions. . . . It is because they are unable to do so that the function and the duty devolve upon their educated and enlightened compatriots to feel, to understand and interpret their grievances and requirements, and to suggest and to indicate how these can be best redressed and met.[31]

Gokhale affirmed repeatedly that the small English-educated class constituted the brain and the voice of the dumb millions of India. Tilak wanted the Congress not only to win the support of the English-educated minority, which numbered scarcely a million, but to penetrate the five millions versed in the vernaculars and even some layers of the unlettered 250 millions. He was not prepared to wait until all these millions could be educated in schools, which the government had in any case neither the funds nor perhaps the will to set up.

The divergence in political outlook between Tilak and the Congress Establishment (of which Gokhale was a member and the ablest spokesman) was sharpened by a clash of personalities. Two decades of factional politics in Poona had left a legacy of suspicion and mistrust. Gokhale had not forgotten or forgiven the ferocity with

[29] Ibid., p. 64.   [30] *Kesari*, 12 Nov. 1895.
[31] H. P. Mody, *Sir Pherozeshah Mehta*, Bombay, 1921, vol. I, p. 258.

which Tilak's adherents and newspapers had pursued Agarkar over the Age of Consent Bill in 1891, and Ranade over the holding of the Social Conference in the Congress pavilion in 1895. In 1897, in the wake of the apology incident, Gokhale himself had been reduced to a political pariah. Innuendoes and recriminations between the two factions in Poona had become a routine. In 1899 there was a direct confrontation; Gokhale contested a seat in the Bombay Legislative Council against Tilak and won it.

Unlike Tilak, Gokhale did not take the game of factional politics in his stride. A misstatement, a harsh phrase, or an unkind innuendo in a newspaper could give him a sleepless night. During the excitement of the Ganapati or Shivaji festivals in Poona he was sometimes ridiculed and maligned in songs and speeches. Tilak may not have been responsible for initiating these attacks on his political rival, but he does not seem to have checked the excessive zeal of his adherents. Gokhale was so unhappy at these recurrent attacks that in 1902–3 he thought of leaving Poona for good and settling in Bombay. Two years later we find Narayan G. Chandavarkar writing to him: 'I have heard with pain and shame of the manner in which your opponents in the Extremist camp have been speaking and writing about and against you.'[32] Gokhale found that whatever he said or did was put in an unfavourable light by his opponents. It was insinuated, for example, that being a Member of the Viceroy's Legislative Council, he felt obliged to do what Lord Minto told him. He was called a 'Vibhishana' who had deserted his brother Ravana to join the enemy's camp. His visits to England were ridiculed. He was accused of wasting time and money, and of pursuing a will-o'-the-wisp.

Because of this long history of conflict, it is not surprising that Gokhale should have entertained a deep mistrust of Tilak and his adherents. An idea of this mistrust may be formed from a letter he wrote to Pherozeshah Mehta on Tilak's offer (made at the Bombay Congress) to raise funds for a Congress Deputation to England.

Gokhale to Pherozeshah Mehta, 25 January 1905: There is one suggestion [regarding] . . . the ten thousand rupees that you have guaranteed for the Bombay Presidency in connection with the expenses for the proposed deputation [to England].

The resolution about the deputation was seconded by Mr Tilak, who has, on several occasions, expressed his readiness to raise the portion that may be allotted to the Deccan for the purpose. . . . take

---

[32] N. G. Chandavarkar to Gokhale, 2 Oct. 1904 (G.P.).

him at his word and ask him to raise about one-third (say, three thousand rupees out of the total). Two points will be gained by your insisting on Mr Tilak taking the share of the burden. In the first instance your personal responsibility will be reduced from ten to seven thousand, and secondly Mr Tilak would be committed definitely and practically to our raising and spending money for the purpose of agitation in England.

I am afraid there will be great difficulty in your actually getting the amount from him, but in that case you will put it out of his power to talk tall and come forward with impractical proposals.[33]

Tilak knew that he was not a *persona grata* with the Moderate group in Bombay. But he was too shrewd a politician to throw down the gauntlet until a suitable opportunity offered itself. The opportunity came with the partition of Bengal in 1905. In December of that year at the Benares Congress, Tilak forged an alliance with the radicals of Bengal. A year later, with the deepening of the political crisis, he felt emboldened to openly challenge the Congress Establishment. Calcutta as the venue of the 1906 Congress offered him an advantage which he was quick to seize.

[33] G.P.

23

The Widening Rift

'You have not returned a day too early', R. N. Mudholkar, the Moderate leader from Berar, wrote to Gokhale on 14 September 1906. 'During your absence events have moved fast, and far into the sea of trouble is the ship of Congress gone.'[1] Mudholkar was referring to dissensions within the Congress organization which were undermining its unity and raising a big question-mark over the next annual session due to be held at Calcutta in December 1906.

It was at the Benares session, over which Gokhale had presided, that the 1906 Congress was invited to Calcutta. Surendranath Banerjea, Bhupendranath Basu and other Bengali Moderates did not take long to realize that it was 'improvident' to have invited the Congress to Calcutta.[2] They were under fire from Bipin Chandra Pal and the young radicals thrown up by the anti-partition agitation. Personal animosities combined with the clash of ideologies to produce a deadlock in the Bengal Congress. No love was lost between Pal and Banerjea, or between Banerjea and Motilal Ghose. There was continual sniping between the *Amrita Bazar Patrika* and the *Bengalee*. Anglo-Indian newspapers added to the confusion by playing off one Congress faction against the other, and the Muslims against the Hindus.

A reception committee for the annual session had been formed at Calcutta early in 1906, but it was much too unwieldy and heterogeneous a body for effective action. Neither the Moderates nor the Extremists were sure of a majority in the reception committee, and the crucial meeting to elect a working committee and the president for the Congress session was put off. Bipin Chandra Pal and his adherents were in touch with Tilak and the Poona Extremists. While Gokhale was in England, Khaparde, Tilak's lieutenant in C.P. and Berar, issued a 'circular' letter proposing Lajpat Rai for the Congress presidency. 'My own idea', Wedderburn told Gokhale, 'would be

---

[1] G.P.   [2] B. Basu to Gokhale, 9 Oct. 1906 (G.P.).

to let Messrs Tilak & Co. to have a trial in the management and honours of the Congress.'[3] This was an eminently sensible suggestion, but wholly repugnant to Pherozeshah Mehta and the Bombay Moderates, who threatened to keep away from the Calcutta Congress if Tilak or any other Extremist leader was elected president.[4]

In September 1906 the situation in Bengal seemed sufficiently menacing to Gokhale to claim his attention immediately after his return from England. He called twice on Tilak, who happened to be in Bombay, and took counsel with Pherozeshah Mehta. A discussion was arranged in Pherozeshah's chambers; among those who were persuaded to attend it was Tilak, but no agreement could be reached. Gokhale planned a visit to Calcutta, but, on second thoughts, decided to send his assistant G. K. Devadhar for a preliminary survey of the situation. Devadhar's telegrams gave a depressing picture. Gokhale shared his misgivings with his friend Krishnaswami Aiyer.

Gokhale to Krishnaswami Aiyer, 29 September 1906: Even if all arrangements for the next Congress are completed in time and the Congress does meet in Calcutta during next Christmas, there will be great trouble about the programme of work. Bipin Chandra Pal and his party are working hard to get a large contingent of delegates on their side and they want to sweep the present programme of the Congress clean off the board and substitute in its place only three resolutions, the first declaring our inherent right to govern ourselves and demanding autonomy, absolute and immediate, free from foreign control; the second calling upon all Congressmen to withdraw their sons and wards from all government institutions and make independent provision for their education so that the rising generation should grow up full of a determination to wrest complete autonomy from England; and the third advocating not only Swadeshism in the industrial field but a comprehensive boycott against everything English . . . so that the only points of contact between the government and the people should be those of violent hatred. This is the programme of the new Bengal Party and they profess they will make no compromise with anyone who proposes to agitate for mere reforms, as the success of such agitation would mean an improved and therefore a prolonged foreign rule. They are claiming Mr Tilak as their leader, though we all know that he does not believe in the practicability of their programme; only as is his wont, he will do nothing to discourage their belief that he is their leader.

When the Congress meets, if it meets at all in Calcutta, we must be prepared for violent scenes and disorderly attempts to make its work

[3] Wedderburn to Gokhale, 8 Aug. 1906 (G.P.).
[4] Samaldas to Gokhale, 14 July 1906 (G.P.).

on old lines impossible. It is sad, inexpressibly sad, that all this should occur at the very moment when the Viceroy and the Secretary of State are contemplating an important step forward. It may be that we are, after all, as an ancient writer says, 'the mere sport of an aimless destiny'.[5]

The crisis in the Congress was partly due to the revolt of the younger generation against its leadership. Gokhale's friend G. A. Natesan, the Madras publisher, argued that the crisis could have been averted by greater flexibility on the part of Pherozeshah Mehta in conceding a democratic constitution for the Congress. That Pherozeshah had sometimes been much too rigid and obstinate was true, but in Gokhale's opinion this could hardly explain, much less justify, the Extremists' behaviour. Natesan's argument provoked Gokhale into perhaps the frankest criticism of his political opponents which he ever made in writing. The fact that he was addressing a friend, in whose discretion he had complete confidence, made this analysis uninhibited.

Gokhale to Natesan, 2 October 1906: I do not think that two at least of the three (Messrs Tilak and Pal) would ever have been really conciliated by any compromise on the subject of a constitution. Mr Pal has never worked for the Congress in the past. He is a very unscrupulous man and inordinately ambitious. Being a very powerful speaker, he does not see why he should not have the same influence in the country as Mr Surendranath [Banerjea] and he is determined to play the role of a leader at all costs. He uses brave words, but behind these words, there is neither courage nor character and, of course, there is no judgement, and I have little doubt that in a year or two, we shall see this man's collapse, whatever noise he may succeed in making temporarily. . . .

Mr Tilak is, of course, in many respects a wholly different kind of man, but he too, I am sorry to say, is afflicted with an ambition to which there are no limits. It is with great reluctance that I say this because I know the great admiration and affection you have for him, and I have no desire to pain you in any way. Moreover, my own relations with him have now been unsatisfactory for a long time and it might easily be said, that my estimate of him was not likely to be charitable or even fair. I make it a rule therefore never to say a word of criticism about him publicly. But in writing to a friend like you, some freedom may be permitted to me which I do not claim on other occasions.

Mr Tilak has a matchless capacity for intrigue and he is not burdened with an exacting conscience. As a result, he is often about to play for his own hand when to all appearances, he is fighting for a

[5] G.P.

principle only. His great talents, his simple habits, his sturdy and dauntless spirit and above all the cruel persecution which he has had to bear at the hands of the Government have won for him the hearts of the millions in all parts of the country. And this general affection and admiration make it comparatively easy for him to play his game.

I think you will agree with me when I say that no man of our time was ever more pure-minded or more humble, more entirely devoted to national welfare and more anxious for conciliation all round than the late Mr Ranade, and yet Mr Ranade in spite of his utmost efforts failed to conciliate Mr Tilak, not only in matters of social reform but in regard to political work also. While therefore Sir Pherozeshah Mehta's unyielding and somewhat dictatorial attitude may be justly deplored, I do not think a greater conciliation on his part would have made any difference as regards Mr Tilak's ambition and his methods.

Lala Lajpat Rai as a public worker is, I think, more selfless than either Mr Tilak or Mr Pal. I am sure that though his name is being freely used by Mr Pal and his party, he is not with them in their views or methods. . . .[6]

By October 1906 the Calcutta session had become an occasion for a trial of strength between the two parties in Bengal. The Congress presidency was the chief bone of contention. The Extremists, led by B. C. Pal and Aurobindo Ghose, favoured Tilak, but the Moderates refused to accept him. The latter then resorted to an unscrupulous manoeuvre. Without formally consulting the reception committee, they cabled an invitation to Dadabhai Naoroji to accept the Congress presidency. After Dadabhai had accepted, the Extremists were presented with a *fait accompli*. The eighty-one year-old leader was held in such high esteem that public opposition to his presidency was unthinkable. Though Pal rudely cabled Dadabhai to keep his hands off the Calcutta session,[7] few members of his party, and least of all Tilak, dared openly to object to the election of Dadabhai.

2

'You have saved us from a crisis', Surendranath Banerjea wrote to Dadabhai when he agreed to preside over the Congress.[8] Little did Banerjea know that the crisis was only just beginning. The Extremists brought large contingents of delegates from Maharashtra, the Punjab and Berar to Calcutta and enrolled a large number of delegates from

[6] Ibid.   [7] Sastri, *Life and Times of Sir Pherozeshah Mehta*, pp. 89–90.
[8] Masani, op. cit., p. 497.

Bengal. Even before the Congress assembled, a fierce controversy broke out over a speech delivered by the Viceroy, while opening the Indian Industrial and Agricultural Exhibition, which was part of the annual Congress ritual. 'I shall at any rate rejoice', said Minto, 'if my presence would contribute to confirm the dissociation of *swadeshi* from political aspirations.' This was a deliberate and gratuitous affront to the Extremists. 'I know', Minto confided to the Secretary of State, 'there was a bitter quarrel on this issue. It seemed rather an opportunity of giving Moderates a pat on the back.'[9] Surendranath Banerjea and his Moderate friends, who invited the Viceroy to open the exhibition, had blundered. Minto's provocative words enabled the Extremists to whip up popular emotion and to raise the political temperature in Calcutta on the eve of the Congress. Public feeling would have been further inflamed had it been known that the proposal to sing the Bande Mataram was dropped from the programme inaugurating the exhibition in deference to the Viceroy's wishes![10]

Throughout the last week of 1906 Calcutta was in turmoil. It was 'a succession of meetings, conferences, private and public discussions'.[11] The Extremists formed themselves into a pressure group, with Tilak, Pal, Khaparde, Aurobindo Ghose and Aswini Kumar Dutt as its leading lights. 'We have a clear majority here', Khaparde noted in his diary, 'and a great deal of local support.'[12] Dadabhai Naoroji summoned the leaders of the two factions to the house of his host, the Maharaja of Darbhangha, for a preliminary discussion. The really contentious resolutions were those on boycott and *swadeshi*. There were heated exchanges between Pal, Khaparde and Tilak on the one hand, and Mehta, Malaviya and Gokhale on the other. The President-elect 'did not open his lips during the proceedings', and said his opinions would be known when his presidential speech was read.

The meeting of the Subjects Committee, where the resolutions for the full Congress session were discussed and amended, was stormy. 'The Extremists are in the ascendant', Motilal Nehru wrote to his son, just as he was about to attend the Subjects Committee meeting, 'and they outnumber the Moderates.'[13] Pherozeshah Mehta was a special target for the Extremists' fury. They objected to his sitting next to the President, and shouted: 'Down with Mehta', 'Kick him

[9] Minto to Morley, 26 Dec. 1906 (M.P.).
[10] *Idem*, 19 Dec. 1906 (M.P.).
[11] Khaparde Diary, 31 Dec. 1906.
[12] Ibid.   [13] Motilal to Jawaharlal, 27 Dec. 1906 (Nehru P.).

out'.[14] Mehta, Malaviya and Gokhale were heckled and booed. The debate on the *swadeshi* and boycott resolutions was extremely acrimonious. The Extremists functioned more or less as a solid bloc. Dadabhai declined to put the disputed resolutions to the vote; the Extremists walked out in protest and threatened to challenge the resolutions in the plenary session.

The following morning, as the time for the plenary session approached, tension rose to a high pitch. Fortunately, before it was too late, Daji Abaji Khare, a delegate from Bombay, arranged a private discussion in which Tilak, Mehta and others joined. Tilak was unyielding. 'You would not and could not have treated me so in Bombay', Mehta told Tilak. 'If provoked to it', retorted Tilak, 'we would show you a sample even in Bombay.'[15] A compromise was hurriedly hammered out; the resolutions on the partition of Bengal, *swadeshi* and boycott were re-phrased and secured a smooth passage in the open session.

The re-phrasing of the resolutions did not unite the minds and hearts of the antagonists. The desperate expedient of inviting the octogenarian Dadabhai from England to preside over the Congress staved off an open rupture in the Congress, but it did not bring the two factions really closer. Indeed, if a new synthesis had to be worked out between the 'Old' and the 'New' parties, Dadabhai was hardly the man for it. Undoubtedly, he was, as Gokhale put it, 'the foremost Indian of our time, the man without self or stain', but he was not fit to play the role of an umpire or peacemaker. Apart from the fact that his powers were failing, he was wholly committed to the Moderate strategy: indeed he was one of its authors, and had preached and practised it far too long to think of an alternative, or even of any modification of it. He was far too removed from the new winds which had swept young India off its feet. Ironically, just before he left England, he was canvassing for a 'safe' seat in the House of Commons, and Wedderburn was trying to get him nominated to the Secretary of State's Council.[16]

Dadabhai's presidential speech shocked the Anglo-Indian press. The *Civil & Military Gazette* concluded that 'the veteran agitator in his old days had gone over to the Extremists'. The *Englishman* complained that Dadabhai, who had been invited by the Moderates to

[14] Sastri, op. cit., p. 90.
[15] Khaparde Diary, 31 Dec. 1906.
[16] Gokhale to H. A. Wadya, 1 Nov. 1906 (G.P.).

quench the flames of hatred against British rule in India, had used kerosene for the purpose.

Dadabhai's presidential address, despite its mention of the magic word *swaraj* (self-government), was in fact not a revolutionary statement. It began in a pedestrian fashion with quotations from British Liberals, John Bright, Henry Fawcett, Campbell-Bannerman and John Morley. It appealed to the spirit of Queen Victoria's Proclamation of 1858 and sought support in the pronouncements of former British Prime Ministers. It made out a case for self-government, but some of the arguments may sound curious today, such as the statement that Indians were British citizens entitled to all the rights of British citizens 'as if born and living in England' from the moment they came under the British flag.[17] Dadabhai conceded that the Congress had not achieved much during the first twenty years of its life, but struck a note of optimism for the future because of the Liberal revival in England. He argued that petitions to the British Parliament and press were not a form of 'mendicancy', but claims for rights and justice. There was no such thing as a 'settled fact' in British politics; measures defeated in the British Parliament could be revived and passed under pressure of public opinion. This had happened with the abolition of slavery, the game laws, and the extension of franchise, and could happen in the case of reforms for India. 'The fact that we have more or less failed', said Dadabhai, 'is not because we have petitioned too much, but that we have petitioned too little.'[18]

This was a reiteration of the traditional Moderate creed. Arguing from the same old premises, Dadabhai had come to the same old conclusions. It is true that he used some hard-hitting expressions, but there was a strange contradiction between his verbal vehemence and his staid adherence to sober constitutional politics. 'What we do not understand', the *Indian Social Reformer* once wrote about Dadabhai, 'is arguing for revolution, and asking for, say, the separation of executive and judicial functions.'[19] Ironically, some of the stronger passages in his presidential speech owed their retention in it to an accident. Dadabhai sent the text of his address to Wacha, and asked him to show it to Pherozeshah Mehta before it was printed. Wacha, in a fit of absent-mindedness, sent it off to Calcutta without waiting for Mehta's comments. Mehta was furious: he wanted to tone down parts of Dadabhai's address, but it was too late.[20]

---

[17] *Congress Presidential Addresses*, First Ser. 1885–1916, Madras, 1935, p. 719.
[18] Ibid., p. 739.   [19] *Indian Social Reformer*, 2 Oct. 1904.
[20] C. Setalvad to Gokhale, 16 Dec. 1906 (G.P.).

As the president of the Congress and its committees, Dadabhai was hardly effective. It was one thing to command reverence from a distance of six thousand miles; it was another to arbitrate between contending factions, swayed by political passion and personal rivalries. It is true that he was personally spared by the Extremist hecklers, but he could hardly have enjoyed the role of a passive chairman, who could neither reconcile nor control the conflicting pressures. The *Bande Mataram*, the voice of the Bengali Extremists, published, on the opening day of the Congress session, an article entitled 'The Man of the Present and the Man of the Future'. It was an unflattering comparison of Dadabhai Naoroji with Tilak. Dadabhai was described as 'worn and aged, bowed down with the burden of half a century of toils and labour, . . . a man of the past, reminding us of a generation that is passing away, ideals that have lost their charm, methods that have been found to be futile, and energy and hope once buoyant and full of life, which now live on only a wearied and decrepit old age, phantom-like, still babbling exploded generalities and dead formulas.'[21]

The Calcutta Congress revealed that the respect and even the awe in which the Founding Fathers of the Congress had long been held were fast evaporating. Pherozeshah Mehta had to swallow insults from schoolboys; Surendranath Banerjea was humiliated by the discovery that he was no longer the eloquent charmer he had been. When he raised his voice to command attention, the students shouted him down. 'What, in my own city, it has come to this!' he shrieked. 'Yes', the Pal-ites shouted back, 'it has come to this.'[22]

3

The Extremists had reasons to be satisfied with the results of the Calcutta Congress. 'The Congress has emerged', the *Mahratta* wrote on 6 January 1907, 'triumphant and rejuvenated'. Even the *Bande Mataram* recognized that 'all that the forward party has fought for has in substance been conceded'.[23] The new party had emerged as a strong, coherent and powerful force; it had thwarted—what it believed to be—determined attempts to jettison or water down the Congress programme and had kept the Moderates at bay. The Moderates left Calcutta with mingled feelings of bewilderment, humi-

[21] *Bande Mataram*, 26 Dec. 1906.   [22] Sastri, op. cit., p. 91.
[23] *Bande Mataram*, 31 Dec. 1906.

liation and dismay. It was not so much the resolutions on *swadeshi* and boycott, but the way they were pushed through that worried them. Gone was the genteel decorum of a gathering which had hitherto conducted itself as if it was an unofficial Parliament of India. Acrimonious argument and open conflict had replaced quiet diplomacy and consensus through friendly negotiations.

The cracks in the Congress, papered over at Calcutta, were soon to be revealed and indeed widened. While still at Calcutta, Tilak ridiculed the Moderate creed and its exponents. He recalled that Dadabhai Naoroji had spent twenty-five years of his life in England in an effort to 'convince the English people of the injustice that is being done to us'. He had worked hard, held conversations with Secretaries of State and Members of Parliament, but with what result?

He has come at the age of eighty-two to tell us [Tilak said] that he is bitterly disappointed. Mr Gokhale, I know, is not disappointed. He is a friend of mine and I believe that this is his honest conviction. Mr Gokhale is not disappointed, but is ready to wait another 50 years till he is disappointed like Mr Dadabhai. He [Gokhale] is young, younger than myself and I can very well see that disappointment cannot come in a single interview, from interviews which have lasted for a year or so.[24]

Persistent criticism and ridicule by the Extremists alarmed the Moderates. The Extremists had already made a place for themselves in Bengal, Maharashtra, Berar and the Punjab. Would the Moderates lose the rest of the country to the 'New Party'? It was not merely a question of which party would be supreme in the Congress. The stakes, as a Moderate colleague reminded Gokhale early in 1907, were much higher.

R. N. Mudholkar to Gokhale, (n.d.) *January 1907:* But the present is not a mere fight for titular leadership, but is a fight for the establishment of certain principles, for the organization of certain definite methods of work. . . . They [the Extremists] believe in and preach the 'revolutionary' methods for driving from India the foreign devils, who have usurped sway there. Mr Khaparde almost semi-publicly talks of a war and an insurrection which might be expected in a couple of years, and the year 1913 is confidently mentioned by him as one which will see the end of British rule in India . . . it is a duty we owe to ourselves, to our country and to our God to expose the true character, aim and objects of the new school . . . they are

[24] *Tilak's Writings and Speeches,* p. 40.

dangerous lunatics from whose wild and fanatical teachings our people have to be protected.[25]

Mudholkar argued that the immediate task of the Moderates was to win the minds and hearts of the student community. 'They are the coming men. Let us "capture" them before the Extremists approach them. . . . The U.P. and the Madras Presidency are not yet appreciably affected by the Extremist views. . . . Let us save these two provinces for the present . . . [and] take the wind out of the sails of the Extremists.'

It was as a part of this counter-propaganda campaign that Gokhale planned his tour of the Punjab and the U.P. early in 1907. He arrived at Allahabad on 3 February and received a warm welcome. As he came out of the railway station, an enthusiastic crowd of students shouted '*bande mataram*', and insisted on unhorsing and dragging the carriage in which Gokhale was to proceed to the house of his host, Tej Bahadur Sapru. Gokhale tried to dissuade them; he threatened to go back to Calcutta, but the students had their way. On the following day, he delivered a lecture on the 'Work Before Us'. Motilal Nehru, who was in the chair, wrote to his son, Jawaharlal, that Gokhale's lecture was 'a masterpiece of close reasoning and sound commonsense expressed in the best and purest English'.[26] It is not surprising that this lecture should have thrilled the intelligent, hard-headed and prosperous élite of Allahabad. Gokhale began by pointing out the fundamental facts of the Indian situation:

On one side [was] the bureaucracy, a small body of foreign officials, who held in their hands practically a monopoly of all political power. These men, who had behind them the vast power of a mighty empire, have built up in the course of the century an elaborate and imposing fabric of their rule in the country. . . . On the other side, they had the vast mass of the people of the country lying inert and apathetic, except when under the sway of a religious impulse . . . deplorably divided and sub-divided with hardly any true sense of discipline, plunged in abject poverty and ignorance, and wedded to usages and institutions which, whatever their value for purposes of preservation, were not exactly calculated to promote vigorous, sustained or combined action for purposes of progress. Between the two, there stood the educated class with its number steadily growing, already exercising extensive influence over the mass of the people. . . . This class, at one time so well disposed to British rule, was daily growing more sullen and discontented, resenting the non-fulfilment of solemn promises, feeling keenly the humiliation of its subject position and

[25] G.P.   [26] Motilal to Jawaharlal, 7 Feb. 1907 (Nehru P.).

was determined to attain for itself a political status worthy of the self-respect of civilized people.[27]

Gokhale went on to spell out his political creed. On his part, he wanted his country to take its proper place among the great nations of the world, in politics, industry, religion, literature, science and the arts. 'I want all this', he added, 'and feel at the same time that the whole of this aspiration can, in its essence and its reality, be realized within this Empire.' The French in Canada and the Boers in South Africa had found an honourable place in the British Empire; so could the Indians. Despite occasional lapses—and some of them most lamentable lapses—the genius of the British people, 'as revealed in history, is on the whole made for political freedom, for constitutional liberty'.[28]

Self-government was the goal; constitutional agitation was the means of reaching it. Constitutional agitation was not to be narrowly conceived; in Gokhale's view it embraced even passive resistance and the non-payment of taxes; only violence and revolution fell outside its ambit. But everything that was constitutional was not necessarily wise or expedient.[29] Tilak and his party were wrong in suggesting that constitutional agitation had failed in India. The people of India, argued Gokhale, had not exhausted even a thousandth part of the possibilities of real constitutional agitation.

The Congress could have achieved much more if it had been able to command greater zeal from its adherents. 'Political privileges could not be had for the mere asking', Gokhale affirmed. 'They had cost other peoples prolonged struggles.' It was true that the British bureaucracy in India was impervious to constitutional agitation. But it was amenable to pressure from the British democracy. That was why work in England was an integral part of the Congress programme. But nine-tenths of the work lay in India. Much remained to be done to bridge the gulf between Hindus and Muslims and between different sections of the Hindu community, and to develop a strong and high type of character and discipline, and finally, to cultivate an intense feeling of nationality above caste, creed and class.

After explaining the Moderate creed and strategy, Gokhale exposed the holes in the Extremist doctrine. It was being suggested by the Extremists that the people should have nothing to do with the government of the country and should achieve everything by the

[27] Karve & Ambekar, op. cit., vol. II, p. 216.
[28] Ibid., p. 217.   [29] Ibid., p. 218.

simple expedient of a universal boycott, the real significance of which they only vaguely understood. The implications of an industrial boycott were grave enough: it postulated a deliberate sacrifice on the part of the people in buying indigenous articles which were of poorer quality and priced higher than imported goods. There was also the stupendous problem of setting up new industries to dispense with imports. The talk of a general or 'political' boycott was sheer madness. It was impossible within a measurable time to set up national schools and colleges on a scale sufficient to replace institutions aided or run by the government. The boycott of local bodies, legislative councils and government service was simply suicidal. The object of the Indian people, Gokhale argued, 'should be to seek steadily to increase what little powers of administration and control they possessed', rather than to lose what they had secured after years of agitation and struggle.[30]

4

Compared with the presidencies of Bombay and Bengal, the United Provinces were a political backwater, thanks to the entrenched orthodoxy of the Hindus, a conscious isolationism of the Muslims, and the existence of a powerful landed aristocracy loyal to the Raj. Nevertheless, Gokhale's visit was surprisingly successful. 'I met Gokhale privately', Harcourt Butler, the Commissioner of Lucknow, told Dunlop-Smith, the Viceroy's private secretary, 'at a dinner given by the Raja of Mahmudabad, the leading Muhammedan noble of these parts and one of the proudest. Another Taluqdar, a C.I.E., a friend of Europeans, presided at his meetings. There was remarkable enthusiasm for Gokhale in public.'[31] Butler went on to suggest that Gokhale should be appointed Education Member of the Viceroy's Executive Council. The Governor, Sir J. P. Hewett, testified to the 'favourable impression' left by Gokhale: 'Both Hindus and Muslims have been struck by his moderation. The student class are said to have fallen peculiarly under his influence. . . . Mr Gokhale has too by his personality made a very favourable impression & on the whole, the impression is as much personal as political.'[32]

Gokhale had an equally cordial welcome in the Punjab. On arrival

[30] Ibid., p. 221.   [31] H. Butler to Dunlop-Smith, 24 March 1907 (M.P.).
[32] J. P. Hewett to Minto, 24 Feb. 1907 (Minto P.).

at Lahore on 15 February, he was taken in a huge procession, 'with bands playing, banners flying and crowds becoming hoarse with wild cheering'. The young men of the city, mostly students, insisted on drawing his carriage through the decorated streets of Lahore, punctuated with welcome arches. The procession took three hours to cover the three miles from the Lahore railway station to the house of Lajpat Rai, where Gokhale stayed.

The following day, Gokhale spoke in the 'Town Hall Quadrangle' with Jogesh Chandra Chatterjea, the president of the local Indian Association, in the chair. On 17 February the students presented him an address of welcome printed on '*swadeshi* Lahore silk'. They paid a tribute to his dedication to the cause of education, his deep interest in the youth of India and his freedom from barriers of caste, creed and race, and went on:

We feel, Honoured Sir, that your whole life is one continuous living lesson to each and every one of us. . . . We know we [in the Punjab] have been asleep and are left behind in the race. But thanks to the selfless devotion of patriots like yourself we have at last been shaken out of our lethargy. Enliven and strengthen our faith. . . . Preach unto us . . . the Gospel of Liberty . . . a liberty self-earned, though slowly accomplished. . . .[33]

Mian Fazal-i-Hussain, Secretary, 'Indian Muslim League', who was one day to play a prominent role in the public life of the Punjab and indeed of India, sought Gokhale's views 'on the methods of bridging over the gulf which unfortunately separates the two communities'.[34]

A remarkable feature of Gokhale's tour of the Punjab and the U.P. was the enthusiasm it evoked in the Muslim community. The British officials were puzzled and even disturbed by the response of the Muslim nobility of Lucknow and the students of Aligarh College to Gokhale.[35] Speaking to the students at Aligarh, Gokhale argued it was a bad thing that European professors should supervise higher learning. Soon after his visit to Aligarh, there was a showdown between the students on the one hand, and the European Principal and the College Trustees on the other. The tension in the college long antedated Gokhale's visit, but the Lt-Governor's appraisal was that it had 'at least supplied the match which caused the explosion'.[36]

Gokhale was pleased with his reception in the U.P. and the Punjab.

[33] *Panjabee*, 20 Feb. 1907.
[34] Fazal-i-Hussain to Gokhale, 15 Feb. 1907 (G.P.).
[35] Hewett to Minto, 24 Feb. 1907 (Minto P.).   [36] Ibid.

'The affection that the people are lavishing on me on all sides is beyond words. How the heart swells with gratitude at the thought of "What a Return for How Little!"' Enthusiastic audiences and admiring crowds did not however sweep Gokhale off his feet. His speeches contained hard facts, cool reasoning and subdued optimism. He did not blame all the ills of India on the British. Nor did he pretend to know an easy way out of complex political and economic problems. In his view, the question was 'one not of what was theoretically perfect, but what was practically possible. It was further a question not merely of dreams, but also of "muscle and character, of capacity, of organization and sacrifice".' Nation-building was nowhere an easy task; in India especially it was beset with formidable difficulties. India was at a stage of evolution when achievements were bound to be small, and disappointments frequent; while future generations would serve India by their successes, 'we of the present generation must be content to serve her merely by our failures'. These arguments may have struck forty-five year-old Motilal Nehru as the 'soundest commonsense in the purest English', but they could hardly be expected to enthuse the young radicals whose patriotism had been inflamed by the partition of Bengal and the heady wine of Extremism jointly brewed by Tilak, Pal and Aurobindo Ghose.

Soon after Gokhale's return to Calcutta it was obvious that it was his personality, rather than his politics, which had made him such a success with the students. Motilal Nehru, elected to preside over a predominantly Moderate provincial conference at Allahabad soon after Gokhale's visit, confided to his son, 'What I am particularly afraid of is the student class . . . no sober or serious thinker can expect to secure an uninterrupted hearing from an audience composed of this element.'[37] In March 1907 C. Y. Chintamani was complaining to Gokhale that the student leaders of the U.P. were 'inviting people from outside, preaching boycott, insulting the local leaders and so on'.[38]

The Moderate counter-propaganda campaign had only limited success. The inherent weakness of the Moderate party was that it had little tangible to show for its pains. More than a year had passed since the Liberal Government assumed office, but the partition of Bengal remained unaltered, and the issue of constitutional reforms practically unopened. This unconscionable delay was undermining

[37] Motilal to Jawaharlal, 24 January 1907 (Nehru P.).
[38] Chintamani to Gokhale, 15 March 1907 (G.P.).

the credibility of the Moderate leadership, and reinforcing the case of their opponents. 'Unless concessions are promptly announced', Gokhale warned the Imperial Legislative Council in March 1907, 'and steps taken to give immediate effect to them, they would, I fear, lose half their efficacy and all their grace'.[39]

'The handle of the lever', as Wedderburn put it, was, however, in London. By March 1907, Wedderburn was reduced to despair by Morley's inaction. 'The silence of Mr Morley is so extraordinary and so mischievous', he wrote to Gokhale, 'that I feel that something must be done to draw him out.'[40] Wedderburn wrote to Morley, requesting an interview, stressing the increasing alienation of educated India and the possibility of the Moderates, 'the party of peaceful and ordered progress', being swamped by their more militant opponents.

It was not until 30 April 1907 that Morley received Wedderburn. The forty-five minutes' conversation left Wedderburn with 'the impression of a weary man; his sympathies are with us, but he finds it difficult to bear up against the weight of this great bureaucracy which has had everything its own way for so long'.[41]

Wedderburn's impression was to be tragically confirmed within a week, when the Secretary of State found himself defending, against his better judgement, the drastic measures of his subordinates in India to cope with a crisis chiefly of their own making.

---

[39] Patwardhan & Ambekar, op. cit., vol. 1, p. 123.
[40] Wedderburn to Gokhale, 14 March 1907 (G.P.).
[41] *Idem*, 2 May 1907 (G.P.).

24

Crisis in the Raj

While Gokhale and Wedderburn were scanning the political horizon for a generous gesture from the Liberal Government, India was hit by a political storm which threatened to cut the ground from under the feet of the Moderate leadership. The storm was caused by the arrest on 9 May 1907 of Lajpat Rai, the most prominent Congress leader of the Punjab and his deportation, without a trial, to Burma. The weeks which followed this drastic step were among the tensest and most strenuous of Gokhale's life. He had to batter against the wall of official prejudice; his own aims and motives were impugned by the authorities in Simla and London, who were led to believe that the Punjab was riddled with sedition and a second mutiny imminent.

On 4 May 1907 the Government of India received a report from Sir Denzil Ibbetson, the Lt-Governor of the Punjab, describing the political situation in the province as 'exceedingly serious and exceedingly dangerous'.[1] He referred to the deep feeling in Lahore in the wake of the prosecution of the editor of the nationalist newspaper, *The Panjabee* (started by Lajpat Rai) and to the tension in several towns such as Rawalpindi, Ferozepore, Amritsar and Batala. The most disconcerting feature of the unrest was that it was penetrating the countryside. The Punjab Government had received reports of strikes of minor revenue officials and the withholding of the land revenue by peasants, of officers on tour being denied carriages and other conveniences, and of policemen being pilloried and adjured to quit the service of an alien government. 'Everywhere', Ibbetson wrote, 'people are sensible of a change, of a new air, a *nai hawa* which is blowing through men's minds.' He believed Lajpat Rai to be the brain behind the agitation, called for his immediate deportation—along with another 'agitator' Ajit Singh —to Burma, and urgently sought additional powers for district officers to curb public meetings and seditious writings.

[1] Home Pol. 148–235, Aug. 1907 (NAI); also in V. C. Joshi (ed.), *Lajpat Rai: Autobiographical Writings*, pp. 228–40.

Ibbetson's report came as a bolt from the blue to the Government of India. They had never suspected that the situation in the Punjab was so critical. They knew of course that all was not well with that province, which had been ravaged by plague, and was suffering from a scarcity of labour, crop-failures and rising prices. The introduction of a 'Land Colonization Bill' in the local legislature had added to the discontent. The authors of this bill, Financial Commissioner James Wilson and his colleagues, were sincere in their desire to make the twenty-year old Chenab colony a model one.[2] They sought to restrict the right of transfer of land by sale or inheritance to money-lenders and absentee landlords living in towns. Punitive fines, recoverable in the same fashion as land revenue, were to be imposed for failure to plant trees, or to observe sanitary or building regulations. However well-meant these stringent measures may have been, they aroused deep misgivings: after all, their actual enforcement rested in the hands of petty officials who were known to be corrupt. By a strange coincidence, soon after introducing this controversial bill in the local legislature, the Punjab Government sanctioned a substantial increase—in some cases as high as fifty per cent—in water rates in the districts of Amritsar, Gurdaspur and Lahore. This was done at a time when the supply of canal water was irregular and crops had failed. Early in 1907, when Gokhale was touring the Punjab, agrarian discontent was already coming to the surface. A number of protest meetings were held in the Chenab colony. On 29 January, three thousand peasants were present at a meeting at Sangla. On 3 February, and again on 27 March, there were demonstrations at Lyallpur. Among those who spoke at Lyallpur were Lajpat Rai and Ajit Singh. Immediately after the meeting on 27 March, Lajpat Rai left for the United Provinces. Ajit Singh stayed on, and fanned the flames of discontent, but his role in this agitation was not so important as was made out later. Indeed, a significant feature of this agitation was that it was led by local men, who rose to fame overnight and were soon to be forgotten: Ramchand and Shahabuddin, lawyers and land-owners of Lyallpur, and Sirajuddin, a former post office employee, who ran the Zamindars' Association and edited the hard-hitting *Zamindar*.

British officers in the Punjab, whether in the districts or the secretariat, were trained in the tradition of 'iron rule' and 'no nonsense'.

[2] N. G. Barrier, 'Punjab Disturbances of 1907' in *Modern Asian Studies*, I, IV, 1967, p. 356.

They missed the true significance of the discontent. Sir Charles Rivaz, who was the Lt-Governor of the Punjab until March 1907, belittled the agitation as a 'put-up job' by the lawyers of Lahore, and pushed the bill through his Legislative Council a few days before he left. Sir Denzil Ibbetson, who succeeded him, belonged to the Punjab cadre, and was imbued with its traditions. He postponed the enhancement of the water rate in the three districts of the Central Punjab, but decided not to make any change in the Land Colonization Bill. He did not underrate the discontent in the Chenab colony, but he misread its manifestations. Seditious ariticles in newspapers and bold speeches at public meetings seemed to him to be danger-signals of a mass uprising, 'a second mutiny', calling for urgent and drastic action.

2

Lord Minto and at least two of his colleagues on the Executive Council, E. N. Baker and Harvey Adamson, were not quite convinced by Ibbetson's arguments, but they swallowed their qualms. Until March 1907, Ibbetson himself had been a member of the Viceroy's Executive Council; he had served in the Punjab for many years and could well be expected to know what he was talking about; he was the man on the spot, and it seemed only decent not to let him down. In the imperial mythology, the Punjab was one of the most sensitive parts of the Indian Empire; it accounted for more than a third of the Indian Army; it seemed 'criminal' to condone in it the slightest sign of sedition. On 6 May the Viceroy's Executive Council accepted the Lt-Governor's recommendations. Three days later Lajpat Rai was arrested, put in a special train and deported to Burma without trial under the half-forgotten Regulation III of 1818. Ajit Singh was arrested on 2 June. An ordinance was promulgated, banning public meetings in certain districts, and a telegram, based largely on Lt-Governor Ibbetson's report, was sent off to Morley to apprise him of the 'crisis' in the Punjab.

The alarming tone of the telegram had the desired effect on Morley, who immediately endorsed the action of the Government of India. In the House of Commons he spoke of the 'emergency' that had arisen in India. He attributed Lajpat Rai's arrest not to any legitimate agitation against any reasonable grievances, but to the promotion of sedition, deliberately and insidiously aimed at the inflammable Sikhs. Haldane, the Secretary of State for War in the Liberal Cabinet, declared that the arm of the Crown in India was stronger than it had been fifty years earlier at the time of the Mutiny. Anglo-India worked itself up into a frenzy. The *Civil & Military Gazette* of Lahore published wild stories about Lajpat Rai having collected a hundred thousand men to attack the Lahore Fort on 10 May 1907, the fiftieth anniversary of the Mutiny. Detachments of British cavalry and artillery paraded the streets of Lahore. The British press carried sensational reports about the events in the Punjab. The *Daily Mail* alleged that an incipient uprising, in which Lajpat Rai was to be the Maharaja of the Punjab, had been nipped. The *Evening Standard* published sensational stories about a riot in Delhi; it was alleged that the crown of Queen Victoria's statue had been struck off, and European women missionaries insulted by their 'ayahs'. *The Times* wondered whether the Government of India was strong enough to deal with the 'crisis'. King Edward VII thought it necessary to administer a royal admonition to Morley for taking the riots in India too casually. 'One would have thought', Morley wrote to the Viceroy, 'that Rawalpindi was a scene of fire and sword, carnage and rape (yes, almost), as if it had been siege of Magdeburg in the Thirty Years War.'[3]

Anglo-Indian die-hards drew their own moral from the 'Punjab disturbances': if the Raj was to be saved, native newspapers and agitators must be silenced; if any constitutional reforms were to be conceded, they would have to be accompanied by an increase in the size of the British garrison in India.

Minto was pleasantly surprised at the ready support he received from the Secretary of State. In fact, Morley's first reaction to Lajpat Rai's deportation was hostile, but his advisers talked him into defending the men on the spot. This defence went further than Anglo-India had even dared to hope. Dunlop-Smith, the private secretary to the Viceroy, detected a 'Cromwellian ring' in Morley's comments on the Punjab.[4] There is no doubt that Morley was deeply disturbed by the news as it came to him through official channels. He wondered whether other provinces would go the way of the Punjab. 'Pray tell me', he asked the Governor of Bombay, 'what you hear of Poona and its inhabitants. If they don't make any sign I shall think that the coup at Lahore had been a real deterrent.'[5] Early in July, Morley was

[3] Morley to Minto, 9 May 1907 (M.P.).
[4] Gilbert, *Servant of India*, p. 90.
[5] Morley to Lamington, 17 May 1907 (Lamington P.)·

suggesting the despatch of troops to East Bengal to forestall a violent outbreak.[6]

Little did Morley know that the crisis in the Punjab had been magnified, if not created, by the transmission of panic from the secret service men to district officers, from district officers to the Lt-Governor, from the Lt-Governor to the Viceroy, and from the Viceroy to the Secretary of State. Immediately, its effect in the eyes of the British public was to tar all Indian politicians with the same brush. Even Ripon, Morley's colleague on the Liberal Cabinet, and a reputed friend of Indian aspirations, thought it necessary to warn Wedderburn: 'I hope men like Mr Gokhale will understand that no British Government can tamper for a moment with anything like real sedition.'[7]

3

Gokhale was in Calcutta when Lajpat Rai was arrested. The news came as a great shock to him. He had known Lajpat Rai for many years, and admired his ability and patriotism. During the summer of 1905, when the two men toured England as Congress delegates, they had been thrown together a great deal. They did not always see eye to eye on every issue, but they had developed a mutual respect and affection. In February 1907 Gokhale visited the Punjab at the invitation of Lajpat Rai, and stayed with him at Lahore. There was hardly an aspect of the Indian situation on which they had not exchanged views. 'Again and again, he and I have discussed our aims,' wrote Gokhale in a 1600-word letter to the *Times of India* on 21 May 1907, 'our hopes, our methods of work, and there never has been any substantial difference of opinion between us. His language was at times a trifle strong—this must necessarily be a matter of temperament—but his aims and methods have always been strictly constitutional.'

Gokhale had no doubt that the Punjab Government had been misled by the police and the secret service. It was true that Lajpat Rai had addressed a protest meeting against the Colonization Bill at Lyallpur and visited Rawalpindi to help some of his friends who had been hauled up by the local authorities for sedition. But all this was part of the day's work for a lawyer and a politician: by no stretch of

[6] Gilbert, op. cit., p. 90.
[7] Wedderburn to Gokhale, 27 June 1907 (G.P.).

imagination could it be regarded as 'revolutionary' activity. Gokhale affirmed in his letter to the *Times of India*:

The Government had misjudged the volume and character of the unrest prevalent in the Punjab. . . . People in this country believe and will continue to believe that there never was any real chance of a second mutiny, and that Lala Lajpat Rai has been sacrificed to the nervous apprehension that suddenly seized the authorities.

Gokhale's diagnosis of the situation in the Punjab was to be confirmed by events, but in May 1907 the government was in no mood to appreciate it. Indeed anyone who sprang to Lajpat Rai's defence was himself likely to fall under a cloud. Gokhale knew the risk he was running. But for him it was not merely a question of redeeming the honour and restoring the liberty of a friend, but of saving the Moderate-led Congress and indeed the political future of India. If the government could get away with such arbitrary action, it would vindicate the Extremist thesis that the British were beyond redemption. 'Lajpat Rai's deportation', Gokhale wrote to Wedderburn on 24 May, 'has literally convulsed the country from one end to the other. All sorts of hard things are being said about Mr Morley, and we have so far practically nothing to urge on the other side.' There was, Gokhale added, 'a great apprehension in the country that the bureaucracy in India will take advantage of recent events to put pressure on Mr Morley to abandon the contemplated reforms'.[8]

In Gokhale's mind, the fate of Lajpat Rai came to be linked with that of the constitutional reforms. He hurried from Calcutta, where he had heard the news, to Poona, and from Poona to Matheran, where Pherozeshah Mehta was holidaying. Gokhale proposed a memorial to the Viceroy demanding Lajpat Rai's release; it was to be signed by non-official members and ex-members of the Imperial and provincial legislative councils, ex-presidents of the Congress and ex-chairmen of provincial conferences. He planned a visit to Simla to plead for Lajpat Rai with the Viceroy and other high officials. If—as seemed likely—he was unable to convert the Government of India, he proposed to appeal to British public opinion and Parliament by organizing an influential delegation consisting of R. C. Dutt, Surendranath Banerjea, Nawab Syed Mohammed Bahadur of Madras and himself.

Gokhale had mailed copies of his letter to the *Times of India*, to the Viceroy's private secretary and some members of his Executive

[8] Gokhale to Wedderburn, 24 May 1907 (G.P.).

Council. 'I half begin to wonder', Morley wrote to Minto, 'whether Gokhale is not at heart such a revolutionist as Pal, etc., and as determined to belittle and disparage sensible and steady reforms as Tilak or Lajpat.'[9] Some of the British officials, haunted by the spectre of a second mutiny, went so far as to lay the responsibility for the crisis at Gokhale's door: his visit to the Punjab was alleged to be the match which had set the political tinder ablaze in that province. Minto wrote to Morley:

As to Gokhale, I can only say that if he chooses to play with fire, he must be prepared to take the consequences. We can't afford to allow him to tamper with the army. . . . Malik Umar Hyat Khan told me that he held Gokhale chiefly answerable for what had occurred in the Punjab, that it was his arrival there, and his speeches there which set everything in a blaze. I believe this is to a great extent true. I am thoroughly disappointed in Gokhale. I had liked what I had seen of him & believed he was honest at heart. But the part he has played of late has disgusted me. . . .[10]

Minto was so worked up that he felt sorry that he had not vetoed Gokhale's re-election to the Imperial Legislative Council.[11] He decided not to include him in the Factories Commission not only because, 'with his ability and eloquence, he might exert too great an influence on his colleagues', but also because 'his appointment would be strongly disapproved and misunderstood by many of our most loyal and native supporters. They look upon Gokhale as an arch-traitor.'[12]

This persistent denunciation could not but poison the mind of the Secretary of State against Gokhale. Morley expressed concern at the prospect of Gokhale visiting England to plead for Lajpat Rai. 'This will make plenty of trouble for me', he wrote on 20 June 1907. 'I dare say because he [Gokhale] is a master of plausibility and his speeches and argumentation will have an effect upon my slightly motile Radical friends both in the H[ouse] of C[ommons] and on the platforms in the country.'[13] Three weeks later when Herbert Risley, one of the senior officers of the Government of India, called at the India Office, Morley asked him whether Gokhale was extremely simple or extremely crooked. 'I told him', Risley reported to the Viceroy, 'what

[9] Morley to Minto, 18 July 1907 (M.P.).
[10] Minto to Morley, 7 Aug. 1907 (M.P.).
[11] *Idem*, 10 July 1907 (M.P.).
[12] *Idem*, 12 Sept. 1907 (M.P.).
[13] Morley to Lamington, 20 June 1907 (Lamington P.).

I told H.E. in Simla, and he seemed to agree that the facts did not point to simplicity or good faith.'[14]

It is not surprising that at the very time, when he had become the *bête noire* of the British official world, Gokhale should have unwittingly embarrassed E. N. Baker, the only member of the Viceroy's Executive Council who had been friendly with him. In a letter to Wedderburn, Gokhale had innocently quoted a remark by Baker, that Congress agitation might be more fruitful in England than in India. Wedderburn, who had occasionally been passing on Gokhale's letters to Morley to give him an 'Indian view of Indian affairs', did not foresee Baker's predicament, of being summoned by the Secretary of State to explain why he had incited an Indian politician to organize political agitation in England. This was a wholly perverse view of what had actually happened, and Minto required all his tact and skill to defend Baker.

Minto to Morley, 26 December 1907: [Baker] is I know intimate with Gokhale and has no doubt often discussed the political position with him. Gokhale must be well-acquainted with his views, and quite possibly he may have told Gokhale that his opinions might have more chance of acceptance at home than in India.

I fancy Gokhale has very often been told to air his views in England for the sole purpose of getting rid of him here! But even if Baker did say anything of the sort, that is a very different thing from encouraging Gokhale to wage war against His Majesty's Government.[15]

5

Gokhale's plan for an 'influential' memorial on behalf of Lajpat Rai ran into unexpected difficulties. Some of the leading men who were to sign it were not prepared to treat Ajit Singh on a par with Lajpat Rai even though both had suffered at the hands of the government. Pherozeshah Mehta had endorsed the idea of the memorial when Gokhale had met him at Matheran. But Pherozeshah was no admirer of Lajpat Rai, and seems to have had second thoughts. 'My draft has been with him', Gokhale confided to a friend on 19 August, 'for more than three weeks, but as yet he makes no sign of returning it, and without his cooperation, the memorial is bound to be a failure. . . . This is most annoying to me personally, but it is Sir

---

[14] Risley to Dunlop-Smith, 19 July 1907 (Minto P.).   [15] M.P.

P. M. Mehta's way and it is no use quarrelling with what cannot be helped.'[16]

Gokhale's fear that Lajpat Rai's deportation was only the first manifestation of the government's panic proved true. In 1907, as in 1897, the Anglo-Indian press clamoured for a curb on 'seditious' writings and speeches. The Viceroy with the powerful support of the Commander-in-Chief, Lord Kitchener, proposed a stringent press law. But Morley, with the backing of the British Cabinet, stood firm against any such proposal despite a strongly worded warning from the King that 'the freedom of the press, although an undoubted boon to a free people under self-government, is apt to be abused by a people under the autocratic government of another race.' [17]

Morley had declined to muzzle the press, but was persuaded to permit the curtailment of rights of assembly. The ordinance restricting public meetings in the Punjab and Bengal issued in May 1907 was due to expire six months later. In October 1907 the Government of India introduced the Seditious Meetings Bill in a special session of the Imperial Council at Simla. The Select Committee was made to report within a week and the bill was rushed through the Council. Gokhale savagely assailed it. He traced its genesis to 'the exaggerated importance attached to the utterances of a few visionaries', and the official exploitation of 'every accidental circumstance to represent an agitation for reforms or removal of specific grievances as a movement of revolt'.[18] To him the saddest part of the story was that the Secretary of State for India had fallen a victim to these misrepresentations. 'What was sedition?' he asked, and answered:

There are those [among European officials] who think that unless an Indian speaks to them with 'bated breath and whispering humbleness', he is seditious. There are those who do not go so far but who still think that anyone who comments adversely on any of their actions, or criticizes the administration in any way or engages in any political agitation is guilty of sedition.[19]

With a permanent official majority, the passage of the bill was assured, but it was significant that all the three Indian members present in the Imperial Council, even the Tikka Sahib of Nabha belonging to a loyal princely family, voted against it.

The Seditious Meetings Bill was passed on 1 November 1907. Three days later the Viceroy called Harvey Adamson, the Home

[16] Gokhale to S. Ray, 19 Aug. 1907 (Ray P.).
[17] Sidney Lee, *King Edward VII: A Biography*, London, 1925, vol. II, p. 318.
[18] Karve & Ambekar, op. cit., vol. II, p. 23.   [19] Ibid., p. 32.

Member, to discuss the release of Lajpat Rai. On 5 November, Minto wrote to Morley that he had decided to order the release of Lajpat Rai and Ajit Singh.

I can say [Minto wrote] that I have always had grave doubts as to the justice of Lajpat's imprisonment. We were asked by Sir Denzil [Ibbetson] to act at once in the face of immediate danger. . . . I cannot say that I look upon the performance of the Punjab Government at that time with any admiration. Lajpat is undoubtedly a man of high character, & very much respected by his fellow countrymen & if when I was asked to arrest him, I had known what I do now, I should have required much more evidence before agreeing.[20]

The stand which Gokhale had taken five months earlier in his letter to the *Times of India* had at last been vindicated. Well might Morley exclaim: 'Ibbetson has been weighed in the balance and found utterly wanting.'[21]

As we have already seen, Minto had been deeply disturbed by Ibbetson's report on the Punjab early in May, and ordered—rashly as it turned out—the deportation of Lajpat Rai. But the Viceroy had not been wholly convinced by Ibbetson's arguments. On 26 May he had vetoed the hated Punjab Colonization Bill 'as a very faulty piece of legislation—legislation which would be inadvisable at any time, but which at the present moment, if it becomes law, would add fuel to the justifiable discontent which has already been caused.'[22] Ibbetson and his advisers failed to see that the discontent in the Punjab countryside was rooted in specific grievances and that its leaders were not professional politicians but local men who were destined to fade from public view as suddenly as they had emerged. The viceregal veto on the Punjab Colonization Bill transformed the atmosphere in the province overnight. When Ibbetson returned to India after two months' leave, he was surprised and embarrassed by expressions of public gratitude for the repeal of the bill. The detractors of the Lt-Governor and alien rule had turned into admirers of British justice.

The bubble of the second mutiny had at last been pricked. The 'riots' in Rawalpindi and Lahore ('Babu riots', as an English newspaper called them) had been vastly exaggerated. Most of the accused in the Rawalpindi trials were acquitted. Hans Raj Sawhney, Gurdas Ram and other leaders of Rawalpindi were hardly the stuff of which

[20] Minto to Morley, 5 Nov. 1907 (M.P.).
[21] Morley to Minto, 8 Nov. 1907 (M.P.).
[22] M.P.; also in Sri Ram Sharma, *Punjab in Ferment*, Delhi, 1971, p. 417.

heroes are made: their patriotism was not passionate enough to let them stake their liberty and professional fortunes on it. Lajpat Rai had noticed—even before his arrest on 9 May—a tendency in the Rawalpindi lawyers to avoid him.[23] After Lajpat Rai's arrest, the demoralized 'gentry' of Lahore, Rawalpindi and other towns made an unseemly scramble to propitiate the authorities.[24] The Sikhs re-affirmed their loyalty and pointed out that Ajit Singh was not a Sikh. The Arya Samaj sent a memorial claiming to be a wholly religious body, and disavowing interest in politics. What the *Panjabee* wrote about Ferozepore was true of most other towns in the Punjab in the summer of 1907: 'The town is practically asleep. Nobody even [dares] to hold religious gatherings, not to say political meetings. The word political is heard from detectives only.'[25]

The events of 1907 showed that while the Government of India had little imagination, the politicians of the Punjab—and perhaps other provinces—had little stamina to withstand the repression by the government. One of the most caustic and yet perceptive comments on the events of 1907 was made within a week of Lajpat Rai's arrest by the forty-six year-old Motilal Nehru, then a 'Moderate' leader of Allahabad, to his son:

an impartial observer cannot help noticing a change of tone which amounts to a confession of cowardice. The advocates of Swaraj have made themselves scarce. The heads of the different communities are anxious to show their loyalty to the Government. The arrest and deportation of Lajpat Rai unjustifiable and inexcusable as it is has shown what stuff our countrymen are made of. It is nothing but a storm in a tea-pot, and it is all over now—only we are put back half a century. The forces which were slowly and silently working for the good of the country have received a sudden check. For all this we have to thank the Extremist fools.[26]

To Motilal, as to other 'Moderate' Congressmen, it seemed that indiscreet words and actions of Extremist writers and speakers were giving a handle to the Anglo-Indian bureaucracy for stalling constitutional reforms, invoking repressive measures, discrediting all political agitation and undermining the position of the educated élite as represented by the Indian National Congress.

[23] L. Rai, *The Story of My Deportation*, Lahore, 1908, p. 23.
[24] *The Panjabee*, 31 Aug. 1907.   [25] Ibid., 28 Aug. 1907.
[26] Motilal to Jawaharlal, 17 May 1907 (Nehru P.). 'I regret', D. E. Wacha wrote to Dadabhai Naoroji on 10 May 1907, 'that our extremist friends by their intemperate speeches and other acts make the government hostile. The sins of a few are visited on the whole country.' (D.N.P.).

25

Road to Surat

While Gokhale grappled with the crisis caused by Lajpat Rai's deportation, another and a more serious crisis which was to have far-reaching consequences was brewing in the Congress. At the Calcutta session in December 1906 it had been decided, at the request of the Moderate leaders of the Central Provinces, to convene the next Congress session at Nagpur. This invitation was in fact a Moderate manoeuvre to prevent the Congress from being held at Lahore, where the Extremist influence had been growing since the partition of Bengal. G. M. Chitnavis and his friends, who controlled Congress affairs in the Central Provinces, felt sure of their influence in Nagpur, but they failed to foresee that this influence could be offset by contrary pressures from Maharashtra and Berar where Tilak and Khaparde commanded wide popular support.

In February 1907 the provincial Congress committee and the reception committee of the Congress session met at Nagpur to elect their office-bearers. Chitnavis was elected president of both the committees, and B. S. Moonje, one of the local Extremist leaders, was elected joint general secretary of the reception committee. The harmony between the two factions did not last long. The Extremists stepped up a propaganda offensive against the Moderate leaders, acquired control of a local Hindi paper, the *Desh Sewak*, and decided to publish a Hindi edition of the *Kesari* from Nagpur. The Moderates decided to start an Anglo-Marathi paper of their own from Nagpur. There was an unseemly competition in enrolling new members and raising funds. The Extremists made no secret of their ambition to elect Tilak president of the session. The Moderates were emphatic that they would not accept Tilak. Despite their numerical majority in the local Congress organization, the Nagpur Moderates were, however, at a disadvantage. Their leader, G. M. Chitnavis, had neither the courage nor the stamina to assert himself in a crisis. As early as July 1907 he had thrown up the sponge, and suggested to

Gokhale the abandonment of the annual Congress session and its replacement by a meeting of selected individuals at Nagpur or at some central place.[1] Gokhale considered Chitnavis's proposal impracticable.

Who is to select the individuals? [he asked Chitnavis]. Who, according to your idea, should form this year's Congress? The All India Congress Committee could not undertake this responsibility, as it has no power to do any such thing. No, the only way before us is to face the crisis in December next. That this year's crisis is the gravest that has so far confronted us is without doubt.[2]

In 1907, as in the preceding year, the presidency of the Congress promised to become an occasion for a trial of strength between the rival factions.

We say it clearly [a Moderate journal[3] wrote] Mr Tilak has made himself impossible for a position of so much responsibility as the presidentship of the Congress at a grave crisis such as the country is passing through at present, and that his election may mean nothing less than the secession of the most experienced, most trusted and most competent leaders of the movement in every part of the country.

The Moderates were agreed on excluding Tilak, but not on who should preside over the Nagpur Congress. Pherozeshah Mehta was an obvious choice for a session which threatened to be stormy, but he had already presided over the Congress thrice. He proposed the name of Nawab Syed Mohammed Bahadur of Madras as an overdue gesture to south India and to the Muslim minority.[4] Gokhale favoured Rash Behari Ghose, not only because he was an eminent lawyer and an eloquent speaker, but because his election could 'keep on our side a considerable body of Bengali delegates, who otherwise may work and vote with the new party in the Congress'.[5]

The meeting of the reception committee, which was to elect the president of the Congress and make arrangements for it, took place in the Town Hall at Nagpur on 22 September 1907. A jeering crowd of local students and rowdies greeted the Moderate leaders as they arrived for the meeting. The 500-odd Moderates allowed themselves to be bullied by a tiny but vociferous group of Extremists who pre-

---

[1] G. M. Chitnavis to Gokhale, 18 July 1907 (G.P.).
[2] Gokhale to Chitnavis, 7 Aug. 1907 (Chitnavis P.).
[3] *Hindustan Review*, April 1907.
[4] H. S. Dickshit to Gokhale, 10 Sept. 1907 (G.P.).
[5] Gokhale to H. N. Apte, 11 Sept. 1907 (G.P.).

vented Chitnavis, the president of the reception committee, from taking the chair and pushed through the election of its own members to the executive committee. The Moderates were flabbergasted. They had never faced such a situation before. Chitnavis lost his nerve and washed his hands of the Congress session. The Moderate predicament was explained to Pherozeshah Mehta by Gokhale's friend Mudholkar, one of the Moderate leaders intimately concerned with the Congress affairs of the Central Provinces and Berar.

R. N. Mudholkar to Pherozeshah Mehta, 2 October 1907: The extremists, though there are only a few of them on the Reception Committee, are active, energetic, bold and unscrupulous. They have captured the executive committee, because the Moderates were most of them pusillanimous, inactive and indolent. Though the Moderates had about 500 present at the meeting of the 22nd September, they were thoroughly cowed down and nonplussed by the rowdyism of about 2 or 3 dozen extremists. The Nagpur Koshtis have long been known to be a turbulent lot and the Nagpur school boys and college boys have been for years more or less unruly. These mischievous elements have been set in motion against the Moderates, and excepting a few of these, the majority are afraid of attending any meeting . . . the rowdies of Nagpur, from the L.L.B.s and the M.A.s down to the Koshtis and . . . ruffians, will do all they can to prevent a smooth session of the Congress if their idol Tilak is not made President. I was warned that the mob would not only hoot or pelt at our President and leading members, but that serious personal injury would be done to them. Now there is none at Nagpur who has the courage and firmness to take a bold stand against threats like these, and to adopt measures for putting down this unruly disposition. Under these circumstances the only course open to us is to change the venue of this year's Congress. . . .

We must avoid disgraceful scenes. We must as far as possible save ourselves from a situation in which for sheer self-protection we shall have to meet physical force by superior physical force or seek the aid of the police or the magistracy. It is said that there is a great jubilation among European officials over this fight among Congressmen, and several of the most thoughtful men of Nagpur fear that an order under section 144 Cr.P.C. may be suddenly issued to put a stop to the meeting of the Congress.[6]

2

Gokhale had been watching the developments at Nagpur with deep concern. He was not only (with D. E. Wacha) a joint general

[6] G. P. (A copy was sent by Mudholkar to Gokhale.) See also Chitnavis' letter of 21 Oct. 1907 to Wacha in P. Mehta P.

secretary of the Indian National Congress and a member of its Central Standing Committee, but also on intimate terms with Moderate leaders of the Central Provinces and Berar—Chitnavis and Mudholkar, who looked up to him for advice and support against (what they believed to be) the machinations of the Nagpur Extremists under the inspiration of Tilak and Khaparde. Soon after the 22 September meeting, Chitnavis resigned from the chairmanship of the reception committee. The Extremists had gained control of the executive committee (of the reception committee) and seemed to be in a defiant mood. They rebuffed overtures from the local Moderates, but relented when an emissary came from Bombay to negotiate a compromise. They agreed to the representation of both the parties on the executive committee, and to leave the choice of the Congress president to the Standing Committee of the Congress. The negotiations, however, broke down on the somewhat complicated and sordid issue of the disposal of the funds which had been collected for the Congress session. The Nagpur Extremists argued that the decision on this matter could only be taken by the 'Rashtra Mandal', which had raised the funds. They undertook, however, to persuade that body to advance money to the reception committee on the condition that it would ultimately be refunded out of any savings which might be left at the end of the Congress session. The refund was, however, to be waived if Tilak was elected Congress president. In other words, the Nagpur Extremists offered a financial bait to the Moderates to secure their agreement to Tilak's election.[7]

The Nagpur imbroglio filled Congress leaders throughout the country with deep foreboding. Was this the 'New Spirit' of which the Extremists had been speaking so eloquently? The indiscipline, intimidation and violence which characterized the proceedings of the reception committee of the Congress at Nagpur could shatter the fabric of nationalist politics built patiently over a quarter of a century. As the Moderates looked at the political scene, they could not help feeling that the Extremists had done a good deal of damage already. The Hindu–Muslim tension in East Bengal, the divisions in the ranks of the educated élite all over the country, the stiffening of the British attitude as indicated by Lajpat Rai's deportation, and the inevitable setback to constitutional reforms seemed to be the first bitter fruits of Extremist tactics, which had reduced the organization of the annual Congress session to a nerve-racking exercise.

[7] Chintamani to Gokhale, 20 Oct. 1907 (G.P.).

The Moderates' frustration and anger were sharply expressed in a letter to a Bombay paper, *Jame-Jamshed*, by H. A. Wadya, a confidant of Pherozeshah Mehta.

The accounts of the doings at Nagpur of the Extremists and their misguided followers from school and college make it imperative [wrote Wadya] that the Moderates should assert themselves if the Congress is to be saved. . . . It is impossible any longer to keep patience with the strange paralysis that has overcome those who should lead the Moderates to confront and withstand the worst enemies of our cause—the Extremists. What is it we are waiting for? Have we not seen or realized enough? Are we still to prattle vainly of discipline and unity? The only discipline these men have known and shown is to proceed from abuse to assault, and to impose by brute force the policy they cannot enforce by argument. The union of these men with the Congress is the union of a diseased limb to a healthy body, and the only remedy is surgical severance, if the Congress is to be saved from death by blood poisoning.[8]

In a crisis the Moderates were wont to look up to Pherozeshah Mehta for a lead, but this time they looked up to him in vain. 'The oracle', Wadya wrote to Gokhale on 2 October 1907, 'is dumb.'

The oracle spoke a month later, with his usual firm accents. On 10 November Pherozeshah held a meeting of the Central Standing Committee of the Congress in his palatial house in Bombay. Among those present were Gokhale and Wacha, the two joint general secretaries, Vijayaraghavachariar from Madras, Daji Abaji Khare, M. A. Jinnah, G. D. Parekh, Ambalal Sakerlal from Bombay, Tilak and Khaparde. The last two were the only representatives of the Extremists. The Nagpur Extremist leaders, B. S. Moonje, A. B. Kolhatkar and N. R. Alekar, accompanied Tilak, but Pherozeshah Mehta, who was in the chair, did not allow them to attend the meeting on the ground that they were not members of the Central Standing Congress Committee. The Committee was informed that it was not possible to hold the Congress session at Nagpur. Vijayaraghavachariar suggested a compromise to enable the two parties at Nagpur to work together. He proposed that the executive committee (of the reception committee) be reconstituted with an equal number of representatives of the two parties, but with a majority of 'outsiders' to be nominated by the Central Standing Congress Committee, and that the Nagpur Extremists should hand over the moneys collected for the Congress session. When Khaparde raised objections to this

[8] Copy enclosed with H. A. Wadya to Gokhale, 2 Oct. 1907 (G.P.).

proposal on behalf of the Extremists, Pherozeshah sent for a deputation of Gujarati gentlemen who were waiting in an adjacent room. They offered to hold the Congress session at Surat. The offer was accepted by all those who were present, with the exception of Tilak and Khaparde, who did not vote.

After the meeting Tilak seems to have had second thoughts. He persuaded Khaparde and the Nagpur Extremists to accept the terms proposed by Vijayaraghavachariar.[9] Next morning, two emissaries of Tilak called on Wacha, the joint general secretary of the Congress on behalf of the Nagpur Extremists and agreed to the reconstitution of the executive committee and to leaving the choice of the Congress president to the Central Standing Committee of the Congress. This was clearly a climb-down for the Extremists, but it had come too late. Wacha declined to commit himself without consulting Pherozeshah. Pherozeshah was averse to the reopening of the issue. 'It is too late now,' Wacha wrote to Gokhale on 12 November, 'and the irreconcilables must repent of their extreme folly and obstinacy. I think they have been excellently served. I am not at all sorry for what has happened. It is a stern lesson [to the Extremists].'

Pherozeshah Mehta had, in the graphic words of Aurobindo Ghose, 'juggled' the Congress into Surat.[10] 'Gujarat', wrote the *Kesari*, 'is a private street of Mehta & Co. and according to the adage which says that every contemptible dog becomes important in his own street . . . the Moderates will no doubt preponderate in the Surat Congress.'

3

The decision to hold the Congress session at Surat was taken on 10 November 1907. There were barely six weeks for the session to begin. A reception committee was quickly formed at Surat and Gokhale attended the meeting at which the president of the Congress session was to be elected. The Extremists proposed Lajpat Rai, who had just been released from Mandalay. Lajpat Rai admired Tilak and was sceptical of the Moderate strategy, but he was averse to becoming a pawn in the game of factional politics; he declined to be the presidential candidate of a single faction, or to encourage the project of an exclusively Extremist Congress at Nagpur.[11] The Moder-

[9] Khaparde Diary, 10 & 11 Nov. 1907.
[10] *Bande Mataram*, 17 Dec. 1907.
[11] L. Rai to Gokhale, 3 Nov. 1907 (G.P.).

ates were in a majority in the reception committee at Surat and carried through the election of Rash Behari Ghose, whose candidature had, incidentally, been supported by all the provincial Congress committees except that of Berar.

The change in the venue of the Congress session from Nagpur to Surat did not avert a collision between the two parties. Politically Surat was a backwater and a Moderate stronghold, but there was nothing to prevent the Extremists from mustering their supporters from other provinces. 'Khaparde, Moonje & Co.', Gokhale was warned on 23 November, were planning to take hundreds of rowdies from Nagpur.[12] If the Moderates were not to be outvoted, they would have to produce a thousand Moderate delegates of 'the right stuff and metal' from Gujarat, besides ensuring sizable contingents from the Deccan and other provinces. Tension at Surat rose to a fever pitch. Several days before the Congress was scheduled to meet, Khaparde was in Surat, haranguing the local public. 'Mr Khaparde is daily preaching here', wrote one of the secretaries of the reception committee to Gokhale. 'The mob only attend these lectures. No people of higher social rank go there.'[13] The meetings of the Extremists were well attended; the one on the day of Tilak's arrival was attended by at least seven thousand people. The Extremist camp in the Congress was fast filling up. On 24 December, Khaparde noted in his diary: 'We number over 600'.[14] Extremist orators denounced the policy of 'mendicancy' of their opponents, and declared their resolve not to permit any backsliding from the resolutions passed by the Calcutta Congress. On 24 December, a conference of Extremist delegates was held at Gheekantawadi with Aurobindo Ghose in the chair. Some of the speakers decried the idea of any deal with the Moderates and demanded an exclusively Extremist Congress.

Tilak did not support these counsels of despair. 'Now I feel', he is reported to have said, 'I shall one day bring round this very Congress to my way of thinking. As we do not have a majority today, we must compromise with the Moderates and keep ourselves in the Congress itself.'[15] Tilak may have sincerely desired a *modus vivendi* with the Moderates; his tactics were, however, calculated to defeat this object. Persistent denunciations of Moderate leadership and policies in the press and on the platform, frantic competition with the Moderates

[12] Mudholkar to Gokhale, 23 Nov. 1907 (G.P.).
[13] M. Nanabhai to Gokhale, 20 Dec. 1907 (G.P.).
[14] Khaparde Diary, 24 Dec. 1907.
[15] S. L. Karandikar, *Lokamanya Bal Gangadhar Tilak*, Poona, 1957, pp. 261–2.

in the enrolment of delegates, and the allegations of an imminent betrayal of the nationalist cause by the Moderate leadership could hardly create a climate for a compromise. On 24 December, two days before the Congress was to be inaugurated, came the news of the attempt on the life of Allen, the Collector of Dacca. The Moderates were deeply disturbed by this news. History was repeating itself. In 1907, as in 1897, the country was confronted with a vicious circle of repression, terrorism, and counter-terrorism. Moderate leaders saw a logical connection between the reckless propaganda of the Extremists and the wild aberrations of impressionable youth. The Dacca outrage steeled them in their resolve to stand no further nonsense from their political opponents.

4

As the 1600 delegates and 800 visitors trooped into the huge Congress pavilion on the bank of the Tapti on 26 December, there was a latent tension and an air of vague expectancy, but no one could have predicted the course of events. An enthusiastic ovation greeted Lajpat Rai, who had recently returned from a six-month deportation to Burma and Dr Rutherford, a British Liberal, who had specially come from England to attend the session as a friendly observer. Then came the presidential procession, including Rash Behari Ghose, the president-elect, Pherozeshah Mehta, Wacha, Gokhale and other leaders. Tribhovandas N. Malvi, chairman of the reception committee, read his welcome address, and then Ambalal Sakerlal Desai formally proposed that Rash Behari Ghose should take the presidential chair. Ghose had in fact already been elected by the reception committee on the recommendation of all the provincial Congress committees except one: Desai's proposal at the plenary session was thus merely part of an annual ritual, but it evoked cries of protest from a section of the audience. Surendranath Banerjea, whose appearance on the Congress platforms was usually a signal for hushed silence, rose to second the proposal but was shouted down. As the hostile demonstration showed no signs of subsiding, the chairman of the reception committee suspended the sitting for the day.

Never had the inaugural Congress meeting been interrupted in this unseemly fashion. The Congress usually lasted for only three days, and the loss of a day was a serious matter. Nevertheless, the Congress met again on the following day at 1 p.m. and the proceedings were resumed where they had been broken off on the previous day. Surendranath Banerjea was able to conclude his speech. Motilal Nehru of Allahabad was then called upon to support the proposal for the election of Rash Behari Ghose. Meanwhile, a section of the audience was visibly restive and interjecting objections. Just before the commencement of the session, Tilak had sent a note to T. N. Malvi saying that he wished to address the delegates on the proposal for the election of the president after it had been seconded. After waiting vainly to be called by the chairman, Tilak rushed to the dais and insisted on his right to move an amendment. Neither Malvi, the chairman of the reception committee, nor Rash Behari Ghose, the president-elect, allowed him to speak. Tilak refused to be ruled out of order. He insisted that Ghose had not yet been elected president, and that he (Tilak) had every right to appeal for a decision to the delegates. Tilak stood defiantly on the platform, while the Congress pavilion resounded with rival shouts of 'shame, we don't want you to speak', and 'he must speak; he must be allowed to speak'. Rash Behari Ghose tried to read his presidential address, but his voice was drowned in the growing tumult. The transition from words to blows did not take long: 'a flying missile', a shoe, hit Pherozeshah Mehta and Surendranath Banerjea, the Moderate leaders seated on the dais. This was followed by the brandishing of sticks and the unrolling of turbans, the breaking of chairs and bruising of heads; the crowning humiliation occurred when the police came and cleared the hall.

The responsibility for the Surat fiasco was to be fiercely debated for months. The Moderates published their own version of the events at Surat on the evening of 27 December 1907; it was signed, among others, by Rash Behari Ghose and Gokhale. The Extremist version came out four days later over the signatures, among others, of Tilak and Aurobindo Ghose.

In the eyes of the Moderates, Tilak was the villain of the piece. They charged him with a deliberate plot to wreck the Surat session. The fact is that no one was more unhappy than Tilak at the turn events had taken. On 28 December, at the instance of Motilal Ghose of the *Amrita Bazar Patrika*, Tilak tried to appease his opponents by writing what amounted to a letter of regret, waiving his opposition to the election of Rash Behari Ghose, invoking the spirit of 'forget and forgive', and offering his cooperation to preserve the unity of the party. Motilal Ghose took the letter personally to the Moderate camp, but was (to use his own words) 'simply howled out by the

Moderate leaders, headed by Sir Pherozeshah Mehta'.[16] Aurobindo Ghose, who was in the thick of the fray at Surat, wrote many years later, that 'to no one was the catastrophe so great a blow as to Mr Tilak. He did not love the "do-nothingness of that assembly [the Indian National Congress], but he valued it both as a great national fact and for its unrealized possibilities. . . ." '[17]

If Tilak was misunderstood, he was himself largely to blame. A strange inconsistency and even vacillation seem to have characterized his attitude to the Congress in 1906 and 1907. At the Calcutta session he took a tough line and, only at the last minute, agreed to a compromise which gave the Extremists what they wanted and staved off an open confrontation with the Moderates. Tilak's followers hailed the Calcutta Congress as an Extremist triumph, but immediately afterwards, he launched a tirade against the Moderate leaders. In the early months of 1907, he does not seem to have exercised a moderating influence on his hotheaded adherents, Moonje, Kolhatkar and the others, who brought the work of the Congress reception committee at Nagpur to a standstill. Nor does Tilak seem to have pulled up his followers for the disgraceful scenes at the meeting of the reception committee held on 22 September, which convinced the Moderates that it was impossible to hold the Congress at Nagpur without the protection of the police. Tilak's posture at the crucial meeting of the Central Standing Committee in Pherozeshah Mehta's house on 10 November was also inconsistent. He did not at first agree to a compromise suggested by Vijayaraghavachariar, and when he did decide to accept the terms, it was too late.

There is no reason to doubt Tilak's sincerity when he argued later that at Surat he had tried hard for a reconciliation with his political opponents through intermediaries like Lajpat Rai and Surendranath Banerjea. The Moderates could hardly be blamed for not taking these overtures seriously. While Tilak was throwing his peace-feelers, Khaparde and Aurobindo Ghose, his close associates, were haranguing the people of Surat on the iniquities of the Moderate leadership, casting doubts on their bona fides and accusing them of a design to wriggle out of the resolutions passed at the Calcutta Congress twelve months earlier. Even after the session commenced, Tilak did not do all he could have done to prevent a catastrophe. Indeed, he himself

[16] P. Dutt, *Memoirs of Motilal Ghose*, Calcutta, 1935, p. 173.
[17] S. B. Bapat, *The Reminiscences and Anecdotes of Lokmanya Tilak*, Poona, 1925, p. 18.

started the argument and provided the provocation which in the surcharged atmosphere prevailing in the Congress pavilion led to a mêlée. It is true that on the following day Tilak was prepared to 'forget and to forgive', but in the eyes of the Moderates he had lost his credibility.

The Extremist stance *vis-à-vis* the Congress Establishment had been changing repeatedly. Initially at Nagpur, the issue between the two factions was the composition of the executive committee (of the reception committee) and the choice of the president of the Congress session. Then came the argument about the disposal of the funds collected for the session. From November onwards, the main Extremist grievance seemed to be the shifting of the venue from Nagpur to Surat. After Lajpat Rai declined to stand and almost all the provincial Congress committees had approved of the election of Rash Behari Ghose, the argument on the Congress presidency should have ended. But it was revived at Surat, and the Extremists alleged that Rash Behari Ghose had in the past used undignified expressions about them in a speech in the Imperial Legislative Council. They also alleged that the Moderates were engaged in a deliberate plot—to which Gokhale was supposed to be a party—to whittle down the resolutions passed at the Calcutta Congress the previous year. This criticism seemed odd, coming as it did from a seasoned congressman like Tilak, who had been attending the Congress sessions for nearly two decades and knew the established ritual and procedures. The Congress resolutions were drafted by the reception committee, but were subject to discussion, amendment and approval by the Subjects Committee, which met after the inaugural session. The Subjects Committee was the proper forum for seeking a consensus behind the scenes and preserving the façade of party unity. Unfortunately, at Surat the Congress broke up without the two factions getting an opportunity to reconcile their differences in the Subjects Committee.

Tilak was a cool and hard-headed politician. It is possible that at Surat he intended to repeat the tactics he had employed at Benares in 1905 and at Calcutta in 1906: to raise the political temperature, pose a few burning issues, whip up the fervour of his adherents, take a tough line in informal negotiations or even in the Subjects Committee, and when thwarted, threaten to carry the controversy to the arena of the plenary session. This technique of negotiating from a 'position of strength' had paid off at Benares and Calcutta, but Tilak failed to see that by the end of 1907 the patience of his opponents had been exhausted. It is also clear that at Surat, Tilak signally failed to discipline his lieutenants, whose hatred of Pherozeshah Mehta, suspicion of Gokhale and contempt for the Moderates as a group, were obvious to all. Lajpat Rai, who was committed neither to the Moderate nor to the Extremist camp, wrote eighteen months after the Surat fiasco, that

instead of leading his party, Tilak had allowed himself to be led by some of its wild spirits. Twice on my request at Surat he agreed to waive his opposition to the election of Dr Rash Behari Ghose and leave the matter of the four Calcutta resolutions to the Subjects Committee, but the moment I left him he found himself helpless before the volume of opinion that surrounded him.[18]

Lajpat Rai's impression was to be dramatically confirmed many years later by no less a person than Aurobindo Ghose, one of the leading men in the Extremist camp at Surat. 'Very few people know', Aurobindo Ghose wrote, 'that it was I (without consulting Tilak) who gave the order that led to the breaking of the Congress and was responsible for the refusal to join the new-fangled Moderate Convention. . . .'[19] For Aurobindo this was not an act of vandalism but a deliberate effort 'to mend or end' the Indian National Congress. The political struggle of a subjugated people, he argued, demanded an inner struggle rather than a fictitious unity. He deduced from the experience of the Italian and American revolutions that in any contest between the Moderates and the Extremists 'one or the other must be crushed or prevail before the unity of a regenerated nation can replace the false unity of acquiescence in servitude'.[20]

It is doubtful if Tilak would have gone the whole hog with Aurobindo. Despite his passionate hatred of foreign rule, Tilak was acutely aware of the realities of political life in India. It is important to remember that Extremism was far from being a coherent ideology. There was all the difference in the world between the robust realism of Tilak, the volatile flamboyance of B. C. Pal, and the messianic romanticism of Aurobindo Ghose. And there were Extremists who were not very far, ideologically, from the Moderates. Keir Hardie's definition of the Indian Moderate being 'extreme in moderation', and of the Indian Extremist being 'moderate in extremism', was particularly applicable to Gokhale and Tilak.

[18] V. C. Joshi (ed.), *Lajpat Rai: Writings and Speeches*, vol. 1, p. 180.
[19] *Sri Aurobindo on Himself and on the Mother*, Pondicherry, 1953, p. 82.
[20] *Bande Mataram*, 27 Oct. 1907.

Twelve years later, in December 1919, Tilak emphatically denied that at Surat his party was for *swaraj* or self-government at one blow. In a letter to the *Bombay Chronicle*, he recalled that 'on behalf of the nationalists I was then pressing for a Resolution embodying a very very moderate scheme of self-government, for immediate adoption by the Congress . . . my only fault at that time was to anticipate by a few years, the Government and the Moderates [in the adoption of the Montagu–Chelmsford reforms of 1919].'[21]

5

Immediately after the Surat Congress, the Extremist mood was one of righteous indignation. So was that of the Moderates, but in their case it was also tinged with a feeling of relief. 'The surgical severance' of the 'diseased limb' which Wadya, the Bombay Moderate, had recommended in the *Jame-Jamshed* had at last come about. Pherozeshah Mehta told a representative of the *Times of India* soon after the Surat Congress that the separation between the two parties was inevitable if the Congress was not to 'submit itself to the rule of the Extremists', whose aspirations were 'unreasonable and unrealizable and were such that the bulk of the Congress would not work on their lines'.[22] Pherozeshah was particularly pleased at the exclusion of Tilak, whose politics were anathema to him and whose barbed shafts in the *Kesari* and the *Mahratta* had deeply wounded him. Tilak's influence 'among reputable people' in provinces other than Maharashtra seemed to Pherozeshah 'to rest on the fact that he managed to hang on to the Congress. Now that the split has come, people would find him out.'[23] Pherozeshah's reaction was not untypical of the Moderates as a group. Motilal Nehru had expressed to his son deep suspicions of Extremist motives and tactics just before the Surat Congress.[24] Madan Mohan Malaviya went to the length of saying that he would not like to be seen again on any platform with Tilak.[25]

Gokhale's reaction was different from that of most of his fellow Moderates. His suspicion of the Extremists, and particularly of Tilak, was deep enough. He had been in the heart of the cold war

---

[21] *Bombay Chronicle*, 13 Dec. 1919.
[22] J. R. B. Jejeebhoy, *Some Unpublished and Later Speeches and Writings of the Hon. Sir Pherozeshah Mehta*, Bombay, 1918.
[23] Ibid. [24] Motilal to Jawaharlal, 20 Dec. 1907 (Nehru P.).
[25] G. K. Devadhar to Gokhale, 16 Jan. 1908 (Devadhar P.).

between the two factions in the Congress since 1905. The squabbles at Nagpur had caused him much anxiety. As early as May 1907 he had written to a friend: 'But if the split must come, let it come. I think that almost anything is preferable to the present situation in which wild and irresponsible men, who can think and talk daily of nothing but turning the "Feringhee" out of the country, seem to be dragging us along with them. I fear that the tail has been allowed to wag the dog too long.'[26] His apprehensions about the fate of the Congress continued even after the decision to change the venue of the Congress from Nagpur to Surat. 'The truth is', he wrote to a friend on 22 November 1907, 'that the patriotism & sense of discipline & responsibility which are necessary to work successfully such a vast organization as the Congress do not yet exist in the country.'[27] A month later as he was preparing to leave for Surat he noted: 'An open split at the forthcoming Congress seems now inevitable and no one can say what our course in the immediate future is going to be.'[28] At Surat it was not Gokhale, but Pherozeshah who was in command of the Moderate camp, but Gokhale's influence during those critical days was, on the whole, cast on the side of moderation. On the first day of the Congress, H. W. Nevinson, the correspondent of the *Manchester Guardian*, found Gokhale 'distressed, anxious, harassed with vain negotiations and sleepless nights'. On the following day, during the last tumultuous scenes at the ill-fated session which split the Congress for a decade, Nevinson noted that Gokhale was 'restraining the rage of the Moderates, ingeminating peace if ever man ingeminated peace. Mr Gokhale, sweet-natured even in extremes, stood beside his old opponent, flinging out both arms to protect him from the threatened onset.'[29] And finally, when the split came, it filled Gokhale more with sorrow than anger. He confessed that he had been shocked by 'the utter unscrupulousness and malignity' of the attacks by a section of the Extremists, and the 'malevolent' attacks on him personally in the *Bande Mataram* and the *Amrita Bazar Patrika* which had 'published day after day telegrams about me which are a concoction, pure and simple, without a word of truth in them'.[30] All this was an indication to him that 'our national character has to be raised from even a lower depth than we had thought when

[26] Gokhale to Chitnavis, 7 Aug. 1907 (Chintnavis P.).
[27] Gokhale to Ray, 22 Nov. 1907 (Ray P.).
[28] *Idem*, 20 Dec. 1907 (Ray P.).
[29] H. W. Nevinson, *The New Spirit in India*, London, 1908, p. 257.
[30] Gokhale to Ray, 2 Jan. 1908 (Ray P.).

we took our most pessimistic estimate of it'.[31] Deeply disgusted as he was with the Extremists, Gokhale foresaw, with far more prescience than many of his fellow Moderates, the great dangers of a schism in the nationalist ranks. Nearly ten weeks before the Surat Congress he confided to William Wedderburn: 'If a split does come it means a disaster, for the Bureaucracy will then put down both sections without much difficulty.'[32]

The first British official to react to the Surat split was the District Magistrate of Surat, who immediately telegraphed to the Governor of Bombay: 'Indian National Congress Meeting today became disorderly, blows being exchanged. President called on police to clear assembly room and grounds. Order now restored. None reported seriously hurt. No further disturbance anticipated.'[33] The casual, matter-of-fact tone of this message would have shamed both the Moderates and the Extremists if they had been able to see it. Three weeks later, on 15 January 1908, Minto told Morley that the 'Congress collapse' at Surat was 'a great triumph for us'.[34] Morley, with his experience of Ireland, knew better; almost prophetically he told the Viceroy that, despite their immediate eclipse, the Extremists would eventually capture the Congress.

Unlike most of his Moderate colleagues, Gokhale felt neither jubilation nor relief at the disastrous conclusion of the Surat Congress. He felt 'like one who has been blown up into high air with the fort he was guarding & who descends on earth to find himself surrounded only by ruins. But the feeling will pass away in due course, and meanwhile there is so much to do if only to gather ruins before the others, better equipped for the task, begin the work of reconstruction.'[36]

6

Nineteen hundred and seven had been a year of trials for Gokhale. The strain of the Calcutta Congress, the debate in the Imperial Council, the propaganda war with the Extremists, the problems of

[31] Ibid.
[32] Gokhale to Wedderburn, 11 Oct. 1907 *in* Morley to Minto, 31 Oct. 1907 (M.P.).
[33] Telegram from Dist. Magistrate, Surat, to Sec., Jud. Dept., Bombay Govt., 27 Dec. 1907. Report of the Disturbance at the Indian National Congress Meeting at Surat, Bombay Govt. Jud. Dept. 1908 (1), vol. 98.
[34] Minto to Morley, 5 Jan. 1908 (M.P.).
[35] Morley to Minto, 27 Dec. 1907 (M.P.).
[36] Gokhale to Ray, 23 Jan. 1908 (Ray P.).

running the Servants of India Society and the uncertainty of the political situation had told on his health even before the bombshell of Lajpat Rai's deportation fell. In April, he was confessing to a 'sad and empty feeling'. In June, he suffered a grievous bereavement: his elder brother Govind, who had brought him up after the death of their father, was taken seriously ill. Gokhale rushed to his bedside at Kagal, their ancestral village, took him for treatment to the nearest town, Miraj, but all efforts to save Govind's life proved unavailing, and he passed away on 21 June.

Gokhale's domestic affairs could hardly have been in greater disarray than in the summer of 1907. One of his sisters was at Belgaum with his younger daughter. His other sister was in the Karve's Widows' Home. His elder daughter was a resident-student in the Female High School at Poona, and now after the death of his brother Govind, the responsibility for looking after his widowed sister-in-law and her four young sons fell on him. The cup of his grief brimmed over. 'I have been bearing suffering', he wrote to a friend on 9 August, 'but I have been brought well-nigh to a breaking point.' In October, he described his health as 'well-nigh shattered'. He suffered from insomnia, and then a disorder of the liver. In September the short rail journey from Poona to Bombay had exhausted him to such an extent that, by the time he arrived at his destination, he was 'more dead than alive'.

From this depth of physical and mental suffering Gokhale was pulled up by new tasks and challenges in the autumn of 1907. The recrudescence of plague in Poona led him to organize a relief committee. G. K. Devadhar, one of the young men who had joined the Servants of India Society, became its secretary and Gokhale its chairman. It was arduous and dangerous work, but important for the unfortunate people of Poona who had repeatedly suffered from the ravages of the epidemic. In October Gokhale attended the special meeting of the Imperial Council at Simla which was to discuss the Seditious Meetings Bill. The prospect of registering a public protest against the government's repressive policy infused fresh energy into him. The closing weeks of 1907 found him in the midst of the political storm which was to wreck the Congress. He returned from Surat thoroughly exhausted and chastened. The Extremists' tirades against him in the press and their uninformed criticism hurt him, but he consoled himself with the thought that he had lived the greater part of his life and done the greater part of his work amidst general misunderstanding; in any case he had never expected much visible success for his work during his lifetime. 'So let them call me insincere or timid or anything else they like. I do my work because I love my country & I feel amply rewarded by the opportunities I have of doing it. This is the only rock on which one should build in public life. Whoever builds on anything else builds on sand.'[37] His thoughts were, however, already turning to the task of salvage and reconstruction of the Congress. Ironically, the burden of reconstruction was to fall more on him than on the Moderate stalwarts of Bombay, who had been the loudest at Surat in advocating 'political surgery' on the 'diseased Extremist limb'. From Surat Pherozeshah Mehta and Rash Behari Ghose returned to their lucrative legal practice, Wacha to his mill, Surendranath Banerjea to his editorial chair, and the other Moderate leaders to their professional and domestic chores. It was left largely to Gokhale, untrammelled by personal and professional ties, to devise plans for nursing the Congress back to health.

[37] *Idem*, 14 Feb. 1908 (Ray P.).

26

Reforms on the Anvil

In the heat and dust raised by the deportation of Lajpat Rai and the Moderate–Extremist conflict, the issue of constitutional reforms seemed to have receded to the background. But it was soon to dominate the political scene again. Towards the end of August 1907, the Government of India's dispatch of 21 March 1907 to the Secretary of State on constitutional reforms was published, and the decision to appoint two Indians to the Secretary of State's Council announced. Early in September 1907, a Royal Commission was appointed to report on decentralization of the Indian administration.

These announcements failed to evoke much enthusiasm in India. The 'Simla proposals'—as the Government of India's dispatch to the Secretary of State came to be known—were based on the recommendations of a sub-committee of the Viceroy's Executive Council. The committee had been instructed to report on the enlargement of legislative councils to 'the fullest extent possible [consistently] with the necessary authority of the Government', the creation of a separate electorate for the moneyed and landed classes in order to provide 'the requisite counterpoise' to the influence of the professional classes, and the formation of an Imperial Advisory Council (consisting of ruling chiefs and territorial magnates) whose proceedings were to be private, informal and confidential. 'It would be a curious piece of irony', wrote the *Statesman*, 'if at a time when the Government of which he [Mr Morley] is a member are preparing an attack upon English feudalism, as represented by the House of Lords, he should have originated the doctrine that the salvation of India is to be found in the exaltation of the landed aristocracy.'

That the Government of India should have thought of banking upon the princes, landlords and other vested interests in the face of growing unrest may seem odd in the light of later history. It was, however, quite in accord with the philosophy of the British ruling

¹ Note, 15 Jan. 1908 of Dunlop-Smith (M.P.).

class in India, which Minto had readily imbibed, and which he modified only slightly under the dual pressure of Indian discontent and Morley's exhortations. It was on Minto's advice that Morley chose for his Council, not well-known public figures like R. C. Dutt and Nawab Syed Mohammed Bahadur, but K. G. Gupta, a not particularly brilliant member of the I.C.S., and Syed Husain Bilgrami (Nawab Imad-ul-Mulk), a retired civil servant from Hyderabad. Whatever value these gestures had for Indian public opinion was largely lost after the deportation of Lajpat Rai, and the enactment— in the teeth of non-official opposition—of the Seditious Meetings Bill.

The Surat Congress would have pronounced its verdict on the 'Simla proposals', had it not ended in a pandemonium. A fortnight later, when Gokhale was in Calcutta, he called on the Viceroy and urged him to accelerate the constitutional reforms. The Extremists, he told Minto, had been discredited at Surat, and would cease to be a factor of any importance in Indian politics if the constitutional reforms were framed to satisfy the reasonable aspirations of the educated classes. In March, while speaking on the budget in the Imperial Council, Gokhale returned to the same theme. He referred to the 'sense of irritation and disappointment' caused by certain words and actions of Morley, whom educated Indians had learnt to look upon as a philosopher-statesman. 'Whatever reforms are taken in hand,' he said, 'let them be dealt with frankly and generously. And let not the words "too late" be written on every one of them. For while the Government stands considering, hesitating, receding, debating within itself, . . . opportunities rush past it which can never be recalled. And the moving finger writes, and having writ moves on.'[2] It was a sober speech, but the Viceroy, who was in the chair, took it amiss. 'Gokhale had a cut at you', Minto wrote to Morley, 'which provoked me and I dealt with what he had said somewhat testily. . . . Gokhale came afterwards to see Dunlop-Smith, professing to be hurt at what I had said . . . perhaps I was too hard on him.'[3] This incident showed once again Minto's ambivalence: he was attracted by Gokhale's ability, but repelled by his spirit of independence. A few days later, Minto told Morley that Gokhale's note to the Decentralization Commission 'was as good as anything I have seen'.[4]

---

[2] Patwardhan & Ambekar (eds.), op. cit., vol. I, p. 138.
[3] Minto to Morley, 2 April 1908 (M.P.).
[4] *Idem*, 13 May 1908 (M.P.).

In another letter, while discussing the choice of the first Indian member of the Viceroy's Executive Council, Minto conceded that Gokhale was 'by far the ablest of that school whom we know', but added that he 'could not trust him. I don't know what there is behind him. . . . He is too a Maharatta Brahmin which means a great deal.'[5]

Morley complimented Minto on giving a 'rap on the knuckles' to Gokhale.[6] Fortunately this incident did not become the starting point for the kind of hostile campaign which had brought Gokhale to a standstill during his visit to England in 1906. Much had happened in the intervening two years to raise Gokhale's stock in the eyes of the Secretary of State. Morley had never been a great admirer of the civil service, but he never forgave it for the way it misled him—and the Viceroy—over the deportation of Lajpat Rai. Morley knew enough of imperial history to realize the damage done by the 'men on the spot' in misleading opinion at home and violently irritating opinion in the colonies. 'After all', he told the Viceroy, 'it is not you nor I, who are responsible for [Indian] unrest, but the over-confident and overworked Tchinovniks who have had India in their hands for 50 years past.'[7]

2

In 1906 Morley had been reluctant to overrule his senior advisers in the India Office; two years later, he felt able to assert himself. Dunlop-Smith, the Viceroy's private secretary, after meeting Arthur Godley (who had a quarter of a century's experience in the India Office), wrote in June 1908: 'Poor old Godley was most pathetic. . . . He said—he almost whined—that his position is very different from what it was . . . that all power has been taken away from him and he is not allowed to use his influence with other men. Godley said that Lord Morley is the most autocratic and most vain person he had seen. He will not recognize also that there is any British public in India or that men in the [civil] service can think for themselves.'[8]

In the summer of 1908, Morley had reasons to be impatient with the bureaucrats who surrounded him in London and Minto in Simla. There had been an inordinate delay in the formulation of the reforms. With his political instinct sharpened by his sense of history, and

---

[5] *Idem*, 11 June 1908 (M.P.).
[6] Morley to Minto, 23 April 1908 (M.P.).
[7] *Idem*, 17 June 1908 (M.P.).   [8] Gilbert, op. cit., p. 158.

particularly by the history of Ireland, Morley saw that the early passage of reforms was an acid test of the efficacy of the constitutional method in India and that further delay could completely alienate the educated classes. It seemed to him that the Surat Congress signified not the final defeat of the Extremists, but merely a breathing space for the Moderates, and that the Moderates were likely to be swamped by the Extremists unless they could show some tangible fruits for their labours.[9]

The 'Simla Scheme' had been a great damper for the Moderates, but Morley let it be known to their spokesmen in England (such as Wedderburn) that the Government of India's dispatch of 21 March 1907 was not the last word on the issue of Indian reform, and was subject to revision in the light of criticism.[10] Unaware of the genesis of the 'Simla Scheme', Indian public opinion tended to attribute it to Morley and to hold him responsible for its defects. This was not only unfair to Morley but harmful to the Indian cause. Wedderburn pleaded with his Indian friends not to alienate Morley. He had no doubt that the Secretary of State's mind was still open on constitutional reforms. Morley's position in the Liberal party and the Cabinet was unassailable: to incur his ill-will would be suicidal.

Wedderburn to Gokhale, 28 February 1908: It is quite clear to my mind that the only chance of getting valuable concessions is by Mr Morley's goodwill . . . the best help our Parliamentary friends [in England] can give us is by using friendly and encouraging pressures in the right direction. . . .

No advocate going to a court of appeal would open his case by denouncing & insulting the judge. Now in the present instance Mr Morley is practically sole ultimate judge. He may have (& has) his weaknesses, he may be timid and vain, but what do we stand to gain for India by ceaselessly charging him with these defects & assuming that he has abandoned the principles of a lifetime? All this is bad tactics.

It was primarily in order to influence Morley and the Liberal party in favour of constitutional reforms that Wedderburn and the British Committee of the Congress asked Gokhale to visit England. He arrived on 10 May 1908. To a Reuter correspondent, who met him at the Charing Cross Station, he said that his visit was in connection with the Indian Government's reforms scheme and he hoped to see Morley and other prominent men. A few days before his arrival,

[9] Morley to Minto, 27 Dec. 1907 (M.P.).
[10] Wedderburn to Gokhale, 6 Feb. 1908 (G.P.).

Morley had become Viscount Morley of Blackburn. Wedderburn was not worried by Morley's elevation to the House of Lords. 'I have let Mr Morley know', Wedderburn wrote to Gokhale on 24 April, 'that you are coming. On the whole I think it is advantageous that he is moving to the House of Lords. It would have been disastrous if he had left just when his plans were maturing—he had to choose between the House of Commons & the India Office and his choice seems to imply that he means to do something.'[11]

Gokhale met Morley on 22 May. The meeting lasted an hour and a quarter. 'We parted', Gokhale wrote home, 'with a good understanding. He has promised to consult me freely at every stage of the progress of the reforms proposals, and he has assured me that before the year is over, the reforms would not only be formulated but carried out.'[12] A few days later, while Gokhale was at Liverpool, he received an urgent letter from the Secretary of State for India asking him to see him at once. He hurried back to London and went to the India Office where he had 'a most important and on the whole highly satisfactory interview with him [Morley]. It was worth one's while to have come to this country for this interview, if for nothing else.'[13] On 12 June, Gokhale noted that Morley had 'begun slowly to assert himself'.[14] He found him cordial and responsive. The doors of the India Office seemed open to him at all times. 'The whole atmosphere', he noted, 'is friendly to me personally.' Morley seems to have been drawn to the young professor-politician from Poona. In one of his asides, he once confessed that he was not attracted by Orientals— 'Gokhale being an exception, if any'.[15] Morley's cordiality may have stemmed from political calculation. Gokhale's intimate knowledge of Indian politics and economics could be useful to the Secretary of State in refuting the arguments of the reactionaries in the India Office and the Tory party. Morley may also have hoped to use Gokhale to soften the edge of the small critical group of radical Liberals in the Commons led by Sir Henry Cotton.

On 16 June, Gokhale was invited for a confidential luncheon discussion in the India Office, with T. Buchanan, the Under-Secretary of State for India and four members of the India Council, Walter Lawrence, Theodore Morison, Lawrence Jenkins and S. A. Bilgrami.[16] The initiative for his meeting seems to have come from

[11] G.P.   [12] Gokhale to Patwardhan, 29 May 1908 (G.P.).
[13] *Idem*, 12 June 1908 (G.P.).   [14] *Idem*, 2 June 1908 (G.P.).
[15] Morley to Minto, 18 Feb. 1909 (M.P.).
[16] Gokhale to Patwardhan, 19 June 1908 (G.P.).

Theodore Morison, but it could hardly have been arranged without Morley's approval. For an Indian politician, such attention from the India Office was a singular compliment. 'You may take it from me', Gokhale wrote to his disciples in Poona, 'that it [the meeting] has strengthened our position in the India Council.'[17]

Meanwhile, in consultation with Wedderburn and the British Committee, Gokhale addressed a meeting of the Indian Parliamentary Committee and interviewed some prominent British statesmen, including Lords Ripon, Courtney, Reay, Welby and Fitzmaurice. He was also the chief guest at a dinner given by H. W. Nevinson of the *Manchester Guardian*, which was attended by the leading Liberal journalists, including A. G. Gardiner and H. W. Massingham. Wedderburn was delighted that Gokhale had an opportunity of 'getting at the brain of the Liberal Party in London'.[18]

By the middle of July, Gokhale was predicting that the reforms would take final shape before the Indian National Congress met at Madras in December.

Gokhale to Vamanrao Patwardhan, 10 July 1908: It is almost certain (of course this is strictly confidential) that an important Indian reform Bill will be introduced in Parliament in December next and the whole scheme of reforms will be roughly settled in October & November. On December 2, I shall leave for India so as to arrive in time for the next Congress. It is considered here of the utmost importance that I should be present at the next Congress and convey a message of hope to the constitutional party. . . .[19]

3

Gokhale's optimism was somewhat tempered by the news from India. While he was on his way to England, an outrage had occurred at Muzaffarpur in Bihar. The wife and daughter of a European barrister were killed by a bomb really intended for D. H. Kingsford, the District Magistrate, who had incurred much notoriety in Calcutta for awarding savage sentences in political cases. Of the two young men who were arrested after the Muzaffarpur outrage, one shot himself, and the other made a confession which led to the discovery of an ammunition dump and the trial of thirty young men in what came to be known as the Maniktola Conspiracy case. Gokhale read the news at Marseilles. This was not the first time that a major political crisis had occurred in his homeland as soon as he left it. In

[17] Ibid.   [18] *Idem*, 6 Aug. 1908 (G.P.).   [19] G.P.

1897, it had been the plague operations; in 1905, the Bengal partition; in 1906, the Barisal affair. And now it was this senseless assassination which threatened to put the clock back in India, and to make Gokhale's task in England doubly difficult. If the vicious cycle of repression and retaliation continued, where was the room for sane counsels of the Moderate party? Would not the Anglo-Indian lobby in England counter his pleas for reforms by raising the spectre of anarchy in India? Gokhale took the earliest opportunity of sharing his misgivings with his disciples:

I am really sorry [he wrote] that I should be out of India at such a grave juncture. There is some fatality connected with my visits to this country [England]. Every time I come here, something happens in India and throws the country into a state of wild excitement. . . . I fear [he added] that there will now be a fierce outburst of repression for the next two or three years, it will be a case of repression on one side and crime on the other. Ultimately, I have no doubt, crime will be stamped out, or the violence of the extreme section of the Extremists will get exhausted, but meanwhile men like ourselves can do very little useful work & we shall be compelled merely to helplessly look on. . . . It is not difficult at any time to create disorder in our country—it was our portion for centuries—but it is not easy to substitute another form of order for that which has been evolved by Englishmen in the course of a century. . . .[20]

The immediate result of the Muzaffarpur tragedy, as Gokhale had foreseen, was an Anglo-Indian clamour for the tightening of screws on Indian politicians and newspapers. 'The danger', the Viceroy wrote to the Secretary of State, 'is a very real one. It is a personal danger such as British men and women do not talk of, but they know it.'[21] Minto feared that the European population might panic and take the law into its own hands. The *Englishman* was indeed making ominous suggestions on 'self-defence' by Europeans. The government lost no time in summoning the Imperial Council at Simla and rushing through an 'Explosives Bill' based on an English Act of 1853. The debate lasted for less than two hours. On the same day was passed the Indian Newspapers (Incitement to Offences) Bill, which gave the executive wide powers to curb 'seditious' writings. The rigour of this bill was fortunately moderated by the intercession (at the request of Wedderburn) of Lord Ripon, who was Morley's colleague in the British Cabinet.[22] These modifications in the press

[20] Gokhale to Patwardhan, 15 May 1908 (G.P.).
[21] Minto to Morley, 14 Sept. 1908 (M.P.).
[22] Ripon to Morley, 29 May & 1 June 1908 (Ripon P.).

bill, Morley assured the Viceroy, would make it easier for the Moderates to resist the Extremist attack. 'Such an attack', he wrote, 'is sure to come and it is our business, as I think, not to do anything that will give substance to extremist taunts and reproaches against their moderate opponents.'[23]

In 1908, as in 1897, the ruling race in India was alarmed, and traced a direct connection between political terrorism and incendiary writings in the press. Once again, the victim of the panic of the Anglo-Indian community was Tilak. Immediately after the Muzaffar-pur outrage, he had denounced it publicly. This did not, however, save him from a prosecution by the Bombay Government for two articles in the *Kesari*, which had commented on the Muzaffarpur tragedy. He was arrested in the last week of June. The trial began on 13 July before Justice Davar of the Bombay High Court. Tilak defended himself with great courage, skill and dignity, but was sentenced on 22 July to six years' imprisonment. It is significant that the trial was held not in Poona, where the *Kesari* was published, but in Bombay, and while it was in progress, Tilak was detained in an improvised lock-up in the High Court building. Nevertheless, the city of Bombay was in a turmoil for a fortnight. The mill workers of Bombay went on strike on 25 July; out of 84 mills, as many as 76 stopped working. The strike spread to railway workshops; black flags with Tilak's photographs went up in the streets; motor-cars and carriages carrying Europeans were stoned. British troops were called out. The Governor, Sir George Sydenham Clarke, conferred with prominent businessmen of Bombay and was disconcerted by the discovery that most of them at heart sympathized with Tilak. 'The business natives', he wrote, 'seemed not to have a vestige of political instinct.'[24] Vishnu Bhatvadekar, a friend of Gokhale, wrote to him from Bombay that the government 'had sought to crush Mr T [Tilak] by a portentous prosecution, but they have only succeeded in making him a greater hero and martyr than ever'.[25]

The news of Tilak's arrest, the packed jury, the savage sentence, and the violent sequel in Bombay caused Gokhale deep concern. His heart went out to his old political rival in his hour of trial. Even from a distance of six thousand miles Gokhale could also see that these events boded ill for the cause of constitutional reform and the future of the Moderate party.

[23] Morley to Minto, 28 May 1908 (M.P.).
[24] G. Clarke to Minto, 27 July 1908 (Minto P.).
[25] V. Bhatvadekar to Gokhale, 3 July 1908 (G.P.).

Gokhale to Vamanrao Patwardhan, 17 July 1908: The telegraphic summaries of Mr Tilak's defence have made a very good impression on friends of India in this country. This is the real Tilak, as he was and would be but for the pernicious influence of those around him. . . .

23 July 1908: This morning's papers contain telegrams about the shocking sentence inflicted on Mr Tilak. There is of course no doubt that he will be brought back and set free after things quiet down, if & when they quiet down.

Still the conviction and sentence will really be a great blow to our party, for part of the resentment against the Government is likely to be directed also against us.

Gokhale to Natesan, 24 July 1908: Yesterday's papers contained the news of Mr Tilak's conviction and sentence.

I wonder what is going to happen next. It is useless to talk of reforms at a time like the present & I fear the public in India will be in no mood to appreciate them when they are produced.[26]

Gokhale's worst fears were soon confirmed. Bhatvadekar noted that the Tilak case had strengthened rather than broken the Extremists: 'The excitement caused by the press prosecutions [of the *Kesari* and the *Kal*] has made [the work of the Moderate Party] more than ever difficult . . . local feeling is strong and people are yet hardly prepared to listen to the voice of reason.'[27] An ugly sequel to Tilak's trial was a whispering campaign against Gokhale, who was alleged to have conspired with Morley to get his rival out of the way. The *Bande Mataram* of Calcutta and the *Hindu Panch* of Poona gave currency to such insinuations. 'The rumour', in Bhatvadekar's words, was 'too puerile to be seriously considered, but some of our Extremist friends are worse than children. The *chawl* politicians in Bombay are loudly abusing you, P. M. Mehta & my brother & in fact all the Moderates as being responsible for the prosecution.'[28] It was not only irresponsible hot-heads who helped to spread this rumour; Tilak's devoted colleague and legal adviser, G. S. Khaparde, and the Extremist leader of Bengal, Bipin Chandra Pal, who were both in England that summer, seem to have joined in the smear campaign against Gokhale. The public indignation against the government was thus partly diverted to Gokhale and the Moderates. During the Ganapati festival in Poona in 1909, songs were composed to depict

[26] G.P.   [27] Bhatvadekar to Gokhale, 21 Aug. 1908 (G.P.).
[28] Ibid.

Gokhale as the murderer of Tilak.[29] At a public meeting in London, his detractors planned to pelt him with rotten eggs, but the plan did not materialize.[30] There was even talk among Extremist youth of assassinating Gokhale.

This was not the first time that Gokhale's opponents had hit below the belt. He had bitter memories of the 1890s, of the days of the Age of Consent Bill, of the Poona Congress, and the plague operations. 'The malevolence of these men', he wrote, 'is no new thing. It has pursued me for years past with a virulence which I alone know. . . . The truth is that bulk of our educated countrymen have as yet neither a true sense of justice nor true manliness nor magnanimity.'[31]

The charge that Gokhale had persuaded Morley to order Tilak's arrest was of course baseless.

Gokhale to Vamanrao Patwardhan, 25 September 1908: . . . As I have told you before the whole accusation is a despicable & malevolent fabrication. I never had any talk whatever with Lord M about Mr Tilak before the prosecution. I had a talk with him afterwards & in that, I expressed my deep regret at the prosecution & pointed out its great unwisdom. I know as a fact that Lord M was himself greatly distressed when he learnt about Mr Tilak's arrest, though, of course, this must be kept confidential. . . .[32]

Despite an impression to the contrary prevailing in India at the time, the initiative for the prosecution had come not from Morley, nor even from Minto, but from Sir George Clarke, the Governor of Bombay, who seems to have acted against the advice of his own senior officers. From the private correspondence of Morley with Minto and Clarke, it is now clear that Morley not only did not initiate action against Tilak, but doubted its wisdom. After reading one of the allegedly incriminating articles in the *Kesari*, Morley was not convinced that a prosecution was 'inevitable'. He noted that the jury which tried Tilak was composed of seven Europeans, two Parsis and not a single Hindu. After referring to 'a packed jury', Morley wrote to the Viceroy: 'I suppose the sentence will be heavy—and at all events heavy enough to produce a good deal of exasperation in

[29] 'A meeting of the Poona citizens was held with Mr Govind V. Kanitkar, retired sub-judge, in the chair. Mr H. N. Apte moved: "This meeting strongly denounces some of the songs sung before large mixed audiences of students, women and children by several *melas*, and particularly by the Sanmitra Samaj Mela, as containing vile criticism and false, unfounded and filthy charges against our respected fellow townsman, the Hon. Mr Gokhale, and other gentlemen and institutions." ' *The Times*, 1 Nov. 1909.
[30] H. M. Bose to Gokhale, (n.d.), presumably Feb. 1909 (G.P.).
[31] Gokhale to Patwardhan, 2 Sept. 1909 (G.P.).   [32] G.P.

the Mahratta mind & to make the Moderate game much harder to play.'[33]

One of the worst offenders in maligning Gokhale was the Marathi *Hindu Panch*. It charged him with secretly visiting Government House at night in order to conspire with the Bombay Governor, with poisoning the mind of Morley against Tilak in England, and playing 'the role of Iago' in the Tilak case. Gokhale's friends, infuriated by such allegations, suggested legal action against the *Hindu Panch*. Gokhale cabled his concurrence from England, but the disciple of Ranade was soon having qualms of conscience. He wrote on 20 September:

I do not mind confessing that I have been feeling somewhat sad since despatching that telegram on Monday last. . . . Somehow I feel that I have not been quite loyal to the teachings and principles of my departed master [Ranade] in asking you to proceed against the offending journals as I have done. But while the heart is sad, the brain tells me that the course I have urged is the only course left open to me. Our public is so gullible that it simply swallows such stories.[34]

There was an interesting sequel to the prosecution of the *Hindu Panch*. Its proprietor, Krishnaji Kashinath Phadke, was at first defiant, but his press was confiscated by the government and he was rendered penniless. Gokhale sent for him and helped him with a a subsistence allowance for several years. Phadke was deeply moved by Gokhale's magnanimity and repented the part he had played in the smear campaign against him.

4

Incessant work and worry took their inevitable toll. By July 1908, Gokhale's health was failing. Dr Walter Carr, who had examined him earlier in May, expressed his concern at Gokhale's diabetes, which was mild, but 'such apparently mild cases are liable at any time, sometimes without any obvious reason, to become exceedingly severe. I saw last autumn a man who had been passing sugar for about 15 years, who suddenly developed symptoms and died in three weeks.' 'I fear', Dr Carr went on, 'that he [Gokhale] may sacrifice his health to his politics.'

[33] Morley to Minto, 16 July 1908 (M.P.).
[34] Gokhale to Patwardhan, 25 Sept. 1908 (G.P.).

At Wedderburn's suggestion, Gokhale agreed to spend three weeks at Vichy for treatment, another four weeks in Switzerland for 'after care', and to return to London in early October. Gokhale's holiday at Vichy began well, but was marred by an injury to his left arm which caused him acute suffering and compelled him to return to London. Since the pain continued, an X-ray was taken and a bone fracture was discovered. The discovery came too late: the arm was henceforth permanently weakened and the wrist became crooked. 'I am thankful', he wrote, 'it is the left arm and not the right.' The deformity could have been avoided if Gokhale had had an X-ray taken immediately after the accident. His passive resignation to suffering and reluctance to seek medical help promptly was not new; it had brought him to death's door in 1897 when he had injured his chest on his way to England and borne the pain in silence until his friend Wacha sent for a doctor.

Once in London, Gokhale had things other than his health to worry about. The news from India again became disturbing. There were fresh outrages. On 7 November an attempt was made on the life of Sir Andrew Fraser, the Governor of Bengal. Two days later a sub-inspector of police was murdered. On 13 November the statue of Queen Victoria was defaced, and on the same day nine persons in Bengal, including Aswini Kumar Datta, were deported under Regulation III of 1818. The British and Anglo-Indian newspapers clamoured for drastic measures. Morley refused to panic, or to withhold the constitutional reforms. On the contrary, he realized that the reforms had to be hastened if they were to conciliate the educated classes. 'I understand from a friend', Morley told Minto in November 1908, 'who has seen Gokhale that impatience is quite lively in India—because the chance of Moderates holding their own against Extremists when the Congress meets in the last week of December depends on their being able to show that we have our scheme actually ready for Parliament.'[35]

In April 1908, the Moderates held a meeting of the 'Convention' Committee at Allahabad and framed a constitution for the Indian National Congress, which was intended to provide it with elected committees and yet, by excluding the Extremists, insure it against the repetition of the internal convulsions which had culminated in the tragedy of Surat. Gokhale played a leading role in the drafting of the new Congress constitution, but he had to leave for England imme-

[35] Morley to Minto, 12 Nov. 1908 (M.P.).

diately afterwards. The recrudescence of political terrorism, the resultant repression by the government, and the Tilak trial brought political activity in India to a low ebb. With Tilak and Aurobindo Ghose in jail, and Khaparde and Bipin Chandra Pal in England, the Extremists were almost leaderless. In the wake of the popular indignation which swept the country following the Tilak trial, the Moderates also suffered a setback. They had the misfortune of being a party with able leaders but few workers. The new electoral machinery approved by the Allahabad Convention called for a great deal of organizational effort, but there was hardly anyone to take it up seriously. Gokhale was urged by some of his Bombay friends to return to India and to put some life into the organization with the help of his Servants of India.

It was not only Gokhale's friends who were appealing to him to return. Sir George Clarke, the Governor of Bombay, seems to have been rattled by the terrorist outrages and the intense excitement in his province caused by Tilak's arrest and imprisonment.

Dear Mr Gokhale [he wrote on 7 August 1908]
Will you forgive me for writing frankly to you? I feel strongly that your right place is in India at this juncture & if your health would permit it, your return would be an advantage in every way. I have no time to write about the recent events about which you will not agree with me. I will only ask you to believe [Tilak's arrest] was absolutely necessary. . . . The party of violence has developed much more rapidly than you can know and this has become a serious danger to the peace of India.
What we need now is a leader who will dissociate himself from futile visions which, if realized, would ruin India, who will act as a check on the party of violence, who will tell the truth plainly to the people, and who will work, critically it may be, with us in carrying out a series of gradual reforms. For India, it is now a question of orderly evolution, or of red revolution which would set back the clock for 50 years. I venture to think . . . that you alone can take the position I have indicated. . . .[36]

It was unusual for a British Governor to address an Indian politician in these terms. Sir George Clarke had only recently ordered the arrest of Tilak; in coming years he was to prove no friend of Indian aspirations. But in 1908, while his daughter Violet was alive, he impressed many Indian observers with his sympathy and sensitivity to public feeling. It is difficult to say whether he was sincerely seeking

[36] Clarke to Gokhale, 7 Aug. 1908 (copy of the original which seems to have been sent by Gokhale to Wedderburn) (G.P.).

Gokhale's help in stabilizing the political situation, or merely trying to win over the ablest spokesman of Indian aspirations with soothing words. Gokhale was, however, not the man to play another man's game, and before long Sir George Clarke was to be his severest critic in official circles in India.

Gokhale himself was keen to return to India; the affairs of his Society and of his party urgently required his presence. In September, he was complaining of 'homesickness'. But he could hardly leave England until the reforms scheme had taken shape. The 'Simla proposals' of the Government of India had to be purged of their conservative and even reactionary features. The Council of Notables, a feudal concept, had to go; the increase in the size and powers of the legislative councils had to be such as to impress the educated classes; the administration had to be decentralized and Indian opinion associated with it. Above all, a dramatic gesture such as the undoing of the partition of Bengal or the appointment of an Indian to the Viceroy's Executive Council was imperative if the faith of the Indian educated classes in British bona fides was to be restored.

With his better perspective of history and greater distance from the Indian bureaucratic machine, Morley viewed the reforms as a rallying point for those Indians who wanted to tread the constitutional path. By 1908, the Liberal party, after losing several bye-elections, was feeling shaky, and there were possibilities of the dissolution of Parliament and a general election. Morley did not have much time in which to get his reforms through. He had largely overcome the resistance of the Government of India by alternately lecturing and coaxing Minto through his weekly letters. In October 1908 he appointed a committee of his (India) Council, with Sir David Barr as Chairman, and gave it a twelve-point poser to cover the major points at issue in the scheme of constitutional reforms. The committee expressed unanimity on all the points except three. These were: the appointment of an Indian to the Viceroy's Executive Council, non-official majorities in the provincial legislative councils and the appointment of Indian members on the Governor's Executive Councils at Bombay and Madras. On these issues the majority of the members of the committee of the India Council shared bureaucratic fears rather than Indian aspirations.[37] On 27 November Morley sent off his despatch to the Government of India, and on 17 December made his statement on the reforms in the House of

[37] Report of the Special Committee, 12 Oct. 1908, signed by David Barr (M.P.).

Lords. Morley thus kept his promise to Gokhale that the reforms would be announced before the Indian National Congress met for its annual session at Madras. Their last meeting on 2 December was very cordial.

I had a farewell talk with Gokhale on Wednesday [wrote Morley]. He thinks he will never come to England again; no more work to be done for India here; must work in his own country; this is the moment of crisis; if nothing comes of our attempt, then the Extremists will have their own way: confusion, danger, ruin will follow—his tone both attracted and impressed me. He promises very confidently a good reception for our Reforms by the Congress.[38]

Just when the Indian constitutional cauldron was beginning to boil, Gokhale received an invitation to visit the United States and address the Civic Forum of New York in March 1909 on 'The National Movement in India'. The Civic Forum was an important non-political platform; among those who had addressed it were Taft and Bryan, the two U.S. presidential candidates in 1908, and the leader of the Liberal Party in the Russian Duma. 'It is a great opportunity', Gokhale wrote home in July, 'to state our case to the civilized world.'[39] By December 1908, he had given up the idea of going to the United States. He had been away from India for more than six months; he had plenty to do at home, and the news of student unrest and terrorist outrages disturbed him deeply. It seemed hardly feasible to return again in the spring not only for the passage of the Reforms Bill in Parliament, but for a visit to America.

5

Three months before the Congress was scheduled to meet at Madras, Gokhale had impressed upon Krishnaswamy Aiyer the importance of making the session a spectacular demonstration of the strength and unity of the Moderate party, its adherence to constitutional methods and willingness to work the new reforms in a spirit of cooperation with the government. He suggested that the honour of presiding over the session should go to Pherozeshah Mehta, 'the foremost constitutionalist',[40] but it was actually conferred on Rash Behari Ghose, the president-elect of the Surat session which had dissolved in chaos.

[38] Morley to Minto, 4 Dec. 1908 (M.P.).
[39] Gokhale to Patwardhan, 10 July 1908 (G.P.).
[40] Gokhale to K. Aiyer, 25 Sept. 1908 (G.P.).

Compared with the preceding three sessions at Benares, Calcutta and Surat, the Madras Congress (December 1908) was a tame affair. The inner tensions which had brought the confrontation between the Moderates and Extremists to a head a year earlier were absent; the Extremists were in fact conspicuous by their absence. The proceedings were placid, almost dull. There seemed to be a conscious effort not to do anything that would antagonize the government, embarrass Morley, or cast doubts on the loyalty of the educated classes, while the reforms were on the anvil of the British Parliament. A resolution on *swadeshi* was passed, but 'boycott' was not even mentioned. The proceedings began (to quote from the official record of the Madras Congress) with the 'Indian National Anthem' sung to the tune of 'God Save the King', and ended with 'cheers for the King-Emperor, Lord Morley and Lord Minto'. The first resolution of the Congress tendered 'loyal homage' to His Gracious Majesty, the King-Emperor, and respectfully welcomed 'the message sent by His Majesty to the Princes and People of India on the Fiftieth Anniversary of the Memorable Proclamation issued in 1858 by his Illustrious Mother, Victoria the Good'. Rash Behari Ghose in his presidential speech refuted Anglo-Indian insinuations about Congress loyalty to the Raj. 'We must be mad', he said, 'if we were really disloyal. . . . Our loyalty is above all suspicion. . . .'[41]

The Congress expressed the 'deep and general satisfaction of the country' and gratitude to Morley and Minto for the proposed reforms, which were described as 'a large and liberal instalment . . . needed to give the people of this country a substantial share in the management of their affairs and to bring the administration into closer touch with their wants and feelings'. Surendranath Banerjea, who moved this resolution, described the reforms scheme as the 'crowning triumph of constitutional agitation' and described Morley as the 'Simon de Montfort of the future Parliament of India'.[42] 'Henceforth the executive will not be able to control all provincial legislation', said Rash Behari Ghose. 'In a word, we shall now have something like a constitutional government in the place of an autocratic and irresponsible government.'

Strangely enough, the one man in that assembly who knew more about these constitutional reforms than anyone else did not speak on this resolution. It was only towards the end of the session, when

[41] *Report of the Proc. of the Twenty-third Indian National Congress held at Madras*, p. 38.   [42] Ibid., p. 49.

a formal motion of thanks to Hume and Wedderburn was moved, that Gokhale expressed his views on the reforms scheme. Though he considered it 'a fruition of 23 years of Congress effort', he agreed that all that it had done was to 'modify' the bureaucratic administration. The admission of Indians to the Councils of the Secretary of State, the Viceroy, and the provincial Governors had given India a 'reasonable access to the seats of highest power and authority'. Even though the new legislative councils had limited powers, the non-official majorities in the provincial councils provided a 'preventive control' over provincial legislation. True, the veto of the government remained. To question that, argued Gokhale,

is not to understand the working of constitutional government. Even the House of Commons works under what may be called a veto, viz. the practical veto of the House of Lords and the theoretical veto of the Sovereign. They are a self-governing people and yet they bear all the inconveniences of this double veto. Let us grow to the full bounds of the new opportunities and it will be time enough to talk of circumscribing the veto. . . . None of us wants to be satisfied with things as they are, but we must prove that we can bear these responsibilities, before we ask for more.

Hitherto, they had been engaged in agitation from outside; henceforth they would be engaged in 'responsible association' in administration. 'There is plenty of scope for growth here, and as we grow and discharge the responsibility that devolves on us properly, I am sure there will be progress further and further towards our having what may be called a responsible administration.'[43]

Gokhale knew that Morley's statement on the reforms was only the opening shot in his campaign. There were strong vested interests hostile to the reforms in Britain, which were bound to exploit issues like 'boycott' and partition of Bengal, and embarrass Morley while he piloted the reforms through the British Parliament. It was on Gokhale's advice that the Madras Congress maintained a discreet silence on these vital but controversial issues.

Gokhale's speech put the reforms in perspective, forestalled criticism of their rather modest aims, soothed public feeling excited by anarchical outrages and repressive legislation, and promised the support of educated India for the reforms. Morley was delighted by the verdict of the Madras Congress, which had (he noted) 'done all that we had a right to expect and will do a good deal to justify our

[43] Ibid., p. 137.

policy in both persevering with the reforms and in making them liberal'.[44]

Gokhale was not alone in expressing enthusiasm for the reforms. On 6 January 1909, a week after the Madras Congress, Morley wrote to Minto that R. C. Dutt and K. G. Gupta, who had dined with him, were jubilant at the way the Moderates had rallied to the defence of the reforms, and insisted 'that it will last for ever & that you have now a national party more or less committed to constitutional ways'. Three months later, Dadabhai Naoroji assured Minto and Morley that Indians would remember with gratitude their names for having courageously and sincerely made a beginning towards raising India to the status of a self-governing member and real partner in the British Empire.[45] The *Hindustan Review*, edited by Sachchidananda Sinha, eloquently summed up the optimistic mood of the Moderates:

Loyal patriotism has triumphed over unreasoning fanaticism . . . the better mind of the people as well as of those in authority has prevailed over the narrow-minded and short-sighted extremists among Anglo-Indians and Indians alike. In all this, gratitude compels us to assign the greatest credit to the great scholar and statesman [Morley] who presides over the destinies of India.[46]

---

[44] Morley to Minto, 31 Dec. 1908 (M.P.).
[45] Naoroji to Minto & Morley, 3 April 1909 (M.P.).
[46] *Hindustan Review*, Dec. 1908, p. 609.

27

Climax

'We have now fairly raised the curtain', Morley wrote on 18 February 1909, 'and our play has begun. The Councils Bill was read formally a first time in H. of L. [House of Lords] last night.'[1] The second reading was postponed by a couple of days to enable Curzon to take part in the discussion. Morley noted that his audience, including as it did a number of former Viceroys and Governors, was 'rather brilliant, and very attentive, but not over-sympathetic...'[2] Lords Reay and Ampthill supported the bill, but Lords Macdonell, North-cote, Harris and Sandhurst were critical. Lansdowne did not agree that the bill was a natural development of the Act of 1892: 'it was not a step forward but a plunge forward, and a plunge which will lead us we cannot tell where'. Morley observed that Curzon hated 'the bill and the whole policy of which the bill is the instrument'. To Curzon the enlargement of the councils was a 'revolutionary change'. He saw great risks in dispensing with official majorities in the pro-vincial legislative councils. He did not see why the Executive Councils of the Viceroy and the Governors should be thrown open to Indians. To obtain Indian advice in India, said Curzon, it was not necessary to put a man into the Viceroy's Cabinet. The territorial electorates proposed in the bill were also unacceptable to him. These, he feared, would be manipulated by the Hindus. The right of asking supple-mentary questions was an avoidable burden on the civil service, who were 'dictators' and not 'debaters'. He also opposed the extension of Governor's Executive Councils to provinces other than Bombay and Madras, where they already existed.[3]

Two months before he spoke in the House of Commons, Curzon had warned Arthur Balfour, the leader of the Conservative party, against the 'looming crisis in India'. Morley was, wrote Curzon,

[1] Morley to Minto, 18 Feb. 1909 (M.P.).
[2] *Idem*, 25 Feb. 1909 (M.P.).
[3] *Debates on Indian Affairs*, House of Lords, session 1909, 9 Edward VII, London, 1909, pp. 21–39.

in active communication with the leaders of the Native party, particularly Gokhale, who has been two or three times to England to interview him and to whom he gave assurances that have transpired in India, and in his public speeches and replies to questions he constantly interjected passages that gave encouragement to the Indian agitators and led them to think that he would finally come down upon their side. . . . While the Constitution-mongers have been working and disputing, the extreme men have taken the law into their hands [resulting] in press vituperation, violence, crime and assassination.[4]

Curzon's fear that Morley had fallen under Gokhale's spell was widely shared by the Anglo-Indian lobby in London. In his speech in the House of Lords, Lansdowne, in an obvious reference to Gokhale, had a dig at Morley:

I am sure the noble Viscount [Morley] recollects a passage in Boswell in which it is related that at one time, Dr Johnson was in the habit, I think on Sunday evenings, of frequenting the house of Dr John Campbell. But in time he came to the conclusion that it was better for him no longer to frequent the doctor's society, because he said he was convinced that the shoals of Scotsmen to be found there would, whenever 'he did anything well', immediately remark, 'Aye, aye! he must have learnt that from "Cawmell".' I leave the noble Viscount opposite to apply the moral which I seem to detect in that little story.[5]

The attack on Morley—and Gokhale—was not confined to good-humoured sallies in Parliament. In March 1909, *The Times* lent its correspondence columns to a campaign against Gokhale by publishing letters whose authors signed themselves as 'Thirty years Service' and 'Suum Cuique'. They drew attention to a note by Gokhale, which had been published in the *Friend of India* and was stated to have been given to the Secretary of State for India in September 1908. They saw a great deal of resemblance between the proposals outlined in Gokhale's note, and the clauses of the Indian Councils Bill introduced by Morley in the House of Lords. They alleged that Morley had, at Gokhale's bidding, gone beyond the recommendations of the Government of India on several vital points. They argued that the reforms had been wrung from the Secretary of State for India by the leaders of the agitating classes. 'Who was the author of the reforms?', they asked. 'Is the skeleton to be clothed, is the

---

[4] Curzon to Balfour, 11 Dec. 1909 (C.P.).
[5] *Debates on Indian Affairs*, House of Lords, session 1909, 9 Edward VII, London, 1909, p. 214.

cheque to be filled in on the counsels of the Government of India, or on those of Mr Gokhale?'[6]

Morley could not leave such insinuations unanswered in the House of Lords.

What do people mean [he asked] when they say that reforms were wrung from the Secretary of State by an Indian political leader—a certain Indian political leader known to some of your Lordships?... Now Mr Gokhale, who is well known as a prominent and responsible spokesman of a very highly important section or branch of Indian opinion, came to see me at the India Office before the Despatch of the Government of India of October last reached this country. I wound up our conversation with a request, which I have made to other people, that he would be so good as to write on a sheet of notepaper his views as to the reforms which he and his friends desired, and he did so. Did I stop there? The very self-same process I went through with a spokesman of the Mahomedans. . . . I may say that I never had any communication whatever after that, which, I think, was on some day in September—with Mr Gokhale until the day before he left this country—after my Despatch had gone—when he called to say goodbye. . . . No proceeding was ever more strictly in order, was ever more above board. . . .[7]

Charged by the Tory Opposition—and in the columns of *The Times* —with a conspiracy against the British Raj, it was natural that Morley should have played down Gokhale's contribution to the reforms. These had of course not been 'wrung' by Gokhale, but his advice had definitely contributed to the liberalizing of some of the clauses in the bill. Gokhale himself came to Morley's rescue by under-rating his own part in the formulation of the proposals. Speaking in the Imperial Council at Calcutta on 29 March 1909, he belittled not only his own contribution but also Morley's, and attributed nine-tenths of the scheme to the Viceroy whom the Tory Opposition could scarcely disown. 'The fact is', he argued, 'that the path of constitutional reform in India is extremely narrow, and those who want to advance along that path have no choice but to have in view more or less the same stages and almost the same steps.' To Morley, Gokhale paid a handsome tribute as 'one who has taught so highly, and to whose name such great honour attaches even in distant lands'. It would have been a sad thing for humanity if his tenure of office, as Secretary of State for India, had produced nothing more than de-

[6] *The Times*, 11 March 1909.
[7] *Debates on Indian Affairs*, House of Lords, session 1909, 9 Edward VII, London, 1909, pp. 210–11.

portations and Press laws. Gokhale was glad, however, that Morley's 'great Liberalism has been amply and strikingly vindicated even in so difficult a position as that of the head of a vast bureaucracy'.[8]

The Tory majority in the House of Lords did not like the bill but, as Morley noted, 'they did not dare to take the responsibility of throwing it out; and so they have to be content with attempts to nag and whittle it away'.[9] In these attempts, the Conservatives had one important success in the House of Lords: clause 3, which empowered the creation of executive councils to assist the Governors of what were known as major provinces, was deleted. This clause was, however, re-introduced in an amended form by the House of Commons, where the Liberal Government had a comfortable majority. Despite fierce attacks by Balfour, Percy and other Conservative members, the bill was passed by the House of Commons.

2

Curiously enough, the most controversial part of the reforms was one which had not been included in the Indian Councils bill: the appointment of an Indian to the Viceroy's Executive Council. The 'Native Member' was, Morley noted, at the back of the minds of most members of the Lords and the Commons, even when they were talking of other things.[10] For nearly three years, Minto and Morley had been debating whether to throw open the highest executive posts under British rule to an Indian. The proposal had been stoutly resisted by a majority of Minto's colleagues, by the India Council in London, by the Tory Opposition, by *The Times* and, not least, by King Edward VII. Morley was informed on 12 March 1909 from Biarritz, where His Majesty was holidaying:

The King regrets that he cannot change his views on this subject. . . . He remains, however, of opinion that this proposed step is fraught with the greatest danger to the maintenance of the Indian Empire under British rule . . . as . . . at the last meeting of the Cabinet Council the Government were unanimous on the subject, the King has no other alternative but to give way much against his will. He, however, wishes it clearly to be understood that he protests most strongly at this new departure.[11]

On 20 March the royal assent was received and four days later it

[8] Patwardhan & Ambekar (eds.), op. cit., vol. I, p. 153.
[9] Morley to Minto, 5 March 1909 (M.P.).   [10] Ibid.
[11] S. Lee, *King Edward VII: A Biography*, London, 1927, vol. II, p. 385.

was announced that S. P. Sinha, the Advocate-General of Bengal, would succeed Erle Richards as the Law Member of the Viceroy's Executive Council.

'It is a proud day', Gokhale wrote to Dunlop-Smith, Minto's private secretary, 'in the lives of us Indians today.'[12] A few days later, Gokhale told the Imperial Legislative Council that he had been touched by Morley's reference to Sinha as 'one of the King's equal subjects. . . . This phrase has touched a chord in Indian hearts which will keep vibrating for some time.'

Within three months of its introduction in the House of Lords, the Indian Councils Bill had completed its parliamentary passage. 'The immortal Bill is through', Morley reported to Minto on 21 May. For this consummation much of the credit must go to Morley. He had carefully planned the reforms, wrestled with the diehards in his own Council in London, worn down the opposition of the bureaucracy in Calcutta, and withstood the calumnies of the Tory Party and the Anglo-Indian lobby. He had, however, made one cardinal blunder for which he was to pay dearly. He failed to heed the warning of Sir Henry Cotton not to leave too much of the shaping of the bill in the hands of the officials. Morley simply followed the precedent set by the framers of the Councils Bill of 1892 of leaving the details to be filled in by the Government of India. Morley should have known that his critics in India were looking for loopholes in his scheme to frustrate it. As early as February 1909, Lansdowne, a former Viceroy and a severe critic of the Bill in the House of Lords, was banking on 'the general scope of the regulations', and hoping that the Secretary of State (for India) could be induced to 'go out of his way to be reassuring'.[13] Lansdowne, whose son had recently married the Viceroy's daughter, was told by Minto that his real object had been 'to ensure representation of classes we thought had hitherto been left out in the cold & who represented a real solid stake in the country'. In other words, the reforms were intended to bolster the feudal nobility and other loyalist groups. 'In fact, I always thought', Minto confided to Lansdowne, 'our proposals are very conservative in many ways, and was surprised at the good reception they met with from Congress circles.'[14] Minto did not like the idea of members of legislatures being elected, but he also realized that it was no use pitting himself against the Secretary of State for India and the Liberal

[12] Gokhale to Dunlop-Smith, 24 March 1909, *in* Gilbert, op. cit., p. 186.
[13] Lansdowne to Minto, 26 Feb. 1909 (Minto P.).
[14] Minto to Lansdowne, 18 March 1909 (Minto P.).

majority in the House of Commons. 'We shall have to trust', the Viceroy wrote, 'to a careful creation of electorates and disqualification [of potentially hostile candidates].'[15] The framing of the regulations under the bill was thus an opportunity for the bureaucrats in Simla and London to recover some of the ground they had been compelled to yield to Morley. There were safeguards enough for the Raj even in Morley's scheme: the Imperial Legislative Council had an official majority; the provincial councils had limited powers—which were further subject to the veto of the Governor—and the Imperial Council had concurrent powers to legislate for the provinces. All this did not, however, seem adequate to Minto and the Government of India. They wanted to have the power of approving a candidate even after he had been elected. A long and bitter debate ensued between the Viceroy and the Secretary of State by letter and cable on the disqualification of those who had been deported under Regulation III of 1818. The Viceroy finally won his point. The whole purpose of non-official majorities in the provinces was undermined by increasing the proportion of non-official nominated members, who could be depended upon to vote with the official bloc. The reforms were thus whittled down by the framers of the 'regulations'. Unfortunately for Morley, while he had acquired a fair understanding of the Indian political scene, he did not have enough mastery of administrative details to avoid the pitfalls which the senior civil servants in Simla and London contrived for him. Again and again, questions which were presumed to have been settled were re-opened. Again and again, whatever little was conceded by the Parliament was delayed and diluted by the 'experts'. As late as October 1909, Minto was telling Morley that it would be another year before the reforms could be implemented.[16] Morley was fighting a lone and losing battle, though he did not know it. The 'regulations' framed under the Indian Councils Act were to destroy part of his work. On one issue, the formation of electorates for the reconstituted legislatures, Morley himself was a party to the process of destruction. His anxiety to ensure a safe passage for the bill was skilfully and successfully exploited by the Anglo-Indian lobby acting in concert with Muslim League leaders in London.

[15] Ibid.

[16] 'Your telegram about Regulations', Morley wrote to Minto on 14 October 1909, 'has just been placed in my hands, and the last words of it positively make my hair stand on end—"postponement for another year"!!! If that catastrophe happens, we had better throw up the sponge.' (M.P.).

28

Origins of Muslim Separatism

When Gokhale was being initiated into the politics of the Deccan in the late 1880s, the first confrontation had already taken place between Indian nationalism as represented by the Indian National Congress, and Muslim separatism as represented by Sir Syed Ahmed Khan and other Muslim leaders. Only two Muslim delegates attended the first Congress session in 1885; the number rose to 33 at the second session in 1886, and 79 at the third session in 1887, over which a prominent Muslim leader of Bombay, Badruddin Tyabji, presided. The bulk of the Muslim élite in India, however, followed Sir Syed's lead and kept away from the Congress. It was Sir Syed's thesis that representative institutions designed for 'homogeneous' societies of the West would not suit India, where the Hindu superiority in numbers, education and wealth amounted to 'a game of dice in which one man had four dice and the other only one'.[1] Even if the Muslim disadvantage in numbers could be offset by some electoral jugglery, Sir Syed doubted whether the democratic process could work satisfactorily in India.

Let us suppose [he said] that a rule is laid down that half the members [of the Indian legislature] are to be Muhammadans, and half Hindus, that the Muhammadans and the Hindus elect their own men. Now I ask you to pardon me for saying something, which I say with a sore heart. In the whole [Muslim] nation there is no person who is equal to the Hindus in fitness for the work [in the Councils].[2]

The fear that Muslims would not be able to hold their own in elective bodies and competitive examinations seems to have moulded the political philosophy of Sir Syed. He pooh-poohed the idea that Indians could ever rule themselves. He considered it India's good fortune that she had fallen under the domination of Britain rather than that of Russia, Germany or France. 'Every one would admit',

[1] S. Mohammed, *Writings and Speeches of Sir Syed Ahmad Khan*, Bombay, 1972, p. 210.   [2] Ibid.

he asserted, 'that their governments are far worse, nay, beyond comparison worse, than the British Government. It is therefore necessary that for the peace of India and for the progress of everything in India, the English Government should remain for many years—in fact for ever.'[3]

The acceptance of British rule as a reality, and even as a beneficent reality, was not confined to Sir Syed in the closing decades of the nineteenth century. The Hindu and Parsi élites, which formed the backbone of the Congress, also accepted British rule, but they wanted progressively to Indianize its administration, and to make it responsive and even responsible to Indian opinion. To Sir Syed, however, the idea that senior appointments should be conferred on highly educated Indians ('Bengalees' as he called them) for merely passing the Indian Civil Service competitive examination seemed absurd. 'Do you think', he asked, 'that the Rajput & fiery Pathan who are not afraid of being hanged or of encountering the swords of the police or the bayonets of the army could remain in peace under the Bengalees?'[4] No less absurd in his view was the idea of subjecting the Government of India to popular control. Was there any instance in the history of the world, he asked, in which a nation, after conquering and ruling over another, had bestowed representative institutions on its 'conquered people'?[5] The principle of democracy, Sir Syed argued, was

not adapted to a country in which one foreign race has conquered another. The English have conquered India and all of us along with it. And just as we [Muslims] made the country [India] obedient & our slave, so the English have done with us. Is it then consonant with the principles of empire that they [the British] should ask us whether they should fight Burma or not?[6]

Sir Syed ridiculed the idea that a man of 'low caste or insignificant origin',[7] who had taken a university degree and had the necessary ability, should have a seat in a legislative council. A seat in the legislative council of the Viceroy was, observed Sir Syed, 'a position of great honour and prestige. None but a man of good breeding can the Viceroy take as his colleague, treat as his brother and invite to entertainments at which he may have to dine with Dukes and Earls.'[8]

Sir Syed was haunted by the memories of the revolt of 1857 and

---

[3] Ibid., p. 185.   [4] Ibid., p. 209.   [5] Ibid., p. 186
[6] Ibid., p. 187.   [7] Ibid., p. 204.   [8] Ibid., p. 205.

the harm it had done to the interests of the Muslim community. He was afraid that political agitation would lead to turmoil and Muslims would incur the wrath of their British rulers. His innate conservatism, his isolation from the progressive political thought of the day, and his conviction of the backwardness of his own community led him to lean increasingly on British support. He was not alone in propounding this parochial philosophy; almost simultaneously, other influential Muslim leaders in Bengal, like Abdul Latif and Syed Ameer Ali, had rejected the proferred hand of Surendranath Banerjea, and decided to organize educated Muslims on a separate platform.

It would be unjust to ascribe Sir Syed's political philosophy wholly to British inspiration, but he found willing and zealous supporters among the British. Foremost among them were the successive principals of the Anglo-Muhammedan College, Aligarh, Theodore Beck, W. A. Archbold and Theodore Morison. Through the columns of the *Aligarh Institute Gazette* and of Anglo-Indian papers, such as the *Pioneer*, these European principals of the Aligarh college drove home the point that the 'parliamentary form of government made no sense in a country containing two or more nations tending to oppress the numerically weaker'. Indian nationality, argued Beck, was 'but a shadow'.[9]

2

It must be acknowledged that Muslim opposition to the Indian National Congress in these early years was stronger and more stubborn than the Congress leaders then—and for many years later— were prepared to recognize. Muslim opposition, or at best indifference, to the Congress was exploited by its enemies. Writing to a Muslim friend (Kazi Shahabuddin), Dadabhai Naoroji bewailed in 1887:

How your action has paralysed not only our own efforts, but the hands of our English friends. . . . In the House of Commons, I think, Mr Bright has stoutly urged the necessity of an examination in India to put us on an equality with English candidates. Today when he would and could have urged the same thing with ten times the force, he feels himself staggered, and owing to your opposition he feels puzzled and cannot help us. What a blight you have thrown upon our future and how you have retarded our progress for a long time to come![10]

[9] *Aligarh Institute Gazette*, 30 April 1887, p. 485.
[10] Masani, *Dadabhai Naoroji*, p. 256.

At the suggestion of Badruddin Tyabji who presided over the 1887 session, the Congress had bound itself not to discuss at its annual meetings any subject to the introduction of which the Hindu or Muslim delegates as a body objected, 'provided, however, that this rule shall refer only to subjects in regard to which the Congress has not already definitely pronounced its opinion'.[11] Even this self-denying ordinance failed to attract many Muslims to the Congress, the composition of which continued to be predominantly Hindu. The Congress proceedings and resolutions do not, however, betray the least communal bias. Indeed, during the first twenty years of its existence, the Congress was dominated less by Hindus than by Parsis like Dadabhai Naoroji, Pherozeshah Mehta and D. E. Wacha, whom even their worst enemies never accused of a communal outlook. This did not affect the stance of Sir Syed or his adherents. They flatly repudiated the concept of an Indian nationality, and questioned the wisdom of curtailing the British monopoly of power and patronage in India. Indeed, Sir Syed and Principal Beck of the Aligarh College were honorary secretaries of the 'Indian Patriotic Association', established in August 1888 to carry on propaganda against the Congress in Great Britain, and 'to strive to preserve peace in India and to strengthen the British rule'.[12] This Association petitioned against Bradlaugh's Bill in 1889, and opposed the extension of the elective principle to the legislative councils. In December 1893 the Muhammedan Anglo-Oriental Defence Association was founded at Aligarh, 'to discourage popular and political agitation among the Muhammedans and to support measures "calculated to increase the stability of the British Government" '.[13] The demands of this association included claims for 'proper representation' for Muslims in legislative councils, and municipal and district boards, and the abolition of competitive examinations. In 1896 a memorandum was sent to the British friends of Aligarh for *equal* representation of Muslims and Hindus in the legislature of the North-Western (later the United) Provinces whose Muslim population constituted only fourteen per cent of the total.

The head-on clash between the Congress led by A. O. Hume and Muslim opinion led by Syed Ahmed occurred during the years 1887–8, just when the Congress had incurred the bitter hostility of

[11] *Report of the Fourth Indian National Congress held at Allahabad*, p. 88.
[12] M. S. Jain, *The Aligarh Movement*, Agra, 1965, p. 124.
[13] Ibid., pp. 127–8.

the British Government in India. During the succeeding sixteen years, the Congress organization had somewhat languished. The partition of Bengal galvanized it into activity in 1905, but it also created a situation in which the fears of the Muslim community and the interests of the British Raj converged. To the adherents of the Congress the partition of Bengal seemed a sinister British plot designed to weaken a politically conscious province, but to the Muslim middle class it seemed to create a Muslim majority province which opened new vistas of education, employment and prosperity for them. The victory of the Liberal party in Britain, which thrilled nationalist India, only aroused misgivings in the minds of the Muslim élite and the British bureaucrats to whom elective institutions in India were anathema.

We have already seen how Minto and his colleagues at once distrusted and feared Morley, the new Secretary of State for India. Throughout the summer of 1906 the Congress leaders, including Gokhale (who was in London), waited with bated breath for a momentous announcement from Morley on the political future of India. Morley's statement, when it came, was far too cautious to gladden the hearts of the Congress leaders, but even its guarded reference to the reform of legislative councils seems to have alarmed the Muslim leaders. They had observed Sir Syed's advice to shun nationalist politics but knew that even Sir Syed had not been able to prevent the passage of the Indian Councils Bill of 1892. What was there to prevent Morley from sponsoring another instalment of constitutional reforms which could have the effect of strengthening the Hindus *vis-à-vis* the Muslims? The announcement that the Viceroy was about to constitute a committee of his Executive Council to frame a reforms scheme seemed ominous. There may have been a good case for Muslims eschewing politics in the late 1880s, but its validity in 1906 sounded doubtful. The Muslim leaders did not want to remain passive spectators of events.

Morley delivered his budget speech in the House of Commons on 26 July. Nine days later, Nawab Mehdi Ali Khan—better known as Mohsin-ul-Mulk—who had succeeded Sir Syed Ahmed Khan as secretary of the Aligarh College, wrote in a letter to W. A. J. Archbold, the Principal of the Aligarh College, then spending the summer vacation at Simla:

You must have read and thought over John Morley's speech on the Indian budget. It is very much talked of among the Mohammedans of India, and is commonly believed to be a great success achieved by the 'National Congress'. You are aware that the Mohammedans always feel a little disappointed and young educated Mohammedans seem to have a sympathy for the 'Congress', and this speech will produce a great tendency in them to join the 'Congress'. . . . I have got several letters drawing attention particularly to the proposal of 'elected representatives' in Legislative Councils. . . . If the new rules now to be drawn up introduce 'election' on a more extended scale, the Mohammedans will hardly get a seat, while the Hindus will carry off the palm by dint of their majority.[14]

Mohsin-ul-Mulk sounded Archbold on the possibility of presenting a memorial to the Viceroy to draw his attention to the 'consideration of Muslim rights'.

That the sixty-nine year-old Mohsin-ul-Mulk, a loyal adherent of Sir Syed Ahmed, should have taken fright at the prospect of concessions to the Congress by the Liberal Government in Britain is not at all surprising. Five years earlier, on 20 October 1901, a meeting of leading Muslims of upper India held at Lucknow had resolved to form 'a representative association' for the protection of their political and social rights.[15] The project, through the inertia and mutual jealousies of its sponsors, was however still-born. British friends of the Muslims, including Principal Morison, warned them to adhere to Sir Syed's line and to keep away from politics. Five years later, Principal Archbold (who had succeeded Morison) and British officials gave a helping hand in organizing the Muslim community for a political purpose. This volte-face was due to a change of circumstances. The possibility of Muslim youth being swept off their feet in the highly charged atmosphere in the wake of the partition of Bengal was as unwelcome to the British officials as to the older leaders of the Muslim community.

Mohsin-ul-Mulk's letter to Archbold was written on 4 August. Within three days it had not only reached Minto at Simla, but had been forwarded to the Secretary of State for India. 'I have not had time to think over the advisability of receiving the proposed deputation', Minto wrote, 'but am inclined to do so.'[16]

That the representative of the British Crown in India should receive a political deputation consisting of members of only one community would have seemed preposterous to Curzon. In February 1901, he had

[14] Mohsin-ul-Mulk to Archbold, Aug. 1906, enclosed with Minto to Morley, 8 Aug. 1906 (M.P.).
[15] *Aligarh Institute Gazette*, 1 Aug. 1903, p. 2.
[16] Minto to Morley, 8 Aug. 1906 (M.P.).

turned down the request of Nawab Muhammed Hyat Khan of the Punjab for a separate deputation from 'the Muhammadens of India to present an address to H. M. the King-Emperor'. 'It would be difficult, if not impossible', wrote the Viceroy's private secretary to the Nawab, 'to select one community or the members of one religion, in preference to another, as entitled to proceed to England and to present the address in person.'[17] Never in the twenty-one year history of the Indian National Congress had a Viceroy received a deputation from it. In 1906, however, there were good reasons for the Viceroy to oblige Mohsin-ul-Mulk and his friends. It was evident that the new Secretary of State was inclined to conciliate the educated classes, and to consider some of the demands of the Indian National Congress which threatened the monopoly of British power and privilege in India. The Viceroy and his advisers were already thinking of using the princely order and landed aristocracy as a counterpoise to to the Congress. They could not but welcome any indication on the part of the Muslim community to challenge the claims of the Hindu educated classes which formed the backbone of the Congress. It is difficult to say how far Muslim youth was really exposed to the infection of sedition in the summer of 1906, but this possibility was shrewdly played up by Archbold to win the sympathy of Dunlop-Smith and other British officials close to the Viceroy. On 10 August, Denzil Ibbetson, a member of the Viceroy's Executive Council, advised Minto to 'receive the deputation and answer them sympathetically'. The educated Mohammedans, Ibbetson wrote, 'are the most conservative element' in Indian society, and it would be 'a calamity' if the younger generation of Mohammedans were driven 'into the arms of the Congress party'.[18] On 10 September, Dunlop-Smith confided to his diary: 'What I want to stop is these young Mohammedans forming small societies all over India. Once they start the game they can make us really anxious.'[19]

The 'Fuller Episode' became another reason for making a conciliatory gesture to the Muslim community at this time. Sir Bampfylde Fuller, the indiscreet and obdurate Governor of Eastern Bengal and Assam, had brought about his own downfall, but he had come to be regarded as a patron of the Muslim community. His virtual dismissal shocked Muslim leaders in Bengal. They needed to be reassured that

[17] Walter Lawrence to Nawab Mohammed Hyat Khan, 1 Feb. 1901 (C.P.).
[18] Ibbetson to Dunlop-Smith, 10 Aug. 1906 (Minto P.).
[19] Gilbert, op. cit., p. 56.

the government would continue to keep a benevolent eye over Muslim interests, especially in the newly created province and had no intention of reversing the partition of Bengal.

3

Meanwhile the drafts of the memorial to the Viceroy were being debated by Muslim leaders. A draft prepared by Syed Husain Bilgrami was circulated to the members of the deputation and to some British officers who 'took kindly interest in matters connected with the Muhammadens'.[20] One of these British officials was Harcourt Butler, then Commissioner of Lucknow. He was in the confidence of two key figures in this drama, Mohsin-ul-Mulk, Secretary of the Aligarh college and Dunlop-Smith, the Viceroy's private secretary. A letter from Butler to Erle Richards, the Law Member (who was in Simla), written on the very day the Muslim leaders met in Lucknow, mirrors the hopes and fears not only of the Muslim élite, but of its British friends.

Harcourt Butler to H. E. Richards, 16 September 1906: Delegates from all India are now assembled in Lucknow to pass the draft memorial to the Viceroy.

Mohsin-ul-Mulk sees me daily & has shown me his confidential correspondence on the subject.

Great diversity of views prevails. The majority attach much more importance to getting more appointments than to getting more seats in council. The former affect many, the latter few. They are mixing the two up together in one memorial. The Hindus are waiting to pounce. They are deeply exasperated at the open partisanship shown by the Anglo-Indian Press.

The difficulty of the situation is increased by the fact that no one [Mahommedan] has a practical scheme. The whole business from Fuller's retirement to now has been organized by Mohsin-ul-Mulk & Imdad ul Mulk in a hurry. . . .

The whole memorial is being hacked about hourly, & there may be another plan tomorrow. There is no cohesion & no one to lead. . . . Mohsin-ul-Mulk has himself no idea what will happen. He will try to please all.[21]

Butler noted the strong 'anti-Hindu feeling' among the Muslim leaders assembled in Lucknow. 'That', he wrote, 'is about the only common platform that they have.' He formed a poor opinion of the

---

[20] Mohsin-ul-Mulk to H. Butler, 2 Sept. 1906 (Butler P.).
[21] Butler to Erle Richards, 16 Sept. 1906 (Butler P.).

Muslim leaders and their capacity for organization, and feared that they would fall out among themselves. 'I have been in touch', Butler summed up, 'with several movements of late years, but I have not yet come across so sketchy a movement as this. However, it will grow.'[22]

The memorial in its final form reflected the highest common denominator of Muslim demands. As Butler had correctly forecast, Mohsin-ul-Mulk tried 'to please all'. Most of the thirty-five signatories to the memorial, headed by His Highness the Aga Khan, belonged to the titled and landed gentry, the Nawabs, the Khan Bahadurs and the C.I.E.s. It is true that some of them such as Hakim Ajmal Khan, Syed Ali Imam, and Abdur Rahim represented the rising urban Muslim middle class, but the tone of the deputation was set by the feudal elements, who were proud to flaunt their loyalty to the Raj. The memorial included almost every demand that could possibly be made in 1906 upon the British Government on behalf of the Muslim community *vis-à-vis* the Hindus. However, its primary object seems to have been to prevent the extension of the elective principle to the legislatures, and if that was not possible, to find some means of offsetting the numerical inferiority of the Muslims. The memorialists argued that representative institutions of the European type were new to India and that the greatest care, forethought and caution were necessary, if these institutions were to be successfully adapted to the social, religious and political conditions obtaining in India; that in the absence 'of such care and caution, their adoption is likely among other evils to place our national interests at the mercy of an unsympathetic majority'.[23] They conceded that the sixty-two million Muslims formed no more than one-fifth of the population of India, but argued that they were, nevertheless, more numerous than the entire population of any first class European power, except Russia.

We venture, indeed, with Your Excellency's permission, to go a step further, and urge that the position accorded to the Mohammedan Community in any kind of representation, direct or indirect, and in all other ways affecting their status and influence, should be commensurate not merely with their numerical strength, but also with their political importance and the value of the contribution which they make to the defence of the Empire; and we also hope that Your Excellency will in this connection be pleased to give due consideration to the position which they occupied in India a little more than a

[22] Ibid.   [23] The Muslim Address to the Viceroy, para 8 (M.P.).

hundred years ago, and of which the traditions have naturally not faded from their minds.[24]

From these premises it was but a step to argue that Muslim electors should form a separate electoral college of their own, and the Muslim community should be awarded more seats in expanded legislative councils than its numbers warranted.

It is doubtful whether most of the members of the deputation had any clear conception of the composition or functions of legislative councils; they were probably more interested in the other demands outlined in the memorial, such as that for posts in the 'Gazetted and Subordinate and Ministerial Services of all Indian Provinces'. The memorial mentioned that there were Hindu judges on the various High Courts in India, but no Muslim. 'Qualified Mahommedan lawyers, eligible for these appointments', the memorialists pointed out, 'can always be found.' At least half a dozen candidates were to be found among the signatories to the Memorial. It was further suggested that if one or more Indians were appointed to the Viceroy's Executive Council, 'more than one Mohammedan . . . will be found in the country, fit to serve with distinction'.

4

On 1 October 1906, the Muslim Deputation was granted an audience by the Viceroy. He had been advised by Archbold and Dunlop-Smith to give a 'reassuring reply'. The whole issue of the expansion of legislative councils and the structure of the electoral system was then being examined by a sub-committee of the Executive Council, which had yet to reach any conclusions. Strangely enough, Minto, whose comments on complicated matters were usually ambiguous and evasive, did not hesitate to tread tricky constitutional ground, and to pronounce on fundamental issues. He began by appreciating 'the representative character' of the deputation and hailed his guests as 'the descendants of a conquering and ruling race'. He readily endorsed the thesis that representative institutions of the European type were entirely new to the people of India and their introduction required great care, forethought and caution. Above all, with unusual alacrity, he conceded the major demands of the memorialists:

The pith of your address, as I understand it, is a claim that, in any system of representation, whether it affects a Municipality, a District

24 Ibid., para 5.

Board or a Legislative Council, in which it is proposed to introduce or increase an electoral organization, the Mohammedan community should be represented as a community. You point out that in many cases electoral bodies as now constituted cannot be expected to return a Mohammedan candidate, and that if by chance they did so, it could only be at the sacrifice of such a candidate's views to those of a majority opposed to his own community, whom he would in no way represent, and you justly claim that your position should be estimated not merely on your numerical strength, but in respect to the political importance of your community and the service it has rendered to the Empire. I am entirely in accord with you.[25]

The Viceroy's reply was not given on the spur of the moment; its tenor and content had been debated by his advisers for weeks. On 20 September, Dunlop-Smith had informed Butler that he had been preparing notes for the Viceroy's reply, and expected 'criticism among the Hindus & Calcutta press will howl. I don't think that will much matter.'[26] Immediately after the departure of the deputation, Minto confided to Lawley, the Governor of Madras, 'I have only a few minutes ago replied to the Muhammedan Deputation. Their address was moderate and excellent, but very difficult to answer without tumbling into quicksands.'[27] Minto knew what he was doing; if he tumbled into 'quicksands' he took a calculated risk. Immediately, his object was to win over the Muslim community and prevent it from going the Congress way.

J. R. Dunlop-Smith to Harcourt Butler, 2 October 1906: The Deputation has come & is going. . . . H.E. took infinite trouble with his reply . . . his trouble was justified as it was a most important gathering—quite unique. It meant the Ms [Muslims] declared to the H.E. that they would not join the Congress, that they preferred appealing to their Ma Bap to stumping the country & that they realized in some measure the difficulties of ruling this country. . . .[28]

Dunlop-Smith echoed the satisfaction of the official world in Simla at acquiring a new stick with which to beat the 'Congress-wallahs'. The Anglo-Indian and even the British newspapers could hardly conceal their glee at the performance of the Muslim deputation. *The Times* went to the length of describing the memorial (a hotch-potch of sectional demands for reservation of jobs and seats in elective bodies) as 'the only piece of óriginal political thought which

---

[25] Earl of Minto, *Speeches*, Calcutta, 1910, pp. 65–70.
[26] Dunlop-Smith to Butler, 20 Sept. 1906 (Butler P.).
[27] Minto to Lawley, 1 Oct. 1906 (Minto P.).   [28] Butler P.

has emanated from modern times.'[29] Even the Liberal Secretary of State observed that the Muslim Deputation had embarrassed British friends of the Indian National Congress in the House of Commons, as it prevented them from 'any longer presenting the Indian Government as the ordinary case of the bureaucracy versus the people'.[30]

By the end of the week, Mohsin-ul-Mulk had been given an opportunity of meeting the sub-committee of the Viceroy's Council, which was considering the problem of constitutional reforms, and of presenting to it far-reaching demands for exclusive and weighted Muslim electorates in provincial and central legislative councils. Mohsin-ul-Mulk was delighted. This was his finest hour. He thanked the Viceroy for putting 'a new heart' into the Muslim community, and for making 'a historic declaration of the policy of the Indian Government'.[31]

The full implications of the Muslim Deputation of October 1906 did not unfold themselves immediately. As Hindu–Muslim differences grew, the nationalists tended to see in the deputation the thin end of the wedge which was to divide the Indian subcontinent in 1947. The events of 1906 were seen as part of an Anglo-Muslim plot to thwart Indian nationalism. The *Amrita Bazar Patrika* (3 October 1906) described it as 'a got-up affair fully engineered by interested officials'. Seventeen years later the Khilafat leader, Maulana Mohamed Ali, in his presidential address to the Coconada Congress in 1923 described the deputation to Minto as a 'command performance', arranged at the instance of the government. We know a lot more about the deputation than Mohamed Ali did fifty years ago. There is no doubt now that the initiative in organizing the deputation came from Mohsin-ul-Mulk and his friends. Morley's budget speech in the House of Commons was a warning bell to those Muslim leaders who believed that every little gain to the Hindus could only be a corresponding loss to the Muslims. That this line of thinking should have appealed to the Muslim mind, especially in northern India, should not surprise anyone familiar with Muslim politics and newspapers at the turn of the century. The Muslim intelligentsia had a deep distrust of the Hindu majority, was opposed to purely territorial representation on the basis of population, and tended to take its cue from the Anglo-Indian press. The Muslim response in India and England was thus predictable. What is surprising is not that the

[29] *The Times,* 2 Oct. 1906.
[30] Morley to Minto, 26 Oct. 1906 (M.P.).
[31] Mohsin-ul-Mulk to Dunlop-Smith, 7 Oct. 1906 (B.P.).

Muslim leaders should have wanted to lead a deputation and submit a memorial to the Viceroy, but that they should have been so warmly welcomed and given such wide-ranging assurances so hastily on constitutional issues of which the full implications were yet to be worked out by the Viceroy and his advisers.

There has been much speculation about the role of Principal Archbold in this affair. His presence at Simla, and his access to the Viceroy's private secretary and members of the Executive Council were undoubtedly useful to Mohsin-ul-Mulk. But it is evident from Archbold's letters in August 1906 that, far from taking a cue from the British officials at Simla, he had, in the initial stages, to use his persuasive skill to convince them that the Muslim leaders meant well and were not up to any mischief. He drew attention to the excited state of Muslim feeling after the resignation of Lt-Governor Fuller, and how it needed a sedative from the Government. He gave assurances on behalf of his Muslim friends that they would not say or do anything 'which was in the slightest degree disloyal or objectionable'.[32]

There is evidence that it was the 'Fuller Episode' which provided the immediate provocation for the Muslim initiative in 1906. In a letter to Erle Richards, Butler traced the genesis of the proposal for the Muslim deputation to the Viceroy: 'Mohsin-ul-Mulk gives Khwaja Yusuf Shah of the Punjab [Amritsar, I believe] the credit for starting the business on Fuller's resignation. He telegraphed Mohsin-ul-Mulk, & Mohsin-ul-Mulk and Imad-ul-Mulk [Syed Bilgrami] did the rest. "I was asleep", said Mohsin-ul-Mulk in his address, "& the Khwaja Saheb woke me".'[33]

While the lead was undoubtedly taken by the Muslim leaders themselves, Butler's encouragement and guidance to Mohsin-ul-Mulk at Lucknow, and Principal Archbold's advocacy at Simla, Dunlop-Smith's sympathy in the Viceroy's entourage, and Erle Richards' support on the Executive Council all helped to contribute to the success of the deputation. Without this influential official backing, the deputation would have had little political significance.

It is not difficult to guess the motives of the Viceroy and his principal lieutenants. Minto was under pressure from nationalist elements in India, and from Morley in England to initiate a scheme of constitutional reforms. He was not really convinced of the wisdom

[32] W. A. J. Archbold to Dunlop-Smith, 9 Aug. 1906 (Minto P.).
[33] Butler to H. E. Richards, 23 Sept. 1906 (B.P.).

of such a scheme, but felt he could not stall it indefinitely. He and his advisers were thinking hard on how to neutralize any concession they might be compelled to make to nationalist opinion on the reform of legislative councils. The government's dilemma in regard to the Imperial Legislative Council was succinctly posed by H. Earle Richards to Butler: 'Under present conditions it is essential that the Government should have a majority; it would not do in practice for the Government to be dependent on the votes even of the European non-official Members. As long as we are an absolute Government we must retain absolute power.'[34] It was in the interest of the government to strengthen elements on whose loyalty it could count. 'We must preserve & develop a landed aristocracy', Butler suggested, 'and work through it if we wish to keep an absolute govt. in India. . . .'[35] Against this background it is not surprising that the Muslim community should have been viewed by the British policy-makers in the same light as the princes and the landed class, as a possible counterpoise to the educated Hindu.

Curiously, the Congress leaders were slow to grasp the full significance of the Simla Deputation. Most of its demands so obviously contradicted the axioms of representative government, as practised in England, that the *Advocate*—the pro-Congress newspaper of Lucknow—'refused to believe that any British statesman will give countenance to such a movement'.[36] The *Advocate* was not alone in misreading the motives of the Aligarh politicians or underrating the potentialities of an Anglo-Muslim alliance. Even Tilak's colleague, N. C. Kelkar, the editor of the *Mahratta*, expressed his satisfaction in the *Hindustan Review* at the fact that the isolation of the Muslim community, dating from Sir Syed's time, was breaking and asserted that even a mere political aspiration in the Mohammedans was a national asset for all India. 'We for one can find it in us to rejoice', added *Kelkar*,

if as a reward for not joining the Congress, the Mohammedans are appointed to the memberships of the Supreme Executive Council. A Mohammedan Governor of a province would be still more welcome. The Mohammedans are surely a fine martial race; why not appoint a Mohammedan to a high post in the army? They say that Mr Ameer Ali has a better chance of being appointed to a vacant post in Mr Morley's Council than Mr R. C. Dutt. All right; that is equally welcome. What is of importance to every broad-minded lover of

[34] Richards to Butler, 11 Sept. 1906 (B.P.).
[35] Butler to Richards, 16 Sept. 1906 (B.P.).   [36] *Advocate*, 20 Sept. 1906.

India just at this time is to push on the boundary line of political privilege; who the actual occupant of the outpost is, whether Hindu, Mohammedan or a Parsee, is a secondary matter.[37]

The 'Simla Deputation' did not settle everything. The available evidence indicates that both Muslim leaders and high officials of the Government of India saw the deputation as an insurance against future risks. The government was taking precautions against a possible defection of the Muslim educated class, particularly the younger generation, to the Congress; the Muslims were insuring themselves against a possible Hindu dominance if the legislatures were leavened with a larger elective element. By October 1906, the Government of India had not yet worked out the full implications of larger legislative councils with increased Indian representation. The preparation of a precise scheme was to take months and years and, before it could be adopted, it had to run the gauntlet of the Viceroy's Executive Council, the Secretary of State for India and his Council, and finally the British Parliament. Minto's assurances had gladdened the hearts of Mohsin-ul-Mulk and his friends, but even the Viceroy does not seem to have realized the precise implications of these assurances. The Muslim leaders themselves were not quite clear or coherent on what they wanted. The omnibus memorial to the Viceroy included almost every conceivable political demand that could have been made at that time by the Muslim élite.

No responsible man who has talked freely with me [Butler wrote] expects to get all they are asking for. But the trouble is that the rank & file will swallow the memorial whole, & the opposition of the Hindus will make any falling short of the requests by the Govt. wear the appearance of a concession to the enemy. My experience in this country is that extreme requests put forward come in time & in the face of religious feeling, to be regarded as the irreducible minimum.[38]

Butler was shrewd enough to perceive the immediate advantages and long-term risks—from the British point of view—of a separate Muslim electorate. He wrote on 23 September 1906:

I do not believe that any scheme for it would ever get through the Secretary of State, even if it got so far, which I gather, is unlikely. Nor do I think it is desirable *per se*. It is well perhaps for us that Hindus & Mohammedans should be unable to take continuous concerted action as Orangemen and Catholics in Ireland. But separate electorates would mean constant irritation & excitement. And when

---

[37] *Hindustan Review*, Dec. 1906, pp. 443–4.
[38] Butler to Richards, 23 Sept. 1906 (B.P.).

excitement is in the air, the attitude of both the parties to the govt. tends to take its pitch & tone from the prevailing excitement.[39]

5

The 'Simla Deputation' had more far-reaching consequences than its sponsors had dared to hope. The Viceroy's cordial response had (in the words of Mohsin-ul-Mulk) put new heart into the Muslim community. The Aga Khan had talks with the Viceroy and other high officials in Simla. Mohsin-ul-Mulk was given access to the sub-committee of the Executive Council which was formulating proposals for constitutional reform. The members of the delegation from East Bengal were separately received by Dunlop-Smith and assured that the partition would not be undone, and Muslim interests in the new province would be fully safeguarded. It is not clear how far these talks at Simla concerned the setting up of a separate political (Muslim) party, but before the end of October the Aga Khan had laid his cards on the Viceregal table.

In order to reach the definite objects mentioned by the Deputation, [he wrote to Dunlop-Smith], I have asked all the members ... to form a permanent committee, and I have given to my old friend Nawab Mohsin-ul-Mulk, who, as you know, is a most loyal and zealous Mohammedan, certain instructions regarding the methods by which he is to proceed. . . . I have also asked him not to move in any matter before first finding out if the step to be taken has the full approval of the Government privately, as otherwise, unintentionally, he might be led to do something or other that would leave the Government in an inconvenient position.[40]

Within two months of the Aga Khan's letter the All India Muslim League was born at Dacca. Delegates, who had come from various provinces to attend the All India Muhammedan Educational Conference, met in a separate session and decided to form the All India Muslim League. Syed Husain Bilgrami, who had prepared the draft of the memorial to the Viceroy, spoke at this meeting and affirmed that 'time and circumstances made it necessary for Muhammedans to unite in an association so as to make their voice heard above the din of other vociferous parties in India and across the wide seas to England'.[41] He warned his co-religionists that unless Muslims united

[39] Ibid.
[40] Aga Khan to Dunlop-Smith, 29 Oct. 1906, *in* Gilbert, op. cit., p. 57.
[41] S. R. Wasti, *Lord Minto and the Indian Nationalist Movement*, Oxford, 1964, p. 78.

and worked in 'loyal unison' with the government, they would be 'submerged by the Hindu flood'.[42]

Among the professed objects of the Muslim League were the promotion of loyalty to the British Government, and protection and advancement of Muslim interests. One of its first resolutions denounced the agitation against the partition of Bengal.

The formation of the Muslim League was acclaimed by the Anglo-Indians. The *Englishman* predicted that the League 'will provide an effective answer to the Congress as well as affording an avenue for the publication of Mahommedan aspirations'.[43] The *Times of India* noted the happy circumstances of the formation of the League 'on the safe and sure rock of loyalty to the British Raj'. The Prince of Wales, the future King George V, wrote: 'I see Mr Naoroji has been holding forth before the National Congress and inciting them to agitate until they get what he calls "their rights". The Muhammedan movement is indeed most satisfactory and ought to have a salutary effect upon these Bengal agitators. . . .'[44]

The Times [London], in a slightly sceptical vein, asked whether the new party would make for peace. The question seemed hardly necessary in 1906. There was no doubt about the amenability of the leader of the new party. The Aga Khan had already promised the Viceroy that every important step by the League would be taken in consultation with the government. The Nawab of Dacca, who had played host to the inaugural meeting of the League at Dacca, was deeply attached to the British connection by interest as much as by sentiment; he was to be rescued from bankruptcy by the government in 1907[45] and honoured with a K.C.I.E. The loyalty of Mohsin-ul-Mulk was unquestionable. Syed Husain Bilgrami (Imad-ul-Mulk) was a former civil servant and an aspirant for high office under the Crown, and Syed Ameer Ali, a long-time opponent of the Congress who was to play a crucial role in the events of these years, was before long to be rewarded with a membership of the Privy Council.

[42] Ibid.   [43] *The Englishman*, 1 Jan. 1907.
[44] Prince of Wales to Minto, 1 Jan. 1907 (Minto P.).
[45] Minto to Morley, 8 May 1907 (M.P.).

29

Gokhale and the Communal Problem

Nearly three months before the Viceroy received the Muslim deputation, indeed even before Mohsin-ul-Mulk sought the assistance of Principal Archbold in arranging an interview with the Viceroy, Gokhale, in a speech in London, had hailed the awakening of the Muslims of Aligarh to the necessity of political agitation as a significant sign of the times. 'It is most improbable', he told the East India Association, 'that the Aligarh programme when drawn up will be found to be substantially different from the Congress programme, and though the new organization may maintain its separate existence for a while, it must inevitably merge itself sooner or later into the larger and older organization of the National Congress.'[1]

Gokhale's optimism was to be belied by events; in July 1906, he could have hardly foreseen the chain of events which was to culminate in the formation of the All-India Muslim League before the end of the year. His own freedom from religious passion and prejudice made it easier for him to get on with Muslim politicians, but it also somewhat disabled him from anticipating their moves. Schooled in the politics of Ranade, he was wholly free from regional and religious parochialism: 'I am neither a Hindu, nor a Muslim' was how Ranade described himself in his presidential address to the All India Social Conference at Lucknow in 1899. Gokhale never diverged from the catholic line of his master. 'The India of the future', he affirmed, 'could not now be only a Hindu India or a Muhammedan India; it must be compounded of all the elements which existed in India—Hindu, Muhammedan, Parsee, Christian, aye, and the Englishman who adopted India as his country.'[2] Some of Gokhale's best friends were to be found among the Parsis and Gujaratis of Bombay. In Poona, his home town, where religious passions occasionally rose high, Gokhale's influence was invariably cast on the side of restraint.

[1] Karve & Ambekar (eds.), op. cit., vol. II, pp. 351–2.   [2] Ibid., p. 393.

This had brought him, and other adherents of Ranade much odium. In the early 1890s when Poona and parts of Maharashtra were in the grip of Hindu–Muslim tension and disturbances, Gokhale had tried to pour oil on troubled waters. As a member of the Bombay Legislative Council and later of the Imperial Council, he had made it a point to champion national rather than sectarian interests. 'Your ideals are and must be', the Aga Khan wrote to Gokhale, 'the ideals of every Indian who is honest and thoughtful. . . .'[3] The promotion of 'cordial goodwill and cooperation among the different communities' was embodied in the constitution of the Servants of India Society which Gokhale had personally drafted. Every 'Servant of India' was required to 'regard all Indians as brothers' and to 'work for the advancement of all, without distinction of caste or creed'.

There are few references to the Hindu–Muslim problem in Gokhale's early writings and speeches, because the problem was not in the forefront of Indian politics at the turn of the century. After the initial confrontation between Sir Syed Ahmed and the founding fathers of the Congress, the educated section of the two communities learnt to move in their own separate grooves. Their paths did not really cross until after the partition of Bengal. The partition may not have been deliberately conceived by Curzon as a measure for playing off the two communities against each other, but after the launching of the massive agitation for the reversal of the partition, high British officials, especially in the newly created province of East Bengal and Assam, headed by Sir Bampfylde Fuller, increasingly sought Muslim support to offset a political pressure which was predominantly Hindu. Sir Bampfylde's quip about the Muslim community being his 'favourite wife' could be laughed away. But in his *Studies of Indian Life and Sentiments* published in 1910, he frankly explained why he looked upon Muslims as the natural allies of the British Raj. 'By their religion and political ideas, they [Indian Muslims] are less disposed than the Hindus to dissent from the assumptions which lie at the root of Imperial authority.'[4]

2

The partition of Bengal exacerbated the relations between the two communities in that province: it also accelerated the polarization

---

[3] Aga Khan to Gokhale, n.d., but probably Jan. 1906 (G.P.).
[4] B. Fuller, *Studies of Indian Life and Sentiments*, London, 1910, p. 349.

within the Congress. An open clash between the Moderates and the Extremists was staved off at Calcutta in December 1906, but in the succeeding year the two factions were again poised for a head-on collision. Gokhale's tour of northern India at the beginning of 1907 was part of the Moderate offensive to rally the educated classes to the Congress. This tour was remarkable for the response he was able to evoke from the Muslim community, particularly among its youth. Muslims turned up in large numbers to attend his meetings at Lucknow, Aligarh, Meerut, Lahore and other places. At Lucknow he was entertained to breakfast by twenty Muslim leaders including Nawab Mohsin-ul-Mulk, the prime mover of the Simla deputation. The Raja of Mahmudabad, the most important Muslim landowner in the province, gave a dinner in Gokhale's honour, and Syed Nabi-ullah, a leading barrister and a member of the Simla deputation, took the chair at the public meeting addressed by Gokhale at Lucknow. At Aligarh, a thunderous welcome awaited him; the students un-horsed his carriage and pulled it through the streets to the College Hall amidst shouts of 'Gokhale Zindabad' (Long Live Gokhale). Gokhale seems to have been deeply moved by the warmth of the reception. Dr Syed Mahmud, then a student at Aligarh, later recalled that Gokhale turned to Mohamed Ali, the future Khilafat leader, who had taken him to Aligarh, and said: 'I shall now die a happy man. When I see young Musalmans with so much enthusiasm for me and for India, little doubt remains in my heart that India will get freedom soon.'[5]

Perhaps the highest compliment from the Muslim community came to Gokhale at Lahore, when he was invited by the Muslim League to deliver a lecture on Hindu–Muslim relations. There was no problem, Gokhale declared, which was more important for the future of India, and none that required greater tact, forbearance and judgement for its solution than that of Hindu–Muslim relations. 'I now propose to examine this question', he went on, 'in a spirit entirely free from prejudice and passion and I trust that you will follow me in the same spirit.'[6] He admitted that the relations between the two communities were 'most unsatisfactory'. In a brief historical survey he recalled the coming of Islam to India, the confrontation between Hinduism and Islam, the proselytizing zeal of early Muslim invaders, the emergence of an Indo-Muslim polity, the rise and decline of the

[5] Interview with Dr S. Mahmud, 6 Aug. 1966, Oral History (NMML).
[6] *Tribune*, 24 Feb. 1907.

Mughal Empire, the challenge from the Rajputs, the Marathas and the Sikhs and, finally, the British conquest. 'The British came', said Gokhale, 'at a time when the Muslims were sullen and the Hindus uncertain, and the antagonism between the two communities was in evidence here, there and everywhere, and in its worst form.' That tradition of antagonism had survived; it often lay dormant in wide areas of the country, but could at the smallest provocation become active again.

Gokhale described the basic equation between the two communities. The Muslims were in a minority in all provinces except in the Punjab, and in the newly created province of East Bengal and Assam. They had lagged behind in education: only three per cent of the Muslim population could read and write in the vernacular as against five per cent of the Hindus. In higher education, the Hindus were even better off: one in 300 Hindus knew English as against one in 600 Muslims. All the advantages, however, were not with the Hindus. The Muslims were less burdened with the divisions and subdivisions of caste and sect. Sixty million Muslims could indeed be more effective in practice than two hundred million Hindus. Gokhale had, however, no doubt that the two communities could pull together. They had not only common interests, but suffered from common disabilities. The Arms Act in British India applied equally to Muslims and Hindus. The Muslims in South Africa were not spared the indignities heaped upon the Hindus. He urged the Hindus to realize their special responsibilities for improving the relations between the two communities. They had the advantage of numbers, education, and wealth; it was their duty to understand the genuine fears of the Muslim minority, and to treat it with tact and forbearance. The whole atmosphere could be transformed if only a few Hindus voluntarily devoted themselves to the service of the Muslim community. The Muslims on their part had to realize that the struggle of the Indian people for their rights was 'not a religious but a national struggle'; the political set-up of the future would be on national, not on religious lines. Muslims could sympathize with the Pan-Islamic movement, but they must remember that the national ideal was spreading all over the world, that the 'Young Turks' were all for Turkey, the Egyptians for Egypt and the Persians for Persia. It did not speak well for the Muslims that they should have left the fight for India's rights to the Hindus. 'The Mahomedans of India', said Gokhale, 'must also accept India as their country and it is then that they will be able to realize their highest ideal.' 'Certain forces' were trying to keep the two communities apart. 'Some of you', he warned his predominantly Muslim audience, 'may like to side with the officials, many of whom will like to have you on their side, but you should remember that men [the British] who love patriotism and liberty cannot but despise you. There may be small favours, but when a certain limit is reached, you too will not be allowed to go further.'[7]

Gokhale had spoken candidly, but he had spoken from the heart. The spontaneity and warmth of the Muslim response delighted him as much as it surprised and disturbed the authorities. Only four months earlier, Harcourt Butler, the Commissioner of Lucknow, had testified to the bitter anti-Hindu feeling among the Muslim politicians of northern India. In February–March 1907 they seemed to be vying with each other in admiring and entertaining Gokhale. Butler and his friends were assailed by fresh doubts and fears. Would Muslim youth slide down the slippery road of political extremism? Was the Muslim middle-class about to make common cause with the Hindus? Was it possible that the antagonism between the two communities would be overlaid by a common hatred of the British Government? Soon after Gokhale's visit to Meerut, the Hindus opened a refreshment room for Muslims during 'Mohurrum', and the Muslims reciprocated by serving refreshments to the Hindus during the 'Holi' festival. 'This augurs well for future', wrote a correspondent to Gokhale, 'and is entirely due to your recent visit.'[8]

3

Gokhale's tour did not prove to be a magic wand. Indeed, even while he was making his triumphal progress in the United Provinces and the Punjab, events in East Bengal had moved to a tragic climax. As we have already seen, the partition of Bengal had ranged the Hindus and Muslims in that province on opposite sides. Though as late as November 1906, Surendranath Banerjea was assuring Gokhale that he could get up a memorial against the partition exclusively signed by Muslims, the fact was that the Muslims of East Bengal, especially those belonging to the landowning and professional classes, quickly acquired a vested interest in the administration of the new province. British officials in Dacca, and in the districts of East Bengal, harassed by the anti-partition agitation, were not averse to

[7] Ibid.   [8] Babulal Vakil to Gokhale, 2 March 1907 (G.P.).

playing upon the natural antagonism of the Muslim peasantry to Hindu landlords and upon the jealousy of Muslim lawyers and landlords towards their Hindu rivals. Ambitious politicians like the Nawab of Dacca saw new vistas of power and patronage open before them. The virtual dismissal of Sir Bampfylde Fuller came as a blow both to Muslim politicians and British officials, and brought them even closer.

Early in 1907 Gokhale received disquieting reports from East Bengal. He had sent V. S. Srinivasa Sastri (who had recently joined the Servants of India Society) to tour East Bengal and study the conditions there. Sastri reported that, except for the Muslim weavers (*Jolas*) and a few educated young men, the bulk of the Muslim community was opposed to the *swadeshi* movement. 'I find it hard to believe, but it seems to be the truth', Sastri told Gokhale, 'that such thorough opposition to the country's cause is the work of a band of Maulvies paid by the Nawab of Dacca and helped by the police.'[9] There was no doubt of the British officials' partiality towards the Muslim community in East Bengal. Indeed, accusations of official connivance at Muslim rowdyism against the Hindus were made not only in the Hindu press, but before Dunlop-Smith, the private secretary to the Viceroy, by an influential deputation consisting of the Maharaja of Darbhanga, Surendranath Banerjea, A. Chaudhury, Narendra Nath Sen, Nawab Syed Amir Husain and Sayid Shams-ul-Huda, who requested the government to wean away local officials from their blatant partisanship and policy of playing off Muslims against Hindus.[10]

Conditions in East Bengal did not, however, improve. In May 1907 Gokhale spent a fortnight in Calcutta to personally assess the situation. On his return to Poona, he summed up his impressions in a letter to Wedderburn.

Gokhale to Wedderburn, 20 May 1907: I think the responsibility for the unhappy disturbances in East Bengal lies with all the three parties —the Hindus, the Mohammedans and the officials—though necessarily in varying degrees. The anti-Partition agitation which is confined mostly to the Hindus is naturally resented by the officials who are still smarting under a sense of humiliation in connection with Sir B. Fuller's resignation. The wild talk in which some of the more

[9] T. N. Jagadisan (ed.), *Letters of The Right Honourable V. S. Srinivasa Sastri*, Bombay, 1963, p. 7.
[10] Note of Dunlop-Smith, 13 March 1907 (M.P.). See also Gilbert, op. cit., p. 76.

irresponsible speakers on the Hindu side have been indulging on the subject of Independence, or Swarajya without British control as they call it, is also naturally setting the officials against the Hindu community. . . . There is also no doubt that the officials have allowed the impression to spread (and have even openly encouraged it) that the Hindus were in their bad books and that the Mohammedan community was the special object of their favour and patronage. There is also no doubt that when the present disturbances first began, there was a marked tendency to wink at Muslim rowdyism and leave the Hindus more or less to their fate. . . . A number of Muslim rowdies have been preaching for some time a holy war against the Hindus, not on account of the boycott, but on religious grounds. The red pamphlet which I have seen myself and which is of a most inflammatory character has been circulated, broadcast throughout the province and in this pamphlet, the Mohammedans are called upon to rise and destroy the Hindus, so that the glory of Islam be once more re established.

I mention these things not to urge anything against the Musalmans, because these charges and counter-charges between the two communities are harmful to the real interests of both, and the quarrel is deeply painful and humiliating to those whose hopes for the future of the community lie in the two communities working together. . . . I do not wish even now to blame them [the Muslims of East Bengal] for they are ignorant and fanatical and know no better, but I want you to see clearly the unfairness of the Government . . . the whole affair has been most unfortunate and it has put the clock of progress back by several years.[11]

The events in East Bengal were soon to be overshadowed by the political crisis caused by the deportation of Lajpat Rai in May 1907. For the rest of the year Gokhale tried, on the one hand to stem official panic and repression, and on the other to prevent a paralysis of the Indian National Congress from internecine strife. Important, and even critical, as these developments may have been, they were in the long run only a red herring across Gokhale's path. The real goal on which he had set his heart was the reform of the legislatures to open a new chapter in Indo-British relations. Not until April 1908 was he able to leave for England to mobilize support for this reform.

[11] G.P.

30

Separate Electorates

An event destined to change the face of the Indian sub-continent occurred four days before Gokhale's arrival in England in 1908, but was scarcely noticed at the time. This was the opening of a branch of the All-India Muslim League at 42 Queen Anne's Chamber, Westminster. The president—and the prime mover—of the London branch was Syed Ameer Ali, a barrister and a former judge of the Calcutta High Court, who had consistently advised his co-religionists to take to western education, but to keep clear of the Indian National Congress. Like Syed Ahmed Khan, he counted on British support to win for Muslims a greater share of government jobs and council seats. Curzon did not think much of Ameer Ali as a judge. However, Ameer Ali's stock with his community stood high, and obviously he had political ambition. Though a Bihari settled in Calcutta, he had kept in touch with Muslim politics in the upper provinces; it is not without significance that in one of the earlier drafts of the memorial prepared for presentation to Minto in 1906, Ameer Ali was named as the ideal choice for a Muslim representative on the Secretary of State's Council in London.[1]

In cultivating Tory politicians and Anglo-Indian officials and ex-officials, Ameer Ali found a useful ally in the thirty-two year-old Aga Khan. Successive Viceroys, Governors of Bombay and Secretaries of State for India had delighted to favour the Aga Khan, even though he struck them as a 'smart young man about town' or 'a denationalized Eastern'.[2] There were good reasons for the Aga Khan's popularity in official circles. He was rich; he was influential in his community, and he was very willing to oblige the government. In March 1902, while recommending him for a G.C.I.E., Lord Northcote, the Governor of Bombay, confided to the Viceroy: 'Your Foreign Office has recently (last year) asked me to make use of him

[1] Draft Memorial drawn up for private perusal and approval of Members only by Nawab Imad-ul-Mulk (Butler P.).
[2] Minto to Morley, 28 March 1907 (M.P.).

under certain contingencies of a confidential nature, and he has expressed his readiness to do all he can.'[3] Northcote's successor, Lord Lamington, aptly described the Aga Khan as 'ex animo, a favourer of our rule'.[4] In the summer of 1906, the Aga Khan seemed briefly to be under a cloud for hobnobbing with Gokhale,[5] but the India Office soon discovered that its fears were groundless. It was the Aga Khan who was chosen to head the Muslim Deputation to Minto in October 1906, and it was his 'permanent' presidency of the newly formed Muslim League which gave to that organization the hallmark of Muslim loyalty to the Raj in the first four years of its existence.

The Aga Khan and Ameer Ali were in close touch while the Minto–Morley reforms were being discussed in England in the latter half of 1908. They were anxious to bring off the best possible deal for their community. In April 1908, a few weeks before Gokhale arrived in England, Ameer Ali assured Wedderburn of the basic identity of interests between Hindus and Muslims, and expressed the hope that the differences on details could be resolved.[6] These differences on 'details' became the subject of heated controversy after the reforms were published on 17 December 1908. The London branch of the Muslim League launched a fierce attack on the scheme of electoral colleges proposed by Morley; in this attack it received warm support from Conservative newspapers and politicians in England, and Anglo-Indian officials and journalists in India. Curzon and Lansdowne in the House of Lords, and La Touche, Edgerley and Theodore Morison in the India Council were highly critical of the likely effect of the electoral colleges on the position and loyalty of Muslims. Of Morison, a former Principal of the Aligarh college, Morley wrote that 'he would rather have no Reforms at all than such as might be taken to place the Muslims at a disadvantage'.[7]

2

In 1931 when Gandhi was in London for the Round Table Conference, Lady Minto asked him if he remembered her name. 'Remember your name!', exclaimed Gandhi. 'The Minto–Morley reforms have been our undoing. Had it not been for the separate electorates then

[3] Northcote to Curzon, 19 March 1902 (C.P.).
[4] Lamington to Morley, 21 June 1906 (Lamington P.).
[5] See chap. 21, *supra*.
[6] Ameer Ali to Wedderburn, 12 April 1908 (G.P.).
[7] Morley to Minto, 20 Aug. 1909 (M.P.).

established, we should have settled our differences by now.' 'You forget, Mr Gandhi,' replied Lady Minto, 'that the separate electorates were proposed by your leader and predecessor, Mr Gokhale.' 'Ah!', Gandhi replied, 'Gokhale was a good man, but even good men may make mistakes.'[8]

That Lady Minto's memory should have misled her on events which had occurred twenty-three years earlier is less surprising than that Gandhi should have without question accepted the legend of Gokhale's responsibility for the introduction of separate electorates. Gokhale exercised little control over the sequence of events which led to separate electorates. Indeed, in the last phase of the passage of the reforms, he seems to have been overtaken by events rather than shaping them.

Gokhale's attitude to the Muslim community was basically one of sympathy; he did not reject its claim for protection in reformed legislatures out of hand. He knew that in the legislatures set up under the Indian Councils Act of 1892, Muslims had sometimes failed to secure adequate representation, and the deficiency had to be made up by the government through nomination. That the Muslim community should prefer to have elected representatives in councils rather than nominees of the government was obvious enough. It was 'all very well to say', Gokhale told the Madras Congress, 'that the end we have in view is absolute unity in the country, union among all different elements . . . , but we have to deal with the existing facts as they are'.[9] It was this recognition of 'facts as they are' which had led him to suggest in his note of September 1908 to the Secretary of State on constitutional reforms[10] that of the twenty-five elective seats in the Imperial Council twenty-one should be filled by an electorate common to all communities, and four seats should be reserved for special Muslim constituencies. For provincial councils, Gokhale recommended that half their members should be elected from territorial constituencies 'without distinction of caste and creed', a quarter from constituencies representing 'special interests', and the remainder should be nominated by the Governor of the province. In Gokhale's scheme separate electorates had thus a limited role, that of supplementing deficiencies in Muslim representation

[8] Countess of Minto, *India, Minto and Morley (1905–1910)*, London, 1934, p. 20.
[9] *Report of the Proc. of the Twenty-Third Indian National Congress held at Madras*, p. 137.
[10] Karve & Ambekar (eds.), op. cit., vol. II, p. 288.

caused by the operation of general electorates. This approach practically coincided with that of the sub-committee of the Viceroy's Executive Council (the Arundel Committee) on the advice of which the Government of India framed its (Simla) proposals in 1907. The scheme announced by Morley on 17 December 1908, however, made a radical departure in favour of 'electoral colleges' to which a fixed number of Muslims and Hindus were to be returned 'in the ratio of population'; these 'colleges' were later to elect members of the provincial councils in like proportions.

The combination of joint electorates and proportional representation was obviously intended to serve the twofold purpose of securing equitable Muslim representation, and preserving harmonious relations between the two communities. The bulk of the Muslim educated class was, however, in no mood to accept joint electorates. At its annual session at Amritsar in December 1908 the All-India Muslim League denounced the scheme of electoral colleges as a betrayal of the Muslim community. The spectre of a 'Muslim revolt' was conjured up by the Anglo-Indian press in India, and the Tory press in England. On 31 December 1908 *The Times* [London] published a cable from its Bombay correspondent that the protest of the Muslim League against the electoral colleges was echoed by 'all Indian Muslims'. Two weeks later, *The Times* referred to Muslim discontent in India and reported: 'The approaching Muharrum is awaited with anxiety in Calcutta.' Morley was unprepared for this storm. The electoral scheme was one of the twelve issues on which he had sought the advice of his departmental committee in the India Office; he had swiftly accepted its recommendations, and the details of the scheme had been worked out by Lord MacDonnell. The volley of Muslim protests, Tory taunts, and Anglo-Indian insinuations surprised and even unnerved Morley. This new development could endanger not only the passage of the Indian Councils Bill through the House of Lords (which had a Conservative majority) but also the realization of his cherished proposal for appointing an Indian to the Viceroy's Executive Council. To William Lee-Warner, a member of his Council whose ultra-conservative views had in recent months begun to jar on him, Morley now turned for help to make 'my peace with the Muhammedans'. He also sought the advice of his lifelong friend Sir Alfred Lyall, who had long experience of India and advised him to conciliate the Muslims.[11]

[11] A. Lyall to Morley, 4 Feb. 1909 (M.P.).

On 27 January 1909 Morley received a Muslim League deputation headed by Ameer Ali, who pleaded for a Muslim member on the Viceroy's Executive Council, for separate electorates, and a larger representation in legislatures for the Muslim community than its population justified to 'suit its political importance'. In his reply, Morley tried to appease Ameer Ali, though on the issue of Muslim electorates he was vague and self-contradictory. Morley was uneasily aware that Ameer Ali and the Aga Khan had deliberately contrived the row; though he talked of 'taking care that in picking up Musalmans we do not drop our Hindu parcels',[12] he had in fact already decided to give in to the combined pressure from Muslims and Anglo-Indians. 'The Muhammedans demand', Morley told the House of Lords on 23 February 1909, '. . . the election of their own representatives on these councils in all the stages. . . . Secondly, they want a number of seats somewhat in excess of their numerical strength. These two demands we are quite ready and intend to meet in full.'[13]

From joint electorates with proportional representation for the two communities, Morley had swung to the other extreme of separate electorates and weighted representation for Muslims. He had thus gone further in meeting the demands of the Muslim League than even the Government of India had proposed. Arthur Godley and others in the India Office were glad that old India hands led by William Lee-Warner had been able to re-assert their influence over Morley. Morley's volte-face was due more to the immediate pressures operating on him than to a cool consideration of the issues at stake. His Council's sympathy with the Muslim League may have helped to tilt the balance in its favour.[14]

Morley's statement of 23 February 1909 was a signal triumph for Ameer Ali and his friends in London, who immediately seized upon the words 'in all stages' in Morley's statement, and called for separate electorates in local bodies, universities, special constituencies and chambers of commerce. The Viceroy and his colleagues were embarrassed by this aggressive posture.[15] A number of Muslim leaders, including Syed Ali Imam, the president of the Muslim League for the year, were accordingly summoned to Simla and advised not to

[12] Morley to Minto, 21 Jan. 1909 (M.P.).
[13] Viscount Morley, *Indian Speeches 1907–1909*, London, 1909, p. 126.
[14] Many years later, Morley told V. S. S. Sastri that he 'held out long against separate electorate for Mohammedans, but yielded on finding that he could not otherwise carry his reforms'. Sastri, *Thumb-nail Sketches*, Madras, 1904, p. 51.
[15] Minto to Morley, 10 June 1909 (M.P.).

make extravagant demands. Ali Imam was dispatched post-haste to London to act as a brake on Ameer Ali and the Aga Khan.

3

Instead of seeking to restrain Muslim League politicians in London, the Viceroy could have spent his time more usefully in supervising his own senior civil servants who were drafting the regulations for the Indian Councils Bill. When the regulations were published, they seemed to have been designed not so much to implement Morley's reforms as to emasculate them. Sweeping powers to disqualify candidates were vested in the heads of provincial governments. Non-official majorities in the provincial legislatures became farcical, with the increase in the number of nominated members who could always be relied upon to vote with the government. Above all, the electoral arrangements were so devised as to punish the very class which had worked for them. The non-Muslim educated classes received a raw deal. The novel concept of 'political importance of the Muslim community' led to glaring anomalies in the composition of the new councils. In the United Provinces, where Muslims constituted only 14 per cent of the population, they secured the same representation in the Imperial Council as the 85 per cent Hindus; in the provincial council they bagged 7 out of the 20 elective seats. It was the same story in most other provinces. No less invidious was the discrimination in franchise. In Calcutta, a Muslim teacher drawing Rs 50 a month could vote, but a Hindu professor drawing Rs 500 could not. Even Gokhale, who had consistently pleaded for generosity to the Muslim minority, was scandalized by the blatant discrimination.

G. K. Gokhale to Sir William Wedderburn, December 1909: There is no doubt that except in Mohammedan circles, the regulations have caused very great dissatisfaction throughout the country. . . . The Mohammedan representation in the Viceroy's Council is so excessive as to be not only unjust but monstrously unjust. . . . For the next three years, out of four members which this presidency [Bombay] will send to the Viceroy's Council, three will be Mohammedans, and this when they are only one-fifth of the population of this presidency! No wonder that even a man like Sir Pherozeshah feels disgusted and would like, as he said to me the other day, to wash his hands of the whole affair!

  Again take the Punjab. There are to be three men from the Punjab in the Viceroy's Council and it is not improbable that to begin with all three may be Mohammedans! The Hindus will probably have sometimes no representation and sometimes only one! And this when they are about half the population of the province, and in point of education, wealth and public spirit by far the more advanced!

. . . everywhere more representation has been given to Moham-medans than they are justly entitled to. But what hurts the other communities even more than the excessive representation of Moham-medans is the great difference in the franchise conferred on the Mohammedans and the others. Thus in the city of Bombay while every Mohammedan who has an annual income of £135 has a vote in the election of a member to the Council, no Hindu or Parsee, however wealthy or whatever his position in other respects, has a vote unless he is a member of the three of four bodies which have been called upon to return a member. And it is the same throughout the country. The distinction is too glaring and hurts very much in practice.[16]

The regulations, Gokhale added, 'have virtually killed all enthusi-asm for the scheme in the country except among the Muhammedans'. Paradoxically, Morley, who had done more than anyone else in the government to hasten the reforms, was primarily responsible for this dismal result. He committed the fatal blunder of framing only a skeleton Councils Bill leaving the details to be filled in by a civil service whose antipathy to the reforms was an open secret. The civil service frustrated in detail what the Viceroy and the Secretary of State had conceded in principle. The 'regulations' for working the reforms alienated the Hindu middle class whom Morley had wanted to 'rally'. Through his inept meddling with the electoral arrange-ments, the Secretary of State had introduced into the Indian body politic a canker which was to grow and cause immense future com-plications. Morley did not realize that he had been duped by the Anglo-Indian lobbies in England and India. Many Europeans in India (Chief Justice Jenkins told Morley in September 1909) who championed the Muslim demands did so 'because they consider it the most effective mode of thwarting your scheme'.[17] 'From all I hear,—and on the spot one is in a position to hear much—I incline to the view that the Muhammedan demand was prompted in the first instance from other sources, and has been skilfully engineered.'

In this final phase of the constitution-making process, Gokhale himself was more a spectator than an active participant. His own attitude to Muslim franchise vacillated a good deal. In his note to Morley in September 1908 he had recommended separate electorates,

[16] G.P.   [17] L. Jenkins to Morley, 15 Sept. 1909 (M.P.).

but only marginally to correct any inadequacies which might arise in Muslim representation through common electorates. At the Madras Congress in December 1908, while allaying Muslim fears, he had defended Morley's joint electoral colleges. In January 1909 he was quoted by Minto as saying that he would not insist on the retention of [Morley's] electoral colleges if Muslim opinion was opposed to them.[18] In March 1909, while speaking in the Imperial Council, he took his stand on a high pedestal. What did it matter, he asked, if one community had a few more seats than the other? After all, the last word in the new councils would rest with the government, and non-official members would only have opportunities of exercising influence, rather than power. Gokhale's dispassionate, almost judicial, posture won him a compliment from the Viceroy, but it disabled him from throwing his weight against the machinations of the Anglo-Muslim lobby. Both Minto and Morley persuaded themselves that Gokhale would not object to separate electorates. If Gokhale had denounced the extravagant demands of Ameer Ali and his friends as soon as they became known in January 1909, Morley may have been forewarned of the pitfalls ahead. Unfortunately, Gokhale was not only slow in appreciating the potentialities of the Anglo-Muslim alliance, but also seems to have suffered from a strange paralysis of will even after most of his own colleagues had seen through the game. As late as May 1909, he was advising his friend Krishnaswami Aiyer not to work up an agitation against separate electorates through the All-India Congress Committee. 'I have reasons to believe', he wrote, 'that the Viceroy and the Home Member are annoyed at the line recently taken by the Mohammedans of Lucknow and other places in India. Any agitation on our part at this juncture may have the effect again of driving the Government of India and the Mohammedan community into each other's arms.'[19] It is true that Minto was at this time annoyed with Ameer Ali and the Aga Khan for their strident propaganda in London, but it was rather naïve of Gokhale to imagine that the Viceroy and his I.C.S. colleagues would fight Muslim communalists on behalf of nationalist India. This was an occasion which called not for quiet diplomacy but a protest, even a vehement protest. In July 1909, on behalf of the Bombay Presidency Association, Pherozeshah sent a strongly worded telegram to the government against communal

[18] Private telegram from Viceroy to Sec. of State, 15 Jan. 1909 (M.P.).
[19] Gokhale to K. Aiyer, 18 May 1909 (G.P.).

electorates. The telegram was drafted by Gokhale;[20] yet he deliberately refrained from a strong public expression of his views. Evidently he thought his association with the reforms in their formative stage, and particularly in 1908 during his meetings with Morley, had laid him under a certain obligation to defend the reforms scheme *in toto*. He failed to see that the electoral arrangements for Muslims were viewed by the Europeans in India not merely as a defence of Muslim interests, but also of the Raj against the nationalist challenge. Lovat Fraser, the editor of the *Times of India*, confided to the private secretary of the Viceroy in July 1909: 'Men like the Aga Khan plainly feel that in pressing for large separate treatment for Mahommedans, they are fighting our battle much more than their own. We have far more to lose than the Muslims by an *entente* between Islam and Hinduism.'[21]

That separate electorates constituted the thin end of the wedge between the two communities was at once seen by some shrewd observers of the political scene. In March 1909, Motilal Nehru noted that Hindu–Muslim antagonism had grown, and 'our Anglo-Indian friends have distinctly scored in this matter, and no amount of Council reform will repair the mischief'.[22] Equally prophetic was the verdict of the veteran R. C. Dutt, who, like Gokhale, had set much store by the reforms and indeed laboured for them. He predicted:

When the history of this cleavage will come to be written, the responsibility of those who fomented it, and the folly of those who accepted it, will be recorded. . . . The Muslims have sung to the tune played to them, and think a separation from their own countrymen will raise them in power and dignity! But Tory papers in England and the Anglo-Indian papers have fooled them to the top of their bent; the *Times* had endeavoured to separate the Northern States from the Southern during the Civil War in America. There, the *Times* failed—the Americans knew better than to be divided. But our simple Muslim compatriots have been easily gulled and separation has been decreed.[23]

In fairness to Ameer Ali and the Aga Khan, it must be said that they were the only party in this controversy who knew what they

[20] 'British rule in India, the Association begs leave to remind the Government, is based on the principle of equal treatment for all communities without distinction of race or creed. The present policy of favouring one community at the expense of the others strikes at the root of that principle and is bound to produce disastrous results.'
[21] Quoted by Gilbert, op. cit., p. 202.
[22] Motilal to Jawaharlal, 25 March 1909 (Nehru P.).
[23] R. C. Dutt to Gokhale, 28 June 1909 (G.P.).

wanted and set out to attain it with single-minded purpose. Morley
—and the Moderates in the Congress— vaguely aimed at the conciliation of the educated classes which clamoured for constitutional
reforms and a share in political power. The British bureaucracy in
India was at heart opposed to reforms, but was prepared (as was the
Viceroy) to accept them if effective safeguards for the Raj could be
built into the Indian Councils Bill. Ameer Ali and the Aga Khan
were, however, concerned only with the strengthening of the position
of their community *vis-à-vis* the Hindus. This limited objective they
were able to achieve in 1909 by shrewdly exploiting the Congress
leaders' eagerness for and the Anglo-Indian fear of the reforms.

31

Anticlimax

On 25 January 1910 Gokhale attended the first meeting of the Imperial Council after its reconstitution under the Act of 1909. The new Council was very different from the one Gokhale had known for eight years. British officials and their nominees maintained their majority, but the number of members had more than doubled. There were more Indian members and there were greater opportunities for the discussion of official policies and resolutions. The new seating arrangement imparted to the council the appearance of a deliberative chamber rather than that of an official committee. Minto gave a vivid pen-picture of the inaugural meeting to Morley.

Minto to Morley, 27 January 1910: It was an impressive sight. The room itself had a fine old-world look about it, and two small galleries —my own invention for strangers and for the Press—worked in very well with the general surroundings. My chair is placed under a picture of Warren Hastings, and on each side of the room to my right and left hang large full-length portraits of Cornwallis, Dalhousie, Wellesley and my great-grandfather. Members are seated on green leather benches, slightly raised above each other and facing me in horseshoe shape. The proceedings are opened by taking the oath of allegiance and when one saw the seats filled with British Officials in their sombre frock coats and with Indians in many-coloured turbans one realized that the occasion was a memorable one, full of meaning for the future.[1]

Minto's inaugural speech was (he told Morley) 'very well received and the applause (a thing hitherto unheard of in the Council room, I am told) amounted to a demonstration'. His satisfaction was somewhat tempered by news of attempts on the lives of government officials. Just before the meeting of the Imperial Council, a police inspector was shot down within the precincts of the Calcutta High Court. In November 1909 an attempt was made on the Viceroy's own life; it was, as he put it, 'a pretty near thing'.[2] A series of terrorist

---

[1] Minto to Morley, 27 Jan. 1910 (M.P.).
[2] Minto to Lawley, 18 Nov. 1909 (Minto P.).

outrages took place in 1909; of these the most sensational was the assassination in London of Sir William Curzon Wyllie, the political A.D.C. to the Secretary of State for India, by an Indian student, Madan Lal Dhingra. A note recovered from Dhingra immediately after his arrest read: 'I believe that a nation unwillingly held down by foreign bayonets is in a perpetual state of war. Since open battle is rendered impossible, I attacked by surprise . . . since cannon could not be had, I drew forth and fired a revolver.'

The assassination of Curzon Wyllie was publicly denounced by most educated Indians, but there were exceptions. On 17 July 1909, a letter appeared in *The Times* from Shyamji Krishnavarma, the proprietor of 'India House' and the *Indian Sociologist* in London, to say that he approved of Dhingra's action and regarded its author as 'a martyr in the cause of Indian independence'. Edward VII, to whom Morley reported the incident, was furious and recorded that 'the sooner the Indian students are sent back to their own country the better. They fall into bad hands and return to India to sow sedition.'[3]

Anglo-Indian reaction to these outrages was a demand for stern measures. There was a clamour for martial law from the Europeans in Bengal. 'We are very much nearer the declaration of Martial law', Harcourt Butler, the Education Member of the Viceroy's Council wrote home, 'than most people think.'[4] Minto set his face against these counsels of despair. He realized, however, that he had to do something spectacular to reassure the European community. This he did by the extension of the Seditious Meetings Act of 1907 to the whole of India, and by permitting the introduction of a Press Bill in the Imperial Council to strengthen the hands of local officials.

2

On 4 February 1909, Herbert Risley, the officiating Home Member, introduced a Press Bill which authorized district officers to demand securities from newspapers and printing presses. To Gokhale it seemed 'a cruel irony of fate' that one of the first measures placed before the reformed central legislature should have been for the curtailment of the liberty of the press. The forfeiture of securities and even confiscation of the printing presses was made an almost wholly executive act, against which an appeal lay only to a special tribunal

---

[3] S. Lee, op. cit., vol. II, p. 382.
[4] Butler to Mrs Griffin, 5 Aug. 1909 (Butler P.).

of High Court judges. The Government of India betrayed an indecent haste in pushing the bill through the Imperial Legislative Council. The normal process laid down in the standing orders of the council was suspended and the bill passed in four days.

Gokhale did not deny that 'a rash' of assassinations, conspiracies and dacoities in the country had created a difficult situation for the government. He did not deny that a section of the Indian press had been irresponsible, but pointed out that the Anglo-Indian press was equally, if not more, provocative and mischievous. In the eyes of the Indian public the distinction between official and non-official members of the ruling race tended to get blurred. 'Many of my countrymen imagine', said Gokhale, 'that every Anglo-Indian pen that writes in the press is dipped in Government ink.'[5]

Gokhale had appended a minute of dissent to the report of the Select Committee on the Press Bill. When the bill came before the Imperial Council, he moved a number of amendments all of which were lost by the combined strength of the official and nominated members. To the surprise of everyone, however, when the division took place, Gokhale did not vote against the bill. His inconsistency came in for much criticism at the time, but we know now that he had reasons for his decision which he could not disclose at the time. The Law Member of the Viceroy's Executive Council at that time was S. P. Sinha, whose appointment as the first 'Native Member' had been made by Morley with the support of Minto despite stubborn official opposition in Britain as well as in India. Sinha did not like the original draft of the Press Bill at all, and threatened to resign. Sinha's resignation on a political issue, within a few days of the meeting of the 'reformed' Imperial Council, would have cast doubts on the wisdom of constitutional reforms in India, and embarrassed both Minto and Morley. The Viceroy held anxious consultations with Sinha, Gokhale and the Chief Justice, Lawrence Jenkins. He persuaded his colleagues on the Executive Council to agree to tone down the bill and to include in it a provision for judicial review. Sinha agreed not to press his resignation if Gokhale promised not to oppose the bill. Gokhale felt that Sinha was unreasonable in imposing such a condition. While it was incumbent upon Sinha as a member of the highest executive body in the country to support the government, non-official members of the Imperial Legislative Council, such as Gokhale, were free to express their views and to vote

[5] Karve & Ambekar (eds.), op. cit., vol. II, p. 63.

against particular measures. It was only when Sinha seemed bent on carrying out his threat of resignation that Gokhale decided not to vote against the bill.[6] Gokhale may have thus saved the Viceroy, the Secretary of State, and Sinha from embarrassment, and the cause of Indian constitutional reforms in Britain from a shattering blow, but he exposed himself to much public obloquy. 'What business had Gokhale to enter into a pact with Sinha?', asked Pherozeshah Mehta. 'Sinha knew his own business. Why should the representative of the Bombay Presidency [Gokhale] go out of his way and stand shoulder to shoulder with Sinha, taking a large part of the odium on himself?'[7] Unlike Pherozeshah, Gokhale viewed the crisis in terms of the larger interests of the Congress and the country. Unlike Pherozeshah, he had worked hard for four years to overcome the obstacles to the reforms. If the first Indian member of the Executive Council actually resigned so soon, it could only confirm the Anglo-Indian legend about the irresponsibility of Indian leaders; the impact on the British press, public and Parliament (on whom, as against the bureaucracy, rested hopes for further reforms) could be disastrous.

Gokhale's chivalry cost him dear. The public was unaware of what had gone on behind the scenes. The fact that at this time his influence was openly cast against the 'physical violence' party in the country added to his unpopularity. Soon after the passage of the Press Bill, the Viceroy expressed his concern for the safety of Gokhale and Sinha. 'I see them', he wrote to the Secretary of State, 'in greater danger than our own people. They are both plucky fellows and dislike precautions being taken on their behalf, in fact even have refused to allow them. But I am anxious about them—particularly just now, when there are conditions which may encourage reprisals.'[8]

Six months later, the government convened the Imperial Legislative Council at Simla to extend for a further period of five months the Seditious Meetings Act of 1907 (curbing the rights of public assembly) which was due to lapse on 1 November 1910. Gokhale feared this extension was only a prelude to a permanent incorporation of this obnoxious measure in the statute book. This legislation which he described as 'draconian',[9] had been applied rather unimaginatively

---

[6] For an 'inside' story of this incident see S. P. Sinha's letter, 12 April 1921 to Secretary, the Servants of India Society, and C. Y. Chintamani's note dated 2 July 1925 to V. S. S. Sastri (G.P.).

[7] Sastri, *Pherozeshah Mehta*, p. 60.

[8] Minto to Morley, 17 Feb. 1909 (M.P.).

[9] Karve & Ambekar (eds.), op. cit., vol. II (Pol.), p. 42.

and harshly. Innocuous meetings had been prohibited, and some district magistrates had even gone to the length of dictating the resolutions to be passed at the meetings.

Gokhale did not see any justification for these 'extraordinary' powers for curtailing the freedom of association; the condition of the country in 1910 was not the same as it had been three years earlier. 'The air has been largely cleared', he told the Imperial Council. 'The wild elements, which by their reckless careering have been a source of so much anxiety, have well-nigh exhausted themselves.' The country was returning to a normal state of things; what it needed was not 'the heavy hand of coercion, but the gentle touch of conciliation and sympathy, of forbearance and oblivion . . . to obliterate bitter memories and start the country on a career of prosperity and progress'.[10]

Gokhale's appeal fell on deaf ears, partly because the government was not as optimistic about the immediate future as he was, and partly because it distrusted Gokhale. Gokhale was a Moderate, but he was not moderate enough for the guardians of the Raj. Few British officers in India were capable of appreciating the large perspectives and lofty aspirations for Indo-British partnership which animated Gokhale. As late as December 1909, no less a person than F. M. Vincent, Bombay's Commissioner of Police, described Gokhale as 'a disciple of Tilak'.[11] Early in 1910 after the first session of the new Imperial Council, the Bombay C.I.D. forwarded a report on a meeting at which

the Hon'ble Mr Gokhale privately discussed with the Honourables Mr Dadabhai, Sir Vithaldas, Sir Sassoon David, Mohammed Ali Jinnah, Mazhar-ul-Haq and several other members, the desirability of organization and division of work in the Council in such a manner that at least two members should devote themselves to studying and mastering the details of each department of the Government. . . . [The] discussion resulted in an agreement to the effect that they should organize opposition on the lines mentioned above, and should . . . persuade Government to legislate, taking into consideration chiefly the well-being of the Indians, and that if they failed to persuade Government, they should resign in a body. . . .[12]

About the same time, Minto commended to Morley the choice of R. W. Carlyle as the Revenue Member of the Viceroy's Executive

[10] Ibid., p. 45.
[11] F. M. Vincent to Du Boulay, 11 Dec. 1909, Home Pol. (Confdl.) Proc., Jan. 1910, Nos. 100–1, Pt. B. (NAI).
[12] Secret Abstracts, 1910, C.I.D. Bombay, para. 1477, p. 609.

Council on the ground that he knew 'privately of an intended attack in which Gokhale is interested on the whole of our revenue system, and it is all important that we should be well prepared to meet it'.[13]

3

In the closing months of Minto's viceroyalty, Gokhale noticed that instead of a relaxation in the wake of the Minto–Morley reforms, there was a stiffening on the part of the administration. This he attributed to the new Home Member, J. L. Jenkins, who had been 'lauded up by the Anglo-Indian papers as a "strong man", and was trying to play up to the reputation'.[14] An example of bureaucratic obtuseness came to Gokhale's notice when the Central Hindu College, Benares, and its founder Mrs Annie Besant found themselves in trouble. An article by her in the *Central Hindu College Magazine* incurred the displeasure of J. P. Hewett, the Lt-Governor. Babu Bhagavan Das, the Honorary Secretary of the college, was sent for by the Collector of Benares and threatened with a prosecution under the Press Act. The Commissioner of Benares went further: he summoned the members of the managing committee of the college to his house, admonished them, and directed them to dissociate themselves from Mrs Besant. Even a veiled threat of withdrawing recognition from the Central Hindu College was held out.

Mrs Besant immediately dashed off a letter to Gokhale and sought his intercession.[15] 'I am extremely obliged to you for your most valuable good offices', she wrote a few days later. 'I have had a kind letter from H.E. [His Excellency] and an assurance from Colonel Pinhey [Private Secretary to the Viceroy] that the whole thing is dropped.'[16]

Minto's refusal to permit the prosecution of Mrs Besant, his visit to Benares to see her college, and his presence in 1910 at the opening of the 'Minto Park' in Allahabad, where the limelight fell on Congress leaders like Madan Mohan Malaviya and Motilal Nehru, did not endear the retiring Viceroy to the European community in India.[17] Anglo-Indians had never really taken kindly to Minto's modest constitutional reforms, or forgiven him for his refusal to

[13] Minto to Morley, 26 May 1910 (M.P.).
[14] Gokhale to Wedderburn, 9 Sept. 1910 (G.P.).
[15] A. Besant to Gokhale, 23 Feb. 1910 (G.P.).
[16] *Idem*, 12 March 1910 (G.P.).
[17] J. P. Hewett (Lt-Governor of U.P.) to Curzon, 24 Sept. 1910 (C.P.).

impose martial law as a reprisal for attacks on European officials. The Europeans of Calcutta made no secret of their sullen antagonism to Minto. He did not receive a farewell dinner in Calcutta from the mercantile community, the Bengal Club or even the senior civil servants. Nor did the Byculla Club in Bombay (which had given a dinner to every outgoing Viceroy except Ripon) entertain Minto. These studied insults by men of his own race hurt Minto deeply, but they raised his stock with educated India. Some Congress leaders even thought of launching an agitation for the extension of Minto's viceroyalty in order that the constitutional reforms might have a fair chance of success. The Indian élite of Bombay arranged a magnificent reception in his honour when he arrived there to sail for England in November 1910. Gokhale attended the reception where Indian politicians and editors vied with each other in lavishing compliments on the retiring Viceroy. It was forgotten for the moment that it was Minto who had rejected out of hand appeals for the reversal of the partition of Bengal, sanctioned the deportation of Lajpat Rai, abridged the liberty of association and the press, and allowed the constitutional reforms of 1909 to be undermined by his subordinates. Luckily for Minto, Indian public opinion tended to give much of the credit for the reforms to him, and the discredit for their imperfections to his advisers, such as Ibbetson, Risley, Adamson and Jenkins. The *Hindustan Review* voiced the feeling of the politicially-conscious class in the autumn of 1910 when it included Minto among the great Viceroys of India, 'whose names are remembered with gratitude and affection as benefactors and friends—Bentinck, Canning and Ripon'.[18]

[18] *Hindustan Review,* Oct.–Nov. 1910, p. 487.

32

A House Divided Against Itself

If the 'reformed' legislatures belied Gokhale's hopes, the 'reformed' Congress proved a still greater disappointment. He had returned from the Surat Congress more in sorrow than anger, but most of his Moderate colleagues were in a bellicose and vindictive mood. 'Mr Tilak and his followers', Krishnaswami Aiyer wrote in the *Madras Standard* in January 1908, 'are like a diseased limb gangrened to the core, which ought to be amputated.'[1] Two months later Tilak called on R. C. Dutt and pleaded for a *rapprochement* between the two parties. 'All that he got from me', Dutt wrote to Gokhale, 'was my firm declaration that if the Moderates recede now from their published "creed", they will be committing political suicide.'[2]

Immediately after the Surat fiasco, the Moderates had decided to hold a meeting of the 'Convention Committee'. This meeting took place at Allahabad on 18 and 19 April. Dr Rash Behari Ghosh presided. Of the fifty-five prominent Moderates present, one-third had come from Bengal, Bombay and the United Provinces, five from the Punjab, and only one each from Madras and Berar. Even though the Extremists were excluded and the press was not allowed, the Moderate leadership did not have a smooth sailing. There were serious differences of opinion. The discussions were lively and occasionally heated. The Bengal Moderates, backed by the delegates from the Punjab, were anxious not to bang the door against the re-entry of the Extremists. They urged that the Congress Constitution be framed in terms which the Extremists could also accept. They proposed that the next Congress session due in December 1908 should be deemed a continuation of the session 'adjourned' at Surat. These proposals were turned down by the Moderate leaders, who were in no mood to 'forget and forgive' what had happened at Surat. They desired, in the words of Pherozeshah Mehta, a 'resuscitated, renovated, reincar-

[1] Quoted in *Amrita Bazar Patrika*, 9 Jan. 1908.
[2] R. C. Dutt to Gokhale, 11 March 1908 (G.P.).

nated Congress'.[3] However, they were not prepared to make any compromise on the basic character and complexion of the Congress organization, 'a constitutional body aiming at a steady reform of the constitution of the Indian Government and its administrative methods so as gradually and increasingly to Indianize it'. No quarter was to be given to those who deviated from constitutional agitation, or advocated the severance of India's connection with Britain.

Ironically enough, the very Moderate leaders who had stubbornly resisted the idea of a written constitution for the Congress before 1905, now favoured very elaborate rules for the composition and functioning of the party at the sub-divisional, district, provincial and national levels. They went to absurd lengths in prescribing the procedure for the annual Congress sessions. For example,

> every member of a sitting of the Congress or of the Subjects Committee shall be bound (a) to occupy a seat in the block allotted to his province, (b) to maintain silence when the President rises to speak or when another member is in possession of the House, (c) to refrain from hisses or interruptions of any kind or indulgence in improper and un-Parliamentary language, (d) to obey the chair, (e) to withdraw when his own conduct is under debate.[4]

The shadow of the Surat Congress seemed to linger over the Allahabad Convention. The uppermost, albeit the unspoken, thought of the Moderate leaders was: 'It shall not happen again.'

The most controversial part of the new constitution was Article 1 on the aims and methods of the organization. The goal of the Congress was defined as 'the attainment by the people of India of a system of government similar to that enjoyed by the self-governing Members of the British Empire, and a participation by them in the rights and responsibilities of the Empire on equal terms with other Members'. This goal was to be attained by 'constitutional means', by bringing about 'a steady reform of the existing system of administration', and by promoting national unity, fostering public spirit and developing the intellectual, moral, economic and industrial resources of the country. It was not so much this creed as the condition that it must be accepted in *writing* that galled the Extremists, who were convinced that the Allahabad Convention had deliberately framed the rules in such a way as to make it difficult for them to rejoin the Moderate-dominated Congress.[5]

[3] *Hindustan Review*, April 1908, p. 393.
[4] Rules for Conduct of I.N.C. Meetings adopted at Allahabad (G.P.).
[5] *Mahratta*, 26 April 1908.

2

Gokhale attended the meeting of the Convention Committee at Allahabad and took an active part in its proceedings. Since he planned to leave for England soon afterwards, his resignation from the post of Joint General Secretary of the Congress was accepted. During the next few months, the Congress organization began to languish. The reasons for this are not far to seek. The 'gangrened limb'—as some Moderates bitterly described the Extremist faction— had been lopped off at Surat, but the surgical operation had done no good to the patient. It seemed as though the Congress had been drained of all vitality. The Allahabad Convention produced an elaborate constitution. It prescribed the elective procedures for Congress committees from the *taluk* Congress Committee to the All-India Congress Committee. But who was to set up all these committees, and who was to run them? The Congress had few full-time workers. Most Congress leaders might find time to dash off a letter to the editor of a newspaper, or to address a meeting in the local town-hall, but they were averse to organizational work. For such work, Gokhale often received requests to depute his Servants of India, who travelled the length and breadth of the country, collecting subscriptions for *India*, providing succour to famine-stricken areas, and helping to organize provincial and annual Congress conferences. There were, however, not enough Servants of India to go round. The Moderate party was not only short of workers, but in 1908 it also suffered a severe setback in the wake of the Government's repressive measures against Extremists and 'terrorists'. Some of the simmering popular indignation against this repression recoiled on the Moderates. Conscious of their unpopularity, the Moderates tended to lie low. This political quiescence was most inopportune at a time when Gokhale, Wedderburn and the British Committee in London were mobilizing pressure on Morley to initiate constitutional reforms in the teeth of Tory and Anglo-Indian obstruction. The Indian National Congress had to put up a façade of unity and strength if it was to win any tangible concessions from the British Government and the Parliament. The next Congress session was scheduled to be held in Madras. Gokhale urged his friends to 'make it an eventful one'.[6] Seasoned politician as he was, Morley realized the value of the Congress support for his Councils Bill. He saw to it that his statement on the re-

[6] Aiyer to Gokhale, 25 Sept. 1908 (G.P.).

forms was issued before Gokhale returned to India and the Congress assembled at Madras. The Congress leaders reciprocated Morley's gesture. The Madras Congress hailed the Indian Councils Bill which Morley had introduced in the House of Lords as 'a large and liberal instalment'.

The Madras Congress was the first wholly 'Moderate' Congress. The Extremists were absent. The constitution framed by the Allahabad Convention was endorsed. The proceedings in the Subjects Committee and the plenary session were smooth; there was no recrimination, no clash of policies or personalities, no last-minute compromises. Early in 1909 Gokhale assured an English correspondent that the proportion of real extremists among the educated classes in India, who were keen on a separation from England, had been reduced to no more than 'two or three per cent at the outside', and the number of 'desperate physical violence party' did not exceed 'a few hundreds in the whole country'. Thanks to the announcement of the reforms scheme, the feeling throughout the country seemed to Gokhale to be 'one of deep and general satisfaction'.[7]

Gokhale was too sanguine. Morley's Reforms Bill had yet to run the gauntlet of both Houses of the British Parliament, and the 'regulations' which were to fill in vital details had still to be framed. It is true that the Extremists had suffered an eclipse, but this was largely due to the witch-hunt initiated by the government against them. Tilak had been sentenced to six years' imprisonment and deported to Burma. When Aurobindo Ghose returned to Calcutta in 1909 after a year in the Alipore Central jail, he noted the change in the popular temper. He observed:

When I went to jail the whole country was alive with the hope of a nation, the hope of millions of men who had newly risen out of degradation. When I came out of jail, I listened for that cry, but there was instead a silence. A hush had fallen on the country and men seemed bewildered; for instead of God's bright heaven full of vision of the future that had been before us, there seemed to be overhead a leaden sky from which human thunders and lightnings rained.[8]

Lajpat Rai, a shrewd observer of the political scene, noted in the *Panjabee* in July 1909 that the Extremists had been 'well-nigh crushed', but warned that their extinction would be a grave menace

[7] Gokhale to Jenkins, 29 Jan. 1909 (G.P.).
[8] Sri Aurobindo, *Speeches*, Pondicherry, 1952, pp. 51–2.

to the future of the Congress itself.[9] The Surat split had reduced 'the position of the Congress to an organization run by a section of the educated Hindus in the name of the united nation'.[10]

By the autumn of 1909, Gokhale was himself driven to these dismal conclusions. Gone was the optimism he exuded at the Madras Congress only a few months earlier. Reactionary officials, dissidents within the Congress and political terrorists outside it had upset not only the political equilibrium, but threatened the very existence of the Congress.

Gokhale to William Wedderburn, 24 September 1909: I fear one of our numerous disintegrations has overtaken us again—this time it is the national movement that appears to be going to pieces, throwing us back on Provincialism and one grieves to find that there is no influence available anywhere in the country, capable of staying the process. The organization evolved by Mr Hume out of the material prepared by a succession of workers in different parts of the country is crumbling to pieces and the effort of the nation's heart and mind that brought us together in that organization seems to have almost exhausted itself. The split at Surat, followed by the vigour with which the Government came down on the Extremists everywhere, has turned the whole Extremist party into active enemies of the national constitutional movement. And the 'Moderates' placed between the officials and the Extremists have not the necessary public spirit and energy of character to hold together effectively for long, though they are numerically strong in the country. In addition to the incessant attacks of the Extremists, the conduct of the Bengal Moderates is hastening the disintegration of the national movement. Bengal really has no leader on our side. Surendranath Banerjea is an orator, but he has no great courage or backbone, and he cannot keep in hand the unruly pack whom he professes to lead. Moreover there is no doubt that the position of the constitutional party has been rendered practically impossible by the Government's refusal to reconsider partition [of Bengal] and the continued incarceration of the deportees.[11]

The Bengal Moderates objected to the election of Pherozeshah Mehta as president of the 1909 Congress which was to meet at Lahore. They denounced separate and excessive Muslim representation in the new Councils and talked of seceding from the All-India Congress. The reception committee of the Lahore Congress was reported to be riddled by divisions. Lajpat Rai pronounced the temper of the Punjab unfavourable for the Congress session, and

[9] V. C. Joshi (ed.), *Writings and Speeches,* vol. 1, p. 181.
[10] Ibid., p. 182.   [11] G.P.

suggested that it should be called off. Pherozeshah Mehta, the president-elect, fearing a repetition of the Surat fiasco, declined to preside. It seems Pherozeshah expected Gokhale to take his place.[12] Gokhale had, however, no desire to step into the breach. Having lashed out at both the Extremists and the 'terrorists', he was only slightly less unpopular at this time than Pherozeshah Mehta himself. It was not Gokhale but Madan Mohan Malaviya who presided over the Lahore Congress, at which the Congress fortunes seemed to have reached their nadir.

Gokhale to Wedderburn, 30 June 1910: [The Lahore Congress] was the poorest gathering on record. Bengal had all but seceded. The bulk of the Punjab was not only indifferent, but actively hostile. The attendance from other Provinces too was unsatisfactory. There were two main causes of this. One was opposition to the Congress constitution framed at Allahabad on the part of many, who in their views and convictions are more with us than with the Extremists, but who think that the constitution stands in the way of a reunion on the Congress platform of all parties in the country. The other was the feeling that has no doubt been rapidly spreading in the Hindu community since last year that the Congress has done no good to it, that while it bore the brunt of the struggle all these years, the Muhammedans have walked away with the greater part of the spoils, and that it was necessary for Hindus now, first and foremost, to look after their own interests, as distinguished from those of the Muhammedans.[13]

3

The Lahore Congress (December 1909) revealed the tensions between the government and the Congress, the Hindus and the Muslims, the Moderates and the Extremists. The reforms had lost their glamour even before they had actually been launched, and there was hardly any prospect of the constitutional issue being reopened for at least a decade. Meanwhile, something had to be done to contain the racial and religious bitterness and to arrest the demoralization and dissension within the Congress. If the next Congress could meet in London, the presence and prestige of the founding fathers of the Congress, Hume, Naoroji and Wedderburn, could infuse fresh life into it. But it was not easy to convene a session in London. Not only was it expensive, but the religious and caste prejudices of the orthodox Congress delegates also posed problems. Some of these prob-

[12] F. M. Vincent, Police Commissioner, Bombay to Du Boulay, P. S. to Gov. of Bombay, 11 Dec. 1909, Home Dept. (Confdl.), Pol. (B), 1910, Proc., Jan., Nos. 100–1.   [13] G.P.

lems could be solved by chartering a steamer to carry the Congress delegates from India to London. However, the proposal of a Congress session in London fell through when Wedderburn pointed out that, with a general election in the offing, the British public would be too preoccupied with domestic issues to bother about Indian problems.

If it was not possible for the Congress to go to London, could not some of its founding fathers come out to India? Unfortunately, Hume and Naoroji were too old and frail to respond to this proposal, but Wedderburn gallantly offered to preside over the Allahabad Congress in December 1910. He was seventy-three, had chronic bronchial trouble and a weak heart. Gokhale offered to serve as his secretary while he was in India. This helped to revoke the 'veto' of Wedderburn's wife and doctor on the trip to India. 'What is most needed', Gokhale wrote to Wedderburn, 'is a centre, such as your presence will supply, round which the old Congress elements of the country may re-gather with the old faith revived and strengthened.'[14]

That a septuagenarian Scotsman, a former member of the I.C.S., should have been called upon to play the role of a saviour of the Indian National Congress in 1910 may seem odd today, but the honour was well-deserved. Wedderburn's devotion to the cause of India was total; he had grudged it neither time nor money. 'My most intimate friend', was how he had once addressed Gokhale; the compliment could have been reciprocated with equal warmth and sincerity. They had thought and laboured together for the Indian National Congress for thirteen years, but Wedderburn's attachment to India long antedated Gokhale's emergence on the political scene. 'For the last twenty-five years', Gokhale told the Allahabad Congress, 'he has fought for us in England as no other man of our time has done ... his abounding love for the people of this country, love that has stood all tests, such tests as Indians themselves will not be able to stand. Certainly his love for India was more than that of most Indians and certainly more than that of any Englishman.'[15] Of these twenty-five years, no less than twenty coincided with the ascendancy of the Conservative party in Britain. However heavy the odds against him and against India, Wedderburn never lost hope. His philosophy of life was epitomized in the words of his friend Wilfrid Lawson: 'We must hope all things, but expect nothing.'[16] Wedderburn had spent

[14] Ibid. [15] Karve & Ambekar (eds.), op. cit., vol. III, pp. 308–9.
[16] *Speeches and Writings of Sir William Wedderburn*, p. 15.

many years in India and had no illusions about the benevolence of the British bureaucracy. 'The question between the official and the non-official', he once wrote, 'is one between the rulers and the ruled, and I have always believed in the wisdom of Sancho Panza, who said that in the everlasting quarrel between the muleteers and the mules, the mules on the whole are in the right.'

The mission of reconciling Hindus and Muslims, Moderates and Extremists, officials and non-officials, which had brought this old Briton to India was delicate and difficult. But in December 1910 certain forces were working towards a reconciliation. Hindu–Muslim tension had been aggravated by the Minto–Morley reforms. 'I doubt indeed', the Lt-Governor of the U.P. told the Viceroy in January 1910, 'whether the relations of the two communities have ever been much worse during the whole of my 32 years in India.'[17] The very accentuation of this tension had, however, brought forth its corrective.

Gokhale to Wedderburn, 9 September 1910: Here we have lost a great deal of ground during the last two years, and I fear it will be a long time before the mischief is undone. I think some Muslim League leaders have now begun to realize the far-reaching character of the harm which they have done and there is a distinct decline in the influence exercised by its more bigoted and fanatical leaders. However, in this matter the first advance will have to come from the Mahommedans. The number of Hindus who are anxious for a reconciliation is not large. The bulk of the community is full of sullen resentment. I had an interesting letter two months ago from the Aga Khan. . . . It is full of pious wishes for better relations, but no definite suggestions are made.

If the Aga Khan and Mr Ameer Ali heartily join in a movement for reconciliation, something may be effected; but I doubt if they will do so, and I also doubt if the Anglo-Indians who have so long backed them will let them enter on such negotiations.[18]

The Aga Khan and Ameer Ali were inclined to agree to a truce in 1910. They had scored a great success in 1909 and won concessions beyond their hopes. The next instalment of constitutional reforms was in any case far off. The growing tension between the two communities served no purpose, and was in fact frowned upon by British officials, who may not have yearned for Hindu–Muslim unity, but did not want an overt conflict either. In the last months of his viceroyalty, Minto realized that the pendulum had swung too far in

[17] J. P. Hewett to Minto, 13 Jan. 1910 (Minto P.).
[18] G.P.

favour of the Muslims; he tried in his own way to redress the balance.
The Muslim leaders took the hint and expressed a willingness to help
alleviate communal tension. Their mood was mirrored in a letter to
the new Viceroy by Valentine Chirol, the correspondent of the *Times*,
who was on the friendliest terms with Ameer Ali and his friends in
London.

Valentine Chirol to Hardinge, 9 November 1910: I dined last night
with the Aga Khan and had a very interesting talk with him.
 . . . It was largely to obviate this danger of [the Muslims being
organized politically and drifting into the Congress camp] that he
started the Muslim League which had of course exasperated the
Hindu politicians. The antagonism between the two communities was
now the greater danger, . . . and he was anxious to do something to
mitigate that antagonism . . . he was thinking about a small Congress this winter between a few Mahommedan leaders and some of the
more moderate Hindu leaders, including Gokhale, for whom he has
a very profound personal regard, which might be held at Bombay to
see what steps can be taken to remove the danger of actual collision
between the two communities and to discuss the questions in which
they might loyally work together.[19]

This Hindu–Muslim conference actually took place at Allahabad
on 1 January 1911 immediately after the Allahabad Congress. It was
attended (with William Wedderburn in the chair) by about a hundred delegates, including more than forty Muslims, who had just attended a Muslim League session at Nagpur, and come to Allahabad
in a special train. The Aga Khan spoke on behalf of the Muslim
community, and Babu Sarada Charan Mitra on behalf of the
Hindus. A good deal of steam was let off on the issues of communal representation in legislatures, the language question, Muslim
education, cow killing and music before mosques. It was decided to
appoint a committee of sixteen (eight Hindus and eight Muslims)
to examine these controversial issues. After the composition of the
committee had been announced, a strange but memorable scene took
place. There was a demand from the audience that Gokhale's name
be added to the joint committee. 'But I am a Hindu', Gokhale protested; 'that will make too many Hindus.' The audience shouted
back: 'We do not care whether you are a Hindu or not. You are a
friend of us all. We wish that you should be on the Committee.'[20]
Thus it was that Gokhale became the seventeenth member of this

[19] H.P.
[20] *Speeches and Writings of Sir William Wedderburn*, pp. 510–11.

24

committee, the precursor of the many 'unity conferences' which were
to follow during the next thirty years, and which were to belie the
hopes of their sponsors.

Compared with the Hindu–Muslim problem, the Moderate–
Extremist conflict presented less difficulty at Allahabad. Expelled
from the Congress and hunted by the government, the Extremists
were in no position to challenge the Moderates' control of the party.
The Moderate 'dissidents' from Bengal and the Punjab, who had
brought the previous Congress session at Lahore to the verge of a
crisis, were more amenable at Allahabad. This was largely due to
Wedderburn's tact, and capacity for ironing out differences.

Of Wedderburn's self-imposed tasks of reconciliation none was
more difficult than that of bringing together officials and non-
officials. Here again, there were forces subtly working towards a
rapprochement. Deep as their disappointment with constitutional reforms was, the Congress leaders knew that there was no prospect of
the British Parliament making any changes in the near future; and
they had to make the best of a bad bargain. Meanwhile, it was
important to rescue the country from the vicious circle of terrorist
outrages and official reprisals which boded ill for its political progress. Indeed, soon after after the 'reformed councils' were launched,
Gokhale's mind was turning to constructive tasks outside the
legislatures.

Gokhale to Wedderburn, 29 April 1910: We propose to devote all our
energies [of the Servants of India Society] now to educating and
organizing public opinion on the necessity of universal elementary
education, on technical, industrial and agricultural education, improved sanitation, the growth of cooperative movement, the relief of
agricultural indebtedness and the development of local self-government. This is a large programme and it will tax our energies to the
utmost. In addition to this some Members are going to devote themselves to the spread of higher education among women, the promotion of harmony between Hindus and Muhammedans and work
among the depressed classes. We cannot expect any large constitutional changes for the next ten years or so now; meanwhile the work
we have taken in hand will amply repay itself and prepare the
ground for the next advance.'[21]

This programme was non-controversial, almost apolitical; all
communities, all parties and even the government could contribute
to its success. In his presidential speech at Allahabad, Wedderburn

[21] G.P.

urged British officials to work the Minto–Morley reforms 'in an ungrudging, even a generous spirit and to facilitate the return of the country to normal conditions by dispensing with extraordinary executive powers'. Wedderburn called for the restoration of the 'old friendly relations', and harked back to 'the views of the older generation of administrators—Elphinstone and Malcolm, Munro and Macaulay—who foresaw with gladness the day of India's emancipation'.

It is unlikely that the Viceroy and his advisers were impressed by these exhortations. They had no intention of winding up the Indian Empire, but they badly needed a breathing space. King George V, who had recently succeeded his father, had expressed a desire to visit India, and a political truce seemed essential to create a tranquil atmosphere for the visit. Lord Hardinge, the new Viceroy, accepted the advice of Crewe, the Secretary of State, and agreed to receive a Congress deputation, which included Gokhale and was headed by Wedderburn. The deputation expressed its gratitude for the Minto–Morley reforms and reiterated innocuous demands such as the extension of elementary education. The Viceroy's reply was courteous, but cautious. The Congress leaders were, however, carried away by their own enthusiasm for a *rapprochement* with government. To Wedderburn and the Moderate leadership, the Allahabad Congress seemed a spectacular success. Wedderburn hopefully forecast a phase of constructive cooperation in Indian politics. On his way to England he wrote to Henry Cotton, his colleague on the executive of the British Committee of the Congress, about

the better understanding between the Indians and British extended to the unofficial Anglo-Indian community and press, e.g. as shown in the Calcutta Club, where English & Indians meet on friendly terms; as also at the St Andrew Dinner, where the Chairman strongly advocated amicable cooperation in developing Indian resources. I have had the opportunity of meeting most of the important people, including the Viceroy, the C. J. [Chief Justice], the Lt-Governor, the Members of the Viceroy's Executive Council, both English and Indian & most of the Legislative Councillors, and there is clearly a feeling that the condition of antagonism should end & a period of constructive cooperation should be initiated. Our Congress friends are very strong on this point; they practically have the control of the independent element in the new Councils and they see their way to some really good work for the people if they can maintain and even improve the present amicable relationships with the authorities.[22]

[22] Wedderburn to H. Cotton, 9 Jan. 1911 (G.P.).

33

Détente

Gokhale's policy of general conciliation, which the Allahabad Congress had endorsed, happened to fit in with the changes in the British official hierarchy. Morley had resigned from the Liberal Cabinet in September 1910. By that time the constitutional reforms which he had piloted through the British Parliament had already lost much of their glitter. His inflexible stand on the partition of Bengal and his ostensible support to the repressive measures of the Minto regime during the years 1907–10 had damaged his prestige in nationalist circles in India.

Not many tears were, therefore, shed over Morley's departure from the India Office. Little was known in India about his successor, the Earl of Crewe, except that he was a Liberal and receptive to new ideas. Before retiring, Morley did one last good turn to India: he prevented the appointment of Lord Kitchener as Viceroy in succession to Minto. Kitchener was backed by Minto, Prime Minister Asquith, and King Edward VII, but Morley insisted that the appointment of 'the most famous active soldier of the day' as the Viceroy of India soon after the launching of a scheme of constitutional reforms was ill-advised.[1] It was not Kitchener, but Sir Charles Hardinge, an Under-Secretary in the British Foreign Office, who succeeded Minto.

Hardinge was destined to end his viceroyalty as the *bête noire* of Anglo-India and the Indian Civil Service, but he started well. Harcourt Butler, a member of his Executive Council, noted that the new Viceroy was 'an impulsive man . . . & feels things much, but once he has made up his mind he is forceful—and that is a great merit in a Viceroy'.[2] It is doubtful if Hardinge had any novel or radical ideas on the administration of India to start with; he did not take long to imbibe the prejudices of most of his countrymen in India. In his autobiography, he proudly recalls his last speech in the Imperial

---

[1] P. Magnus, *Kitchener, Portrait of an Imperialist*, London, 1958, p. 247.
[2] Butler to his mother, 12 Aug. 1911 (B.P.).

Legislative Council in which he argued that the self-governing institutions in the British Dominions had been evolved through a process of steady and patient evolution, and that what India required was 'not idealism but practical solutions', and the capacity to 'look facts squarely in the face'.[3] Hardinge's prejudices hardened with age. In 1929, even Lord Irwin's modest declaration on dominion status as a goal for India struck him as dangerously idealistic. Hardinge's private papers indicate that he had little love for or even understanding of Indian politicians and political parties. 'The fact is', he wrote to the Governor of Madras in May 1911, 'that educated people in this country love notoriety and the airing of their views in the press. If their speeches were not reported, they would give up politics.'[4]

There is evidence that the new Viceroy quickly acquired a deep distrust of Gokhale; he tended, in common with most senior British officials, to put the worst possible construction on Gokhale's words and actions. Experienced diplomat as he was, Hardinge knew how to hide his real feelings; unlike Curzon he did not gratuitously tread on the corns of Indian politicians. In emergencies Hardinge ignored the advice of local officials, cut red tape and, through timely intervention, staved off many a crisis. One example of such an initiative was his withdrawal of the 'conspiracy cases' in 1910–11 to create a congenial climate for the Delhi Durbar; another was his astute handling of the Cawnpore mosque affair to regain the confidence of the Muslim community. He knew how to strike the inner chords of India's educated classes. His description of Britain 'as the greatest Mohammedan power in the world'[5] was typical of the man. His public denunciation of the South African government for its repression of the Indian minority in Natal and the Transvaal raised his stock sky-high in India.

Luckily for Hardinge, he came to India at a time when, exhausted by the humiliations of the Curzon regime and the deferred hopes and the final frustrations of the Minto–Morley reforms, the politically conscious classes were longing for a breathing space. As we have seen, Gokhale himself favoured a moratorium on political controversies for a few years, and wanted to concentrate on constructive pro-

[3] Hardinge of Penhurst, *My Indian Years*, London, 1948, p. 141.
[4] Hardinge to A. Lawley, 1 May 1911 (H.P.).
[5] 'After all', Hardinge wrote to Ali Imam, a member of his Executive Council on 14 November 1912, 'Britain is the greatest Mohammedan power in the world, and the Government of India is the greatest safeguard of the Mohammedan religion.' (H.P.).

grammes in which officials and non-officials, Hindus and Muslims, Europeans and Indians could cooperate. A political truce at this time was especially welcome to the new Viceroy because of the proposed visit and coronation of George V towards the end of 1911.

Many eyebrows were raised in Britain[6] when the King expressed a wish to visit India. Was it essential for the British Sovereign to have a coronation in every country of the British Empire? Who was to pay for the grand spectacle if it was to be held in India? And what would be the effect of such a ceremony on a country already seething with nationalist discontent? Curiously enough, the proposal for the royal visit and a Durbar did not provoke much opposition in India. The Imperial Legislative Council was even enthusiastic about it. One Indian member after another (Hardinge wrote home) got up and said that 'they did not mind how much money was going to be spent on the Durbar provided the money was well spent, and in a manner to increase the dignity of the occasion and to show the intense loyalty of the Indian people to their King-Emperor. . . . Not a soul has made one single criticism of the amount set aside in the budget for the expenses of the Durbar.'[7]

The Viceroy sensed 'pacification' in the air, and noted that 'with the prospect of the King's visit in view, an opportunity presents itself for a truce which may never occur again'.[8] Indian tradition linked a coronation with 'boons' from the throne. There were speculations in the press on the 'boons' which the royal visit would bring to India. Even a further instalment of constitutional reforms was considered a possibility! Wedderburn wrote to the Viceroy and the Secretary of State proposing a knighthood for Dadabhai Naoroji. 'He has never expressed such a desire for such a recognition', Wedderburn wrote to Hardinge, 'and I should not press the matter if I did not believe that an honour bestowed on this veteran friend of the British Government would be an important stroke of good policy.'[9] Hardinge was inclined to accept Wedderburn's proposal: 'I am always opposed to giving honours to people who have been opponents of Government because it tends to discourage our supporters, but this case is somewhat special, because Dadabhai's active career has long ended. . . .'[10] The Government of Bombay was, however, firmly opposed to the

[6] C. Cross, *The Liberals in Power 1905–1914*, London, 1963, p. 52.
[7] Hardinge to R. Ritchie, 20 March 1911 (H.P.).
[8] Hardinge to Clarke, 25 Nov. 1910 (H.P.).
[9] Wedderburn to Hardinge, 27 April 1911 (H.P.).
[10] Hardinge to Clarke, 14 Aug. 1911 (H.P.).

proposal and it fell through.[11] About the same time Ramsay Mac-Donald, the future Labour Premier, was sounding out the government on the possibility of releasing Tilak and announcing a general amnesty for political prisoners.

The Delhi Durbar did not bring these 'boons' but it brought an unexpected one. The partition of Bengal, enforced by Curzon in the teeth of bitter opposition in 1905, was annulled, and it was announced that Delhi instead of Calcutta would be the capital of the country. Nationalist India was thrilled. For seven years the partition had been a running sore in Indian politics; it alienated large sections of the intelligentsia, especially in Bengal, from the government; it sucked thousands of students into political agitation; it widened the gulf between Hindus and Muslims; it split the Indian National Congress, brought into being a small but desperate party of violence, and it brought irksome curbs on public meetings and freedom of the press.

Thanks to the official repression on the one hand and the introduction of constitutional reforms on the other, the agitation against the partition of Bengal declined by 1911. Charles Bayley, the Governor of East Bengal, assured the Viceroy that the embers of the partition agitation were 'stone-cold'.[12] Hardinge himself opposed the reopening of this question.

Hardinge to Crewe, 22 February 1911: I can well understand that His Majesty would desire to make some striking announcement at the Durbar . . . and I warmly sympathize with his idea of setting right what has been represented to him as a wrong and as a grievance, but I am quite sure that you will agree with me that an announcement of this kind would alienate the Muhammedan population. . . . What India requires above everything at the present moment is peace and quiet. We do not want fireworks or any political concessions designed to produce an effect. . . . the idea [of the revocation of partition] should be abandoned. To give the slightest hope of any such solution would be simply to provoke a renewal of agitation, which as I have said before is dying down, and will disappear shortly from inanition.[13]

Hardinge's pleas were in vain. The King, who as Prince of Wales had visited India in 1905–6, knew how the partition of Bengal had then convulsed India, and had his way.

The Durbar turned out to be a magnificent spectacle and a poli-

[11] *Idem*, 18 Aug. 1911 (H.P.).
[12] Bayley to Hardinge, 28 Oct. 1911 (H.P.).
[13] H.P.

tical masterstroke. A city of tents was set up to house a quarter million people in Delhi. The King reviewed 50,000 troops and attended a reception in the gardens of the Red Fort. During an interval in the garden party, he and the Queen donned their crowns and royal robes, came out and sat in a conspicuous position on the battlements of the fort from which the people below could see them. The pageantry of the Durbar, the reversal of the partition of Bengal and the allocation of fifty lakhs of rupees for education created an excellent effect on public opinion in India.

Along with other members of the Imperial Legislative Council, Gokhale was present at the Durbar. He saw the opening of a new chapter in Indo-British relations. The Durbar seemed to have dissipated overnight the results of the unpopular measures of the last years of Curzon's regime and of the half-measures of Minto's viceroyalty. With the rankling grievance of the partition of Bengal out of the way, it seemed possible to restore the faith of the educated classes in the sincerity of the Raj and to halt the drift to lawlessness and violence. While the King was on his way back to England, Gokhale drafted a message from 'the Princes and the people of India' to 'the people of Great Britain and Ireland', expressing

cordial goodwill and fellowship, also an assurance of their warm attachment to the world-wide Empire of which they form part and with which their destinies are indissolubly linked. . . . [The Royal visit] has drawn closer the bonds that unite India and England. They are confident that this great and historic event marks the beginning of a new era, ensuring greater happiness, prosperity and progress to the people of India, under the aegis of the Crown.[14]

The message, which was endorsed by the Indian members of the Imperial Legislative Council, was cabled to England to synchronize with the return of the King and the Queen to London. Its felicitous phrases might amuse one today, but they reflected the sentiments of the bulk of the Indian intelligentsia before the first world war who saw no inherent incompatibility between Indian patriotism and loyalty to the British throne. The almost magical effect of the Durbar on India was explained by Gokhale to Wedderburn.

Gokhale to Wedderburn, 25 January 1912: The King-Emperor's visit about the wisdom of which serious misgivings were entertained at one time in many quarters has proved a big and unqualified success.

[14] Gokhale to Scott, 4 Feb. 1912 (H.P.). See also *Gazette of India Extraordinary*, Home Dept., 6 Feb. 1912.

The King has the rare and happy knack of touching on every occasion the right chord and his utterances throughout the visit evoked deep and widespread enthusiasm. His speech on education in reply to an address from the Calcutta University was a masterpiece, and is already regarded by Indians of all classes as a new educational charter for the country. . . .

There is no doubt that the reversal of the partition and the announcement of that reversal at Delhi before the King's visit to Calcutta was a masterstroke of policy. I have been coming to Calcutta personally before the partition and after the partition. The heavy feeling of despair which one felt on all sides here like a pall since Lord Curzon forced his partition measure on Bengal in 1905 has vanished as at some magic touch and one feels things are as they were before 1905—only better.[15]

Gokhale's mood of mingled relief and gratitude was understandable. The six years that had elapsed since the partition of Bengal had been an ordeal for him. The successive annual Congress sessions at Benares, Calcutta and Surat, the Convention at Allahabad, and even the Congress session at Madras had taxed to the utmost his energy, patience and optimism. Now that the partition had been reversed, it seemed possible to dispel the feelings of despair which had swelled the ranks of Extremists and anarchists.[16] The revocation of the partition seemed to vindicate the faith of the Moderate party, and to justify the policy of *détente* which Gokhale and Wedderburn had favoured since 1910. In a sense, this was a personal triumph for Gokhale, who had borne the main burden of guiding and rallying the Moderates since the Surat fiasco. Wedderburn's description of the Delhi Durbar as the 'grandest and the most bloodless revolution in history'[17] may sound odd today, but it echoed the feelings of Gokhale and his Congress colleagues in December 1911.

[15] G.P.
[16] 'The wounds of those terrible years 1906–1909 are really healing', C. F. Andrews wrote to Hardinge, on 5 Feb. 1913 (H.P.).
[17] Wedderburn to Gokhale, 14 Dec. 1911 (G.P.).

34

Leader of the Opposition

Gokhale saw in the 'reformed' legislative councils an instrument of constructive cooperation between the educated classes and the government. These councils, however, proved more conservative than he expected. The Imperial Council had a solid official bloc consisting of seven Executive Councillors, eight representatives of the provincial governments and nineteen officials of the Government of India. Since the government could also count on most of the representatives of the European Chambers of Commerce, the landholding classes and the Muslim community, it had an overwhelming majority in a legislature consisting of only sixty members. Men like Malik Umar Hyat Khan Tiwana, Nawab Zulfiqar Ali of Malerkotla, Kanwar Sir Ranbir Singh of Patiala, the Raja of Pratabgarh, the Prince of Arcot, Maharaja of Burdwan and Abdul Majid of Allahabad took their cue from the government. The stratagem of introducing class and sectional representation had reduced the politically conscious element in the Imperial Council to a tiny minority. There were hardly half a dozen members who shared Gokhale's political outlook, such as the veteran Nawab Syed Mohammed Bahadur from Madras, young M. A. Jinnah from Bombay, Bhupendranath Basu from Bengal, R. N. Mudholkar from Berar, and Sachchidananda Sinha and Madan Mohan Malaviya from the United Provinces.

Towards his Indian colleagues, even those who toed the official line, Gokhale did not adopt a superior or self-righteous attitude. In his private correspondence with the Secretary of State, Minto was referring to Gokhale as the 'leader of the non-officials in the Legislative Council'[1] and Ali Imam, a member of the Viceroy's Executive Council, once described Gokhale as the 'Leader of the Opposition' on the floor of the House.

I know [Gokhale remarked] that my Hon'ble friend meant to be complimentary, when he spoke of me as the 'Leader of the Opposi-

[1] Hardinge to Crewe, 2 Feb. 1911 (H.P.).

tion', but we are far away yet from the time when the Government Members will exchange places with private members in this Council, and until that time comes there can be no regular Opposition here, as the term is understood in Western countries. As a matter of fact, we support the Government here more than we oppose it; and if, on any occasion, we have to differ, it is simply owing to our conscientious conviction that the view of the Government is not correct.[2]

Though there was no organized 'Opposition', Gokhale realized that even the moral influence which the handful of elected members could exercise depended upon their ability to hold together. Gokhale did his best to keep clear of communal and regional controversies. In January 1911, when Madan Mohan Malaviya moved a resolution to correct the imbalance in representation accorded to various communities under the Indian Councils Act of 1909, Gokhale opposed the reopening of the electoral issue. He did not deny that the representation accorded to Muslims was excessive, but pleaded with his 'Hindu brethren to make the best of the situation in the larger interests of the country'.[3]

With its standing majority the government was in a position to carry through any measure it wanted. But it was not insensitive to the criticism of non-official members which, thanks to the newspapers, reverberated in thousands of Indian homes. The Viceroy who combined the roles of the Head of the State, Prime Minister and Speaker, presided over the meetings of the Imperial Legislative Council, except when a senior member of the Executive Council (whom he nominated as Vice-President) relieved him of the duty of presiding over some of the meetings. The discussion of the budget in the 'reformed' council was less perfunctory and no longer confined to the reading of prepared speeches by non-official members in a given sequence on the last day of the winter session. Honourable members could comment upon new taxes, fresh loans and additional grants, and on each head of revenue and expenditure. The Finance Member furnished, together with the budget statement, an explanatory memorandum which was open to discussion, though not to vote.

2

Gokhale was quick to seize the opportunities in the Council for a fuller examination of the country's finances. These opportunities

---

[2] Karve & Ambekar (eds.), op. cit., vol. II, p. 56.   [3] Ibid., p. 78.

seemed to grow after Hardinge's appointment. The new Viceroy wanted to keep the political temperature low, and in this aim he was supported by some members of his Executive Council, Harcourt Butler, Ali Imam, and above all, by Guy Fleetwood Wilson. Fleetwood Wilson had served in the British Treasury and the War Office in London, and had been picked up by Morley for the key post of the Finance Member of the Government of India. He was disliked and distrusted by the Civil Service which regarded him as an interloper. Self-centred, conceited and a man of strong likes and dislikes, he was not an easy person to work with, but he was happily free from the deep-seated prejudices, hauteur and complacency of most senior civil servants. He had heard of Gokhale's ability as a legislator. Fleetwood Wilson recalled later:

The one man I frankly feared was Gokhale, the Gladstone of India. Accordingly I endeavoured to find out what Gokhale's line of attack would be. All and everyone told me that the attempt would be futile, and that any apparent frankness on Gokhale's part would only be a cloak to his real intentions. So I left him severely alone. Imagine my surprise at receiving, on the eve of the debate, a letter from Gokhale, whom I did not even know, to the effect, that as he had good reason to believe that I meant to do my utmost for the good of India, he had no desire to embarrass me and that he, therefore, sent me the notes of the speech he proposed to make ...

Gokhale did not have to regret this gesture. He found Fleetwood Wilson more considerate and accommodating than any of his predecessors. 'We have never found', Gokhale told the Imperial Legislative Council on 25 March 1912, 'Sir Guy Wilson wrapped up in official reserve. He has often presented new points of view to us, and he has himself been always anxious to enter into our feelings and thoughts.'[4] Gokhale was impressed by Fleetwood Wilson's attachment to the Gladstonian principles of economy. For years Gokhale had been pleading for economies in civil and military expenditure. Now there was a Finance Member who was not only prepared to listen to these pleas, but to act upon them. The obvious deference with which Fleetwood Wilson treated Gokhale was not liked by his European colleagues in the government. In February 1912 we find Harcourt Butler telling his mother that Fleetwood Wilson was 'very much under Gokhale's influence'.[5]

The cordiality between Gokhale and Fleetwood Wilson may not

[4] Patwardhan & Ambekar (eds.), op. cit., p. 264.
[5] Butler to his mother, 27 Feb. 1912 (B.P.).

have been wholly disinterested. Fleetwood Wilson may have considered it worth his while to cultivate the one man in the Imperial
Legislative Council, and indeed in the country, who could tear the
financial and economic policies of the government to pieces. On his
part, Gokhale could not but be grateful for being able to put across
the nationalist view of Indian economy directly to the man who was
the custodian of the Government of India's finances.

In January 1911 Gokhale gave notice of a resolution demanding
an enquiry into public expenditure, which had gone up by twenty
crores in ten years. The Finance Member, whom Gokhale had taken
into confidence, told the Viceroy that the Government was on a
weak wicket, and should meet Gokhale half-way.

Guy Fleetwood Wilson to Hardinge, 12 January 1911: Mr Gokhale's
resolution makes it incumbent on your Council to adopt one of the
three courses.
1. To meet it by a simple negative and crush the mover by means of
   official majority. I hardly think anyone would advocate this.
2. To accept the outside enquiry. I am sure no one will agree to that.
3. To set our own house in order individually as well as collectively.
   This is the policy which will I hope commend itself to Your
   Excellency and be supported by our colleagues. . . .[6]

Gokhale withdrew his resolution when the Finance Member gave
the assurance that 'all the members of the Government of India will
during the current year subject the expenditure for which they are
individually responsible to close scrutiny with a view to effecting all
possible economies'.[7] Seven months later, the Viceroy complained to
the Secretary of State that there was 'great professional hostility' to
any reduction in military expenditure and that the Army Department of the Government of India 'itself was frightfully overgrown
and overstocked. I wish half of it could be burnt down, and the
officers sent back to their regiments.'[8] The Finance Member urged a
tough line with the Army Headquarters. 'If Army expenditure could
be reduced', Fleetwood Wilson wrote to Hardinge, 'it will not only
make Your Excellency's position bearable, but will also enable a
development of the country to go on which will greatly redound to
the credit of your viceroyalty.'[9]

Gokhale knew that the national budget was more than a question

[6] F. Wilson P.
[7] *The Times*, 26 Jan. 1911.
[8] Hardinge to Crewe, 24 Aug. 1911 (H.P.).
[9] Wilson to Hardinge, 8 Nov. 1911 (F. Wilson P.).

of accounting and book-keeping, and that financial and economic policies were intimately linked with political issues. This is why he took care to link changes in financial and economic policies with the Indianization of the services, development of agriculture and industries, and decentralization of administration. An apt pupil of Ranade, Gokhale did not ride any economic theory to death, but took his stand on the facts of the Indian economic situation. He favoured a reduction in public expenditure not merely to lighten the burden of taxation, but to find funds for education, sanitation and health. When the Finance Member gave a million pounds for education and sanitation, his comment was: 'But the Hon'ble [Finance] Member does not go far enough. One million is good, but three millions would be better.'[10] Gokhale was enough of an idealist to accept the loss to the Indian exchequer of seven million pounds of the Opium revenue accruing from trade with China. 'It was', he said, 'a stain on our finances because it is drawn from the moral degradation of the people of a sister country.'[11]

Gokhale was conscious of the basic conflict of interests in a 'colonial' economy. An interesting example of this came in March 1911 when Madan Mohan Malaviya moved a resolution for the imposition of a duty on imported sugar to enable the indigenous sugar industry to survive. Gokhale was not opposed to 'protective' duties, but insisted that every proposal for such duties should be judged on its merits. The sugar industry in India was controlled by Europeans. If a thirty per cent import duty on sugar was levied, it was likely to yield two crores of rupees. These two crores, Gokhale said, would be taken out of the pockets of the poor consumers in India.[12] Again, when it was proposed to impose a duty on oil for lighting lamps, official spokesmen argued that the extra expenditure for a family would be no more than four annas per year. 'I accept this calculation', observed Gokhale. 'To my mind four annas per family is a serious addition to the burdens of the poorest classes of this country.'[13]

Gokhale's exposition of financial and economic issues drew high compliments even from the official benches. To listen to Gokhale, Fleetwood Wilson said, was an 'intellectual treat'.[14] His deputy, James Meston, the Finance Secretary, testified to Gokhale's 'lucidity'

[10] Patwardhan & Ambekar (eds.), op. cit., vol. I, p. 213.
[11] Ibid., p. 205.   [12] Ibid., p. 339.   [13] Ibid., p. 163.
[14] Ibid., p. 317.

and extreme firmness. 'Like the late Mr Gladstone', said Meston, 'the Hon'ble Mr Gokhale has the rare and happy knack of making figures interesting and it has been a sincere pleasure to listen to the skill with which he marshalled the figures and inspired life into the dry bones of our statistical returns.'[15] If these compliments were intended to flatter Gokhale into silence they failed in their object. Gokhale continued to express his views without fear or favour, and to pull skeletons out of the Imperial cupboard.

3

In March 1911, the Seditious Meetings Bill was introduced in the Imperial Legislative Council. Enacted in 1907 during Lord Minto's regime, it was to lapse in November 1910, but had been extended, despite Gokhale's opposition, till March 1911. All the provincial governments favoured its retention. Fleetwood Wilson had urged Hardinge to placate Indian opinion and to amend the Act, if he could not scrap it outright. 'I sounded Gokhale in this direction, when he was at Simla', Fleetwood Wilson wrote, 'and I received the impression that if the bill were materially altered, the attitude of the Indian Members might undergo a considerable modification.' The government (with its standing majority) was in a position to push the bill through the Imperial Council, but Hardinge agreed to soften its rigours in deference to the wishes of Gokhale and his friends.

Viceroy to Secretary of State, 2 February 1911: My [Executive] Council unanimously accepted my suggestions. They are strongly of opinion that an [Seditious Meetings] Act is necessary, provided that it is kept in the background as much as possible. The only addition that was made was the suggestion that Sinha, the former Member of [the Executive] Council, and Gokhale the leader of the non-officials in the Legislative Council should be asked to make suggestions as to the amendment of the Act. This proposal we all welcomed, and the Home Member has been charged to get into communication with these two. He has done so and we are to receive their proposals in two or three days. We must be careful not to reduce the Act to an absolute nullity. Still some impression would be made if the amendments to the Act were moved and accepted in open [session of Legislative] Council, so that the non-officials might get the credit of having effected something, and the Government might appear to have made some concession to opinions in the Council.[16]

The amended bill did not meet all of Gokhale's objections, but it

[15] Ibid., p. 311.   [16] H.P.

included some safeguards against the misuse of the special powers by the executive.

During the year 1911–12 elected Indian members moved a number of constructive resolutions. Subba Rao introduced a resolution calling for a commission to consider Indian claims to higher and more extensive employment in the public services. Gokhale himself brought forward a resolution for the creation of District Advisory Councils composed partly of elected and partly of nominated members. He described the district administration in India as 'bureaucratic in character, based upon reports placed from below, and carried on under orders received from above'. He affirmed that the association of the educated classes would contribute to the 'higher purpose of British rule', and enable the people of India to advance with slow but sure and steady steps to a place in their own country in accord with modern ideas of self-respect of civilized beings.[17]

British officials in India could hardly have accepted this conception of the purpose of British Rule. Nor could they have relished Gokhale's grand design of a democratic government: village panchayats at the base, the advisory councils in the districts, representative legislatures in the provinces and a parliament at the apex of the Indian administrative pyramid.

Among other non-official resolutions were those introduced by Vithaldas Thackersey on the currency, by Bhupendranath Basu on the High Courts being placed under the Government of India, and by S. P. Sinha on the separation of the judicial and executive functions.

In February 1912, Hardinge noted that the non-official members of the Legislative Council were having a 'gala time with a number of resolutions that they have brought forward'.[18] His colleagues and subordinates did not consider this a laughing matter. 'Gokhale', wrote the Viceroy's private secretary to Home Member Jenkins on 21 August 1911, 'likes to pose as the defender of the liberties of the people.' Sir George Clarke, the Governor of Bombay, who had at one time admired Gokhale, developed a deep distrust of him. 'Mr Gokhale's schemes', he wrote to Hardinge, 'are generally such as would, if accepted, create ill-will between Government and people. I am not sure whether he realizes this and I have found him apparently frank, but also inscrutable. He is coming to see me to-

---

[17] Karve & Ambekar (eds.), op. cit., vol. II, p. 101.
[18] Hardinge to Crewe, 20 Feb. 1912 (H.P.).

morrow but I shall never get at the back of his brain.'[19] A few months later, Clarke was warning the Viceroy that if

Gokhale were to succeed in saddling the councils with elected majorities we should certainly have trouble. I earnestly hope that no Secretary of State will listen to him for a moment. We have to rule, and if our measures could be defeated by an Indian faction in the Councils, the only recourse left would be to ask the Govt. of India to legislate over our heads and this would reduce the local Councils to futile and objectionable debating societies. Any weakening of the Civil Service will be disastrous and this is Gokhale's object.[20]

Gokhale did not know how deeply these high British dignitaries distrusted him, but he knew his activities were watched. In February 1912, speaking in the Imperial Council, he referred to the police surveillance over him. He had, he said,

always taken it as in the day's work. My life is frankly given to national work and I am free to recognize that the Government may think it necessary to keep in touch with all who are engaged in such work. What we are entitled to expect, however, is that the men who are employed in this duty shall do their work in a less clumsy and offensive manner than that in which they do it at present.[21]

Whatever his misgivings about the new Councils with their larger and more vocal Indian element, Hardinge personally adapted himself to them. 'Our Legislative Council', Hardinge wrote on 14 March 1912, 'has been extremely busy talking. They have not done much good, but I think it is a very good thing that they should be able to air their views and grievances. They will all go so much happier for having been allowed to do this.'[22] One of the measures which had been 'talked out' in the Council was Gokhale's Elementary Education Bill.

[19] Clarke to Hardinge, 9 April 1912 (H.P.).
[20] *Idem*, 5 Oct. 1912 (H.P.).
[21] Karve & Ambekar (eds.), op. cit., vol. II, pp. 111–12.
[22] Hardinge to Clarke, 14 March 1912 (H.P.).

35

Educating the Masses

Gokhale started life as a teacher and taught at the New English School and the Fergusson College for nearly eight years. There was scarcely an aspect of the Indian educational system to which he had not given thought. He had pleaded for the extension of female, technical, and higher education. Above all, he had advocated the diffusion of elementary education among the Indian masses. As early as 1896, when invited to deliver the annual address to the Bombay Graduates Association, Gokhale chose 'Education in India' as his subject. 'To us', he had declared, 'it [the spread of primary education] means the future salvation of our country.'[1] Universal education alone, Gokhale argued, could help the farmer to resist exploitation by the money-lender, to improve sanitation, to shake off superstition, to increase his earning capacity, to take an intelligent interest in public affairs, and to remove the reproach that Indian public life was the monopoly of a tiny minority. In the Imperial Legislative Council he pleaded vigorously for the education of the masses. It seemed to him 'a monstrous and cruel wrong' that millions and millions should be left without the rudiments of knowledge and that 'the joy of that knowledge' should be absolutely unexperienced by them.[2]

In 1910, at the very first meeting of the 'reformed' Imperial Council, Gokhale took advantage of the right given to non-official members to move resolutions, and proposed that 'a beginning should be made in the direction of making elementary education free and compulsory throughout the country, and that a mixed Commission of officials and non-officials be appointed to frame definite proposals'. Though he withdrew this resolution on being assured by the government that his proposals would be carefully considered, Gokhale had succeeded in making elementary education a live issue. It was taken up by the Indian press; it figured in a resolution passed by the Allahabad Congress at the end of the year; it was debated by the All-India

---

[1] Karve & Ambekar (eds.), op. cit., vol. III, p. 166. [2] Ibid., p. 218.

Muslim League at its annual session in Nagpur at about the same time. In November 1910, the Government of India appointed Harcourt Butler, a brilliant young officer of the Indian Civil Service, as the first Member of the Viceroy's Executive Council in charge of a newly created Department of Education. Butler called a meeting of the heads of the provincial education departments in April 1911 to discuss *inter alia* the problem of elementary education.

2

On 16 March 1911, Gokhale introduced his Elementary Education Bill, which incorporated most of the suggestions he had made in the Imperial Council a year earlier. Based largely on the Irish Education Act of 1892 and the English Education Acts of 1870 and 1876, it sought gradually to introduce the principle of compulsion into elementary education. The bill had, as he put it, 'a purely permissive character',[3] to be applied only to selected areas where elementary education had already developed up to a point, and which were to be specially notified by municipalities and district boards. These local bodies, which were to bear part of the expenditure, were to be empowered to levy a special education tax. Compulsion was to be applied only to boys between the ages of six and ten, but it could be extended to girls of the same age-group with the approval of the provincial governments. School fees were not to be charged from parents whose income was less than ten rupees a month, and, to avoid hardship, whole classes or communities could be exempted from the operation of the bill.

Gokhale deliberately brought forward a cautious measure to forestall objections on administrative and financial grounds. His speech in the Imperial Council was closely reasoned. It was a masterly survey of elementary education in India and abroad. He pointed out that in several European countries, the United States of America, Canada and Australia, whole populations could read and write, but in India only 6 per cent of the people were literate. A mere 1.7 per cent of the population went to elementary schools in India, as against 20 per cent in the U.S.A. and western Europe, 11 per cent in Japan and 5 per cent in Russia. The expenditure on elementary education was 16s. per head in the U.S.A., 10s. in England and Germany, 4s. 10d. in France, 7½d. in Japan, 7½d. in Russia, and barely a penny

[3] For text of the bill, see ibid., pp. 106–9.

in India. Elementary education had been made compulsory and free in Great Britain, Ireland, France, Germany, Switzerland, Austria, Hungary, Italy, Belgium, Denmark, Norway, Canada, U.S.A., Australia and Japan; in Holland it was compulsory, but not free. In Russia it was for the most part free, but not compulsory. If illiteracy was to be banished from India within a measurable period, Gokhale saw no escape from some form of compulsion. He pointed out that in 1870, before England introduced compulsion, only forty-three per cent of her children were at school; ten years had sufficed to bring all of them to school. Similarly, Japan had by means of compulsion made elementary education universal within twenty years. The diffusion of education among the Indian masses was in Gokhale's opinion a great national task in which the government and the people could cooperate. He urged the government to adopt elementary education as its own policy, and to provide funds for it as 'Governments in other civilized countries are doing'. He agreed that leaders of Indian opinion, on their part, had to bring to this task energy, enthusiasm and above all the courage to court unpopularity by advocating compulsion.

Gokhale made an impassioned and even indignant attack on the critics of his bill. A Bombay businessman, Sir Sassoon David, had told the Imperial Council that the time for compulsion had not yet come. 'Will he tell us', asked Gokhale, 'how and why it has arrived in Baroda and not in British territory? Will he tell us why, when the Philippino Municipalities have introduced compulsion, our own Municipalities should not?'[4] Harcourt Butler, the Education Member, rejected the analogy of Baroda on the ground that it was 'autocratically' governed. 'Western countries will not do', Gokhale retorted, 'because they are governed democratically! Baroda will not do, because it is governed autocratically! I suppose the Hon'ble Member will not be satisfied unless I produce the analogy of a country governed bureaucratically, and as there is no other country governed as India is, he is safe in insisting on such an analogy, and I must say I give it up.'[5]

3

After the bill had been introduced and circulated, twelve months were to elapse before it could come up before the Imperial Legislative

[4] Ibid., p. 104.   [5] Ibid.

Council again. Gokhale had a year in which to mobilize popular support for his proposals and to break down official prejudice and opposition. The bill was well received by the Indian press, and even by a few Anglo-Indian newspapers such as the *Indian Daily News*, the *Madras Mail* and the *Madras Times*. The Senate of the Madras University, which was the only university senate consulted, expressed itself in favour of the bill. Public meetings were held in several places to support it. Gokhale undertook a tour to educate public opinion. He visited Calcutta, Nagpur and Madras.

The visit to Madras proved the most memorable in this campaign. He had written to V. S. Srinivasa Sastri, his disciple and host in Madras, to avoid processions and public receptions. 'It is impossible', Sastri wrote back, 'to keep the young men from the platform or railway station compound, but we can take care of you and drive you home as fast as decency will allow.'[6] On 22 July, Gokhale addressed a public meeting in the Victoria Town Hall, which was packed to capacity, its 600 seats having been reserved several days in advance. A day earlier, a petition bearing more than a hundred signatures addressed 'to the Hon'ble G. K. Gokhale, C.I.E., Madras', read: 'The Victoria Town Hall can accommodate only 600 persons. But this is a very small fraction of your admirers & sympathizers in this city, we beg that you be pleased to arrange [an] open air meeting. . . .'[7]

An 'open air meeting' was unthinkable in those days. While Gokhale spoke on the problems of education, with the veteran S. Subramania Iyer, a former judge of the Madras High Court, in the chair, thousands waited outside the Town Hall. Next morning another meeting was held in the Victoria Hall by the students of Madras, who presented an address to Gokhale. He spoke to them on 'The Needs and Responsibilities of Public Life'.

The critics of the Elementary Education Bill were not confined to the ranks of British officials. Surendranath Banerjea opposed it, fearing that it would divert funds for elementary education from higher education—in which incidentally he was personally interested. The Bombay Corporation, under the inspiration of Pherozeshah Mehta, passed a resolution which endorsed the objects, but criticized the methods proposed in Gokhale's bill. Pherozeshah wanted the responsibility for elementary education to remain squarely on the shoulders of the Government of India; he feared that devolution of

[6] Sastri to Gokhale, 12 July 1911 (G.P.).
[7] The 'petition' dated 21 July 1911 is preserved in G.P.

this responsibility, even partially to municipalities and district boards, would give the government a pretext for inaction.[8]

Muslim reaction was mixed. Some Muslim newspapers, such as the *Observer* of Lahore, supported the bill. So did the Aga Khan. But Syed Ameer Ali and his friends in London struck a discordant note. Some Muslim politicians—such as Mian Muhammad Shafi of the Punjab—could hardly be expected to take a line which ran counter to the wishes of the government. But already—in 1911— efforts were being made to misrepresent Gokhale's proposals as communal. The secretary of the All-India Muslim League, in a letter to the Home Department of the Government of India, suggested that the sole medium of instruction for Muslim children should be Urdu, that they should be taught the essentials of Islam, that their textbooks should draw upon Islamic sources and be prepared by Muslim writers and approved by textbook committees composed exclusively of Muslims. He went so far as to demand 'a staff of Muslim inspectors to look to the peculiar needs of the community'. Even the supervisory committees envisaged in Gokhale's Bill were to have equal representation of Hindus and Muslims.[9] These extreme demands, the effect of which could only be to accentuate the isolation of the Muslim community from the mainstream of Indian life, could hardly have been taken seriously in 1911. Gokhale was, however, quick to recognize the justice of the demand for instruction in Urdu and other regional languages. He agreed to the introduction of a clause in his bill permitting the use of any Indian language if twenty-five children speaking it attended a school.[10]

4

Gokhale had known all along that because of the standing majority of the official bloc in the Imperial Council, the fate of his bill would ultimately depend upon the attitude of the government. In March 1911, that attitude seemed to him 'cautious, but not unfriendly'. He paid a tribute to the Education Member, Harcourt Butler, who, he said, 'brings to his task a reputation for great practical capacity . . . the Indian sun has not dried the Hon'ble Member and . . . he has not shed those enthusiasms with which perhaps we

[8] Chintamani to Gokhale, 16 Sept. 1911 (G.P.).
[9] Mohammed Aziz Mirza, Hon. Sec., All-India Muslim League to Sec. to Govt. of India, Home Dept., 5 Oct. 1911 (copy in G.P.).
[10] Karve & Ambekar (eds.), op. cit., vol. III, p. 129.

all start in life and without which no high task for the improvement of humanity has even been undertaken.'[11] Butler's rise in the official hierarchy had indeed been meteoric; within three years he had risen from the post of Deputy Commissioner, Lucknow, to that of Education Member of the Viceroy's Executive Council. In 1910–11 he seemed to be enthusiastic about elementary education. Fleetwood Wilson, the Finance Member, was also sympathetic. In February 1911, he told the Viceroy that elementary education 'would make an appropriate—not to say dramatic—concession for announcement by His Majesty' at the Durbar proposed at the end of that year.[12] With the impending loss of revenue from the opium trade with China, the prospects for Indian finance were far from bright, but Fleetwood Wilson favoured the additional expenditure on education, hoping for economies in civil and military expenditure.

In May 1911, Harcourt Butler estimated that the cost of free elementary education throughout India would be rupees fifty lakhs a year. In a comprehensive note (which the Viceroy forwarded to the Secretary of State), Butler drew attention to the growing 'insistence and intensity' of the demand for free primary education. 'Hindus and Muhammedans alike have made it part of their platform', he wrote:

It is advocated in Legislative Councils, at public meetings and in the press by landowners no less than by lawyers; and philanthropists and politicians are starting free institutions, night schools and the like. True, Gokhale's Bill contemplates the payment of fees by parents whose income exceeds Rs 10 per mensem, but the public prefers the abolition of fees to the contingent introduction of the compulsory principle, and that was Mr Gokhale's own attitude in the Imperial Legislative Council a year ago. Personally I regard the provision of free elementary education as a matter of real urgency and vital consequence not only because I foresee that we shall be forced to concede it within a year or two, nor because I think that more than any other measure it will remove the deep-rooted belief in India and outside it, that we are afraid of education and put difficulties in its path, but mainly because the economic and political conditions of the country require it. . . . I am convinced that unless we move in harmony with popular opinion in this matter we shall find control slipping through our fingers.[13]

Butler's appraisal of the elementary education campaign in February 1911 was a measure of Gokhale's success in making it a live

[11] Ibid., pp. 91–2. [12] Wilson to Hardinge, 6 Feb. 1911 (F. Wilson P.).
[13] Note, 13 May 1911, on Free Primary Education, by S. H. Butler, enclosed with Hardinge to Crewe, 1 June 1911 (H.P.).

issue. Even the Viceroy was deeply impressed and told the Secretary of State:

It has become perfectly clear to me from the debate in [the Imperial Legislative] Council on Gokhale's Education Bill, and the comments of the Press that it is absolutely necessary that we should go in for an educational programme . . . [Butler and I] are agreed that our first step should be a campaign against illiteracy and this would be best initiated by free compulsory education. . . . Butler estimates the cost of making elementary education free throughout India at 50 lakhs a year. I think that this money should be found without difficulty and should be the first step in a big educational programme.[14]

At the end of July 1911 Hardinge's optimism was at its peak: he went so far as to express the hope that free elementary education would be introduced in India before he left the country.[15]

Hardinge, Butler and Fleetwood Wilson may have been wholly sincere in their desire to support free and compulsory education for the masses, but they had to reckon with the resistance from the local (provincial) governments to whom mass education spelt mass sedition. The Governor of Bombay warned the Viceroy:

The agitation for education [so far as Primary education is concerned] is of quite recent origin, comes from the people who are anxious to make our Rule impossible. . . . They well realize that their power to stir up discontent would be immensely increased if every cultivator could read. . . . We cannot teach the great mass of people long enough or thoroughly enough to make them *permanently* able even to read and write; but we can, and we shall, do much to promote general discontent. In that part of their calculations the Gokhales are perfectly right.[16]

The Bombay Governor's prejudices and fears were typical of the British ruling class in India. The local governments were on the whole hostile to the bill. Governor Clarke's own government pronounced compulsory elementary education as 'an unwarranted interference with the liberties of the people'. The Bengal government saw no objection to the principle of mass elementary education, but ruled it out on the ground of shortage of money and trained teachers. The Punjab government warned that the majority of the people in that province were opposed not only to compulsory education, but to any education whatsoever. The U.P. government even predicted a

[14] Hardinge to Crewe, 1 June 1911 (H.P.).
[15] Hardinge to Clarke, 28 July 1911 (H.P.).
[16] Clarke to Hardinge, 21 July 1911 (H.P.).

popular uprising if parents were compelled to educate their children! Only the backward province of Baluchistan saw no danger in free and compulsory education.

In July 1911 Wedderburn, at Gokhale's suggestion, organized a deputation headed by Lord Courtney to wait upon Crewe, the Secretary of State for India. Crewe expressed himself as 'wholly sympathetic' to the extension of elementary education and described Gokhale's bill as extremely moderate. Neither the public support of the Secretary of State nor the initial sympathy of the Finance and Education Members of the Executive Council and the Viceroy, however, availed against the massive opposition of the British 'steel frame' in India.

By the beginning of October 1911 Gokhale had sensed that the Government of India would not support his bill, and its fate was sealed.[17] Nevertheless, he decided to put up a fight when the bill came back to the Imperial Council on 18 March 1912. 'The main opposition to the bill', he said, 'has come from official quarters.' He answered objections to the bill, clarified knotty points, allayed fears, and exposed the fallacies of his critics. He conceded special arrangements for teaching the languages of cultural minorities. Of Sir Gangadhar Chitnavis and Nawab Abdul Majid, the two members of the Imperial Legislative Council who had frankly doubted the value of elementary education, Gokhale said that in this attitude they were not singular: 'There are men belonging to this class in other countries —in Western countries—who have the same distrust of mass education.'[18] He reminded Sir Gangadhar that the Elementary Education Bill had been supported by the Nagpur Municipality and Nagpur District Board of which he was the chairman. To another member, Dadabhoy, who had first supported and then turned a critic of the Bill, Gokhale offered his congratulations 'not only on his conversion to official views but to his very manner of expressing those views'. To a European member who said he had visited thousands of primary schools, Gokhale retorted: 'Sir, we have *learnt* in primary schools. We have experience from the inside of these schools.'[19] There were some British officials, Gokhale said, who were against mass education, because they were against all popular progress, and imagined 'in their short-sightedness that every step gained by the people is one lost by them'.[20]

---

[17] Gokhale to Wedderburn, 6 Oct. 1911 (G.P.).
[18] Karve & Ambekar (eds.), op. cit., vol. III, p. 132.
[19] Ibid., p. 142.   [20] Ibid., p. 117.

Harcourt Butler described Gokhale's bill as 'a modest and un-assuming measure . . . full of safeguards', but 'premature'. He paid a tribute to Gokhale for creating an enthusiasm for elementary education, lauded his aims, but did not support his bill. On 19 March 1911, the bill was defeated by 13 votes to 38. 'This bill', Gokhale said, 'thrown out today will come back again and again till on the stepping-stones of its dead selves, a measure ultimately rises which will spread the light of knowledge throughout the land.' On the evening of 18 March there was an official dinner at Calcutta, at which Gokhale sat next to Butler. 'We had a long talk', Butler wrote home. 'He [Gokhale] said that I had made things very difficult for him, but he rejoiced greatly at my enunciation of policy. He had seen the change that had come over the Education Departments in different provinces since I had assumed charge. . . . I never can fathom Gokhale, but tonight at any rate he was very human.'[21]

Gokhale was saddened, but not surprised by the defeat of his bill. As early as October 1911, he had foreseen this possibility and planned his strategy to meet it. He had decided to visit England to canvass support for this bill in the Parliament and the press to overcome the resistance of the British officials in India to mass education. 'It is quite clear to me,' Gokhale wrote to Wedderburn on 6 October 1911, 'with earnest and persistent work both in this country and in England for three or four years, we should get this Bill or something similar to it placed on the statute book.'[22]

The battle for free and compulsory education turned out to be longer and harder than Gokhale had expected. Not till 1917 was the first successful measure (largely based on his bill) for enforcing compulsion in elementary education passed by a provincial legislature. Bombay was the pioneer. The following twenty years saw the enactment of similar laws by the legislatures of other provinces and Indian states.

[21] Butler to Glory, 18 March 1912 (B.P.).
[22] Gokhale to Wedderburn, 6 Oct. 1911 (G.P.).

Book IV

THE LAST PHASE

36

Educating the British

Gokhale had long been thinking of visiting England to canvass support for his education bill. Early in 1912 he had strong reasons for undertaking this trip. His friends were anxious about his failing health, and begged him not to drive himself too hard. 'I wish', he wrote in 1910 to Krishnaswamy Aiyer, 'I could tear myself off from all work as you suggest and I cannot tell you how I long for the *santi* [peace] that you speak of. The time for this, however, is not yet for me. A couple of years may make the situation easier and then I should take the first opportunity to do as you suggest.'[1]

The situation never became easier. Immediately, there was enough for Gokhale to worry about: the repressive legislation in the closing months of Minto's viceroyalty, the legislative business before the expanded Imperial Council, the problems of the divided Congress party, and the beleaguered Indian minority in South Africa. In 1911, while he was waging a strenuous campaign for free and compulsory education, his daughter went through a serious illness. By the end of the year, he was thoroughly exhausted, both physically and mentally. 'It is absolutely necessary in public interest', Wedderburn wrote to him, 'that the question of your health should take the first place & no time should be lost in getting, in Europe, the proper treatment for your trouble.'[2]

Gokhale sailed from Bombay on 3 May 1912. Immediately on arrival in England, he consulted his doctor at Manchester, who ordered complete rest for five weeks. By the end of June, he had improved sufficiently to resume normal activity. In 1912, as in his earlier visits, his confidant and guide was Wedderburn. They were in constant touch, frequently writing to each other and taking counsel together. Occasionally, Wedderburn travelled to London, and conferred with Gokhale at the office of the British Committee of the

---

[1] Gokhale to Aiyer 10 Oct. 1910 (G.P.).
[2] Wedderburn to Gokhale, 28 Feb. 1912 (G.P.).

Congress. The two friends then lunched at the National Liberal Club where Gokhale invariably stayed. Usually they were joined at lunch by a visiting Indian leader, a British politician or a sympathetic civil servant. The day was rounded off by a visit to Westminster if there was a debate on Indian affairs in one of the Houses of Parliament. Occasionally, Gokhale went up to Meredith in Gloucester for a quiet weekend with the Wedderburns. Wherever and whenever they met, Gokhale and Wedderburn had only one thought: India. Wedderburn neither stinted time nor money; all his contacts, all his friendships were meant to promote the Congress cause. He had been disappointed in Morley, but after Morley's departure from the India Office, he cultivated the new Secretary of State, Lord Crewe, and his assistant, Edwin Montagu. He started fraternizing with J. Ramsay MacDonald when he saw the Labour Party was emerging as a factor in British politics. The issues for which Wedderburn fought in England were the issues which stirred Congress leaders in India. From 1905 to 1910, he had concentrated on the partition of Bengal and constitutional reforms. From 1911 onwards, as Gokhale campaigned for elementary education, Wedderburn also began to harp on the iniquity of keeping the Indian masses ignorant.

Wedderburn and Gokhale achieved remarkable *rapport*. 'Do not trouble to write to me', Wedderburn wrote on 9 July 1913, 'except when it is quite convenient. I shall always know that you are working for the best, & I do not know that we ever differed as to what the best is.'[3] One of the happiest moments of Gokhale's life came on 4 July 1912, when at an 'At Home' in London he presented, on behalf of Wedderburn's admirers in India, a necklace to Lady Wedderburn[4] 'as a sincere token of the very high esteem, admiration and affection in which Sir William is universally held . . . and the gratitude we feel for the great and invaluable services he has rendered to India during a lifetime devoted entirely to her service.'

On this occasion, in the presence of a number of Indians resident in London, and British friends of India, Gokhale gave his own appraisal of Indo-British relations as they appeared to him in the summer of 1912. The Minto–Morley reforms seemed to him a 'valuable step in advance even though they did not go far enough'. 'A [machinery] has now been created in India', said Gokhale, 'whereby all our minor grievances can be brought effectively to the notice of the Government without troubling Parliament or the people

[3] *Idem*, 9 July 1913 (G.P.).   [4] *The Times*, 5 July 1912.

of this country [Britain]. For large questions of policy or principle our appeal will still have to be here.'[5]

Gokhale was already looking beyond the Minto–Morley reforms. A fortnight after the presentation of the necklace to Lady Wedder-burn, while speaking at a reception given in his honour by the Indian community in London, Gokhale said that he had never before spoken 'with so much confidence, with so much glad hope in the heart or with a clearer vision of what awaited them in future'.[6] He referred to 'provincial autonomy', took note of British doubts and difficulties, but did not see any ground for discouragement.

For these were matters [he said] that were not so much in the hands of English statesmen, as they were in their [Indians'] own hands. More-over, there were forces mightier than any statesman, mightier than all statesmen put together, that were moulding the destinies of all the East, and of India among the Eastern nations, and if only they [the Indians] would have faith in themselves and were determined to work for their salvation, as they ought, no statement of policy, no interpretation of any passage, no matter from whom it came, could long stand in the way of their just advance.[7]

Indians must remember, in speaking of their political progress, Gokhale observed, that it was not what the English rulers did so much as what they did themselves upon which their future really depended. The aim of the Indian people briefly was a position in India that other people in other parts of the Empire had in theirs. The existing constitutional position was transitional; they had to agitate for elected majorities in the councils. It was in this context of a future self-governing India that Gokhale placed his scheme for elementary education. He had no doubt that India produced men and women who could hold their own against individuals in any country, but the average calibre in India needed to be raised with the help of universal education. The edifice of self-government, he felt, would have to rest not upon a few individuals, but upon the average strength of the people.[8]

2

Gokhale's affirmation in London of the inevitability of Indian self-government was the more remarkable because Lord Crewe, the Secre-

[5] *Speeches of Gokhale*, p. 828.   [6] *The Times*, 20 July 1912.
[7] Karve & Ambekar (eds.), op. cit., vol. II, p. 391.
[8] Ibid., p. 393.

tary of State, had recently ridiculed the school of political thought in India which cherished the dream of dominion self-government: 'I say quite frankly that I see no future for India on those lines. I do not believe that the experiment . . . of attempting to confer a measure of real self-government, with practical freedom from Parliamentary control, upon a race which is not our own . . . is one which could be tried.'[9]

The truth was that the British Liberal party in the years preceding the First World War could no more envisage India without British tutelage than the Tory Opposition or the Government of India. The Viceroy and his colleagues may have resigned themselves to the Minto–Morley reforms, but they wanted no further 'meddling' with the Indian administration by the British Parliament. In a note circulated to the members of his Executive Council, Hardinge gave it as his considered opinion that

Whatever may be the future political development of India, Colonial self-government on the lines of British Dominions is absolutely out of question. . . . We have undertaken the serious and difficult task of guiding the destinies of India and of developing her civilization. Our task is not yet half-completed; and having put our hand to the plough, we cannot turn back. The pace has been quite fast enough of late—it would be wicked to accelerate it at the present moment.[10]

Far from accepting the idea of a representative government for India, Hardinge shuddered at the thought of even a non-official majority in his legislative council. 'When once we have a non-official majority in the Viceroy's Legislative Council', Hardinge wrote to the Governor of Bombay, 'the Viceroy had better pack up his traps & leave the country. His position would be lacking in dignity.'[11]

While reluctant to share power with the Indians, the British Establishment in India—at least in its highest echelons—was not unaware of its own shortcomings. As we have already seen, in the early years of his viceroyalty, Hardinge noticed how overstaffed the Army Headquarters in India was. Occasionally, he penetrated the wall of prejudice erected by the bureaucracy, such as in October 1913, when he ordered that an honorary degree be conferred by the Calcutta University on Rabindranath Tagore. 'I do not care', Hardinge told Carmichael, the Governor of Bengal, 'whether the Criminal Intelligence

[9] 12 House of Lords Debates, 5s, cols. 155–6.
[10] Hardinge's Minute, 1 July 1912, commenting on the secret memorandum of R. Craddock (H.P.).
[11] Hardinge to Clarke, 27 March 1913 (H.P.).

Department give him [Tagore] a bad character or not. I am determined to give him an Honorary Degree. . . .'[12] Harcourt Butler privately confessed: 'We are at present organized for inaction & we ought to be organized for action, because India is moving so fast.'[13] Fleetwood Wilson, the Finance Member, who did not belong to the Indian Civil Service, noticed with the perceptive eye of an outsider how the Anglo-Indian society in Simla and Calcutta was out of touch with the country over which it ruled. Extravagant, self-centred, artificial, it seemed blissfully unaware of the mountain of misery on which it sat; it was hardly conscious that the state revenues were 'wrung from a people who are frequently . . . on the borderland of starvation & who at the best of times have no luxuries & not much comfort'.[14]

The scepticism of a Butler or the cynicism of a Fleetwood Wilson made little difference to the Establishment in the Indian Empire. It was powerful enough to assimilate, or to neutralize the few dissidents who succeeded in infiltrating its ranks. It distrusted Indian politicians and their radical friends in England, and was always thinking of stratagems to frustrate their 'designs'.

3

Intriguing as Gokhale's optimism about the future of his country may have seemed in the summer of 1912, it stemmed largely from the fact that he had discovered a friend and ally in the very heart of the enemy's citadel: Edwin Montagu, the youthful Under-Secretary of State for India, who seemed to be brimming over with energy and ideas. His brilliant mind and his high standing with Prime Minister Asquith enabled him to shed the passive role of his predecessors, who had been content merely to toe the line of the Secretary of State, or to repeat the shibboleths of the dyed-in-the-wool Conservative bureaucrats of the India Office. Montagu asked embarrassing questions. What was preventing the reform of the police, the espionage system and the prisons in India?[15] Why could the expenditure on the civil and military establishment not be cut down? Why should such

[12] Hardinge to Carmichael, 20 Oct. 1913 (H.P.).
[13] S. H. Butler to Mrs Griffin, 3 Aug. 1911 (B.P.).
[14] Wilson to C. Dilke, 9 Nov. 1909 (F. Wilson P.). In a letter to the Bishop of Calcutta, 22 June 1913, Fleetwood Wilson wrote: 'Surely, God never turned India into a grazing ground for the overflow of the middle class of England with no thought of lifting up of those committed to our charge.'
[15] E. Montagu to F. Wilson, 26 Oct. 1911 (F. Wilson P.).

26

a vast country not decentralize administration and go in for provincial autonomy? Why not have a close look at the composition and functions of the India Office itself?[16] Montagu's first visit to India was not to take place until the end of 1912, but this did not prevent him from proposing a radical reconstruction of the India Council; his initiative was to culminate two years later in Lord Crewe's India Council Bill.

When Wedderburn called on Montagu on 25 November 1911, he was pleased to find that Montagu had a high opinion of Gokhale 'both as a reformer & a statesman'. 'I think he said', Wedderburn told Gokhale, 'he had not met you, but had formed this opinion from your speeches and writings.'[17] During the summer of 1912, Gokhale had several opportunities of meeting Montagu, and was thrilled to find in him a fervent friend of India. Montagu's speech in the House of Commons on 30 July 1912 delighted Gokhale. 'In courage & width of outlook & in sympathetic needs of Indian progress', Gokhale wrote to him, 'it will, if I may venture to say so, take rank with some of the most notable utterances that we have had in recent years on India. I can wish nothing better for my country than that you should long remain connected with the Indian administration & that one day you may be placed in supreme charge of it. . . .'[18]

While Gokhale was still in England, a Royal Commission on the Public Services in India was announced. The proposal had in fact been under consideration of the government for some time. In February 1911, while in Calcutta for the winter session of the Imperial Council, Gokhale had been approached by Fleetwood Wilson. 'I feel very strongly', Fleetwood Wilson wrote, that 'a Royal Commission without you on it would be like Hamlet, without Hamlet.'[19] It was not only respect for Gokhale's ability which inspired Fleetwood Wilson to canvass Gokhale's nomination to the Royal Commission.

Fleetwood Wilson to Hardinge, 2 March 1912: It appears to me that it would be an excellent thing if you would ask Lord Crewe to put him on the Commission. In the first place, he will make an excellent Indian member, and I suppose there would be one or two Indians on it. In the second place, he will have to bless the report instead of

[16] 'Note by the Hon'ble Mr E. S. Montagu on Reconstruction of India Council', 20 March 1912, enclosed with Crewe to Hardinge, 21 March 1912 (H.P.).
[17] Wedderburn to Gokhale, 26 Nov. 1911 (G.P.).
[18] Gokhale to Montagu, 31 March 1912 (G.P.).
[19] Wilson to Gokhale, 29 Feb. 1912 (F. Wilson P.).

doing the opposite; and in the third place, it will keep him occupied, and on this I lay great stress. . . .

He is at all times a formidable adversary in debate, and I am afraid that your Executive Council are not too strong in debating capacity. I myself am old and worn out, and in any case I am only available for financial matters. It is quite true that Craddock promises to be first-rate, and Butler is undoubtedly also very good. But when it comes to Carlyle, Ali Imam and Clark, there can be no doubt that Gokhale can eat anyone of them up in five minutes. . . .

The Royal Commission will probably last two years, and I cannot but think that if Gokhale drowns himself in it, which he is sure to do, it will make your position as Governor-General in Council so much pleasanter. . . .[20]

It is difficult to say whether Fleetwood Wilson was double-crossing the Indian Civil Service (for which he had little love) by introducing a Trojan horse into the Public Services Commission, or was double-crossing Gokhale by drawing a red herring across his path. The Viceroy, at any rate, was not convinced by Fleetwood Wilson's machiavellian reasoning. 'You know', Hardinge wrote back, 'I mistrust Gokhale more almost than any man in India, as he is watching for our mistakes, and is the only Indian who knows how to play a waiting game.'[21] Hardinge had explained Gokhale's 'waiting game' to Clarke, the Governor of Bombay:

In my own mind he is looking forward 20 years hence, and he showed his hand once this year in [Imperial] Council, when in discussing his proposals for district councils, he was nettled by something Craddock said, and retorted that what he was trying for was to take over all power from out of the hands of Collectors, saying: 'It is power we want and we shall get it.' He is a dangerous man, because his disloyalty is only to take effect 20 years hence.'[22]

The Viceroy declared himself 'dead against' Gokhale's appointment to the Royal Commission. So did the majority of his Executive Council, including the Indian Member, Syed Ali Imam. 'Ali Imam', Hardinge told Crewe, 'in particular thinks that the inclusion of Gokhale will have a bad effect on moderate Indian opinion. . . .'[23]

The Secretary of State overruled the Viceroy, and Gokhale was included in the Royal Commission, but to offset the influence which he might exercise, an ultra-conservative like Valentine Chirol of *The Times* was made a member of the Commission and an I.C.S. Officer,

[20] H.P. or F. Wilson P.
[21] Hardinge to Wilson, 18 July 1912 (F. Wilson P.).
[22] Hardinge to Clarke, 16/19 April 1912 (H.P.).
[23] Private telegram from Viceroy to Sec. of State, 12 July 1912 (H.P.).

M. S. D. Butler, was appointed its Secretary. Hardinge's misgivings were not dispelled: 'The aim of some of the persons [on the Commission] such as Gokhale and Ramsay MacDonald is simply to destroy the Civil Service, which really means to destroy British administration in India. I feel very strongly on the subject of Gokhale's appointment, as I regard Gokhale the most dangerous enemy of British rule in this country.'[24]

Gokhale could hardly have imagined the deep distrust and even dread with which some members of the Government of India regarded him, but he knew he was no favourite of the Raj. Ever since he had entered politics in the late 1880s, he had been a relentless critic of official policies and a tireless advocate of a new deal for his countrymen. This was hardly a convenient line for anyone who wanted favours from the government. Early in May 1912, just before Gokhale left for England, a rumour was afloat that he might succeed Ali Imam on the Viceroy's Executive Council. Questioned by a correspondent of the *Times of India*, Gokhale contradicted the rumour, and added that 'those engaged in moulding public opinion were more useful outside the government'.[25]

If the membership of the Royal Commission was an honour for Gokhale, it was also a challenge. The exclusion of Indians from posts of responsibility in their own country had long rankled. 'We must live', he had told the Welby Commission in 1897, 'all the days of our life in an atmosphere of inferiority, and the tallest of us must bend, in order that the exigencies of the existing system must be satisfied.' Fifteen years later, he had an opportunity to explore from within the citadel of British bureaucratic power in India, and to seek possible openings for infiltration by his own compatriots. Here at last was a chance of exposing the true nature of Anglo-Indian vested interests —what Wedderburn called the 'Simla Clique'.

Gokhale felt that the composition of the Royal Commission was not unfavourable for a sympathetic consideration of the Indian nationalist case. He wrote to V. S. Srinivasa Sastri on 6 September 1912:

Remember that half a dozen of us Indians, holding Congress views & making recommendations in accordance with our views, could now secure for our recommendations the weight which will attach to the recommendations of men like Lord Islington, Mr Fisher, Mr

[24] Hardinge to Carmichael, 2 Aug. 1912 (H.P.).
[25] *The Times*, 4 May 1912.

MacDonald & Sir Valentine Chirol . . . Our friends in England, who know what these Royal Commissions really mean, are on the whole pleased with the composition of the Commission. Sir William Wedderburn, Sir Henry Cotton, Mr Ramsay MacDonald, Sir Herbert Roberts, all think that in keeping down the civilian element as much as the Government has done & in giving so much prominence to independent element, the Liberal Government have done a good day's work for India. . . .[26]

In 1912 Gokhale did not suspect the latent reserves of resistance in the I.C.S. to the assault on its monopoly. Nor did he foresee that the outbreak of the World War in 1914 would relegate the Public Services Commission to the background, and that he himself would not live to see the labours of the commission completed.

To Gokhale and to friends of India in England, the appointment of the Royal Commission on Public Services seemed another confirmation of the growing political *détente*, and a glimmer of the dawn of a better day for India. Gokhale's inclusion in the Commission reflected the new stature he had acquired. It is true that during the years 1905–8 when he had visited England, he had secured access to the Secretary of State for India, but Morley, conscious of the dislike of the Civil Service for Gokhale (as indeed for all 'agitators'), was reluctant to publicly avow his appreciation of Gokhale's ability. Morley's successor had no such inhibitions. Crewe freely granted interviews to Gokhale, invited him to the annual Imperial dinner, and put him in touch with the Colonial Secretary for discussions on the Indian question in South Africa. Edwin Montagu, the Under-Secretary of State for India, was, if anything, even more deferential to Gokhale. Liberal politicians such as Lord Courtney, and Labour leaders such as Ramsay MacDonald, were cordial. Lord Minto, the ex-Viceroy, and Lord Reay, the ex-Governor of Bombay, were glad to receive Gokhale. James Meston and Fleetwood Wilson, members of the Viceroy's Executive Council, who came home on leave, and Lord Pentland, who was going out to Madras as Governor, made it a point to call on Gokhale in London. Gokhale was approached for letters of introduction by Britons who proposed to visit India, and was consulted by Lord Ampthill and his colleagues on the knotty problem of Indians in South Africa. He was much sought after. 'I heard from Lady Primrose', wrote one of his Indian acquaintances in London, 'you were out when Sir Henry [Primrose] called, &

---

[26] Gokhale to Sastri, 6 Sept. 1912 (G.P.).

she said she hoped you will lunch with her on Sunday next. Sir Patrick Playfair has also asked me to ask you why you have not let him know you were in London & he also added, "Tell Mr Gokhale, does he see only Burra Sahebs here?" '[27] Gokhale's movements figured in the social column of *The Times*, along with those of the Royalty, the Ministers of the Crown and other celebrities.

The attention paid to Gokhale in London was an eyesore to Anglo-India. 'I am afraid', the Viceroy wrote while Gokhale was still on his way to England in May 1912, 'at what Gokhale may succeed in doing in England. He is extremely plausible & he will find plenty of Radical M.P.s to agree with every wildcat scheme that he may prepare for India.'[28] A month later, Fleetwood Wilson who was on leave in England, after meeting Gokhale, wrote to Lady Hardinge: 'He dresses in the smartest of English clothes, frock-coat, high hat, patent-leather boots and all the rest of it. He has turned very white in this country, and he looks more like a Portuguese financier than anything else. . . . I am quite sure he is full of mischief.'[29] Fleetwood Wilson's comment was obviously spiced to please Lady Hardinge, who shared the prejudices of the Viceregal entourage against Gokhale. Actually, Gokhale had been keeping very poor health and, when Fleetwood Wilson met him, he had just completed a regimen of rest and treatment under the advice of his doctor. On 8 August 1912, *The Times* announced: 'Mr Gokhale left London yesterday for Vichy, whence he goes to Switzerland. He returns to this country on September 28 and leaves a few days later for South Africa. Before his departure he discussed the Indian South African problem with Viscount Gladstone [Governor-General of South Africa].'

[27] D. C. Jehangir,' 26 June (prob. 1912) to Gokhale (G.P.).
[28] Hardinge to Clarke, 9 May 1912 (H.P.).
[29] Wilson to Lady Hardinge, 5 June 1912 (F. Wilson P.).

37

Gandhi and Gokhale

On 3 September 1893, Ranade read a paper on 'Indian Foreign Emigration' before the third conference of the Industrial Association of Western India. 'Few people are aware', he observed, 'of the comparative magnitude of relief . . . afforded to our surplus population, and of the magnificent field for extension [of emigration], which is opening before our vision in the possibilities of the future. In this respect the expansion of the British Empire is a direct gain to the mass of the population of this country.'[1]

This paper was published in the *Quarterly Journal of the Poona Sarvajanik Sabha* of which Gokhale was then the editor, but it is doubtful if he gave a second thought to the problem of Indian emigration until 12 October 1896 when M. K. Gandhi, a young barrister practising at Durban, came to Poona and called on him. Their first meeting has been graphically described by Gandhi in his autobiography. Gandhi had approached Gokhale with some diffidence. Gokhale, only three years older than Gandhi, had already been in nationalist politics for nearly a decade; he had been secretary of the Sarvajanik Sabha and a joint secretary of the Reception Committee of the 1895 (Poona) Congress. He was known to be a protégé of the great Ranade. Gokhale took an instant liking to the youthful and modest barrister from South Africa, and treated him with an easy informality. He showed him round the Fergusson College, and promised to help in arranging a meeting in Poona to express sympathy with the Indian immigrants in Natal.

The first meeting with Gokhale left Gandhi, to use his own words, 'exultantly happy'.[2] Earlier, Gandhi had been courteously received by Pherozeshah Mehta in Bombay and Bal Gangadhar Tilak in Poona, but he was somewhat awed by them. Pherozeshah reminded him of

[1] M. G. Ranade, 'Indian Foreign Emigration' *Sarvajanik Sabha Quarterly Journal*, Oct. 1893, p. 3.
[2] M. K. Gandhi, *Story of my Experiments with Truth*, Ahmedabad, 1945, p. 221.

the Himalayas, and Tilak of the ocean, but Gokhale was 'the Ganges. One could have a refreshing bath in the holy river. The Himalaya was unscalable, and one could not easily launch forth on the sea, but the Ganges invited one to its bosom.'[3] Six days later Gandhi wrote his first letter to Gokhale, urging him to take up the question of the Indians overseas. 'The question affects', he wrote, 'not only South African Indians, but Indians in all parts of the world outside India. . . . I submit that our great men should without delay take up this question. Otherwise, within a very short time there will be an end to Indian enterprise outside India.'[4]

When he returned to Natal in January 1897, Gandhi was nearly lynched by a European mob in the streets of Durban. This provoked a strongly worded article in *India* (the journal of the British Committee of the Congress) from Gokhale, unfolding a tale 'which no right-minded Englishman ought to read without a feeling of deep shame and indignation'. It struck him as a curious irony of fate that in 1897, the year of the Diamond Jubilee of Queen Victoria, it had been brought home forcibly to the Indian people that, after all, they were 'only British slaves and not British subjects', and that it was 'idle on our part to expect justice or fair treatment where it does not suit the interests of Englishmen to be just or fair'.[5]

The meeting between Gandhi and Gokhale in October 1896 was far too brief to permit an intimate interchange of views. The opportunity for this came five years later, when after the Boer War Gandhi decided to leave Natal and practise law at Bombay. In December 1901, he was in Calcutta to attend the annual Congress session. Once again, he felt overawed by the eminent leaders of the Congress but, thanks to Gokhale's support, he succeeded in piloting his resolution on the plight of 'British Indians' in South Africa through the Subjects Committee and the plenary session of the Calcutta Congress.

After the Congress session was over, Gandhi decided to spend some time in Calcutta. The India Club, where he took a room, was Gokhale's favourite haunt for a game of billiards. Noticing that Gandhi was inordinately shy and retiring, Gokhale told him, 'You have to stay in this country, and this sort of reserve will not do. You must get into touch with as many people as possible. I want you to do Congress work.' Gokhale invited him to be his guest, and the

[3] Ibid., p. 220.
[4] *Collected Works of Mahatma Gandhi*, vol. II, p. 90.
[5] *India*, June 1897.

month that Gandhi spent under his roof in Calcutta set the seal on what was to be their lifelong friendship. Gokhale himself had not long been in Calcutta; his first budget speech in the Imperial Legislative Council in March 1902, which was to raise his political stock sky-high, had not yet been delivered. But already he enjoyed great prestige as a scholar-politician. Gandhi has left a fascinating pen-picture of Gokhale: 'To see Gokhale at work was as much a joy as an education. He never wasted a minute. His private relations and friendships were all for public good. All his talks had reference only to the good of the country, and were absolutely free from any trace of untruth or insincerity. India's poverty and subjection were matters of constant and intense concern to him.'[6] This admiration was reciprocated in equal measure by Gokhale. At a public meeting held in Albert Hall in Calcutta on the 'Indian problem in South Africa' on 19 January 1902, Gokhale paid a tribute to Gandhi which was remarkably perceptive. Gokhale recalled his first meeting with Gandhi and his impression of Gandhi's 'ability, earnestness and tact and also ... his manner, at once so gentle and yet so firm'. Gandhi (Gokhale said) was 'made of the stuff of which heroes were made'. He had proved that the fiercest opposition could be overcome and the bitterest misunderstanding removed, if only they were true to themselves and worked in a correct, selfless, straightforward manner, and did not return insult for insult, abuse for abuse. 'If Mr Gandhi settled in this country', continued Gokhale, 'it was the duty of all earnest workers to place him where he deserved to be, at their head.'[7]

Gandhi could not help feeling that Gokhale was too lavish in his praise. 'It is my honest opinion—and I yield to no one in my honesty', he protested to Gokhale, 'that you have appraised my services to the country altogether too generously.'[8] Gandhi's own attitude to Gokhale had a large element of hero-worship. Indeed, Gandhi felt towards Gokhale as Gokhale had felt towards Ranade. Both Gandhi and Gokhale were, however, too intelligent and honest not to be aware of their intellectual and temperamental differences. Gokhale was amused by Gandhi's food-fads, his enthusiasm for nature-cure, scepticism towards science, technology and western political institutions, his idealization of simple village life, and his

---

[6] M. K. Gandhi, op. cit., p. 286.   [7] *Indian Mirror*, 26 Jan. 1902.
[8] Gandhi to Gokhale, 30 Jan. 1902, in *Collected Works of Mahatma Gandhi*, vol. III, p. 224.

insistence on travelling in third class by rail and by trams in Calcutta. The word '*satyagraha*' was not to be coined for another four years, but Gandhi was already talking in terms of conquering hatred by love. Before the year was out, Gandhi had been recalled by his compatriots in South Africa to resume the struggle on their behalf. Gandhi and Gokhale were not to meet again for ten years, but the reservoir of mutual respect and affection built up in 1902 never ran dry.

2

Before leaving India Gandhi had implored Gokhale to keep an eye on the Indian question in South Africa. He discovered that the Indian settlers had to free themselves not only from the old chains with which they were shackled in Natal but from the new chains forged for them in the Transvaal by the new Briton–Boer partnership. The British victory in the Boer War did not improve the lot of the Indians; on the contrary, the anti-Indian laws of the Boer regime were compiled in a handy manual and enforced more thoroughly. Gandhi kept up the campaign of Indian protest against racial discrimination. An essential feature of his strategy was the mobilization of public opinion in India. 'All that is needed', he wrote in the *Indian Opinion* of 28 September 1907, 'is to focus the energy of different organizations and organs of opinion in India and to bring the weight of this solid influence to bear on Lord Minto; then the Indian question [in South Africa] cannot but be solved in accordance with the principles of justice and humanity.'[9] Gandhi counted on a series of pressures; the pressure of Indian opinion on the Viceroy, the pressure of the Viceroy and the Government of India on the British Government, and the pressure of the British Colonial Office and public opinion on the South African colonies. For this strategy, Gandhi could not have a better ally than Gokhale. Gokhale could stir educated India, and had access to the Viceroy and high British officials; he had influential friends in London through whom he could seek the support of the India Office and the Colonial Office. From Johannesburg Gandhi continually plied Gokhale with questions and requests. Would Gokhale recommend some promising young Indians prepared to work as teachers in South Africa? Would he contribute articles to the *Indian Opinion* (which Gandhi himself

[9] *Collected Works of Mahatma Gandhi*, vol. VIII, p. 255.

was editing) or suggest correspondents who would write about events at home? Finally, could he ask questions in the Imperial Legislative Council to focus the limelight on specific problems of the Indians overseas? In the columns of *Indian Opinion*, Gandhi kept track of Gokhale's tours and speeches in India and England, and hailed him as a model patriot, parliamentarian, educationist and reformer. On his part, Gokhale never failed to spring to the defence of his friend and the cause with which he was so completely identified. On 2 November 1905, for his lecture to the Lambeth Radical Club in England, Gokhale chose the problem of Indians in South Africa. The lecture made a deep impression on George Godfrey, one of Gandhi's close colleagues. 'You cannot imagine the gratitude of the Natal Indian Congress and the British-Indian Association of the Transvaal', wrote Godfrey, 'when I report the great and good work you are doing for them here in England.'[10] Two years later, when Gandhi launched his *satyagraha* campaign in the Transvaal, Gokhale cabled his good wishes: 'Following struggle closely, anxious interest, deepest sympathy, admiration. Trust securely Divine Will.' Gandhi proudly published the cable in the *Indian Opinion* and expressed the hope that it would raise the spirit of every Indian to the highest degree of courage. 'That Prof. Gokhale has sent the cable means that the whole of India will now be roused and will run to our rescue.'[11]

Unfortunately, India was not roused deeply enough to come to the rescue of her beleaguered children in South Africa. From 1901 onwards, the Indian National Congress passed a resolution every year denouncing the policies of the governments and Europeans of South Africa, but very little in the way of informed comment or active help was forthcoming. This was partly due to the fact that the politically-conscious classes in India were almost wholly absorbed by the exciting sequel to the partition of Bengal, the antagonism between the Government and educated India, the tug-of-war within the Congress between the Extremists and the Moderates, and the controversies in India and Britain surrounding the passage of the Minto–Morley reforms. By 1909, the internal convulsions within the Congress party were over, the reforms had taken shape, and the political temperature had come down. By 1909 Gandhi's own struggle had reached a critical stage, and he badly needed the support of his countrymen.

[10] G. Godfrey to Gokhale, 3 Nov. 1905 (G.P.).
[11] *Collected Works of Mahatma Gandhi*, vol. VII, p. 240.

3

By 1909 the Indian campaign in South Africa was causing serious anxiety to Gokhale. Of the 8,000 Indian adults resident in the Transvaal, no less than 7,500 had taken part in the *satyagraha* campaign, and more than 2,500 had been imprisoned. The losses suffered by Indian merchants were estimated at five million rupees. Gandhi had given up his legal practice, and spent all his savings on the movement. All these sacrifices did not, however, bring the Indians visibly nearer their goal. The colonial governments and the European minority of South Africa seemed as determined as ever to preserve white domination. The British Government, anxious for a British–Boer accord, was reluctant to intervene. In 1906 Morley, the Liberal Secretary of State for India, had vainly tried to link the mitigation of the rigours of the Anti-Asiatic ordinance with a loan to the Transvaal. Three years later, when Gandhi called on Morley in London, he was asked if public opinion in India was really concerned about the lot of the Indian immigrants in South Africa.[12] Gandhi realized how vital the mobilization of Indian public opinion for his cause was, and decided to send to India H. S. L. Polak, an English Jew and a barrister, who had long been his friend and colleague in the Transvaal.

M. K. Gandhi to Gokhale, 23 July 1909: By the time this reaches you, Mr Polak will have been in India. Our work here is very difficult; this, however, will be no news to you. I merely mention it by way of introduction in order to enable me to ask you if you can spare time to give special attention to it.

I am anxious that our leaders should realize the national importance of the struggle. . . . We will continue to suffer in the Transvaal until justice is granted, but we have a right to expect much more than we have yet received from the Motherland.[13]

On 9 September 1909, at a public meeting in Bombay's Town Hall (which was attended by Polak) Gokhale moved a resolution calling upon the British Government and Parliament to prevent continued injustice and ill-treatment of His Majesty's Indian subjects in the Transvaal, and urging the Government of India to stop further recruitment of Indian labour for South Africa. It was at this meeting that Gokhale referred to the 'indomitable Gandhi, a man of tremen-

---

[12] Gandhi to H. S. L. Polak, 30 July 1909, in *Collected Works of Mahatma Gandhi*, vol. IX, p. 322.
[13] *Collected Works of Mahatma Gandhi*, vol. IX, p. 308.

dous spiritual power, one who is made of the stuff of which great heroes and martyrs are made'.[14] Gokhale traced the connection between what was happening in South Africa and India: 'The root of our present troubles in the colonies', Gokhale observed, 'really lies in the fact that our status is not what it should be in our own country. Men who have no satisfactory status in their own land cannot expect to have a satisfactory status elsewhere. Our struggle for equal treatment with Englishmen in the Empire must therefore be mainly carried on in India itself.'[15]

Gandhi had instructed Polak to place himself entirely under Gokhale's guidance. Gokhale spared no pains to make Polak's visit a success. He took the initiative in organizing an influential committee to raise funds for the hard-pressed *satyagrahis*. He vetted a pamphlet, *The Indians of South Africa*, written by Polak, and had it published by his friend G. A. Natesan, the Madras publisher. Gokhale and his disciples in the Servants of India Society arranged for Polak to meet influential people in different parts of the country and to address public meetings. These meetings were organized at Delhi, Benares, Faizabad, Lahore and other places. The Benares meeting was addressed by Annie Besant and the Lahore meeting by the local Anglican Bishop. Ratan J. Tata, the industrialist, contributed Rs 25,000 to the fund. Gokhale appealed for a lakh of rupees at the Lahore session of the Indian National Congress in December 1909. 'What is a lakh of rupees', he asked, 'compared to the sufferings that they [the South African Indians] have cheerfully borne for the sake of our country and our honour?... It is your duty to come to the assistance of these people ... you are on trial, the whole of our nation is on its trial, our patriotism, public spirit and our sincerity, all of them are on their trial before God and Man in this matter.'[16]

In February 1910, Gokhale successfully piloted a resolution through the Imperial Legislative Council calling for a ban on recruitment of indentured labour. 'The time has come not merely for making representations,' observed Gokhale; 'the time has come for retaliation.'[17] The following year, a ban was imposed on recruitment of indentured labour for Natal; six years later it was extended to labour intended for all overseas colonies.

---

[14] Karve & Ambekar (eds.), op. cit., vol. II, pp. 409–10.
[15] Ibid., pp. 415–16.   [16] Ibid., p. 425.
[17] Ibid., p. 423.

4

Polak's visit helped to educate the Indian intelligentsia on the struggle of the Indian minority in South Africa, but it also had an unexpected result: Polak's comments on Gandhi's personality and philosophy of life at once fascinated and disturbed Congress leaders. The fact was that hardly any of them except Gokhale knew Gandhi, and even Gokhale had not met him for seven years during which Gandhi's radicalism had become more pronounced. Gandhi was a radical in the true sense of the word, always trying to get to the root of every problem and asking 'awkward' questions.

Gandhi's radicalism had found a dramatic expression in 1906 in his campaign of passive resistance, or *satyagraha*, as he called it. A series of articles in the Gujarati section of the *Indian Opinion*, later published as a pamphlet entitled *Hind Swaraj* (Indian Home Rule), revealed that Gandhi was evolving not only a new technique for resolving social and political conflicts, but his own peculiar philosophy of life. *Hind Swaraj* made nonsense of the assumptions, aspirations and beliefs of the educated middle class and its leaders in India. British rule in India, Gandhi asserted, was due to Indian weakness. 'The English have not taken India; we have given it to them. They are not in India because of their strength, but because we keep them.'[18] English education which the Indian élite had always hailed as a gift from God appeared to Gandhi in a different light: it had 'enslaved the Indian people'. Gandhi argued that India had no use for the English language, English civilization, English machinery. Nor did he consider the English political system as worth emulating.[19] He prescribed passive resistance as the panacea for India's ills; as 'an all-sided sword, it can be used anyhow; it blesses him who uses it and him against whom it is used'.[20] It is not surprising that the Law Member of the Viceroy's Executive Council should have considered *Hind Swaraj* 'by M. K. Gandhi of Johannesburg' as 'a most pernicious publication'. The Government of India banned its entry into India 'by sea or land'.[21]

Hind Swaraj confirmed British suspicions of Gandhi which long antedated its publication. 'I hear of good grounds for suspecting', Morley had written to Minto on 12 November 1908, 'that Mr

[18] M. K. Gandhi, *Hind Swaraj*, Ahmedabad, 1938, pp. 42–3.
[19] Ibid., pp. 27–33. [20] Ibid., p. 127.
[21] Notification by G.O.I., Dept. of Commerce & Industries, 30 July 1910. See Home Dept., 1910, Pol. A, Proc. 96–103.

Gandhi really is aiming less at claiming rights in Africa than in finding fresh fuel for the smouldering fires in India.'[22] The insinuation that Gandhi's struggle in South Africa was being fomented and financed by Indian Extremists was, of course, without any foundation. Gandhi's political contacts in India were confined to the Moderate party. Indeed in 1909, when he sent Polak to India, he advised him to keep clear of Extremists, and to take instructions only from Gokhale.

Polak brought with him a typed copy of the English translation of *Hind Swaraj* for Gokhale. Gokhale's immediate reactions are not on record, but he could hardly have appreciated a thesis which contradicted every single tenet of his own political creed. *Hind Swaraj* had a strangely utopian and even idiosyncratic flavour; it bore the mark of Gandhi's personality. It was derived from Gandhi's own philosophy and experience rather than from any clear-cut ideology. Gokhale was not convinced by Gandhi's logic, but he was not disturbed by it to the same extent as most of his colleagues in the Moderate-led Congress were. This was due partly to Gokhale's feeling that Gandhi's ideas had developed in an alien country in response to an extraordinary situation, and would correct themselves when he returned to India. Gandhi had foreseen that *Hind Swaraj* would not meet with Gokhale's approval. 'The opinions expressed by me in the booklet', Gandhi wrote to Gokhale, 'are personal to me. Though they have been matured in the course of the struggle [in South Africa], they have nothing to do with it at all. . . .'[23] In 1909, the crucial issue was that of the survival of the Indian community in South Africa and how much support it could obtain from India. At the Town Hall meeting held in Bombay on 9 September 1909, Gokhale had not only paid a high tribute to Gandhi, but committed what was almost a sacrilege for a Moderate Congressman: he had justified passive resistance as a political weapon. 'I think,' Gokhale said, 'and I say this deliberately, that in the circumstances of the Transvaal, passive resistance such as that organized by Mr Gandhi is not only legitimate, but is a duty resting on all self-respecting citizens.'[24] Since 1905 'Passive Resistance' had been a plank in the Extremist programme, and was associated in the minds of the Moderates with the dangerous politics of Tilak, B. C. Pal and

[22] Morley to Minto, 12 Nov. 1908 (M.P.).
[23] Gandhi to Gokhale, 2 May 1910, in *Collected Works of Mahatma Gandhi*, vol. X, p. 239.
[24] Karve & Ambekar (eds.), op. cit., vol. II, p. 414.

Aurobindo Ghose. Few Moderate leaders were prepared to go so far as to legitimize passive resistance.

As Polak went round the country explaining Gandhi's views, Congress leaders saw that passive resistance was Gandhi's panacea not only for South Africa but for India as well. Deliberate defiance of 'constituted authority' and of laws was something which few Moderate Congressmen, most of whom were lawyers, could stomach. Many of them were ambivalent towards Gandhi: they were attracted by his heroism and sacrifices, but bewildered by his political philosophy. This ambivalence led towards the end of 1911 to an imbroglio which came close to irretrievably damaging Gandhi's cause in South Africa and his friendship with Gokhale.

5

The annual Congress session for 1911 was to be held in Calcutta and be presided over by Ramsay MacDonald, the British Labour leader. Unfortunately his wife was taken seriously ill, and by September 1911 it was clear that he could not come over to India in December. Satyananda Basu, one of the leaders from Bengal, wrote to Gokhale to enquire if Gandhi should be asked to preside. Gokhale replied that personally he would be happy if the honour was conferred on his friend, but he was not sure that Gandhi would be able to come out or even whether he 'still believed in the Congress programme'.[25] In any case, it seemed proper to Gokhale that Gandhi should be consulted before his name was proposed. The Secretary of the Bengal Congress Committee then sent the Natal Congress a cable which was vaguely worded and misled both the Natal Congress and Gandhi into believing that he was being invited to preside over the Congress. Gandhi cabled his consent, and the Reuter flashed the news. The muddle was complete when a majority of provincial committees voted for R. N. Mudholkar, the Congress leader from Berar, and the Bengal Congress Committee which had originally proposed Gandhi's name changed its preference in favour of Sir Henry Cotton.

It is not difficult to see why Gandhi should have found so little support in the provincial Congress Committees or among Moderate Congressmen. 'I am positive', C. Y. Chintamani wrote to Gokhale on 24 October 1911, 'that I should not vote for Mr Gandhi, who may

[25] Gokhale to Chintamani, 26 Oct. 1911 (G.P.).

preach or support passive resistance in which, according to Mr Polak, he profoundly believes. I may say that the idea of honouring Mr Gandhi was present in our minds last year, but we felt that it would be injudicious to elect him after hearing Mr Polak about his opinions.'[26] Gokhale was convinced that the Bengal Congress had handled the whole affair very clumsily: it should either not have proposed Gandhi's name for the Congress Presidency, or seen it through. If there was a contest, and Gandhi was defeated, it was likely to give a handle to his political opponents and to damage the cause for which he was fighting in South Africa. 'The situation as regards Gandhi', Gokhale wrote to Chintamani, 'is very awkward, but for his sake and for the sake of the cause identified with his name, we must extricate him from it with the best grace we can.' Gokhale advised the Secretary of the Indian National Congress to exclude Gandhi's name from the list of candidates on the ground that he would not be able to come out even if elected.

'I cannot tell you', Gokhale wrote to Gandhi, 'how sorry I am for the whole incident. I feel that your name was unnecessarily dragged into a controversy and left there exposed to unnecessary criticism. However, the one comfort of your friends is that you yourself are too calm in spirit, too selfless and too fully conscious of the real triviality of such things to worry about what has happened.'[27] Thanks to Gokhale's candour and Gandhi's magnanimity, this incident was soon forgotten, and did not affect their relationship; on the contrary it was just at about this time that the phase of their closest cooperation began.

Gandhi had been pleading with Gokhale for many years to pay a visit to South Africa. The visit was intended to boost the morale of the Indian community fighting for its survival, but also to afford Gokhale a little respite from the unceasing strain of public work in India and England. When Gokhale visited England in the autumn of 1905, Gandhi had urged him to visit South Africa before returning to India via the Cape of Good Hope. This was not possible as Gokhale completed his tour of England just in time to sail for India. In 1909, writing from London, Gandhi repeated the invitation.

Gandhi to Gokhale, 11 November 1909: In his last letter Polak tells me that overwork and anxiety have ruined your health and that plain-spokenness has endangered your life. I venture to suggest that

[26] Chintamani to Gokhale, 24 Oct. 1911 (G.P.).
[27] Gokhale to Gandhi, 3 Nov. 1911 (G.P.).

27

you should come to the Transvaal and join us. . . . I have moved very freely among our countrymen here [in London] and I notice extreme bitterness against you. Most consider that violence is the only method for securing any reform. In the Transvaal we are trying to show that violence is futile and that the proper method is self-suffering, i.e. passive resistance. If therefore you came to the Transvaal, publicly declaring that it was your intention to share our sorrows, and therefore to cross the Transvaal border as a citizen of the Empire, you would give it a worldwide significance, the struggle will soon end and your countrymen will know you better. . . . If you would come and if you are left untouched, and I am free, I should deem it a great privilege to nurse you. If you are arrested and imprisoned, I should be delighted. . . .[28]

Gandhi had a penchant for high drama, but it is doubtful if the prospect of imprisonment in a Transvaal prison appealed to Gokhale. It was not until October 1912 that Gokhale was able to pay a visit to South Africa.

Early in 1912 the Government of South Africa was making anxious enquiries about Gokhale's visit. It feared that his presence would stiffen the Indians' attitude. The Secretary of State for India and the Viceroy had their own anxieties; they were disturbed by the possibility of Gokhale himself being subjected to some of the humiliations against which his countrymen in South Africa were fighting. Crewe wrote to Hardinge on 2 August 1912:

Some uneasiness is felt in many quarters about the visit of Gokhale to South Africa. The view taken of a brown man varies in many places; at Capetown there would be no difficulty. But he would very likely be turned out of a tram-car—though not nowadays off the pavement,—either at Johannesburg or Durban. I had Sir R. Solomon here, and the principal public men, both British and Dutch, are being written to, asking them to have Gokhale looked after, and given a railway compartment and a carriage to drive in if possible.[29]

Gokhale had a foretaste of racial discrimination even before he left for South Africa. He had arranged to sail by the s.s. *Saxon* from Southampton on 5 October 1912. The Union Castle Company, which owned the ship, insisted that he should pay for a whole cabin, as no white man was likely to travel with him in the same cabin. Gokhale was beside himself with anger. 'I have so far made nine voyages' between this country and India in P & O Company's

[28] Gandhi to Gokhale, 11 Nov. 1909, in *Collected Works of Mahatma Gandhi*, vol. IX, pp. 531–2.
[29] Crewe to Hardinge, 2 Aug. 1912 (H.P.).

steamers, he wrote, 'and never has such an insult been offered to me. It is not the extra money demanded that I mind so much as the injustice or humiliation involved in it.'[30] Gokhale's protest, backed by an intervention from Whitehall, led the shipping company to waive the condition.

Thanks to the hints thrown by the British Colonial Office to the Pretoria government and by some British politicians to their friends in South Africa, Gokhale's visit went off without any unpleasant incident. Among those who greeted him on arrival at Cape Town on 22 October 1912 was an official of the Immigration Office with a letter from the Minister of Interior extending 'on behalf of the [South African] Government welcome on your arrival in South Africa'. The same evening a reception was given in the Cape Town City Hall, with the Mayor in the chair. Gokhale was interviewed by the editor of the *Cape Times*, and met European politicians of both parties.

From Cape Town, Gokhale went to Beaconsfield, Kimberley and Johannesburg, New Castle, Ladysmith, Maritzburg, Durban, Phoenix. The enthusiasm of the Indian community knew no bounds. At Johannesburg the address presented to him was engraved on a heart-shaped plate of gold from the Rand mounted on Rhodesian teak, resembling a map of India and Ceylon. A vegetarian banquet was held in his honour; covers were laid for 400 guests, including 150 Europeans, 'a novel experience for so many Europeans to sit at the same table'.[31]

The cordiality of the European response was partly due to Gandhi's effort to keep racial rancour out of his struggle, and partly to the impression made by Gokhale on the saner section of the European community. Senator Schreiner, a South African politician, was so impressed that in 1913, while speaking on the second reading of the Immigration Restriction Bill in the South African Parliament, he described Gokhale as 'one of the greatest men of the time'. The South African Government and the bulk of the European community were, however, too hard-headed to be swept off their feet.

On 14 November 1912 Gokhale saw Prime Minister Botha, and two other ministers, Smuts and Fischer, at Pretoria, the Union capital. After the interview he told Gandhi: 'Everything has been settled. The Black Act will be repealed. The racial bar will be re-

[30] Gokhale to Union Castle Co., 24 July 1912, (G.P.).
[31] Gandhi, *Satyagraha in South Africa*, Madras, 1928, p. 402.

moved from the emigration law. The tax will be abolished.' 'I doubt it very much', Gandhi replied. 'You do not know the ministers as I do.'[32]

In retrospect it seems that the gulf between the Indian and the European points of view had really not been spanned, or if the bridge existed, it was only in the imagination of well-meaning Europeans and Indians who were eager for some kind of *modus vivendi* in South Africa. Lord Ampthill, a former Governor of Madras, and a friend of the Indian cause in South Africa, congratulated Gokhale on achieving results which could 'not have been attained in any other way than by the personal influence which you are so fortunately able to exercise, and certainly not by any number of eloquent despatches or speeches in the several Parliaments concerned'.[33] In fact, the Indian problem in South Africa, with its racial and economic overtones, was far too complex to be solved by gestures of goodwill.

Gokhale's trip was important more for the effect it had on Gandhi and the Indian community than on the government and people of South Africa. Gandhi saw Gokhale after eleven years, and was shocked to see the deterioration in his health. The programme drawn up for Gokhale was much too strenuous, but Gandhi was continually in attendance, providing as much relief as was possible in the circumstances. During these three weeks Gandhi's affection and respect for Gokhale grew. He observed with admiration the working of Gokhale's mind like a sensitive and precise instrument, his capacity for taking infinite pains, mastery of facts, his innate courtesy and uncanny flair for striking the right note on every occasion. 'I listened to every speech made by Gokhale', Gandhi wrote later, 'but I do not remember a single occasion when I could have wished that he had not expressed a certain idea or had omitted a certain adjective.'[34]

Gokhale paid a great tribute to Gandhi at a gathering of Indians and Europeans at Johannesburg, referring to him as 'the pure and indomitable spirit that dwelt in that frail-looking frame, that glorified what it touched, would break but never bend in a just and righteous cause'. Gokhale did not, however, pretend to appreciate all the bees in his host's bonnet. While visiting Tolstoy Farm, Gokhale, who was weak and tired, was made to walk the one-and-a-half miles from the railway station, and caught a chill. Gandhi prepared some soup for him, but the kitchen was so far off that it was cold by the

[32] Ibid., p. 408. [33] Ampthill to Gokhale, 15 Jan. 1913 (G.P.).
[34] Gandhi, *Satyagraha in South Africa*, p. 403.

time it was taken to Gokhale's cottage. Gandhi and his companions slept on the floor at Tolstoy Farm. A bed was offered to Gokhale, which he refused. 'You all seem to think', he gently rebuked Gandhi, 'that you have been born to suffer hardships and discomforts and people like myself have been born to be pampered by you.' When Gandhi offered to iron a scarf given to Gokhale by Ranade, he replied: 'I can trust your capacity as a lawyer, but not as a washerman.' Despite the deep bond of affection between the two men, Gokhale was sometimes puzzled by the romantic ideas of his host, but he felt confident that contact with the realities of life in his homeland would bring him down to earth.

Of one remarkable trait of Gandhi, Gokhale saw further evidence: he could evoke intense loyalty for public causes from a great variety of people. That he should have won the devotion of H. S. L. Polak, Hermann Kallenbach and other Europeans for fighting against white domination was a remarkable phenomenon. If Gandhi returned to India and joined the Servants of India and evoked a similar enthusiasm in the youth of India, would it not change the face of the country? Gandhi decidedly was one of those ideal missionaries Gokhale had been looking for when he founded the Servants of India Society. Gandhi could, however, return to India only after the South African crisis was resolved. What was required was the redress of the main Indian grievances by the South African Government. And this redress seemed to be in the offing after Gokhale's interview with the Union ministers in Pretoria in November 1912. On the return voyage to Zanzibar, Gokhale talked to Gandhi at length about the affairs of the homeland and analysed for him the characters of important leaders of Indian opinion. This analysis, Gandhi wrote thirteen years later, 'was so accurate that I have hardly perceived any difference between Gokhale's estimate and my own personal estimate'.[35]

Gokhale had expected 1913 to be a year of reconciliation in South Africa; it proved to be the year of crisis.

---

[35] Ibid., p. 409.

38

Crisis in South Africa

Gokhale returned from South Africa on 13 December 1912 in a mood of sober optimism. He told a correspondent of the *Times of India* that he had been heartened by the desire he had noticed in a section of the European population in South Africa in favour of a reasonable settlement of the Indian grievances. Bombay gave Gokhale a magnificent welcome. On 14 December 1912 a meeting was held in his honour at the Town Hall which was packed to capacity; hundreds, unable to gain admission, waited outside. Jamsetji Jejeebhoy, the Parsi baronet, presided and among those present were Jehangir B. Petit, H. A. Wadya, Ibrahim Rahimatoola, K. Natarajan, the editor of *Indian Social Reformer*, Ratan Tata, the industrialist, and Stanley Reed, the editor of the *Times of India*. Pherozeshah Mehta was, however, conspicuous by his absence. As early as 1896 he had presided over a meeting in Bombay addressed by Gandhi, then an unknown visitor from Natal, but Pherozeshah had never really bothered much about the Indians in South Africa. In December 1912 he was annoyed with Gandhi and Gokhale for acquiescing in the restriction of Indian immigration by the South African Government. Pherozeshah's grievance was relayed to Gokhale by a common friend.

H. A. Wadya to Gokhale, 15 December 1912: I had no time to tell you yesterday about my visit to Sir Pherozeshah. . . . He repeated the story about *Gandhi's surrender*. And he looked upon our meeting [to honour Gokhale] as a public acquiescence in such [a] surrender. . . . He was not generous in his . . . remarks. He would give no thought to Gandhi's sacrifices (he called it only a *sentimental* matter) nor to the sufferings of the poor people there. Let *them* disappear from South Africa, but *let not the door* [of Indian immigration] *be closed.* . . .[1]

In his speech at the Town Hall meeting, Gokhale, without naming

[1] G.P.

Pherozeshah, answered critics who had picked up the cry of 'open door to South Africa'. What was the use, Gokhale asked, of 'theoretical equality' before the law, if in practice European officers manning the Immigration Departments in South Africa would not admit any Indian? Was it not wiser to allay European fears of an 'Asian flood', agree to limit immigration, and try to ensure an honourable existence for those Indians who were already in South Africa? What was important was not immigration of further indentured labour from India, but the liberation of those already in South Africa from the three-pound poll tax and vexatious curbs on the choice of profession, place of work, admission to schools and travel within and outside South Africa. The charges of 'weakness' and 'betrayal' against Gandhi cut Gokhale to the quick. He challenged Gandhi's critics to follow up their words with deeds:

Start a dignified agitation if you have the stuff in you; go about the country, make the kind of sacrifices that Mr Gandhi and others have made, and then insist upon free immigration into South Africa. It is all very well to sit at home and criticize men like Mr Gandhi. God knows that most of us are poor enough clay, and when once in a way a man rises amongst us, here we are sitting quiet at home and criticizing him and tearing him to pieces in the manner that some of us are doing.[2]

The Indian problem in South Africa became an irritant in the relations between Gokhale and Pherozeshah in the same way as the question of a Congress delegation to England had become in 1905. With all his respect for Pherozeshah, Gokhale was almost driven to despair by his superior, impatient and off-hand manner of treating complex issues. Ten months later, when the crisis in South Africa had further deepened and Gokhale, against the advice of his doctors, was touring the country in support of Gandhi's struggle, Pherozeshah was still sulking and quibbling. K. Natarajan of the *Indian Social Reformer*, who vainly tried to enlist Pherozeshah's support, informed Gokhale: 'Sir Pherozeshah Mehta said that he had wished to talk over the matter with you, but you did not give him the opportunity. ... Mr Gokhale has taken up the question and as he is so cold about consulting us, we do not wish to interfere.' One of Pherozeshah's grievances against Gandhi turned out to be that he had not published an account of the moneys already sent to him from India![3]

[2] Karve & Ambekar, op. cit., vol. II, p. 463.
[3] K. Natarajan to Gokhale, 7 Oct. 1913 (G.P.).

2

The hope that Gokhale's visit to South Africa would be a turning-point in the solution of the Indian question proved illusory. The improvements which Gokhale and Gandhi had expected in the Immigration Regulation Bill were not realized. Nor was there any relaxation in the rigorous administration of the discriminatory laws against the Indians. The Union Government continued to tighten the screws. In February 1913, the 'South African British-Indian Committee' in London represented to the Colonial Office that 'the policy of obstruction' followed by the South African administration was 'not due to the idiosyncrasies of individual officers, but that it is a part of a deliberate plan to make the position of even old-established Indians intolerable, and to prevent others in India from returning to their homes in South Africa'.[4]

Meanwhile, Gokhale was doing all he could to stave off a collision in South Africa. He was educating Indian opinion and was in constant touch with W. H. Clark, the Commerce Member of the Viceroy's Executive Council, who dealt with the problem of Indians overseas. During the summer of 1913 when he was in London to attend the sittings of the Public Services Commission, Gokhale met almost everyone who could be of help to Gandhi's cause. He had meetings with Lord Ampthill, the chairman of the South African British-Indian Committee, Earl Crewe, the Secretary of State for India, and L. Harcourt, the Colonial Secretary. He suggested that the Government of India should send an official mission to South Africa, including James Meston or Harcourt Butler.[5] His pleas were in vain.[6] The Immigration Act fell short not only of the hopes of the Indian community, but also of the promises made to it by the South African authorities three years earlier; even the right hitherto enjoyed by the South African-born Indians to enter Cape Colony was taken away. The three-pound poll tax was not abolished. For its repeal Gokhale had pleaded with South African ministers, whom he had met at Pretoria in November 1912. He had come away with the impression that they were conscious of the iniquity of this tax as well

[4] M. E. Polak, Asst. Hony. Sec., South African British-Indian Committee to Colonial Office, 27 Feb. 1913, vol. 1225, J & P (IOL).
[5] Crewe to Hardinge, 11 July 1913 (H.P.).
[6] Crewe to Gokhale, 19 July 1913 (enclosure to letter dated 28 Oct. 1913 from F. H. Lucus, P.S. to Sec. of State for India to Du Boulay, P.S. to the Gov. of Bombay.).

as of its negligible financial value—the net proceeds being less than £10,000. Later Smuts denied that any assurance had been given to Gokhale.[7] Gokhale contradicted Smuts and quoted from the statements made by members of the Natal Parliament published in the *Natal Advertiser*. The stark reality was that the three-pound tax had failed in its professed object of inducing the Indian labourer to return to India but tended to compel him to re-indenture. This was exactly what the sugar planters of Natal (some of whom were members of the South African Parliament) wanted. Botha and Smuts did not feel strong enough to make any substantial concessions to the Indian community as they themselves were under attack from the right wing of their own party led by Hertzog, the fanatical champion of Afrikaner ideals and interests. Wrote the *Friend*, Bloemfontein, the organ of the Hertzog faction (3 December 1913):

The Indian in South Africa accepts one compromise only as an assistance to gain another. The agitation against the £3 tax and the raising of the labour grievances in Natal are merely red herrings drawn across the trail. The Asiatic demand is for full rights, political and otherwise, with the European. It is a demand that South Africa cannot concede, and the sooner the door is banged, bolted and barred upon it, the better.[8]

The majority of Europeans in South Africa seemed impervious to the Indian grievances. Some of them went so far as to say that Gandhi had hired passive resisters in South Africa with funds raised in India, and that his real game was to help 'Mr Gokhale and his friends in their political campaign in India'. The India Office, prompted by Gokhale and even by the Government of India, was sympathetic to Gandhi's cause, but it was powerless. The Colonial Office was reluctant to intervene, partly because of the logic of colonial self-government, and partly because it was not convinced of the justice of the Indian case. 'The attitude of the Indians', Governor-General Herbert Gladstone wrote on 18 September 1913 to Crewe, the Secretary of State for India, 'has been so inconsiderate, and their demands so exorbitant that a conciliatory response on the part of the Ministers can hardly be anticipated.'[9]

The frustration of the Indian community reached its peak when the Cape Supreme Court ruled that, with the exception of marriages

[7] W. K. Hancock, *Smuts, The Sanguine Years 1870–1919*, Cambridge, 1962, p. 342.   [8] D. Chaplin to Hardinge, 11 Dec. 1913 (H.P.).
[9] Gladstone, Gov.-Gen., South Africa to Sec. of State for India, 18 Sept. 1913, vol. 1266, J & P (IOL).

celebrated according to Christian rites, or those registered by the Registrar of Marriages, all marriages were illegal. This reduced the wives of Indian residents, as one of them put it, to the status of concubines.

It became clear to both Gandhi and Gokhale in the summer of 1913 that the Indians in South Africa would soon have to fight for their very survival. Gandhi took Gokhale into his confidence on his next *satyagraha* campaign, which was to be 'a very bitter and prolonged one'.

Gandhi to Gokhale, 20 June 1913: So far as I can judge at present, 100 men and 30 women will start the struggle. As time goes on, we may have more. . . .
  I do not expect to raise much cash, but I do not anticipate any difficulty about getting sufficient food and clothing by begging. . . . If no funds arrive unasked from India or elsewhere, we shall perform our wanderings on foot and no money will then be spent on telegrams and cables. . . .
  The struggle is expected to last for a year. . . . We are making provision for an indefinite prolongation. . . .
  My prayer to you is: please do not worry about us, do not beg for funds publicly and do not injure your health for the cause. The prayer is selfish. I am anxious to meet you in the flesh in India, work under you and learn, may I say, at your feet.[10]

It was all very well for Gandhi to ask Gokhale not to 'worry', but Gokhale knew he had a part to play in the struggle which was about to begin. He decided to interrupt his work on the Royal Commission in England and to sail for India. His friends were aghast at this decision. His health was at a low ebb and it was the worst time of the year for sailing through the Red Sea. Wedderburn begged him not to forget the interests of the 250 million people of India for the sake of the tiny Indian minority of 100,000 in South Africa. The racial issue in South Africa in any case was hardly susceptible to an early solution. 'Your health and strength (& life)', wrote Wedderburn, 'are the best asset the Indian people have at present, and you will be doing them a great wrong if you do not preserve them in their interest.'[11]

3

Gokhale did not return to India a day too soon. Events in South Africa were moving fast. On 23 September 1913, sixteen *satyagrahis*

[10] G.P.
[11] Wedderburn to Gokhale, 13 June 1913 (G.P.).

from Phoenix in Natal, including Mrs Gandhi, were arrested for entering the Transvaal from Natal without a permit, and were jailed. A few days later, a party of eleven women from Tolstoy Farm in the Transvaal crossed into Natal without a permit, and proceeded to Newcastle; before they were arrested, they had persuaded the Indian miners to go on strike. The European mineowners forced out the miners and their families from their quarters by cutting off water and electricity. Gandhi decided to march this motley crowd—2,037 men, 127 women and 57 children—from Newcastle to a point on the Transvaal border. On 6 November, he was arrested and three days later the miners were stopped, herded into special trains and sent back to Natal, where the government hit upon an ingenious device for working the mines and at the same time punishing the strikers. The mine compounds were declared 'outstations' of the Dundee and Newcastle jails! The mineowners' European staff were appointed jail wardens. To complete the cruel joke, work in the mines was made part of the sentence! The miners refused to be forced underground; they were brutally whipped, fired upon and treated with the utmost cruelty. The news of this ruthless repression provoked spontaneous strikes in the north and west of Natal where Indian labourers came out of plantations and mines. The South African government adopted a policy of 'blood and iron'. Racial prejudice and vested interests combined to inflict a savage punishment on the poor Indian labourers, who were chased back to work in the mines by mounted military police. Gandhi himself was awarded a sentence of nine months' hard labour and made to dig stones and sweep the compound in Volksrust jail. Summoned as a witness in a case, he was made to walk to the court with handcuffs on his hands and manacles on his feet.

Gokhale was deeply disturbed by the news from South Africa. On 25 October, he addressed a public meeting at Bombay, and called for a ban on the import of coal from South Africa and for other retaliatory measures. He defied the advice of his doctors, and toured the country to raise funds for the support of the families of the *satyagrahis* who were in jail. Gokhale felt that the people of India were on trial. When his friend G. A. Natesan, the Madras publisher, sent him a paltry donation of Rs 100 for the Indians in South Africa, Gokhale administered a severe rebuke:

Gokhale to Natesan, 9 November 1913: We have to find for this struggle, which, mark you, is going to be a life-and-death struggle, a sum of £20,000 in three or four months from all India. Other

nations have from time to time to go to war, when they find themselves compelled to make enormous sacrifices in men and money.
We in this country have no occasion to go to war and therefore we
are never called upon to make sacrifices of that nature on that scale.
Our patriotism invariably goes with soft and easy living, brave
words. . . .

I am writing like this because I feel angry with you that you should
have subscribed only Rs 100 yourself when our brothers and sisters
are undergoing untold suffering at the hands of a brutal and unscrupulous enemy and new-born babies are dying in concentration
camps. . . .

I am sure you will not think it improper for me to mention to you
that out of my small resources—I have only about Rs 7000 of my
own laid by—I have already given Rs 1000 to the Bombay Committee, and I will give another thousand if I find it necessary. Nay,
I will give the whole of this Rs 7000 to the cause before I say to Mr
Gandhi that no more money can be sent from this country, while
he needs it.[12]

Among those who threw themselves into the fund-raising campaign
were Jawaharlal Nehru, a young barrister of Allahabad, and C.
Rajagopalachari, a thirty-five year-old lawyer, who sent a remittance
of Rs 1500 from the district of Salem. Valentine Chirol, Gokhale's
colleague on the Public Services Commission, and no friend of
Indian nationalism, contributed five pounds. 'Few Englishmen', he
wrote to Gokhale, 'who take a genuine interest in the welfare of India
& have faith in the value of the British connection both for India and
for the Empire, can fail to have been moved by the statement you
made in Bombay.'[13] Even Lord Willingdon, the Governor of Bombay,
wanted to contribute to the fund. 'I wish I could help that,' he wrote
to the Viceroy, 'but fear you won't allow me. I had a long talk with
Gokhale the other day, . . . I like him; he is very frank and seemed
quite honest.'[14]

Meanwhile the situation in South Africa moved to a tragic climax.
With the news of mass arrests, floggings and shootings, a wave of
horror ran through the length and breadth of India. On 19 November, *The Times* wrote an editorial, 'From Bad to Worse in South
Africa', and pointed out that almost the whole Indian population of
Natal (about 150,000), which slightly outnumbered the white population, was involved in the demonstrations against the Union Government. *The Times* commented upon the non-violent character of

[12] G.P.
[13] V. Chirol to Gokhale, 3 Nov. 1913 (G.P.).
[14] Willingdon to Hardinge, 8 Nov. 1913 (H.P.).

Gandhi's campaign: two thousand-odd Indians, who had crossed without a permit into the Transvaal, had allowed themselves to be arrested by only forty policemen. It called for 'a sympathetic redress of the Indian grievances', and suggested that the Government of India should send a representative for negotiations with the Union ministers[15]—a suggestion which Gokhale had privately made to the Government of India several months earlier.

On the very day of the publication of *The Times'* editorial, Gokhale telegraphed the Viceroy that he should summon an emergency session of the Imperial Legislative Council to discuss the crisis in South Africa. Gokhale personally called upon Butler, the Education Member, at Delhi, repeated the demand for an emergency session, and sought an assurance that students in India would not be prevented from raising funds for their compatriots in South Africa.[16] Gokhale's appeal to his countrymen evoked an astonishing response. There were protest meetings in the principal towns, and the remarkable thing was the presence of a large number of students and members of the Muslim community, which had so far kept away from such demonstrations. A strong nationalist impulse moved the Indian intelligentsia, obliterating for the moment barriers of caste, creed and political affiliation. On 14 November 1913, when Gokhale addressed a meeting in Bradlaugh Hall at Lahore, he 'received an enthusiastic ovation', which lasted for several minutes, cheers being called again and again and enthusiastically given. Among those who were present were the poet Mohammed Iqbal, Nawab Sir Zulfiqar Ali, Justice Shah Din and Lala Lajpat Rai. There were more meetings: at Lahore on 17 December, presided over by Mian Mohammed Shafi; at Allahabad on 19 December with Nawab Abdul Majid in the chair. A students' meeting at Calcutta on 14 December was addressed by Gokhale. The Maharaja of Burdwan took the chair at a meeting at Calcutta at which the speakers included Surendranath Banerjea. Pherozeshah Mehta and the Aga Khan spoke at Bombay, Motilal Nehru and Tej Bahadur Sapru at Allahabad. For the first time Indian women joined in a political demonstration, and held meetings to express their indignation against the treatment of Indians overseas. The Viceroy was impressed by the strong feeling in the country; he was advised that 'there had been no movement like it since the Mutiny'.

Lord Hardinge had an uncanny sense of the public mood in India.

[15] *The Times*, 19 Nov. 1913.
[16] Butler to Hardinge, 20 Nov. 1913 (H.P.).

On 20 November he cabled to his counterpart in Pretoria, Governor-General Gladstone, to urge on his government 'the use of methods common to civilized countries in dealing with strikes'.[17] Gladstone accused Gokhale of making monstrous allegations and charged that the atrocity stories were 'invented in India'. Hardinge found it difficult to swallow the South African government's thesis that the passive resistance and strikes in Natal had been engineered from India, and that it was all a conspiracy between Gandhi and Gokhale to undermine the British Raj. 'The Indians do not in reality ask much', Hardinge told Gladstone. 'They do not ask for unrestricted immigration. All they ask for is a fair treatment for those Indians who have been admitted into South Africa and had added to its prosperity.'[18]

Finding private protests of little avail, Hardinge was driven to the conclusion that 'it was only by opening the eyes of the world to the treatment of the Indians that there was any chance of obtaining redress'.[19] On 23 November 1913, while replying to an address presented to him by the Mahajana Sabha of Madras, he referred to the allegations that the 'movement of passive resistance in South Africa had been dealt with by measures which would not for a moment be tolerated in any country that claims to call itself civilized'. Hardinge affirmed that the Indian resistance in South Africa had 'the sympathy of India—deep and burning—and not only of India, but of all those who, like myself, without being Indians themselves, have feelings of sympathy for the people of this country'.[20]

Hardinge's speech provoked a storm of protest in Pretoria and London, but it proved a sedative for the inflamed Indian opinion. The mounting indignation in India against the racialist regime in South Africa did not turn upon Britain. Indeed, the protest meeting at Lahore on 14 November addressed by Gokhale is reported to have 'ended with three cheers for Mr Gandhi, Mr Gokhale and the King-Emperor'.[21]

4

The Viceroy's protest on behalf of India, 'prompt, public and

---

[17] Telegram, Viceroy of India to Gov.-Gen. of South Africa, 19 Nov. 1913 (H.P.).
[18] Hardinge to Gladstone, 20 Dec. 1913 (H.P.).
[19] Hardinge to Ampthill, 23 Dec. 1913 (H.P.).
[20] Hardinge of Penhurst, *Speeches*, vol. 2, p. 132.
[21] *Tribune*, 16 Nov. 1913.

emphatic', embarrassed the South African Government. With public opinion in India, Britain, and indeed the whole world roused by Gandhi—and Gokhale—the South African ministers seem to have had second thoughts. Smuts, who (in the words of his biographer) never learnt 'to disentangle the feelings of fascination, admiration and irritation which Gandhi's words and actions aroused in him at different times',[22] was in favour of conciliating the Indian minority. The Union Government announced the appointment of an Inquiry Commission headed by Justice Solomon and released Gandhi on 18 December 1913. Gandhi welcomed an inquiry, but objected to the composition of the Commission: it did not include any Indian, and two of its members, Wylie and Esselen, were notorious for their anti-Indian bias. Gandhi refused to have anything to do with such a Commission, and announced his resolve to resume passive resistance on 1 January 1914 if all Indian prisoners, 'not convicted of violence', were not set free, and a member acceptable to the Indian community was not appointed to the Commission. The prospect of the renewal of the struggle, with ruthless repression by the South African authorities, and its inevitable repercussions on India, drove the Viceroy to despair. Hardinge begged Gokhale to persuade Gandhi not to boycott the Solomon Commission. He offered to send to South Africa a senior I.C.S. Officer, Sir Benjamin Robertson, Chief Commissioner of the Central Provinces and a former Secretary in the Commerce Department, which dealt with the problems of Indians overseas. Unhappily, Gokhale was at this time immobilized in Poona with a malady diagnosed as 'the accumulation of fluid in the cavity of the heart', which compelled him to lie flat on his back. The Viceroy was anxious for a relaxation of tension in India. Gandhi, with thousands of his adherents still in South African prisons, would not, however, budge an inch from what he believed to be points of principle. The deepening crisis, as it seemed to Gandhi, Gokhale and the Viceroy, may be glimpsed from some of the telegrams exchanged by them in December 1913.

Viceroy to Gokhale, 23 December 1913: The news contained in Reuter's telegrams strikes me as very unsatisfactory, and the attitude assumed by the Indian leaders as likely to alienate the sympathy of many true friends of India in South Africa and exasperate public opinion . . . the only way out now seems to be for Gandhi to announce that, in view of the mission of a representative of the Govern-

[22] Hancock, op. cit., p. 346.

ment of India to South Africa, he and his friends will accept the Commission as at present constituted.[23]

Gandhi to Gokhale, 23 December 1913: . . . Great efforts being made by Local Government discredit agitation which is assuming almost uncontrollable proportions. My firm conviction that mass people so indignant that if attempts were made ask them accept present Commission, they would kill leaders. . . . It is patent present Commission designed not grant relief but gain time, hoodwink public.[24]

Viceroy to Gokhale, 24 December 1913: . . . I have received a telegram from the Secretary of State in which he says that there is no prospect of demands formulated by Gandhi for reconstitution of Commission and release of passive resistance prisoners being granted. If passive resistance is renewed, Union Government will be compelled to put law in motion to quell disturbance and will have support of entire European community. In that event neither His Majesty's Govt nor I would be able to intervene in favour of Indians. . . .[25]

Viceroy to Gokhale, 25 December 1913: I ask you to make a further representation to Gandhi in my name to modify his present attitude of which the consequences to his followers may be very serious. . . .[26]

Gokhale to Gandhi, 25 December 1913: . . . I fully understand position as explained by you, but notwithstanding this repeat my conviction your present course a grave mistake, and implore you once again find some way meet Viceroy's wishes, as otherwise you throw away enormous advantages not likely to be secured again. . . . If Indian community South Africa feels itself entitled support of Indian Government, surely Government entitled some consideration be shown its wishes. Do find some way out; please cable urgent.[27]

Gandhi to Gokhale, 25 December 1913: Understand your feeling. Would give my life if that might help. This struggle independent of temporal power. Solemn declaration in God's name. Sunday irrevocable. Question was asked before administration of oath. I said no human being could induce alteration in declaration once solemnly made. Feel we are gaining ground here, but whether or not and whether after loss Viceroy's sympathy which you apprehend, we retain or lose hold on masses, struggle must continue till the few perish in attempt. Throughout this long spiritual struggle we have hitherto successfully upheld above vital principle.[28]

Gokhale to Viceroy, 28 December 1913: Gandhi promises not renew

[23] H.P.
[24] *Collected Works of Mahatma Gandhi*, vol. 12, pp. 288–9.
[25] H.P.
[26] H.P.
[27] Quoted in Gokhale's telegram to the Viceroy, 25 Dec. 1913 (H.P.).
[28] H.P.

struggle till Sir Benjamin has had one week there after arrival. . . .
While I am glad to get at least this small promise from Gandhi, I feel
I must acquaint Your Excellency with my fear, born of my knowledge of Gandhi, that no power on earth will move him if he has
taken an oath. . . .[29]

Benjamin Robertson sailed on 1 January 1914. Gokhale was too
ill to go to Bombay to see him before his departure, but from his
sickbed he dictated a note, which, besides recapitulating the issues at
stake, contained a vignette of Gandhi. 'He is a thoroughly straightforward, honourable and high-minded man,' wrote Gokhale, 'and
though he may at times appear obstinate and even fanatical, he is
really open to conviction.' Gokhale requested Robertson to treat
Gandhi with the same confidence with which, 'I venture to think,
you would have treated me, if I had been in his place'.[30]
Robertson's experience in the Commerce Department of the
Government of India was of little use to him in the extraordinary
situation in which he found himself in South Africa. He was incapable
of understanding the *satyagraha* struggle and its leader. 'Altogether a
most extraordinary person, very subtle-minded and always ready to
change his ground at a moment's notice . . . he has a terrible amount
of conscience and is very hard to manage', was Robertson's description of Gandhi to the Viceroy.[31] Gandhi's distrust of Robertson was
equally deep and even the South African ministers did not seem eager
for his mediation.[32]
It was not the official envoy of the Viceroy, but Gokhale's personal
envoy who was to take a hand in the negotiations which culminated
in the Gandhi–Smuts agreement. C. F. Andrews, a young English
missionary and teacher at St Stephen's College, Delhi, had telegraphed to Gokhale in November 1913 and offered to go out to
South Africa. By the end of the month he was, along with his friend
W. W. Pearson, on the high seas. On 1 January 1914 he arrived at
Durban and was greeted by Polak, whom he had met in India. Polak
introduced him to 'a slight ascetic figure dressed in a white dhoti and
kurta of such coarse material as any indentured labourer might wear.'
Andrews bent swiftly down and touched Gandhi's feet.[33] This instinctive gesture of reverence to an 'Asiatic' scandalized the local Europeans, and the editor of a local newspaper personally protested to

[29] G.P.   [30] Gokhale to B. Robertson, 31 Dec. 1913 (G.P.).
[31] Robertson to Hardinge, 4 Feb. 1914 (H.P.).
[32] C. F. Andrews to Gokhale, 23 Jan. 1914 (G.P.).
[33] B. Chaturvedi & M. Sykes, *Charles Freer Andrews*, London, 1949, p. 94.

Andrews, who reminded him that Christ and St Paul and St John were also 'Asiatics'.

Andrews and Gandhi became friends and were soon calling each other 'Mohan' and 'Charlie'. Andrews grasped at once—what the Viceroy and even Gokhale had failed to grasp—that the Indian community in South Africa, which had made enormous sacrifices, could not be pushed into a compromise against its will. Emily Hobhouse, the English lady noted for her valiant protests against the scandals of the concentration camps for Boer women and children, was then in South Africa, and in touch with both Gandhi and Smuts.[34] The international situation at the end of 1913 seemed full of dangerous possibilities. Smuts and Botha had thus good reason to want a truce on the home front. They were impressed by Gandhi's chivalrous gesture in calling off the resumption of *satyagraha*, when the South African government was embarrassed by a strike on the railways and in the mines. Andrews brought his healing touch to the negotiations and helped to sort out some of the knotty issues. Gandhi acknowledged Andrews' contribution to the settlement (the Gandhi–Smuts agreement) by describing it as the 'joint work' of Andrews and himself.[35]

On 25 January 1914, Gandhi cabled to Gokhale that the provisional agreement with Smuts had been reached and passive resistance was to be suspended pending legislation in the next session of Parliament.

[34] Ibid., p. 100.
[35] Gandhi to Gokhale, telegram, 22 Jan. 1914.

39

The Last Battle

While the South African crisis was at its height, Lord Willingdon, the Governor of Bombay, wrote enthusiastically to Lord Hardinge about a meeting he had had with Gokhale. 'I am glad', Hardinge replied on 14 November 1913, 'that you saw Gokhale and that you like him. I like him too. But my confidence in him has certain limitations. I know what his ultimate aims & objects are, although he bides his time, & these are inconsistent with the prolongation of the British Raj.'[1]

That the Viceroy should have expressed such distrust of Gokhale at a time when he was receiving the fullest cooperation from him in tackling the crisis of the Indian minority in South Africa may seem surprising. This distrust was, however, not new. It had been entertained all along not only by Hardinge, but by his predecessors, Minto and Curzon, who had reacted to Gokhale with a peculiar mixture of admiration, suspicion and irritation. At the end of 1913, Hardinge had reasons to be annoyed with Gokhale because of the strongly nationalist line he was taking on the Public Services Commission. The commission was inquiring into the methods of recruitment, systems of training and terms and remuneration of imperial and provincial services in India. To Gokhale, and indeed to all politically-conscious Indians, the commission was not merely an instrument for securing a few more posts or slightly better terms for their countrymen, but a potential weapon for breaking the British monopoly of the higher levels of administration in India.

Ever since its inception, the Indian National Congress had been demanding equal opportunities for Indians for entry into the higher services: at the very first Congress session held at Bombay in 1885 Dadabhai Naoroji had moved a resolution calling for a simultaneous entrance examination for the I.C.S. in India and England. Despite persistent Indian agitation, this demand had not been conceded.

[1] Hardinge to Willingdon, 14 Nov. 1913 (H.P.).

Even a resolution of the House of Commons in 1893 on the subject was not implemented by the Government. Four years later, in his evidence before the Welby Commission, Gokhale protested against the virtual exclusion of the sons of the soil from the higher echelons of the administration in India.

The excessive costliness of the foreign agency is not, however, its only evil. There is a moral evil which, if anything, is even greater. A kind of dwarfing or stunting of the Indian race is going on under the present system. We must live all the days of our life in an atmosphere of inferiority, and the tallest of us must bend. . . . The upward impulse, if I may use such an expression, which every schoolboy at Eton or Harrow may feel, that he may one day be a Gladstone, a Nelson, or a Wellington, and which may draw forth the best efforts of which he is capable, that is denied to us.[2]

There was no appreciable improvement in the Indian representation in the higher services during the next fifteen years. Gokhale reverted to this theme from time to time in and outside the Imperial Legislative Council. When he was invited to serve as a member of the Royal Commission on the Public Services in 1912, it seemed a heaven-sent opportunity to breach the bureaucratic citadel from within. Dadabhai Naoroji, now in his eighty-seventh year, who had all his life vainly clamoured for a simultaneous competitive examination for the I.C.S. in India and England, was delighted at Gokhale's inclusion in the Public Services Commission. 'You are the man of the day', he wrote to Gokhale,

the hope of India, and if the result of the present Public Services Commission is not a distinct assertion of the necessity of giving full effect to the Act of 1833 as recommended by the India Office Committee of 1860, it will be a great misfortune for India, especially if *you* did not firmly fight for the result and allowed yourself to be drawn into the details of the service as it exists at present. This is exactly the dodge by which the Anglo-Indians put us off for 80 years and will continue to do so for other many 80 years . . . the question of the simultaneous examination should be uncompromisingly fought by you in the Commission. Till this change is made in the present policy of bleeding India . . . there is no hope for the prosperity of India. . . .[3]

2

We have already seen how fiercely Gokhale's appointment to the Public Services Commission was resisted by the Viceroy and his

[2] Patwardhan & Ambekar (eds.), op. cit., vol. I, p. 488.
[3] Naoroji to Gokhale, n.d. (presumably July 1912) (G.P.).

advisers in India and by the Anglo-Indian lobby in London. From the day the Commission started its work, some of its members, such as Chirol, Ronaldshay, Himmick and Madge, who were the partisans of the Tory or Civil Service views, felt that Gokhale was a thorn in their side. The Viceroy, who was kept posted by Chirol with the goings-on in the Commission, was disconcerted by the favourable impression Gokhale seemed to be making on Lord Islington, the Chairman of the Commission. 'The Commission is playing Gokhale's game admirably', Hardinge wrote in a private letter to Crewe, the Secretary of State, on 6 February 1913, 'and that is what I have always feared.'[4] Early in June, Chirol complained to Hardinge that Islington 'had gone over bag and baggage to the Gokhale camp', that he was inclined to agree to a separate examination for the I.C.S. in India, and was even 'talking of satisfying political aspirations of the Indian educated classes'.[5] Islington himself confided to the Viceroy that his object was to carry Gokhale with him on 'a compromise scheme', which would provide sufficient safeguards in the interests of British rule, but also afford a fair chance to the various communities and provinces of India to be adequately represented. 'You will agree, I am sure,' Islington added, 'that it is of importance to secure Gokhale's adhesion, provided this can be done without undue sacrifice of British interests.'[6] Hardinge warned Islington that what was at stake was not merely the allocation of a few posts, but the future of the British Raj.

Lord Hardinge to Lord Islington, 1 September 1913: I could not agree to a reduction of a single European of the cadre of the Civil Service. To reduce the existing number of European Civil Servants would, in my opinion, result in the weakening of the administration and the diminution of its British character. These are two eventualities that must be avoided at all cost. . . .
   As regards recruitment of Indians for the Civil Service, I would infinitely prefer to see them recruited from the Provincial Services. . . . As regards a compromise with Gokhale, I am not in favour of any compromise which will weaken the administration, and which, I know, to be Gokhale's aim. Knowing Gokhale's past history, and remembering the language used by him in [Imperial] Council on one occasion when he let himself go in a temper, I know perfectly well that his aim and object is practically to destroy the Civil Service and

[4] Hardinge to Crewe, 6 Feb. 1913 (H.P.).
[5] Chirol to Hardinge, 6 June 1913 (H.P.).
[6] Islington to Hardinge, 14 Aug. 1913 (H.P.).

get the executive power entirely in the hands of Indians. In fact he used words to that effect in Council.[7]

The Viceroy's warning seems to have had the desired effect. Chirol reported to him that Islington was adopting a more cautious attitude towards Gokhale.

By the winter of 1913, a fundamental cleavage between the Indian and European members became obvious. Gokhale was shocked by the volte-face of Ramsay MacDonald, the Labour leader, who was believed to be a friend of India, and would indeed have presided over the Calcutta Congress in 1911 but for his wife's serious illness. MacDonald's apostasy reduced the alignment in the Commission to purely racial lines. All the British members seemed to have banded together, while Gokhale had the support of the other two Indian members. Chirol wrote to Hardinge:

I must say that the line he [Gokhale] has taken this year has lowered enormously my opinion of him. . . . Whilst the ugly bitterness he has from time to time betrayed, his avowed and offensive distrust of Government and his open imputations of bad faith, past and prospective, upon all British authorities in India, have very much shaken my confidence in his sincerity and his professed acceptance of the necessity of maintaining British rule and influence.[8]

What particularly galled Chirol and his friends was that under Gokhale's influence, the Muslim member of the Commission, Abdur Rahim, refused to toe the official line. 'As for Abdur Rahim,' wrote Chirol, 'he has been simply Gokhale's stalking horse. . . . An extreme Hindu Nationalist could not have been more oblivious of Mahomedan interests.'[9] Even the Aga Khan, who had always been ready to ingratiate himself with the British Government, and was regarded as a pillar of the Raj, seemed to have been suddenly bitten by the patriotic bug. In his evidence before the Royal Commission on 3 March 1913, he pleaded for the Indianization of the Civil Service and the I.C.S. examination being simultaneously held in India and England. He was reluctant to be drawn into a discussion of Hindu–Muslim antagonism.[10]

---

[7] H.P.

[8] Chirol to Hardinge, 31 July 1914 (H.P.).　　　　[9] Ibid.

[10] Chirol and some British members of the Commission were shocked by the Aga Khan's evidence. Chirol to Hardinge, 24 March 1913 (H.P.) See also *Royal Commission on the Public Services in India, Appendix to the Report of the Commissioners*, vol. VI, London, 1914, pp. 54–69.

3

It is a strange paradox that just when Gokhale's work on the Royal Commission was causing deep annoyance to the Viceroy, he should have been offered a knighthood. On 16 June 1914, he received a letter from Lord Peel, the Under-Secretary of State, that the Viceroy had recommended him for promotion to a Knight Commander of the Indian Empire, that Lord Crewe, the Secretary of State for India, had endorsed the recommendation, and the King had approved of it. Gokhale replied the following day, expressing his grateful appreciation of the honour proposed to be conferred on him, but pleading that he 'would much prefer . . . to continue under my present simple designation. May I hope that Lord Crewe will understand this wish which, I may state, is based largely, though not entirely, on personal grounds.' Gokhale gave a fuller explanation of his motives to Lord Peel when he called on him at the India Office. A knighthood accorded ill with the simplicity of life to which all members of the Servants of India Society were pledged. Gokhale also felt that the title would compromise his position as a member of the Royal Commission, which had yet to submit its report.

It is doubtful if any Indian had ever before declined an honour like the K.C.I.E., but Gokhale's refusal was taken in good part by the Viceroy and the Secretary of State. Gokhale's friends and disciples appreciated his courage of conviction; their reaction was echoed by Srinivasa Sastri: 'You would be more honoured with the honour refused than with it accepted.'[11]

The Viceroy confided to the Secretary of State that he had proposed the honour for Gokhale, 'entirely due to the very real assistance and advice that he offered me in the South African question'.[12] Gratitude may not have been the only or even the primary motive of the Viceroy. A knighthood would raise Gokhale in the official warrant of precedence; it could also lower him in the eyes of some of his countrymen. 'Sir Gopal Krishna Gokhale' might not be able to command the prestige of Mr Gopal Krishna Gokhale. One wonders if the Viceroy remembered the words of Fleetwood Wilson, his one-time colleague on the Executive Council, in justification of Gokhale's inclusion in the Royal Commission. 'I entirely agree with you in your estimate of Gokhale,' Fleetwood Wilson had written to Hardinge on

[11] Sastri to Gokhale, 9 July 1914 (G.P.).
[12] Hardinge to Crewe, 25 June 1914 (H.P.).

1 September 1912, 'but my humble policy *ab initio* has been to make him through himself less of a power amongst his own people. Indians never forgive one of their own who accepts the badge of servitude, & Gokhale will perforce have to remain on our side of the fence.'[13] Fleetwood Wilson had miscalculated: Gokhale did not 'accept the badge of servitude', nor go over to the Anglo-Indian side of the fence.

4

Gokhale was far from well when the offer of knighthood came. Ill-health had prevented him from participating in the final stages of the only serious but abortive move made in the constitutional sphere between 1909 and 1917. This move which concerned the reform of the India Office was largely inspired by Edwin S. Montagu, the Under-Secretary of State for India. Montagu had confidentially raised the question of reforming the India Office in 1912. He was being continually urged to take an initiative by William Wedderburn, who was in close touch with Gokhale. Both Wedderburn and Gokhale knew that the glow of optimism engendered by the Indian Councils Act of 1909 had already faded. The 'regulations' framed by the Government of India had neutralized much of the advance implicit in the Minto–Morley scheme. The distribution of seats in the legislatures between elected and nominated members, between officials and non-officials, and between Hindus and Muslims had been so contrived as to tilt the balance against the nationalist element. The enlargement of the non-official representation in the Councils had thus made them scarcely more effective from the Indian point of view. The Decentralization Commission from which Gokhale and R. C. Dutt had hoped for much took an unconscionable time in submitting its report. Its recommendations were halting and half-hearted; the bureaucratic structure of administration remained intact.

The stark fact was that while Anglo-India was bent on preserving its monopoly of place and power, the Liberal government itself was not convinced of the justification for Indian self-government. When the plans for the construction of the new capital at Delhi were under consideration, Edwin Montagu pleaded for a fine chamber for the Imperial Legislative Council. Secretary of State Crewe rejected the

[13] Wilson to Hardinge, 1 Sept. 1912 (F. Wilson P.).

plea out of hand, 'telling him that names and forms mattered more' than he supposed, that 'a number of . . . advanced [Indian] politicians . . . regard parliament as the goal of their ambition; that no colour should be given to any notion that we favour their hopes'.[14] Crewe wanted it to be made plain that the Indian Legislative Council would continue to be 'the Viceroy's Council, and the circumstances and the surroundings should emphasize the fact'.[15] That an Indian parliament was an impossible dream was not a secret shared between the Secretary of State for India and the Viceroy; indeed, the former told the House of Lords in 1912: 'The idea of an Indian Dominion is a world as remote as any Atlantis or Erewhon that ever was thought of by the ingenious brain of an imaginative writer.'[16]

The constitutional position in India had thus been frozen for some time, and it was obvious to Wedderburn and Gokhale that other avenues would have to be explored for an advance in the interim period. One of these avenues was the Indianization of the higher services for which Gokhale was fighting within the Royal Commission. Another was the weakening of the stranglehold of the 'old India hands' on the India Office. 'The antagonism to Indian interests', Wedderburn wrote to Gokhale on 13 November 1913,

is not essentially either national or racial, but professional, the interest of the official monopolists being to decry their outside competitors, & poison public sentiment in England against them by charges of sedition, etc. It is the same thing as in Russia and Ireland, where the permanent officials are the enemies of popular aspirations. We must have a systematic propaganda to make our Parliamentary friends understand the real merit of the case & to realize that the interests of India as represented by the [Indian] reformers, are identical with those of this country & especially that 'unrest' is the direct result of retrogressive & oppressive action of the official faction & would disappear if Liberal principles were courageously applied.[17]

Wedderburn felt that the most effective single step towards weakening the bureaucratic monopoly of power in India would be to make the India Council in London more responsive to Indian opinion. Prompted by him, Montagu worked out a scheme for the reconstitution of the Council. Besides canvassing support in the Liberal party in Britain for this scheme, Wedderburn wrote to the leaders of the Congress in India to work up an agitation for it. In December

[14] Crewe to Hardinge, 5 July 1912 (H.P.).　　　[15] Ibid.
[16] 12 House of Lords Debates, 5s., col. 745.
[17] Wedderburn to Gokhale, 13 Nov. 1913 (G.P.).

1913 the Karachi Congress passed a resolution on the reform of the Council of the Secretary of State for India, and decided to send a deputation to England. The deputation included M. A. Jinnah and N. M. Samarth from Bombay, Sachchidananda Sinha from the U.P., and B. N. Sarma from Madras. Gokhale could not join it, but Wedderburn accompanied it. The deputation, of which Jinnah was the spokesman, urged that one-third of the members of the India Council should be elected by the members of the Indian legislatures. A bill was actually introduced by the Secretary of State. It was a modest measure; all that it did was to provide for the selection of the two Indian members from a panel chosen by the non-official members of the central and provincial legislative councils. The bill evoked fierce opposition from the Conservative peers led by Curzon, who described the indirect election of the 'two native gentlemen' as an undesirable and dangerous 'innovation'. The bill, to the relief of the Government of India and the Anglo-Indian lobby in London, was rejected by the House of Lords.

The British in India had their own reasons for not wanting a change in the composition of the Secretary of State's Council and for its continued manning by retired civil and military officers rather than by Indian or British politicians. The Viceroy himself let the cat out of the bag. Hardinge wrote to Crewe on 22 May 1912:

As long as there are persons like yourself and Morley at the India Office no rash experiments will be attempted, but who will say what might happen if a Socialist Government were in Office?... I should be sorry if the policy of His Majesty's Government in India were to depend on the views of a few Parliamentary faddists with no real knowledge of India and the Indian people.[18]

Evidently, one of the functions of the India Council—from the point of view of the guardians of the Raj—was to prevent a radical Secretary of State from running amuck.

5

The proceedings of the Royal Commission put a greater strain on Gokhale than he had expected. The South African visit in October–November 1912 had stretched his physical and nervous strength to the limit; it was not only the heavy schedule, but the fear of aggravating an already tense situation, which weighed on him. On his

[18] Hardinge to Crewe, 22 May 1912 (H.P.).

return to India, he had to plunge into the work of the Royal Commission, which spent the winter months of 1912–13 in holding its meetings at Madras, Calcutta, Rangoon, Delhi, Bombay, Nagpur, Bankipore, Lucknow and Lahore. The continual travelling and the tedious sessions were bad enough. What was worse was the arrogance of the European witnesses in expatiating on the unfitness of Indians for higher posts, which cut Gokhale to the quick. He needed all his alertness, patience and skill in cross-examining these witnesses and exposing their pride and prejudice. No wonder that at the end of the day, he should have often felt completely exhausted.

In May 1913, Gokhale travelled with the Royal Commission to England and attended its meetings in that country. However, as the crisis in South Africa deepened, he decided to return to India in September. The three months which followed were among the most strenuous of his life. He constantly kept in touch with Gandhi. He toured India to mobilize moral and financial support for him. He bombarded the Viceroy with letters and cables urging intercession on behalf of the harassed Indian minority with the South African and British governments. He secured the sympathy of the Indian press. All this had to be done at a time when he was himself far from well. Indeed, in December 1913 and January 1914, he conducted this campaign from his sick-bed in Poona.

The South African crisis was apparently resolved happily by the end of January 1914. Early in February 1914, against the advice of his doctors, Gokhale rejoined the Royal Commission when it visited Bombay. 'I do not know', Dr Mrs Bahadurji wrote to Gokhale, 'how to induce you to see the force of [the argument for] taking rest quite so long; for you politicians think the country will all fall to pieces without you. . . .'[19] In 1914 the Royal Commission returned to England and Gokhale decided to go with it. His friends, particularly Wedderburn, felt that this visit to England was essential for rest, medical treatment and the 'cure' at Vichy which always seemed to rally Gokhale, even if temporarily. A letter which Gokhale wrote from Vichy to his disciples in Poona revealed how very ill he was.

Gokhale to H. S. Deva, 21 May 1914: The writing of this letter is in itself some evidence of the improvement that has taken place in me, for I could not have written such a letter till this week. Of course, I am now feeling very very tired and the pulse, which was 86 when I began writing this letter, has gone up to 103. Dr Bright has forbidden

[19] Bahadurji to Gokhale, 3 Jan. 1914 (G.P.).

my doing anything with the pulse above 94. But it was worthwhile doing this for the sake of the pleasure which I know the letter will give you and other members [of the Servants of India Society].[20]

The following day Gokhale received elaborate instructions from Dr Bright. He was to watch his pulse carefully during an interview and, if it went above ninety-four, to stop talking. He was to see no one without a previous appointment, and never to see more than one person at a time. He was not to see more than four persons in a day, and no interview was to exceed ten minutes. Exciting topics of conversation were to be avoided altogether, and no special invitation of any kind was to be accepted. Dr Bright might as well have ordered Gokhale to retire from politics!

The visit to Vichy seemed once again to have had a magical effect on Gokhale. All the serious symptoms began to disappear and by the middle of June, he was able to walk for half an hour. He returned to London, and took up his residence in the National Liberal Club. But after a few active days, his health began to deteriorate again. Jivraj Mehta, a brilliant young doctor, was continually in attendance upon Gokhale. In April he had him examined by Dr Hadley, an eminent consulting physician. We have a first-hand report by Jivraj Mehta on Gokhale's health:

Gokhale's heart has given way under great strain and it will take weeks and weeks before it could be recovered to some extent. . . . He suffers from cardiac dyspepsia, occasional palpitation and great general exhaustion. Occasionally he gets a sinking and choking sensation with a tendency to faint after some extra exertion. But as you can well understand, Mr Gokhale would not like the servants or any one of us to do any work for him and thus would unduly exert himself, e.g. lifting bags, putting luggage in order, walking about in rooms, which give no rest to the heart.[21]

Obviously in this state of health, the National Liberal Club was not the ideal place for Gokhale. Fortunately, Ratan Tata, the Indian industrialist, and his wife were in England at this time and invited him to stay with them at Twickenham, a splendid and invigorating place with plenty of fresh air. The river was close by, and the garden was in full bloom. Gokhale had complete rest; he was not allowed to leave his room or to receive visitors, but there were a few exceptions, one of them being Sarojini Naidu, who came to see him almost daily. Though herself a semi-invalid, she was lively, loquacious, scintillat-

[20] G.P.
[21] J. Mehta to Deva, 10 April 1914 (G.P.).

ing. She seemed to bring with her a breath of fresh air. As she crossed the threshold of Gokhale's sick-room, she would ask with a smile: 'Am I to be a stimulant or a sedative today?' Gokhale's invariable reply was: 'Both'. 'And this one word', Sarojini Naidu wrote later, 'most adequately summed up the need of a sinking heart and overburdened brain through these anxious and critical weeks.'[22]

At Twickenham, Gokhale had the company of the Tatas, and besides Dr Jivraj Mehta, was attended on by Dr Mrs Bahadurji, the physician of the Tata family. Dr Mehta pleaded with Gokhale to give up the work of the Royal Commission altogether, and thus allow his heart to recoup. Gokhale did not agree; he returned to London on 21 July, and decided to visit Vichy again for a change of air and treatment. On 24 July he left for Vichy. He arrived there accompanied by Dr Jivraj Mehta on 30 July. Unfortunately he had an attack of cardiac asthma, and was feeling very low when he arrived at Vichy. Within three or four days, however, he was on his feet again. Among those who were staying in Hôtel du Parc et Majestie at Vichy at this time were the Maharaja of Baroda, Dr Bahadurji, and M. B. Chaubal, one of Gokhale's colleagues on the Public Services Commission. The company was congenial, the weather was invigorating, and Gokhale looked forward to a few quiet weeks of rest and treatment. But this was not to be. When he reached Vichy, Europe had already moved to the brink of disaster. On 1 August, Germany declared war on France; two days later, she invaded Belgium. On 4 August, Britain declared war on Germany.

Though Vichy was not close to the border with Belgium or Germany, it immediately felt the impact of the war. With total mobilization under way, the normal tenor of life was disturbed. Gokhale had no funds; no remittance was forthcoming from Thomas Cook & Sons, his travel agents in London. Nor was it easy to secure a return passage. It was only after the India Office in London had sought the intervention of the British Foreign Office that the French authorities arranged for the return of Gokhale, the Gaekwad of Baroda and other Indians stranded in Vichy.

6

Twenty years before the First World War, Allan Octavian Hume had told a public meeting, held in Bombay to bid him farewell, that

[22] *Speeches and Writings of Sarojini Naidu*, 1st ed., p. 50.

if a war broke out and England was involved, he hoped the Indian people would give 'united and ungrudging support to the British people. . . . Yes, in the noblest sense of the word, a great war would be India's opportunity—opportunity for proving that if in periods of peace she clamours, at times somewhat angrily, for equal civil rights, in the hour of war, she is ever ready and anxious to accept equal military risks.' Hume's prophecy was fulfilled at least in the first weeks of the war. 'I trust', Dadabhai Naoroji wrote to the Viceroy on 10 August 1914, 'this the greatest struggle for liberty, honour and righteousness will end gloriously to the credit of England and the good of humanity.'[23] Three days later, Pherozeshah Mehta declared at Bombay that all races and religions 'are merged in one general and universal denomination—the proud denomination of loyal and devoted subjects of the British Crown. As such we are met together to lay at the feet of our august sovereign, our beloved King-Emperor, our unswerving fealty, our unshaken allegiance and our enthusiastic homage.'[24] Surendranath Banerjea spoke in a similar vein at Calcutta. M. K. Gandhi, whose arrival in London *en route* to India coincided with the outbreak of the war, decided 'for the sake of the motherland and the Empire, to place his services at the disposal of the authorities', and took the lead in organizing an ambulance unit from among Indian residents in England.

In December 1914, the Indian National Congress, meeting at Madras, passed a resolution conveying 'to His Majesty the King-Emperor and the people of England its profound devotion to the Throne, its unswerving allegiance to the British connection, and its firm resolve to stand by the Empire at all hazards and at all costs'. The Congress expressed its gratitude and satisfaction at the despatch of the Indian expeditionary force to the theatre of war, 'affording the people of India an opportunity to fight shoulder to shoulder with the people of other parts of the empire in the defence of the rights and justice and the cause of the empire'. Lajpat Rai, the *bête noire* of the Europeans in India, publicly invited the cooperation of the people of India 'in the world struggle'. 'Whatever may be said against the [British] rule,' he wrote, 'from a purely Indian point of view, it cannot be denied that British rule in India is a monument of British genius for government and for their general sense of justice.'[25] The

[23] Naoroji to Hardinge, 10 Aug. 1914 (H.P.).
[24] Jeejeebhoy, *Speeches and Writings of Pherozeshah Mehta*, pp. 466–7.
[25] *Tribune*, 16 Oct. 1914.

Governor of Bombay gleefully reported to the Viceroy on 5 August that Tilak, who had recently been released from jail, 'has given us no trouble here at all, and I hear rumours that he wishes to make the *amende honorable* to Government and be a good boy'.[26] On 30 August 1914, the *Mahratta* came out with a letter to the editor from Tilak that 'our sense of loyalty and desire to support the government is both inherent and unswerving', that it was the duty of every Indian, 'be he great or small, rich or poor, to support and assist His Majesty's Government to the best of his ability'. Tilak denounced political violence unambiguously and denied that his attitude was in any way hostile to the British Government. 'That has never been my object,' he declared, 'I may state once for all that we are trying in India, as the Irish Home Rulers have been doing in Ireland, for a reform of the system of administration and not for the overthrow of government.'[27]

Curiously enough, the despatch of Indian troops to European theatres of war did not evoke the opposition in India which it was to do twenty-five years later. On the contrary, it was welcomed. Tilak's own paper, the *Mahratta*, wrote on 4 October 1914: 'Indian hearts will be thrilled to know that Indian troops have landed in France.' The award of the first Victoria Cross to an Indian soldier made banner headlines in the Indian press, and was greeted with great enthusiasm in the country as a shining example of Indian valour.

In November 1914, just before he left England, Gokhale had urged the Secretary of State to open the King's Commission to Indian youth. The same point was driven home by C. F. Andrews in a personal letter to the Viceroy: 'There is nothing in the world that Indian students of the noblest type feel more bitterly', Andrews wrote, 'than this refusal to recognize their manhood.'[28]

When the Imperial Legislative Council met, the elected Indian members vied with each other in avowing their loyalty to the British connection. Surendranath Banerjea suggested that the cost of the Indian expeditionary force should be borne, contrary to precedents, by the Indian exchequer. Within six months of the outbreak of war, seven divisions of infantry, and two divisions and two brigades of cavalry had left India. In addition, twenty batteries of artillery and twenty-two batteries of British infantry, altogether 80,000 British

---

[26] Willingdon to Hardinge, 5 Aug. 1914 (H.P.).
[27] Letter from Tilak to Editor, *Mahratta*, 30 Aug. 1914.
[28] C. F. Andrews to Hardinge, 19 Dec. 1914 (H.P.).

officers and soldiers and 210,000 Indian officers and men were despatched to the various theatres of war. The idea of Indian troops fighting shoulder to shoulder with British troops in European battle-fields was not liked by some of the guardians of the British Raj, but in the face of the German peril they had to swallow the bitter pill. 'So', wrote Sir Valentine Chirol in November 1914, 'we have got to throw every trained man we have into this appalling melting pot, whether white, brown or black. Of course we shall have to pay pretty heavily afterwards from the political point of view. But this is not the moment we can even think about ulterior consequences.'[29] Shrewd British administrators did not take the Indian professions of loyalty at their face value. 'India is behaving well on the whole', Harcourt Butler wrote to his uncle, Montagu Butler. 'Quite a lot of the loyalty is genuine, but amongst the educated classes there is, so many of them tell me, real pleasure at a German victory. They do not want to see Germans here; they do not want to see us crushed; but they do want to see us humbled. It is I suppose a natural feeling for a race subject to alien rule, rather for the more advanced section in it.'[30]

The improvement in the relations between the British Government and the Indian educated classes produced by the German peril was not to last long, but while it lasted it had some curious results. In January 1915 the Viceroy, accompanied by the Bombay Governor Willingdon, paid a visit to Villa Versova near Bombay to see Dadabhai Naoroji. The Indian mood of enthusiastic loyalty and the British mood of self-satisfaction at the avowal of this loyalty was soon to pass. The war took a heavy toll and the myth of the invincibility of British arms was broken. Muslim loyalty was strained by the entry of Turkey in the war on the side of Germany. Rising prices, the famine, the 'flu, the terrorist outrages, reports of armed risings with or without German instigation, all added to the political ferment in the country.

Gokhale's own view of the war in these early months of 1914–15 was no different from that of Dadabhai Naoroji, Pherozeshah Mehta, Surendranath Banerjea, and others. He had been distressed by the initial German victories. 'I do hope', he wrote to Dr Deva on 11 September 1914, 'the end to this business would soon be reached. Germany and Austria are bound to be smashed. The only question is how long will it take to smash them.'[31] Immediately, the war had an

[29] Chirol to Butler, 19 Nov. 1914 (B.P.).
[30] H. Butler to M. Butler, 10 Dec. 1914 (B.P.).
[31] Gokhale to Deva, 11 Sept. 1914 (G.P.).

impact on the Public Services Commission. It resumed its sittings in London in August, but its work no longer seemed important. Gokhale's thoughts were already turning homeward.

Gokhale to Dr Deva, 28 August 1914: I am very sorry not to be in India in these grave times. But so long as there is a possibility of the Commission continuing its work, I can't leave London. Later, there may be difficulty in getting a passage to India, but I will try my best to be now back in India, & I may say I have now no heart in the work of the Commission.[32]

Sarojini Naidu, who was still in England and meeting Gokhale frequently, found him oppressed by a sharp sense of exile, and haunted by a deep nostalgia not only for the physical surroundings, but the spiritual texts and lore of his motherland. She was startled by Gokhale's frequent allusions to old Sanskrit writers. It was as if Gokhale sensed that he had not long to live, and wanted to hasten home to die among his own people. 'I do not think we shall meet again', he said as he bade her good-bye. 'If you live, remember your life is dedicated to the service of the country. My work is done.'[33]

Whatever the war with Germany may have done, it failed to melt the hearts of the British members of the Public Services Commission, who were united in opposing the views of their three Indian colleagues. Even Ramsay MacDonald failed to play up. 'I am very sorry', Wedderburn wrote to Gokhale, 'that Mr Ramsay MacDonald has disappointed you & hope he may yet see the error of his ways.'[34] The Commission reached a virtual deadlock which the British members tended to attribute to Gokhale's obstinacy. 'Gokhale had been very restive of late', Chirol wrote to the Viceroy on 7 October 1914, 'and intimated to the Chairman and to some of my colleagues that it seemed to himself hopeless that any report based upon the conclusions arrived at by the majority last summer could satisfy him or his fellow-Indians; and that he proposed to return to India at once, for he and his two other Indian colleagues might just as well draft their minority report out there when it was all over.'[35]

The fundamental question for Gokhale was the position of Indians in the administration of their own country. He demanded that the Indians' share in the Indian Civil Service should be at least thirty-five to forty per cent; the British members of the Commission were

[32] G.P.
[33] *Speeches and Writings of Sarojini Naidu*, p. 52.
[34] Wedderburn to Gokhale, 29 Sept. 1914 (G.P.).
[35] Chirol to Hardinge, 7 Oct. 1914 (H.P.).

not prepared to concede more than twenty-five per cent. Gokhale wanted to raise the proportion of Indians in other imperial and provincial services, and to have Indians and Europeans treated at par. All this was unacceptable to the British members of the Commission, who insisted on preserving the predominance of the European element in the administration.

By October 1914, Gokhale had lost not only hope, but even interest in the Public Services Commission. It was open to him and his two Indian colleagues, Chaubal and Abdur Rahim, to produce a separate minority report. Gokhale wondered, however, if a minority report would serve any really useful purpose. What had the minority report of the Welby Commission achieved? Was it for this dismal result that he had wasted two years of his life and ruined his health?

The war had pushed the question of Indian reforms to the background in Britain. With the terrible holocaust in Europe, it looked somewhat absurd to haggle over the percentage of posts in the various departments of the Government of India. The public, the press and the Parliament were too preoccupied with the survival of Britain to take interest in the niceties of Indian administration. Futile as his stint on the Public Services Commission turned out to be, it was not without its lessons. A few days before Gokhale left England, Wedderburn had told him: 'one chief lesson taught is that a [royal] commission will always be packed & that for inquiries we should always try for a parliamentary Committee'.[36] Wedderburn, who had done his utmost to support Gokhale, went on to make an extraordinarily perceptive comment which put the problem of Indian representation in the public services in perspective. 'Please do not worry too much about [the] Royal Commission', he wrote to Gokhale; 'the great thing we need is the subordination of the bureaucracy to the people, and this is not within the terms of its [the Commission's] reference.'[37]

[36] Wedderburn to Gokhale, 29 Oct. 1914 (G.P.).
[37] *Idem,* 10 July 1914 (G.P.).

40

No Reunion

When Gokhale returned to India in November 1914, three months
after the outbreak of the war, it was still too soon for people to
visualize the tremendous changes the war was to bring about. However, many thinking people felt that in the face of the world crisis
the country should stand united. There had already been a thaw in
Hindu–Muslim relations as a sequel to the Balkan wars, and a
rapprochement between the All-India Muslim League and the Indian
National Congress was on the cards. But the gulf which divided the
Moderates and the Extremists within the Congress remained
unbridged.

As we have already seen, the Moderate victory at Surat had been
a pyrrhic one.[1] The Extremists had been thrown out of the Congress,
but with them had gone a good deal of the élan it had acquired in the
wake of the partition of Bengal. The annual Congress session once
again became a tame affair. The heroic efforts of Wedderburn and
Gokhale to infuse new life into the Congress organization at the
Allahabad session in 1910 achieved little. The following year, when
the Congress met at Calcutta, the *Modern Review* noted the 'long
rows of empty benches in the visitors' gallery'.[2] Bhupendranath Basu,
who presided over the session, found it necessary to refute the argument that after the recent expansion of the legislative councils the
Indian National Congress had become a superfluous body. The
1912 Congress session at Bankipore in Bihar was, if anything, even
more lifeless. It was attended by no more than 207 delegates, of
whom 53 came from Bihar and 42 from Bengal. Bombay sent only
9 delegates, including 3 from the Servants of India Society, and the
Punjab was represented by only 4 Congressmen. Some of the Bihar
leaders had been keen on electing Gokhale as president of the
Bankipore session, but were persuaded to spare him[3] because of the
responsibilities he had assumed in connection with the Indian prob-

---

[1] See above, chap. 32. [2] *Modern Review*, Jan. 1912, p. 123.
[3] Wedderburn to M. M. Malaviya, 5 Sept. 1912 (G.P.).

lem in South Africa and the Public Services Commission. Gokhale
went to Bankipore, but had to leave immediately after the inaugural
session to attend a meeting of the commission.

During the next two years Gokhale was almost wholly preoccupied
with the work of the Public Services Commission. He had to spend
several months at a stretch in England, and even when he was in
India, he was touring with the commission, sitting up late at night,
ploughing through the minutes of evidence, preparing questions for
cross-examination of witnesses and notes for discussion with his
colleagues. All this left him little time for politics, but he was uneasily
aware that all was not well with the Congress.

As we have already seen, Gokhale's own reaction to the 'Surat
Split' had been one of resignation rather than of elation.[4] The
exclusion of the Extremists brought peace to the Congress, but it was
the peace of the grave. During the Allahabad session in December
1910, when Gokhale acted as Wedderburn's private secretary, he
acquired a more sympathetic insight into the Extremist point of
view. It seemed to him that the Extremists had learnt their lesson,
and that most of them were ready to accept the Congress creed as
defined by the Allahabad Convention of 1908. They professed willingness to rejoin the Congress, but could not bring themselves to entreat
their opponents to enrol them as members of the existing Congress
committees, or to affiliate their own organizations to these committees. They proposed that the pre-Surat practice of electing delegates to the annual sessions at public meetings should be revived.
Gokhale gave the problem much thought. He formulated the terms
of a compromise and placed them before the Subjects Committee of
the Calcutta Congress in 1911: delegates to the Congress session were
to be elected by all public bodies which accepted the creed and
methods of the Congress, or by public meetings held under the
auspices of such bodies. The proposal passed through the Subjects
Committee with an overwhelming majority, but the opposition of the
Bombay Moderates, such as Wacha, was so vehement that Gokhale
decided not to move the resolution at the plenary session. A year
later, when the proposal again came up for discussion at Bankipore,
Gokhale was not present. It was adopted in a somewhat mutilated
form: the right of electing Congress delegates was restored to public
meetings, but only to those which were under the auspices of the existing Congress committees. Since these committees were controlled

[4] See above, chap. 25.

by the Moderates, the decision amounted to the retention of the *status quo*. The grievance of the Extremists remained unredressed.

2

In November 1914, when Gokhale returned from England, the prospects of ending the feud in the Congress suddenly seemed to brighten. The war was itself an important reason for a reappraisal of the position. When the fate of the British Empire and India hung in the balance, the niceties of electoral arrangements for the annual Congress sessions seemed relatively unimportant. A few weeks before the outbreak of the war, Tilak was released from jail. His early statements were extraordinarily moderate; his public avowal of constitutional methods seemed to narrow the gulf between him and his opponents in the Congress. One of Tilak's chief lieutenants, N. C. Kelkar, met Gokhale soon after his return to Poona, and assured him that their party was eager for a *rapprochement* with the Moderates. Motilal Ghose, an exponent of Extremist views, but a friend of both Tilak and Gokhale, advised the latter to throw his weight in favour of a united Congress.

Motilal Ghose to Gokhale, 15 November 1914: My heart weeps for the motherland. . . . I am anxious that you & Tilak should shake hands & embrace each other as brothers. . . . I know you bear no malice or ill-will to him. I further know that, even if you have any cause for offence, you are generous enough to forgive & forget, especially at the present critical moment. As you are in a more favourable position, it would be a graceful act for you to [make an] advance. If he rejects, the people will blame him & bless you. But I believe he will appreciate your motive. . . . The so-called Bengali leaders are now fossils. It is Mahratta intellect and patriotism which must save the country. If you and Tilak make up . . . there is yet hope for India.[5]

That Gokhale's stand *vis-à-vis* the Extremists was not rigid was known. 'So far as Mr Gokhale is concerned', Tilak wrote[6] to his friend, G. S. Khaparde, on 22 November 1914, 'he would favour the idea of a compromise, but [the Pherozeshah] Mehta party is opposed and will vote against us in the Subjects Committee.'[7]

[5] G.P. [6] Tilak to Khaparde, 22 Nov. 1914 (Khaparde P.).
[7] 'For God's sake', Pherozeshah Mehta wrote to Bhupendranath Basu, 'let us have done with all inane and slobbery whine about unity where there is really none.' Quoted in H. P. Mody, *Sir Pherozeshah Mehta, A Political Biography*, 1921, vol. II, p. 549.

The 1914 session of the Congress was to be held at Madras and, if the Extremists were to attend it, there was not much time to lose. The initiative for negotiations was taken by Mrs Besant, who was keenly aware of the impact the world war was likely to make on Indian politics. She had met Gokhale in England, and corresponded with him immediately after his return to India. She came to Poona on 5 December 1914 and stayed as Gokhale's guest in the Home of the Servants of India Society. She had fruitful talks with both Gokhale and Tilak before returning to Madras on 7 December. The same evening, Subba Rao, the Secretary of the Congress, who had been participating in these talks, went to Bombay to see Pherozeshah Mehta. Pherozeshah was not at all enthusiastic about the move for a compromise made by Mrs Besant with Gokhale's tacit support. He was firmly opposed to election of delegates to the Congress by public meetings, but was prepared to accept the affiliation of a few public bodies, such as Poona's Sarvajanik Sabha, in order to allow Tilak and his friends to come in.

Subba Rao returned to Poona on 8 December and had another meeting with Tilak, which proved disastrous. What passed between Subba Rao and Tilak was disputed later, but Subba Rao prepared a brief summary of Tilak's views, and had it corrected by Tilak himself. According to this document, Tilak had told Subba Rao that

the Extremists or Nationalists form the advanced wing of the Congress. Their attitude is one of constitutional opposition to the Government, while that of the Moderates or Constitutionalists is one of cooperation with the Government. Though the ideal of both is the same, namely self-government within the Empire, the difference between them lies in the methods adopted by them for reaching the goal. The Nationalists are and have been willing to join the Congress, but they feel they are humiliated by the way in which the Congress Constitution was framed, especially with reference to the election of delegates. They do not want to come into the Congress through the present Congress Committees. . . . They wish to join the Congress only if separate and independent constituencies . . . are created, which should automatically have the right to elect delegates, either at meetings of such bodies, or at public meetings convened under their auspices. If this is done, it is their intention to take steps to widen the door of elections as before to all public meetings, if necessary, and get recognition of these methods by educating public opinion and working for and securing a majority in the Congress, if possible.

Subba Rao's account of his conversation with Tilak came as an eye-opener to Gokhale, who had assumed all along that the compromise he had sponsored was to be the final solution of the dispute between the two parties. Gokhale could not help feeling that Tilak had 'learnt nothing and unlearnt nothing during all these years'.[8] As a concession to the Extremists, Gokhale was willing to permit public meetings to elect delegates to the annual Congress session, but these meetings were to be held under the auspices of Congress Committees or of public bodies affiliated to them. Tilak had made it clear to Subba Rao that he regarded this concession only as a step towards the election of delegates by *any* public meeting, as had been the practice in the pre-Surat Congress days. Subba Rao's version was corroborated by Professor Bijapurkar and N. C. Kelkar, who had been present at the talk with Tilak. Gokhale came to the conclusion that he had been proceeding on wrong premises, that there had really been no change of heart in Tilak, that the re-admission of the Extremists would virtually mean the opening of the Pandora's box which had been closed with extreme difficulty at Surat in December 1907. He decided to take into his confidence his friend Bhupendranath Basu, the Bengali Moderate leader, who was to preside over the Madras Congress during the Christmas week.

Gokhale to Bhupendranath Basu, 14 December 1914: I regret . . . to say that the statement of his position made by Mr Tilak to Mr Subba Rao last week has shaken me altogether as regards the advisability of the relaxation in rules that I have favoured these three years. My hope was that if we enabled the seceders by such relaxation to come in, they would, having seen the impossibility of political action on any other lines, co-operate with us in furthering the programme of the Congress by present methods. That hope has, however, been shattered. Mr Tilak has told Mr Subba Rao frankly and in unequivocal terms that though he accepts the position laid down in what is known as the Congress creed, viz. that the aim of the Congress is the attainment of self-government within the Empire by constitutional means, he does not believe in the present methods of the Congress which rest on association with Government where possible, and opposition to it where necessary. In place of these he wants to substitute the method of opposition to Government, pure and simple, within constitutional limits—in other words a policy of Irish obstruction.

We on our side are agitating for a larger and larger share in the Government of the country—in the Legislative Councils, on Municipal and Local Boards, in public services and so forth. Mr Tilak wants to address only one demand to the Government here and to

[8] G.P.

the British public in England, viz. for the concession of self-government to India, and till that is conceded, he would urge his countrymen to have nothing to do with either the public services or Legislative Councils and Local and Municipal Boards. And by organizing
obstruction to Government in every possible direction within the
limits of the laws of the land, he hopes to be able to bring the administration to a standstill, and to compel the authorities to capi-
tulate. . . .

He has explicitly told Mr Subba Rao that he gives us fair warning
that this is his purpose in seeking re-admission into the Congress
fold, and that once he is inside, he will strive first for effecting such
changes in the rules as will throw open election of delegates practically to everybody as before 1907 and then for getting the Congress
to endorse his programme by securing at its sessions the attendance
of a majority of delegates of his way of thinking.

The unfettered right to elect delegates at public meetings resolved
itself in practice, wrote Gokhale,

largely into a question of delegates' fees and travelling expenses for
a certain number of Mr Tilak's followers. Should he succeed in this,
I feel almost certain that it will be the end of the Congress. . . . But
even if he does not succeed in securing the majority, it will virtually
mean a return to a state of things that prevailed in 1906 and 1907
when all our energies had to be given to preventing Mr Tilak and
other Extremist leaders from capturing the Congress, involving a
strain that was well-nigh intolerable.[9]

Gokhale's health did not permit him to go to Madras during the
Christmas week but he advised Basu to work for the postponement
of the question of a compromise between the two parties for another
year. Negotiations could, however, be resumed a year later, if
definite assurances were forthcoming from Tilak and his friends.

Gokhale's letter was marked 'confidential', but Basu referred to it
at the meeting of Subjects Committee at Madras, and dwelt on the
basic differences of the (Moderate) Congress leaders with Tilak on
such issues as boycott. Mrs Besant, who had assumed the role of a
mediator between the two parties, thereupon telegraphically called
for Tilak's comments. 'I have never advocated boycott of Government', Tilak wired back. 'Prominent Nationalists [Extremists] have
served and are serving in Municipalities and Legislative Councils and
I have fully supported their action both privately and publicly.' The
Moderate leaders were not convinced by Tilak's protestations, and
feared that Mrs Besant was meddling with matters which she did not

[9] G.P.

quite understand. The initial enthusiasm for a compromise at the Madras Congress, voiced by Subramania Iyer, Motilal Ghose, and even by Bhupendranath Basu, faded away.

Gokhale made no secret of his views when one of his rare meetings with Tilak took place at Poona on 19 December. He reported to Basu:

I told him frankly that after his statement to Subba Rao, which he practically confirmed in his conversation with me, it was impossible for me to support the idea of a compromise any more, and that with the views and intentions he entertained, it was best from the standpoint of the interests of the Congress that he should remain outside that body.

3

The Madras Congress decided to defer a decision on the re-entry of the Extremists for a year. Since the 1915 Congress session was to be held at Bombay, the stronghold of Pherozeshah Mehta, the Extremists realized that the door had again been banged against them. In their frustration they poured out the vials of their wrath on Gokhale. They charged him with deliberately sabotaging the move for a compromise. He was accused of 'stabbing Tilak in the dark', by writing a confidential letter to the president of the Madras Congress. On 21 January 1915 Tilak himself wrote to Gokhale to inquire if he had written a letter to the Reception Committee of the Madras Congress on the amendment of the Congress Constitution, suggesting that Tilak, after re-entering the Congress, proposed to adopt the boycott of the government and methods of Irish obstruction. Gokhale replied the same day:

My dear Balvantrao,
  It is quite untrue that I wrote a letter to the Reception Committee or any of its officers at Madras. What I did do, however, was to write a private letter to Babu Bhupendranath Basu at Calcutta in reply to a letter from him soon after Subba Rao's visit to Poona, and explained at some length why it was impossible for me to support any more the amendment [of the Congress Constitution] which I had myself suggested to Mrs Besant. . . . My change of attitude was due to the statement made by you to Mr Subba Rao. . . . A copy of this letter was sent confidentially to Mrs Besant, with a request that she should know why I could not continue my support to the proposed amendment. The words 'boycott of Government' are not in that letter. The words 'Irish obstruction' certainly are. You should have

no difficulty in recalling your conversations with Mr Subba Rao. Mr Subba Rao was staying with me when those conversations took place, and he gave me a detailed account of all that passed between you and him. My letter was shown, before it was despatched, to Prof. Vijapurkar who was present during your interviews with Mr Subba Rao. . . . Finally you will remember that these opinions and intentions were repeated by you personally to me when I had a talk with you a few days later, and I stated frankly to you that with these views and intentions it was clearly best that you should remain outside the Congress.

To Gokhale it seemed there was something ominous about Tilak's letter and the minatory tone of the articles in *Kesari* and the *Mahratta*. It was bad enough that Gokhale, who had tried for three years, against heavy odds, for the readmission of the Extremists into the Congress, should have figured as a saboteur of a compromise between the two parties. But Poona was thick with rumours and recriminations, reminiscent of the days of the Age of Consent controversy of 1891, the Poona Congress in 1895 and the Surat Split in 1907. The mounting tension was too much for Gokhale with his failing health. He pulled himself together to write long letters to Bhupendranath Basu, Subba Rao, Annie Besant and even to important newspapers to refute the allegations against him, and to set the record straight. As Gokhale unburdened himself to Mrs Besant (whose enthusiasm for a united Congress had landed him in this controversy), memories of a quarter of a century's conflict with his political antagonist flooded back. He recalled the battles he had fought against Tilak, and why it had not been possible for the Extremists and Moderates to work together.

Gokhale to Mrs Besant, 5 January 1915: You say if Tilak tries to give trouble again, we shall fight and put him down. That is not an easy fight . . . certainly not one to be lightly entered on again. The two parties are not evenly matched. There is naturally a good volume of anti-foreign feeling—expressed and unexpressed—in the country and it loads the scales heavily on Tilak's side. We have to ask our countrymen to be reconciled to foreign domination—even though it be as a transitional arrangement—and our propaganda has to rest on one of its sides on some measure of faith in the sense of justice of British democracy. Tilak has no difficulty in ridiculing the latter as 'mendicancy', and denouncing the former as pusillanimous and unpatriotic cringing to the authorities. The number of men who can form a sound political judgment in the country is not large. But you can find any number of unthinking men filled with an honest but vague feeling for the emancipation of the country, ready to follow any plausible leader, whom in their heart of hearts they believe to be wholly against the foreigner.

It was with the help of such a following that Tilak captured the Poona Sarvajanik Sabha, the work of Ranade's hands, and destroyed its usefulness in less than twelve months [the Government placing it under a ban because of its excesses]. It was with the help of such a following that he nearly wrecked the Congress at Poona in 1895. And finally it was with the help of such a following that he actually wrecked the Congress at Surat in 1907.

I was one of his principal antagonists in all these three contests, and I know what he can do with his following and what he cannot. But who has ever said that democratic methods can at once be applied today in this ancient land, caste-ridden and priest-ridden for long long centuries? You ask why should we keep the door closed against a large number of men who are not likely to give trouble for the sake of one man who may give trouble? But you cannot ignore the fact that this one man is their foremost leader.[10]

The explanation apparently had some effect; Mrs Besant implored Gokhale not to worry. 'You must guard your body for future work,' she wrote on 23 January 1915, 'and your life is a thousand times more important than Tilak's presence in, or absence from, the Congress.'

There were rumours in Poona that Tilak might initiate legal action against Gokhale for misrepresenting him in his letters to Bhupendra-nath Basu. Tilak's statement that he had never favoured boycott of the government intrigued his critics. Understandably, in the midst of a world war when the government had assumed vast powers and political activity was at a low ebb, Tilak could hardly be expected to advocate boycott as he had done during the years 1905–7. When Tilak demanded the publication of Gokhale's letter to Bhupendra-nath Basu, Gokhale offered to show the letter to him and to publish it if he still insisted on it. Gokhale was sure that publication would not suit Tilak; the statement that he had never been in favour of the boycott of the British Government could indeed damage his militant image.

Gokhale apologized to Mrs Besant for writing at such length about Tilak. 'As I said to you personally here the other day, I have no wish to treat Tilak ungenerously. In fact, it goes greatly against my grain to take the line I am often forced to take. But by my bitter experience ranging over nearly 30 years now, I have learnt that not generosity but caution has to be the keynote of our dealings with him.'[11]

[10] G.P.   [11] Gokhale to A. Besant, 26 Jan. 1915 (G.P.).

The negotiations for the readmission of the Extremists to the Indian National Congress in the winter of 1914–15 proved abortive. Mrs Besant burnt her fingers[12] in her very first political venture in India. The acrimonious debate which followed raised the political temperature in Poona, infuriated the Extremists and left a bitter taste in Gokhale's mouth, and probably hastened his end.

[12] 'One thing I have learnt about her,' wrote N. Subba Rao to Gokhale on 1 Jan. 1915, 'and that is that we cannot be too careful in dealing with her.' Rao to Gokhale, 1 Jan. 1915 (G.P.).

41

Last Days

The outbreak of the war in Europe, the deadlock in the Royal Commission, and the failure of the negotiations initiated by Annie Besant for a united Congress combined to make the political landscape in early 1915 a bleak one, but Gokhale was not unduly depressed. Ever since the partition of Bengal, Indian politics had been tricky and unpredictable. But he had never given up hope; this was partly due to the fact that he took long-term views and could thus take setbacks and failures in his stride. He had a firm conviction that ultimately the destiny of India would be moulded by her people and particularly by the younger generation. 'Our best material', he would tell his English friends, 'is in our country.'[1]

It was to harness the youth to patriotic service that Gokhale had founded the Servants of India Society. The Society was never far from his thoughts. At one time he considered giving up all other work, including his membership of the Imperial Legislative Council, to devote all his time to the Society. This he could not do, but he was never happier than when in the Poona Home of the Society. During his long absences from India in connection with Minto–Morley reforms and the Public Services Commission, he wrote long letters giving his disciples all the news and much good advice. The Society had started with four members in 1905; the number rose to eight in 1907, to ten in 1908 and to twenty-seven in 1915. Branches of the Society were opened in Madras in 1910, in Nagpur and Bombay in 1911, and in Allahabad in 1913. Gokhale talked of enrolling at least one 'Servant of India' for each of the 275 districts in the country. However, he found the recruitment and training of even twenty-odd members of the Society a tremendous task. He was extremely rigorous in his selection of new entrants. A university degree and an aptitude for, if not actual experience of, public work were essential qualifications. No one was admitted as a member until after he had

[1] Bahadurji to Gokhale, 25 Sept. 1913 (G.P.).

seen something of the kind of life he was expected to lead, and had been adjudged suitable by Gokhale himself. The subsistence allowance was Rs 30 a month; it was raised to Rs 50 after the first five years. The earnings of the members (including Gokhale's savings from his allowances as a member of the Legislative Council) went to the Society.

As the First Member of the Society, Gokhale kept a vigilant eye on the members. The conduct of each member was carefully observed; the atmosphere in the headquarters of the Society was almost that of a college hostel, if not of a monastery. The members were allowed to marry, but families were not allowed to stay in the Home of the Society. Even Gokhale's two motherless daughters stayed in a small house with his widowed sister close to, but outside, the premises of the Society. We get a glimpse of the goings on in the Society's Home at Poona from the diary kept by Srinivasa Sastri, who seemed to be functioning in 1909 as the second-in-command (Second Member).[2]

Diary of Srinivasa Sastri, 3 July 1909
F.M. [First Member] asked me today to be strict about Mr Devadhar. Somebody had told him of his being late twice at night during his absence.

5 July 1909
Obtained leave for Kaikini to go to Bombay to consult a doctor. Goes in the afternoon today & returns Wednesday morning, as F.M. is to address us that evening.

6 July 1909
F.M. is to discourse on Finance on Friday. Debate led by Vaze on 'The Brahmans–Non-Brahmans'. Kaikini has returned.

11 July 1909
Admission in the morning of Messrs. Deole, Kunzru and Kaul . . .

16 August 1909
In the evening Mr G. [Gokhale] called us all together in his room & made a programme for each member.

8 September 1909
Some talk with Mr G. led to Mr Patwardhan's absence last night & Devadhar's frequent irregularities. At once they were sent for and rated in my presence. I feared it might lead to unpleasantness, but, thank God, both took it well.

From Sastri's diary, we find that Majli, one of the probationers, overstayed his leave and was reported to the First Member. He was

[2] NMML.

pulled up and he apologized, but resigned after a month. Sastri himself was upbraided by Gokhale for leniency to other members. Even Devadhar and Patwardhan, two of the founder members of the Society, were occasionally on the mat. The fact is that the standard of performance and discipline was much too exacting for some of the young men. Majli left in August 1909 and so did Deshpande. Another member, J. Krishna Rao, was weaned away by his father and father-in-law. A Muslim member, Syed Haider Hussain, who had joined the Society, found its discipline much too rigorous, resigned, and took a government job in Bihar.

On 12 July 1909 Sastri noted in his diary that the First Member wanted 'to give our little arrangements a stiff formal character. Needs Committee, Library Committee, General Advice Committee! I am to be convener of the two latter, & have two Proceedings Books.' Two days later, Gokhale wrote to Principal Paranjpye, requesting him to allow one of the newest members, H. N. Kunzru, to attend Professor Kale's lectures on economics in the Fergusson College.

In the Poona Home of the Society, the programme included debates in some of which Gokhale himself participated. Among the subjects debated were the 'Political Creed of the Servants of India Society', the 'Practicability of the Colonial Swaraj', the 'Principles of Social Reform', 'Native States', the 'Merits of a Congress Session in London', the 'Indian Police', 'Race Prejudice'. Occasionally, Gokhale delivered lectures on such subjects as 'Indian Finance as it is and as it should be', 'Our Work' and the 'Drain Theory'.

It was Gokhale's ambition to train these young men in the habits of ascetic simplicity, intellectual curiosity, methodical work and discipline, such as he had himself acquired at Ranade's feet. On 1 October 1910 Gokhale sent his disciples to Versova on the western coast to pay their respects to Dadabhai Naoroji. This was a 'pilgrimage' to instil in them love of the country and reverence for its great leaders. Gokhale insisted that no member of the Society under training should deliver a lecture or write an article without obtaining his approval. He knew the harm done by half-baked opinions of young hotheads. While he was away from India, he shuddered to think of the consequences of an indiscreet word or action on the part of any Servant of India. In 1908, when there was an outburst of terrorism in India, he wrote from London: 'It is most necessary that every one of the members [of the Society] should realize fully a special responsibility resting on us all. Tell Deodhar that he should keep his own enthusiasm & that of his two colleagues under the control of sound judgment.'[3]

The Servants of India were engaged in a variety of political and social activities: organizational work for the Indian National Congress, journalism, education and social reform. In Poona the Society ran *Dnyanaprakash*, which was edited by Patwardhan. Later it acquired *Hitavada* of Nagpur and the *Hindustan* of Lucknow. The Society received calls for help in emergencies of all kinds. In 1907, it helped organize a campaign against plague in Poona. Devadhar acted as the secretary of the Plague Relief Committee. In 1908–9, after the adoption of the new Congress constitution at Allahabad, the members of the Society were called upon to help in forming district Congress committees. Their assistance was sought for making arrangements for the annual Congress sessions. They collected funds for the British Committee of the Congress in London and subscriptions for its journal, *India*. When Wedderburn's biography of A. O. Hume, published soon after the death of the 'Father of the Congress', found few buyers, the Servants of India were called upon to push the sales. When Gokhale launched his Education Bill, some of the 'Servants' toured the country to mobilize public support for compulsory and free elementary education.

The Society had acquired a high standing in the country, but the responsibility of running it (the annual expenditure had gone up to Rs 40,000) had been a heavy burden on Gokhale. There were occasions when the Society ran out of funds and Gokhale had to request friends for contributions to keep it going. His failing health added to his concern about the future of the Society. As early as 1909 we find Srinivasa Sastri conveying Gokhale's anxiety to one of Gokhale's best friends.

Srinivasa Sastri to Krishnaswami Aiyer, 22 June 1909: . . . An eminent English doctor has told him that diabetes goes smoothly for some years, but once it takes a wrong turn—may gallop & finish the patient in a short time. . . .

He asks me what will happen to the Society after him, & whether it will turn out that he has been too bold to start it. 'I will do all I can while I live; but you get Krishnaswami to take it up after me, will you?'

One great cause of his condition is the embarrassment of our finance. The Press has been mismanaged all this time & though nothing is beyond repair, I fear we are very much to the worse.

[3] Gokhale to Patwardhan, 26 June 1908 (G.P.).

Matters have been nearly put right, but at what cost to the health & peace of mind of Mr. G. [Gokhale], I may best describe by saying that he once said he realized the condition of those that commit suicide.[4]

The government's attitude to the Servants of India Society varied from the contemptuous to the critical. As we have already seen, the immediate reactions to its formation from the Viceroy downwards were far from cordial. A. T. Arundel, the Home Member, predicted that, despite initial enthusiasm during the lifetime of its founder, the Society would be wrecked by internal disputes, especially about money.[5] 'If this Society survives and is widely patronized', Curzon wrote on 18 July 1905, 'it may turn out to be a very formidable organization exclusively devoted to political ends and only imperfectly masked under the assumption of loyalty to British rule.'[6]

With such official preconceptions, it was only natural that the 'Servants of India' should have been subjected to police surveillance, even when they were engaged in such innocent activities as famine relief. In one of his speeches in the Imperial Council, Gokhale mentioned an incident in which a police detective not only trailed a Servant of India in the United Provinces, but insisted on 'sitting in the coach box of the hackney carriage engaged by him [the Servant of India] for going about'.[7] In 1911, Srinivasa Sastri, who was in charge of the Madras Branch, fell foul of the Dewan of Mysore and was told in no uncertain terms that the Society was regarded as disloyal by the State.[8]

With the political *détente* in the viceroyalty of Hardinge, official hostility to the Society somewhat softened. Guy Fleetwood Wilson, the Finance Member, visited Poona and saw the Society at work.

The College buildings [he wrote] are of a superior character, the library is of the very first class and all the arrangements appeared to have been well thought out from every standpoint, including sanitation. The members number fifteen, and the permanent assistants five, making twenty-one in all, including Mr Gokhale. All the men I saw, who seemed to be between 20 and 30 years of age, impressed me most favourably. They had frank, open countenances, seemed quite at their ease, spoke with perfect freedom, and were altogether as nice as I should wish to meet anywhere.[9]

[4] V. S. S. Sastri P.
[5] Home Pub. Dep. No. 48, July 1905 (NAI).   [6] Ibid.
[7] Karve & Ambekar, op. cit., vol. II, p. 112.
[8] T. N. Jagadisan (ed.), *Letters of the Right Honourable V. S. Srinivasa Sastri*, Bombay, 1963, p. 34.
[9] G. F. Wilson, *Letters to Nobody 1908–1913*, London, 1921, p. 75.

Fleetwood Wilson had long conversations with the members individually and with Gokhale, but confessed that he could not get a clear idea of what the 'ulterior object' of the Society was. Fleetwood Wilson's difficulty stemmed from his own ambivalence. Like many of his other countrymen in India, he could admire Gokhale, tolerate and even appreciate his work for intellectual elevation and social reform, but became instantly suspicious of any leader or organization professing to train 'political missionaries'.

When its members were in residence at Poona under Gokhale's benign eye, the Servants of India Society resembled a political academy with a course of instruction in history, economics, public finance, law and journalism. Such an organization may have been redundant in a western country with long-established political institutions, but it had a useful role in India. The Society was, however, very different from the *ashrams* which Gandhi had set up at Phoenix and Tolstoy Farm in South Africa, and was to set up at Sabarmati and Sevagram. The *ashrams* of the Mahatma (who was training *satyagrahis* and not parliamentarians) emphasized ascetic simplicity and moral discipline rather than intellectual development and political culture. Even while he was in South Africa, Gandhi had been repelled by the academic and highbrow orientation of Gokhale's Society; he feared it would get out of touch with the realities of Indian life. Gandhi's misgivings grew after Henry Polak's visit to India in 1909–10. While still in South Africa, Gandhi seems to have had an uneasy feeling that he might not fit into the Servants of India Society when he returned to India.

Gandhi to Gokhale, 27 February 1914: If there is a settlement in March, I propose to leave for India in April. I shall have with me probably about 20 men, women and children who will live with me. These will include the schoolchildren who are likely to come. I do not know whether you will want me to live at the Servants of India Society quarters in Poona or how.... I am entirely in your hands. I want to live at your feet and gain the necessary experience....

My present ambition you know. It is to be by your side as your nurse and attendant. I want to have the real discipline of obeying someone whom I love and look up to.[10]

In the autumn of 1912, when Gandhi and Gokhale had envisaged that the former would join the Servants of India Society, both were aware of the intellectual gulf between them, but they hoped to bridge

---

[10] *Collected Works of Mahatma Gandhi*, vol. XII, pp. 360–6.

it with mutual affection and trust in each other. As soon as the settlement of the South African issue was in sight, Gandhi placed his services at Gokhale's disposal. But it was not until 9 January 1915 that Gandhi actually returned to India. Three days later, there was a party in Bombay in his honour at the residence of Jehangir Petit. Gandhi did not announce his future programme, but disclosed that he would be guided by 'his guru', the 'Hon'ble Mr Gokhale'. Gandhi had already promised Gokhale that for the first twelve months in India he would 'keep his ears open and his mouth shut'.

A few days' stay in Poona brought it home to Gandhi that Gokhale's enthusiasm for his admission to the Servants of India Society was not shared by most of its members, who feared that there was too great a divergence between Gandhi's ideals and methods and those to which the Society was pledged. As the decision on his admission was likely to take time, Gandhi planned a visit to Rajkot, Porbandar and Santiniketan. On 14 January 1915 there was a farewell party in Gandhi's honour in the Society's premises. Only fruits and nuts were served. Gokhale was not feeling well, but insisted on attending the party and fainted. He did not have long to live.

3

When the First World War broke out in 1914 few people could have foreseen that it would last for four years. Indeed, the common belief was that it would all be over by the end of the year. It was, however, obvious that things would never be the same again and Indo-British relations would have to be readjusted. Shrewd British administrators were already applying their minds to post-war problems. Lord Willingdon, the Governor of Bombay, requested Gokhale to suggest constitutional reforms which he considered essential and immediately practicable.

Willingdon to Gokhale, 26 January 1915: Many thanks for your letter. ... By all means let the matter wait until next month [when] we can discuss. I have told the Viceroy that you were going to prepare some notes of your views for me. He expressed a great desire to see them. If you don't object, I should very much like to send them to him.

In the meantime, I hope you will have a talk with Aga Khan. He is most interesting on his experiences & would I think be an assistance to you. ... [11]

[11] G.P.

Before he set down his views on paper, Gokhale wanted to consult not only the Aga Khan, but also Pherozeshah Mehta who was still one of the best-respected leaders of the Indian National Congress. It was not easy for the three to meet. Gokhale was too ill to leave Poona, the Aga Khan had his own preoccupations, and the ageing Pherozeshah Mehta was himself not very mobile. As Willingdon seemed to be in a hurry, Gokhale decided, on 17 February, to prepare a rough draft of a scheme which could become the basis for further discussion with Pherozeshah and the Aga Khan.

The draft,[12] which Gokhale pencilled two days before his death, envisaged provincial autonomy for the provinces. The Governor of each province was to be assisted by an Executive Council consisting of three Indians and three Europeans. Each province was to have a legislature consisting of 75 to 100 members, of whom 80 per cent were to be elected. While all laws—and the budget—were to pass through provincial legislature, the Governor retained the right of veto, and the members of his Executive Council did not require the support of the majority in the legislature to remain in office. Wider powers for taxation and borrowing were, however, to be given to the provincial governments. The Legislative Council at the centre was to be enlarged, and to have more powers, but the principle of an official (or rather nominated) majority was to be maintained. If a provincial legislature declined to enact laws which the government regarded essential in the vital interests of the province, they could be passed by the central legislature over the head of the provincial legislature. Such occasions were, however, expected to be few; this provision was obviously inserted to reassure the authorities and to overcome their reluctance to concede provincial autonomy. The Government of India was to be largely freed from the control of the Secretary of State for India—especially in fiscal matters. The India Council in London, it was proposed, would be abolished, and the position of the Secretary of State for India was to approximate as far as possible that of the Secretary of State for the Colonies.

These constitutional changes, which Gokhale outlined in his draft, have been called his 'political testament'. They were nothing of the kind. Gokhale was not framing the outline of a model constitution for India. He was not defining the political goal of nationalist India, nor even writing an article for a newspaper. He was simply spelling out, at the request of the Bombay Governor, a scheme which could

[12] G.P.

be expected to run the gauntlet of the provincial governments, the Government of India and the British Parliament, be acceptable to the British Government and yet satisfy political India in 1915. The scheme was modest enough, but British opinion was not ready for more liberal measures. Having only recently spent several months in England with the Royal Commission on the Public Services, Gokhale knew the obstacles in the way of any radical change. In 1914, the House of Lords had even rejected Lord Crewe's modest bill for indirect election of the Indian members to the India Council, and the House of Commons had turned down an innocuous proposal for an Executive Council to assist the Lt-Governor of the United Provinces. Early in 1915, Indian politics were quiescent, and the course of the war and the ferment it would generate could hardly be predicted. Nevertheless, it is a remarkable fact that this draft on post-war reforms, hurriedly pencilled by Gokhale in February 1915, already anticipated the tenor of the Montagu–Chelmsford Reforms, which the British government was to concede four years later, after its hands had been practically forced by the cumulative pressure of political and economic discontent created by the war and its aftermath.

4

The drafting of the outline of constitutional reforms on 17 February must have required a great effort of will-power on Gokhale's part. His health was badly shattered even when he had landed at Bombay in November 1914. Cardiac asthma, aggravated by his seventeen year-old diabetes, the tedium and tension of the long sittings on the Royal Commission and the English winter had played havoc with his constitution. He may well have looked forward to some quiet and rest at Poona, but soon after his return, he was drawn into the acrimonious parleys on the re-admission of the Extremists to the Congress. 'The fact is', Gokhale wrote to N. Subba Rao, the Secretary of the Indian National Congress, 'I have taken out of my system during the last week more than my system could stand.' Gokhale had indeed been making a heavy overdraft on his physical and mental reserves for a long time, and had little reserve strength. During the summer of 1914, when he was in England, his condition had been a source of constant anxiety to his friends. Even visits to Vichy for rest and cure had ceased to work the wonders they had done in previous years. He continually suffered from attacks of 'suffocation' at night. From 13 February these attacks recurred during daytime, and his condition grew worse. On Friday, 19 February, his condition became critical. That afternoon he said with a smile, 'I have been seeing the fun on this side so long, now let me go and see it on the other.' The end came at 10.25 p.m.

Two hours earlier he had taken leave of those of his faithful Servants of India who were in Poona. To Anantrao Patwardhan, the keeper of the Aryabhushan Press, he said: 'I have often scolded you. Please tell me before I die that you have forgiven me.' He gave instructions for the formation of a 'trust' (out of the royalties accruing from his arithmetic book) and its utilization for the education of his daughters and the children of the Servants of India. He bade farewell to his daughters, and to his friends Bijapurkar, Paranjpye and others. 'He did all this', Dr Deva wrote, 'as if it was an ordinary affair and that he happened to be changing his present abode for another. . . . He was conscious to the last. . . . In my practice extending to over twenty-four years I have never seen a man die as peacefully as that.'[13]

[13] Deva's Note, 27 Feb. 1915, circulated to Wedderburn & others (G.P.).

42

'The Greatest Indian'

'Mr Gokhale was the greatest leader that India has ever produced,' wrote the *Statesman* on 21 February 1915, 'perhaps her greatest man.'[1] A few days later, at a memorial meeting in London, Sir Krishna Gupta, a member of the India Council, referred to Gokhale as the greatest Indian of his time. Obituaries and memorial tributes often need to be discounted, but there is no doubt that at the time of his death, and indeed for nearly a decade before it, Gokhale occupied a unique place in the public life of India. 'You know', Mrs Besant had pleaded with him in 1914, 'that India cannot spare you and a month or two of rest may mean years of work.'[2] 'You must remember', wrote Rabindranath Tagore in December 1913, 'that for a man like you to live is in itself a service to your country—for your life is not merely useful, it is a light to others.'[3] In November 1913, when her own life hung precariously in the balance, the poetess Sarojini Naidu sent 'a message of love and gratitude' to Gokhale: 'You have been a beacon light of hope to the young generation.'[4] She was reflecting the feelings of many others, of Motilal Nehru, Tej Bahadur Sapru, C. Y. Chintamani, M. R. Jayakar, M. A. Jinnah and, above all of M. K. Gandhi of South African fame, who was to mourn Gokhale's death by walking barefoot for a year.

It was no mean achievement for a man who had started life without the advantages of birth or fortune to have attained such pre-eminence. Gokhale had forged his way to the forefront of Indian politics by 1902, but from 1905, when he presided over the Benares Congress, until his death in 1915, he was, to use the expressive phrase of Mohammed Ali (the future Khilafat leader), the 'First Moderate'.[5]

Gokhale owed his rise primarily to his own outstanding ability,

---

[1] *Statesman*, 21 Feb. 1915.
[2] A. Besant to Gokhale, 12 May 1914 (G.P.).
[3] R. Tagore to Gokhale, 9 Dec. 1913 (G.P.).
[4] S. Naidu to Gokhale, 28 Nov. 1913 (G.P.).
[5] A. Iqbal (ed.), *Select Writings and Speeches of Maulana Mohammed Ali*, Lahore, 1944, p. 6.

industry and public spirit. His ambition to excel in everything he attempted, whether it was a college examination, a magazine article, a public speech or a game of billiards, had turned him early in life into an assiduous student of politics. He was lucky enough to serve his political apprenticeship under Ranade, who instructed him in the principles of a humane, liberal and secular nationalism, besides giving him a thorough grounding in Indian politics and economics. To be Ranade's protégé was an obvious asset. The Bombay Moderates, led by Ranade's friend, Pherozeshah Mehta, who disliked and distrusted Tilak, were glad to find in Gokhale an able Maharashtrian politician who could act as a counterweight to Tilak. Gokhale owed his election to the Imperial Legislative Council—which proved to be a turning-point in his political career—largely to the support he received from Pherozeshah Mehta. Again, it was Wedderburn—another friend and admirer of Ranade—who helped Gokhale shape into a successful unofficial envoy of his country to England. Wedderburn initiated Gokhale into the mysteries of British politics and introduced him to ministers, politicians, editors and officials in London who were concerned with Indian affairs. Gokhale shed his early shyness and diffidence and learnt to be at home in England, addressing public meetings in London and the provinces, briefing friends of India in Parliament, crossing swords with Anglo-Indian officials and interviewing British ministers in Whitehall.

The clarity, conviction and courage with which he spoke up for his country raised Gokhale's stock with the Indian educated classes. What impressed them was not the 'moderation', but the sharpness of Gokhale's indictment of the policies of the government. The fact that this indictment rested on carefully marshalled facts and arguments made it all the more powerful. As they read or heard Gokhale, educated Indians felt that he was articulating their own inmost thoughts and aspirations. They also saw in Gokhale an embodiment of personal sacrifice and dedication, which they admired, but could not bring themselves to emulate.

Gokhale vowed himself to voluntary poverty for life, first as a member of the Deccan Education Society, and then as the First Member of the Servants of India Society. He viewed politics not as the pursuit of power or influence on behalf of individuals or groups, but as a lever for the regeneration of his country. This idealistic conception of politics seemed to fit in with the needs of a subject race struggling to be free; it did not sound hypocritical when it was expounded by a man whose words never went beyond his deeds. Gokhale saw how well trained and organized the British bureaucracy in India was; he saw what little chance there was of challenging its monopoly of power without enlisting an equivalent measure of talent, training and discipline in the nationalist ranks. This was why he set out to build a cadre of 'political missionaries' through the Servants of India Society.

In India, more than perhaps in any other country, a charisma tends to grow around a public figure who is seen to be utterly selfless. Gokhale's call for renunciation struck answering chords among his countrymen. Not only did he live a simple and austere life, but in the long years of negotiation and discussion preceding the Minto–Morley reforms, he never sought the slightest advantage for himself. He was remarkably free even from that occupational disease of politicians—vanity and self-advertisement. When it was suggested to him during his visit to Madras in 1907 that he should lay the foundation-stone of a new building, Gokhale protested that he deserved no such honour, that too much was made of the too little done by public figures in India, and that men like him had 'to think of the vast work that lies in front of them compared with what little they may have been privileged to attempt'.[6]

It was this extraordinary self-effacement which led R. P. Paranjpye to remark that Gokhale's 'patriotism was pure gold with no element of dross in it'.[7] Lovat Fraser, the editor of the *Times of India*, who was no friend of Gokhale, but saw something of him in London during his last years, noted that he had 'in his heart spiritual hunger. From his youth he was vowed to poverty, and when one met him clad in silk hat and frock-coat in the lobby of the House of Commons, one knew that he secretly loathed these trappings. His mild and gentle eyes shone with the light of soaring thoughts, and only his love of country kept him to his self-appointed path.'[8] The dinner tables of London—in the words of Cobden—may have had their 'insidious attractions for the simple-minded',[9] but they failed to seduce Gokhale. Till the last he continued to fight tenaciously for a better future for his country. And till the last he remained the *bête noire* of successive Viceroys, and high officials in Calcutta, Simla and London.

[6] Gokhale to G. A. Natesan, 18 July 1907 (G.P.).
[7] *Servant of India*, 25 Feb. 1937.
[8] *The National Review*, 1915, pp. 310–11.
[9] Thornton, op. cit., p. 255.

2

It was not only the British bureaucracy which questioned Gokhale's bona fides. In Maharashtra, and especially in Poona, he was often maligned by his political opponents as a traitor or a coward. It was all part of a political vendetta which stemmed from personal rather than ideological animosities. In this vendetta Gokhale—like his mentors Agarkar and Ranade before him—was generally at a disadvantage. His antagonist, Tilak, with the halo of recurrent imprisonments in British jails, and as the reputed defender of the Hindu faith and orthodoxy, enjoyed a charismatic appeal in Maharashtra which Gokhale and his fellow-Moderates, with their constitutional methods and secular philosophy, could never attain. In the Marathi press, there was a continual sniping at Gokhale; he was lampooned by cartoonists, and vilified in malicious verses sung in the Ganapati festival processions in Poona. For this smear-campaign, Tilak may not have been directly responsible, but he does not seem to have done very much to stop it. Between the rival parties in Poona—the Moderates and the Extremists—it was almost a thirty years' war, sometimes 'cold', sometimes 'hot', which was to end (and even then not completely) only with Gokhale's death in 1915. While Gokhale's body was being consigned to the flames on the afternoon of 20 February, Tilak paid a magnificent public tribute to Gokhale,[10] but the Extremist bitterness towards Gokhale may be glimpsed from the entry in the diary of G. S. Khaparde (a friend and follower of Tilak), on the same day: 'In the Bar Room I heard that Gopal Krishna Gokhale died yesterday night. I am sorry he did not live long enough to endure the consequences of his double-dealing and roguery.'[11]

The tragedy of Gokhale, as his friend, K. Natarajan of *Indian Social Reformer*, graphically described it, was that 'a proud and sensitive spirit was forced by the stress of self-imposed duties to expose itself to frequent galling wounds'.[12] Gokhale shed some of his hypersensitivity after the terrible ordeal of the 'apology incident' in 1897, but he never developed a thick enough skin. He would have suffered less if he had not thought of politics as a game to be played according to the rules of Westminster. He would have suffered less if he had

---

[10] 'This diamond of India, this jewel of Maharashtra, this prince of workers, is taking eternal rest on the funeral grounds. Look at him and try to emulate him.'

[11] Khaparde Diary, 20 Feb. 1915.

[12] *Indian Social Reformer*, 21 Feb. 1915.

possessed the stoicism of his master, Ranade, the nonchalance of his rival, Tilak, or the egotism of his eminent contemporary, Pherozeshah Mehta.

As it was, the never-ceasing duel with his political opponents in Poona was a great strain on Gokhale's dwindling reserves of physical and nervous energy. Indeed, had it not been for his election to the chairmanship of the municipality of Poona, he would have left Poona for good and settled in Bombay in 1902. Fortunately, after his election to the Imperial Council, he had ceased to be a man of Poona or of Bombay. His influence extended beyond the bounds of the Deccan and western India; he came to be respected as much in Calcutta and Madras as in Lahore and Allahabad. No other Indian politician of the time, with the possible exception of Dadabhai Naoroji at the turn of the century, commanded such high prestige among the Indian élite outside his own province. The fact is that most Congress leaders were bogged down in local politics and controversies: this was as true of Pherozeshah Mehta and D. E. Wacha in Bombay as of B. G. Tilak in Maharashtra, Surendranath Banerjea and B. C. Pal in Bengal, G. S. Khaparde and R. N. Mudholkar in Berar, and Lajpat Rai in the Punjab. Gokhale, who had outgrown regional and sectarian loyalties early in his life but had failed to strike strong roots in his home region, Maharashtra, was well suited for a role on the national stage.

It was characteristic of Gokhale that in Bombay his best friends and hosts were not Maharashtrian Brahmans, but Gujarati and Parsi families, and that the two 'trustees' he nominated to look after his daughters after his death were both Gujaratis. His Servants of India were recruited from different provinces; his successor, Srinivasa Sastri, was a South Indian. He was one of the few Congress leaders who continued to carry some weight with the Muslim community. And despite the nagging official suspicion of his motives, the more far-sighted Englishmen learnt to recognize in him a bridge-builder between India and Britain. 'The most statesmanlike mind I have known', was the verdict of H. W. Nevinson, the well-travelled correspondent of *Manchester Guardian*.[13] To Sir Henry Cotton, a former Chief Commissioner of Assam and a member of the British Committee of the Congress, Gokhale seemed 'an ideal interpreter between India and England'.[14] G. P. Gooch, the British historian and Liberal

[13] *Indian Review*, March 1915, p. 207.
[14] *India*, 12 March 1915.

member of Parliament, who had an opportunity of coming into contact with 'almost all the leading performers on the Indian stage' before and after the First World War, records in his memoirs that he was most impressed by Gokhale in whom he saw 'not only a great Indian, but a citizen of the world'.[15]

3

Gokhale had begun his life as a teacher; he loved English literature and especially English poetry. He had in some ways the approach of a scholar to politics. His speeches and conversation had a fine literary flavour, but it would be wrong to think of him as an intellectual who had strayed into public life. Even though he was conscientious about his teaching chores, his heart was always in politics, with all their excitement and heartache. Neither academic laurels nor the seductions of authorship could divert him from his self-imposed tasks in public life. He declined to serve as principal of the Fergusson College, and even his project of writing a biography of Ranade had to give way to the urgent claims of public duties. With his increasing immersion in politics, Gokhale gave up physical exercise and the hobbies of his youth. Politics became a constant preoccupation, almost an obsession with him. He had little time for personal affairs. His two motherless daughters—who lived not far from the Home of the Servants of India Society—saw little of him. No wonder he should have found it impossible to take even the first yoga lessons on the concentration of the mind. 'Directly he set himself to the task,' a friend recalled, 'visions of blue books and government resolutions appeared before him to distract his attention.'[16]

Gokhale's consuming interest in politics stemmed from his passionate patriotism. He hated foreign rule, but he did not blame all the ills from which India suffered on the British. He wanted her to shake off the shackles of social and economic backwardness as well as of political subjection. He wanted to turn the encounter with the Raj into an opportunity for building a secular, modern and democratic society. The task was formidable. 'I sometimes think', he wrote, 'that no country in the world has been called upon to face such a problem as ours.' The inculcation of discipline and team-work

[15] Gooch, op. cit., p. 128.
[16] V. G. Apte *in* 'Reminiscences of Hon. Mr. Gokhale', *Modern Review*, April 1915, p. 502.

seemed to him essential prerequisites for a healthy political life. 'Our public life is weak', he observed, 'because our public spirit is weak.'[17] And public spirit required the subordination of individual gain and convenience to the collective good.

'We are most of us in India . . .', Gokhale said, 'a somewhat dreamy race. . . . Dreams have their importance in shaping aspirations for the future, but in practical matters, we have to be practical men.'[18] He called for honest, unremitting application to the work in hand. It was characteristic of him that he should have advised the young graduates of Bombay, aspiring to enter public life, to make a beginning by cleaning the dust from the books of the Royal Asiatic Society Library.[19]

Gokhale's political ideals were the ideals of the founding fathers of the Congress. The chief formative influence in his life was, of course, Ranade, who, in turn, had been inspired by the example of Dadabhai Naoroji. Gokhale used to describe himself 'as an intellectual grandson of Dadabhai Naoroji'.[20] There was a striking unanimity among the early leaders of the Congress in their approach to politics. Gokhale's own contribution to (what may be called) the Moderate Congress ideology was to impart to it greater clarity, coherence and sophistication.[21] He was no defender of the *status quo* in the political, social or economic sphere. Nor did he idealize the masses; in accordance with the liberal thought of the time, he considered literacy as a *sine qua non* for an intelligent interest in politics. If he assumed that there would be no franchise for the illiterate masses in his country, it was not for all time. Indeed, one of the avowed objects of his campaign for free and compulsory education was to bring the mass of the Indian people more effectively into the

---

[17] G. K. Gokhale, *Public Life in India, Its Needs and Responsibilities,* Bombay, 1922, p. 10.

[18] *Report of the Proc. of the Twenty-third Session of the Indian National Congress held at Madras on 28, 29 and 30 Dec. 1908,* Madras, 1909, p. 138.

[19] Limaye (ed.), op. cit., pts. II & III, pp. 160–1.

[20] P. C. Ray, *Autobiography of an Indian Chemist,* Calcutta, 1958, p. 100.

[21] 'Till that sober and patient politician, Mr Gokhale, formulated his idea of expansion within the Empire, there were in evidence in the Congress camp only crude, undefined and often conflicting aspirations. The fluent but the unsubstantial pathos of Mr Banerji's long drawn eloquence, the vehement and senile insistence of Mr Dadabhai Naoroji's denunciations, and Sir Pherozeshah's spicy oratory, coupled even with the thousand-and-one resolutions of twenty sessions of the Congress, failed to give one a clear idea of what was needed as a general remedy, though they created a vague sense of universal suffering and made audible the resonance of more or less unmusical sounds where all spoke and few cared to hear.' (Mohammed Ali in 1907, quoted in *Selected Writings and Speeches of Maulana Mohammed Ali,* Lahore, 1944, p. 6.)

mainstream of national life. That he should have always felt an affinity with the unprivileged millions among his countrymen is not surprising; he had himself sprung from them. In his youth, he had known the pinch of poverty, and all his adult life he had lived simply, almost austerely. 'The sadness of an Indian village', wrote one of his British colleagues on the Public Services Commission, 'was never very far from him.'[22]

4

Gokhale's exposition of the nationalist case was almost invariably a notable achievement and occasionally a triumph. But the same cannot be said of his management of men and events. In the Indian National Congress, he never tried to organize a personal following: even when his prestige was at its peak, he commanded more respect than authority. The result was that at crucial moments, such as at the Surat Congress in December 1907, he could exercise only a limited influence on the course of events. During the same year, when communal disturbances occurred in East Bengal, he hastened to Calcutta and stayed there for a fortnight, but his role was no more than that of a distressed observer. Two years later, on the crucial issue of separate electorates, he was completely outplayed by the Aga Khan–Ameer Ali group. If the South African crisis of 1913–14 had a happier ending, the credit for it was largely due to Gandhi.

As a politician, Gokhale seems to have suffered from the defects of his virtues. His complete freedom from racism, communalism and casteism predisposed him to underrate the strength of these dark forces in others. His instinctive aversion to acrimonious controversy, his extreme sensitivity to criticism and his natural disinclination to hit back at his enemies often placed him at a disadvantage. His lofty ideal of 'spiritualizing' politics was practicable only in small groups; it enabled him to kindle the pure flame of patriotism in some of the finest young men and women who came under his spell, but it could not protect him against the savage assaults of his political opponents or the calculated stratagems of the hard-headed guardians of the Raj. His faith in the virtues of rationality and moderation may have been admirable, but it was a fallible guide in a world largely swayed by irrationality and expedience. Gokhale, however, shared

[22] H. A. L. Fisher in *The Nation*, 27 Feb. 1915.

this faith with most of his great contemporaries among the Moderates. To assess his achievements and limitations it is essential to see him in the context of the Moderate era, which was more or less conterminous with his own political career.

43

The End of an Era

Within nine months of Gokhale's death, the Moderates suffered another shattering blow. Pherozeshah Mehta died on 5 November 1915. Most of the Congress veterans were dead or dying. Telang, Ranade, Bonnerjee, Badruddin Tyabji, R. C. Dutt, Ananda Charlu, Anand Mohan Bose and A. O. Hume had already gone. Old Dadabhai Naoroji, living in retirement near Bombay, lingered on awhile, and Wedderburn gallantly carried on the work of the British Committee of the Congress until his death in 1918. But the Moderate era had really ended.

The Moderates had taken India half-way to freedom, but circumstances conspired to deprive them of the credit for it. The sudden radical turn which nationalist politics took, first in the wake of the partition of Bengal, and then with the advent of Gandhi on the political scene, helped to foster the myth that the Moderates were political 'mendicants', woolly-headed and weak-kneed politicians who only petitioned and prayed to the British for petty concessions, instead of demanding *swaraj* (self-government). To this myth was added another. The Moderates came to be denigrated as representatives of a small, urban, educated minority which had been fighting for its own class interests.

These myths were the more readily accepted because later generations found it difficult to visualize the heavy odds against which the founders of the Indian National Congress had to contend. The evolution of an Indian nationality was not so simple or inevitable a phenomenon as it may seem today. But for the skill and tenacity of a few able and outstanding men, Indians and Britons, it might have been delayed, if not halted altogether. True, by the middle of the nineteenth century, the Bengalis had taken to British administration, the Parsis and Gujaratis to British commerce, and the Punjabis to the British–Indian army, but the task of fusing these diverse elements in a common mould was a formidable one. The intellectual ferment created by the contact with the West, the common administrative structure imposed by the British and the social and economic pressures of a colonial economy were all impelling different communities and regions of the sub-continent into closer contact—or collision. However, Indian unity was the cherished aspiration of only a tiny minority which dared to think and look ahead. Most Indians, even educated Indians, habitually thought in terms of their castes and localities; their rulers would have liked them to continue to do so.

In retrospect, the foundation of the Indian National Congress in 1885 and its survival into the twentieth century appear to be miracles. But for the energy, perseverance and shrewdness of A. O. Hume, it may have been difficult to provide a common channel for incipient Indian nationalism, and to protect it in those early years against erosion from within and without. For the next thirty years no Congressman could mention Hume without deep emotion. Hume had the courage (as Bhupendranath Basu told the Bankipore Congress in 1912)

to conceive and carry out what great Emperors and Empires in the past had failed to do. He conceived the great idea of binding together the different people and nationalities and communities and creeds of India into one common nation. . . . Who do you think had the power in the early days of the eighties, to bring together men unknown to each other, from Bombay, from Madras, from the Punjab, from Bengal, from the United Provinces?[1]

2

Once they came together, Congressmen from different parts of the sub-continent did not take long in developing a broad identity of outlook. Their vision of India's future was shaped not only by their image of her past, but of the past of England. It seemed to them that after centuries of political disunity, social stagnation and economic backwardness, India had, at last, an opportunity of imbibing from the West the spirit of progress and reform, and of winning her due place in the comity of nations. In this great adventure they looked forward to guidance and support from the English people, 'a nation, not only one of the greatest on earth, but also one of the most progressive'.[2] They viewed English history as the continual unfolding

[1] *Report of the Proc. of the Twenty-seventh Indian National Congress held at Bankipore on the 26, 27 and 28 Dec., 1912*, p. 50.
[2] R. C. Dutt, *England and India*, London, 1897, p. 121, quoted in *India*, Dec. 1897.

of constitutional liberty and individual freedom broadening from precedent to precedent—a theory popularized by Whig historians, especially Macaulay. If the founders of the Congress did not have this theory ready-made in their textbooks on British history, they would have had to invent it. For they needed it badly when, soon after the foundation of the Congress, it became obvious that the guardians of the British Raj in India looked askance at it.

These British officials were appalled, when they were not amused, by the suggestion that representative institutions evolved over several centuries in England should be transplanted to India. The suggestion seemed as absurd as the idea of an elephant feeling at home in the Scottish mists, or a banyan tree growing in London's Parliament Street. To most Britons in India, men like Hume and Wedderburn were, at best, cranks and, at worst, traitors. Congress leaders like Dadabhai Naoroji, W. C. Bonnerjee, Ranade and Pherozeshah Mehta struck the official world as irresponsible fire-brands or scheming politicians out to undermine the Raj. The resolutions passed by the Congress at its annual sessions did not appear as innocuous to the government as they may strike us today. The demand for holding the entrance examination to the I.C.S. simultaneously in India and in England, and for the grant of commissions to Indians in the army directly threatened the British monopoly of higher ranks of civil and military services. The separation of the judicial from executive functions was seen as an attempt to weaken the authority of the district officer—the king-pin of the administration. The call for larger and more powerful legislative councils was seen as an inroad into the functions of the Government of India and the British Parliament. The insistence on a lower duty on salt, a higher minimum for income tax, and the repeal of Arms Act seemed sheer political demagogy. The demands for the enforcement of prohibition, a ban on prostitution and police reform may have seemed innocent, but even their acceptance was not without its hazards to the prestige of the government. 'For a century', a former British Cabinet Minister warned in 1892, 'the Englishman has behaved in India as a demi-god. . . . Any weakening of this confidence in the minds of the English or of the Indians would be dangerous.'[3] Twenty years later, a senior British official, after the experience of a lifetime in India, wrote in the same vein, reminding his countrymen that their 'rule in India rested not so much upon our strength, as upon prevailing ideas of our strength.

[3] V. G. Kiernan, *The Lords of Human Kind*, London, 1969, p. 55.

. . . For this reason a policy of concession, of compromise is exceedingly dangerous.'[4]

Within a couple of years of the founding of the Congress, it became obvious that the official hierarchy in India was implacably hostile to it, and that, if the Congress was to survive as a political body, it would have to appeal to the British public over the head of the Government of India. This necessitated not only the setting up of a branch of the Congress in London, but a careful modulation of Congress policies and propaganda which would carry conviction to the saner section of opinion in England. With a hostile administration in India and an unsympathetic Tory regime in England, it would have been foolish for the Congress to alarm its enemies unduly and to invite repression which it was in no position to resist. We may not doubt the sincerity of the Congress leaders' professions of loyalty to the Empire during these early years, but there was apparently a conscious effort to disarm British suspicions. Speaking at the Allahabad Congress in December 1888, K. T. Telang denied that the Congress was agitating for a democratic government: 'We have not asked for Parliamentary institutions which England has got after many centuries of discipline; we have not asked for the power of the purse; and we have not asked that the British Executive should be brought under subjection to us.'[5] A similar denial was made by Surendranath Banerjea in a speech in London in April 1890, when he affirmed that the Congress or the educated classes did not want democratic government. 'We do not think India is ripe for it yet,' said Banerjea, 'nor do we want Home Rule . . . we [only] press for the reform of the legislative councils which impose taxes and make the laws.'[6]

Such 'sweet reasonableness' was evidently intended to reassure English opinion. 'If we honestly expect the English nation will do its duty towards us', Dadabhai Naoroji had exhorted the Congress in 1886, 'we must prove ourselves worthy by showing that we are never unreasonable, never violent, never uncharitable. We must show that we are earnest, but temperate, cognizant of our rights, but respectful of those of others. . . .'[7]

This posture of studied moderation fitted in with the political

[4] B. Fuller, *Studies of Indian Life and Sentiment*, London, 1910, p. 347.
[5] C. L. Parekh, *Eminent Indians of Indian Politics*, Bombay, 1892, p. 275.
[6] Ibid., p. 96.
[7] Report of the Second Indian National Congress held at Calcutta on the 27, 28 & 30 Dec. 1886 (n.p., n.d.), p. 112.

conditions in the last quarter of the nineteenth century. It was bound to change when these conditions changed. For one thing, the appeals to the democratic conscience of England seemed to fall on deaf ears: the Congress went on passing virtually the same resolutions year after year. For another, the tensions generated in the last years of Curzon's viceroyalty affected the rank-and-file of the Congress. Even before the partition of Bengal forced its hands, the Congress leadership was being pushed towards a more purposeful and aggressive stance. The prospect of a general election and a Liberal victory in England in 1904–5 boosted the Congress morale. It was a sign of the times that when Gokhale arrived in England early in September 1905, he affirmed self-government to be the goal of the Congress.

3

The strategy of the Indian National Congress during the first twenty years of its life was well adapted not only to its equation with the British, but to the internal limitations and contradictions of Indian nationalism in its nascent stage. It was no small achievement for the Congress to have survived the long spell of Tory ascendancy in England and official displeasure in India. It was no small achievement that the Congress had belied the hope of Anglo-India that it would 'totter to its fall'.[8] By steering clear of the potentially disruptive issue of social reform, by rotating the venue of the annual sessions among the principal towns of the sub-continent, by choosing the Congress presidents in turn from different provinces and communities, and by evolving a well-understood ritual for its annual sessions and unwritten conventions for evolving a political consensus, the Congress had securely established its position as an all-India political body. At times public enthusiasm seemed to flag and the Congress ran short of funds. At times it was riven by personal and factional rivalries and differences, but—with the exception of the crisis of 1907—these differences were as a rule reconciled and a façade of unity maintained. It is true that the Congress was dominated by the numerically small urban educated class, especially lawyers, teachers and journalists, but it did not become the champion of a small privileged section. The Congress thought of itself as the brain and conscience of the people of India as a whole. Few of the Congress resolutions could fairly be attributed to the class or

[8] Curzon to Hamilton, 18 Nov. 1900 (C.P.).

sectional interests of those who attended or dominated its annual sessions. Such demands, as those for the reduction in land revenue and salt duty, an increase in the minimum level of income on which tax was leviable and the separation of the judiciary from the executive, were obviously in the interest of the common man. So was the demand for free and compulsory elementary education. There were few industrialists in the Congress in these years and the proposal for protection of indigenous industries could hardly be in the interests of the urban middle class, which would have had to pay higher prices for articles it consumed. True, there were a few issues—such as those of the extension of permanent settlement and the opposition to the Punjab Land Alienation Act—on which some Congress leaders seemed to favour the propertied classes; but these were rare exceptions which do not invalidate the generalization that the Congress did not become an instrument for the aggrandizement of any particular class or community.

The real weakness of the Congress in these early years lay not in its strategy or tactics—which were indeed well-adjusted to the political realities of the time—but in its failure to function as an effective political organization between its annual sessions. Efforts to put new life into the Congress had begun even before the partition of Bengal. The partition stirred the stagnant pools of Indian politics. The massive Liberal victory in Britain coincided with the end of Curzon's viceroyalty, which seemed to have been the darkest hour before the dawn.

1906 was the year of hope. The dream of the founders of the Congress—the Moderate dream—seemed on the point of realization. It was a dream in which Britain was seen as India's mentor. Slowly but steadily, the people of India were to be associated with the governance of their country; as they learnt to shoulder the responsibilities entrusted to them, more and more power was to devolve upon them until India acquired the status of a self-governing dominion within the British Empire. The Moderates looked upon the British Empire very much as we look upon the United Nations today. The British Empire seemed not only a guarantee of security in a world made increasingly insecure by the competing imperialisms of Germany, Russia and Japan, but also a valuable link with the western world for those cultural, technological and commercial interchanges which were essential to usher India into the twentieth century.

4

The decade 1905–1915 was ideal for the realization of the Moderate dream. Throughout this period, a Liberal Government was in power in Britain, and Indian politics were dominated by the Indian liberals, the Moderates. The Moderate leaders did all they could to create the 'right atmosphere' in India to enable the Liberal party in Britain to do something big for India: they fought and even expelled the Extremist faction from their ranks when its propaganda seemed likely to hurt the cause of reform. The Moderate dream, however, was not realized. The constitutional reforms were not only delayed, but doled out in pitifully small doses. One by one, the idols of the British Liberal party fell from the Moderate pedestal. The stark truth was that India hardly figured on the agenda of the Liberal party in 1905. Neither its leadership nor its rank-and-file wanted a radical change in India. John Morley's initial doubts, hesitations and vacillations were doubtless due to the contrary pressures which operated on him. But his liberalism—which conditioned him against encroachments on the freedom of the press and arbitrary arrests and deportations—did not go far enough to embrace the possibility of self-government for oriental races. It was with mingled bewilderment and shock that the Moderates discovered that the Liberal party was in no hurry to usher in a millennium in India. Gokhale hit the nail on the head in 1908 when he told W. S. Blunt that Morley was 'more for personal than [for] national liberty'.[9]

The Moderates' image of 'British Democracy'—as opposed to the British bureaucracy in India—was also romantic. To a generation which bitterly and passionately disputed the Irish claim that Ireland was a nation, the idea of launching India on the road to self-government could hardly have made sense. The fact is that the British public did not bother about India, except when a famine, a riot or the threat of a mutiny made headlines in the newspapers. The annual debate on the Indian estimates continued to take place year after year in a virtually deserted House of Commons. With the exception of a small and committed core of M.P.s, briefed by Wedderburn and Gokhale, the Liberal party took little interest in Indian affairs. The Liberal leaders did not want to make India a party issue. Indeed, immediately after taking office Prime Minister Campbell-Bannerman had declared: 'It has been a pretty unbroken rule, a wise rule that

[9] Wilfrid Scawen Blunt, *My Diaries*, London, 1920, pt. 2, p. 229.

we assuredly shall not be the first to break, to keep questions of the internal administration of India outside the arena of party politics.'[10] Curiously, the attitude of the Liberal and Conservative parties towards India did not really differ on fundamentals. They were all for strong and impartial government, for justice between Indian and Indian, and even between Indian and Briton. The Liberals were probably more willing than the Conservatives to agree to the widening of the base of the legislatures, or to the appointment of Indians to a few high executive posts; their object, however, was not to transfer authority to Indian hands but merely to provide safety-valves for political discontent.

Between the aspirations of the Moderate leadership in India and the objectives of Liberal statesmen in Britain was thus a wide gulf which could not be bridged by courteous phrases. This gulf was widened by the fact that India could not be ruled from London. The cadre of professional civil servants, the 'men on the spot' in India who prided themselves on being 'realists', looked askance at constitutional reform. Many of them doubted whether the British parliamentary system was worth emulating. James Fitzjames Stephen, a former Law Member of the Viceroy's Council, had argued in his book *Liberty, Equality, Fraternity* (1873) that the English parliamentary system paralysed executive government, and was a hindrance to good government even in its homeland.[11] To transplant such a system to India seemed madness. The primary concern of British officials in India was the preservation of the Raj. 'We must realize', Bampfylde Fuller wrote in 1910, 'that we are foreigners in the country, and that a foreign Government cannot, in the nature of things, command much popular sympathy.'[12] Even in the first decade of the present century, the shadow of the mutiny of 1857 lingered, 'a kind of phantom standing behind official chairs'.[13]

The European community in India was prone to periodical attacks of mutiny-phobia. As we have already seen, in 1907 the Punjab Government worked itself—and the Government of India—into a panic which proved to be wholly unjustified. A year later, in the wake of a few terrorist outrages, there was a clamour for the imposition

[10] *India*, 29 Dec. 1905. It was the same Campbell-Bannerman who had said earlier that good government could never be a substitute for government by the people themselves.
[11] Quoted by G. R. Searle, *The Quest for National Efficiency*, Oxford, 1971, pp. 30–1.
[12] Fuller, op. cit., p. 339.
[13] M. Darling, *Apprentice to Power*, London, 1966, p. 116.

of martial law in Bengal. In such a crisis, every Briton, from the Viceroy downwards, persuaded himself to believe that he was defending an Imperial outpost. 'The Raj will not disappear in India', Minto wrote to Morley in 1908, 'as long as the British race remains what it is, because we shall fight for the Raj as hard as we have ever fought if it comes to fighting, and we shall win as we have always won.' Minto looked for the safety of the Raj to the 'allegiance of conservative forces . . . the Indian princes, the commercial community, the Muhamedans, and the Indian staff of public services'.[14] A more candid, if a somewhat more machiavellian, programme for the defence of the Indian Empire was outlined in a minute recorded by one of Minto's colleagues on his Executive Council in April 1910, a few months after the Minto–Morley reforms had been launched:

The immediate political objective [wrote Harcourt Butler] is, no doubt, different in the different Provinces. In the Deccan and in Southern India we have to help in breaking the power of the Brahmins. In Bengal we have to watch and counter the influence of the religious ascetics. . . . In the Punjab we have to utilize the divisions in the Arya Samaj. . . . In the United Provinces, we have to retain and build up the loyalty of orthodox Hinduism centred at Benares, Ajudya, Allahabad, Muttra, Hardwar. And generally we ought to assist the land-owning and agricultural classes to hold their own. . . . 'Blow hot and cold', said the Nizam to me, 'but never forget your strength.' . . . There will always be a certain movement against the aliens. We require all our strength and prudence. We must make friends. We must reward loyalty and make it pay.[15]

One of the greatest dangers to the Raj, in the eyes of the British officials in India, emanated from the contacts of the Congress leaders with British politicians. It was not merely that embarrassing questions could be asked in the House of Commons and critical comments appear in British newspapers. The Government of India felt unable to deal with political agitation with the requisite severity. We get an insight into the official dilemma in the diary of Dunlop-Smith, Minto's private secretary, who lamented in 1906 that

At present we have in England a highly democratic Government subject to frequent fits of sentimentalism. They would never tolerate the amount of repression that would be necessary for a successful campaign against the press or seditious . . . brawlers. No House of

[14] Minto to Morley, 27 May 1908 (M.P.).
[15] Note on Political Discontent enclosed with Minto to Morley, 28 April 1910 (M.P.).

Commons would ever stand the amount of repression necessary to make the present unrest inaudible.[16]

Dunlop-Smith and his friends were resourceful men and did not throw up the sponge. They knew how to 're-educate' every new Viceroy and Governor who came from England. They could not hold off the passage of legislative reforms through the British Parliament, but they knew how to defeat in practice what was conceded in principle. They framed regulations which were ostensibly designed to implement the Minto–Morley scheme, but actually undermined it. They neutralized even the 'momentous' decision of the appointment of an Indian to the Viceroy's Executive Council by taking major decisions outside the Council. The admission of an Indian, Harcourt Butler wrote in 1915, 'had made [executive] council government on the old lines quite impossible. We are solving things in a truly British way. We admit Indians to our Councils and then relegate the Councils to insignificance.'[17]

It is obvious that the Moderates underrated the built-in resistance in the Raj to 'peaceful penetration' by purely constitutional means. The path of constitutional evolution taken by Canada and Australia was not easily available to India. 'The average Englishman,' Gokhale once remarked, 'whatever his faults, has the grace to feel honestly ashamed of an injustice when brought to his mind.'[18] This may have been true enough in day-to-day administration, or in personal relationships, but when it came to questions impinging on the safety or interests of the Raj, Englishmen were not so ready to oblige. The Empire would not give way under the weight of reasoned indictments and damning statistics, even if they were culled from government reports and Blue Books.

There was, thus, no meeting of minds between the Liberal Establishment in Britain and the Indian liberals as represented by the Moderates in the Indian National Congress. The constitutional reforms of 1909 were a great disappointment. The report of the Decentralization Commission proved a damp squib. The Elementary Education Bill on which Gokhale had pinned high hopes was scotched by official hostility. Even a mild measure for the reform of the India Council in London failed to get through Parliament. Gokhale felt thoroughly disillusioned with the Public Services Commission.

[16] Gilbert, op. cit., p. 59.
[17] Butler to Glory, 1 Aug. 1915 (B. P.).
[18] *India*, 31 May 1912.

By 1910, he and Wedderburn had practically written off the Liberal party, and switched their hopes to the Labour party. They began to look up to Keir Hardie and Ramsay MacDonald, as they had done to Ripon and Morley. But Labour was not yet a power in Britain.

The Moderate dream of an Indo-British partnership, in which Britain was to help India come into her own, thus remained unrealized. Indeed, given the political realities of the time on both sides of the water, the dream was unrealizable. There was little prospect of Britain assuming the responsibility for grooming India into a self-governing Dominion. True, in August 1917, two-and-a-half years after Gokhale's death, the Government of India, under new pressures generated by the global war, announced the 'progressive realization of responsible government in India' as the goal of their Indian policy. But this goal seemed so remote at the time that most Britons and Indians continued to think of the Raj as a virtually permanent phenomenon.

5

Early in 1915 when Gokhale passed away, the Moderates still dominated the Congress and indeed the political life of the country. But their position was really much weaker than it seemed at the time. The Moderate rank-and-file was apathetic; its leadership was passive; there were few workers and scarcely any money in the Congress coffers. The British Committee in London and its journal *India* again verged on bankruptcy. Even the annual Congress sessions failed to evoke much enthusiasm. It was obvious that if the Congress was to play a vital role in Indian politics, it needed a new orientation, a new method and even a new leadership.

In 1914–15, most observers would have agreed that if the Moderates lost their hold on the Congress, it would fall into the lap of the Extremists. Tilak and his adherents had certainly more fight in them; but they had hardly any new ideas. With the exception of Aurobindo Ghose (who had retired from politics to Pondicherry in 1910), almost all the Extremist leaders had grown under the shadow of the founding fathers of the Congress. On critical occasions, such as during the partition of Bengal, their degree of alienation from the Raj was greater, and their language was stronger, but most of them did not really think in terms radically different from those of the Moderates.

Their attitude to the Empire was ambivalent; despite their indictment of British officials and administrators, they did not really think of giving up constitutional methods or breaking all ties with Britain. It is significant that Tilak's approach to the Montagu–Chelmsford reforms in their final stages bore a striking resemblance to that of Gokhale to the Minto–Morley reforms. In December 1919, Tilak advocated the acceptance of the Montagu–Chelmsford reforms on the ground that the British Government had its own difficulties and limitations arising from the aftermath of the war. The people of India, exhorted Tilak, should

put into their pocket whatever they got [from the British Government] by the left hand, while the right hand stood extended asking for more. Let us agitate, let us ally with those in England who understand . . . our own need. . . . There was enough work to be done in England. I want you to come forward and do it in England as well as in India.[19]

Tilak was using the same arguments, almost the same words, which Gokhale had used eleven years earlier while commending the Minto–Morley reforms to the Madras Congress.

Even if Tilak had not died in August 1920, it is doubtful whether he would have taken any new initiatives or suggested any new methods. The Extremists had run out of steam and even out of ideas. While they could command a resounding rhetoric, they had not (as the experience of Bengal and Maharashtra in 1908–10 revealed) discovered the art of converting rhetoric into political techniques and organization. It was obvious that the Raj was not going to wilt under the barbed shafts of the *Kesari* or the hard-hitting prose of the *Bande Mataram*.

If the Extremists could not provide an effective alternative to the Moderates, the physical violence party was even less able to do so. Engaged in dark and daring deeds, its members operated in small, isolated and secret groups. Though imbued with religious fervour, they were poorly led, ill-equipped, and riddled by mutual jealousies. In the midst of a huge unarmed (and peace-loving) population, pitted against a mighty Empire, continually hunted by the secret service, these ardent young men, with their hit-and-run tactics, could hardly become a coherent political force in a vast sub-continent.

If force was to be ruled out in the Indian context, was argument the only alternative? Winston Churchill is reported to have told an Indian visitor in 1909: 'Stick to your arguments; they must sap the

[19] *Bombay Chronicle*, 8 Dec. 1919.

position. Don't try force, because we've got it, and you haven't!'[20]
The Moderate strategy had, indeed, solely relied on the arts of per-
suasion. 'The dripping of water', Wedderburn once told Gokhale,
'pierces the hardest rock.'[21] Thirty years of patient argument had,
however, not visibly pierced the rock of Anglo-Indian opposition.
The Extremists had invoked the more powerful weapons of boycott
and passive resistance in 1905–7, but these weapons were used neither
with much skill nor with much tenacity, nor on any considerable
scale. They could hardly be invoked in the midst of the Great War
when the government had armed itself with extraordinary powers.

Tilak and his friends were determined to rehabilitate themselves in
the Congress. They were re-admitted in 1916, and shortly afterwards
succeeded in dominating the Congress. In 1918 another 'Surat'—in
the reverse—was staged: this time it was the Moderates' turn to be
squeezed out of the Congress. The Extremists' triumph did not last
long. With the advent of Gandhi in 1919, they found themselves in
the political limbo. The non-cooperation programme of 1920 bore a
superficial resemblance to the Extremist programme of 1905–7, but
Gandhi's methods, style and scale of operation were vastly different.
Tilak died in August 1920 just when the non-cooperation campaign
was being launched, but most of the Extremist leaders, B. C. Pal,
G. S. Khaparde, N. C. Kelkar and others, found it difficult to fall
into line with Gandhi. Nor were they able to stop the Gandhian
avalanche. The Mahatma's mixture of millennial patriotism, religious
asceticism, romantic anarchism, and deep humanity fascinated and
bewildered the Indian political élite as much as it perplexed and
angered British officials, but it gave him unprecedented popular
appeal. The appeal of the older leaders had been largely restricted:
that of Ranade and Tilak to Maharashtra, of Surendranath Banerjea
and Aurobindo Ghose to Bengal, of Pherozeshah Mehta and Wacha
to Bombay, of M. M. Malaviya to the U.P., of Lajpat Rai to the
Punjab. It is true that the influence of Dadabhai Naoroji and
Gokhale in their prime transcended provincial boundaries, but even
then it did not extend beyond the English-educated urban middle
class. Gandhi was the first political leader who was able to penetrate
the deeper layers of Indian society throughout the length and breadth
of the country. He employed new symbols and slogans which appealed to the minds and hearts of millions of men and women who

[20] F. Mackarness to Gokhale, 11 May 1911 (G.P.).
[21] Wedderburn to Gokhale, 8 Sept. 1910 (G.P.).

had hitherto remained practically untouched by politics. No other Indian politician had shown such a genius for spotting and enlisting for the nationalist cause so many men and women of varying talents and temperaments. No other leader had possessed such a flair for organization. Within a year, Gandhi had solved a problem which had repeatedly baffled the Moderate leadership for thirty years: the problem of converting the Congress from a three-day annual spectacle into a militant political party capable of functioning throughout the year.

Most of the older leaders—Moderate as well as Extremist—felt unable to jump on to the Gandhian bandwagon. Surendranath Banerjea, D. E. Wacha, Bhupendranath Basu, Srinivasa Sastri, Sankaran Nair, C. Y. Chintamani, M. A. Jinnah and Tej Bahadur Sapru refused to deviate from what they believed to be the true Congress ideals and methods. But their influence rapidly declined; they were soon reduced to the position of armchair critics of the political scene. Some of them, such as Sapru and Sastri, occasionally acted as 'honest brokers' between Gandhi and the government. Gandhi treated them with great respect. He did not ridicule them, nor did he denigrate the liberals. He recognized the debt he owed to the Moderate veterans and especially to Gokhale. They had familiarized their countrymen with the concept of Indian nationality. They had left in the Indian National Congress an instrument which, when refurbished, became a powerful weapon in the nationalist armoury. No less serviceable was the ideal the Moderates bequeathed to their successors, of a humane, secular and democratic nationalism which remained the ideal of the Indian National Congress under the more vigorous and successful leadership of Gandhi and Nehru.

Bibliography

A. GOVERNMENT RECORDS

Specific reference to official records of the India Office, the Government of India (National Archives of India) and the Bombay Government will be found in the footnotes on the relevant pages.

B. PRIVATE PAPERS

The list of collections consulted in India, the U.K. and U.S.A. is given below:

PAPERS IN INDIA

National Archives of India, New Delhi

Gopal Krishna Gokhale Papers.
Khaparde Diaries.

Nehru Memorial Museum & Library, New Delhi

G. G. Agarkar Papers.
G. M. Chitnavis Papers.
G. K. Devadhar Papers.
Pherozeshah Mehta Papers.
G. A. Natesan Papers.
Dadabhai Naoroji Papers.
Nehru Papers.
R. P. Paranjpye Papers.
S. Ray Papers.
V. S. Srinivasa Sastri Papers.
Assorted diaries of V. S. Srinivasa Sastri.
Bal Gangadhar Tilak Papers (microfilm).

Gandhi Memorial Museum & Library, New Delhi

M. K. Gandhi Papers.

PAPERS IN THE U.K. & U.S.A.

India Office Library, London

Ampthill Collection. Papers of Lord Ampthill as Governor of Madras, 1900 to 1904 and as *ad interim* Viceroy, 1904.
Butler Collection. Papers of Sir Spencer Harcourt Butler.
Curzon Collection. Papers of Marquess Curzon of Kedleston.

Elgin Collection. Papers of the ninth Earl Elgin as Viceroy, 1894 to 1899.

Fleetwood-Wilson Collection. Papers of Sir Guy Fleetwood-Wilson, Finance Member of the Viceroy's Executive Council, 1908 to 1913.

Hamilton Collection. Papers of Lord George Hamilton as Secretary of State for India, 1895 to 1903.

Harris Collection. Papers of Baron Harris as Governor of Bombay, 1890 to 1895.

Hirtzel, F. A. Diary, Home Miscellaneous Series, no. 864, 6–9.

Kilbracken Collection. Papers of Sir Arthur Godley (later first Baron Kilbracken of Killegar) as permanent Under-Secretary of State for India, 1883 to 1909.

Lansdowne Collection. Papers of the fifth Marquess Lansdowne as Viceroy, 1888 to 1894.

Lytton Collection. Papers of the first Earl of Lytton as Viceroy, 1876 to 1880.

Morley Collection. Papers of Viscount Morley as Secretary of State for India, 1905 to 1910 and 1911.

Temple Collection. Papers of Sir Richard Temple, Governor of Bombay, 1877 to 1880.

National Library of Scotland, Edinburgh

Minto Collection. Papers of Lord Minto, Viceroy of India, 1905 to 1910.

British Library, London

Campbell-Bannerman Papers.

Ripon Papers. Papers of Lord Ripon, Viceroy of India, 1880 to 1884.

Cambridge University Library, Cambridge

Hardinge Papers. Papers of Lord Hardinge, Viceroy of India, 1910 to 1916.

Duke University Library, Durham (U.S.A.)

Lamington Collection. Papers of Lord Lamington, Governor of Bombay.

C. PUBLISHED SOURCES (PRIMARY)

(i) Specific reference to the reports of political, social and other organizations, proceedings of central and provincial legislatures in India, and the debates in the British Parliament are given in the footnotes on the relevant pages.

(ii) *Collections of Speeches and Documents*

Afzal Iqbal, comp. & ed. *Select Writings and Speeches of Maulana Mohamed Ali.* Lahore: Shaikh Muhammad Ashraf, 1944.

Bhavsinhji, comp. *Speeches of His Excellency the Right Honourable Baron Hardinge of Penshurst, Viceroy and Governor-General of India.* 2 vols. Madras: Ganesh, 1915.

Chintamani, C. Yajnesvara, ed. *Indian Social Reform: Being a Collection of Essays, Addresses, Speeches etc. with an Appendix.* Madras: Thompson, 1901.

———. *Speeches and Writings of the Honourable Sir Pherozeshah M. Mehta.* Allahabad: Indian Press, 1905.

Chiplunkar, Vishnu Krishna. *Nibandhmala*. Ed. Vasudev Vinayak Sathe. Edn. 3. Poona: S. N. Joshi, 1926. (Marathi) (Articles from 'Nibandhmala', monthly, published between 1874 and 1881).

Chitalia, Karsandas Jagjivandas. *Some Incidents from the Life of Gokhale*. Poona: Arya Bhushan Press, 1936.

Curzon, George Nathaniel. *Lord Curzon in India: Being a Selection From His Speeches as Viceroy and Governor-General of India, 1898–1905* . . . London: Macmillan, 1906.

——. *Place of India in the Empire, being an Address Delivered before the Philosophical Institute of Edinburgh . . . on October 19th, 1909*. London: J. Murray, 1909.

Elgin, Earl of. *Speeches by the Earl of Elgin, Viceroy and Governor-General of India, 1894–1899*. Calcutta: Superintendent of Government Printing, 1899.

Gandhi, M. K. *Collected Works*. Vols. 2–13. Delhi: Publications Division, 1959–64.

Gokhale, Gopal Krishna. *Speeches*. Edn. 3. Madras: G. A. Natesan, 1920.

——. *Speeches and Writings*. 3 vols. Bombay: Asia Publishing House, 1962–7.

Vol. 1. *Economic*. Ed. R. P. Patwardhan & D. V. Ambekar.

Vol. 2. *Political*. Ed. D. G. Karve & D. V. Ambekar.

Vol. 3. *Educational*. Ed. D. G. Karve & D. V. Ambekar.

Jagadisan, T. N., ed. *Letters of the Right Honourable V. S. Srinivasa Sastri*. Edn. 2. Bombay: Asia Publishing House, 1963.

Jeejeebhoy, J. R. B., ed. *Some Unpublished and Later Speeches and Writings of the Honourable Sir Pherozeshah Mehta*. Bombay: the author, 1918.

Joshi, G. V. *Writings and Speeches of Honourable Rao Bahadur G. V. Joshi*. Poona: Dinkar Ganesh Joshi, 1912.

Joshi, Vijaya Chandra, ed. *Lajpat Rai: Autobiographical Writings*. Delhi: University Publishers, 1965.

——. *Lajpat Rai: Writings and Speeches*. 2 vols. Delhi: University Publishers, 1966.

Kaikini, L. V., ed. *Speeches and Writings of Sir Narayan G. Chandavarkar*. Bombay: Manoranjak Grantha Prasarak Mandali, 1911.

Kolasker, M. B., ed. *Religious and Social Reform: A Collection of Essays and Speeches by Mahadeva Govind Ranade*. Bombay: Gopal Narayan & Co., 1902.

Mandlik, Vishvanath Narayan. *Writings and Speeches, with a Sketch of His Life by Damodar Ganesh Padhye*. Bombay: Native Opinion Press, 1896.

Minto, Earl of. *Speeches*. Calcutta. Superintendent, Government Printing, 1911.

Morley, John Viscount. *Indian Speeches, 1907–1909*. London: Macmillan, 1909.

Naidu, Sarojini. *Speeches and Writings of Sarojini Naidu*. Madras: G. A. Natesan [1918].

Naoroji, Dadabhai. *Speeches and Writings*. Edn. 2. Madras: G. A. Natesan [1886].

Pal, Bipin Chandra. *Speeches delivered at Madras*. Madras: Ganesh, 1907.

Pitale, Balkrishna Nilaji, comp. *Speeches and Addresses of Sir H. B. E. Frere*. Bombay: Naro Krishna Dumale, 1870.

Pradhan, Ganesh Prabhakar, ed. *Agarkar-Lekh-Sangraha*. New Delhi: Sahitya Akademi, 1960. (Marathi) (Selections from the writings of Gopal Ganesh Agarkar).

Ranade, Mahadev Govind. *Essays on Indian Economics: A Collection of Essays and Speeches*. Edn. 2. Madras: G. A. Natesan, 1906.

——. *Miscellaneous Writings of the Late Hon'ble Mr. Justice M. G. Ranade.* Bombay: Ramabai Ranade, 1915.

Shan Mohammad, comp. & ed. *Writings and Speeches of Sir Syed Ahmad Khan.* Bombay: Nachiketa Publications, 1972.

Sharma, Sri Ram. *Punjab in Ferment*. 3 vols. in 2. New Delhi: S. Chand, 1971.

Telang, K. T. *Selected Writings and Speeches*. 2 vols. Bombay: Manoranjan Press [1916].

Tilak, Bal Gangadhar. *His Writings and Speeches*. Madras: Ganesh [1918].

Vidwans, M. D., ed. *Letters of Lokamanya Tilak*. Poona: Kesari Prakashan, 1966.

Vivekananda, Swami. *Complete Works*. 8 vols. Calcutta: Advaita Ashrama, 1962–4.

Wedderburn, William. *Speeches and Writings*. Madras: G. A. Natesan [1918].

(iii) *Newspapers and Serials*

Aligarh Institute Gazette. Aligarh.
Amrita Bazar Patrika. Calcutta.
Bande Mataram. Calcutta.
Bengalee. Calcutta.
Bombay Chronicle. Bombay.
Hindu. Madras.
Hindustan Review and Kayastha Samachar. Allahabad.
India. London.
Indian Mirror. Calcutta.
Indian Nation. Calcutta.
Indian Opinion. Phoenix, Natal.
Indian Social Reformer. Madras, Bombay.
Indu Prakash. Bombay.
Kesari. Poona.
Leader. Allahabad.
Mahratta, Poona.
Modern Asian Studies. London.
Modern Review. Calcutta.
Panjabee. Lahore.
Pioneer. Lucknow.
Quarterly Journal of the Poona Sarvajanik Sabha. Poona.
Reports on Native Newspapers. Bombay.
Statesman. Calcutta.
The Times. London.
Times of India. Bombay.
Tribune. Lahore, Ambala, Chandigarh.

D. PUBLISHED SOURCES (SECONDARY)

Abhyankar, Ganesa Raghunath. *Gopal Krishna Gokhale Yanche Charitra*. Poona: Arya Bhushan Press, 1926. (Marathi)

Adams, William Wheen Scovell. *Edwardian Portraits*. London: Secker & Warburg, 1957.

Aga Khan. *Memoirs: World Enough and Time*. London: Cassell, 1954.

Ahmad Khan, Saiyid. *Review on Dr. Hunter's 'Indian Musalmans': Are They Bound in Conscience to Rebel Against the Queen?* Benares: n.p., 1872.

Ambekar, Bapuji Martand. *Hari Narayan Apte Yanchen Sankshipt Charitra*. Poona: n.p., 1922. (Marathi)

Atmaprana, Pravrajika. *Sister Nivedita of Ramakrishna-Vivekananda*. Calcutta: Sister Nivedita Girls' School, 1961.

Aurobindo, Sri. *Bankim—Tilak—Dayananda*. Calcutta: Arya Publishing House, 1940.

——. *On Himself and on the Mother*. Pondicherry: Sri Aurobindo Ashram, 1953.

——. *Open Letter to His Countrymen*. Calcutta: Manmohan Ghose, 1909.

——. *Uttarpara Speech*. Edn. 4. Calcutta: Arya Publishing House, 1943.

Ballhatchet, Kenneth. *Social Policy and Social Change in Western India, 1817–1830*. London: Oxford University Press, 1957.

Banerjea, Surendranath. *Nation in Making*. Bombay: Oxford University Press, 1963. Reprint of 1925 edn.

Bapat, S. V., ed. *Reminiscences and Anecdotes of Lokamanya Tilak*. 3 vols. Poona: the author, 1924–8.

Bhandarkar, Ramakrishna Gopala. *Note on the Age of Marriage and its Consummation According to Hindu Religious Law*. Poona: Arya Vijaya Press, 1891.

Bhate, Govind Chimnaji. *History of Modern Marathi Literature, 1800–1938*. Poona: the author, 1939.

Bhatia, B. M. *Famines in India: A Study in Some Aspects of the Economic History of India, 1860–1945*. Bombay: Asia Publishing House, 1963.

Blunt, Wilfrid Scawen. *My Diaries: Being a Personal Narrative of Events, 1888–1914*. 2 pts. London: Martin Secker, 1919–20.

Bose, Bipin Krishna. *Stray Thoughts on Some Incidents in My Life*. Calcutta: Das Gupta & Co., 1919.

Buckland, C. E. *Dictionary of Indian Biography*. London: Swan Sonnenschein, 1906.

Butler, Harcourt. *India Insistent*. London: William Heinemann, 1931.

Chandavarkar, Ganesh L. *Wrestling Soul: Story of the Life of Sir Narayan Chandavarkar*. Bombay: Popular [1955].

Chaturvedi, Benarsidas & Sykes, Marjorie. *Charles Freer Andrews: A Narrative*. London: George Allen & Unwin, 1949.

Chesney, George. *Indian Polity: A View of the System of Administration in India*. Edn. 3. London: Longmans Green, 1894.

Chirol, Valentine. *Indian Unrest*. London: Macmillan, 1910.

Clarke, George Sydenham. *My Working Life*. London: John Murray, 1927.

Colebrook, Thomas Edward. *Life of the Honourable Mountstuart Elphinstone . . .* 2 vols. London: John Murray, 1884.

Colvin, Auckland & Hume, A. O. *Audi Alteram Partem: Two Letters on Certain Aspects of the Indian National Congress Movement*. Simla: Station Press [1888].

Cotton, Henry. *Indian and Home Memories*. London: T. Fisher Unwin, 1911.

——. *New India or India in Transition*. London: Kegan Paul, 1904.

Cross, Colin. *Liberals in Power, 1905–1914*. London: Barrie & Jenkins, 1963.

Curzon, Marchioness of Kedleston. *Reminiscences*. London: Hutchinson, 1955.

Damle, P. R. *Gopal Krishna Gokhale*. Poona: Kesari Press, 1961.

Das, M. N. *India Under Morley and Minto: Politics Behind Revolution, Repression and Reforms*. London: George Allen & Unwin, 1964.

Dayaram Gidumal. *Life and Life-work of Behramji J. Malabari: Being a Biographical Sketch, with Selections from His Writings and Speeches on Infant Marriage and Enforced Widowhood, and also His 'Rambles of a Pilgrim Reformer'.* Bombay: Education Society's Press, 1888.

Deccan Sabha, Poona: Golden Jubilee Celebration. Poona: Deccan Sabha, 1957.

Devadhar, G. K. *Servants of India Society*. Poona: Arya Bhushan Press, 1914.

Dongerkery, S. R. *History of the University of Bombay, 1857–1957*. Bombay: University of Bombay, 1957.

Douglas, James. *Book of Bombay*. 2 vols. Bombay: Bombay Gazette Press, 1883–6.

Dutt, Paramananda. *Memoirs of Moti Lal Ghose*. Calcutta: Amrita Bazar Patrika Office, 1935.

Dutt, Romesh Chandra. *Economic History of British India under Early British Rule from the Rise of the British Power in 1757 to the Accession of Queen Victoria in 1837*. London: Routledge & Kegan Paul, 1902.

Elphinstone, Mountstuart. *Report on the Territories Conquered from the Paishwa, submitted to the Supreme Government of British India*. Calcutta: Government Gazette Press, 1821.

Farquhar, J. N. *Modern Religious Movements in India*. Ind. Edn. Delhi: Munshiram Manoharlal, 1967. First pub. 1918.

Fraser, Lovat. *India Under Curzon and After*. London: William Heinemann, 1911.

Full and Authentic Report of the Tilak Trial (1908): Being the only Authorised Verbatim Account of the whole Proceedings with Introduction and Character Sketch of Bal Gangadhar Tilak together with Press Opinion. Bombay: N. C. Kelkar, 1908.

Fuller, Bampfylde. *Studies of Indian Life and Sentiment*. London: John Murray, 1910.

Gandhi, M. K. *Gokhale: My Political Guru*. Ahmedabad: Navajivan Publishing House, 1955.

——. *Hind Swaraj or Indian Home Rule*. Rev. edn. Ahmedabad: Navajivan Press [1938].

——. *Satyagraha in South Africa*. Tr. from the Gujarati by Valji Govindji Desai. Edn. 2. Ahmedabad: Navajivan Publishing House, 1950.

——. *Story of My Experiments with Truth*. Tr. from the Gujarati by Mahadev Haribhai Desai & Pyarelal Nair. 2 vols. Ahmedabad: Navajivan Publishing House, 1927–9.

Geddes, Patrick. *Life and Work of Sir Jagadis C. Bose*. London: Longmans Green, 1920.

Gilbert, Martin. *Servant of India: A Study of Imperial Rule from 1905 to 1910 as Told Through the Correspondence and Diaries of Sir James Dunlop-Smith*. London: Longmans, 1966.

Gokhale, Purushottam Pandurang. *Namdar Gopal Krishna Gokhale Yanche*

Charitra. Poona: Nilkanth Prakashan, 1966. (Marathi) (Life of Gopal Krishna Gokhale).

Gooch, G. P. *Under Six Reigns*. London: Longmans, 1958.

Gopalakrishnan, Panikkanparambil Kesavan. *Development of Economic Ideas in India, 1880–1950*. New Delhi: People's Publishing House, 1959.

Gore, John. *King George V: A Personal Memoir*. London: John Murray, 1948.

Graham. G. F. I. *Life and Work of Syed Ahmed Khan*. Delhi: Idarah-i Adabiyat-i Delhi, 1974. Reprint of 1885 edn.

Gupta, Jnanendra Nath. *Life and Work of Romesh Chunder Dutt* . . . London: J. M. Dent, 1911.

Gupte, Kashinath Shrikrishna. *Bombay Land Revenue Code with Rules* (*Bombay Act V of 1879*) *with Explanatory and Critical Notes, Exhaustive Commentary, etc.* Poona: the author, 1934.

Hamer, D. A. *John Morley: Liberal Intellectual in Politics*. London: Oxford University Press, 1968.

Hamilton, George Francis. *Parliamentary Reminiscences and Reflections, 1868–1906*. 2 vols. London: John Murray, 1917–22.

Hancock, W. K. *Smuts: The Sanguine Years, 1870–1919.* Cambridge: Cambridge University Press, 1962.

Hardinge of Penshurst. *My Indian Years, 1910–1916: Reminiscences*. London: John Murray, 1948.

Heimsath, Charles H. *Indian Nationalism and Hindu Social Reform*. Princeton: Princeton University Press, 1964.

Hoyland, John Somervell. *Gopal Krishna Gokhale: His Life and Speeches*. Calcutta: Y.M.C.A. Publishing House, 1933.

Humayun Kabir. *Muslim Politics, 1906–1942*. Calcutta: Gupta Rahman & Gupta, 1943.

Huttenback, Robert A. *Gandhi in South Africa: British Imperialism and the Indian Question, 1860–1914*. Ithaca: Cornell University Press, 1971.

Indian Opinion: Souvenir of the Hon'ble Gopal Krishna Gokhale's Tour in South Africa, October 22nd–November 18th [*1912*]. Johannesburg: Transvaal Leader [1912].

Infant Marriage and Enforced Widowhood in India: Being a Collection of Opinions, for and against, Received by Mr. Behramji M. Malabari, From Representative Hindu Gentlemen and Official and other Authorities. Bombay: Voice of India Printing Press, 1887.

Jagadisan, T. N., ed. *My Master Gokhale: A Selection from the Speeches and Writings of Rt. Hon'ble V. S. Srinivasa Sastri*. Madras: Model Publications, 1946.

——. *Thumb-nail Sketches: A Selection from the Writings and Speeches of the Right Hon'ble V. S. Srinivasa Sastri*. Madras: S. Viswanathan, 1946.

Jagadisan, T. N. & Shyamlal, eds. & comps. *Thakkar Bapa: Eightieth Birthday Commemoration Volume*. Madras: the compilers, 1949.

Jain, M. S. *Aligarh Movement: Its Origin and Development, 1858–1906*. Agra: Sri Ram Mehra & Co., 1965.

Javadekar, Shankar Dattatreya. *Adhunik Bharat: Bharat ke Rashtriya Evam Sanskritik Vikas Ka Itihas*. Tr. from the Marathi by Haribhau Upadhyaya. New Delhi: Sasta Sahitya Mandal, 1961. (Hindi) (Modern India).

Jayakar, M. R. *Story of My Life.* 2 vols. Bombay: Asia Publishing House, 1958–9.

Joshi, V. S. *Vasudeo Balvant Phadke: First Indian Rebel against British Rule.* Bombay: D. A. Marathe, 1959.

Kale, Vaman Govind. *Gokhale and Economic Reforms* . . . Poona: Arya Bhushan Press, 1916.

Kanetkar, M. S. *Tilak and Gandhi: A Comparative Character Sketch.* Nagpur: n.p., 1935.

Karan Singh. *Prophet of Indian Nationalism: A Study of the Political Thought of Sri Aurobindo Ghose, 1893–1910.* London: George Allen & Unwin, 1963.

Karandikar, S. L. *Lokamanya Bal Gangadhar Tilak: The Hercules and Prometheus of Modern India.* Poona: the author [1957].

Karmarkar, D. P. *Bal Gangadhar Tilak: A Study.* Bombay: Popular, 1956.

Karve, D. D., tr. *New Brahmans: Five Maharashtrian Families.* Berkeley: University of California Press, 1963.

Karve, Dattatraya Gopal. *Ranade: The Prophet of Liberated India.* Poona: Arya Bhushan Press, 1942.

Kelkar, Narsinha Chintaman. *Life and Times of Lokamanya Tilak.* Tr. from the Marathi by D. V. Divekar. Madras: S. Ganesan, 1928.

——. *Pleasures and Privileges of the Pen.* Ed. Kashinath N. Kelkar. Poona: the editor [1929].

Kellock, James. *Mahadev Govind Ranade: Patriot and Social Servant.* Calcutta: Association Press, 1926.

Kiernan, V. G. *Lords of Human Kind: European Attitudes towards the Outside World in the Imperial Age.* London: Weidenfeld & Nicolson, 1969.

Kodanda Rao, P. *Gokhale and Sastri.* Mysore: Prasaranga, 1961.

Kunzru, H. N., ed. *Gopal Krishna Devadhar.* Poona: Servants of India Society, 1939.

Lajpat Rai. *Story of My Deportation.* Lahore: Panjabee Press, 1908.

Lee, Sidney. *King Edward VII: A Biography, etc.* 2 vols. London: Macmillan, 1925–7.

Limaye, P. M., comp. *History of the Deccan Education Society, 1880–1935.* Poona: Deccan Education Society, 1935.

Magnus, Philip Montefiore. *Kitchener: Portrait of an Imperialist.* London: John Murray, 1958.

Maharashtra, State Committee for History of the Freedom Movement in India. *Source Material for a History of the Freedom Movement in India.* Vols. 1 & 2. Bombay: Directorate of Printing & Stationery, 1957–8.

Mankar, G. A. *Sketch of the Life and Works of the Late Mr. Justice M. G. Ranade.* 2 vols. Bombay: Caxton Printing Works, 1902.

Masani, R. P. *Dadabhai Naoroji: The Grand Old Man of India.* London: George Allen & Unwin, 1939.

Mathur, D. B. *Gokhale, a Political Biography: A Study of His Services and Political Ideas.* Bombay: Manaktala, 1966.

Mazumdar, Amvika Charan. *Indian National Evolution: A Brief Survey of the Origin and Progress of the Indian National Congress and the Growth of Indian Nationalism.* Edn. 2. Madras: G. A. Natesan, 1917.

Mehrotra, S. R. *Emergence of the Indian National Congress.* Delhi: Vikas, 1971.

——. *India and the Commonwealth, 1885–1929.* London: George Allen & Unwin, 1965.

Minayeff, I. P. *Travels in and Diaries of India and Burma.* Tr. from the Russian by Hirendranath Sanyal. Calcutta: Eastern Trading Co., n.d.

Minto, Mary Caroline, Countess of. *India, Minto and Morley, 1905–1910: Comp. from the Correspondence between the Viceroy and the Secretary of State . . . with Extracts from Her Indian Journal.* London: Macmillan, 1934.

Mody, H. P. *Sir Pherozeshah Mehta: A Political Biography.* 2 vols. Bombay: The Times Press, 1921.

Mohamed Ali. *Thoughts on the Present Discontent.* Bombay: Bombay Gazette Steam Press, 1907.

Morley, John Viscount. *Recollections.* 2 vols. London: Macmillan, 1918.

Mosley, Leonard. *Curzon: The End of an Epoch.* London: Longmans Green, 1960.

Mukherjee, Haridas & Mukherjee, Uma. *'Bande Mataram' and Indian Nationalism, 1906–1908.* Calcutta: Firma K. L. Mukhopadhyay, 1957.

Naidu, Sarojini. *Reminiscences of Mr. Gokhale.* Poona: Arya Bhushan Press, 1915.

Naik, V. N. *Indian Liberalism: A Study.* Bombay: Padma Publications, 1945.

Nanda, B. R. *Mahatma Gandhi: A Biography.* London: George Allen & Unwin, 1958.

——. *The Nehrus: Motilal and Jawaharlal.* London: George Allen & Unwin, 1962.

Naoroji, Dadabhai. *Poverty and Un-British Rule in India.* London: Swan Sonnenschein, 1901.

——. *Poverty of India: Papers and Statistics.* London: Vincent Brooks, Day & Co., 1878.

Natarajan, K. *Gopal Krishna Gokhale: The Man and His Message.* Bombay: Vaibhav Press, 1930.

Natarajan, S. *Lalubhai Samaldas.* Bombay: Yeshanand Publications [1941].

Nevinson, Henry W. *New Spirit in India.* Delhi: Metropolitan, 1975. Reprint of 1908 edn.

Nurullah, Sayyid & Naik, J. P. *History of Education in India during the British Period.* Bombay: Macmillan, 1943.

Pal, Bipin Chandra. *Memories of My Life and Times.* 2 vols. in one. Edn. 2. Calcutta: Bipinchandra Pal Institute, 1973.

Paranjpye, R. P. *Gopal Krishna Gokhale.* Poona: Arya Bhushan Press, 1915.

Parasnis, S. R. *Na Gopal Krishna Gokhale Yanche Charitra.* Poona: S. N. Joshi, 1933. (Marathi) (Life of Gopal Krishna Gokhale).

Parvate, T. V. *Gopal Krishna Gokhale: A Narrative and Interpretative Review of His Life, Career and Contemporary Events.* Ahmedabad: Navajivan Publishing House, 1959.

Pattabhi Sitaramayya, B. *History of the Indian National Congress, 1885–1947.* Delhi: S. Chand, 1969. 2 vols. Reprint of the earlier edn.

Phatak, Narhar Raghunath. *Adarsh Bharatsevak: Gopal Krishna Gokhale Yanche Charitra.* Bombay: Mauj Prakashan, 1967. (Marathi) (Ideal Servant of India: Life of Gopal Krishna Gokhale).

——. *Nyayamurti Mahadev Govind Ranade Yanche Charitra.* Edn. 2. Poona: Nilkanth Prakashan, 1966. (Marathi) (Life of Justice Mahadev Govind Ranade).

Polak, H. S. L. *Hon'ble Mr. Gokhale in South Africa*. Poona: Servants of India Society, 1912.

Pradhan, G. P. & Bhagwat, A. K. *Lokamanya Tilak: A Biography*. Bombay: Jaico Publishing House, 1959.

Pratt, H. *India's Rights: An Open Letter to Hon'ble G. K. Gokhale*. London: A. Bonner, 1905.

Rajendra Prasad. *Autobiography*. Bombay: Asia Publishing House, 1957.

Ram Gopal. *Lokamanya Tilak: A Biography*. Bombay: Asia Publishing House, 1956.

Ranade, Ramabai. *Ranade: His Wife's Reminiscences*. Tr. from the Marathi by Kusumavati Deshpande. Delhi: Publications Division, 1963.

Ratcliffe, S. K. *Sir William Wedderburn and the Indian Reform Movement*. London: George Allen & Unwin, 1923.

Ravinder Kumar. *Western India in the Nineteenth Century: A Study in the Social History of Maharashtra*. London: Routledge & Kegan Paul, 1968.

Ray, P. C. *Life and Experiences of a Bengali Chemist*. Calcutta: Chuckervertty, Chatterjee, 1932.

Ronaldshay, Earl of. *Life of Lord Curzon: Being the Authorized Biography of George Nathaniel, Marquess Curzon of Kedleston*. 3 vols. London: Ernest Benn, 1928.

Sane Guruji. *Namdar Gokhale-Charitra*. Edn. 2. Poona: Venus Prakashan, 1966. (Marathi) (Life of Gopal Krishna Gokhale).

Shahani, T. K. *Gopal Krishna Gokhale: A Historical Biography*. Bombay: R. K. Mody, 1929.

Smith, Wilfred Cantwell. *Modern Islam in India: A Social Analysis*. London: Victor Gollancz, 1946.

Srinivasa Sastri, V. S. *Life and Times of Sir Pherozeshah Mehta*. Madras: Madras Law Journal Press, 1945.

——. *Life of Gopal Krishna Gokhale*. Bangalore City: Bangalore Printing & Publishing Co., 1937.

Subba Rao, K. *Revived Memories*. Madras: Ganesh, 1933.

Tahmankar, D. V. *Lokamanya Tilak: Father of Indian Unrest and Maker of Modern India*. London: John Murray, 1956.

Temple, Richard. *Men and Events of My Time in India*. London: John Murray, 1882.

Thornton, Archibald Paton. *Imperial Idea and its Enemies: A Study in British Power*. London: Macmillan, 1963.

Tinker, Hugh. *Foundations of Local Self-Government in India, Pakistan and Burma*. Ind. edn. Bombay: Lalvani Publishing House, 1967.

Turnbull, Eleanor Lucia & Turnbull, Harold George Dalway. *Gopal Krishna Gokhale: A Brief Biography*. Trichur: V. Sundra Iyer & Sons, 1934.

Tyabji, Husain B. *Badruddin Tyabji: A Biography*. Bombay: Thacker, 1952.

Wacha, Dinshaw Edulji. *Reminiscences of the Late Honourable Mr. G. K. Gokhale*. Bombay: H. T. Anklesaria, 1915.

Wasti, Syed Razi. *Lord Minto and the Indian Nationalist Movement*. Oxford: Clarendon Press, 1964.

Wedderburn, William. *Allan Octavian Hume: Father of the Indian National Congress, 1829–1912*. London: T. Fisher Unwin, 1913.

Wilson, G. F. *Letters to Nobody*. London: John Murray, 1921.

Wolpert, Stanley A. *Tilak and Gokhale: Revolution and Reform in the Making of Modern India*. Berkeley: University of California Press, 1962.

Yajnik, Indulal K. *Shyamaji Krishnavarma: Life and Times of an Indian Revolutionary*. Bombay: Lakshmi Publications, 1950.

Zacharias, H. C. E. *Renascent India: From Rammohan Roy to Mohandas Gandhi*. London: George Allen & Unwin, 1933.

Index

Abdul Latif, 322
Abdul Majid, 378, 393, 429
Abdur Rahim, 328
Adamson, Harvey, 229, 270, 276, 360
Aden, 12, 112, 195
Advocate, 333
Afghanistan, 19, 26, 228
Africa, 12
Aga Khan, the, 215; on the Servants of India Society, 235–6; and the Muslim Deputation to Minto, 328; and the foundation of the All-India Muslim League, 335–6; on Gokhale's ideals, 338; estimate of, 344–5; works for separate electorates, 348–53; and the Allahabad Conference, 368–9; and Gokhale's Elementary Education Bill, 390; 429; evidence before Public Services Commission, 438; 467–8, 478
Agarkar, Gopal Ganesh, 26–9, 31–3, 67, 72, 148–9, 152, 251; conflict with Tilak, 34–7, 77, 246; 251; influence on Gokhale, 38
Age of Consent Bill, 19, 75–8, 83, 246, 251, 305, 458
Ahmednagar, 41
Aiyer, V. Krishnaswami, 171, 175, 212, 219, 254, 310, 351, 361, 397, 464
Ajit Singh, 268–70, 275–6
Ajudhianath, Pandit, 173
Ajudya, 488
Alekar, N. R., 283
Ali, Syed Ameer, 322, 333, 336, 344–5, 348–9, 351–3, 368–9, 390, 478
Aligarh, 265, 323, 337, 339
Aligarh College, 265, 322, 327, 345
Aligarh Institute Gazette, 322
Alipore Central Jail, 364
All India Muhammedan Educational Conference, 335

All-India Muslim League, *see* Muslim League
All India Social Conference, 152, 337
Allahabad Congress, 67, 70, 367, 369, 371–2, 386, 483
Allahabad Convention, 307–8, 361–3, 366, 377, 452
Amherst, Lord, 16
Amir Husain, Nawab Syed, 342
Ampthill, Lord, 154, 182, 192, 314, 405, 420
Amraoti, 114, 116, 164
Amrita Bazar Patrika, 77–8, 138, 145–6, 155, 157, 203, 212, 253, 287, 292, 331
Andrews, C. F., 433–4, 447
Anglo-Afghan War, 12
Anjuman Association, 105
Anti-Imperialist League of America, 218
Apte, Hari Narayan, 8, 106, 132, 149, 154, 162, 219, 305
Apte, V. S., 30, 35–6, 67
Archbold, W. A., 322, 324–5, 329, 332
Arms Act, 340
Arundel, A. T., 213, 465
Arya Bhushan Press, 51 n. 2, 174
Arya Samaj, 79, 488
Asquith, Herbert Henry, 199, 372, 401
Asquith, Mrs, 224
Assam, 108, 192, 243, 326, 340
Australia, 175, 387–8, 489
Ayerst, Lt O. E., 107–9

Bahadur, Sri Ram, 133
Bahadurji, Dr Mrs, 443, 445
Baker, E. N., 214, 229, 270, 275
Balfour, Arthur, 187, 194, 224, 314, 317
Baluchistan, 393
Bande Mataram (periodical), 245, 260, 292, 304

Bande Mataram (slogan & song), 202, 243, 257

Banerjea, Surendranath, 45, 99, 137, 155, 160, 162, 187, 189, 194, 202–3, 243–4, 249, 253, 255–7, 260, 273, 286–8, 295, 311, 341–2, 365, 389, 429, 446–8, 475, 477, 483, 492

Banerjee, Justice Gurudas, 184, 190

Banerji, Kali Charan, 190

Bangladesh, 191

Bankipore, 443, 451–2

Bankipore Congress, 451, 481

Bapat, S. B., 210

Barisal, 216, 243, 302

Baroda, 90, 218, 245, 388

Barr, Sir David, 309

Barrow, Maj.-Gen. E., 229

Basu, Bhupendranath, 254, 378, 384, 451, 453, 455–9, 481, 493

Batala, 268

Bayley, Sir Charles, 375

Beck, Theodore, 322–3

Bedford College for Women, 100

Belgium, 338, 445

Benares Congress, 173, 190–1, 196, 201–11, 252, 289, 416, 471

Bengal, 14, 16, 23, 42, 57, 75, 108, 115, 145, 147, 149, 162, 166–7, 184, 193–4, 197, 201, 203, 209, 213, 232, 243, 245, 254, 256–7, 261, 276, 279, 304, 307, 322, 336, 338, 355, 361, 370, 375–6, 378, 392, 416–17, 451, 461, 475, 480–1, 488, 490

Bengal, Partition of, 191–4, 196–7, 201–2, 204, 208, 210, 212, 214, 228, 245, 249–50, 252, 258, 266, 302, 324–5, 327, 336, 341, 360, 365, 372, 375, 377, 398, 411, 484–5

Bengalee, 178, 192, 253

Bennett, F. J., 114, 120, 130, 209

Bentinck, Lord William, 125, 360

Berar, 164, 190, 192, 206, 253, 256, 261, 279, 285, 361, 378, 416, 475

Besant, Annie, 79, 359, 413, 454, 456–61, 471

Beveridge, Surgeon-Capt. W. W. O., 103–4

Bhagavan Das, 359

Bhandarkar, R. G., 31–2, 59, 76, 151, 185

Bhanu, C. G., 118

Bharati, 149

Bhatvadekar, Vishnu, 129–30, 303–4

Bhide, V. M., 84, 105

Bhownaggree, Sir Mancherjee, 113, 129

Bihar, 191–2, 301, 451

Bijapurkar, V. G., 149, 455, 458, 470

Bilgrami, Syed Husain, 297, 300, 314, 327, 332, 335–6

Birmingham, 216

Bishambhar Nath, Pandit, 206

Bithur, 9–10

Bloemfontein, 425

Blunt, W. S., 486

Boer War, 408, 410

Bombay, 3, 5–7, 17–18, 21, 40, 58, 64, 67, 80–1, 91, 102, 105, 121, 131, 133, 145, 150, 153–4, 158, 160, 164, 167, 187, 192, 207, 242, 245, 247, 251–2, 258, 283, 291, 294, 303, 309, 314, 337, 347, 349–50, 360–1, 368, 397, 400, 407, 412, 415, 422, 427–8, 435, 442–3, 447–8, 451, 461, 467, 469, 475, 477, 481, 492

Bombay Chronicle, 291

Bombay Congress (1904), 68, 187, 248–9

Bombay Graduates Association, 63, 386

Bombay Guardian, 106

Bombay High Court, 19, 25, 91, 160

Bombay Legislative Council, 113, 119, 122, 125, 127, 130–1, 150

Bombay Literary Society, 18

Bombay Presidency Association, 19, 58, 90, 114, 188, 351

Bombay University, 7, 18, 21, 63, 95, 122

Bonnerjee, W. C., 45, 141, 160, 162, 166, 188, 480, 482

Bose, Anand Mohan, 147, 202, 480

Bose, B. K., 134, 185

Bose, Jagdish Chandra, 146–7,

Botha, General Louis, 425, 434
Bradlaugh, Charles, 68, 88, 92, 224, 241
Brahmo Samaj, 79
Bright, John, 6, 88, 241, 259, 443–4
British Colonial Office, 419
British Committee of the Indian National Congress, 88, 98, 101–2, 105, 158–9, 166–7, 169, 188–9, 196, 200, 204, 216, 219, 224, 241, 299, 301, 371, 391, 408, 464, 490
British India Association of the Transvaal, 411
Brodrick, St John, 193–4, 199
Bryan, W. J., 310
Buchanan, T., 300
Burdwan, Maharaja of, 378, 429
Burke, Edmund, 6, 61–3, 88, 208, 223, 241, 248
Burma, 73, 247, 268, 270
Butler, Harcourt, 264, 327–8, 330, 333–4, 341, 355, 372, 380, 387–8, 390–2, 394, 401, 403, 429, 448, 488–9
Butler, M. S. D., 404
Butler, Montagu, 448

Calais, 94, 115, 149
Calcutta Congress, 69, 260, 266, 288, 452
Calcutta University, 183, 400
Cambridge, 94, 100, 115, 196, 216
Campbell-Bannerman, Sir Henry, 194, 208, 225, 255, 259, 486
Canada, 155, 175, 263, 387–9, 489
Candy, Sir Edward, 196
Canning, Lord, 125, 360
Cape Colony, 424
Cape Times, 419
Cape Town, 418–19
Carlyle, R. W., 358, 403
Carr, Dr Walter, 306
Central Hindu College Magazine, 359
Central Provinces, 123, 164, 167, 190, 206, 279, 431
Chandavarkar, N. G., 73, 123, 153, 251
Charing Cross, 195, 299

Charlu, P. Ananda, 164, 249, 480
Charter Act (1833), the, 99
Chatfield, Prof., 19
Chatterjea, Jogesh Chandra, 265
Chatterjee, Bankim Chandra, 79
Chatterton, Principal, 183
Chaubal, M. B., 445, 450
Chaudhury, A., 342
Chenab Colony, 269–70
China, 382, 391
Chintamani, C. Y., 138, 174, 190, 223, 266, 357, 416–17, 471, 493
Chiplonkar, S. H., 43
Chiplunkar, Krishna Shastri, 28–9
Chiplunkar, Vishnu, 28–30
Chirol, Valentine, 369, 403, 405, 428, 437–8, 448–9
Chitnavis, G. M., 279–81, 393
Chitpavan Brahmans, 4, 8–9, 13–14, 17–18, 26, 40, 114, 235, 239
Chittagong, 192
Chota Nagpur, 191
Christina, Sister Greenstidel, 148
Churchill, Randolph, 91
Churchill, Winston, 199, 491
Civic Forum of New York, 310
Civil and Military Gazette, 258, 271
Clarke, Sir George, 161, 303, 308–9, 384–5, 392, 400, 424
Clarke, Violet, 308
Cobden, 473
Coconada Congress, 331
Coleridge, Lord, 199
Colonization Bill, 269–70, 272, 277
Colvin, Sir Auckland, 77
Congress, Central Standing Committee of the, 282–4
Congreve, Mrs, 66, 94
Cooch Behar, 108
Cotton, Sir Henry, 187, 189, 200, 224–5, 227, 234, 238, 318, 371, 405, 416, 475
Courtney, Leonard Henry, 188, 199, 226, 301
Craddock, Reginald, 403
Cranbrook, Lord, 12
Crawford, A. T., 51, 53

Crewe, Lord, 188, 371, 375, 398, 402–3, 405, 418, 424–5, 439–42, 469
Cromer, Lord, 224, 237
Curzon, Lord, on Gokhale, 3, 121, 135–6, 141–2, 146, 149, 156, 158, 166, 168; and Servants of India Society, 176, 465; and the Indian National Congress, 182; opposed by Gokhale, 127, 183–6; and partition of Bengal, 191–4; 195, 197, 209, 212, 226–8, 233; opposes Indian Councils Bill, 314; criticizes Gokhale, 315; 325, 338, 345, 373, 375–7, 435, 442, 485

Dacca, 192, 286, 335–6, 341
Dadabhoy, Sir Maneckji, 358, 393
Daily Mail, 107–8, 271
Daily News, 195
Dalhousie, Lord, 354
Darbhanga, Maharaja of, 134, 257, 342
Date, S. V., 83
Datta, Aswini Kumar, 257, 307
Davar, Justice D. D., 303
David, Sassoon, 358, 388
Dayananda, Swami, 79
Deccan College, 5–6, 8, 16, 26, 36, 60, 63–4, 183
Deccan Education Society, 24, 31–2, 34–5, 37–8, 60, 63–4, 72, 77, 91, 118, 149–50, 170, 472
Deccan Sabha, 86–7, 105–6, 116
Deccan Star, 28
Delhi Durbar (1903), 181; (1911) 373–7, 391
Deole, 462
Desai, Ambala Sakerlal, 283, 286
Desh Sewak, 279
Deshmukh, Gopal Hari, 17–18, 20, 36, 55
Deva, Dr H. S., 443–9, 470
Devadhar, G. K., 173, 254, 294, 462–3
Dharwar Social Conference, 152, 169
Dhavle, S. B., 62
Dhingra, Madan Lal, 355

Dhulia, 24
Dickshit, H. S., 129
Digby, William, 56, 58, 94, 139
Dilke, Charles, 218, 224, 226
Dnyanaprakash, 17, 63, 113, 173, 464
Dongri Jail, 32
Douglas, James, 82
Dravid, N. A., 173, 202
Du Boulay, J. H., 176
Dublin, 63, 98
Duff, Grant, 62
Dufferin, Lord, 156
Dundee, 180, 427
Dunlop-Smith, 212–13, 229, 234, 264, 271, 297–8, 318, 326–7, 329–30, 332, 335, 342, 488–9
Durban, 408, 419
Dutt, R. C., 94, 125; on Gokhale's election to Imperial Legislative Council, 147; on revitalizing the Congress, 164–5; 167, 178; on the Curzon regime, 185–6; 206, 218, 237, 273, 297; on Minto-Morley reforms, 313, 333; on separate electorates for Muslims, 352, 361, 440, 480

East Bengal, 193, 237, 240, 243, 272, 282, 326, 340–3, 375, 478
East India Association, 216
East India Company, 9, 14, 23
Edward VII, King, 181, 271, 276, 317, 355, 372
Egypt, 237
Elementary Education Bill, 387–94, 464
Elgin, Lord, 98, 102, 156, 178, 188, 225–6
Ellis, E. R., 184
Ellis, J. E., 216, 218
Elphinstone College, 6–7, 9, 19, 21, 61, 160
Elphinstone, Mountstuart, 14, 18, 125, 371
Emerson, 45
Englishman, 226, 258, 302, 336
Eton, 100, 177, 436
Evening Standard, 271

Fabian Society, 198
Factories Commission, 274
Fawcett, Henry, 88, 224, 259
Fazal-i-Hussain, Mian, 265
Federation Hall, 202
Fergusson College, 31–3, 36, 59–67, 115, 128, 149–50, 170, 386, 407, 476
Fergusson, Sir James, 25, 30–1, 51, 60, 111
Ferojkhan, Nawab Abdul, 105
Ferozepore, 268, 278
Fisher, H. A. L., 404, 419
Fitzmaurice, Lord, 226, 301
Fowler, Sir Henry, 89, 156, 188, 194, 225–6
France, 225, 320, 388, 445
Franklin, Benjamin, 101
Fraser, Lovat, 138, 180, 352, 473
Fraser, Sir Andrew, 192, 307
Freeman, 63
Frere, Bartle, 21
Friend of India, 315
Fuller, Bampfylde, 192, 237, 243, 326, 332, 338, 342, 487

Gaikwad of Baroda, 41
Ganapati festival, 81–3, 247, 474
Gandhi, M. K., 46; visits Poona, 58; meets Gokhale, 59; 138; on Gokhale, 148; 162, 228; on separate electorates, 345–6; relations with Gokhale, 407–21; Gokhale's defence of, 422–3; Gokhale's support to, 424–34; 443; attitude to First World War, 446; and Servants of India Society, 466–7; 471, 480; and the Moderates, 492–3
Gandhi–Smuts Agreement, 433–4
Ganesh Khind, 107
Ganges, 9, 202, 245
Gardiner, A. G., 301
George V, King, 209, 231, 336, 371, 374
Germany, 320, 387–8, 445, 448–9, 485
Gheekantawadi, 285
Ghosal, J., 148
Ghosal, Sarla, 148–9
Ghose, Aurobindo, 157, 163, 244–5, 248, 256–7, 266, 284–5, 287–8, 290, 308, 364, 416, 490, 492
Ghose, Lal Mohan, 165
Ghose, Manmohan, 160
Ghose, Motilal, 77, 113, 145–6, 212, 253, 287, 453, 457
Ghosh, Rash Behari, 190, 285–7 289–90, 295, 310–11, 361
Gladstone, Herbert J., 406, 425, 430
Gladstone, William Ewart, 51, 207–8, 223, 226, 380, 383
Gloucester, 98, 216, 398
Godfrey, George, 411
Godley, Sir Arthur, 189, 199, 234–5, 237–8, 298, 348
Godubai, 74
Gokhale, Gopal Krishna, birth, 4; ancestry, 4; education 5–7; teacher at New English School, 7–8; joins Deccan Education Society, 31–2; relations with Agarkar and Tilak, 34, 38; relations with Ranade, 43–4; and politics in Poona 51–8; first meeting with Gandhi, 58–9; as professor in Fergusson College, 60–3; relations with Principal Selby, 64; family life, 65–6; controversy over social reform, 72–8; and 1895 (Poona) Congress session, 83–4; resigns from Sarvajanik Sabha, 85–7; meets William Wedderburn, 90–3, 100; gives evidence before Welby Commission, 88–101; 'apology incident', 102–17; member Bombay Legislative Council, 119–27; death of his wife, 128; elected to Imperial Legislative Council, 128–31; president, Poona Municipality, 131–2; reactions to first speech on the budget, 134–42; life in Calcutta, 145–9; retires from Deccan Education Society and Fergusson College, 149–50; declines leadership of social reform movement, 152–3; gives up plans for a parliamentary career in England, 165–6; operation to revitalize Congress, 164–8; foundation

of Servants of India Society, 169–76;
opposition to Universities Reform
Bill and Official Secrets Bill, 185–6;
visits Britain, 188–90, 195–201; and
Partition of Bengal, 191–4, 197;
presides over Benares Congress
session, 190–1, 204–11; and Minto,
212–15, 233; visits Britain, 215–17;
meetings with Morley, 100, 199,
218–19, 228–9, 233–9; distrusted by
Minto, 233; attitude to revolutionaries, 241–2; Partition of Bengal
and the 'Extremist' party, 243–4;
relations with Tilak, 245–56; and
Calcutta Congress, 256–62; tour of
U.P. and Punjab, 262–6; reaction to
Lajpat Rai's deportation, 272–8;
attitude to the Moderate–Extremist
conflict and the Surat Split, 279–95
passim; discussions with Morley
on constitutional reforms 299–300,
309; reaction to Tilak's prosecution,
305; and Sir George Clarke, 308–9;
invitation to visit the U.S.A., 310;
attends Madras Congress (1908),
310–13; Tory criticism of, 314–16;
on Sinha's appointment to Viceroy's
Council, 318; and the Communal
Problem, 337–43; and Separate
Electorates, 346–52; opposes repressive legislation, 355–8; inter-
cedes on behalf of Mrs Besant, 359;
on the Lahore Congress (1909), 366;
role at the Allahabad Congress,
367–70; distrusted by Hardinge, 373,
435, 437; on Delhi Durbar (1911),
376–7; 'Leader of the Opposition'
in Imperial Legislative Council,
378–84; suspected by Governor
Clarke, 385; on education for the
masses, 387; introduces Elementary
Education Bill, 387–94; on India's
political future, 399; member, Royal
Commission on Public Services, 403;
relations with Gandhi, 408–18;
visits South Africa, 419–21; defends
Gandhi, 423; mobilizes official and

public opinion in favour of Gandhi's
struggle, 424–34; differences with
British members of Royal Commission, 434–8, 449–50; declines
knighthood, 439–40; health, 442–5;
and Sarojini Naidu, 444–5, 449; on
First World War, 448; attitude to
re-admission of Extremists to the
Congress, 451–3; failure of negotiations with Tilak, 454–60; and the
Servants of India Society, 461–7;
drafts outline of constitutional reforms immediately required, 467–9;
estimate of, 471–3; attacks on, 474;
death, 469–70, 475–8

Gokhale, Govind, 4–8, 294
Gokhale, Kashibai, 66, 294
Gokhale, Krishnarao, 4–5, 8
Gokhale, N. V., 205
Gokhale, Radhabai, 65–6, 128
Gokhale, Satyabhama, 4
Gokhale, Savitribai, 65
Gokuldas Tejpal Sanskrit College, 91
Golden Temple, 181
Goldingham, Lt, 140
Goldsmith, Oliver, 70
Gooch, G. P., 218, 475
Grant, Robert, 15
Granta, 196
Garud, D. S., 119, 120–1
Grey, Sir Edward, 224
Gujarati, 113, 205
Gupta, K. G., 297, 313, 471
Gurdas Ram, 277
Gwalior, 11

Haldane, Richard, 199, 271
Hamilton, Lord George, 3, 21, 99,
102–3, 108–9, 139, 156, 158, 181, 236
Harcourt, Sir William, 52, 424
Hardie, Keir, 218, 290, 490
Hardinge, Lord, 369, 371–2; reaction
to Indian nationalists, 373–4; 381;
on Gokhale's opposition to Seditious Meetings Bill, 383; 384–5; on
Tagore, 400; opposes appointment
of Gokhale to Public Services Com-

mission, 402–4; 406, 418; and Indian agitation in South Africa, 429–33; distrust of Gokhale, 435, 437–8; opposes reform of India Council, 442; 465

Harris, Lord, 53–5, 60, 80, 314

Hastings, Warren, 98, 354

Hawthornwaite, Prof., 7

Hertzog, J. B. M., 425

Hewett, J. P., 231, 264, 359

Himmick, Murray, 437

Hind Swaraj, 414–15

Hindu College, 15–16

Hindu Panch, 304, 306

Hindustan Review, 154, 313, 333, 360

Hirtzel, F. A., 235–8

Hitavada, 464

Hobhouse, Emily, 434

Hongkong, 104

Hume, Allan Octavian, on Poona, 39; 42, 44; visits Poona, 55–6, 58, 67; appeals to public opinion in India and Britain, 88, 92, 100–1, 111; on the 'apology incident', 114; on self-government for India, 155, 158; Dadabhai Naoroji on, 159; 162, 165, 173, 188, 190, 204, 224, 242, 312, 323; Gokhale on, 365; 366–7; on India and Britain, 445–6; 464; and the foundation of the Congress, 480–2

Hunter, W. W., 30, 62, 99

Husain, Syed Haider, 463

Hydari, Akbar, 138

Hyndman, H. M., 200

Ibbetson, Denzil, 268 70, 277, 326, 360

Ilbert Bill, 19, 51

Imam, Syed Ali, 328, 348, 378, 380, 403

India, 92, 158, 166, 188, 241, 408, 464, 490

India Council, 235, 244, 301, 317

India Office, 298, 300, 316, 401, 425, 439–40, 445

Indian Antiquary, 19

Indian Association, Calcutta, 90

Indian Association, Lahore, 188

Indian Councils Act (1892), 122, 129, 133

Indian Councils Act (1909), *see* Minto–Morley Reforms

Indian Daily News, 139, 389

Indian National Congress, 1, 19, 24, 33, 39–40, 64, 67, 69, 71–2, 77, 83–4, 88, 92, 116, 130, 154, 157, 159–60, 162, 175, 187, 194, 230–1, 245, 248, 336, 413, 480–1, 484, 489

Indian Parliamentary Committee, 88, 110–11, 216, 225, 301

Indian People, 174

Indian Opinion, 410–11, 414

Indian Social Reformer, 148, 158, 259, 422–3, 474

Indian Sociologist, 241–2, 355

Indian Spectator, 113

Indu Prakash, 21, 157

Immigration Regulation Bill, 424

Ireland, 25, 207, 299, 388, 441, 447

Irving, Henry, 99

Irwin, Lord, 373

Islington, Lord, 404, 437

Iyengar, T. Bhashyam, 230

Iyer, G. Subramania, 90, 206, 457

Iyer, S. Subramania, 389

Iqbal, Mohammed, 429

Jame-Jamshed, 283, 291

Japan, 213, 387–8, 485

Jayakar, M. R., 174–5, 471

Jefferson, Principal, 19

Jehangir, Petit, 467

Jejeebhoy, Sir Jamsetji, 422

Jenkins, J. L., 359

Jenkins, Lawrence, 300, 350, 356, 360, 384

Jinnah, M. A., 187, 283, 358, 378, 442, 471, 493

Johannesburg, 410, 414, 419–20

Joshi, Ganesh Vasudeo, 40

Joshi, Ganesh Vyankatesh, 43–4, 61, 63, 78, 86, 90, 97, 137

Joshi, N. M., 173

Justice, 224

Kagal, 4, 6, 8, 294
Kaiser-i-Hind, 113
Kal, 176, 304
Kale, Prof., 463
Kallenbach, Hermann, 421
Kanilkar, V. H., 32
Kanitkar, Govind V., 305
Kanpur, 9–11
Karachi Congress, 442
Karve, D. K., 6, 61, 72, 74
Keay, J. Seymour, 219
Kelkar, N. C., 36, 86, 131, 149, 333, 453, 455, 492
Kesari, 31–2, 34, 65, 77, 80, 86, 104, 118, 176, 205, 246–7, 279, 284, 291, 303–5, 458
Kevalkar, Krishnabai, 66
Keynes, J. M., 196
Khan, Hakim Ajmal, 328
Khan, Nawab Muhammed Hyat, 326
Khan, Sir Syed Ahmed, the political philosophy of, 320–1; relations with the British, 322–3; 324, 325, 338, 344
Khaparde, G. S., 209, 245, 253, 257, 261, 279, 282–5, 288, 304, 308, 453, 474–5, 492
Khare, Daji Abaji, 127, 258, 283
Khatidarkar, V. V., 115
Kingsford, D. H., 301
Kitchener, Lord, 213, 229, 239, 276, 372
Kolhapur, 4, 5–6, 10–11, 21, 32, 62, 90–1, 234
Kolhatkar, A. B., 283, 288
Kotluk, 4
Krishna, Dr Bhalchandra, 123, 127
Krishnavarma, Shyamji, 241–2, 355
Kunte, M. M., 28
Kunzru, H. N., viii, 173, 462–3

La Touche, James, 345
Labour Party, the British, 219, 398
Ladysmith, 419
Lajpat Rai, 157, 161, 163, 187–8, 203, 209–11, 224, 243, 253, 256, 265, 268–70, 272–9, 282, 284, 286, 288–90,

294, 296–8, 360, 364–5, 429, 446, 475, 492
Lambeth, 98
Lamington, Lord, 176, 232, 239, 345
Lancashire, 180
Land Alienation Act, 485
Lansdowne, Lord, 75–6, 80, 314–15, 318, 345
Law, Edward, 134, 139–40, 184
Lawley, Arthur, 233, 330
Lawrence, Walter, 112, 146, 300
Lawson, Wilfrid, 367
Leader, 174
Lee-Warner, William, 235–8, 347–8
Liberal Party, the British, 88, 92, 156, 187–8, 199–200, 208, 223–6, 400, 486
Liberty, Equality, Fraternity (1873), 487
Limbdi, 241
Liverpool, 300
Livingstone, David, 224
Lloyd George, David, 199
London, 15, 66, 105, 158–9, 227, 233–4, 242, 244, 267–8, 298, 300–1, 305, 307, 315, 319, 324, 344–5, 348–9, 351, 355, 366, 390, 397–9, 405–6, 412, 417–18, 424, 437, 441–2, 445–6, 449, 463–4, 468, 471, 473, 483
London Review, 178
London School of Economics, 173
Lucknow, 264, 325, 337, 339, 341, 391, 443
Lyall, Sir Alfred, 347
Lyallpur, 269, 272
Lytton, Lord, 12–13, 26

Macaulay, T. B., 21, 28, 62, 183, 223, 248, 371, 482
MacDonald, J. Ramsay, 218, 375, 398, 404–5, 410, 438, 449, 490
MacDonnell, Lord, 314, 347
Madge, W. C., 437
Madholal, Munshi, 206, 210
Madras, 42, 90, 133, 154, 162, 167, 173, 182–3, 190, 255, 262, 283, 301, 309–10, 315, 361, 363–5, 377–8, 389, 420, 430, 442–3, 446, 454, 456, 461, 465, 473, 475, 481

Madras Congress Session (1903), 154–5, 162, 165–6, 168; (1908), 311–13, 346, 457

Madras Mail, 389

Madras School of Arts, 183

Madras Standard, 361

Madras Times, 389

Madras University, 389

Mahajana Sabha, 90, 430

Maharaja of Baroda, 445

Maharashtra, 3, 8–9, 16–17, 20, 25–6, 31, 38–9, 54, 65, 121, 204, 206, 246, 256, 261, 279, 475, 491

Mahmud, Syed, 339

Mahmudabad, Raja of, 264, 339

Mahratta, 31–2, 34, 63, 83, 113, 205, 260, 291, 333, 447, 458

Malabari, B. M., 74–7

Malaviya, M. M., 164, 257–8, 291, 359, 366, 378–9, 382, 492

Malcolm, John, 14, 371

Malerkotla, 378

Malvi, T. N., 286–7

Manchester, 196–7, 397

Manchester Guardian, 110–11, 116, 292, 301, 475

Mandalay, 247, 284

Mande, Krishnarao Bapu, 85

Mandlik, V. N., 18–20, 36

Maniktola Conspiracy Case, 301

Maritzburg, 419

Marshman, John Clark, 62

Massingham, H. W., 301

Matheran, 273, 275

Max Müller, F., 75, 79

Mazhar-ul-Haq, 358

Meerut, 339, 341

Mehta, Dr Jivraj, 445

Mehta, Pherozeshah, M., 44–5, 51, 58, 63, 84–5, 91, 123, 125–31, 134, 154, 159, 161–5, 188–9, 204–5, 211, 215, 245–6, 249–51, 254–60, 273, 275, 280–1, 283–4, 286–8, 290–2, 295, 304, 310, 323, 349, 357, 361, 365–6, 389, 407, 422–3, 429, 446, 448, 453, 457, 468, 472, 475, 477, 480, 482, 492

Meredith, George, 98, 227, 398

Meston, James, 382, 405, 424

Mill, John Stuart, 19–20, 32–3, 62, 100, 208, 223, 226

Milner, Lord, 224

Minto, Lady, 229, 345–6

Minto, Lord, 221–3; Gokhale on, 214, 297–8; and Morley, 226–9; response to Indian nationalism, 229–32; attitude to Gokhale, 233–4; 239, 241, 251, 257; and the Punjab crisis, 270–1, 274–5; 277; on the Surat Congress, 293; 297–8, 302, 305, 307, 309, 311, 313, 317–19; Simla Deputation, 324–36 *passim*; 351, 354–6, 358; farewell to, 360, 372, 376, 378, 397, 405, 410, 414, 435; on the British Raj, 488

Minto–Morley Reforms, 314, 318–19, 324, 345–6, 349, 353, 359, 368, 371, 373, 398–400, 411, 440, 461, 473, 488–9, 491

Mitra, S. C., 369

Modern Review, 451

Mohamed Ali, 331, 339, 471, 477

Mohammed Bahadur, Nawab Syed, 190, 273, 280, 297

Mohsin-ul-Mulk (Mehdi Ali Khan), Nawab, 324–8, 331–2, 334–7, 339

Montagu–Chelmsford Reforms, 291, 469, 491

Montagu, Edwin, 398, 401–2, 405, 440–1

Monteath, James, 125

Moonje, B. S., 279, 283, 285, 288

Morison, Theodore, 300–1, 322, 325, 345

Morley, John, meets Gokhale, 100; 199–200; Gokhale on, 208; and Gokhale, 218–19, 405; relations with Minto, 226–33; discussions with Gokhale, 234–40; 241, 259, 267; reaction to Lajpat Rai's deportation, 270–6; 293; and reform of legislatures, 296–303; 309–11, 313, 314–19; and arrest of Tilak, 305; 307, 324, 345; and separate electorates, 347–53; 354–6, 358, 363, 372, 398; meets Gandhi, 412; 414, 442, 486, 488, 490

Morning Leader, 195

Morning Post, 108

Moses, S. M., 130

Mudaliar, Koopooswamy, 105

Mudholkar, R. N., 160, 164, 190, 219 253, 261–2, 281–2, 378, 416, 475

Muhammedan Anglo-Oriental Defence Association, 323

Mukherjee, Asutosh, 234

Munro, Thomas, 125, 371

Murlidhar, Lala, 160

Muslim Deputation, 329, 335, 337, 344, 345, 347, 386–7, 390, 451

Muslim League, All-India, 335, 337, 339, 344, 345, 347, 348, 368–9, 390, 451

Mutiny (1857), the, 10–11, 46, 80

Muttra, 488

Muzaffarpur, 301, 303

Mymensingh, 192

Mysore, 465

Nabha, Tikka Sahib of, 276

Nabiullah, Syed, 339

Nagpur, 279–80, 282–5, 288–9, 292, 387, 389, 393, 443, 461, 464

Naidu, Sarojini, 444–5, 449, 471

Nair, Sankaran, 493

Namjoshi, G. M., 36

Nana Saheb, 10

Nanabhai, M., 285 n. 13

Naoroji, Dadabhai, 42, 44–5, 49, 51; visits Poona, 57–8; 67, 87; member Welby Commission, 89; 91, 94–5, 98, 101–2, 111, 114, 118–19, 129, 136, 154, 157; on the British Committee of the Congress, 159; 162, 165–6, 188, 190, 195, 200, 204; receives Gokhale, 195, 216; 228, 241; appeals to Tilak, 248–9; presides over Calcutta Congress, 256–61; 278; on Minto-Morley reforms, 313; on Muslim attitude to the Congress, 322–3; 336, 366–7, 374,

435; on First World War, 446; visited by Governor of Bombay, 448; 463, 475, 477, 480, 482–3

Nasik, 24

Natal, 93, 373, 408, 413, 422, 425, 427

Natal Advertiser, 425

Natal Indian Congress, 411, 416

Natarajan, K, 148, 422–3, 474

Natesan, G. A., 214, 255, 413, 427

National Liberal Club, 99, 198–9, 398, 444

National Social Conference, 24, 83–4, 152–3

Native Opinion, 18

Natu, Sardar Tatya Sahib, 81

Nawab of Dacca, 342

Nehru, Jawaharlal, 61, 95, 131, 262, 428, 493

Nehru, Motilal, 257, 262, 266, 278, 287, 291, 352, 359, 429, 471

Nevinson, H. W., 172, 244, 292, 301, 475

Newcastle, 419, 427

New English School, 7–8, 29–30, 34–5, 60, 149, 386

Nivedita, Sister, 147–8

Northcote, Lord, 124, 140–1, 314, 344–5

North–West (United) Provinces, 80, 167, 190–1, 203, 206, 231

Norton, Eardley, 190

Nugent, John, 123

Nulkar, K. L., 52

Observer (Lahore), 390

O'Connor, T. P., 99

O'Donnell, C. J., 225

Official Secrets Bill, 185–6

Orissa, 191–2

Oxford, 216

Padumji, Dorabji, 131

Pal, Bipin Chandra, 23, 147, 154, 244–5, 253–7, 266, 274, 290, 304, 308, 415, 475, 492

Palmerston, Lord, 229

Pandit, Shankar Pandurang, 50

Panjabee, 268, 278, 364
Paranjpye, R. P., 69, 94, 115, 152, 166, 170, 463, 470, 473
Parekh, G. D., 283
Parnell, Charles Stewart, 25
Partab Singh, Raja, 230
Patiala, 378
Patwardhan, A. V., 118, 173, 301, 304, 462–4, 470
Peel, Lord, 439
Peile, Sir James, 95–7
Pentland, Lord, 405
Peshwa, the, 2, 9, 14, 25, 42, 62, 247
Petit, Bomanji Dinshaw, 130
Petit, Jehangir B., 423
Phadke, Krishnaji Kashinath, 306
Phadke, Wasudeo Balwant, 11–12, 23–5
Phillips, C. R., 103
Phoenix, 418, 427, 466
Pinhey, Col., 359
Pioneer, 92, 322
Plague Committee, 103–15, 113
Playfair, Sir Patrick, 406
Polak, Henry, 412–17, 421, 433, 466
Pondicherry, 490
Poona, 6–9, 11–12, 14–15, 17, 21, 24, 25, 27, 29–31, 36, 38–9, 41–3, 52–9, 63, 66–7, 71–4, 77, 78, 81, 83–5, 107, 109–12, 115, 119, 121–2, 124, 131–2, 145, 151, 153, 195, 205, 214, 237, 246–7, 250–1, 271, 273, 294, 300–1, 303–4, 338, 407, 431, 443, 454, 457, 459–61, 463, 465–7, 474–5
Poona Congress (1895), 83–5, 155, 305 407, 458
Poona English College, 16–17
Poona High School, 28, 30, 51
Poona Sarvajanik Sabha, 24, 37, 40–2, 48, 53, 55–7, 67–8, 71, 90, 105, 116, 128, 130, 159, 164, 407, 459
Porbandar, 467
Prabhakar, 17
Presidency College (Calcutta), 146
Press Bill, 355–7
Pretoria, 419, 421 424, 430

Primrose, Henry, 405
Prince of Arcot, 378
Prince of Wales, 206, 209–10, 231, 233
Punjab, 162, 167, 204, 206, 233, 256, 261–2, 264–5, 268–74, 276, 278, 326, 341, 349, 361, 365, 370, 392, 475, 481, 488, 492
Pusa, 179

Quarterly Journal of the Poona Sarvajanik Sabha, 43–4, 54, 63, 67, 74, 77, 85–7
Queen's Proclamation (1858), 67, 182

Rahimatoola, Ibrahim, 130, 150–1, 422
Rajagopalachari, C., 428
Rajaram College, 5–6, 62
Rajendra Prasad, 174
Rajkot, 407
Ramabai, Pandita, 33–4, 50, 73, 106
Ramakrishna Mission, 148
Ramakrishna Paramahansa, 79
Ramchand, 269
Ramoshis, 11
Rana, S. R., 241–2
Ranade, Mahadev Govind, 4; education, 21; on British rule in India, 22–3; official distrust of, 24–5; 27, 29, 31, 36; and the Poona Sarvajanik Sabha, 40–3; and Gokhale, 43–4; estimate of, 45–50; 51, 57, 61, 63; on social reform, 74; controversy with Tilak, 76–8, 81–6; foundation of the Deccan Sabha, 86–7, 89–91; on Gokhale, 90, 101; 93, 98, 105, 120; Gokhale's tribute to, 126; 128, 130, 137; relations with Gokhale, 151–3, 159, 167, 191, 205, 251, 256, 306; attitude to communal problems, 337–8; on Indian emigration, 407; 409, 421, 459, 463, 472, 474–5; biography of, 476; 477, 480, 482, 492
Ranbir Singh, Sir Kanwar, 378
Rand, W. C., 103–4, 107–10, 112, 118
Rangoon, 443

Rao, J. Krishna, 463
Rao, K. Subba, 84, 384, 454–8, 469
Rashtra Mandal, 282
Ratcliffe, Samuel, 213
Ratnagiri, 4, 18, 26
Ravenscroft, E. W., 24–5
Rawalpindi, 268, 271–2, 277–8
Ray, Prafulla Chandra, 146
Ray, Sarla, 172, 201 n. 28, 293 n. 36
Reay, Lord, 51–5, 75, 188, 199, 226, 301, 314, 405
Reddy, C. R., 196
Reed, Sir Stanley, 422
Regulation III of 1818, 270, 319
Rhodes, Cecil, 224
Richards, Erle, 318, 327, 332–3
Ripon, Lord, 19, 51, 55, 92, 108, 132, 178, 188–90, 199, 225–6, 236, 272, 301–2, 360, 490
Risley, Sir Herbert, 192–3, 229, 274, 355, 360
Rivaz, Sir Charles, 270
Roberts, Herbert, 225, 405
Robertson, Sir Benjamin, 431
Ronaldshay, Lord, 437
Rosebery, Lord, 224
Round Table Conference, 345
Roy, Raja Rammohun, 16, 46
Royal Asiatic Society, 18–19, 477
Royal Commission on the Public Services in India, 402, 404–5, 436, 439, 441–3, 449–50, 452, 461, 478–89
Royal Commission on Indian Expenditure (Islington Commission), *see* Welby Commission
Russia, 184, 213, 310, 320, 328, 387, 441, 485
Rutherford, Dr, 286

Sabarmati, 466
Samaldas, Lallubhai, 129, 163, 166, 189
Samarth, N. M., 442
Sandhurst, Lord, 103, 105–8, 110–11, 113, 118, 121, 123–4, 129, 314
Sangla, 269

Santiniketan, 467
Sapru, Tej Bahadur, 262, 429, 471, 493
Sardesai, G. S., 72
Sarkar, Jadunath, 78–9
Sarma, B. N., 442
Sastri, V. S. Srinivasa, 6, 161, 173, 342, 357 n. 6, 389, 404, 462–5, 475, 493
Sathe, Shivram Hari, 43
Sawhney, Hans Raj, 277
Schreiner, Senator, 419
Seditious Meetings Bill, 276, 294, 297, 355, 357, 383,
Selby, F. G., 36, 64, 149, 183
Sen, Narendra Nath, 342
Servants of India Society, 64, 132, 168, 170–2, 174–6, 191, 205, 215, 235, 242, 294, 308, 338, 357, 363, 370, 421, 439, 451, 454, 461, 466–7, 472, 476
Sevagram, 466
Shafi, Mian Muhammad, 390, 429
Shah Din, Justice, 429
Shahabuddin, 269
Shahabuddin, Kazi, 322
Shams-ul-Huda, Sayid, 342
Shinde, V. R., 33
Shivaji, 9, 40, 42, 46, 82; Shivaji Festival, 83, 245, 247, 251
Sholapur, 41, 90
Simla, 3, 88, 139, 145, 183, 227, 229, 232, 235, 268, 273, 276, 294, 298, 302, 319, 324–5, 330, 332, 335, 348, 357, 383, 401, 473
Simon de Montfort, 311
Sind, 18, 121–2
Singh, Ranbir, 378
Sinha, S. P., 318, 356–7, 384
Sinha, Sachchidananda, 313, 378, 442
Sircar, Nilratan, 146
Smuts, General Jan Christian, 419, 425, 431, 434
Social Democratic Federation, 200
Solomon, R., 418, 431
South Africa, 58, 148, 228, 263, 397, 406, 408, 410, 412–35, 443, 466, 471

Southampton, 418
Spectator, 178, 236
Spencer, Herbert, 19–20, 32–3, 75, 115
St Stephens College, Delhi, 433
Standard, 99
Statesman, 213, 243, 296, 471
Stephen, Sir James Fitz-James, 177, 487
Sudharak, 33–4, 37, 63, 67, 77–8, 118, 152
Surat, 102, 279, 284–5, 287, 289–93, 297, 299, 307, 310–11, 361–3, 365, 377, 451, 455, 458–9, 478, 492
Switzerland, 215, 307, 388, 406

Taft, W. H., 310
Tagore, Rabindranath, 146, 148, 400, 471
Tamhanmala, 4
Tata, J. N., 160
Tata, Ratan J., 413, 422, 444
Telang, Kashinath Trimbak, 19–20, 31, 36, 51, 73–4, 480, 483
Temple, Sir Richard, 12–13, 25, 40–1
Thackersey, Vithaldas, 358, 384
Thakkar, A. V., 173–4
Thana, 24
Tibet, 228
Tilak, Bal Gangadhar, ancestry and education, 26–7; foundation of New English School, 29–30; and Agarkar, 27–8, 31–7; and Gokhale, 37–8; 43, 52, 58, 61, 67, 72–3; controversy on Age of Consent Bill, 76–8; and the Ganpati and Shivaji festivals, 81–2; conflict with Ranade, 83–4; and Sarvajanik Sabha, 85–7; 103, 107, 112, 113, 118; contest with Gokhale for membership of Bombay Council, 119–22, 123, 130–1, 140, 145, 161, 163, 205, 209; political stance before and after the partition of Bengal, 245–52; 254, 255–6; and Calcutta Congress (1906), 257–61; 266, 274, 279–84; and Surat Congress (1907), 284–91; arrest and trial, 303–8; 358, 361, 364, 375, 407–8, 415, 447; on

First World War, 447; controversy with Gokhale on readmission of Extremists to Congress, 458–9; relations with Gokhale, 474–5; 490–2
The Times, 52, 63, 111, 236, 271, 315–17, 330, 336, 347, 352, 355, 369, 403, 406, 429
Times of India, 30, 52–4, 60, 63, 65, 114, 120, 122, 127, 130, 180, 209, 272–3, 277, 291, 336, 352, 404, 421, 428–9, 470
Tiwana, Malik Umar Hyat Khan, 274, 378
Tolstoy Farm, 420, 427, 466
Transvaal, the, 373, 410–12, 415, 418, 429
Trevelyan, C. P., 218
Turkey, 448
Tweedmouth, Lord, 188
Twickenham, 444
Tyabji, Badruddin, 51, 160, 320, 323, 480

Union Castle Company, 418
United States, 48, 310, 352, 387–8
Universities Bill, 185, 195
Universities Commission, 184

Vaidya, D. G., 119
Varma, Munshi Ganga Prasad, 160, 203
Vaze, S. G., 462
Versova, 448, 463
Vichy, 307, 443–5, 469
Victoria, Queen, 80, 106, 156, 181, 271, 408
Vidyasagar, Iswarchandra, 74
Vijayaraghavachariar, C., 283–4, 288
Vincent, F. M., 112, 358
Vivekananda, Swami, 73, 79, 147–8
Volksrust Jail, 427

Wacha, D. E., 21, 66, 84, 89–90, 93–4, 99, 112, 160, 162, 165, 188–9, 259, 278, 281, 283–4, 286, 295, 307, 323, 452, 475, 492–3

Wadya, H. A., 166, 283, 291, 422
Warren, Countess of, 99
Wedderburn, J., 91
Wedderburn, Lady, 398–9
Wedderburn William, 31, 44; president, Bombay Congress, 67–8; member, Welby Commission, 89–90; and India, 91–3; relations with Gokhale, 98–102; and the British Committee of the Congress, 88, 158–9, 162, 165–7; correspondence with Curzon, 182; 187–90, 196, 200, 204, 216, 218, 224–6, 228, 236, 242, 253, 258, 267–8, 273, 275, 293, 299–302, 307, 312, 342, 345, 349, 363; presides over Allahabad Congress, 366–71; 374–7, 393–4; relations with Gokhale, 397–9, 402, 405, 426; and reform of India Council, 380, 440–2, 482, 486, 490, 492

Welby Commission (Royal Commission on Indian Expenditure), 47, 93–8, 101–2, 137, 228, 436
West Bengal, 191–2
Westminster Gazette, 195
Westropp, Chief Justice, 19
Willingdon, Lord, 435, 448, 467–8
Wilson, Guy Fleetwood, 380–3, 391–2, 401–2, 405–6, 439–40, 465–6
Wilson, James, 269
Wood, Sir Charles, 183
Wordsworth, Principal, 7, 31
World War, First, 467, 476
Wyllie, Sir William Curzon, 355

Yeravda, 12

Zamindar, 269
Zanzibar, 421
Zulfiqar Ali, Nawab, 378, 429